European Commission Decisions on Competition

European Commission Decisions on Competition provides a comprehensive economic classification and analysis of all European Commission decisions adopted pursuant to Articles 101, 102, and 106 of the FEU Treaty from 1962 to 2009. It also includes a sample of landmark European merger cases. The decisions are organized according to the principal economic theory applied in the case. For each economic category, the seminal Commission decision that became a reference point for that type of anticompetitive behavior is described. For this, a fixed template format is used throughout the book. All subsequent decisions in which the same economic principle was applied are listed chronologically. This book complements the most widely used textbooks in industrial organization, competition economics, and competition law to which detailed references are offered. It contains source material for teachers, students, and scholars of competition law and economics, as well as practising competition lawyers and officials.

FRANCESCO RUSSO works as a competition lawyer at Bonelli Erede Pappalardo and is a member of the Italian Bar. He is a visiting researcher at the Amsterdam Center for Law and Economics (ACLE).

MAARTEN PIETER SCHINKEL is Professor of Competition Economics and Regulation at the Department of Economics of the University of Amsterdam and Co-director of the Amsterdam Center for Law and Economics (ACLE). He is a visiting professor at the College of Europe in Bruges.

ANDREA GÜNSTER is a post-doctoral researcher in economics at the Professorship for Intellectual Property of the ETH Zurich. She is a visiting researcher at the Amsterdam Center for Law and Economics (ACLE).

MARTIN CARREE is Professor of Industrial Organization in the School of Business and Economics of Maastricht University. He is the current Head of the Department of Organization and Strategy.

European Commission Decisions on Competition

Economic Perspectives on Landmark Antitrust and Merger Cases

FRANCESCO RUSSO

MAARTEN PIETER SCHINKEL

ANDREA GÜNSTER

MARTIN CARREE

CAMBRIDGE
UNIVERSITY PRESS

CAMBRIDGE UNIVERSITY PRESS
Cambridge, New York, Melbourne, Madrid, Cape Town, Singapore,
São Paulo, Delhi, Dubai, Tokyo, Mexico City

Cambridge University Press
The Edinburgh Building, Cambridge CB2 8RU, UK

Published in the United States of America by Cambridge University Press, New York

www.cambridge.org
Information on this title: www.cambridge.org/9780521117197

© Francesco Russo, Maarten Pieter Schinkel, Andrea Günster, and Martin Carree 2010

First published 2010

A catalogue record for this publication is available from the British Library

Library of Congress Cataloguing in Publication data
European Commission decisions on competition : economic perspectives on landmark antitrust
and merger cases / Francesco Russo . . . [et al.].
   p.   cm.
Includes bibliographical references and index.
ISBN 978-0-521-11719-7 (hardback)
1. European Commission.   2. Antitrust law – European Union countries – Cases.   3. Consolidation
and merger of corporations – Law and legislation – European Union countries – Cases.
I. Russo, Francesco, 1978–   II. Title.
KJE6456.E938   2010
343.240721 – dc22   2010006632

ISBN 978-0-521-11719-7 Hardback

Contents

Figures

Tables

Abbreviations

ADSL	asymmetric digital subscriber line
ATC	average total cost
AVC	average variable cost
CFI	Court of First Instance
DCF	discounted cash flow
DG	Directorate-General
DG Comp	European Commission Directorate-General for Competition
DSL	digital subscriber line
EC	European Community
ECJ	European Court of Justice
ECMR	European Community Merger Regulation
ECR	European Court Reports
ECSC	European Coal and Steel Community
EEA	European Economic Area
EEC	European Economic Community
EMA	European Medicines Agency
ENCORE	Economics Network for Competition and Regulation
EPO	European Patent Office
EU	European Union
EUA	European Unit of Account
FEU Treaty	Treaty on the Functioning of the European Union
ICN	International Competition Network
IFTRA	International Fair Trade Practice Rules Administration
IO	industrial organization
IP	intellectual property
IPRs	intellectual property rights
ISP	internet service provider
LAN	local access network
M&As	mergers and acquisitions
NCA	national competition authority
OJ	*Official Journal of the European Union*
PPDs	published prices to dealers
PPRS	pharmaceutical price regulation scheme
R&D	research and development
RPM	resale price maintenance
SIEC	Significant Impediment of Effective Competition
SME	small and medium-sized enterprise
SO	statement of objections
SPC	Supplementary Protection Certificate
TO	telecommunications operator

Table of legislation

Council regulations

Commission regulations and decisions

Directives

Council Directive 65/65/EEC of 26 January 1965 on the approximation of provisions laid down by Law, Regulation or Administrative Action relating to proprietary medicinal products [1965] OJ 22/369

Commission Directive 80/723/EEC of 25 June 1980 on the transparency of financial relations between Member States and public undertakings [1980] OJ L 195/35

Council Directive 89/104/EEC of 21 December 1988 to approximate the laws of the Member States relating to trademarks [1989] OJ L 40/1

Commission Directive 90/338/EEC of 28 June 1990 on competition in the market for telecommunication services [1990] OJ L 192/10

Commission Directive 96/2/EC of 16 January 1996 amending Directive 90/338/EEC with regard to provisions regulating mobile and personal communications [1996] OJ L 20/59

Directive 2001/83/EC of the European Parliament and of the Council of 6 November 2001 on the Community code relating to medicinal products for human use [2001] OJ L 311/67

Directive 2003/55/EC of the European Parliament and of the European Council of 26 June 2003 concerning common rules for the internal market in natural gas repealing Directive 98/30/EC [2003] OJ L 176/57

Commission Directive 2005/81/EC of 28 November 2005 amending Directive 80/723/EEC on the transparency of financial relations between Member States and public undertakings as well as on financial transparency within certain undertakings [2005] OJ L 312/47

Notices and guidelines

Commission Notice concerning the assessment of cooperative joint ventures pursuant to Article 85 of the EEC Treaty [1993] OJ C 43/2

Commission Notice concerning agreements, decisions, and concerted practises in the field of cooperation between enterprises [1968] OJ C 75/3

Commission Notice on the non-imposition or reduction of fines in cartel cases [1996] OJ C 207/04

Commission Notice on the definition of the relevant market for the purposes of Community competition law [1997] OJ C 372/3

Commission Guidelines on the method of setting fines imposed pursuant to Article 15(2) of Regulation No. 17 and Article 65(5) of the ECSC Treaty [1998] OJ C 9/3

Commission Notice on the concept of full-function joint venture [1998] OJ C 66/1

Commission Notice on the concept of concentration [1998] OJ L C 66/5

Commission Notice on the concept of undertakings concerned [1998] OJ C 66/14

Commission Notice on calculation of turnover [1998] OJ C 66/25

Commission Notice on the application of the competition rules to access agreements in the telecommunications sector, OJ C 265/2 [1998]

Commission Guidelines on vertical restraints [2000] OJ C 291/1

Commission Guidelines on the applicability of Article 81 to horizontal co-operation agreements [2001] OJ C 3/2

Commission papers and communications

Communication from the Commission The return to viability and the assessment of restructuring measures in the financial sector in the current crisis under the State Aid rules, [2009] OJ C 195/9

FEU Treaty provisions on competition

Article 101

1. The following shall be prohibited as incompatible with the common market: all agreements between undertakings, decisions by associations of undertakings and concerted practices which may affect trade between Member States and which have as their object or effect the prevention, restriction or distortion of competition within the common market, and in particular those which:
    (a) directly or indirectly fix purchase or selling prices or any other trading conditions;
    (b) limit or control production, markets, technical development, or investment;
    (c) share markets or sources of supply;
    (d) apply dissimilar conditions to equivalent transactions with other trading parties, thereby placing them at a competitive disadvantage;
    (e) make the conclusion of contracts subject to acceptance by the other parties of supplementary obligations which, by their nature or according to commercial usage, have no connection with the subject of such contracts.
2. Any agreements or decisions prohibited pursuant to this article shall be automatically void.
3. The provisions of paragraph 1 may, however, be declared inapplicable in the case of:
    – any agreement or category of agreements between undertakings,
    – any decision or category of decisions by associations of undertakings,
    – any concerted practice or category of concerted practices,
    which contributes to improving the production or distribution of goods or to promoting technical or economic progress, while allowing consumers a fair share of the resulting benefit, and which does not:
    (a) impose on the undertakings concerned restrictions which are not indispensable to the attainment of these objectives;
    (b) afford such undertakings the possibility of eliminating competition in respect of a substantial part of the products in question.

Article 102

Any abuse by one or more undertakings of a dominant position within the common market or in a substantial part of it shall be prohibited as incompatible with the common market in so far as it may affect trade between Member States.

Such abuse may, in particular, consist in:

(a) directly or indirectly imposing unfair purchase or selling prices or other unfair trading conditions;
(b) limiting production, markets or technical development to the prejudice of consumers;
(c) applying dissimilar conditions to equivalent transactions with other trading parties, thereby placing them at a competitive disadvantage;

(d) making the conclusion of contracts subject to acceptance by the other parties of supplementary obligations which, by their nature or according to commercial usage, have no
connection with the subject of such contracts.

Article 106

1. In the case of public undertakings and undertakings to which Member States grant
   special or exclusive rights, Member States shall neither enact nor maintain in force
   any measure contrary to the rules contained in this Treaty, in particular to those rules
   provided for in Article 18 and Articles 101 to 109.
2. Undertakings entrusted with the operation of services of general economic interest or
   having the character of a revenue-producing monopoly shall be subject to the rules
   contained in this Treaty, in particular to the rules on competition, in so far as the
   application of such rules does not obstruct the performance, in law or in fact, of the
   particular tasks assigned to them. The development of trade must not be affected to such
   an extent as would be contrary to the interests of the Community.
3. The Commission shall ensure the application of the provisions of this Article and shall,
   where necessary, address appropriate directives or decisions to Member States.

Table of equivalences

The article numbering of the Treaty (now Treaty on the Functioning of the European Union, FEU Treaty) has recently been subject to a comprehensive renumeration by the Treaty of Lisbon, entered into force on 1 December 2009. It had previously been already renumbered by the Treaty of Amsterdam, entered into force on 1 May 1999. Therefore, over time, the Commission has been using different numbering. It is important to have that in mind when reading the decisions as well as the other documents referring to the articles of the Treaty in order to not be confused.

In the book the old numbering is maintained only within the quoting of a Commission decision. Otherwise, even if describing older cases the new numbering is used.

Original numbering	Treaty of Amsterdam numbering	New numbering (Treaty of Lisbon)
Article 3(f) – later also 3(g)	Article 3(1)(g)	Repealed, in substance replaced by Article 3(3) EU Treaty read in conjunction with the Protocol no. 27 on Internal market and competition attached to the EU and FEU Treaties
Article 5	Article 10	Repealed, in substance replaced by Article 4(3) EU Treaty
Article 85	Article 81	Article 101
Article 86	Article 82	Article 102
Article 90	Article 86	Article 106

Acknowledgments

This book is the fruit of a long process, with inputs by many. The idea to disclose the content of the rich publications by the European Commission on its competition decisions in the *Official Journal of the European Union* (OJ) for use in teaching was originally Stephen Martin's. In the period he taught at the University of Amsterdam (January 2000 to June 2002) he initiated the collecting of OJ publications on Commission decisions that made interesting case material in an applied industrial organization (IO) course. The project was structurally sponsored for several years by the Economics Network for Competition and Regulation (ENCORE), then directed by Jeroen Hinloopen and Jules Theeuwes.

At the end of 2005, the project was redirected and combined with the ongoing joint research that three of us, Maarten Pieter, Martin, and Andrea, had started earlier, in 2001, at Maastricht University. In that project, sponsored by METEOR, the research school of the Faculty of Economics and Business Administration of Maastricht University, all Commission decisions since 1957 on antitrust were consistently cataloged in a large data set to be disclosed for quantitative analysis. This allowed for a consistent identification of "landmark cases from an economic point of view."

Further support from ENCORE from 2006 onwards helped finance Francesco's full-time engagement in the project. His involvement in the editing of the second edition of Floris Vogelaar's *The European Commission Rules: Landmark Cases of the European Courts and the Commission* created fruitful synergies. Meanwhile, Jeroen Hinloopen and Jules Theeuwes endorsed the project with further advisory input on economics. Floris Vogelaar advised on aspects of European competition law.

The extensive data set on EU competition decisions – which also served as a basis for the survey statistics presented in the introductory chapter of the book – was continuously cleaned up and perfected in order to be complete and correct on all selected cases. We developed a template format according to which we describe all the cases that were identified as "landmark" in the sense of establishing the application of a specific economic theory for the first time in an EU decision. Completion required another two years of continuous work and further financial support from the Amsterdam Center for Law and Economics (ACLE).

The book classifies all the formal antitrust decisions of the European Commission. It is a short history of half a century of European competition law enforcement. The collection of formal decisions is complete up to and including December 2009. The book is intended for intensive use by the competition policy community: teachers in competition law and industrial organization, as well as scholars, practitioners in the competition authorities, companies and their advisors, economic consultants, and legal counsel.

Apart from the people already mentioned above, we are indebted to Jakob Rüggeberg and Marie Goppelsröder for painstakingly editing early versions of the manuscript. Joris Bijvoet and Norman Bremer worked on the case data file, in particular on appeals revisions. Yevgeniy Stotyka, Ivana Sucur, and Charlotte Heilmann assisted in the collection of materials and description of a number of cases. Patrick van Cayseele, Kati Cseres, Ron Kemp, Valerie Korah, Jarig van Sinderen, Floris Vogelaar, Mike Walker, Jan Kees Winters, and participants of the March 2007 ENCORE workshop at the Netherlands Competition Authority (NMa) in The Hague and the June 2007 ENCORE Research & Education Day at the University of Amsterdam, provided valuable comments on earlier versions of the book. We are especially indebted to Wouter Wils, Marco Haan, Bert Schoonbeek, Lars-Hendrik Röller, Bojan Šporar, Stephen Martin, Ioannis Kokkoris, Bruce Lyons, and five anonymous referees for their valuable and detailed comments. Hagar Rooijakers, and later Audrey Peters, Britta Duiker, Marieke Wagter and Chandra Doest gave secretarial support. Scott Parris and Chris Harrison of Cambridge University Press provided vital editorial support in the final stages of publication.

Naturally, however, we remain solely responsible for any remaining omission in this book.

We are also indebted to the Archivi Guttuso Association for having made our inspired front cover possible. We are happy and honoured they supported our project.

Andrea acknowledges the hospitality of the ACLE to work on the book in Amsterdam. Francesco thanks his colleagues at Bonelli Erede Pappalardo's Antitrust, Regulatory and European Law department for their continuous stimulus in the better understanding of competition matters. We are grateful to Giancarlo Russo, Carla Nuis, Konrad and Marie-Theres Günster, and Jasperina Carree-van Veen for their patience and support during the completion of this volume.

FR, MPS, AG, and MC
Amsterdam
March 2010

1   Introduction

An active protection of competition in and across Member States was recognized in the Treaty of Rome of 1957 as an important fundament for a unified European Economic Community (EEC). The importance of economic analysis in European competition policy has increased over the history of its enforcement. European competition law enforcement is an active area where law and economics meet. This book presents a systematic analysis and classification of all formal decisions adopted by the European Commission in antitrust cases between 1962, when European competition policy became effective, due to the adoption of Regulation 17,[1] and 2009. Included are all Commission decisions pursuant to Articles 101 (agreements and concerted practices), 102 (abuse of dominance), and 106 (special or exclusive rights granted to undertakings by Member States) of the Treaty on the Functioning of the European Union (FEU Treaty).[2] The book also contains a chapter on mergers and acquisitions (M&As) landmark cases dealt with by the European Commission. Finally, the book lists the decisions the Commission adopted in case of lack of due cooperation by the undertakings involved in antitrust proceedings.

The leading principle in classifying and presenting the decisions in this book is the economic issue central to a case. We have drawn up an extensive list of mainstream economic theories of anticompetitive behavior, and describe the first and landmark European Commission decision in which that type of behavior was at the core of the analysis. This book brings together "economic landmark cases." A decision is considered to be an economic landmark decision if it is the first decision in which the Commission adopted and applied a particular economic argument or principle, an application which was confirmed in later decisions thus becoming a reference point for that type of (anti)competitive behavior. Where changes to the economic application in the decision have been made – for example, in response to rulings in appeals – these modifications are described as well. In addition, all subsequent decisions in which the Commission applied the same economic concept are set out chronologically. The book provides a complete and coherent picture of the evolution of the Commission's economic approach to competition law.

The book is organized to allow users rapid access to all information provided with reference to each of the economic issues analyzed. A standard template systematically provides the same type of information for each of the topics discussed. The respective sections describe a category of economic principles underlying the Commission decision. We provide references to the economic and legal literature, as well as European legislation, accompanied by lists of all related Commission decisions.

This book is a reference guide for courses in industrial organization (IO). Lecturers can find which Commission decisions relate to a large variety of topics typically taught in IO courses. The

---

1   Regulation No. 17: First Regulation Implementing Articles 85 and 86 of the Treaty [1962] OJ 13/204, English special edition OJ [1959–62] 87.
2   That is, Articles 81, 82 and 86 until the adoption of the Treaty of Lisbon in 2007 (entered into force in December 2009) and Articles 85, 86, and 90 until the adoption of the Treaty of Amsterdam in 1997 (entered into force in May 1999). Both Treaties re-enumerated the articles.

book will also benefit master and PhD students specializing in the IO field. In addition, it may be of interest to economists and lawyers in their academic and professional activities, be it in a competition authority, a firm, or in academia.

In the description of the cases, the aim is not to make a normative evaluation of the Commission's approach, nor to assess its conformity with the orientation generally adopted by economists concerning certain behavior. Rather, the scope of the book is limited to presenting interpretations given by the European Commission, and more generally by EU competition law, to a number of types of market behavior possibly creating anticompetitive effects.

The information on all such decisions taken by the European Commission in relation to antitrust was collected from the official decision documents as published by the Commission in the *Official Journal of the European Union* (OJ). The first decision is from 1964, after which a total of 544 formal decisions were taken, up to and including all decisions adopted until 31 December 2009.[3] Landmark decisions presented have been confirmed in substance by the European Courts. Although in some cases reductions of fines have been granted, the appeal courts – i.e. the European Court of Justice (ECJ) and the Court of First Instance (CFI, currently named General Court after the Lisbon Treaty has entered into force) – have confirmed the Commission's assessments in principle in all the cases discussed here. As such, the decisions have become case law of EU competition law and the Commission has recalled and confirmed an orientation previously expressed by the Courts in their later judgments. Only in rare circumstances (e.g. predatory pricing), have the Courts intervened to partially modify the approach of the Commission. This happened in issues that were deemed highly controversial and were fiercely debated at the time. Throughout the book, in paragraphs (c) and (e) of the presentation of the relevant cases, it is mentioned if the decision triggered a further clarifying or modifying jurisprudential intervention.

A somewhat different approach has been adopted in the choice of landmark decisions on mergers. Merger control in Europe has recently been object of incisive intervention by the ECJ and the CFI. To describe the current position of EU law on mergers without taking account of these recent judicial developments would be missing a core part of the development of case law. Therefore, we chose to present decisions as landmark cases sometimes not because of their content, but rather because they led to, or were the result of, judicial intervention by the European Courts which established important principles for the Commission to take into consideration in merger control.

In order to survey the high level of production of formal decisions by the European Commission, we have restricted our analysis in several ways. On antitrust, only those decisions formally adopted by the Commission under Article 101, 102 and 106 FEU Treaty have been analyzed. Decisions adopted under the European Coal and Steel Community Treaty (ECSC Treaty), decisions ordering interim measures, (dis)comfort letters, decisions rejecting complaints, decisions concerning the air transport sector, and the commitments decisions adopted pursuant to Article 9 of Regulation No. 1/2003 have been excluded. Furthermore, notices published pursuant to Article 19(3) of Regulation No. 17 (which concerned the hearing of interested third parties in case of envisaged adoption of a negative clearance decision but is no longer in force), the so-called Carlsberg's

---

3   The book lists a total of 576 decisions, as it includes also those adopted by the Commission in case the companies provided incomplete, false, or misleading information, or did not duly cooperate with the Commission in the course of the proceedings. There is only one example of an infringement decision also including a fine for procedural reasons. The case *Theal/Watts* (*Theal/Watts* Commission decision 77/129/EEC [1977] OJ L 39/19, Case IV/28.812) involved a vertical agreement preventing parallel imports notified by the parties, but with incorrect information about the underlying agreement. The two companies were fined ECU 25,000 for procedural errors and the agreement was prohibited.

notices about notified cooperation agreements, which invited interested third parties to submit observations, and the notices published pursuant to Article 27(4) of Regulation No. 1/2003 in case of intended adoption of a decision pursuant to Article 9 of the same Regulation have not been included either.

Furthermore, only a subset of all Commission decisions concerning M&As has been included. The large number of European merger decisions – over 3,500 since the Merger Regulation was adopted in 1989, almost all of which were clearance decisions – makes a consistent overview of all of them beyond the scope of this book.[4] We present only selected landmark merger decisions. Among those, the cases extensively described explain the position of the European Commission and, more generally, of EU law concerning different potential effects of mergers on competition. In addition, the rare cases of mergers treated under Article 102 FEU Treaty before 1989, which were treated as cases of dominance, have all been included in the book. Finally, decisions adopted pursuant to the State aid rules of the EU Treaty are not included in the book.[5]

This introductory chapter is organized as follows. In section 1.1, a brief description of European competition policy is presented together with descriptive statistics and several highlights of European Commission competition decisions. Section 1.2 lays out the organization of the materials and the structure of the book. Section 1.3 provides guidance to instructors on how to use the book in graduate courses.

1.1 A brief history of European competition policy

1.1.1 Institutional and legal framework

European competition policy is a highly visible element of EU policy. The foundation of European competition law was laid in 1957 in the Treaty of Rome establishing the European Economic Community (EEC). Since 1957, the Treaty of Rome has been amended several times, the latest major amendments being made by the Treaty of Lisbon in 2007, which entered into force on 1 December 2009.[6] As a result of those changes, the institutional and normative structure of the EU is now based on two core treaties: the Treaty on European Union (EU Treaty) and the Treaty on the Functioning of the European Union (FEU Treaty). The EU Treaty sets out the rules establishing the objectives, tasks, and institutions governing the EU, the introductory part is dedicated to the principles inspiring it. Article 3(3) identifies as one of the general objectives of EU the achievement of "a highly competitive social market economy." The provision is further clarified by the Protocol No. 27 attached to the Treaties that, recalling the wording of previous versions of the EU Treaty, states that "the internal market as set out in Article 3 of the Treaty on

---

4   Council Regulation (EEC) No. 4064/89 etc. of 21 December 1989 on the control of concentrations between undertakings [1989] OJ L 395/1. The first Merger Regulation, as subsequently amended by Council Regulation (EC) No. 1310/97 [1997] OJ L 40/17, has been substituted by Council Regulation (EC) No. 139/2004 on the control of concentrations between undertakings [2004] OJ L 24/1.

5   Articles 107–109 FEU Treaty. State aid has only recently come under the influence of the "more economic approach," see Röller, L.-H., H. W. Friederiszick, and V. Verouden, "European State Aid Control: An Economic Framework," in P. Buccirossi (ed.), *Advances in the Economics of Competition Law*, Cambridge, MA: MIT Press, 2008.

6   After the referendum of 2005 in France and the Netherlands rejecting the adoption of the newly drafted "European Constitutional Treaty" that had been signed in June 2004 in Rome by the Head of State and Government of the (then) twenty-five Member States, the institutional reforms in the EU suffered a slowdown only partly overcome in the European Council of June 2007 in which Member States, under the German Presidency of the Council, agreed upon partial reform of the EU Treaty. The final outcome of that agreement has been a substantial amendment to the EU and EC Treaties signed in Lisbon by the twenty-seven EU leaders on 13 December 2007 (the "Treaty of Lisbon") that brought to an end several years of negotiations about institutional reforms. After a long and turbulent ratification process (which suffered a slowdown after Ireland, as a result of a referendum held in 2008, initially rejected its adoption), the Lisbon Treaty finally entered into force on 1 December 2009.

European Union includes a system ensuring that competition is not distorted." The competition rules are set out in Articles 101–106 of the FEU Treaty.[7]

The system of EU law provided by the Treaties entitles the Commission to a monopoly position on the proposal of new or additional legislation. Legal acts are subsequently to be adopted by the European Council, together with the European Parliament. In several amendments, the European Parliament has obtained wider power in the legislative process. The FEU Treaty today provides for different systems for the adoption of legislative acts (Regulations and Directives).[8] In case of competition law, Article 103 FEU Treaty explicitly refers to the consultation procedure for the adoption of "the appropriate regulation or directives to give effect to the principles set out in Articles 101 and 102." Under the consultation procedure, the Council, acting by a qualified majority, can adopt legislative acts on a proposal from the Commission after having consulted the European Parliament. The Commission is only entitled to adopt implementing legislation when so empowered by the Council. The Council of the European Union is composed of the competent ministers from the national governments, representing the interests of the Member States. Council or Commission regulations and decisions are legally binding. Regulations do not need to be transposed into national legislation and are immediately enforceable. In contrast, directives, which are addressed to Member States and provide for legislative goals to be achieved rather than the means to achieve them, need to be implemented by Member States in their national legal system within a time limit established in the same directive. In contrast, Notices and Guidelines, which are usually adopted by the Commission to express its interpretation of certain rules or its orientation towards certain circumstances, serve only as guidance and are not legally enforceable.

The European Commissioner for Competition watches over the rules established in European competition law. He or she is assisted by the Directorate-General (DG) for Competition and acts in close cooperation with the national competition authorities (NCAs) of the various Member States. Formal decisions as well as notices and guidelines are adopted by the European Commission as a whole, at the proposal of the Commissioner for Competition.

The history of European competition law enforcement is shorter than that of the US Department of Justice's Antitrust Division. Nonetheless it is no less lively. In recent years, the European Commission has been very active in promoting competition. This is not only due to the growth of the number of countries that are members of the EU.[9] Enforcement has also become stricter, as exemplified by an increase in recent fines and new and stringent fining guidelines. Furthermore, in recent years the Commission has introduced anticartel units as well as adopting and revising a leniency program and settlement procedure.

European competition policy is increasingly relying on economists to advise in cases. Since September 2003, the Commission has a Chief Economist position at DG Comp (the Commission

---

7   The current numeration of the articles has been adopted by the Treaty of Lisbon entered into force in December 2009. Prior to that, the original numeration set by the Treaty of Rome (where competition rules were provided in Articles 85–90) had already been changed by the Treaty of Amsterdam where competition rules were in Articles 81–86.

8   The procedure in which the Parliament is recognized to have more power is the co-decision procedure pursuant to Article 294 of the FEU Treaty. The other main legislative procedure is the cooperation procedure ex Article 252 of the Treaty. Other procedures recognizing more minor power of intervention by the Parliament in the adoption of legislation are the consultation procedure and the assent procedure.

9   The six founding Member States were Belgium, Federal Republic of Germany, France, Italy, Luxembourg, and the Netherlands. In 1973, Denmark, Ireland, and Great Britain entered the EEC. In 1981 Greece became the tenth Member State. In 1986, Spain and Portugal joined the EEC. In 1995, the Member States became fifteen with the accession of Austria, Finland, and Sweden. In 2004, the Czech Republic, Cyprus, Estonia, Latvia, Lithuania, Hungary, Malta, Poland, Slovenia and Slovakia became members of the EU. Member States became twenty-seven after the last enlargement of January 2007, in which Romania and Bulgaria became members of the EU.

Directorate-General for Competition). The office is supported by a team of IO economists. The Commission has adopted a more economic and effects-based approach in its decisions.[10] This has been triggered by an increased need to justify the benefits of competition, by advances in IO thinking, and by the close scrutiny exercised by European Courts.[11] In addition, the Commission increasingly relies on outside economic advice. The Commission is furthermore open to novel enforcement methods that are suggested by law and economics research. In 2006, for example, it refined the method for imposing fines for breaches of Article 101 and in 2008 adopted a system of direct settlement as a further enforcement instrument in case of antitrust violations.[12] On the whole, awareness of the seriousness of the social effects of competition law infringements in Europe is increasing.

DG Comp prepares decisions in three broad areas: antitrust, merger, and State aid cases. The Commission's sector and individual investigations, decisions, interpretations, and opinions often have far-reaching implications for industry structure and individual firms. The Commission decisions are daily news in international media, they involve many firm representatives, competition lawyers, and economic consultants. Recent examples of high-profile cases include the fine of 497 million Euros imposed in 2004 on Microsoft Corporation for abuse of dominance, the record-breaking cartel fine of 1,328 million Euros imposed in 2008 on four car glass producers, the Commission's decision to block the merger between General Electric and Honeywell, which had already been approved by the US competition authorities, and the Commission's strict application of the State Aid rules to government aids to financial institutions in distress during the latest financial crisis.[13]

In this section, we briefly review fifty years of European competition law enforcement.[14] Subsection 1.1.2 briefly describes how the European competition rules evolved and what they currently are. Subsection 1.1.3 presents a brief descriptive history of their enforcement, with some trends over time. Subsection 1.1.4 contains summary statistics on the investigative process of the Commission. Subsection 1.1.5 focuses on remedies and sanctions for infringements of European competition rules.

1.1.2   European competition policy and rules

Article 101(1) FEU Treaty establishes the prohibition of agreements and concerted practices among undertakings affecting trade between Member States when restrictive of competition within the common market. An official investigation under Article 101(1) can lead to the finding

---

10 See Röeller and Stehmann (2005).

11 In 2002, with a series of significant judgments, the CFI annulled three Commission decisions clearing mergers since affected by "a series of errors of assessment" concerning in particular the economic evidences. The cases were Case T-342/99 *Airtours plc* v. *Commission* [2002] ECR II-2585; Case T-5/02 *Tetra Laval* v. *Commission* [2002] ECR II-4381, and Case T-310/01 *Schneider Electric* v. *Commission* [2002] ECR II-4071. These three judgments were among the elements that triggered the wide-ranging reform of merger policy in 2004.

12 See Commission Notice on the method of setting fines imposed pursuant to Article 23(2)(a) of Regulation No. 1/2003 [2006] OJ C 210/2, and Commission Notice on the conduct of settlement procedures in view of the adoption of Decisions pursuant to Article 7 and Article 23 of Council Regulation (EC) No. 1/2003 in cartel cases [2008] OJ C 167/01.

13 See Communication from the Commission The return to viability and the assessment of restructuring measures in the financial sector in the current crisis under the State Aid rules, [2009] OJ C 195/9.

14 This section is based in part on Carree, Günster, and Schinkel (2010), and some of the sources used in that study, including Davies, Driffield, and Clarke (1999), Lauk (2002), and Gual and Mas (2005). Information on mergers also refers to Lindsay (2006). The more than 100-year-old history of competition policy enforcement in the United States since the passing of the Sherman Act in 1890 has been a rich source of empirical analysis and learning, including Corwin (1992), Gallo, Dau-Schmidt, Craycraft, and Parker (1994, 2000), Lin, Baldev, Sandfort, and Slottje (2005), Ghosal and Gallo (2001), and Martin (2007). Data on Commission decisions adopted in 2009, included in the book, are not part of this section.

of an infringement. When the Commission adopts an infringement decision, it has the right to impose remedies and/or sanctions according to Council Regulation No. 1/2003.[15]

Article 101(3) grants the possibility of an exemption conditional on industry or market circumstances, when agreements (i) contribute to improving the production or distribution of goods or to promoting technical or economic progress, (ii) allow consumers a fair share of the resulting benefit, (iii) impose restrictions on competition only when indispensable for the attainment of those objectives, (iv) do not afford undertakings concerned the possibility of eliminating competition in respect of a substantial part of the products in question. Examples of exemptions that have been granted are to industries in structural crisis, that were temporarily allowed to form cartel agreements. This has happened only twice, during the oil shock in the early 1980s and in 1993.[16] Article 101(3) also facilitates licensing and joint venture creation or shared patent agreements with the intention to foster innovation.

Article 102 FEU Treaty prohibits abuse of dominant positions on markets. Article 102 comprehends several types of potential abuses summarized under one heading, including excessive pricing and price discrimination, tying, bundling, and predatory pricing. All cases that have been decided under Article 102 have been infringements, with the exception of one case involving minority shareholder agreements before the introduction of the Merger Regulation.[17]

Finally, Article 106 addresses monopolistic behaviors that are in principle similar to behaviors falling under Article 102, the difference being that dominance is authorized, maintained, or fostered by a Member State regulation. Article 106 has been central in the liberalization of State monopolies.

The antitrust enforcement process in the EU started with the implementation of Council Regulation No. 17. This Regulation constituted the basis for the Commission to adopt decisions establishing: (i) an infringement of Article 101(1) or 102 FEU Treaty; (ii) an exemption from the applicability of Article 101(1) FEU Treaty when the conditions laid down in Article 101(3) FEU Treaty were satisfied; or (iii) declaring the non-applicability of competition rules to a certain agreement (negative clearance). All Commission decisions are possibly subject to judicial review by the European judicatures. Regulation No. 17 also laid down the legal foundation for the Commission to start investigations (Articles 11, 12, 14 and 19); for individuals to lodge complaints with the Commission concerning undertakings' allegedly anticompetitive behaviors, and for firms to file notifications about their own agreements and concerted practices (Articles 4 and 5). Moreover, Regulation No. 17 established the power for the Commission to impose fines and remedies upon firms infringing Articles 101(1) or 102 FEU Treaty (Articles 15 and 16).

In May 2004, Regulation No. 1/2003 replaced Regulation No. 17. It confirmed and strengthened the powers granted to the Commission by Regulation No. 17 and introduced the possibility for the Commission to close the investigations, accepting commitments proposed by the parties (Article 9).

Regulation No. 1/2003 constituted a turning point for competition law in Europe as it abolished the notification system provided by Regulation No. 17 under which firms were obliged to notify any potentially anticompetitive agreement(s), upon which the Commission would take a formal decision, alternatively a negative clearance, an exemption decision, or an infringement decision. Since Regulation No. 1/2003 became effective, the notification system has been replaced by the

---

15   Regulation No. 1/2003 on the implementation of the rules on competition laid down in Articles 81 and 82 of the Treaty [2003] OJ L 1/1. Until May 2004, the Commission's enforcement power were provided by Council Regulation No. 17: First Regulation Implementing Articles 85 and 86 of the Treaty [1962] OJ 13/204, English special edition OJ [1959–62] 87.
16   See European Commission, *XXIII Report on Competition Policy* 1993, p. 49.
17   *Metaleurop SA* Commission decision 90/363/EEC [1990] OJ L 179/41, Case IV/32.846.

"directly applicable exemption" system. This implies that firms entering in an agreement must self-determine the existence of the conditions for the applicability of Articles 101(1) and 101(3) FEU Treaty.[18] Undertakings no longer need to notify the agreement to the Commission and depend on it to determine whether they qualify for an exemption pursuant to Article 101(3). The abolishment of the obligation to notify every agreement potentially covered by Article 101(1) has significantly reduced the number of cases that the Commission needs to investigate.

Since 1962, DG Comp has been divided into sector-specific units screening industries for anti-competitive conduct. In 1998, the first anticartel unit was formed, with about twenty specialized officials. This unit deals with cartel formation throughout all sectors of the economy. The set of enforcement instruments of DG Comp had been extended in 1996 with the introduction of the leniency program, which aimed to encourage participants of cartels to inform the authorities of their involvement in an undetected collusive arrangement in exchange for a full or partial reduction in fines.[19] After a revision in 2002, and most recently again in 2006, a substantial number of leniency applications have been made to the Commission and fine discounts have been given accordingly in the majority of cartel decisions.[20] With the revised leniency program, the Commission installed a second cartel unit. Furthermore, in 2008 the Commission introduced a settlement procedure to settle cartel cases through a simplified procedure, according to which firms acknowledging their involvement in the cartel under investigation are granted a 10 percent fine reduction.[21]

DG Comp has undergone some important reorganization during its existence. The Commissioner for competition has always been one of the most powerful positions in the Commission. The impact of enforcement prepared by DG Comp (formerly DG IV) has grown steadily during the last three decades under Commissioners Andriessen, Sutherland, Brittan, Van Miert, Monti, and Kroes. Over the years, the complexity of economic content in competition cases increased. In response, the European Commission strengthened its in-house economic expertise with the creation of the revolving-door position of Chief Competition Economist and its support team of economists. In addition, the Economic Advisory Group on Competition Policy, a group of leading academic advisors, was formed. These developments, together with increased international cooperation with antitrust agencies worldwide through transatlantic agreements and the International Competition Network (ICN), have advanced an effects-based approach to the Commission's decisions on antitrust.

Until Council Regulation No. 1/2003, the Commission exercised predominance over NCAs. Merger control was the main exception, it was mainly a national issue until the first EC Merger Regulation of 1989 was approved. From 1986 onwards, NCAs could also decide on purely national clear-cut cases under Article 101(1), 102, and group exemption regulations.[22] However, NCAs were not allowed to grant exemptions under Article 101(3).

Regulation No. 1/2003 operated an important decentralization of the enforcement competences fully involving NCAs and national Courts in the application and execution of Articles 101 and 102. Accordingly, the Commission is statutorily no longer the sole executor of European competition

---

18 Pursuant to Article 1 of Regulation No. 1/2003 "1. Agreements, decisions and concerted practices caught by Article 81(1) of the Treaty which do not satisfy the conditions of Article 81(3) of the Treaty shall be prohibited, no prior decision to that effect being required. 2. Agreements, decisions and concerted practices caught by Article 81(1) of the Treaty which satisfy the conditions of Article 81(3) of the Treaty shall not be prohibited, no prior decision to that effect being required. 3. The abuse of a dominant position referred to in Article 82 of the Treaty shall be prohibited, no prior decision to that effect being required."

19 Commission Notice on the non-imposition or reduction of fines in cartel cases [1996] OJ C 207/4.

20 Commission Notice on immunity from fines and reduction of fines in cartel cases [2006] OJ C 298/17.

21 See Commission Notice on the conduct of settlement procedures in view of the adoption of Decisions pursuant to Article 7 and Article 23 of Council Regulation (EC) No. 1/2003 in cartel cases [2008] OJ C 167/01.

22 See European Commission, *XVI Report on Competition 1986*, p. 52.

law but instead a member of a network of European competition authorities with which it cooperates in the enforcement of competition rules. The Commission also cooperates with national Courts.[23] However, NCAs and national Courts cannot take decisions that run counter to (other) decisions already adopted by the Commission.[24] As for Article 106 – i.e. cases addressed to Member States – it is important to note that the Commission is the only European authority implementing these Treaty provisions.

To give an example of the work division among cases after the introduction of decentralization, in 2004 the Commission dealt with 150 out of a total of 707 investigations opened pursuant to EU rules. France led in the activity list of the NCAs with 111 investigations, followed by Germany with 74, The Netherlands with 51, Hungary with 44, and finally Denmark with 41.[25] In addition to decentralization, the Commission has recently focused on the introduction of a legal system facilitating private litigation with the 2008 White Paper.[26]

Next to changes in the regulatory framework, the institutional system of the EU has undergone several changes in the last four decades. In 1989, the Court of First Instance (CFI, now "General Court") became the institution dealing with (first instance) appeal proceedings relating to competition cases. From then onwards, the ECJ has only been responsible for appeal proceedings involving Member States and appeal proceedings of second instance exclusively on legal grounds. The first discussions on the introduction of the CFI had already taken place in 1981.[27]

Over the history of European competition law enforcement, some early regulations were set up to exempt certain sectors from the application of EU competition law.[28] An early example is Council Regulation No. 141 of 1962, exempting the transport sector. Certain sectors such as transport, motor vehicle distribution, communication, banking, and energy have continuously received special treatment.[29] These sectors used to be characterized by state monopoly in most European countries. Former state monopoly sectors involving networks or high entry barriers received critical regulatory attention in the late 1990s.[30]

Additional block exemption regulations were issued, mainly in the 1980s, not covering a specific sector but rather focusing on a specific economic conduct. The large backlog of notifications that the Commission had to deal with, which had accumulated throughout the 1960s and 1970s, forced the Commission to reconsider its decision making system. In the early 1980s the backlog was more than 4,000 pending cases, many of which had little or no restrictive effect on competition. The Commission had to speed up its decision making process.

The Commission therefore introduced block exemption regulations for certain forms of economic conduct, as well as with small and medium-size enterprises (SMEs), in part in an attempt to alleviate its workload in the 1980s. Council Regulation No. 19 of 1965 and Commission Regulation No. 67 of 1967 were the first block exemption regulations setting standards for

---

23   See in particular Articles 5 and 6 of Regulation No. 1/2003, Commission Notice on cooperation within the Network of Competition Authorities [2004] OJ C 101/43, and Commission Notice on the cooperation between the Commission and the Courts of the EU Member States in the application of Articles 81 and 82 EC [2004] OJ C 101/54.

24   See in particular Article 16 of Regulation No. 1/2003.

25   European Competition Network (2007) http://ec.europa.eu/comm/competition/ecn/index_en.html.

26   Commission White Paper – Damages actions for breach of the EC antitrust rules, COM (2008) 165, published on 2 April 2008 on DG Comp website.

27   See European Commission, *XI Report on Competition 1981*, p.28.

28   The power to adopt such a kind of Regulations (and Decisions) is provided by Article 103 EU Treaty.

29   See, as an early examples among others, European Commission, *II Report on Competition Policy 1972*, p. 70.

30   See Communication from the Commission to the Council, the European Parliament, the European Economic and Social Committee and the Committee of the Regions on the Review of the EU Regulatory Framework for electronic communications networks and services SEC(2006) 816 and SEC(2006) 817 of 29 June 2006. See also DG Comp report on the energy sector inquiry SEC(2006) 1724 of 10 January 2007.

patent licensing and exclusive distribution cases, respectively, to be considered eligible for an exemption. In the first half of the 1980s, more than ten block exemption regulations were adopted for specialization and research and development (R&D) joint ventures, exclusive distribution, and purchasing agreements, as well as patent and know-how licensing agreements.[31] Furthermore, at the end of the 1990s the Commission adopted a general block exemption regulation covering all kinds of vertical agreements considered to have a minor impact on competition.[32] In the same period, the Commission adopted new and more economically oriented exemption regulations for R&D, specialization, and technology transfer agreements.[33]

More generally, in 1997, the Commission adopted the "*de minimis doctrine*" establishing that, hardcore restrictions aside, agreements between either competitors with less than 5 percent market share or non-competitors with less than 10 percent market share would be considered of minor importance, thus not appreciably restricting competition (the thresholds were raised to 10 percent and 15 percent, respectively, in 2001).[34] All of this helped to speed up the decision making process and clear the Commission's large backlog of more than 4,000 notifications, which had accumulated in the 1960s and the 1970s. At the same time, however, the increasing number of Member States joining the EU brought more cases to the Commission's attention.

In 1989, after intense and long debate, the first Merger Regulation was approved.[35] It filled a gap that had characterized European competition law until then. The few merger cases treated so far had been analyzed via an extensive interpretation of Article 102.[36] However, this had already been judged to be inappropriate by the ECJ in 1969.[37] The first proposal for a regulatory framework on M&As dates back to 1973. As the Council and the Parliament were not fully convinced by this draft version, it took another sixteen years and four amendments in 1981, 1984, 1986, and 1988 until the European Community Merger Regulation (ECMR) was approved jointly by the three institutions in 1989. Since 1998, this Regulation has also applied to full-function joint ventures previously decided under Article 101.[38]

The 1989 Merger Regulation gave the Commission the discretion to preemptively scrutinize the effect on competition of envisaged mergers and prohibit those potentially creating or strengthening a dominant position on the relevant market. It provides a system of mandatory notifications that is similar to the one provided by Regulation No. 17 in case of agreements under Article 101. The first Merger Regulation was revised in 2004.[39] The new Merger Regulation – which maintained a notification requirement – widened the scope for assessing the restrictive effects of mergers.

---

31 They led to a great deal of use of comfort letters by the Commission. A "comfort letter" is a weak form of negative clearance that postpones further investigations with the promise that, should the notified agreement later be found to be an infringement, it would be treated leniently.

32 Regulation No. 2790/1999 on the application of Article 81(3) of the Treaty to categories of vertical agreements and concerted practices [1999] OJ L 336/1.

33 Regulation No. 2958/2000 on the application of Article 81(3) of the EC Treaty to categories of specialization agreements [2000] OJ L 304/3. Regulation No. 2659/2000 on the application of Article 81(3) of the EC Treaty to categories of research and development agreements [2000] OJ L 304/7. Regulation No. 772/2004 on the application of Article 81(3) of the Treaty to categories of technology transfer agreements [2004] OJ L 123/11.

34 Commission Notice on agreements of minor importance which do not appreciably restrict competition under Article 81(1) of the Treaty establishing the European Community (*de minimis*) [2001] OJ C 368/13.

35 Council Regulation (EEC) No. 4064/89 etc. of 21 December 1989 on the control of concentrations between undertakings [1989] OJ L 395/1.

36 The most significant of these cases is *Continental Can Company* Commission decision 72/71/EEC [1972] OJ L 7/25, Case IV/26.811. The handful of merger decisions adopted before the endorsement of the first Merger Regulation is listed in the introduction to chapter 8, see *infra*.

37 European Commission, *I Report on Competition 1971*, pp. 16 and 23.

38 Council Regulation (EC) No. 1310/97 of 30 June 1997 amending Regulation (EEC) No. 4064/89 on the control of concentrations between undertakings [1997] OJ L 40/17.

39 Council Regulation (EC) No. 139/2004 on the control of concentrations between undertakings [2004] OJ L 24/1.

Particularly, while in the first regulation only concentrations that created or strengthened a dominant position with a consequent impediment of effective competition were prohibited, under the new Article 2(3) of the new Merger Regulation, no merger – at least in case of non-coordinated effects[40] – that in any way significantly impedes effective competition in the internal market is likely to be cleared by the Commission.[41] Both in Phase I of a merger investigation and in Phase II of the procedure, the merging firms can propose remedies and commit to comply with them. The Commission will consider whether the proposed commitments are sufficient to overcome its competition concerns. If so, the Commission can declare these proposed remedies binding upon the undertakings and clear the merger conditional on those divestments, as well as other conditions and obligations.[42] The 2004 revision of the Merger Regulation also introduced the possibility of an efficiency defence.

The system of merger control in Europe is based on a jurisdictional division of competences between the Commission and the NCAs. The Merger Regulation applies only when certain threshold requirements concerning the merging firms are satisfied (i.e. the merger needs to have a *Community dimension*) and only if the merger results in a lasting change in the control of the undertakings concerned.[43] Otherwise, only national legislations may apply. Nonetheless, the Merger Regulation provides a system of case referrals between the Commission and the NCAs. In circumstances in which the notified merger might specifically affect a national market or a part thereof, the Commission can refer the case to the NCA of the Member State concerned.[44] In cases of Member State(s) dealing with a merger without a Community dimension but still affecting trade between Member States and threatening to affect competition in the State(s) involved, Member State(s) can request the Commission to examine the concentration.[45] If in the opinion of the merging parties a merger affects a market in only one particular Member State, the parties can ask the Commission to refer the whole or part of the case to the competent NCA. Similarly, if a merger does not have a Community dimension but affects competition in at least three Member States, so that it is subject to revision under three different national merger legislations, the parties can ask the Commission to deal with the case rather than the individual NCAs.[46]

1.1.3   Commission decisions over time[47]

Figure 1.1 shows the number of decisions adopted by the Commission pursuant to Articles 101, 102, and 106 FEU Treaty as well as decisions adopted for procedural reasons from 1964 to 2008. In the first few years after the approval of Regulation No. 17, the Commission published only a few competition decisions. Thereafter, their number rose steadily over the years.

---

40   Recital 25 of the introduction of the Merger Regulation states: "... The notion of 'significant impediment of effective competition' in Article 2(2) and (3) should be interpreted as extending, beyond the concept of dominance, only to anticompetitive effects of a concentration resulting from the non-coordinated behavior of undertakings which would not have a dominant position on the market concerned."

41   This is determined by the so-called SIEC test, for Significant Impediment of Effective Competition. See Article 2(3) of the Merger Regulation.

42   See Commission Notice on remedies acceptable under Council Regulation (EC) No. 139/2004 and under Commission Regulation (EC) No. 802/2004 [2008] OJ C 267/1.

43   See in particular Articles 1 and 3 of the Merger Regulation.

44   See Article 9 of the Merger Regulation.

45   See Article 22 of the Merger Regulation.

46   See Articles 4(4) and 4(5) of the Merger Regulation.

47   Carree, Günster, and Schinkel (2010) provide a complete analysis of the European Commission's antitrust decisions up to and including 2004. The case file analyzed for this book includes all relevant decisions up to and including December 2009.

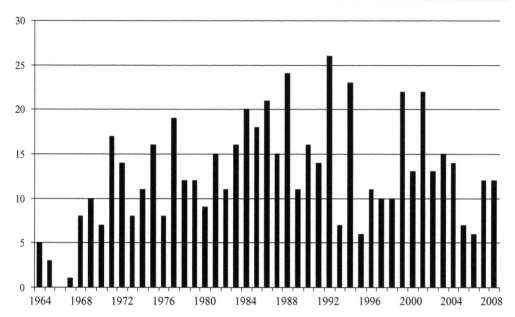

Figure 1.1 Total number of antitrust Commission decisions, 1957–2008.

At the end of the 1980s, the growth in cases over the years stagnated, after which there is a substantial drop in the 1990s.

The early upward trend reflects DG Comp's growing legitimacy and jurisdiction. The reduction in the total number of published decisions in the 1990s may be explained by the measures introduced to reduce the Commission's workload, such as the block exemption regulation systems discussed above. Another possible explanation may be a stronger reliance on the instrument of comfort letters instead of official decisions in this period. In addition, NCAs received more power and responsibility over the years, dealing with a fair share of cases even prior to Council Regulation No. 1/2003. In particular, from the early 1990s onwards, national authorities took over a fair share of cases whose effects were mostly limited to the respective national markets. In addition, during the early 1990s, DG Comp was further burdened with tasks to enforce the new merger control regulation, effective as of 1989. This may well have tied up a number of DG Comp case handlers, leading to decreased numbers of antitrust cases being taken up. From 1997 on, an amendment to the Merger Regulation also decreased the number of antitrust cases by taking over full-function joint ventures.[48]

Towards the end of the 1990s, the total number of formal Commission decisions on antitrust increased again. In 1998, DG Comp created a special anticartel unit. Furthermore, the first leniency notice became effective, which stimulated parties to come forward and report possible infringements to the Commission for it to investigate.

---

48 See Council Regulation (EC) No. 1310/97 of 30 June 1997 amending Regulation (EEC) No. 4064/89 on the control of concentrations between undertakings [1997] OJ L 40/17.

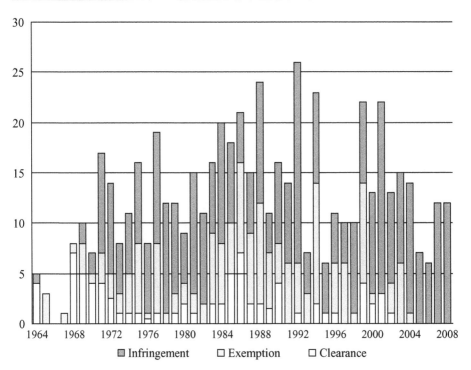

Figure 1.2 Types of formal Commission decisions, 1957–2008.

The first antitrust decision by DG Comp on record deals with a vertical agreement between two German companies, Grosfillex and Fillistorf, notified to the Commission in 1959.[49] The arrangement was given negative clearance under Article 101(1), under the responsibility of Walter Hallstein, in March 1964. Another four decisions followed that year. Though Regulation No.17 entered into force in February 1962, the Commission needed two years to use its enforcement powers for the first time. With only another four decisions in total in the years 1965–7, the number rose to eight in 1968. In the year 1971, with seventeen decisions, enforcement for the first time overshot what would become the average of almost thirteen decisions per year in the Commission's effective policy period between 1962 and 2008.

Figure 1.2 categorizes the official decisions by type: infringement, exemption, or negative clearance. In the early stages of EU competition law enforcement, the Commission concluded its official investigations by mainly issuing negative clearances and exemptions. The first infringement found is in September 1964 in the Commission's fourth decision, the *Grundig–Consten* case.[50] After twenty months of investigation, the agreement between the two firms was decided a breach of Article 101(1) FEU Treaty, and ordered to be discontinued. This first adverse finding was appealed to the ECJ. After almost two years, the Court largely upheld the decision, as the first appeal ruling in European antitrust, in June 1966.

Only in July 1969 did the Commission find an infringement again, in the so-called *Quinine* case, which became a landmark decision due to the fact that the Quinine cartel was the first decision in which, apart from an injunction, fines were levied, totaling ECU 500,000.[51] A breach

49   *Grosfillex & Fillistorf* Commission decision 64/233/EEC [1964] OJ L 64/915, Case IV/61.
50   *Grundig-Consten* Commission decision 64/566/EEC [1964] OJ L 64/2545, Case IV/3344.
51   *Quinine* Commission decision 69/240/EEC [1969] OJ L 192/5, Case IV/26.623.

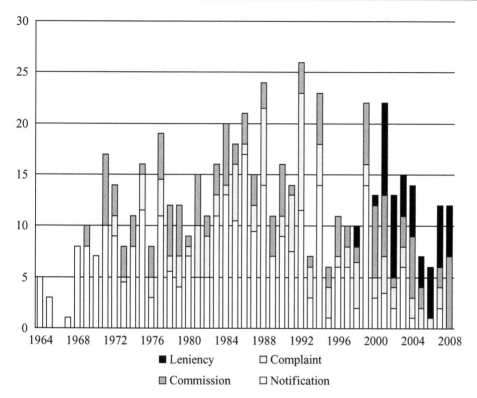

Figure 1.3 Report route of formal Commission decisions, 1957–2008.

of Article 101(1) was found, in form of horizontal market sharing, quota arrangements, and price fixing, in the Commission's first investigation on its own initiative. This second adverse finding was appealed in three distinct ECJ cases by ACF Chemiefarma, Buchler & Company as well as Boehringer Mannheim. The ECJ essentially confirmed the Commission decision.

Figure 1.2 shows that from the early 1970s onwards, the number of infringements found increases substantially relative to exemptions and negative clearances. The figure reveals that the relative number of negative clearances has decreased while the number of exemptions has remained constant. Given that a negative clearance is granting protection from future investigations on the notified arrangement, whereas exemption is given for only a limited amount of time, one way to interpret the trend between the two could be that the Commission gradually moved towards a weaker form of clearance. This is in line with the Commission's continued efforts to use its means of regulation more extensively, motivated by an urge to reduce the administrative burden and produce quicker clearance for notifications awaiting a decision. Substituting comfort letters for negative clearance decisions started in the early 1990s, by which time the majority of conduct-specific block exemption regulations had already been adopted.

Figure 1.3 displays the report route of the investigations resulting in a formal decision. It reveals that leniency indeed formed a large stimulation of cases from 1998 onwards. Two years after the introduction of the leniency program, *British Sugar*[52] was the first decision in which a leniency claim played a role. The percentage of decisions that originated in, or in which the proceedings were facilitated by, leniency claims of one or more parties to the agreements to all cases

---

52   *British Sugar* Commission decision 1999/210/EC [1999] OJ L 76/1, Cases IV/33.708, 33.709, 33.710, 33.711.

since 1996 is 23 percent. Proponents of the availability of leniency often take this high number as a measure of the program's success. The information provided by the parties in their applications can certainly speed up proceedings. One of the European cartel cases that was most swiftly dealt with is *Fine Art Auction Houses*,[53] the first cartel decision made under the revised 2002 leniency notice after only half a year of investigation in 2002.

Another clear trend is that more decisions originate from the Commission's own initiative and the role of notifications in bringing on cases that eventually lead to a formal decision has been small since the turn of the century. It seems that DG Comp was well prepared, therefore, for the abolition of the notification requirement that occurred in May 2004. Official decisions on cases brought to the Commission by complaints, since the mid 1970s, have been a fairly constant share of all decisions.

Complaints are considered an essential source of information by the Commission. Regulation No. 1/2003 provides in Article 7 that "those entitled to lodge a complaint ... are natural or legal persons who can show legitimate interest and Member States." In that regard, the Commission has been recognized as having discretionary power in handling complaints. In particular, the Commission is not obliged either to give a decision or to conduct an investigation on the subject matter of the complaint. It is rather entitled to reject a complaint for lack of Community interest, thus applying different degrees of priority to the cases it handles. The Commission is only obliged to examine carefully the factual and legal circumstances brought to its attention by the complainant(s) and to state reasons why it decides to close the file relating to a complaint if it did so. The reasons have to be stated in a (subject to appeal) written decision after having given the complainant(s) the opportunity to make known its view in writing.[54] The data suggest that initially potential complainants needed some time to become aware of the possibility to complain about alleged anticompetitive behavior of rivals or suppliers. We note though that presumably part of the decisions that are registered as Commission's own initiative were in fact complaints by parties that preferred to remain anonymous.

Figure 1.4 shows the relative size of six (economically) motivated types of arguments in Commission decisions. Apart from Article 102 and 106 cases, these are four Article 101 decisions: horizontal constraints, licensing, vertical restraints, and joint ventures. A few cases are procedural decisions. These include Commission decisions adopted pursuant to Article 11 (Commission right to ask for information) and Articles 15–16 (Commission right to impose fines) of Regulation No. 17. These correspond – notwithstanding the differences – to the current articles 18, 23, and 24 of Regulation No. 1/2003. According to these articles, the Commission is entitled to ask for information and more generally due cooperation from firms during antitrust investigations. The Commission might impose fines in case of lack of due cooperation and/or provision of incorrect, incomplete, or misleading information. In the book, these decisions are listed in Annex I and are not analytically scrutinized since they do not have any economic rationale.

Since the adoption in 1989 of the Merger Regulation, some 3,500 mergers have been assessed by the Commission.[55] The 1989 Merger Regulation provides for a strict timeline which the Commission has to respect in its assessment of the proposed concentration. The initial investigation, the so-called Phase I investigation, which follows a notification, has to be concluded by the Commission within twenty-five working days. If the Commission finds that the merger raises serious

---

53 *Fine art auction houses* Commission decision 2005/590/EC [2005], Summary of the decision in OJ L 200/92, Case COMP/E-2/37.784.

54 See Case T-24/90 *Automec II* [1992] ECR II-2223; Case T-114/92 *Bemin* [1995] ECR II-147 and Regulation 773/2004 relating to the conduct of proceeding by the Commission pursuant to Articles 81 and 82 of the EC Treaty [2004] OJ L 123/18, Articles 5–8.

55 The data regarding merger cases presented in the text are based on statistics on European merger control as published by DG Comp on its website: http://ec.europa.eu/comm/competition/index_en.html. The data refer to the period from September 1990 to June 2007.

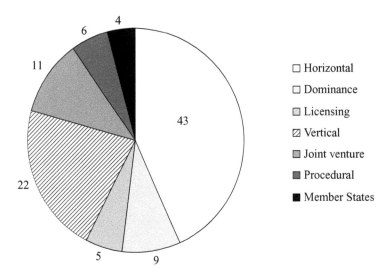

Figure 1.4 Formal Commission decisions, by economic conduct, percent.

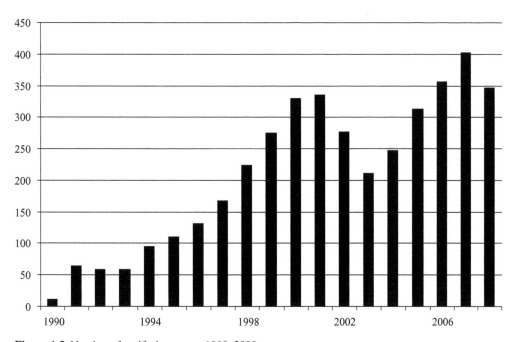

Figure 1.5 Number of notified mergers, 1990–2008.

concerns as to its compatibility with the common market, it can decide to initiate a deeper Phase II investigation. This gives the Commission ninety working days more to verify whether the merger is compatible with the internal market or whether it should be blocked.[56] Figure 1.5 shows the number of notified mergers per year since 1990. Of all notified mergers since 1990, 94 percent

56   See Article 6 in relation with Article 10 and Article 8 in conjunction with Article 10 of the Merger Regulation.

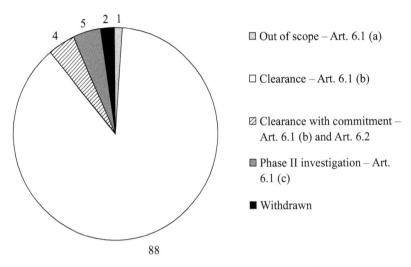

Figure 1.6 Conclusion of Phase I merger investigations, percent.[57]

were cleared in Phase I. Only 5 percent of notifications went on to a Phase II investigation. In a small number of cases (1 percent) the Commission referred the notified merger to the competent NCA under the referral system described above.

Within the Phase I investigation, the Commission can decide, as established in Article 6 of the Merger Regulation, that the proposed merger is compatible with the common market or that it raises serious doubts and deserves further investigation. The Commission can clear the merger unconditionally, or conditional to commitments and obligations on the merging parties. In case the merger does not have a Community dimension, or the proposed operation does not imply a lasting change in control, the Commission can declare the inapplicability of the Merger Regulation. Figure 1.6 is a pie chart of the outcome of all Phase I inquiries of the Commission since 1990. Figure 1.6 also includes cases in which the notification was withdrawn by the parties.

Finally, figure 1.7 displays the outcome of all Phase II investigations since 1990. As established in Article 8 of the Merger Regulation, after an in-depth analysis, the Commission can decide to clear the merger with or without remedies, or declare the merger incompatible with the common market and block it. Prohibition decisions have been rather rare: 20 in total since 1990.[58]

1.1.4 Enforcement of the competition rules

One interesting measure of DG Comp activity in its decision making is the duration of an investigation over time. Figure 1.8 presents the difference in months between the final decision date and the starting date of the official investigation in all antitrust decisions, excluding mergers. Figure 1.8 shows the average case duration in months for each year.

---

57   In total, there have been 3,978 decisions in the Phase I Merger Investigations in the period 1990–2008.
58   For a complete list of the Commission's prohibition decisions see, *infra*, Annex III.

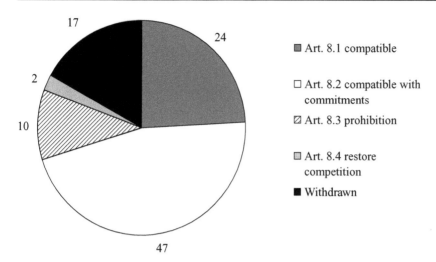

Figure 1.7 Conclusion of Phase II merger investigations, percent.[59]

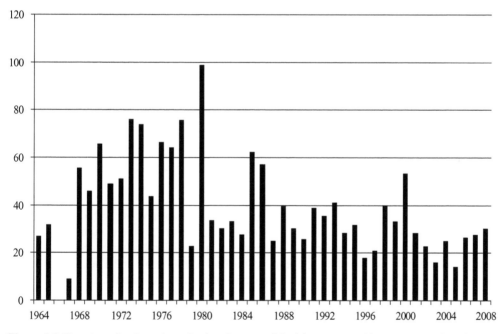

Figure 1.8 Duration of antitrust investigations by year of decision, measured in average number of months, 1957–2008.[60]

59   In total, there have been 191 decisions in the Phase II Merger Investigations in the period 1990–2008.

60   For the following cases it is not possible to retrieve the opening date of the investigation and therefore, they have been excluded from the analysis: *Sodium gluconate* Commission decision of 2 October 2001, Case COMP/36.756, withdrawn on 19 March 2002 and *Jungbuzlauer* its follow-up case; *Fasteners and attaching machines* Commission decision of 19 October 2007, not yet published, Case COMP/39.168; *Greece* Commission decision of 5 March 2008, published on DG Comp website, Case COMP/38.700.

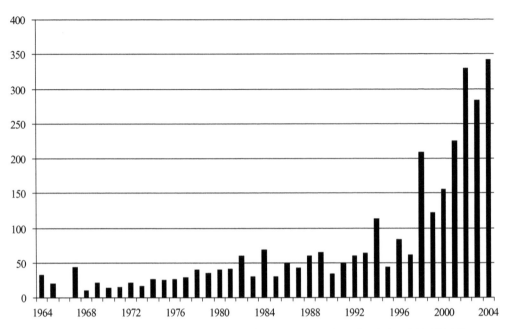

Figure 1.9 Length of decision documents, measured by average number of recitals, 1957–2004.[61]

Clearly, once enforcement got under way from the late 1970s onwards, there has been a downward trend in the average number of investigating months from around sixty in the 1970s to an average of about thirty months per formal decision in the 1990s. These numbers appear high, but they are influenced by some individual cases that took an exceptionally long time. For example, the peak in 1980 is largely due to three cases that had already been notified in the 1960s. Related to the duration of the investigation is the cases' backlog standing over time at DG Comp. During the 1970s, as we have seen, a backlog of about 4,000 cases had evolved, which was only reduced in the 1980s in part because notified agreements had expired. About 1,000 cases were closed in a short period of time. Thereafter, a steady decline of the backlog took place until 1992, when the stock of investigations was again around 1,000.

Another statistic that conveys information about the enforcement process is the length of a final decision. We measured this length by the number of recitals in the official publication, see Figure 1.9. The Commission numbers the paragraph in its decisions, which each contain a separate part of the analysis. Therefore, the length of the decisions in terms of the number of their paragraphs conveys some information on the complexity of the case. As with the mean duration, the number of paragraphs is averaged over all cases of a particular year.

Clearly, from fairly brief decisions in the 1970s, the average number of recitals grew exponentially. In the early years, a case is on average three or four pages long. In 2002, the average length of the fourteen official decisions is about fifty pages with the case of *Plasterboard*, for example, pushing the yearly mean to an all-time high of more than 300 paragraphs per case. In about 106

---

61   Since the majority of decisions have not been published we cannot retrieve the lengths of the decision documents in the form of recitals until 2008. Out of forty-eight decisions taken in the period 2005–8, only thirteen decisions have been published. Figure 1.9 thus ends with the year 2004. For the following infringement decisions it is not possible to retrieve the number of recitals of the decision document and therefore, they have been excluded from the analysis: *Sodium gluconate* Commission decision of 2 October 2001, Case COMP/36.756, withdrawn on 19 March 2002 and *Jungbuzlauer* its follow-up case.

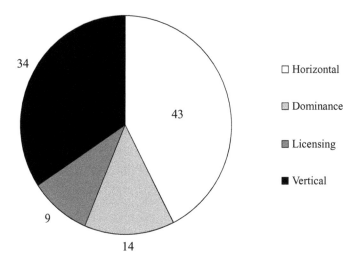

Figure 1.10 Infringement decisions, by economic conduct, percent.[62]

pages, the Commission establishes a hardcore cartel and fines all companies involved a total of 478 million Euros. Since then, the average length of decisions, especially in hardcore cartel cases, remains very high.

On the one hand, one may expect that later cases can rely on earlier developed case law and can therefore be dealt with more swiftly. Also, in cases that involve leniency one might expect that a less extensive justification of the decision would suffice. On the other hand, in part as a result of appeals procedures, the Commission is expected to justify its infringement decisions in more detail. This has raised requirements in terms of precision in the factual description and in the economic and legal argumentation made by the Commission. In addition, the average number of recitals may have increased due to a selection bias, as the Commission almost exclusively publishes infringement decisions in recent years. Furthermore, in cartel cases, the length of the decision is a function of the number of colluders, and the Commission is particularly dedicated to uncovering extensive and therefore harmful collusive arrangements.

Figure 1.10 breaks down the Commission's findings on infringement as a pie diagram. Of all infringements, the main economic violation is horizontal constraints – that is, mostly hardcore cartels. Vertical restraints, as prohibited under Article 101, are the second-largest category, before abuse of dominance. Licensing agreements in breach of Article 101, typically where creating territorial restrictions or exclusive relations denying market access to competitors, represents the last category. In particular, adverse findings concerning licensing vanished after the 1980s.

1.1.5 Remedies and fines

When an infringement of Article 101 or 102 FEU Treaty is found, the Commission can impose remedies pursuant to the rules of Regulation No. 1/2003 (previously Regulation No. 17). Typically, the parties found to have behaved anticompetitively are ordered to discontinue

---

62 In total, in the period 1964–2008, there have been 378 infringements under Article 101 and/or Article 102, including two decisions concerning joint ventures that are not included in the graph.

Table 1.1 Fines imposed for specific economic conduct in million Euros					
	Horizontal	**Dominance**	**Licensing**	**Vertical**	**Procedural**
Total fine	12.279,29	1.141,42	11,14	544,29	937,09
Average fine per infringement with fine	115,84	31,71	2,78	13,27	55,12[63]

the particular behavior.[64] The Commission further has the ability to impose fines.[65] The criteria followed by the Commission when calculating the fines – within the legal limit constituted by the 10 percent of firms' annual turnover – are explained in the notice on the imposition of fines.[66] According to the fines notice, the amount of fines is related to the value of sales involved in the infringement as well as to its duration, and adjusted according to aggravating and mitigating circumstances. As described above, firms can escape by applying for immunity from fines or reduction of fines following the rules established in the Commission leniency program.[67] Firms can now also obtain a reduction of fines in the framework of the settlement procedure.[68]

Table 1.1 presents the average as well as the sum of fines according to economic violation for all infringement decisions from 1964 until 2008.

In the early years, fines were often very low, but in the 1990s this changed drastically. As horizontal infringements were most common and often serious (e.g. cartels), it is obvious that this category would exhibit the steepest incline in average as well as sum of total fines. Horizontal conduct involves several companies, which is one explanation for its larger fines compared to dominance cases, where only one firm is fined. It is also the category receiving the highest average fine per case.

Confirmation of these data is given in Figure 1.11, in which the average fine for antitrust infringement over time is shown.[69] The steep increase in the average fine is shown clearly.

1.2   Structure of the book

The book is based on a template-based description of those cases considered to be economic landmark Commission decisions. In addition to an extensive description of each of these identified landmark cases, a complete list of all the Commission decisions in which the same economic argument was applied is provided. As mentioned before, since the Commission approach

---

63   The procedural fines imposed on E.on (break of seals during Commission dawn raids, *E.ON Energie AG* Commission decision of 30 January 2008, published on DG Comp website, Case COMP/B-1/39.326) and *Microsoft* (failure to comply with a previous Commission decision, *Microsoft* Commission decision of 27 February 2008, published on DG Comp website, Case COMP/C-3/ 34.792) under Regulation No. 1/2003 are the reason for procedural fines being so high. E.on and Microsoft received fines of 38 million Euros and 899 million Euros, respectively. Up to then, fines summing to 85,500 Euros had been imposed for procedural reasons, all under Regulation No. 17. Therefore, the average procedural fine, between 1957 and 2007, amounted to 5,700 Euros .
64   See Article 7 of Regulation No. 1/2003.
65   See Article 23 of Regulation No. 1/2003, and previously Article 15 of Regulation No. 17/62.
66   Commission Notice on the method of setting fines imposed pursuant to Article 23(2)(a) of Regulation No. 1/2003 [2006] OJ C 210/2. The latter version of the fines notice replaced the previous Commission Guidelines on the method of setting fines imposed pursuant to Article 15(2) of Regulation No. 17 and Article 65(5) of the ECSC Treaty [1998] OJ C 9/3.
67   Commission Notice on immunity from fines and reduction of fines in cartel cases [2006] OJ C 298/11.
68   Commission Notice on the conduct of settlement procedures in view of the adoption of Decisions pursuant to Article 7 and Article 23 of Council Regulation (EC) No. 1/2003 in cartel cases [2008] OJ C 167/01.
69   See also Bos and Schinkel (2006).

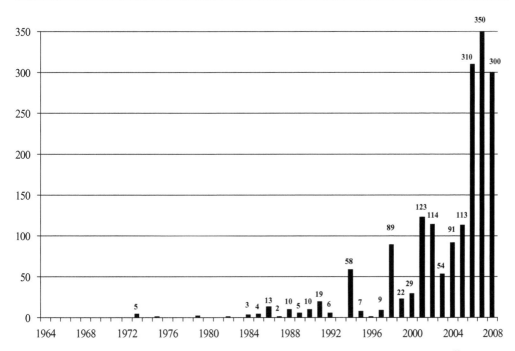

Figure 1.11 Average fine per infringement, with fines measured in million Euros, 1957–2008.[70]

regarding certain types of agreements or conduct evolved over the years, in case of change in the approach initially adopted in the described decision the subsequent landmark decision(s) and their modifications are described as well.

Each of the categorized economic topics is related to a selection of leading graduate books in applied and theoretical Industrial Organization. These are: Bishop and Walker (2009); Carlton and Perloff (2005); Church and Ware (2000); Martin (1994, 2002); Motta (2004); Tirole (1988); Waldman and Jensen (2001). The categorization we present is the result of a combination of the structure of these graduate texts and the Commission's identification of cases. That is, we have taken into account new and interesting categorizations made by the Commission, such as for global alliances (section 6.3) and adopted legislative specificities characterizing the system of EU competition law, as in the decisions described in chapter 8. Our efforts to combine economic texts and Commission decisions has led to a large set of matches, but also to a class of economic rationales specified by the European Commission but not separately analyzed in any of the graduate texts. To the extent that the graduate textbooks discuss forms of anticompetitive behavior on which the European Commission has never based a formal decision, we left them out. Examples of the latter are supply and purchase tie-ins in chapter 2 on horizontal restrictions, and monopsony purchasing in chapter 3 on abuse of dominance. These behaviors could have been infringements of the EU competition rules, but so far never have been.

The Commission decisions are classified into chapters. Each class of economic principle is treated in one chapter. Each of the subcategories is in turn treated in a section (i.e. subchapter). Chapter 2 treats horizontal restrictions, which are subdivided into section 2.1, treating price fixing

---

70   The average amount of fine is stated only if the amount exceeded 1 million Euros. The fine is not inflation adjusted.

cartels, which constitutes the clearest form of hardcore restriction of competition, together with market sharing, treated in section 2.2. They have been consistently opposed by the Commission as strongly restrictive of competition. Section 2.3 deals with bid-rigging and tender fixing and describe their effects on tender markets. Section 2.4, treating structural crisis cartels, introduces possible policy considerations in the enforcement of competition rules. Section 2.5 treats export cartels, together with the possible jurisdictional problems that can arise in Europe in relation to them. Section 2.6 deals with competition concerns that are possibly raised by trade associations. Section 2.7 describes marketing and advertising agreements that can represent *forms* of non-restrictive coordination as well as proper instruments for the implementation of cartels. Section 2.8 illustrates the economics of agreements on standards, and finally section 2.9 covers the exchange of information agreements and gives reasons for the choice to treat them as a separate category of collusion.

Chapter 3 deals with abuse of dominance, and is divided into nine sections. Section 3.1 discusses the clearest forms of exploitative abuse such as excessive pricing, discriminatory sales conditions, and prohibition of resale. Section 3.2 covers loyalty discounts and fidelity rebates, and gives a view of the intense focus placed in Europe on this potential abuse. Section 3.3 describes the Commission's approach to predatory pricing and the difficulties related to its definition. Section 3.4 deals with bundling and tying, constituting one of the more debated behaviors in the literature. Section 3.5 deals with price squeeze, and testifies to the rare application of this economic concept in Commission decisions. Section 3.6 contains decisions about restricting and preventing entry and together with section 3.7, treating refusal to deal and the essential facilities doctrine, is dedicated to highly restrictive exclusionary abuses possibly committed by dominant firms. Section 3.8 handles decisions concerning behaviors aimed at preventing interoperability of standards and networks which are currently highly debated in Europe due to the *Microsoft* case. The last section of the chapter, section 3.9, deals with best price guarantees also known as the "English clause."

Chapter 4 is dedicated to licensing cases. It is divided into two sections dealing with trademarks and branding (section 4.1) and patents and other intellectual property rights (section 4.2).

Chapter 5 examines possible vertical restrictions intervening in the relation between firms. It is composed of seven sections. Section 5.1 treats exclusive dealing and market foreclosure agreements which constitute a reason of particular concern in the European Union due to their possible repercussion on the internal market. Section 5.2 deals with territorial exclusivity and parallel import/export bans, which constitute a clear threat to the achievement of the internal market. Section 5.3 deals with resale price maintenance (RPM), that has always been considered as non-acceptable under EU competition rules. Bundling and tying are discussed in section 5.4 with reference to section 3.4 (where they are described under dominance), in order to recall that the applied economic principles are the same even in case of vertical relations. Selective distribution systems treated in section 5.5 are one of the forms of business cooperation that the Commission has constantly recognized as pro-competitive. Section 5.6 discusses franchising and the partly different approach taken by the Commission compared to economic theory. The last section (5.7), dedicated to discounts and rebates, recalls section 3.2 where the same topic is also discussed under dominance.

Joint ventures and alliances are the subject of chapter 6. They are treated according to a structure differentiating between research and development, treated in section 6.1, and marketing, selling, distribution, and production joint ventures, covered in section 6.2. Finally, taking into account the categorization of such kind of long-lasting agreements made by the Commission, strategic and technological alliances are discussed separately in section 6.3.

Chapter 7 is dedicated to the decisions addressed to Member States pursuant to Article 106 FEU Treaty. Chapter 8 includes a sample of landmark merger decisions including those describing the current approach to mergers in Europe. The decisions dealing with mergers before the entry into force of the first Merger Regulation in 1989 are listed and dealt with in the introduction to the chapter. Section 8.1 describes the approach towards non-coordinated effects in horizontal mergers, while section 8.2 deals with coordinated effects. Section 8.3 describes non-horizontal mergers and gives an example of both vertical and conglomerate merger. In section 8.4, decisions adopted pursuant to Article 101 and 102 FEU Treaty and dealing with minority acquisitions in firms' equity are listed and described. Section 8.5 discusses cases in which specific economic defenses were mounted – in particular, the failing firm defense and the efficiency defense. Finally, in section 8.6 examples are given of structural remedies acceptable under the Merger Regulation in order to make mergers compatible with the common market and eliminate their anticompetitive effects.

An annex (Annex I) lists all the decisions adopted by the Commission in cases of lack of company cooperation during its investigations. The decisions listed in Annex I do not contain any economic reasoning but, nonetheless, have been included for the sake of completeness.

Each chapter is structured according to a fixed template and built up as follows. Section A gives a short introductory summary of the economics related to the topic, including a short description of the chapter's structure. Section B lists the applicable EU legislation. The relevant parts (chapters or paragraphs) of the selected economic graduate texts are given in section C. In addition, in section D, reference is made to four selected leading legal texts: Bellamy and Child (2008); Jones and Sufrin (2008); Ritter and Braun (2005); and Whish (2008). In the references to the selected texts, the wording "not specifically discussed" is used when in the book(s) there are no chapters or paragraphs independently dedicated to the topic treated in the chapter/section. In many cases a subtopic not being discussed in the textbook results from differences in the classification of (anti)competitive behaviors and sometimes the topics are covered in the books in the framework of a broader topic.

In addition, a complete chronological list of all Commission decisions that relate to the specific economic topic of the section is included as section E. Within that list, the landmark decision(s) further discussed in section F or (elsewhere in the book) are highlighted in **bold type** (and cross-referenced). This way, the reader can easily follow the chronological development of the Commission's economic reasoning about the topic. Note that the first economic landmark decision adopted by the Commission very rarely coincides with the first decision adopted concerning a certain type of behavior. The reason for this is that in the decision adopted at the outset of competition law enforcement, the Commission hardly applied any economic rationale and principles in its decisions, and even if it did, it rarely explained or reasoned the axiomatic assumption it had made. Therefore, with the exceptions of few economic principles, only towards the second half of the 1970s did the Commission begin to apply economic reasoning more explicitly and extensively in its decisions. For that reason, the reader will rarely find within the list of all the decisions referring to a certain economic principle the oldest decision to be the landmark decision highlighted, but rather one that was adopted a few years later.

Within the list of decisions referring to a certain economic principle, further cases will be highlighted with a star. These are interesting cases that, although not considered as landmark decisions, are important for the extensiveness of the economic reasoning used by the Commission, or for the specificity of the circumstances in which the cases developed, or also for the impact they had in the development of the debate on competition issues or new policy measures in Europe. Furthermore, in each list, to the decisions that are referenced in the related economics texts (section C), reference is made in brackets to the relevant part(s) of those books.

We have identified an economic landmark decision according to a strict chronological criterion. That is, it often occurs that a later decision is supported by a more extensive economic analysis of the circumstances of the case. In such instances, we did not choose the later case when an earlier decision presented the same fundamental reasoning. Consequently, in some of the landmark decisions the economic argumentation and understanding is only hinted at rather than extensively developed and only in subsequent decisions (usually those we signal with a star) has the principle established in the landmark decision been confirmed and more broadly explained.

When referring to a decision, reference is made to the name of the decision in italics, the number of the decision (which includes the year), the relevant OJ number and pages as well as the case number. This provides the reader with all the information about a decision needed to find further details on the OJ web publication, the DG Comp website, or in the printed version of the decisions available in many libraries.[71] Following the list of the related decisions, we turn to the detailed description of the selected landmark decisions in numbered subsections of section F.

The selected landmark decisions are all presented in the same easy-to-use and comprehensive template. The description of each landmark case relies on two parts. The first part includes the case number, the formal decision adopted by the Commission (negative clearance, exemption, infringement), the addressee(s) of the decision (name of the companies and their nationality), the report route (notification, complaint, or Commission own initiative), the date of the decision, and the member of the Commission in charge of the Competition portfolio. Finally, the relevant product and geographical market are given.

The second part of the description is divided into five paragraphs. Paragraph (a) gives a short summary of the relevant facts, paragraph (b) gives a more detailed description of the report route of the case, paragraph (c) describes the economic argument and understanding adopted by the Commission and which constituted (at least until the possible next landmark decision on that topic was adopted) the line of reasoning the Commission confirmed in later decisions. In paragraph (c) the landmark economic reasoning adopted by the Commission is described and an attempt is made to reproduce, as closely as possible, the exact formal wording used by the Commission. Paragraph (d) lists the fines, the remedies, and the conditions possibly enclosed in the decision. Paragraph (e) indicates (where present) the further developments of the case in the European Courts, namely cases brought either before the CFI (Cases T-) or before the ECJ (Cases C- from 1989 and indicated with no letter until 1989 when the ECJ represented the only appeal instance). Since 1989 there are possibly cases that have been appealed before both Courts.

Annex I to the book lists all the decisions adopted for lack of cooperation of the firms involved in the Commission investigations. Annex II lists all the landmark decisions in the same order as that used throughout the book. Annex III collects all the Commission's decisions declaring a merger incompatible with the common market and thus blocking it, in chronological order. Annex IV lists the subset of landmark merger decisions analyzed in this book, in alphabetical order. Finally, Annex V lists all the decisions adopted by the Commission from 1964 to 2009, in alphabetical order.

---

71   DG Comp website is http://ec.europa.eu/competition/index_en.html. The digital publications of the OJ are available at http://eur-lex.europa.eu/JOIndex.do?ihmlang=en.

1.3 User guide

This book is structured so as to allow easy access to European Commission decisions by economic content. It offers source material for teachers in the preparation of their courses. The book complements the most widely used textbooks in IO, competition economics, and competition law. This allows for easy use in master courses in IO theory and antitrust economics. The book contains a large number of economic theories, many of which will normally be covered in introductory and/or advanced master courses in IO.

To our knowledge, there presently does not exist this kind of systematization and description of Commission decisions in antitrust cases. Jones and Van der Woude (2006) lists, *inter alia*, all Commission decisions on antitrust and merger cases, but does not offer a classification by economic rationale. Vogelaar (2007) focuses on legal landmark cases on competition, primarily judgments of the European Courts (both ECJ and CFI). The collection of decisions that we present is further inclusive of (corrections of) the partial lists in Harding and Gibbs (2005), the Table of Fines appendix in Ritter and Braun (2005), Geradin and Henry (2005), and selected European competition decisions discussed in the legal and economic books referred to throughout the text.[72]

The discussion of each topic is self-contained and organized according to a fixed template. The introduction to the underlying economic theory is offered as a bare minimum and reference is made to the main IO textbooks for a complete coverage of each topic. In addition, the current applicable EU legislation is listed. Detailed summary information on each economic landmark decision is then provided, following the template format. This makes for easy comparison across the decisions. Furthermore, for each topic the book offers a chronological list of European Commission decisions in which that topic was central.

Instructors can use the description of the economic landmark case offered as illustrative class material in teaching the specific economic theory. The organization of the book makes it easy to find the relevant passages for insertion in the course. In addition, the chronological list of cases can be used to base writing assignments or exam questions on. The full text of these decisions can easily be downloaded or copied from the Commission's publications.

---

72 Where a reference text contains a description of a case, we have indicated this after the case number in the list of cases presented in each section of the book (Sections E), in brackets.

2 Horizontal restrictions

A Introduction

The first important category of competition concerns is that of horizontal constraints among firms that have as their object or effect the prevention, restriction, or distortion of competition. This category includes hardcore cartel cases of price fixing and market sharing, but also more sophisticated anticompetitive horizontal agreements such as joint sales agencies, agreements on limiting marketing activities, capacity restrictions and other aspects of production, information sharing on prices and sales, service and distribution agreements, export cartels, and exclusionary practices toward entrants. It further extends to specialization and licensing agreements, trademarks, agreements on (technical) standards, strategic alliances, trade associations, and the joint organization of exhibitions and fairs. While some of these forms of cooperation may have positive welfare effects, they also have an inherent danger of leading to collusion.

Setting up and maintaining a collusive agreement can be difficult, since a number of factors can undermine the successful implementation of a cartel agreement. It is key for cartel success to create trust among its participants. It is generally costly for colluders to monitor and control the behavior of other parties to the agreement. This is important, because each cartel member has an incentive to free ride on the collusive agreement by undercutting the collusive price level to unilaterally increase profits. Therefore, the success of collusion depends among other things on quick detection of deviating behavior and effective punishment mechanisms.

The literature and case law distinguish two types of collusion – explicit and tacit collusion. The latter occurs when firms understand that if they compete less vigorously they can obtain market outcomes guaranteeing higher prices and thus higher profits without any direct interaction or communication to achieve a collusive price. Tacit collusion can occur also at price levels other than the joint profit maximizing level. In order to achieve the fully collusive price, firms can move from tacit collusion to explicit coordination. This would involve some form of explicit communication between them, which in turn might leave evidence of the antitrust infringement. The European cartel laws do in principle not extend to tacit collusion as they require evidence of an explicit cartel agreement. However, the Commission may reduce the risk of tacit collusion by preventing circumstances in which it may arise – for example, through merger control.

The analysis of collusion in modern industrial economics is based on the individual incentive constraints for collusion. According to this approach, firms trade off the gains from collusion against the gains from deviation. The literature recognises a number of factors that contribute to the sustainability of tacit and overt anticompetitive horizontal agreements. These include structural factors, such as a small number of firms, barrier to entry, spare capacity, cross-ownerships and other links among competitors, symmetry in the cost structure, dimension and organization of the firms, product homogeneity, and absent or weak buying power. In addition, transparency of rivals' strategies and actions is important for the existence and the implementation of collusive behavior.

Cartels represent an area of antitrust activity in which the Commission is very active and where the debate on the possible introduction of new instruments to fight cartels is continuously evolving. Recent Commission publications on the method for setting fines, awarding leniency discounts, and negotiating direct settlements demonstrate the priority that the Commission gives to combating hardcore cartels.[1] In recent years, cartel fines have surged to record-breaking levels, while the Leniency Program creates distrust among (potential) cartel members. The possibility to obtain further fine reductions in a settlement provides an incentive to admit guilt and cooperate with the Commission. At the same time, there is an ongoing encouragement by the European Commission of private litigation for damages from breach of antitrust rules that is partly inspired by the US antitrust system. This mix of enforcement instruments is meant to enhance an effective implementation of competition rules against cartels.[2]

This chapter has been set up following the main categories of horizontal cooperation described in the economic literature. The subcategories mainly coincide with the kinds of agreements that the Commission has analyzed over the years and with the most common infringements of competition rules. The sections opening the chapter deal with the most clear-cut cartels. In particular, section 2.1 deals with price fixing, section 2.2 with market sharing and quota cartels, and section 2.3 with bid-rigging. Section 2.5 deals with export cartels. The chapter also includes decisions about forms of horizontal cooperation between (competing) firms that are in the majority of the cases not considered as restrictive of competition by the Commission (i.e. are exempted or granted negative clearance) as well as by economists. These are in particular structural crisis cartels (section 2.4), trade associations (section 2.6), marketing and advertising agreements (section 2.7), the common setting of standards (section 2.8). Finally, a separate section (2.9) is dedicated to exchange of information.

B Applicable EU legislation

Article 101 FEU Treaty

Commission Notice on the definition of the relevant market [1997] OJ C 372/3.

Commission Guidelines on the applicability of Article 81 to Horizontal Co-operation Agreements [2001] OJ C 3/2.

Commission Notice on the method of setting fines imposed pursuant to Article 23(2)(a) of Regulation No. 1/2003 [2006] OJ C 210/2.

Commission Notice on immunity from fines and reduction of fines in cartel cases [2006] OJ C 298/11 (*leniency program*).

Commission Notice on the conduct of settlement procedures in view of the adoption of Decisions pursuant to Article 7 and Article 23 of Council Regulation (EC) No. 1/2003 in cartel cases [2008] OJ C 167/01.

---

1 Commission Notice on the method of setting fines imposed pursuant to Article 23(2)(a) of Regulation No. 1/2003 [2006] OJ C 210/2; Commission Notice on immunity from fines and reduction of fines in cartel cases [2006] OJ C 298/11; Commission Notice on the conduct of settlement procedures in view of the adoption of Decisions pursuant to Article 7 and Article 23 of Council Regulation (EC) No. 1/2003 in cartel cases [2008] OJ C 167/01.

2 See Commission White Paper – Damages actions for breach of the EC antitrust rules, COM (2008) 165, published on 2 April 2008 on DG Comp website.

Commission White Paper – Damages actions for breach of the EC antitrust rules, COM (2008) 165, published on 2 April 2008 on DG Comp website.

C Related economics texts

Bishop and Walker (2009), chapter 5
Carlton and Perloff (2005), chapter 5
Church and Ware (2000), chapter 10
Martin (1994), chapter 6
Martin (2002), chapter 10
Motta (2004), chapter 4
Tirole (1988), chapter 6
Waldman and Jensen (2001), chapters 8 and 9

D Related legal texts

Bellamy and Child (2008), chapters 2, 3, and 5
Jones and Sufrin (2008), chapters 3, 4, and 11
Ritter and Braun (2005), chapters 2, 3, and 8
Whish (2008), chapters 3, 4, 13, and 14

2.1 Price fixing cartels

A Introduction

Price fixing is arguably the most straightforward and clear-cut case of horizontal restriction of competition. It is generally perceived as a hardcore violation of competition rules. The objective is to raise the market price above the competitive level in order to reap economic profits in the form of cartel rents. Agreements to fix prices or the rate of price increases, but also minimum prices, or coordinated and fixed discounts and rebates, are direct means to sustain anticompetitively high prices. Price fixing cartel agreements are often complex and detailed, and can involve overcharges on various price parts, including volume discounts or rebates in addition to unit prices. Cartels often employ price agreements in relatively standardized and homogenous products markets.

B Applicable EU legislation

No special legislation applicable. For applicable legislation see chapter 2, paragraph B.

C Related economics texts

Bishop and Walker (2009), paragraphs 5.07–5.33
Carlton and Perloff (2005), chapter 5
Church and Ware (2000), chapter 10
Martin (1994), chapter 6
Martin (2002), chapter 10
Motta (2004), chapter 4

Tirole (1988), chapter 6
Waldman and Jensen (2001), chapters 8 and 9; chapter 18, paragraph 4

D Related legal texts

Bellamy and Child (2008), chapter 5, paragraph 3(A)
Jones and Sufrin (2008), chapter 11, paragraph 2(C, ii, a and C, iii, b)
Ritter and Braun (2005), chapter 3, paragraph A(2)
Whish (2008), chapter 13, paragraph 3

E Commission decisions in chronological order*

Quinine Commission decision 69/240/EEC [1969] OJ L 192/5, Case IV/26.623 (Martin, 1994,
   p. 200)
Dyestuffs, Matières colorantes Commission decision 69/243/EEC [1969] OJ L 195/11, Case
   IV/26.267 (*) (Martin, 1994, pp. 141–2; Martin, 1994, p. 141; Motta, 2004, pp. 188, 219)
ASPA Commission decision 70/333/EEC [1970] OJ L 148/9, Case IV/299
Carreaux Céramiques (Interest Grouping of German Ceramic Tile Manufacturers) Commission
   decision 71/23/EEC [1971] OJ L 10/15, Case IV/25.107 (Martin, 1994, pp. 181–2)
Nederlandse Cement-Handelsmaatschappij Commission decision 72/68/EEC [1972] OJ L 22/16,
   Case IV/595
Chauffage Central (Central Heating B) Commission decision 72/390/EEC [1972] OJ L 264/22,
   Cases IV/496, 498, 511, 532, 26.238, 26.577
Cementregeling voor Nederland (CRN) Commission decision 72/468/EEC [1972] OJ L 303/7,
   Case IV/581
Cimbel Commission decision 72/474/EEC [1972] OJ L 303/24, Cases IV/242, 244, 245
GISA Commission decision 72/478/EEC [1972] OJ L 303/45, Cases IV/89, 26.349
European sugar industry Commission decision 73/109/EC [1973] OJ L 140/17, Case IV/26.918
   (described in detail as landmark case in section 3.2) (Martin, 1994, p. 142)
Gas water-heaters and bath-heaters Commission decision 73/232/EEC [1973] OJ L 217/34, Case
   IV/25.963
Manufacturers of Glass Containers (IFTRA) **Commission decision 74/292/EEC [1974] OJ L
   160/1, Case IV/400** (Martin, 1994, pp. 164, 183)
Papiers peints de Belgique Commission decision 74/431/EEC [1974] OJ L 373/3, Case IV/426
   (Martin, 1994, p. 181)
Franco-Japanese ballbearings agreement Commission decision 74/634/EEC [1974] OJ L 343/19,
   Case IV/27.095
Preserved Mushrooms Commission decision 75/77/EEC [1977] OJ L 29/26, Case IV/27.039
IFTRA Commission decision 75/497/EEC [1975] OJ L 228/3, Case IV/27.000 (Martin, 1994,
   p. 164)
The Distillers Company Ltd Commission decision 78/163/EEC [1978] OJ L 50/16, Case
   IV/28.282

• Decisions displayed in **bold type** are described in the section. Decisions highlighted with (*) include interesting economic analysis
  by the Commission on the specific topic of the section. Some decisions contain economic reasoning on more than one topic and
  therefore appear in several lists of Commission decisions in chronological order. Reference is made in brackets and **bold type** to the
  relevant section in which the decision is extensively described as a landmark case. When decisions are referenced and/or described
  in some detail in one or more of the economic textbooks, reference in brackets is also made to the relevant part(s) of those texts.

Vegetable Parchment Commission decision 78/252/EEC [1978] OJ L 70/54, Case IV/29.176 (Martin, 1994, pp. 183–4)

FEDETAB Commission decision 78/670/EEC [1978] OJ L 224/29, Cases IV/28.852, 29.127, 29.149

Central Stikstof Verkoopkantoor Commission decision 78/732/EC [1978] OJ L 242/15, Case IV/26.186

BP KEMI-DDSF Commission decision 79/934/EEC [1979] OJ L 235/20, Case IV/29.021

Industrieverband Solnhofener Natursteinplatten eV Commission decision 80/1074/EEC [1980] OJ L 318/32, Case IV/197

Italian Flat Glass Commission decision 81/881/EC [1981] OJ L 326/32, Case IV/29.988 (Bishop and Walker, 2009, 5.07, 5.14; Martin, 1994, pp. 178–9)

SSI Commission decision 82/506/EEC [1982] OJ L 232/1, Cases IV/29.525, 30.000

AROW/BNIC Commission decision 82/896/EEC [1982] OJ L 379/1, Case IV/29.883 (Bishop and Walker, 2009, 5.16)

Vimpoltu Commission decision 83/361/EEC [1983] OJ L 200/44, Case IV/30.174

Cast Iron and Steel Rolls Commission decision 83/546/EEC [1983] OJ L 317/1, Case IV/30.064 (Martin 1994, p. 177)

Nuovo CEGAM Commission decision 84/191/EEC [1984] OJ L 99/29, Case IV/30.804

Flat-Glas (Benelux) Commission decision 84/388/EEC [1984] OJ L 212/13, Case IV/30.988

Zinc Producer Group Commission decision 84/405/EEC [1984] OJ L 220/27, Case IV/30.350

Peroxygen Products Commission decision 85/74/EEC [1985] OJ L 35/1, Case IV/30.907

Fire Insurance (D) Commission decision 85/75/EEC [1985] OJ L 35/20, Case IV/30.307

Milchförderungsfonds Commission decision 85/76/EEC [1985] OJ L 35/35, Case IV/28.930

Wood Pulp Commission decision 85/202/EEC [1985] OJ L 85/1, Case IV/29.725 (*) (Martin, 1994, pp. 142–3; Motta, 2004, pp. 211–19)

Aluminium Commission decision 85/206/EEC [1985] OJ L 92/1, Case IV/26.870

P & I clubs Commission decision 85/615/EEC [1985] OJ L 376/2, Case IV/30.737

Polypropylene Commission decision 86/398/EEC [1986] OJ L 230/1, Case IV/31.149

Roofing Felt Commission decision 86/399/EEC [1986] OJ L 232/15, Case IV/31.371 (**described in detail as landmark case in section** 2.7)

Meldoc Commission decision 86/596/EEC [1986] OJ L 348/50, Case IV/31.204

New potatoes Commission decision 88/109/EEC [1988] OJ L 59/25, Case IV/31.735

Publishers Association/Net Book Agreements Commission decision 89/44/EEC [1989] OJ L 22/12, Cases IV/27.394, 27.393 (Martin, 1994, pp. 522–3)

Flat Glass Commission decision 89/93/EEC [1989] OJ L 33/44, Case IV/31.906

PVC Commission decision 89/190/EEC [1989] OJ L 74/1, Case IV/31.865

LdPE Commission decision 89/191/EEC [1989] OJ L 74/21, Case IV/31.866

Welded Steel Mesh Commission decision 89/515/EEC [1989] OJ L 260/1, Case IV/31.553

Concordato Incendio Commission decision 90/25/EEC [1990] OJ L 15/25, Case IV/32.265

TEKO Commission decision 90/92/EEC [1990] OJ L 13/34, Case IV/32.408

Eurocheque: Helsinki Agreements Commission decision 92/212/EEC [1992] OJ L 95/50, Case IV/30.717

Scottish Salmon Board Commission decision 92/444/EEC [1992] OJ L 246/37, Case IV/33.494

Lloyd's Underwriters Association & Institute of London Underwriters Commission decision 93/3/EEC [1993] OJ L 4/26, Cases IV/32.797, 32.798

Tariff Structures Combined transport of goods Commission decision 93/174/EEC [1993] OJ L 73/38, Case IV/34.494

CNSD Commission decision 93/438/EEC [1993] OJ L 203/27, Case IV/33.407

PVC Commission decision 94/599/EEC [1994] OJ L 239/14, Case IV/31.865

Cartonboard Commission decision 94/601/EEC [1994] OJ L 243/1, Case IV/33.833

Cement Commission decision 94/815/EEC [1994] OJ L 343/1, 33.126, Case IV/33.322

Transatlantic Agreement Commission decision 94/980/EEC [1994] OJ L 376/1, Case IV/34.446

Far Eastern Freight Conference Commission decision 94/985/EEC [1994] OJ L 378/17, Case IV/33.218

SCK/FNK Commission decision 95/551/EC [1995] OJ L 312/79, Cases IV/34.216, 34.179, 34.202

Fenex Commission decision 96/438/EC [1996] OJ L 181/28, Case IV/34.983 (Bishop and Walker, 2009, 5.16)

Ferry Operators Commission decision 97/84/EC [1997] OJ L 26/23, Case IV/34.503

Preinsulated Pipes Commission decision 1999/60/EC [1999] OJ L 24/1, Case IV/35.691

British Sugar Commission decision 1999/210/EC [1999] OJ L 76/1, Cases IV/33.708, 33.709, 33.710, 33.711

TACA Commission decision 1999/243/EC [1999] OJ L 95/1, Case IV/35.134

Greek Ferries Commission decision 1999/271/EC [1999] OJ L 109/24, Case IV/34.446

P&I Clubs Commission decision 1999/329/EC [1999] OJ L 125/12, Case IV/30.373

Europe Asia Trade Agreement Commission decision 1999/485/EC [1999] OJ L 193/23, Case IV/34.250

Reims II + 13 Commission decision 1999/695/EC [1999] OJ L 275/17, Case IV/36.748

FEG and TU Commission decision 2000/117/EC [2001] OJ L 39/1, Case IV/33.884

FETTCSA Commission decision 2000/627/EC [2000] OJ L 268/1, Case IV/34.018

Amino Acids Commission decision 2001/418/EC [2001] OJ L 152/24, Case COMP/36.545/F3

Sodium gluconate Commission decision of 2 October 2001, not yet published, Case COMP/36.756

Graphite Electrodes Commission decision 2002/271/EC [2002] OJ L 100/1, COMP/E-1/36.490 (Bishop and Walker, 2009, 5.07)

Citric Acid Commission decision 2002/742/EC [2002] OJ L 239/18, Case COMP/E-1/36 604

Speciality graphite/PO Commission decision of 17 December 2002, published on DG Comp website, Case COMP/37.667

Vitamins **Commission decision 2003/2/EC [2003] OJ L 6/1, Case COMP/E-1/37.512** (Bishop and Walker, 2009, 5.07, 5.14)

Soda-ash – Solvay/CFK Commission decision 2003/5/EC [2003] OJ L 10/1, COMP/33.133-B

Bank charges for exchanging euro-zone currencies – Germany Commission decision 2003/25/EC [2003] OJ L 15/1, Case COMP/E-1/37.919

Revised TACA Commission decision 2003/68/EC [2003] OJ L 26/53, Case COMP/37.396/D2

Industrial and medical gases Commission decision 2003/355/EC OJ L 123/49, Case COMP/E-3/36.700

Zinc phosphate Commission decision 2003/437/EC [2003] OJ L 153/1, Case COMP/E-1/37.027

Interbrew and Alken-Maes 2003/569/EC [2003] OJ L 200/1, Case IV/37.614/F3

PO/French Beef Commission decision 2003/600/EC [2003] OJ L 209/12, Case COMP/C.38.279/F3

Methionine Commission decision 2003/674/EC [2003] OJ L 255/1, Case C.37.159

Sorbates Commission decision of 1 October 2003, published on DG Comp website, Case COMP/E-1/37.370

PO/Organic peroxides Commission decision of 10 December 2003, published on DG Comp website, Case COMP/E-2/37.857

Methylglucamine Commission decision 2004/104/EC [2004] OJ L 38/18, Case COMP/E-2/37.978

Reims II renotification Commission decision 2004/139/EC [2004] OJ L 56/76, Case COMP/C/38.170

Austrian Banks – Lombard Club Commission decision 2004/138/EC [2004] OJ L 56/1, Case COMP/36.571/D-1

Food Flavor Enhancers Commission decision 2004/206/EC [2004] OJ L 75/1, Case COMP/C.37.671

Carbonless Paper Commission decision 2004/337/EC [2004] OJ L 115/1, Case COMP/E-1/36.212

Electrical and mechanical carbon and graphite products Commission decision 2004/420/EC [2004] OJ L 125/45, Case COMP/38.359

Industrial copper tubes Commission decision 2004/421/EC [2004] OJ L 125/50, Case COMP/38.240

Fee scale of the Belgian architects' association Commission decision of 24 June 2004, published on DG Comp website, Case COMP/38.549

Sodium gluconate Commission decision of 29 September 2004, published on DG Comp website, Case COMP/36.756

Raw tobacco Spain Commission decision of 20 October 2004, published on DG Comp website, Case COMP/C.38.238/B2

Choline chloride Commission decision of 9 December 2004, published on DG Comp website, Case COMP/E-2/37.533

Monochloroacetic acid Commission decision of 19 January 2005, published on DG Comp website, Case COMP/E-1/37.773

Plasterboard Commission decision 2005/471/EC [2005] OJ L 166/8, Case COMP/E-1/37.152

Fine Art Auction Houses **Commission decision 2005/590/EC [2005] OJ L 200/92, Case COMP/E-2/37.784**

Industrial Thread Commission decision of 14 September 2005, published on DG Comp website, Case COMP/38.337

Raw tobacco Italy Commission decision of 20 October 2005, published on DG Comp website, Case COMP/C.38.281/B2

Industrial bags Commission decision of 30 November 2005, published on DG Comp website, Case COMP/F-3/38.354

Rubber chemicals Commission decision of 21 December 2005, published on DG Comp website, Case COMP/F-1/38.443

Hydrogene peroxide and perborate Commission decision of 3 May 2006, published on DG Comp website, Case COMP/38.620

Copper plumbing tubes Commission decision 2006/485/EC [2006] OJ L 192/21, Case C.38.069

Acrylic glass producers Commission decision of 31 May 2006, published on DG Comp website, Case COMP/38.645

Bitumen in the Netherlands Commission decision of 13 September 2006, published on DG Comp website, Case COMP/38.456 (*)

Copper fittings Commission decision of 20 September 2006, published on DG Comp website, Case COMP/38.121

Steel beams (readopted) Commission decision of 8 November 2006, published on DG Comp website, Case COMP/38.907

Synthetic rubber Commission decision of 29 November 2006, published on DG Comp website, Case COMP/38.638

Gas insulated switchgear Commission decision of 24 January 2007, published on DG Comp website, Case COMP/38.899

Elevators and escalators Commission decision of 21 February 2007, published on DG Comp website, Case COMP/38.823 (*)

Netherlands beer producers Commission decision of 18 April 2007, published on DG Comp website, Case COMP/37.766

Fasteners and attaching machines Commission decision of 19 September 2007, published on DG Comp website, Case COMP/39.168

Bitumen suppliers Commission decision of 3 October 2007, published on DG Comp website, Case COMP/38.710

Groupement des Cartes Bancaires Commission decision of 17 October 2007, published on DG Comp website, Case COMP/38.606

Professional videotape producers Commission decision of 20 November 2007, published on DG Comp website, Case COMP/38.432

Flat Glass Commission decision of 28 November 2007, published on DG Comp website, Case COMP/39.165

Chloroprene rubber Commission decision of 5 December 2007, not yet published, Case COMP/38.629

Synthetic rubber producers Commission decision of 23 January 2008, published on DG Comp website, Case COMP/38.628

International Removal Services Commission decision of 11 March 2008, published on DG Comp website, Case COMP/38.543

Sodium chlorate paper bleach producers Commission decision of 11 June 2008, published on DG Comp website, Case COMP/38.695

Aluminium fluoride producers Commission decision of 25 June 2008, not yet published, Case COMP/39.180

Wax producers Commission decision of 1 October 2008, not yet published, Case COMP/39.181

Banana suppliers Commission decision of 15 October 2008, published on DG Comp website, Case COMP/39.188

Marine hose producers Commission decision of 28 January 2009, not yet published, Case COMP/39.406

Calcium carbide and magnesium based reagents Commission decision of 22 July 2009, not yet published, Case COMP/39.396

Concrete reinforcing bar Commission decision of 30 September 2009, not yet published, Case COMP/37.956

Heat stabilisers Commission decision of 11 November 2009, not yet published, Case COMP/38.589

F Economic landmark cases

F.1 *Manufacturers of Glass Containers (IFTRA)* Commission decision 74/292/EEC [1974] OJ L 160/1

Relevance: The first case in which the Commission adopts an economic approach to price competition and collusion. The Commission affirms that competitive behaviors should be based on price competition and that the price charged should be the result of the level of efficiency and viability of a firm. Uncertainty about competitors' behavior and reactions, which are both eliminated in case of price collusion, are also recognized as a structural element of a competitive market.

- Case IV/400
- **Decision:** Infringement of Article 101(1) FEU Treaty

- **Decision addressee(s):**
  - Gerresheimer Glas Aktiengesellschaft, *Federal Republic of Germany*
  - Veba-Glas, *Federal Republic of Germany*
  - H. Heye Glasfabrik "Schauenstein", *Federal Republic of Germany*
  - Himly, Holscher & Co. KG Glasfabrik, *Federal Republic of Germany*
  - Bayerische Flaschen-Glashüttenwerke Wiegand & Söhne GmbH, *Federal Republic of Germany*
  - Carl. Aug. Heinz Glashüttenwerke, *Federal Republic of Germany*
  - Lüner Glashüttenwerke GmbH, *Federal Republic of Germany*
  - Glashüttenwerke Ernst W. Müller Gmbh, *Federal Republic of Germany*
  - Noelle & von Campe Glashütte GmbH, *Federal Republic of Germany*
  - Oberland-Glas Gmbh Glas Fabrik Dr. Harry Wiegand, *Federal Republic of Germany*
  - Spessarter Hohlglaswerke GmbH, *Federal Republic of Germany*
  - Tettauer Glashüttenwerke, *Federal Republic of Germany*
  - Weck Glaswerk GmbH, *Federal Republic of Germany*
  - Verlica-Momignies SA, *Belgium*
  - Bouteilleries Belges Reunies SA, *Belgium*
  - NV Vereenigde Glasfabrieken (United Glasswork), *the Netherlands*
  - Boussois-Souchon-Neuvesel (BSN) SA, *France*
  - Saint-Gobain Emballage SA, *France*
  - Verreries de Blanc-Misseron SA, *France*
  - Verrerie Ouvriere d'Albi SA, *France*
  - Verreries du Puy-de Dôme SA, *France*
  - Bordoni Miva Vetrerie Riunite SpA, *Italy*
  - Aziende Vetraie Italiane Ricciardi AVIR SpA, *Italy*
  - Vetreria Italiana VETR.I. SpA, *Italy*
- **Report route:** Notification for exemption submitted to the Commission on 30 October 1962 by Dr. A.E. Rüdell for the International Fair Trade Practice Rules Administration (IFTRA)
- **Date of the decision:** 15 May 1974
- **Competition Commissioner:** A. Borschette
- **Relevant product market:** Containers in hollow glass (bottles, jars and flasks)
- **Relevant geographical market:** European internal market
- **Description of the case**
  - a. **Relevant facts**

    In March 1955 Belgian, Dutch, and German manufacturers of glass containers (listed above) signed the IFTRA agreement concerning the bottles market, and subsequently also applied it to the Belgian and Dutch markets for jars and flasks. They were joined by five French manufacturers in April 1960 and after initially being limited to the market for bottles, extended the IFTRA rules in 1971 to apply to the production of all glass containers. Italian producers joined the agreement rather sporadically starting in 1961 but terminated their participation in 1971 completely. The implementation of the IFTRA rules was guaranteed through periodical meetings (annual).

    The IFTRA rules were a complex and elaborate set of rules essentially aimed at the maintenance of common prices in each country affected by the agreement, a constant exchange of information among all the signatories about the adopted price and a guarantee of the actual implementation of the rules. The first set of rules (Group A) prohibited the members of the agreement to adopt so-called *unfair practices*. This was *de facto* a prohibition to adopt competitive behavior on price and an obligation to follow the price set by the national producer holding the larger share of the market (*natural price leader*).[3] Under Group A rules the parties were prohibited to sell below cost, to systematically undercut a competitor's price or match its offer, to adopt discriminatory prices (different for different customers) and rebates, to grant special conditions of sales, and to treat bulk sales differently. It was furthermore considered *unfair* and thus prohibited to tie products with an excess of supply to products with scarcity of supply, to imitate trademarks or other distinguished competitors' features with the aim of misleading customers and – above all – to deviate from the price list published. In case of application of discriminatory prices and/or deviation from the published price, to justify its conduct the burden of proof was on the alleged infringer to give a valid reason. Group B rules imposed the obligation to issue public price lists, prohibited predatory pricing and in particular requested a common way to calculate the costs according to *customary rules*.[4] Group C obliged the parties to inform their competitors about their pricing policy. Finally, Group D and E of the IFTRA rules even recognized the right to claim for damages suffered by a competitor in case of *unfair* practices and prescribed the procedure to obtain them through an arbitration panel and in the second instance with recourse to an international Court of arbitration.

Documents concerning the meetings held by the participants to the agreement showed that the two main concerns discussed during those meetings were the fixing of the export prices and the adoption of a reliable system for exchanging information about prices. Regarding the export prices, the system was set in such a way that, adjusting the prices according to the one fixed by the national producer dominating the market and subsequently communicated to the other parties, each party would have not suffered price competition in its own national market. The necessity of a constant flow of information among all parties was emphasized regularly at the IFTRA meetings and it was initially solved through the setting up of *national price information offices* in each country involved. From 1970 it was decided to continue the information flow between the producers directly, "but suspicions should not be aroused that such a direct exchange of information would result in an agreement on the prices to be offered to individual customers."[5]

Furthermore as additional agreements, on the one side the parties established a common system of calculating the prices enabling them to "reach similar if not identical cost curves."[6] On the other side, they also agreed upon the adoption of a delivered-price system according to which areas of distribution in which the producers would have applied the same average transportation costs were established.

---

3   See recital 11 of the decision.
4   See recital 1 of the decision. Emphasis added.
5   Recital 17 of the decision, quote from the minute of one of the meetings held by the parties.
6   Recital 20 of the decision.

The Commission carried out an analysis of the market structure. The glass containers industry as a result was characterized by the presence of few very large actors with a relevant market share (eight main producers in Europe). In each national market there were either a single (monopolist) producer holding an extremely large market share (different for each type of container) or two or three main producers supplying almost the entire market. The manufactured products were largely homogenous. The demand had expanded considerably in the period in question so that on some occasions many producers found themselves with insufficient capacity.[7]

b. Origin of the case

On 30 October 1962 Dr. A.E. Rüdell (the IFTRA lawyer) submitted to the Commission a notification pursuant to Article 4 of Regulation 17 to see the International Fair Trade Practice Rules Administration (IFTRA) be declared exempted from the application of Article 101(1) FEU Treaty by virtue of Article 101(3) FEU Treaty.

c. Economic analysis

The Commission approach toward price fixing agreements has always been very rigorous. The Commission has consistently looked at them as a means of achieving artificially high prices and profits through collusion.

In the present decision the Commission carried out an economically oriented analysis of the anticompetitive effect of a price fixing agreement for the first time.

Starting from the consideration that the IFTRA rules considered as *unfair* the practice of offering prices systematically lower than those of a competitor, the Commission stated that "such provisions thus tend to prevent competitive behavior, such as the practice of the most efficient and viable undertaking offering lower prices than those of its competitors, or applying special prices and discounts to achieve penetration of the market. Within the common market such provisions ensure that a producer . . . will not, in delivering goods in the territory of another party, disturb the price-level in that market, nor apply prices which are lower than those of the IFTRA partner who is considered the local or national price-leader . . . The aim of preventing competition is all the more apparent if it is considered in conjunction with the agreements made between the parties for the exchange of respective price lists, discounts, and terms of trade."[8]

The Commission noted the restrictive effect on competition of such contractual clauses, in particular it stressed that "[b]y such means the possibility of unforeseen or unforeseeable reactions by competitors is sought to be eliminated, thus removing a large element of the risk normally attaching to any individual action in the market."[9]

---

7   For a more detailed analysis of the relevant product market, see recitals 23–31 of the decision.

8   Recitals 35 and 36 of the decision.

9   Recital 43 of the decision. In its early case law the ECJ had already stressed that price fixing collusion led undertakings eliminating all uncertainty between them as to their future conduct and, in doing so, also eliminating a large part of the risk usually inherent in any independent change of conduct on one or several markets. Furthermore it stated that the undertakings in question temporarily eliminated, with respect to prices, some of the preconditions for competition on the market which stood in the way of the achievement of parallel uniformity of conduct. See, Case 48/69 *Imperial Chemical Industries Ltd.* v. *Commission of the European Communities*, recitals 101–103.

The restrictive effect of the rules was strengthened by the agreement on the common calculation of prices that for the Commission ". . . has a direct effect on the process of determining [the] price of each undertaking in question, since it enables the latter to more easily compare their respective prices and thus to coordinate their action on the market."[10]

Finally the delivered price system would have "nullif[ied] any competitive advantage which a producer of glass containers might gain from the proximity to his customers."[11]

The Commission approach to the agreement was to undertake a rigorous analysis of the market's features. In fact, there were many elements facilitating collusion such as the oligopolistic market structure and the homogeneity of the products (of large-scale consumption) that the Commission emphasized. Furthermore the cartel was organized in such a way that detection and punishment of potential cheaters was almost guaranteed (the parties were allowed to claim damages and refer to arbitration panels) and the nature of the products was such that the firms could exclusively compete on price (precisely that kind of competition completely eliminated by the agreement).[12]

d. Fines, remedies, and conditions enclosed
  – Obligations for all the undertakings concerned to bring the infringements to an end.[13]

e. Further developments of the case
  None.

F.2 *Vitamins* Commission decision 2003/2/EC [2003] OJ L 6/1

Relevance: One of the highest fines imposed in the history of European competition law enforcement upon companies involved in a cartel. Confirmation of Commission's increasingly tougher stance on price-fixing (hardcore) cartels.

- Case COMP/E-1/37.512
- **Decision:** Infringement of Article 101 (1) FEU Treaty, imposition of fines
- **Decision addressee(s):**
  – F. Hoffmann – La Roche, *Switzerland*
  – BASF AG, *Germany*
  – Aventis SA, *France*
  – Takeda Chemical Industries Ltd, *Japan*
  – Merck KgaA, *Germany*
  – Daiichi Pharmaceutical Co. Ltd, *Japan*
  – Lonza AG, *Switzerland*
  – Solvay Pharmaceuticals BV, *the Netherlands*
  – Eisai Co. Ltd, *Japan*
  – Kongo Chemical Co. Ltd, *Japan*
  – Sumitomo Chemical Co. Ltd, *Japan*

---

10 Recital 46 of the decision.
11 Recital 48 of the decision. In the same recital the Commission also provided more detailed analysis of the anticompetitive effects of the delivering system.
12 See recital 50 of the decision.
13 For a complete list of all the IFTRA rules considered in breach of Article 101, see Article 1 of the decision.

- Sumika Fine Chemicals Ltd, *Japan*
- Tanabe Seiyaku Co. Ltd, *Japan*
- **Report route:** On 12 May 1999 Rhône-Poulenc (Aventis) applied for leniency pursuant to the *Commission notice on the non-application or reduction of fines in cartel cases*. On 6 July 2000 the Commission decided to initiate a proceeding
- **Date of the decision:** 21 November 2001
- **Competition Commissioner:** M. Monti
- **Relevant product market:** Vitamins A, B1, B2, B5, B6, C, D3, E, H, folic acid, beta-carotene, and carotinoids
- **Relevant geographical market:** Global market
- **Description of the case**
  a. **Relevant facts**

  Between 1989 and 1999 the world's largest vitamins producers listed above devised a set of agreements of different nature and duration, effectively creating a global cartel. By means of their agreements "they fixed the prices for different products, allocated quotas of the same markets, agreed on prices increases, issued price announcement in accordance with their agreements, sold the product at the agreed prices, set up a machinery to monitor and enforce adherence to their agreement, and participated in a structure of regular meetings to implement their plans."[14]

  The market for vitamins was strongly oligopolistic with the world's three leading producers holding a market share in the order of 75–95 percent. La Roche had a 50 percent market share at the time, BASF held 20–30 percent and Aventis 5–15 percent, respectively. Vitamins A and E constituted half of the total market for vitamins. The two main actors of the global market (La Roche and BASF) were active in all vitamins markets with the exception that BASF did not produce vitamins B6 and folic acid. The remaining actors were each active in a fewer number of markets.

  The first cartel, installed in 1989, targeted the markets for vitamins A and E. The structure of the cartel was laid out in detail by senior executives who were responsible for vitamins marketing at La Roche, BASF, Rhône-Poulenc,[15] and Eisai, the four large producers of the world. Together with a group of product managers they determined the size of the relevant markets and agreed between the four of them on quotas "on the basis of their respective achieved sales in 1988."[16] The participants ordered that *price before volumes* be the underlying principle on which the cartel was to be based.

  The structure of the cartel consisted of agreements kept on four different organizational levels of the participating producers and was maintained by regular meetings of representatives from each of the four levels:
  - *Top level.* At the top the cartel was run by senior managers of the participating companies, ensuring that the agreement was supported and devising the overall strategy of the cartel.
  - *Heads of marketing.* Besides attending the top-level meetings, they decided on the practical operation of the agreement and finalized the budget.

---

14 Recital 2 of the decision.
15 Rhône-Poulenc had changed its name to Aventis by the time of the decision.

16 Recital 163 of the decision.

- *Global product marketing level.* At this level there were quarterly meetings of product marketing managers assessing and controlling the implementation of the quota system.
- *Regional product marketing level.* The meetings at this level were organized by the regional management and were held to ensure the implementation of the cartel at a regional level, while taking developments in the relevant market in that region into account and deciding whether to grant special sales conditions to individual customers.

The main purpose of the entire structure was to properly prepare the "budget meetings" (always organized by La Roche) in which the market quota ("annual budget") for each firm was established, the actual sales were compared with the fixed "budget," and where the price increases were set according to the *price before volumes* principle, i.e. usually in steps of 5 percent.[17] For each agreed price increase, the parties chose one firm to announce the increase first before the remaining firms followed. "In this way the concerted price increases could be passed off, if challenged, as a result of price leadership in an oligopolistic market."[18]

The same cartel structure was then used to set up other similar cartels for each of the vitamins listed above.[19] La Roche played the role of leader in all those cartels.[20]

When the Commission adopted the decision, the same set of cartels in the global vitamins markets, had already been prosecuted in the US and Canadian jurisdiction by the competent competition authorities (the Department of Justice and the Canadian Commissioner for Competition).[21]

b. Origin of the case

On 12 May 1999 Rhône-Poulenc announced to the Commission its intention to inform it about its and other undertakings' involvement in a vitamins cartel pursuant to the *Commission notice on the non-imposition or reduction of fines in cartel cases* ("the leniency notice").[22] Following that application for leniency, in the next five months La Roche, BASF, Solvay Pharmaceuticals, Takeda, Daiichi, Tanabe, Eisai, Lonza, and Merck also provided further information to the Commission concerning their participation in the cartel. On 6 July 2000, the Commission decided to initiate proceedings against the cartel.

---

17 For a more detailed description of the cartel's organization and implementation structure, see recitals 160–242.
18 Recital 204 of the decision.
19 For a detailed description of each single cartel, see recitals 243–564.
20 Following a trend developed since the fight against hardcore cartels has been strengthened and since the Leniency Program has been implemented, in order to show the enormous amount of information available about each firm involved and in this way giving a sign to the market to stress further and rapid applications for leniency, in the present decision the Commission provided an extremely detailed description of the cartel's structure and of its organization including the minutes of meetings and the role played by each management sector and each undertaking.
21 Some more details about the investigation carried out in the United States and in Canada are provided by the Commission in recitals 149–157.
22 Commission Notice on the non-imposition or reduction of fines in cartel cases [1996] OJ C 207/04. The first version of the *Leniency Program* was substituted by the Commission Notice on immunity from fines and reduction of fines in cartel cases [2002] OJ C 45/3 and has been further renewed by the more recent Commission Notice on immunity from fines and reduction of fines in cartel cases [2006] OJ C 298/11.

c. Economic analysis

The present decision is particularly relevant because it shows the rigor and strength of the Commission's approach toward price fixing cartels (and hard-core restrictions in general). Since price fixing has been constantly considered detrimental to competition since the very beginning of the enforcement activities of the Commission, in the present decision there are no relevant developments in the economics applied by the Commission in the analysis of the scrutinized agreement. As the Commission remarked, "given the manifestly anticompetitive object of the agreements, it is not necessary for an adverse effect upon competition to be demonstrated."[23]

Still, the *Vitamins* case is particularly interesting because it is the clearest example of the current Commission policy toward cartels.

Evidence of the Commission's current position on hardcore cartels can be found throughout the decision, most notably in the use of aggravating circumstances in setting the fine – i.e. the fact that due to Hoffmann – La Roche's role as a ring leader in the cartel the Commission increased the basic amount of the fine by 50 percent. Similarly, the Commission regarded the involvement of senior management officials as sign of the gravity and significance of the infringement.

The Commission's attitude toward price fixing and attempts to conceal it to prevent detection is conveyed by the tone of its description of the meetings during which the cartel was agreed upon. In recital 218 of its decision the Commission states that "Eisai appears to have rationalized the discussions with competitors in terms of antitrust law by meeting each of the three separately for 20 minutes each: it *disingenuously* calls these meetings "courtesy calls." Whatever ambiguity Eisai may have hoped to engender by this *colorable* device, the effect was negated by its inviting all three competitors to a "joint meeting" immediately afterwards in a restaurant."[24]

d. Fines, remedies, and conditions enclosed

- The Commission imposed the following total fines:

Company	Fine (Euros)
Hoffmann-La Roche	462,000 million
BASF AG	296,160 million
Aventis SA	5,040 million
Takeda Chemical Industries Ltd	37,060 million
Solvay Pharmaceuticals BV	9,100 million
Merck KgaA	9,240 million
Daiichi Pharmaceutical Co Ltd	23,240 million
Eisai Co. Ltd	13,230 million

- The total fines imposed were the result of the reductions granted pursuant to the leniency program. The Commission, in consideration of the cooperation provided, granted to the undertakings involved in the cartel agreement the following reductions:

---

23   Recital 594 of the decision.   24   Emphasis added.

Company	(%)
Hoffmann-La Roche	50
BASF AG	50
Aventis SA	100 and 10
Takeda Chemical Industries Ltd	35
Solvay Pharmaceuticals BV	35
Merck KgaA	15
Daiichi Pharmaceutical Co. Ltd	35
Eisai Co. Ltd	30

 – Obligations for all the undertakings concerned to bring the infringements to an end.

e. Further developments of the case

Case T-15/02 *BASF AG* v. *Commission* [2006] ECR II-213, fines reduction.
Joined Cases T-22/02 and 23/02 *Sumitomo Chemical and Sumika Fine Chemicals* v. *Commission* [2005] ECR II-4065, appeal granted.
Case T-26/02 *Daiichi Pharmaceutical* v. *Commission* [2006] ECR II-713,
fine reduction.

F.3 *Fine art auction houses* Commission decision 2005/590/EC [2005], Summary of the decision in OJ L 200/92

Relevance: The decision reaffirms the Commission's approach toward price fixing as the most serious violation of Article 101(1) FEU Treaty. The decision stresses that anticompetitive cartels can appear in every sector.

 * Case COMP/E-2/37.784
 * **Decision:** Infringement of Article 101(1) FEU Treaty
 * **Decision addressee(s):**
   – Christie's International plc, *United Kingdom*
   – Sotheby's Holdings Inc., *United Kingdom* and *United States of America*
 * **Report route:** Christie's application for leniency
 * **Date of the decision:** 30 October 2000
 * **Competition Commissioner:** M. Monti
 * **Relevant product market:** Market for fine arts auction services
 * **Relevant geographical market:** EEA market
 * **Description of the case**
   a. Relevant facts
   The aforementioned parties are the two main worldwide competitors for the sale on commission of fine arts in auctions. Both undertakings provide further services for the owners of the goods that will be sold in an auction, such as selling expertise, arrangement of the auction, production of a catalogue, and creating pre-sale publicity.
   Both auction houses for fine art held auctions in London and New York but also regularly in Geneva, Zurich, Rome, Amsterdam, Milan, Hong Kong, and Melbourne.[25]

---

25   See recital 5 of the decision.

In the period from April 1993 until February 2000, the parties agreed upon fixing commission fees charged to sellers and on other trading conditions.

In January 2000 Christie's had approached the US Department of Justice and the European Commission, providing them with proof of the cartels' existence. Christie's had applied in both jurisdictions for leniency. The company received leniency while Sotheby's received a fine of 6 percent of its annual turnover, i.e. 20.4 million Euros. Further, the company provided decisive evidence without which the cartel would not have been detected as the Commission had not undertaken any investigation at the time of the disclosure of the information. With regard to the application of the leniency notice, the fines for both parties were reduced by the Commission's decision.

b. Origin of the case

In January 2000 Christie's informed the Commission of the existence of the cartel and applied for leniency.

c. Economic analysis

Within the timeframe of six years and nine months, Christie's and Sotheby's agreed upon particular conditions of business relations toward sellers and buyers. The amount payable by the seller as commission is usually calculated on the "hammer price." The seller's commission was no longer calculated on the "hammer price" but within a newly introduced "sliding scale," meaning that the percentage that was charged to sellers as a commission on the sale changed at certain thresholds.[26] These conditions were merely aimed at achieving an increase in the commission paid by sellers at auction. Due to non-negotiable rates the sellers lost their bargaining capabilities. Regarding buyers, the parties agreed to limit the credit terms to ninety days. Furthermore, the parties reached a consensus upon other trading terms, such as advances paid to sellers, payment conditions, and issuing guarantees for auction results. Moreover, the agreement contained a limitation of their marketing efforts to prevent that one party claimed for itself the leadership in the fine art market or in a certain segment.[27] The cartel led by its nature to a distortion of competition "which is of exclusive benefit to the companies participating in the cartel and is highly detrimental to customers."[28]

The cartel functioned by agreeing on restricting competition on a number of parameters. The two chairmen of both auction houses had been meeting in New York and London where they agreed on price fixing. Regular contacts were upheld by the chief executive officers concerning the cartel. Whenever subjects appeared "to encourage competition between them or otherwise conflict or endanger their agreement not to compete,"[29] the companies exchanged information during meetings or (telephone) conversations.

The agreement of the two most important existing competitors in the fine arts sector worldwide had a huge impact on competition and further on the sales in the EEA and the entire EU. Moreover, the cartel lasted for a period of six years and nine months.[30] The size of the relevant geographical market affected by

---

26   See footnote in recital 9 of the decision.
27   See recital 8 of the decision.
28   See recital 13 of the decision.

29   See recital 10 of the decision.
30   See recital 17 of the decision.

the agreement, and the long duration of the cartel, was stressed by the Commission as an evidence for the gravity of the infringement committed by the two parties.

The coverage of the whole common market and the whole EEA and the fact that both companies participated in the cartel without being compelled by the other party led to large fines, which, however, were subsequently reduced for both companies.

d. Fines, remedies, and conditions enclosed
   –   The Commission imposed the following total fines:

Company	Fine (Euros)
Christie's International plc:	0
Sotheby's Holdings Inc.:	20.4 million

   –   Christie's was the first to inform the Commission of the existence of the cartel. With regard to the full cooperation of Christie's, and their confirmation that the contact with Sotheby's had ended, the Commission applied section B of the "1996 leniency notice."[31] Therefore, the company was granted a 100 percent reduction of the fine.
   –   In light of the cooperation and transfer of relevant information to identify the existence of an infringement, Sotheby's was granted a fine reduction of 40 percent.
   –   Obligations for all undertaking to bring the infringement to an end, in so far as they have not done so. Further the undertakings concerned shall refrain from repeating or adopting any similar behaviors in the future.

e. Further developments of the case
   –   None.

2.2 Market sharing, quota cartels, and specialization agreements

A Introduction

Market sharing and quota fixing agreements enable firms to split the market into different groups of customers, or separate the market into geographical areas and allocate to each firm a certain part of the market. Such agreements are collusive and deemed anticompetitive because they establish an artificial fragmentation of the market with separate *de facto* monopolies in each. By way of the agreement, each firm is able to act unconstrained by competitive forces in a predetermined part of the market and charge (near-) monopoly prices by supplying only to a particular group (or quota) of customers. Such agreements obviously involve the coordinated restriction of output and sales volume so as to create artificial scarcity and induce a consequent price increase. Market sharing is often a preferred mechanism of collusion when there are differences in price structure across suppliers. These differences may be the result of variations in product characteristics and asymmetries in cost structures. In such a scenario, it may be difficult to agree on stable cartel prices. Here, market sharing or quota fixing may achieve a more stable

---

31   Commission Notice on the non-imposition or the reduction of fines in cartel cases [1996] OJ C 207/04, p. 4.

collusive outcome than attempts to fix prices. In Europe, market sharing agreements are viewed as particularly grave infringements, because in addition to creating inefficiencies, they obstruct the integration of the internal market which is one of the main goals of the EU.

Through (unilateral or reciprocal) specialization agreements, firms may refrain from producing a certain good and instead purchase it from the other (competing) party. Specialization can realize economies of scale and scope, as well as achieve quality and technology improvements in the production of specific goods. However, specialization agreements can increase each firm's market power to the point where they supply to the other firm on an almost exclusive basis. There is a strong similarity between market sharing and mutual specialization by firms with large market shares. These arrangements can be thought of as market sharing agreements with markets being separated into different products rather than geographical areas.

Due to the fact that there are subtle differences in the Commission's approach toward the two types of agreements, this section will first describe the landmark decisions on specialization agreements, and then those on market sharing and quota cartels.

B Applicable EU legislation

Specialization agreements entered into by competing undertakings with a combined market share of no more than 20 percent, fall under Regulation No. 2658/2000 on the application of Article 81(3) of the EC Treaty to categories of specialization agreements, [2000] OJ L304/3 (Specialization Agreements Block Exemption Regulation).

Specialization agreements involving the transfer of substantial technology and/or know-how, fall under Regulation No. 772/2004 on the application of Article 81(3) of the Treaty to categories of technology transfer agreements, [2004] OJ L 123/11 (Technology Transfer Block Exemption Regulation).

For agreements not covered by the above-mentioned Block Exemption Regulations, general legislation is applicable (see chapter 2, paragraph B).

C Related economics texts

Bishop and Walker (2009), paragraphs 5.07–5.33
Carlton and Perloff (2005), chapter 5
Church and Ware (2000), chapter 10
Martin (1994), chapter 6
Martin (2002), chapter 10
Motta (2004), chapter 4, specifically paragraph 4.1.1
Tirole (1988), chapter 6
Waldman and Jensen (2001), chapters 8 and 9

D Related legal texts

Bellamy and Child (2008), chapter 5, paragraphs 4 and 5
Jones and Sufrin (2008), chapter 11, paragraph 2(C, ii, b, c and C, iii, c, d)
Ritter and Braun (2005), chapter 3, paragraphs A(3, 4) and B(2)
Whish (2008), chapter 13, paragraph 5 and chapter 15, paragraph 6

E Commission decisions in chronological order•

Nicholas Frères & Vitapro Commission decision 64/502/EEC [1964] OJ L 64/2287, Case IV/95

Transocean Marine Paint Association Commission decision 67/454/EEC [1967] OJ L 163/10, Case IV/223

ACEC-Berliet Commission decision 68/319/EEC [1968] OJ L 201/7, Case IV/26.045

Quinine Commission decision 69/240/EEC [1969] OJ L 192/5, Case IV/26.623 (Martin, 1994, p. 200)

Clima Chappee-Buderus Commission decision 69/241/EEC [1969] OJ L 195/1, Case IV/26.625 (Martin, 1994, pp. 184–5)

Jaz-Peter I **Commission decision 69/242/EEC [1969] OJ L 195/5, Case IV/26.437**

Pirelli-Dunlop Commission decision 69/477 [1969] OJ L 323/21, Cases IV/24.470, 24.471

Julien/Van Katwijk Commission decision 70/487/EEC [1970] OJ L 242/18, Case IV/128, 1968 (Martin, 1994, pp. 180–1)

FN/CF Commission decision 71/222/EEC [1971] OJ L 134/6, Case IV/26.624

Sopelem/Langen Commission decision 72/24/EEC [1972] OJ L 13/47, Case IV/26.418

Nederlandse Cement-Handelsmaatschappij Commission decision 72/68/EEC [1972] OJ L 22/16, Case IV/595

MAN/Saviem Commission decision 72/88/EEC [1972] OJ L 31/29, Case IV/26.612

Wild-Leitz Commission decision 72/128/EEC [1972] OJ L 61/27, Case IV/26.844

Papier Mince Commission decision 72/291/EEC [1972] OJ L 182/24, Case IV/642

Chauffage Central (Central Heating B) Commission decision 72/390/EEC [1972] OJ L 264/22, Cases IV/496, 498, 511, 532, 26.238, 26.577 (*)

Cementregeling voor Nederland (CRN) Commission decision 72/468/EEC [1972] OJ L 303/7, Case IV/581

Cimbel Commission decision 72/474/EEC [1972] OJ L 303/24, Cases IV/242, 244, 245

GISA Commission decision 72/478/EEC [1972] OJ L 303/45, Cases IV/89, 26.349

European sugar industry Commission decision 73/109/EC [1973] OJ L 140/17, Case IV/26.918 (**described in detail as landmark case in section 3.2**) (*)(Martin, 1994, p. 142)

PRYM-BEKA Commission decision 73/323/EEC [1973] OJ L 296/24, Case IV/26.825

Transocean Marine Paint Association Commission decision 74/16/EEC [1974] OJ L 19/18, Case IV/223

Kali und Salz/Kali-Chemie Commission decision 74/17/EEC [1974] OJ L 19/22, Case IV/795 (*)

Manufacturers of Glass Containers (IFTRA) Commission decision 74/292/EEC [1974] OJ L 160/1, Case IV/400 (**described in detail as landmark case in section 2.1**) (Martin, 1994, pp. 164, 183)

Advocaat Zwarte Kip Commission decision 74/432/EEC [1974] OJ L 237/12, Case IV/28.374

Preserved Mushrooms Commission decision 75/77/EEC [1977] OJ L 29/26, Case IV/27.039

IFTRA Commission decision 75/497/EEC [1975] OJ L 228/3, Case IV/27.000 (Martin, 1994, p. 164)

• Decisions displayed in **bold type** are described in the section. Decisions highlighted with (*) include interesting economic analysis by the Commission on the specific topic of the section. Some decisions contain economic reasoning on more than one topic and therefore appear in several lists of Commission decisions in chronological order. Reference is made in brackets and **bold type** to the relevant section in which the decision is extensively described as a landmark case. When decisions are referenced and/or described in some detail in one or more of the economic textbooks, reference in brackets is also made to the relevant part(s) of those texts.

Transocean Marine Paint Association Commission decision 75/649/EEC [1975] OJ L 286/24, Case IV/223

Bayer/Gist-Brocades Commission decision 76/172/EEC [1976] OJ L 30/13, Case IV/27.073

COBELPA/VNP Commission decision 77/592/EEC [1977] OJ L 242/10, Cases IV/312, 366 (Martin, 1994, p. 183)

The Distillers Company Ltd Commission decision 78/163/EEC [1978] OJ L 50/16, Case IV/28.282

Jaz-Peter II Commission decision 78/194/EEC [1978] OJ L 61/17, Case IV/26.437

SNPE-LEL Commission decision 78/571/EEC [1978] OJ L 191/41, Case IV/29.453

Central Stikstof Verkoopkantoor Commission decision 78/732/EC [1978] OJ L 242/15, Case IV/26.186

White Lead Commission decision 79/90/EEC [1979] OJ L 21/16, Case IV/29.535

BP KEMI-DDSF Commission decision 79/934/EEC [1979] OJ L 235/20, Case IV/29.021

Transocean Marine Paint Association Commission decision 80/184/EEC [1980] OJ L 39/73, Case IV/223

Italian Cast Glass **Commission decision 80/1334/EEC [1980] OJ L 383/19, Case IV/29.869**

Italian Flat Glass Commission decision 81/881/EC [1981] OJ L 326/32, Case IV/29.988 (Bishop and Walker, 2009, 5.07, 5.14; Martin, 1994, pp. 178–9)

Navewa – Anseau Commission decision 82/371/EEC [1982] OJ L 167/17, Case IV/29.995

Rolled zinc products and zinc alloys Commission decision 82/866/EEC [1982] OJ L 362/40, Case IV/29.629

Toltecs-Dorcet Commission decision 82/897/EEC [1982] OJ L 379/19, Case IV/30.128

Cast Iron and Steel Rolls Commission decision 83/546/EEC [1983] OJ L 317/1, Case IV/30.064 (Martin 1994, p. 177)

IPTC Belgium Commission decision 83/667/EEC [1983] OJ L 376/7, Case IV/30.671

BPCL/ICI **Commission decision 84/387/EEC [1984] OJ L 212/1, Case IV/30.863**

Flat-Glas (Benelux) Commission decision 84/388/EEC [1984] OJ L 212/13, Case IV/30.988

Zinc Producer Group Commission decision 84/405/EEC [1984] OJ L 220/27, Case IV/30.350

Peroxygen Products Commission decision 85/74/EEC [1985] OJ L 35/1, Case IV/30.907

Aluminium Commission decision 85/206/EEC [1985] OJ L 92/1, Case IV/26.870

Siemens/Fanuc Commission decision 85/618/EEC [1985] OJ L 376/29, Case IV/30.739

Polypropylene Commission decision 86/398/EEC [1986] OJ L 230/1, Case IV/31.149

Roofing Felt Commission decision 86/399/EEC [1986] OJ L 232/15, Case IV/31.371 (**described in detail as landmark case in section 2.7**) (*)

Meldoc Commission decision 86/596/EEC OJ L 348/50, Case IV/31.204

ENI/Montedison Commission decision 87/3/EEC [1987] OJ L 5/13, Case IV/31.055

New potatoes Commission decision 88/109/EEC [1988] OJ L 59/25, Case IV/31.735

Transocean Marine Paint Association Commission decision 88/635/EEC [1988] OJ L 351/40, Case IV/223

Flat Glass Commission decision 89/93/EEC [1989] OJ L 33/44, Case IV/31.906

Decca Navigator System Commission decision 89/113/EC [1989] OJ L 43/27, Cases IV/30.979, 31.394 (**described in detail as landmark case in section 3.8**)

PVC Commission decision 89/190/EEC [1989] OJ L 74/1, Case IV/31.865

LdPE Commission decision 89/191/EEC [1989] OJ L 74/21, Case IV/31.866

Welded Steel Mesh Commission decision 89/515/EEC [1989] OJ L 260/1, Case IV/31.553

Sugar Beet Commission decision 90/45/EEC [1990] OJ L 31/32, Case IV/32.414

Soda-ash – Solvay/ICI Commission decision 91/297/EEC [1991] OJ L 152/1, Case IV/33.133a (*) (Motta, 2004, p. 187)

Soda-ash – Solvay/CFK Commission decision 91/298/EEC [1991] OJ L 152/1, Case IV/33.133b

French-West African Shipowners' Committees Commission decision 92/262/EEC [1992] OJ L 134/1, Case IV/32.450

Quantel International – continuum/Quantel SA Commission decision 92/427/EEC [1992] OJ L 235/9, Cases IV/32.800, 33.335

Cewal, Cowac, Ukwal Commission decision 93/82/EEC [1993] OJ L 34/20, Cases IV/32.448, 32.450 (Motta, 2004, p. 144)

Auditel Commission decision 93/668/EEC [1993] OJ L 306/50, Cases IV/32.031, 32.366, 32.404

Stichting Certificatie Kraanverhuurbedrijf and FNK Commission decision 94/272/EEC [1994] OJ L 117/30, Case IV/B-2/34.179

PVC Commission decision 94/599/EEC [1994] OJ L 239/14, Case IV/31.865

Cartonboard Commission decision 94/601/EEC [1994] OJ L 243/1, Case IV/33.833

Cement Commission decision 94/815/EEC [1994] OJ L 343/1, 33.126, Case IV/33.322

Transatlantic Agreement Commission decision 94/980/EEC [1994] OJ L 376/1, Case IV/34.446

SCK/FNK Commission decision 95/551/EC [1995] OJ L 312/79, Cases IV/34.216, 34.179, 34.202

Preinsulated Pipes Commission decision 1999/60/EC [1999] OJ L 24/1, Case IV/35.691 (*)

TACA Commission decision 1999/243/EC [1999] OJ L 95/1, Case IV/35.134

Amino Acids Commission decision 2001/418/EC [2001] OJ L 152/24, Case COMP/36.545/F3

SAS Maersk Air and Sun-Air Commission decision 2001/716/EC [2001] OJ L 265/15, Case COMP/D.2 37.444 (Bishop and Walker, 2009, 5.07)

Sodium gluconate Commission decision of 2 October 2001, not yet published, Case COMP/36.756

Graphite Electrodes Commission decision 2002/271/EC [2002] OJ L 100/1, COMP/E-1/36.490 (*)(Bishop and Walker, 2009, 5.07)

Citric Acid Commission decision 2002/742/EC [2002] OJ L 239/18, Case COMP/E-1/36.604 (*)

Luxembourg Brewers Commission decision 2002/759/EC [2002] OJ L 352/21, Case COMP/37.800/F3

Speciality graphite/PO Commission decision of 17 December 2002, published on DG Comp website, Case COMP/37.667

Vitamins Commission decision 2003/2/EC [2003] OJ L 6/1, Case COMP/E-1/37.512 (**described in detail as landmark case in section 2.1**) (*) (Bishop and Walker, 2009, 5.07, 5.14)

Soda-ash – Solvay/CFK Commission decision 2003/5/EC [2003] OJ L 10/1, Case COMP/33.133-B

Industrial and medical gases Commission decision 2003/355/EC OJ L 123/49, Case COMP/E-3/36.700

Seamless steel tubes **Commission decision 2003/382/EC [2003] OJ L 140/1, Case IV/E-1/35.860-B**

Zinc phosphate Commission decision 2003/437/EC [2003] OJ L 153/1, Case COMP/E-1/37.027

Interbrew and Alken-Maes 2003/569/EC [2003] OJ L 200/1, Case IV/37.614/F3

O2 UK/T-Mobile UK – UK network sharing agreement Commission decision 2003/570/EC [2003] OJ L 200/59, Case COMP/38.370

PO/French Beef Commission decision 2003/600/EC [2003] OJ L 209/12, Case COMP/C.38.279/F3

Methylglucamine Commission decision 2004/104/EC [2004] OJ L 38/18, Case COMP/E-2/37.978

Sorbates Commission decision of 1 October 2003, published on DG Comp website, Case COMP/E-1/37.370

PO/Organic peroxides Commission decision of 10 December 2003, published on DG Comp website, Case COMP/E-2/37.857

Food Flavor Enhancers Commission decision 2004/206/EC [2004] OJ L 75/1, Case COMP/C.37.671

3G Network sharing Germany Commission decision 2004/207/EC [2004] OJ L 75/32, Case COMP/38.369

Carbonless Paper Commission decision 2004/337/EC [2004] OJ L 115/1, Case COMP/E-1/36.212

Electrical and mechanical carbon and graphite products Commission decision 2004/420/EC [2004] OJ L 125/45, Case COMP/38.359

Industrial copper tubes Commission decision 2004/421/EC [2004] OJ L 125/50, Case COMP/38.240 (*)

Compagnie Maritime Belge (CEWAL) Commission decision of 30 April 2004, published on DG Comp website, Cases COMP/D/32.448, 32.450

Sodium gluconate Commission decision of 29 September 2004, published on DG Comp website, Case COMP/36.756

French beer Commission decision of 29 September 2004, published on DG Comp website on 22 December 2004, Case COMP/C.37.750/B2

Raw tobacco Spain Commission decision of 20 October 2004, published on DG Comp website, Case COMP/C.38.238/B2

Hard Haberdashery-Needles Commission decision of 26 October 2004, published on DG Comp website, Case F-1/38.338

Gaz de France/ENI Commission decision of 26 October 2004, published on DG Comp website, Case COMP/38.662

Choline chloride Commission decision of 9 December 2004, published on DG Comp website, Case COMP/E-2/37.533

Plasterboard Commission decision 2005/471/EC [2005] OJ L 166/8, Case COMP/E-1/37.152(*)

Monochloroacetic acid Commission decision of 19 January 2005, published on DG Comp website, Case COMP/E-1/37.773

Industrial Thread Commission decision of 14 September 2005, published on DG Comp website, Case COMP/38.337

Raw tobacco Italy Commission decision of 20 October 2005, published on DG Comp website, Case COMP/C.38.281/B2

Industrial bags Commission decision of 30 November 2005, published on DG Comp website, Case COMP/F-3/38.354

Copper plumbing tubes Commission decision 2006/485/EC [2006] OJ L 192/21, Case C.38.069

Hydrogene peroxide and perborate Commission decision of 3 May 2006, published on DG Comp website, Case COMP/38.620

Copper fittings Commission decision of 20 September 2006, published on DG Comp website, Case COMP/38.121

Steel beams (readopted) Commission decision of 8 November 2006, published on DG Comp website, Case COMP/38.907

Synthetic rubber Commission decision of 29 November 2006, published on DG Comp website, Case COMP/38.638

Gas insulated switchgear Commission decision of 24 January 2007, published on DG Comp website, Case COMP/38.899

Elevators and escalators Commission decision of 21 February 2007, published on DG Comp website, Case COMP/38.823 (*)

Fasteners and attaching machines Commission decision of 19 September 2007, published on DG Comp website, Case COMP/39.168

Bitumen suppliers Commission decision of 3 October 2007, published on DG Comp website, Case COMP/38.710

Chloroprene rubber Commission decision of 5 December 2007, not yet published, Case COMP/38.629

International Removal services Commission decision of 11 March 2008, published on DG Comp website, Case COMP/38.543

Sodium chlorate paper bleach producers Commission decision of 11 June 2008, published on DG Comp website, Case COMP/38.695

CISAC – European collecting societies Commission decision of 16 July 2008, published on DG COMP website, Case COMP/38.698

Wax producers Commission decision of 1 October 2008, not yet published, Case COMP/39.181

Car glass producers Commission decision of 12 November 2008, not yet published, Case COMP/39.125

Marine hose producers Commission decision of 28 January 2009, not yet published, Case COMP/39.406

E.ON-Gas de France Suez Commission decision of 8 July 2009, not yet published, Case COMP/39.401

Calcium carbide and magnesium based reagents Commission decision of 22 July 2009, not yet published, Case COMP/39.396

Concrete reinforcing bar Commission decision of 30 September 2009, not yet published, Case COMP/37.956

Power transformers producers Commission decision of 7 October 2009, not yet published, Case COMP/39.129

Heat stabilisers Commission decision of 11 November 2009, not yet published, Case COMP/38.589

F Economic landmark cases

F.1 *Jaz-Peter I* Commission decision 69/242/EEC [1969] OJ L 195/5

Relevance: Since the very beginning of EU competition law, the Commission has had a positive approach toward specialization agreements and has recognized the efficiencies deriving from them. Even in the presence of some restrictive effects, the latter are usually outweighed by the efficiencies produced. In this early decision the Commission indicates numerous positive effects produced by such an agreement in particular in case of firms not holding a large market share.

- Case IV/26.437
- **Decision:** Exemption pursuant to Article 101(3) FEU Treaty for ten years
- **Decision addressee(s):**
    - Jaz SA, *France*
    - Peter-Uhren GmbH, *Federal Republic of Germany*
- **Report route:** Notification for exemption submitted to the Commission on 20 March 1967 by Jaz SA
- **Date of the decision:** 22 July 1969
- **Competition Commissioner:** M. Sassen
- **Relevant product market:** Clockwork items
- **Relevant geographical market:** France and Germany
- **Description of the case**
    - a. **Relevant facts**
        Jaz and Peter-Uhren were two producers of clockwork items operating on the French and the German market, respectively. They were both involved in the

production of a number of different products. They reached a reciprocal specialization agreement pursuant to which they would specialize in their primary production and refrain from producing the product in which the other company was specialized. Accordingly Peter-Uhren was to produce big mechanical clock-alarms and Jaz electric clock-alarms and wall-clocks. Simultaneously, they would both continue production of other products.

Next, the two firms not only mutually supplied each other with the product produced under the specialization agreement but were exclusive supplier to each other within the territory of their respective country of origin. Furthermore they guaranteed each other to supply their specialized product to the other firm at prices no less favorable than prices charged to third parties. In addition, they subscribed a non-competition clause according to which they would refrain from buying the product covered by the specialization agreement from third producers for sale in their respective territory. They also agreed upon issuing specialized products which were supplied to be marketed in each country with the matching trademark (Jaz in France and Peter-Uhren in Germany) in order to take advantage of the respective reputation of the trademarks. They also arranged regular exchange of information about production methods and workers' training.

The overall aim of the agreement was the increase of the productivity of their plants and the reduction of the production costs of the products without any restriction in the firms' independence in the setting of their price and export policies.

b. **Origin of the case**

On 20 March 1967 Jaz SA submitted to the Commission a notification pursuant to Article 4 of Regulation No. 17 to see the specialization agreement entered into with Peter-Uhren GmbH be declared exempted from the application of Article 101(1) FEU Treaty by virtue of Article 101(3) FEU Treaty.

c. **Economic analysis**

This early Commission decision is exemplary of the approach of EU competition law toward specialization agreements, in particular as regards agreements entered into by undertakings not holding a large market share.

The Commission carried out a cost benefit analysis of the agreement, weighing the anticompetitive effects against the efficiencies and the increase in the consumer welfare it generated.

The Commission described the foreclosure effects arising from the reciprocal specialization when two companies cease their respective production of goods that they would have been *perfectly able* to produce independently from the cooperation with one other.[32] The two firms would have increased their market power with respect to the specialized product. The restriction of competitiveness in the affected markets was strengthened by the mutually exclusive supply agreement and non-competition clause accompanied by the trademark agreement. They would have diminished both the consumer choice and the prospect of third-party suppliers to provide the companies with the discontinued product.

As mentioned above, the Commission recognized the efficiency gains and consumer benefits commonly attributed to these agreements. Even if it did not

---

32   See recital 6 of the decision. Emphasis added.

perform an in-depth economic analysis in this decision, the Commission laid the basis for a more economic approach to these kinds of agreements that can be traced all the way to the most recent decisions. The Commission stressed in particular that the agreement would have increased the productivity of the two firms' plants, reducing production cost which could lead to an output expansion. Moreover, due to the mutual specialization in the production of their respective primary products the companies would have in all likelihood increased product quality and worker specialization. By means of a trademark and exclusive supply agreements the firms would also be able to improve the distribution process. Finally, the Commission accepted the argument that since the two firms would face strong competition even after the adoption of the agreement they would have to pass on part of the efficiency gains so that consumers would share part of the benefits by way of, for example, lower prices.[33] The Commission therefore concluded that the benefits of the specialization agreement outweighed its restrictive effects.

  d. Fines, remedies, and conditions enclosed
  None.
  e. Further developments of the case
  None.

F.2   *Italian Cast Glass* Commission decision 80/1334/EEC [1980] OJ L 383/19

Relevance: Market sharing and quota agreements have been unequivocally and consistently considered highly restrictive of competition by the Commission throughout the history of EU competition law enforcement. In this decision for the first time the reasoning lays partly on economic concepts. In particular attention is paid to the effect of quotas on price competition.

- Case IV/29.869
- **Decision:** Infringement of Article 101(1) FEU Treaty
- **Decision addressee(s):**
  - Fabbrica Pisana SpA, *Italy*
  - Società Italiana Vetro (SIV) SpA, *Italy*
  - Fabbrica Lastre di Vetro Sciarra SpA, *Italy*
  - Fides-Unione Fiduciaria SpA, *Italy*
- **Report route:** Commission decision of 11 December 1979 to start proceedings on its own initiative
- **Date of the decision:** 17 December 1980
- **Competition Commissioner:** R. Vouel
- **Relevant product market:** Cast glass
- **Relevant geographic market:** Italy
- **Description of the case**
  a. **Relevant facts**
    Fabbrica Pisana SpA (FP) was a wholly owned subsidiary of Saint-Gobain Industries, itself a division of the Saint-Gobain/Pont-à-Mousson group, one of the largest industrial groups in the world and owner of several other companies in Italy, apart from FP, related to the glass market. Fabbrica Pisana had different plants in Italy and it produced many types of glasses.

---

33   See recitals 10–15 of the decision.

Società Italiana Vetro SpA (SIV) was a State-owned glass producer. It never achieved an optimum level of production and its business was strongly export oriented. Fabbrica Lastre di Vetro Sciarra SpA (VS) was a company active exclusively on the cast glass production market. Its products were used mainly in the building industry. Fides-Unione Fiduciaria SpA (Fides), by contrast, was not a glass producer but instead a firm providing management and accountancy services, particularly specialized in supervisory and statistical research activities.

The three cast glass producers held a significant market share on the Italian market; FP held 28 percent, SIV 13 percent, and VS 11 percent.[34]

Cast glass (one of the three types of flat glass) is a product used in different industrial sectors, in particular in the building industry, in horticulture, in furniture production, and in the production of electrical household equipment. Different varieties of cast glass were produced and they were all highly interchangeable.

After investigation the Commission found clear evidence about the existence of an agreement among all the undertakings listed above concerning:
- quantitative sharing of the types of cast glass (quotas)
- exchange of detailed information about all data relating to the manufacturing and marketing of the relevant products
- a system to monitor the correct implementation of the agreement by the parties.

The agreement was formally concluded on 30 March 1976 and included in the "Memorandum on the supervision of the quantities of patterned and wired glass manufactured and sold."[35] The "memorandum fixed the quota on the Italian market for each of the three companies concerned, and also the kinds of cast glass which each undertaking could sell on that market within its quota."[36] A system to repay possible sales exceeding the fixed quota on a quarterly basis was also established.

In some documents attached to the memorandum, the procedures to supervise the implementation of the agreement were described in detail. In particular, each producer involved would have recorded detailed information about the price structure, the products supplied to customers, and the stock movements. Every month, this information was handed over to Fides, the party trusted to monitor the producers' compliance with the quota agreement. In order to carry out this task, special powers were delegated to Fides to demand from the three producers further and more detailed information, in particular about store movements and loading and unloading documents. It was also authorized to enter the offices, factories, and warehouses of the undertakings. The visits made at Fides premises enabled the Commission to establish that the provisions of the agreements were closely adhered to and that Fides diligently fulfiled the task assigned to it.[37]

---

34   The data refer to 1978.
35   See recital I-C-2 of the decision.
36   See recital I-C-2 of the decision.

37   For a detailed description of the documents discovered during the Commission's dawn raids, see recital I-C-7 of the decision.

b. **Origin of the case**

On 11 December 1979 the Commission, on its own initiative, adopted a decision to initiate a proceeding against the above-mentioned undertakings in respect of agreements concluded by them concerning the cast glass market in Italy.

c. **Economic analysis**

The Commission's assessment of quota agreements and market sharing agreements has always been unequivocally severe. In the context of pursuing integration of the European internal market, such agreements typically have the effect to distort integration and all too often have as their very object to prevent the completion of that overall aim. The Commission has made negative appraisals of such agreements persistently throughout the history of EU competition law enforcement. This should come as no surprise as they are explicitly prohibited by Article 101(1)(c) FEU Treaty and are undoubtedly a prime example of *hardcore* violations.

In this decision the Commission described the anticompetitive consequences of the quota fixing agreement. For the first time it explicitly relied on economic concepts while conducting this assessment. It stressed, "the agreements in question were intended to stabilize those undertakings' production and to permit them at least partly to protect the prices of their products from the effects of consumer demand. The manufacturers, having quotas fixed [on] the basis of established market share, no longer had any incentive to reduce their prices to win a larger market share as, if they had done so, they would have forfeited the opportunity of drawing the maximum benefit from their production quotas."[38]

Also the annexed agreement concerning the exchange of information was regarded by the Commission as restrictive of competition.[39]

The benefits of the agreement accrued exclusively to the glass manufacturers; the consumers did not share any part of it. Even if the parties involved claimed that it was merely a specialization agreement in order to react to a structural industry crisis, there would be no positive welfare effects resulting from the agreement possibly justifying the described foreclosures.

d. **Fines, remedies, and conditions enclosed**

 – Obligations for all the undertakings concerned to bring the infringements to an end.

e. **Further developments of the case**

None.

F.3 *BPCL/ICI* Commission decision 84/387/EEC [1984] OJ L 212/1

Relevance: The Commission confirms its positive approach to specialization agreements but makes a deeper economically based analysis of the effects thereof. It refers to cost structures of firms, production processes, efficiency of activities, and welfare increase. Particular attention is paid to the reduction of structural overcapacity deriving from the agreement. Market structure is also described in relation to the agreement's effect on it.

- Case IV/30.863
- **Decision:** Exemption pursuant to Article 101(3) FEU Treaty for fifteen years

---

38   Recital II-A-4.   39   *Idem.*

- **Decision addressee(s):**
  - Imperial Chemical Industries plc, *United Kingdom*
  - BP Chemicals Ltd, *United Kingdom*
- **Report route:** Application for negative clearance and notification for exemption submitted to the Commission on 28 January 1983 by Imperial Chemical Industries plc and on 8 February 1983 by BP Chemicals Ltd
- **Date of the decision:** 19 July 1984
- **Competition Commissioner:** F. Andriessen
- **Relevant product market:** Polyvinyl chloride (PVC) and low-density polyethylene (LDPE)
- **Relevant geographical market:** European internal market
- **Description of the case**
  - a. **Relevant facts**

    BP Chemicals Ltd (BPCL) is a member of the British Petroleum (BP) Group. BP is active in the production of various products related to different industrial areas. Its activities are in oil and gas exploration. Nonetheless, an important part of its business is in the chemical sector.

    Imperial Chemical Industries plc (ICI) is a British company with diversified business activities in different industrial areas. Its production focus however is on chemicals, accounting for 87 percent of its turnover at the time of the decision.

    The products affected by the specialization agreement were PVC and LDPE, petrol–chemical plastics produced by the transformation of derivatives of crude oil. Both parties produced PVC and LDPE and were the United Kingdom's largest ethylene producers, ranking among the most important producers at European level.[40] The European market for petrol–chemical derivates was suffering from considerable overcapacity and an increasing competition from producers outside Western Europe. Consequently many producers were suffering losses at the time.

    BPCL and ICI responded to these market conditions by developing long-term market strategies. The specialization agreement was an essential part of this strategy and a means to achieve their long-term aims. According to the agreement:

    - ICI transferred to BPCL five plants for the production of LDPE together with "all necessary associated plant, equipment and facilities and granted BPCL a license to occupy the LDPE site and to have access necessary in connection with the operation of the LDPE plant and granted on a non-exclusive basis all necessary rights under ICI's patent rights and technical information to enable BPCL to exploit the plant fully. ICI also transferred the goodwill of all its UK LDPE business."[41]
    - ICI agreed to act as the sole agent of BPCL for the operational life of the transferred plants for their operations, care, and maintenance.
    - ICI would have purchased for five years from BPCL a large part of its internal requirement of polyethylene.

---

40   Ethylene is the raw material for the production of derived products such as PVC and LDPE. For a more detailed description of the firms' market position, see recitals 18–20 of the decision.

41   Recital 6 of the decision.

- BPCL concluded a similar agreement with ICI for the transfer of three PVC plants. This part of the reciprocal agreement included neither the supply agreement nor the agent agreement. Nonetheless BPCL agreed to provide ICI with all services ICI could have reasonably requested for the safe and efficient operation of the transferred plants.[42]

In their long-term strategies the two companies had portrayed themselves as having a competitive disadvantage for the production of LDPE (ICI) and PVC (BPCL). They both had eventually considered withdrawing unilaterally from these respective markets. The agreement to swap production enabled ICI and BPCL to get rid of the plants which they were operating relatively inefficiently and implement the market exit strategy. Keeping their part of the promise, BPCL sold most of its modern plants, shut down its remaining PVC plants and thus withdrew completely from the PVC market, effectively implementing the joint strategy. ICI followed suit and shut down its remaining plant in the United Kingdom. They did however keep other LDPE plants outside the United Kingdom in operation.

b. Origin of the case

On 28 January and 8 February 1983 Imperial Chemical Industries plc and BP Chemicals Ltd Application submitted to the Commission an application for negative clearance and a notification for exemption pursuant to Articles 2 and 4 of Regulation 17 to see Article 101(1) FEU Treaty be declared not applicable to a set of agreements or alternatively the same agreements be declared exempted from the application of Article 101(1) FEU Treaty by virtue of Article 101(3) FEU Treaty.

c. Economic analysis

In this decision the Commission confirmed its previous approach but provided a more in-depth economic analysis of the reasoning usually leading it to exempt an agreement on production specialization. In this particular case, the specialization agreement was also an instrument to achieve reduction of overcapacities present in the relevant market. Consistently with its previous approach, the Commission emphasized the competitive restrictions that would have been imposed by the agreement but also stated that the efficiency gains would have outweighed its harmful effects. The agreement would have restricted competition and limited capacity because it entailed BPCL's withdrawal from the production and distribution of PVC and ICI's withdrawal from production and distribution of LDPE. "Competition [was] as a consequence restricted appreciably for both products since each party was an important and active competitor before the agreement."[43] Beyond the obvious direct effect, the parties relinquished the goodwill they had accumulated over time which resembles an implicit non-competition clause arguably creating an indirect but additional restriction of competition. Further anticompetitive effects arose from the "quasi exclusive supply agreements" ICI signed with BPCL and that would have also foreclosed other producers from supplying a significant part of ICI's demand.

After the weighing exercise, the Commission came to the conclusion that although the agreement imposed severe restrictions on competition the benefits accruing to the parties which the agreement allowed would outweigh the harm.

---

42   See recitals 6–12 of the decision.   43   Recital 26 of the decision.

The Commission stated that specializing in the production of one product and keeping each other's customers by mean of the goodwill agreement, the two companies would have increased the loading capacity "both in production of the product in which they [were] specializing and in ethylene. This increased loading [would have] reduced unit costs and [led] to a more efficient production."[44]

In particular the Commission stressed that "this increased plant-loading is particularly important as in the present case where there are high fixed costs such that under-utilization of capacity leads to large increases in unit costs."[45] Furthermore, withdrawing from loss making production and shutting down inefficient plants the parties would have freed resources "to finance long-term investment and research and development rather to cover operating costs"[46] and this would also have been eventually beneficial for consumers. Moreover having acquired each other's most efficient and modern plants they would have specialized in the production of their respective primary production and continued in a more efficient way.

Furthermore, the Commission was concerned about likely *ex post* competitiveness of the market and stressed, in line with its economic approach, that the preservation of competition was particularly important in a market where entry barriers were high and sunk costs particularly relevant. In the relevant market, competition would have been ensured by the "potentially competitive and economically healthy structure of supply in the Community [and by] continued competition between the remaining participating firms."[47] Consequently, consumers would have benefited from the agreement due to the prevailing product variety.

d. **Fines, remedies, and conditions enclosed**
    –   Obligation for ICI to transmit to the Commission a report each three years for the duration of the exemption. The report must indicate ICI's production of LDPE and the sales in the United Kingdom and a breakdown of the sales by status of the purchaser.
    –   Obligation for BPCL to inform the Commission about any future acquisition of plants for the production of PVC in Europe or in any other area available for export in the United Kingdom. Following those potential acquisitions, BPCL shall submit to the Commission a report each three years for the entire period of exemption. The report shall indicate the production by BPCL of PVC and the sales of the same product in the United Kingdom and a breakdown of the sales by status of the purchaser.
    –   Obligation for both parties to inform the Commission about intentions to amend or modify the agreement.

e. **Further developments of the case**
    None.

---

44   Recital 35 of the decision.
45   Recital 36 of the decision.
46   *Idem.*
47   *Idem.*

F.4 *Seamless steel tubes* Commission decision 2003/382/EC [2003] OJ L 140/1

Relevance: Confirmation of the described hardcore restrictive nature of market sharing agreements. The Commission reaffirmed the non-justifiability of such agreements even in markets that have been the object of past protective policy measures of the same Commission or other European institutions. The cost structure analysis carried out by the Commission tends to demonstrate the potential profitability of a competitive race on the relevant market.

- Case IV/E-1/35.860-B
- **Decision:** Infringement of Article 101(1) FEU Treaty, imposition of fines
- **Decision addressee(s):**
  - Mannesmannröhren-Werke AG, *Germany*
  - Vallourec SA, *France*
  - British Steel Ltd, *United Kingdom*
  - Dalmine SpA, *Italy*
  - Sumitomo Metal Industries Ltd, *Japan*
  - Nippon Steel Corporation, *Japan*
  - Kawasaki Steel Corporation, *Japan*
  - NKK Corporation, *Japan*
- **Report route:** Commission decision of 20 January 1999 to start a proceeding on its own initiative
- **Date of the decision:** 8 December 1999
- **Competition Commissioner:** M. Monti
- **Relevant product market:** Seamless carbon-steel pipes and tubes
- **Relevant geographic market:** Global market
- **Description of the case**
  - a. **Relevant facts**

    Mannesmannröhren-Werke AG (MRW), Vallourec SA (Vallourec), British Steel Ltd (BS), and Dalmine SpA (Dalmine) are four large European producers of pipes, tubes, and related steel products. All of the four Japanese companies listed above are among the twenty world's largest steel producers (in particular, Nippon Steel Corporation – NSC – is the second largest steel producer).

    The steel pipe and tube sector includes a wide variety of products which can be split according to the manufacturing process into *seamless* and *welded* steel pipes and tubes. Due to lower production costs and to advanced technology, the demand for welded products had been constantly growing in the last twenty-five years leading up to the Commission investigation. However, the two kinds of products are not entirely interchangeable because for a variety of manufacturing and final goods applications there is no alternative to seamless tubes and pipes.

    The steel market had been the object of several Commission interventions to recover from the effects of a deep crisis which had affected the market since the 1970s coinciding with a continuous fall in demand and collapse of prices. The crisis had generated large overcapacities, low plant utilization, and a price level dissipating company profits. To remedy this situation the Commission adopted a production and delivery quota agreement within the frame of the ECSC Treaty (1977–88).[48] Strict measures restructuring European production

---

48   European Coal and Steel Community Treaty.

capacity had been adopted and an agreement with the Japanese government attaining a voluntary export restraint had also been concluded (1972). Finally, in 1978 "the Commission adopted an agreement with MITI[49] with a view to establish price discipline that would prevent disruption of the Community market and thus ensure the preservation of traditional trade patterns."[50] The market conditions prevalent at the time of the investigation were sustaining substantial global overcapacity.

The demand for manufactured steel products follows the pattern and cyclical swings of the oil market. In fact much of the demand is driven by oil prospecting and extraction firms.

The evidence collected by the Commission during its investigations revealed the existence of a well-thought-out cartel known as the "Euro-Japan club," the aim of which was to ensure a strict and controlled division into national markets. Essentially, each participant to the agreement refrained from selling the relevant products in another participant's national market. These parts of the agreement were referred to as the "fundamentals" disciplining the relations between the subscribers.[51] The cartel members organized two meetings each year. The members of the agreement used to meet at three different levels: presidents, managers, and experts.[52]

Another substantial part of the agreement scrutinized during the Commission's investigations concerned the supply agreement established between BS and the other three European producers involved. According to the agreement, after BS shut down all production of hot-rolled seamless pipes and tubes in 1990, MRW, Vallourec, and Dalmine would supply BS' entire demand for hot-rolled seamless pipes and tubes. By way of that agreement (referred to as the "fundamentals improved") the European producers were able to maintain the United Kingdom as a domestic market and in combination with the main agreement ("fundamentals"), exclude the Japanese competitors from that UK market. On the same market, BS would have in fact acted as if it were still producing the product concerned and consequently prevented the Japanese members of the cartel from supplying the relevant product.

This part of the agreement was to some extent the result of an overall crisis that destabilized the cartel in 1993 and required some reorganization. The most worrying issues for the cartel were the reorganization of the European industry facing the discontinuation of BS, the imminent shut down of Belgium's largest supplier's production facilities and the rise of Latin American producers. Following discussion between all the participants and the candidates from Latin America, the cartel decided to carry on with the agreement and bring in the Latin American producers.[53] The Euro-Japan club stopped its operation in 1995.

b. **Origin of the case**

After having carried out simultaneous investigations in several producers' premises (including of the addressees Mannesmannröhren-Werke, Vallourec, and British Steel) in December 1994, on 20 January 1999 the Commission

49   The Japanese Ministry of International Trade and Industry.
50   Recital 27 of the decision.
51   See recitals 53 ff. of the decision.
52   See recitals 58–60 of the decision.
53   See recitals 83–89 of the decision.

adopted a decision to initiate proceedings against the above-mentioned undertakings for anticompetitive actions in the market for seamless carbon-steel
tubes and pipes.

c. **Economic analysis**

In this decision the Commission reaffirmed its approach toward market sharing agreements, which it had at that time already repeatedly and consistently
established in numerous cases. The Commission stated that "the object of the
agreement was to restrict competition in the common market by providing
that the domestic markets of the different producers . . . should be respected
inasmuch as the supply of seamless pipes and tubes in Member States where
a national producer was established was limited by the other producers party
to the agreement refraining from supplying those markets [and that] the producers, by concerting their action, were able to alter the tonnages of pipes and
tubes which each of them, in the absence of concerted action, would have sold
on the markets of the Member States."[54] At the time this decision was adopted,
the anticompetitive nature of *hardcore* restrictions in the European market,
such as market sharing, was hardly under debate.[55] They were regarded both
as restrictive of competition by object (i.e. regardless of their actual effect on
the market) and as impeding market integration. Accordingly, their restrictive
effects were not described in detail in the decision. The Commission came to
the same conclusion as regards to the supply agreement between BS, Vallourec,
MRW, and Dalmine. It facilitated the separation into national markets and the
protection against foreign competition.[56]

   To an extent, this decision broadens the traditional approach of the Commission because it refers to a market which had been protected by the Commission
until 1990 with political agreements, antidumping measures, and approved
reorganization of capacities, as the Commission recognized the existence of
a crisis. Nonetheless, the Commission firmly rejected the economic argumentation of the parties involved that tried to demonstrate on the one hand that
the Commission had allowed those practices and, on the other hand, that their
non-participation in certain national markets was caused by structural features of those markets. As the Commission pointed out, "the trade measures
adopted . . . were designed to avoid market disruption. While they may have
managed to persuade the Japanese firms not to export to Europe until 1990,
they do not justify the continuation of this policy beyond 1990."[57] Firms are
thus not allowed to prolong policy measures taken by the Commission or
policy makers by means of a mutual agreement. As for the allegedly considerable barriers to entry which would have precluded additional competition in
some markets, the Commission stated that "given the structural overcapacity in
the sector and the high fixed costs, any sale at [a] price above the variable

---

54   Recitals 102 and 106 of the decision.
55   The ECJ had repeatedly stated that in case undertakings did not individually decide their market behavior, but came to a mutual
     understanding to engage in it thereby knowingly substituting practical cooperation between them for the risks of competition, the
     situation would not correspond to normal market conditions and enabled them to maintain the position they had established on the
     market to the detriment of effective free movement of goods in the common market and of the freedom enjoyed by consumers to
     choose their suppliers. See, *inter alia*, Joined cases 40 to 48, 50, 54 to 56, 111, 113 and 114/73 *Coöperatieve Vereniging "Suiker
     Unie" UA* v. *Commission*, recitals 191 and 293.
56   See recitals 110–116 of the decision.
57   Recital 137 of the decision.

costs helps to cover the fixed costs and hence to reduce total production costs. Consequently even markets where the consumption of the products in question was not very great are definitely of interest to all producers."[58] The transportation costs, taking into consideration the percentage of total output exported by the Japanese firms (more than 95 percent) together with the fact that "in shipping the distance is not a factor that determine[s] price,"[59] could not be considered as reducing the attractiveness of the markets in question. Also standards and requirements for national approval were the same all over the world.

The only reasonable explanation for the non-participation on several national markets (European and non-European) was the compliance with the cartel agreement.

d. **Fines, remedies, and conditions enclosed**
   – The Commission imposed the following total fines:

Company	Fine (Euros)
Mannesmannröhren-Werke AG	13,500 million
Vallourec SA	8,100 million
British Steel Ltd	12,600 million
Dalmine SpA	10,800 million
Sumitomo Metal Industries Ltd	13,500 million
Nippon Steel Corporation	13,500 million
Kawasaki Steel Corporation	13,500 million
NKK Corporation	13,500 million

   – In light of the cooperation that Vallourec SA had provided during the investigation, the company was granted a 40 percent fine reduction pursuant to the leniency program.[60]
   – Obligations for all the undertakings concerned to bring the infringements established to an end and to refrain from any future repetition of similar behaviors.

e. **Further developments of the case**
   Case T-44/00 *Mannesmannröhren-Werke* v. *Commission* [2004] ECR II-2223, fine reduction
   Case T-48/00 *Corus UK (anciennement British Steel Ltd)* v. *Commission* [2004] ECR II-2325, fine reduction
   Case T-50/00 *Dalmine* v. *Commission [2004] ECR II-2395,* fine reduction
   Joined Cases T-67/00, T-68/00, T-71/00 and T-78/00, *JFE Engineering, Nippon steel, JFE steel and Sumitomo Metal Industries* v. *Commission [2004] ECR II-2501,* fine reduction
   The ECJ dismissed four further appeals in January 2007.

---

58   Recital 137 of the decision.
59   *Idem.*

60   Commission Notice on the non-imposition or reduction of fines in cartel cases [1996] OJ C 207/04.

2.3 Bid-rigging and tender fixing

A Introduction

In bidding markets sales are concluded through tender processes. Bidding processes are typically used for the tendering of specialty assignments for larger sums of money, such as construction projects. The projects are often specialized and unique, so that there is no regular market for them and bidding allows buyers to compare potential suppliers. Suppliers submit tender bids to win projects. Buyers prefer a large number of firms bidding independently. The firm that submits the winning bid typically supplies the entire tendered project, while its competitors submit their (costly) bids for the project in vain. For the type of markets in which they are used, tenders are a recurrent allocation mechanism in which a relatively small group of suppliers regularly bids against each other.

The combination of high winning stakes, significant bidding costs, and repeated interaction may exert substantial pressure on bidders to collude and so eliminate (or at least soften) price competition. Bid-rigging can lead to *ex ante* market sharing agreements fixing the winning bid or the minimum bid. Often, the agreements include bid-rotation schemes in which cartel members alternate in winning projects. Depending on the auction format, bidding markets can induce collusion, since they are transparent in the sense that the number of bidders is known and the individual bids, including the losing bids, are common knowledge after the auction.

B Applicable EU legislation

No special legislation applicable. For applicable legislation see chapter 2, paragraph B.

C Related economics texts

Bishop and Walker (2009), chapter 12
Carlton and Perloff (2005), not specifically discussed
Church and Ware (2000), not specifically discussed
Martin (1994), not specifically discussed
Martin (2002), not specifically discussed
Motta (2004), paragraphs 4.2.2.2, 4.4.2
Tirole (1998), not specifically discussed
Waldman and Jensen (2001), not specifically discussed

D Related legal texts

Bellamy and Child (2008), chapter 5, paragraph 7(D)
Jones and Sufrin (2008), chapter 11, paragraph 2(C, ii, d and C, iii, e)
Ritter and Braun (2005), chapter 3, paragraph A(2, a)
Whish (2008), chapter 13, paragraph 6

E   Commission decisions in chronological order*

DECA Commission decision 64/599/EEC [1964] OJ L 64/2761, Case IV/71 (**described in detail as landmark case in section 2.5**)

European sugar industry Commission decision 73/109/EC [1973] OJ L 140/17, Case IV/26.918 (**described in detail as landmark case in section 3.2**) (Martin, 1994, p. 142)

Eurotunnel Commission decision 88/568/EEC [1988] OJ L 311/36, Case IV/32.437

Building and Constructions in the Netherlands **Commission decision 92/204/EEC [1992] OJ L 92/1, Cases IV/31.571, 31.572**

EBU/Eurovision System Commission decision 93/403/EC [1993] OJ L 179/23, Case IV/32.150

Preinsulated Pipes Commission decision 1999/60/EC [1999] OJ L 24/1, Case IV/35.691 (*)

Industrial bags Commission decision of 30 November 2005, published on DG Comp website, Case COMP/F-3/38.354

Gas insulated switchgear Commission decision of 24 January 2007, published on DG Comp website, Case COMP/38.899

Elevators and escalators Commission decision of 21 February 2007, published on DG COMP website, Case COMP/38.823

International Removal services Commission decision of 11 March 2008, not yet published, Case COMP/38.543

F   Economic landmark cases

F.1   *Building and Constructions in the Netherlands* Commission decision 92/204/EEC [1992] OJ L 92/1

Relevance: Tender systems recognized as determining a high degree of genuine competition between undertakings. All the efficiencies deriving from such a system are voided by a system providing information exchange about intended tender prices and protection of a commonly selected *entitled* (i.e. winning) firm. In the case of a tender bid process the Commission does not accept the idea of a commonly predetermined price being considered *economically correct*.

- Cases IV/31.571 and 31.572
- **Decision:** Infringement of Article 101(1) FEU Treaty, imposition of fines
- **Decision addressee(s):**
    - Vereniging van Samenwerkende Prijsregelende Organisaties in de Bouwnijverheid, *the Netherlands*
    - Amsterdamse Aannemers Vereniging, *the Netherlands*
    - Algemene Aannemersvereniging voor Waterbouwkundige Werken, *the Netherlands*
    - Aannemersvereniging van Boorondernemers en Buizenleggers, *the Netherlands*
    - Aannemersvereniging Velsen, Beverwijk en Omstreken, *the Netherlands*

- Decisions displayed in **bold type** are described in the section. Decisions highlighted with (*) include interesting economic analysis by the Commission on the specific topic of the section. Some decisions contain economic reasoning on more than one topic and therefore appear in several lists of Commission decisions in chronological order. Reference is made in brackets and **bold type** to the relevant section in which the decision is extensively described as a landmark case. When decisions are referenced and/or described in some detail in one or more of the economic textbooks, reference in brackets is also made to the relevant part(s) of those texts.

- Aannemers Vereniging Haarlem-Bollenstreek, *the Netherlands*
- Aannemersvereniging Veluwe en Zuidelijke IJsselmeerpolders, *the Nether-lands*
- Combinatie van Aannemers in het Noorden, *the Netherlands*
- Vereniging Centrale Prijsregeling Kabelwerken, *the Netherlands*
- Delftse Aannemers Vereniging, *the Netherlands*
- Economisch Nationaal Verbond van Aannemers van Slooperwerken, *the Netherlands*
- Aannemersvereniging "Gouda en Omstreken," *the Netherlands*
- Gelderse Aannemers Vereniging inzake Aanbestedingen, *the Netherlands*
- Gooize Aannemers Vereniging, *the Netherlands*
- 's-Gravenhaagse Aannemers Vereniging, *the Netherlands*
- Leidse Aannemers Vereniging, *the Netherlands*
- Vereniging Markeer Aannemers Combinatie, *the Netherlands*
- Nederlandse Aannemers- en Patronsbond voor de Bouwbedrijven (NAPB Dordrecht), *the Netherlands*
- Noordhollandse Aannemers Vereniging voor Waterbouwkundige Werken, *the Netherlands*
- Oostnederlandse Vereniging Aanbestedings Regeling, *the Netherlands*
- Provinciale Vereniging van Bouwbedrijven in Groningen en Drenthe, *the Netherlands*
- Rotterdamse Aannemersvereniging, *the Netherlands*
- Aannemersvereniging "de Rijnstreek," *the Netherlands*
- Stichting Aanbestedingsregeling van de Samenwerkende Bouwbedrijven in Friesland, *the Netherlands*
- Samenwerkende Prijsregelende Vereniging Nijmegen en Omstreken, *the Netherlands*
- Samenwerkende Patroons Verenigingen in de Bouwbedrijven Noord-Holland-Noord, *the Netherlands*
- Utrechtse Aannemers Vereniging, *the Netherlands*
- Vereniging Wegenbouw Aannemers Combinatie Nederlands, *the Netherlands*
- Zuid Nederlandse Aannemers Vereniging, *the Netherlands*
- Vereniging Nederlandse Aannemers Combinatie, *the Netherlands*

- **Report route:** Application for negative clearance and notification for exemption submitted to the Commission on 13 January 1988 by Vereniging van Samenwerkende Prijsregelende Organisaties in de Bouwnijverheid in respect of the Uniforme Prijsregelende Reglement
- **Date of the decision:** 5 February 1992
- **Competition Commissioner:** L. Brittan
- **Relevant product market:** Construction industry
- **Relevant geographical market:** the Netherlands
- **Description of the case**
  - a. **Relevant facts**

    The Vereniging van Samenwerkende Prijsregelende Organisaties in de Bouwnijverheid (the SPO) was a nationwide association of smaller regional associations of undertakings active in the building and construction sector created in 1963. Occasionally, the admission of individual companies was discussed. Its statutory task was to "promote and administer orderly competition, to prevent improper conduct in price tendering and to promote the formation of economically-justified prices" (Article 3 of the statute).

There were basically two sets of rules provided by the SPO statute: one for the invitation to tender under the restricted procedure (UPR rules) and another for the tendering under the open procedure (UPRO rules).

The rules applied to "all building and construction works to be carried out in the Netherlands and falling within one of the following building and construction sectors:

a) ... residential and non-residential buildings;
b) the drilling, drainage, pipe work and cable laying sector ...;
c) the earthworks, road construction and planting sector ...;
d) the road marking sector ...;
e) the demolition sector;
f) the water-engineering sector ..."[61]

The two sets of rules provided very detailed and precise obligations for the undertakings belonging to the SPO (via their single association of undertakings) and the operating conditions of the UPR(O) system.

The rules were strengthened by the adoption of a *Code of Honour* which was made binding for the SPO members by a decision of the SPO general assembly of 1 October 1980, and which provided obligations and rules for the implementation of a system including sanctions and procedures to be applied in case of deviation.

The system was based on a mutual obligation to provide information each time that an undertaking had the intention of submitting a price tender. After collective negotiations were held this information exchange enabled the member associations to increase the final tender price so as to cover not only the calculation cost carried by each undertaking making a tender offer but also the trade and organizational cost of the association. Essentially, it provided the opportunity to protect the so-called *entitled* undertaking. When the firms fulfilled the obligation to notify their intention to participate in a tender process, the parties involved were called for a meeting organized by the association and were required to attend that meeting.

During the meetings the first decision to be made concerned the question of whether or not to designate an *entitled* undertaking. To that end, participants discussed technical and economic data to be taken into consideration in the comparison of the prices, because "an entitled undertaking can be designated only on the basis of comparable price tenders."[62] All the parties were subsequently requested to submit to the chairman a form containing the *blank figure* of what they would offer in the tender. Subsequently, knowing all bids including the lowest and the respective bidder (whose name was or was not communicated to the others depending on the decision of the meeting) the participants set the price increases in order to reimburse firstly the calculation costs of all the companies involved. The threshold was calculated as a percentage of the value of the contract that, in turn, was calculated on the basis of the average of the proposed tender figures. Usually the added amount was the maximum

61   Recital 6 of the decision.   62   Recital 27 of the decision.

amount allowed by the rules. Secondly an increase of up to 1.5 percent of the lowest proposed figures was decided to cover the operating costs of the organization. At the end of these adjustments "the final prices to be tendered to the client [were] set for each of the participants. The order of sequence of the final price tenders must match that of the initial proposed tender figures. The final price tenders are set by raising each proposed tender figure by the total of the amounts of the increases [provided that these increases do not change the initial order of sequence]. However, with the agreement of the participants which submitted the lowest and the next to the lowest proposed tender figures, the final price tenders of the other participants may be reduced, provided that the order of sequence . . . is not altered. So that the price differences between the tenders submitted to the client do not appear excessive . . . It [was] prohibited to submit to the client a price other than that established at the meeting."[63]

The *entitled* undertaking was at times a different company from the one that offered the lowest price. Nonetheless, it was always granted the exclusive power to negotiate the contract conditions with the client and the opportunity to obtain a price tender increase so that the price differences between the tenders submitted ensure a preferential position for the commonly designated *entitled* contractor. Its protection also extended to subsequent price tenders, for a period of two or five years, depending on the value of the contract. The protection was granted against future tenders in case of both comparable or non-comparable price tenders.[64] In case of infringements, the *Code of Honour* provided for penalties which might amount to up to 15 percent of the value of the construction project in question.

All large and medium-sized Dutch building and construction firms were members of the SPO. The market data showed that almost all contracts that were tendered out in the Netherlands were handled through the SPO.[65] The demand side was "made up of a multitude of public and private sector customers who, either through statutory Requirement or voluntarily, [made] use of tendering system . . . so as to bring competition into play between the suppliers operating on the market, with the aim of obtaining the lowest price possible or the economically most advantageous tender for the work required."[66]

b. Origin of the case

On 13 January 1988 Vereniging van Samenwerkende Prijsregelende Organisaties in the Bouwnijverheid submitted to the Commission an application to see the Uniforme Prijsregelende Reglement cleared (and thus Article 101 FEU Treaty declared inapplicable). Subordinately they submitted a notification for the exemption of the same agreement (issued by the association Erecode voor ondernemers in het Bouwbedrijf and made binding on the undertakings belonging to its member organizations by a decision of 3 June 1980) from the application of Article 101(1) FEU Treaty by virtue of Article 101(3) FEU Treaty. Subsequently, on 26 July 1989, the municipality of Rotterdam lodged

---

63 Recital 38 of the decision.

64 For a more detailed descriptions of the rules implementing the granted protection, see recitals 41 and 51–53.

65 See recitals 18–21 of the decision.

66 Recital 22 of the decision.

a complaint with respect to the above-mentioned rules. With the decision of 7 November 1989 the Commission decided to initiate a proceeding.

c. Economic analysis

In the decision the Commission described all the anticompetitive effects caused by the agreement. First of all it rejected the argument according to which a certain amount of coordination was necessary because of the tendering nature of the market and the consequent exclusion of all non-winning bidders. The Commission stated that "contracts are, for building and construction firms, broadly equivalent alternatives... In addition most of the tenderers... do not have a passive attitude with regards to the market."[67] Being excluded from one tender process would have not meant being excluded from the market as such. The Commission rejected not only the practical argument of buyer power on the demand side because it could not find evidence of its existence but also its theoretical applicability because it would under no circumstances justify collusive behaviors.[68] "A system of invitation to tender is an ideal way to generate competition. This is all the more so with public procurement... designed to create greater transparency... The equality of opportunity thus created for tenderers must not be distorted by a system of concerted action... providing systematically for meetings prior to the submission of price tenders."[69] The Commission also rejected the argument that a tendering process creates *ruinous competition*. Rather, the Commission stated "there is no such a thing as a given price which alone is "the" economically correct price in a specific case: a price which allows an undertaking to cover its costs and achieve a profit margin is a fair price for it, while the same price could mean a loss for another undertaking with higher costs."[70] Similarly, the Commission considered the calculation costs (recovered by each undertaking through the collusive price tender) as constituting general expenses of a company, a general "business cost" which only the bidder submitting the winning bid would be entitled to recover.

The Commission did not accept any justification for fixing the price tender and for sharing the demand side between the SPO members. The systematic and mandatory exchange of information carried out during the meetings would have strongly restricted competition between the members because it would have allowed "each undertaking participating to take account not only of the elements which are liable to determine the costs of its competitors and the choice made by the client, but also of various items of information on the terms of the contract... which it would have not been able to obtain without such exchange of information."[71]

The market sharing was carried out through a system of preferences which was aimed at possibly changing the order of price tenders corresponding to the actual intentions of the tenderers. This was the most obvious anticompetitive effect caused by the agreement, together with the protection granted to the *entitled* undertaking. As the Commission stated, the system "replaces the freedom of choice of the client and his capacity to negotiate with several tenderers [and]

---

67   Recital 73 of the decision.
68   See recital 73 of the decision.
69   *Idem.*

70   See recital 73 of the decision.
71   Recital 81 of the decision.

where non-simultaneous price tenders are involved . . . the system confers on the entitled undertaking a temporary monopoly of two or five years in respect of a given contract and thus prevents competition from operating."[72]

The participants in the SPO system were also enjoying a competitive advantage over non-members of the agreement in as much as, through the exchange of information carried out during the meetings, they could "take account of the risk of any outside competition in establishing the proposed tender figure and the final figures [while a] firm not belonging to the SPO and wishing to submit a price tender is not in a position to measure its competitive economic capacity within the normal framework of a tender by a number of different firms, but is faced with a concerted and flexible tender designed to limit or impede its ability to enter the market."[73] The Commission also considered the flat rate of the reimbursements as not justified by the individual situation of the undertaking concerned. By contrast, it was an unnecessary restriction of competition because it would have prevented the most efficient firms (with low preparatory costs) from making use of their advantage and at the same time dissuaded the less efficient undertakings from improving their productivity.

d. **Fines, remedies, and conditions enclosed**
   - The Commission imposed the following total fines:

Company	Fine (ECU)
Amsterdamse Aannemers Vereniging	1,451,250
Algemene Aannemersvereniging voor Waterbouwkundige Werken	436,500
Aannemersvereniging van Boorondernemers en Buizenleggers	436,500
Aannemersvereniging Velsen, Beverwijk en Omstreken	202,500
Aannemers Vereniging Haarlem-Bollenstreek	337,500
Aannemersvereniging Veluwe en Zuidelijke IJsselmeerpolders	445,500
Combinatie van Aannemers in het Noorden	198,000
Vereniging Centrale Prijsregeling Kabelwerken	180,000
Delftse Aannemers Vereniging	162,000
Economisch Nationaal Verbond van Aannemers van Slooperwerken	184,500
Aannemersvereniging "Gouda en Omstreken"	249,750
Gelderse Aannemers Vereniging inzake Aanbestedingen	996,750
Gooise Aannemers Vereniging	270,000
's-Gravenhaagse Aannemers Vereniging	1,188.000
Leidse Aannemers Vereniging	317,250
Vereniging Markeer Aannemers Combinatie	38,250

(cont.)

---

72   Recital 93 of the decision.   73   Recital 98 of the decision.

Company	Fine (ECU)
Nederlandse Aannemers- en Patronsbond voor de Bouwbedrijven (NAPB Dordrecht)	324,000
Noordhollandse Aannemers Vereniging voor Waterbouwkundige Werken	238,500
Oostnederlandse Vereniging Aanbestedings Regeling	1,116,000
Provinciale Vereniging van Bouwbedrijven in Groningen en Drenthe	474,750
Rotterdamse Aannemersvereniging	2,103,750
Aannemersvereniging "de Rijnstreek"	96,750
Stichting Aanbestedingsregeling van de Samenwerkende Bouwbedrijven in Friesland	384,750
Samenwerkende Prijsregelende Vereniging Nijmegen en Omstreken	200,250
Samenwerkende Patroons Verenigingen in de Bouwbedrijven Noord-Holland-Noord	670,500
Utrechtse Aannemers Vereniging	1,055,250
Vereniging Wegenbouw Aannemers Combinatie Nederlands	4,792,500
Zuid Nederlandse Aannemers Vereniging	3,948,750

– Obligation for all the undertakings concerned to bring the infringements to an end.

e. **Further developments of the case**

Case T-29/92 *SPO and others* v. *Commission* [1995] ECR II-289, appeal dismissed.

In upholding the Commission's decision, the CFI (now "the General Court") stated that the prohibitions laid down by Article 101(1) of the Treaty apply to a system of rules operating within a trade organization which, in relation to contracts in tendering procedures, makes it possible, through agreements between the undertakings concerned, after comparison of the prices that they intend proposing, to designate the undertaking offering the lowest price. The firm will enjoy protection against the risk of submission by its competitors of price tenders adjusted downwards and, therefore, will be the only one authorized to negotiate the content of its tender with the contract awarder. Moreover the CFI ruled that this preference mechanism "... constitutes a sharing of the market in that it is the participants in the meeting who decide which of them is to benefit from protection as the entitled undertaking at a time when competition has not yet taken effect. By so doing, they share the market among themselves to the detriment of the freedom enjoyed by consumers to choose their suppliers ..."[74]

Furthermore the CFI stated that the contract awarder will be deprived of the right to exercise his preferences regarding content and price within

---

74   Recital 183 of the judgment.

each tender and will therefore be limited to choosing between tenders as a whole.[75]

2.4 Structural crises cartels

A Introduction

Grave specific economic circumstances may justify being soft on horizontal constraints. When there is demand failure leading to overcapacity in an industry, firms may need some shelter from competition to avoid a deep structural crisis. This would be exceptional, and cyclical crises should not be mistaken for structural ones. Overcapacity is a normal feature of temporary down-turns, and allowing horizontal constraints would endanger healthy competitive processes. Historically, crises have been grounds for the European Commission to (temporarily) allow horizontal cooperation.

Before exempting horizontal constraints for crisis-related reasons, it is essential to do a careful analysis of alternative resolutions. In this, enforcement agencies may be exposed to quite some political pressure and lobbying by stake holders. There certainly are economic arguments for a social interpretation of the competition rules, as the personal consequences of a crisis can be very severe. Nevertheless, the overriding insight is that the negative long-term effects that cartels can have are large. Allowing crises cartels could, for example, result in inefficient firms remaining in the market to the detriment of the more efficient suppliers. For this and other reasons, allowing crisis cartels is a method of last resort.

B Applicable EU legislation

No special legislation applicable. For applicable legislation see chapter 2, paragraph B.

C Related economics texts

Bishop and Walker (2009), not specifically discussed
Carlton and Perloff (2005), not specifically discussed
Church and Ware (2000), not specifically discussed
Martin (1994), not specifically discussed
Martin (2002), not specifically discussed
Motta (2004), paragraphs 1.2.2.3 and 1.3.2.1
Tirole (1988), not specifically discussed
Waldman and Jensen (2001), not specifically discussed

D Related legal texts

Bellamy and Child (2008), chapter 5, paragraph 4 (5.052)
Jones and Sufrin (2008), not specifically discussed
Ritter and Braun (2005), chapter 3, paragraph A(3)
Whish (2008), not specifically discussed

---

75   Recital 187 of the judgment.

E   Commission decisions in chronological order*

International Energy Agency Commission decision 83/671/EEC [1983] OJ L 376/30, Case IV/30.525

Synthetic Fibres **Commission decision 84/380/EEC [1984] OJ L 207/17, Case IV/30.810** (Martin, 1994, pp. 186–7)

International Energy Agency Commission decision 94/153/EEC [1994] OJ L 68/35, Case IV/30.525

Stichting Baksteen Commission decision 94/296/EEC [1994] OJ L 131/15, Case IV/34.456 (*)

F   Economic landmark cases

F.1   *Synthetic Fibres* Commission decision 84/380/EEC [1984] OJ L 207/17

Relevance: The Commission accepts agreements aimed at overcoming structural over-capacity. The efficiencies possibly generated by such an agreement are recognized. In particular the specialization effect deriving from the agreed capacity reduction, the more efficient relocation of production, the technological advances and the softened social impact of the industry restructuring were given close attention. These types of economic arguments are used for the first time in this decision. Since this kind of agreement has rarely been assessed by the Commission, there are not many analyses that followed the one carried out in this decision.

- Case IV/30.810
- **Decision:** Exemption pursuant to Article 101(3) FEU Treaty for three years
- **Decision addressee(s):**
    - Imperial Chemical Industries plc, *United Kingdom*
    - Courtaulds plc, *United Kingdom*
    - Rhône-Poulenc SA, *France*
    - Enka BV, *the Netherlands*
    - Montefibre SpA, *Italy*
    - Ancifibre SpA, *Italy*
    - SNIA Fibre SpA, *Italy*
    - Enka AG, *Federal Republic of Germany*
    - Bayer AG, *Federal Republic of Germany*
    - Hoechst AG, *Federal Republic of Germany*
- **Report route:** Notification for exemption submitted to the Commission on 10 November 1982 by the parties listed above
- **Date of the decision:** 4 July 1984
- **Competition Commissioner:** F. Andriessen
- **Relevant product market:** Synthetic fibres
- **Relevant geographical market:** European internal market

• Decisions displayed in **bold type** are described in the section. Decisions highlighted with (*) include interesting economic analysis by the Commission on the specific topic of the section. Some decisions contain economic reasoning on more than one topic and therefore appear in several lists of Commission decisions in chronological order. Reference is made in brackets and **bold type** to the relevant section in which the decision is extensively described as a landmark case. When decisions are referenced and/or described in some detail in one or more of the economic textbooks, reference in brackets is also made to the relevant part(s) of those texts.

- **Description of the case**
  a. **Relevant facts**

  In 1982 the undertakings listed above signed an agreement concerning the production of six different synthetic fibres, namely polyamide textile yarn, polyamide carpet yarn, polyester textile yarn, polyamide staple, polyester staple, and acrylic staple.

  The signatories held a large share of total synthetic fibres capacity, i.e. 70 percent in the Western European and 85 percent in the European internal market. The share of the European market for the different products that was supplied by the members of the agreement ranged from 54.6 percent to 77.6 percent.[76]

  The agreement followed a long-term crisis experienced by the European synthetic fibres industry. A decade earlier, in 1972, suppliers had been faced with increasing imports, stagnating demand, and a situation in which the need to invest in larger plants in order to realize economies of scale had resulted in the creation of overcapacity. These factors contributed to a general worsening of market conditions. In 1977, plants were operating on average at 70 percent of their capacity. By means of an earlier time-limited agreement – subsequently not exempted by the Commission – the parties achieved a structural overcapacity reduction of about 20 percent.

  The 1982 agreement was aimed at a combined capacity reduction to allow the producers to operate at 85 percent capacity (a threshold considered economically efficient by the same parties). The parties achieved a total cut in the production of each product and then each single producer provided its own detailed plan. The implementation of the agreement was delegated to an independent trustee entity. The parties guaranteed the retraining and redeployment of the workforce laid off during the industry restructuring process. They committed to not increase output for as long as the agreement was in force (until 1985) as well as declared that they would inform the Commission of any decision taken and of its social and economic results. Simultaneously, the parties would consult each other whenever they perceived major changes in the current situation of the market.

  b. **Origin of the case**

  On 10 November 1982 the parties listed above submitted to the Commission a notification pursuant to Article 4 of Regulation No. 17 to see the agreement be declared exempted from the application of Article 101(1) FEU Treaty by virtue of Article 101(3) FEU Treaty. The agreement was subsequently amended on 9 March and 19 July 1983 in response to observations made by the Commission.

  c. **Economic analysis**

  The restrictive and anticompetitive object and purpose of the agreement was evident and the parties were aware of its anticompetitive nature. The commitment to reduce capacity, to disclose to all other parties the plan to achieve it and to respect the agreed capacity reduction until the expiry of the agreement evidently constituted a collusive attempt to reduce output.

  The Commission recognized the special and generalised crisis affecting the market. The reasons for the overcapacity were identified in rapid technological

---

76   For more detailed data about the market structure, see recitals 6 and 7 of the decision.

advances and in a "demand trend which, though not actually falling, has failed to rise as much as expected."[77]

Having recognized the purpose of the agreement in a capacity reduction allowing the remaining capacity to be used at a more economic level, the Commission analyzed the market conditions and stressed the necessity to intervene where "market forces by themselves had failed to achieve the capacity reduction necessary to re-establish and maintain in the longer term an effective competitive structure within the common market. The producers concerned therefore agreed to organize for a limited period and collectively, the needed structural adjustment."[78]

The Commission described the economic advantages deriving from the agreement and in particular the shedding of the financial burden of having underutilised capacity (and premises) and a strengthening effect which would have allowed the firms to relocate production to the more efficient plants and shut down the less efficient ones. Furthermore "by concentrating on the production of particular products and giving up the production of others, the signatories will tend to become more specialized. Specialization on products for which they have the best plant and more advanced technology will help the parties to achieve optimum plant size and improve their technical efficiency. It will also help them to develop better-quality products more in tune with the user's requirements. The elimination of capital and labor costs of unprofitable activities will make resources available for the capacity that remains in production . . . The coordination plant closures will also make it easier to cushion the social effects of the restructuring by making suitable arrangements for the retraining and redeployment of workers made redundant."[79]

The Commission's analysis does not accept a temporary collusive output reduction to solve the market crisis. Consistently the Commission had already rejected some anticompetitive behavioral clauses contained in an earlier draft of the agreement and had rejected a proposed similar agreement in 1978 because it provided fixed quotas for the participants.[80] It promoted instead the structural capacity reduction that would last favoring not only some of the actors but the entire industry, and would not interfere with the parties' independence in determining output. At the same time, the Commission also took into consideration the consumer benefits arising from the agreement which were identified as more product improvement and variation but only minor price increases.[81]

d. **Fines, remedies, and conditions enclosed**
Prohibition for all the signatories to communicate data on their individual output and deliveries of synthetic fibres to one another.

e. **Further developments of the case**
None.

---

77   Recital 28 of the decision.
78   Recital 31 of the decision.
79   Recitals 35 and 37 of the decision.

80   See recitals 11 and 19 of the decision.
81   See recitals 39–41 of the decision.

2.5 Export cartels

A Introduction

European export cartels are agreements between competitors in the European internal market with the aim to raise the prices of products sold elsewhere in the world. Export cartels are conceptually no different from hardcore cartels, yet the Commission has taken a different approach to them in cases. This relates to the legal importance of jurisdiction in competition law enforcement. The applicability of European competition law depends on the effects on trade *between* Member States.[82] If, as in many decisions in this section, the agreement deals exclusively with collusion affecting exports sold outside the EU market, the competition rules are not applicable.[83] Note that in this the location of production is irrelevant for the applicability of EU competition rules, as long as the product produced by means of anticompetitive practices has an effect on trade between the Member States.

B Applicable EU legislation

No special legislation applicable. For applicable legislation see chapter 2, paragraph B.

C Related economics texts

Bishop and Walker (2009), not specifically discussed
Carlton and Perloff (2005), not specifically discussed
Church and Ware (2000), not specifically discussed
Martin (1994), not specifically discussed
Martin (2002), not specifically discussed
Motta (2004), paragraphs 1.3.2.4 and 4.6
Tirole (1988), not specifically discussed
Waldman and Jensen (2001), not specifically discussed

D Related legal texts

Bellamy and Child (2008), chapter 5, paragraph 4 (5.021–5.022)
Jones and Sufrin (2008), not specifically discussed
Ritter and Braun (2005), not specifically discussed
Whish (2008), not specifically discussed

---

82 See Commission Guidelines on the effect on trade concept contained in Article 81 and 82 of the Treaty [2004] OJ C 101/81.

83 The *effect doctrine* established the applicability of European competition law each time that a conduct affects the natural pattern of trade between Member States regardless of the place where the undertaking(s) involved in that agreement or practice are established or operate. When the agreement produces its effect inside the common market, it can be scrutinized in its possible anticompetitive effects pursuant to EU competition law. The two most relevant ECJ rulings for the clarification of the *effect doctrine* are Case 48/69, *ICI* v. *Commission (Dyestuffs)* [1972] ECR 949 and Cases 89, 104, 114, 116, 117 and 125–129/85, *A. Ahlström Oy* v. *Commission* [1988] ECR 5193 (appeal against the *Wood Pulp* Commission decision 85/2002/EEC [1985] OJ L 85/1, Case IV/29.725).

E   Commission decisions in chronological order*

DECA **Commission decision 64/599/EEC [1964] OJ L 64/2761, Case IV/71**

Alliance des constructeurs français Commission decision 68/317/EEC [1968] OJ L 201/1, Case IV/25.140

Cobelaz-usines de synthèse Commission decision 68/374/EEC [1968] OJ L 276/13, Case IV/565

Cobelaz-cokeries Commission decision 68/375/EEC [1968] OJ L 276/19, Case IV/507

CFA Commission decision 68/377/EEC [1968] OJ L 276/29, Case IV/666

VVVF Commission decision 69/202/EEC [1969] OJ L 168/22, Case IV/597

SEIFA Commission decision 69/216/EEC [1969] OJ L 173/8, 704, Case IV/25.410

Supexie Commission decision 71/22/EEC [1971] OJ L 10/12, Case IV/337

SAFCO Commission decision 72/23/EEC [1972] OJ L 13/44, Case IV/23.514 (Martin, 1994, pp. 182–3)

SCPA – Kali und Salz Commission decision 73/212/EEC [1973] OJ L 217/3, Cases IV/791, 1373, 1374, 1498, 1499, 1500

The Distillers Company Ltd Commission decision 78/163/EEC [1978] OJ L 50/16, Case IV/28.282

Vegetable Parchment Commission decision 78/252/EEC [1978] OJ L 70/54, Case IV/29.176 (Martin, 1994, pp. 183–4)

Central Stikstof Verkoopkantoor Commission decision 78/732/EC [1978] OJ L 242/15, Case IV/26.186 (*)

Floral **Commission decision 80/182/EEC [1980] OJ L 39/51, Case IV/29.672**

Industrieverband Solnhofener Natursteinplatten eV Commission decision 80/1074/EEC [1980] OJ L 318/32, Case IV/197

Siemens/Fanuc Commission decision 85/618/EEC [1985] OJ L 376/29, Case IV/30.739

ANSAC Commission decision 91/301/EEC [1991] OJ L 152/54, Case IV/33.016

Lloyd's Underwriters Association & Institute of London Underwriters Commission decision 93/3/EEC [1993] OJ L 4/26, Cases IV/32.797, 32.798

F   Economic landmark cases

F.1   *DECA* Commission decision 64/599/EEC [1964] OJ L 64/2761

Relevance: This decision represents the first case in which the Commission dealt with an (anticompetitive) export agreement that had produced its effects outside the European internal market. The Commission, therefore, recognized its lack of jurisdiction in assessing the effect on competition of such an agreement. If a cartel does not produce any effect on trade between Member States it cannot be assessed under the rules laid down in Article 101 FEU Treaty.

- Case IV/71
- **Decision** Negative Clearance
- **Decision addressee(s)**:
  - Dutch Engineers and Contractors Association (DECA), *the Netherlands*

- Decisions displayed in **bold type** are described in the section. Decisions highlighted with (*) include interesting economic analysis by the Commission on the specific topic of the section. Some decisions contain economic reasoning on more than one topic and therefore appear in several lists of Commission decisions in chronological order. Reference is made in brackets and **bold type** to the relevant section in which the decision is extensively described as a landmark case. When decisions are referenced and/or described in some detail in one or more of the economic textbooks, reference in brackets is also made to the relevant part(s) of those texts.

- **Report route:** Application for negative clearance submitted to the Commission by DECA
- **Date of the decision:** 22 October 1964
- **Competition Commissioner:** H. von der Groeben
- **Relevant product market:** Civil and hydraulic engineer public works
- **Relevant geographical market:** Non-European market
- **Description of the case**
    a. **Relevant facts**

    The Dutch companies Amsterdamsche Ballast Maatschappij NV, van Hattum en Blankevoort NV, Hollandsche Beton Maatschappij NV, and De Verenigde Bedrijven Bredero NV set up DECA. The statutory goal of the association was to facilitate the participation of its members in civil and hydraulic engineering of public works projects outside Europe.

    Under the DECA agreement, the members were obliged to inform the association when they heard about tenders with a market value above 1 million Dutch guilders. The association would then communicate it to the other parties to the agreement in order to give them the possibility to collaborate in market analysis and in preparation of a possible price tender. If a member had the intention to submit a tender offer higher than 2 million Dutch guilders, it was obliged to inform DECA. The role of DECA was to arrange a meeting with all interested members to determine together the member(s) that would then submit a bid or would share the tender market in question.

    b. **Origin of the case**

    DECA submitted to the Commission an application to see the internal regulation that was approved at the meeting of 2 May 1962 and modified on 15 March 1963 and which regulated its activities, be cleared (and thus Article 101 FEU Treaty declared inapplicable) pursuant to Article 2 of Regulation No. 17.

    c. **Economic analysis**

    The cartel at hand is essentially an export bid-rigging cartel installed by an association that was expressly set up for activities outside the European internal market. The Commission did not analyze the anticompetitive effects arising from the cartel because it was not entitled to enforce Article 101 FEU Treaty. As mentioned in the introduction to this subchapter, agreements or concerted practice producing effects outside the internal market rather than on trade between Member States are not within the scope of application of EU competition rules, irrespective of the effect on competition.[84]

    d. **Fines, remedies, and conditions enclosed**

    None.

    e. **Further developments of the case**

    None.

---

84 An example of this line of reasoning by the ECJ can be found in *Javico International and Javico AG* v. *Yves Saint Laurent Parfums* (Case C-306/96), where the ECJ concluded "that an agreement in which the reseller gives to the producer an undertaking that he will sell the contractual products on a market outside the Community cannot be regarded as having the object of appreciably restricting competition within the common market or as being capable of affecting, as such, trade between Member States" (recital 20 of the judgment).

F.2   *Floral* Commission decision 80/182/EEC [1980] OJ L 39/51

Relevance: Economically based assessment of a cartel aimed at collusive export on the German market (i.e. within Europe thus producing effect on trade between Member States). The Commission bases its negative assessment on the absence of economic restraints justifying common exports via a joint venture agreement, and on the fact that no efficiencies for consumers would derive from the agreement. The described effects are measured in relation to the market (oligopolistic) characteristics.

- Case IV/29.672
- **Decision:** Infringement of Article 101(1) FEU Treaty, imposition of fines
- **Decision addressee(s):**
    - Compagnie Française de l'Azote SA, *France*
    - Générale des Engrais SA, *France*
    - CdF Chimie, Société Chimique des Charbonnages SA, *France*
    - Mr. Franz Schiffer, *Federal Republic of Germany*
    - Floral Düngemittelverkaufsgesellschaft GmbH, *Federal Republic of Germany*
- **Report route:** Commission own initiative and subsequent notification for exemption submitted on 10 July 1978 by the parties listed above
- **Date of the decision:** 28 November 1979
- **Competition Commissioner:** R. Vouel
- **Relevant product market:** Compound fertilizers
- **Relevant geographical market:** Federal Republic of Germany
- **Description of the case**
    a. **Relevant facts**

      On 10 May 1968 Compagnie Française de l'Azote SA (COFAZ), Générale des Engrais SA (GESA) and CdF Chimie, Société Chimique des Charbonnages SA (CdF)[85] – the three largest French producers of compound fertilizers – set up a joint venture with the object of purchasing or manufacturing fertilizers for resale in Germany. The company was named Alfa GmbH and was subsequently renamed Floral GmbH in 1970. Each of the three companies held 30 percent of the shares in Floral and the remaining 10 percent was held by Mr. Schiffer, the appointed managing director of Floral and owner of the Franz Schiffer company being the exclusive distributor of the joint venture products in southern and western Germany.

      The three undertakings concerned in the agreement held more than two-thirds of the French production and more than 10 percent of total European production. Furthermore, exports to Germany accounted for two-thirds of intra-Community French exports and for 38 percent of total French exports. Both the French and the German market were to a large extent dependent on imports and the plants in both countries had some overcapacity.

      The supply to Floral was shared by the three companies, but CdF accounted for 68 percent, GESA for 18 percent and COFAZ for 14 percent, which did not coincide with the correspondent shareholding of each of them.

---

85   At the time the agreement was signed in 1968 the companies involved had a different corporate structure. The structure at the time of the decision was the result of several mergers and inter-firm share acquisitions. See recital 2 of the decision.

The products supplied by the three companies were homogenous and, although they charged the jointly held Floral different prices, they were resold on the German market at a uniform price, uniform terms, and with uniform discounts.[86] The prices charged in Germany at that point were the highest in Europe at both wholesale and retail level.

Until 1974–5, the three companies had been carrying out their export business exclusively through Floral and even afterwards managed to "[channel] the bulk of their exports . . . through their joint subsidiary."[87]

b. Origin of the case

The Commission started investigation on its own initiative. Subsequently on 10 July 1978 the parties listed above submitted a notification pursuant to Article 4 of Regulation No. 17 to see the agreement be declared exempted from the application of Article 101(1) FEU Treaty by virtue of Article 101(3) FEU Treaty. By a decision of 27 September 1978 the Commission decided to initiate a proceeding.

c. Economic analysis

The cartel analyzed in the decision is a price fixing cartel carried out through a joint venture expressly set up to sell the relevant product at a collusive price in a certain geographical area (Germany).

It is an example of an export cartel that is relevant for European competition authorities because it generates effects on trade between Member States and can thus be challenged under the set of rules provided by EU competition law.

The Commission's analysis of the agreement concentrated on the argument that the joint venture was not necessary for the three French producers to enter the German market. The Commission alleged that since all suppliers had idle capacity, disposed of the necessary know-how, and had access to distribution and transport logistics, they would each be capable of supplying the German market without cooperation. Consequently the Commission rejected the existence of "real economic constraints militating in favor of"[88] such an agreement. The Commission challenged the agreement on a number of grounds. It was treated as a restriction of competition because it effectively imposed uniform prices and supply conditions on German consumers, depriving them of the choice among a variety of different offers. Moreover, the Commission regarded as highly unlikely that the three companies would supply other German customers except Floral. Similarly, the Commission rejected claims that the agreement would generate production or distribution efficiencies. Finally, serious doubts arose as to whether the consumers would benefit from an agreement such as the Floral export joint venture.

The agreement significantly affected the trade between Member States. The agreement would in fact regulate the export activities between two States. The Commission was concerned that since the German market for compound fertilizers was already oligopolistic, consisting of few suppliers with large market shares, the existence of the French export cartel would have made the oligopoly even tighter.

---

86 See recital I-6 of the decision.
87 Recital II-1 of the decision.

88 Recital II-2 of the decision.

d. **Fines, remedies, and conditions enclosed**
   – The Commission imposed the following total fines:

Company	Fine (EUA)[89]
Compagnie Française de l'Azote SA	85,000
Générale des Engrais SA	85,000
CdF Chimie, Société Chimique des Charbonnages SA	85,000

   – Obligations for all the undertakings concerned to bring the infringe-
     ments to an end.
e. **Further developments of the case**
    None.

2.6 Trade associations

A Introduction

Trade associations are associations of firms active in the same trade that aim to promote the common interests of their members and the industry as a whole. A trade association generally provides its members with a forum in which to discuss topics of common interests. It organizes trade fairs, conventions, and publications to disseminate information. Associations can serve a number of valuable and legitimate functions, including representation of the association members' point of view to governments, public relations, and lobbying. Trade associations further help to set industry standards, codes of ethics and certifications, as well as run educational programs, and can facilitate cross-fertilization in R&D.

The European Commission nevertheless regards trade associations with a certain amount of suspicion under competition law. In the past, trade associations have been a vehicle to engage in collusive conduct. By facilitating the exchange of market relevant information between its members, trade association meetings may indirectly or directly stimulate collusive behavior. The legitimate meetings may spark a cartel simply by bringing together key competitors. In addition, the articles of association, (binding) recommendations to the members, certifications and qualification standards may (unintentionally) create conditions ideal for (tacit) collusion.[90] This may include the raising of entry barriers as well as installing easy monitoring of compliance with cartel agreements.

---

89 EUA is the acronym for European Unit of Account. It used to constitute the internal accounting unit used for the EEC Member States currencies' exchange. It was then replaced, until the introduction of the Euro, by the ECU (European Currency Unit), adopted by the European Council on 13 March 1979.

90 An example is given in *Verband der Sachversicherer e.V.* v. *Commission* (Case 45/85) concerning a trade association that coordinated its members' activities by means of articles of associations and recommendations to the members. The case concerned so-called "recommendations" which were communicated to the association's members. These recommendations constituted the expression of a concerted practice put into effect by the undertakings affiliated to the association with the object of restricting competition among them.

   The ECJ held that in assessing the recommendations "it is necessary to take account of the nature of the recommendation itself." Although it was described as a "non-binding recommendation," it lays down in mandatory terms a collective, flat-rate and across-the-board increase in premiums. Moreover "the statutes of the association state that it is empowered to coordinate the activities of its members, especially in relation to competition, that the task of the specialist committee on industrial risks is to coordinate the policy of the members with regard to premium rates and that the decisions or recommendations of the committee are deemed to be definitive unless they are referred to the bureau for approval at the request of one of the organs expressly given such a power of reference" (recital 31 of the judgment).

   The ECJ concluded that "it must be stated that the recommendation, regardless of what its precise legal status may be, constituted the faithful reflection of the applicant's resolve to coordinate the conduct of its members on the German insurance market in accordance with the terms of the recommendation" (recital 32 of the judgment).

B Applicable EU legislation

No special legislation applicable. For applicable legislation see chapter 2, paragraph B.

C Related economics texts

Bishop and Walker (2009), paragraph 5.16
Carlton and Perloff (2005), chapter 19, paragraph 3(3)
Church and Ware (2000), paragraph 10.6
Martin (1994), not specifically discussed
Martin (2002), not specifically discussed
Motta (2004), not specifically discussed
Tirole (1988), not specifically discussed
Waldman and Jensen (2001), chapter 9, paragraph 1 and chapter 18, paragraph 9

D Related legal texts

Bellamy and Child (2008), chapter 5, paragraph 8
Jones and Sufrin (2008), chapter 3, paragraph 5(C, iii)
Ritter and Braun (2005), chapter 1, paragraph D(4)
Whish (2008), chapter 3, paragraph 3(B)

E Commission decisions in chronological order•

Transocean Marine Paint Association Commission decision 67/454/EEC [1967] OJ L 163/10, Case IV/223
Eurogypsum Commission decision 68/128/EEC [1968] OJ L 57/9, Case IV/26.352
SOCEMAS Commission decision 68/318/EEC [1968] OJ L 201/4, Case IV/129 (Martin, 1994, p. 182)
Convention chaufourniers Commission decision 69/152/EEC [1969] OJ L 122/8, Cases IV/242, 295
ASPA Commission decision 70/333/EEC [1970] OJ L 148/9, Case IV/299
Cematex Commission decision 71/337/EEC [1971] OJ L 227/26, Case IV/181 (**described in detail as landmark case in section 2.7**)
Vereeniging van Cementhandelaren Commission decision 72/22/EEC [1972] OJ L 13/34, Case IV/324
Gas water-heaters and bath-heaters Commission decision 73/232/EEC [1973] OJ L 217/34, Case IV/25.963
Stoves and Heaters (Haarden- en Kachelhandel) Commission decision 75/358/EEC [1975] OJ L 159/22, Case IV/712
INTERGROUP Commission decision 75/482/EEC [1975] OJ L 212/23, Case IV/28.838
Bomée-Stichting Commission decision 75/781/EEC [1975] OJ L 329/30, Case IV/256

• Decisions displayed in **bold type** are described in the section. Decisions highlighted with (*) include interesting economic analysis by the Commission on the specific topic of the section. Some decisions contain economic reasoning on more than one topic and therefore appear in several lists of Commission decisions in chronological order. Reference is made in brackets and **bold type** to the relevant section in which the decision is extensively described as a landmark case. When decisions are referenced and/or described in some detail in one or more of the economic textbooks, reference in brackets is also made to the relevant part(s) of those texts.

Pabst and Richardz/BNIA Commission decision 76/684/EEC [1976] OJ L 231/24, Case IV/28.980

Centraal Bureau voor de Rijwielhandel Commission decision 78/59/EEC [1978] OJ L 20/18, Case IV/147

FEDETAB Commission decision 78/670/EEC [1978] OJ L 224/29, Cases IV/28.852, 29.127, 29.149

Rennet Commission decision 80/234/EEC [1980] OJ L 51/19, Case IV/29.011

National Sulphuric Acid Association Commission decision 80/917/EEC [1980] OJ L 260/24, Case IV/27.958

IMA Rules Commission decision 80/1071/EEC [1980] OJ L 318/1, Case IV/25.077

Italian Flat Glass Commission decision 81/881/EC [1981] OJ L 326/32, Case IV/29.988 (Bishop and Walker, 2009, 5.07, 5.14; Martin, 1994, pp. 178–9)

VBBB/VBVB Commission decision 82/123/EEC [1982] OJ L 54/36, Case IV/428 (Martin, 1994, p. 532)

Navewa–Anseau Commission decision 82/371/EEC [1982] OJ L 167/17, Case IV/29.995

SSI Commission decision 82/506/EEC [1982] OJ L 232/1, Cases IV/29.525, 30.000

Vimpoltu Commission decision 83/361/EEC [1983] OJ L 200/44, Case IV/30.174

Milchförderungsfonds Commission decision 85/76/EEC [1985] OJ L 35/35, Case IV/28.930

EATE Levy Commission decision 85/383/EEC [1985] OJ L 219/35, Case IV/31.029

London Sugar Futures Market Ltd Commission decision 85/563/EEC [1985] OJ L 368/25, Case IV/27.590

London Cocoa Terminal Market Association Ltd Commission decision 85/564/EEC [1985] OJ L 369/28, Case IV/27.591

Coffee Terminal Market Association Ltd Commission decision 85/565/EEC [1985] OJ L 369/31, Case IV/27.592

London Rubber Terminal Market Association Ltd Commission decision 85/566/EEC [1985] OJ L 369/34, Case IV/27.593

Roofing Felt Commission decision 86/399/EEC [1986] OJ L 232/15, Case IV/31.371 (**described in detail as landmark case in section 2.7**)

International Petroleum Exchange of London Ltd Commission decision 87/2/EEC [1987] OJ L 3/27, Case IV/30.439

GAFTA Soya Bean Meal Futures Association Commission decision 87/44/EEC [1987] OJ L 19/18, Case IV/29.036

The London Grain Futures Market Commission decision 87/45/EEC [1987] OJ L 19/22, Case IV/29.688

The London Potato Futures Market Association Ltd Commission decision 87/46/EEC [1987] OJ L 19/26, Case IV/30.176

London Meat Futures Exchange Commission decision 87/47/EEC [1987] OJ L 19/30, Case IV/31.614

ABI Commission decision 87/103/EEC [1987] OJ L 43/51, Case IV/31.356 (**described in detail as landmark case in section 2.8**)

Baltic International Freight Futures Exchange Ltd Commission decision 87/408/EEC [1987] OJ L 222/24, Case IV/31.764

New potatoes Commission decision 88/109/EEC [1988] OJ L 59/25, Case IV/31.735

Bloemenveilingen Aalsmeer Commission decision 88/491/EEC [1988] OJ L 262/27, Case IV/31.379

Hudson's Bay/Dansk Pelsdyravlerforening Commission decision 88/587/EEC [1988] OJ L 316/43, Case IV/31.424

Publishers Association/Net Book Agreements Commission decision 89/44/EEC [1989] OJ L 22/12, Cases IV/27.394, 27.393 (Martin, 1994, pp. 522–3)

APB Commission decision 90/33/EEC [1990] OJ L 18/35, Case IV/32.302

TEKO Commission decision 90/92/EEC [1990] OJ L 13/34, Case IV/32.408

Concordato Incendio Commission decision 90/25/EEC [1990] OJ L 15/25, Case IV/32.265

Sippa Commission decision 91/128/EEC [1991] OJ L 60/19, Case IV/31.559

IATA Passenger Agency Programmes Commission decision 91/480/EEC [1991] OJ L 258/18, Case IV/32.659

IATA Cargo Agency Programmes Commission decision 91/481/EEC [1991] OJ L 258/29, Case IV/32.792

ASSURPOL Commission decision 92/96/EEC [1992] OJ L 37/16, Case IV/33.100

U.K. Tractor Registration Exchange **Commission decision 92/157/EEC [1992] OJ L 68/19, Cases IV/31.370, 31.446**

Distribution of Railway Tickets by Travel Agents Commission decision 92/568/EEC [1992] OJ L 366/47, Case IV/33.585

Jahrhundertvertrag Commission decision 93/126/EEC [1993] OJ L 50/14, Cases IV/33.151, 33.997

Stichting Certificatie Kraanverhuurbedrijf and FNK Commission decision 94/272/EEC [1994] OJ L 117/30, Case IV/B-2/34.179

Coapi Commission decision 95/188/EC [1995] OJ L 122/37, Case IV/33.686

SCK/FNK Commission decision 95/551/EC [1995] OJ L 312/79, Cases IV/34.216, 34.179, 34.202

Fenex Commission decision 96/438/EC [1996] OJ L 181/28, Case IV/34.983 (*)

FEG and TU Commission decision 2000/117/EC [2000] OJ L 39/1, Case IV/33.884

CECED Commission decision 2000/475/EC [2000] OJ L 187/47, Case IV.F.1/36.718 (**described in detail as landmark case in section 2.8**) (*) (Motta, 2004, pp. 27–8)

PO/French Beef Commission decision 2003/600/EC [2003] OJ L 209/12, Case COMP/C.38.279/F3

Fee scale of the Belgian architects' association Commission decision of 24 June 2004, published on DG Comp website, Case COMP/38.549

Groupement des Cartes Bancaires Commission decision of 17 October 2007, published on DG Comp website, Case COMP/38.606

F Economic landmark cases

F.1 *U.K. Tractor Registration Exchange* Commission decision 92/157/EEC [1992] OJ L 68/19

Relevance: First case in which the Commission emphasized the role played by the association of undertakings in the organization and implementation of the agreement. Particular focus on the exchange of information carried out through the association and on the exclusionary effect generated for firms not member of it.

- Cases IV/31.370, 31.446
- **Decision**: Infringement of Article 101(1) FEU Treaty
- **Decision addressee(s)**:
    – The Agricultural Engineers Association, *United Kingdom*
    – Ford New Holland Ltd, *United Kingdom*

- Massey-Ferguson (United Kingdom) Ltd, *United Kingdom*
- J. I. Case Europe Ltd, *United Kingdom*
- John Deere Ltd, *United Kingdom*
- Renault Agriculture Ltd, *United Kingdom*
- Watveare Ltd, *United Kingdom*
- Fiatagri UK Ltd, *United Kingdom*
- Same-Lamborghini (UK) Ltd, *United Kingdom*

- **Report route:** Notification for exemption submitted to the Commission on 4 January 1988 by the Agricultural Engineers Association
- **Date of the decision:** 17 February 1992
- **Competition Commissioner:** L. Brittan
- **Relevant product market:** Agricultural tractors
- **Relevant geographical market:** United Kingdom
- **Description of the case**
  a. **Relevant facts**

  The Agricultural Engineers Association Ltd (AEA) is the trade association of manufacturers and importers of agricultural machinery of the United Kingdom. The AEA notified to the Commission an information exchange agreement concerning the provision and exchange of information "identifying the volume of retail sales and market shares of eight manufacturers and importers of agricultural tractors on the United Kingdom market."[91]

  The tractor market in the United Kingdom was strongly oligopolistic, with four suppliers (all members of the exchange agreement) holding some 76–77 percent of the market. These four largest suppliers achieved together with the other four (later three) members of the agreement a market share of some 87–88 percent. The remaining market was shared by several small producers. The other main feature of the market was the existence of high barriers to entry. These barriers were firstly created to respond to the requirement to set up and maintain a dense distribution and services network to reach every customer in a timely fashion in case of emergency. Furthermore the market was stagnant, characterized by general overcapacity and with brand loyalty playing an important role. In addition, the UK market did not face any competition from importers from outside Europe.

  The exchange of information system was complex and structured on three different levels in such a way as to disclose aggregate industry data, data identifying the sales of individual competitor members of the agreement, and data on own dealer sales. The aggregate industry data allowed each member to obtain information about the industry sales according to horsepower grouping or by driveline; on a national, regional, local, counties, dealer, or postal code sectors basis. The information provided about each competitor member of the agreement was highly detailed and precise. It concerned the exact volume

---

91   Recital 1 of the decision.

of retail sales and market shares on both a (wider or narrower) geographical basis and according to every specific model sold. Information on the daily and monthly retail sales and market shares of each competitor was also provided. The members of the agreement were aware of the confidential and sensitive nature of the information exchanged and of the circumstance that that exchange was possible only due to a reciprocal exchange of information and confidence.[92] Through the data on dealer sales of own companies, the manufacturers were provided with all details on the import, export, and sales activities of their own dealers throughout the whole United Kingdom

b. Origin of the case

On 4 January 1988 the Agricultural Engineers Association submitted to the Commission a notification pursuant to Article 4 of Regulation No. 17 to see the Exchange Agreement be declared exempted from the application of Article 101(1) FEU Treaty by virtue of Article 101(3) FEU Treaty.

c. Economic analysis

In this decision the Commission focused particularly on the active role played by the trade association (AEA) in the organization and direction of the exchange agreement. Indeed after a period in which the AEA merely functioned as the secretariat of the committee in charge of the implementation of the agreement, the AEA became a permanent forum through which the parties exchanged sensitive commercial information and simultaneously it was responsible for the distribution of the required information among all members of the agreement.

These circumstances constituted a significant restriction of competition, particularly in the light of the market conditions. The exchange of information restricted competition because "it creates a degree of market transparency between the suppliers in a highly concentrated market which is likely to destroy what hidden competition there remains between the suppliers in that market on account of the risk and ease exposure of independent competition action. In this highly concentrated market, "hidden competition" is essentially that element of uncertainty and secrecy between the main suppliers regarding market conditions without which none of them has the necessary scope of action to compete efficiently. Uncertainty and secrecy between suppliers is a vital element of competition in this kind of market."[93] The detailed product and geographic market information on retail sales allowed the parties to establish with accuracy the market position, the performance, and any eventual increase in sales of each competitor, and consequently to limit price competition to the minimum necessary to react to other actors' changes of strategy.[94] "In the absence of the Exchange [agreement], firms would have to compete in a market with some measure of uncertainty as to the exact place, degree and means of attack by rivals. This uncertainty is a normal competitive risk bringing about stronger competition because [the] reaction and reduction of prices cannot be limited to the absolute minimum degree necessary to defend and establish position."[95] The exchange of information raised entry barriers for non-members, i.e. potential market entrants with no prospect of becoming a member, and who would

---

92 See recital 21 of the decision.   94 See recital 42 of the decision.
93 Recital 37 of the decision.   95 Recital 43 of the decision.

be subject to a clear competitive disadvantage in the absence of the detailed market information provided by the AEA.

Furthermore the information provided to each manufacturer on the retail sales of its own dealers, irrespective of whether it provided any information about competitors, would have generated a restriction of trade between Member States because it would have allowed each producer to control (and eventually to impede) parallel import and export activities of their dealers and importers. This was the argument put forth by the Commission to consider this kind of information anticompetitive.

The Commission's assessment of the role of the trade association involved and the consequent exchange of information is based on case-by-case approach. It accordingly performed an analysis of market conditions and the type of information exchanged. In fact, the Commission did not oppose the non-discriminatory exchange of aggregate industry data to all producers through the AEA. The objections that were raised by the Commission concerned on the one hand the role played by the AEA in the collection and provision of detailed data about individual competitors and on the other hand the exchange of such disaggregated data in a highly concentrated and stagnant market. In this decision the Commission did not rule out the possibility that information exchange between competitors might raise concerns of anticompetitive effects also in non-oligopolistic markets. Rather, it established a strong presumption of anticompetitiveness of information exchange among a few firms in a concentrated market. This confirms the Commission's case-by-case analysis of the exchange of information agreements and the fact that the analysis carried out in this landmark decision cannot be considered as establishing *per se* prohibitions or permissions but only a further evolution of the Commission's interpretation of this kind of agreements.

d. **Fines, remedies, and conditions enclosed**
– Obligation for the parties to put an end to the infringement forthwith.
– Obligation for the parties to refrain from any future agreement with the same or similar object or effect.

e. **Further developments of the case**
Case T-34/92 *Fiatagri UK Ltd and New Holland Ford Ltd* v. *Commission* [1994] ECR II-905, appeal dismissed.
Case C-8/95P *New Holland Ford* v. *Commission* [1998] ECR I-3175, CFI judgment upheld.
Case T-35/92 *John Deere Ltd* v. *Commission* [1994] ECR II-957, appeal dismissed. The CFI (now "the General Court") ruled that the AEA functioned as "... an institutional framework enabling information to be exchanged between the traders through the trade association to which they belong and, having regard to the frequency of such information and its systematic nature, it also enables a given trader to forecast more precisely the conduct of its competitors, so reducing or removing the degree of uncertainty about the operation of the market which would have existed in the absence of such an exchange of information . . ."[96]

96 Recital 52 of the judgment.

Case C-7/95 *John Deere Ltd* v. *Commission* [1998] ECR I-3111, CFI judgment upheld.

2.7 Marketing and advertising agreements

A Introduction

Producers advertise their goods to inform potential customers about product features, price, quality, and distribution points, all with the aim of increasing demand. Advertising is an important dimension of competition. Apart from being informative, advertising campaigns are known to help create brand loyalty in markets with differentiated products. Since advertising is expensive and companies will generally only invest in it if it is profitable, advertising appears to be effective in increasing demand and/or reducing its price elasticity. The overall welfare effects of advertising are ambiguous, however. To the extent that advertising informs customers about new products and services to enjoy, it is often beneficial. If advertising is largely persuasive and aimed at stealing business from rivals, competing firms may find themselves spending marketing budgets wastefully, yet unable to unilaterally reduce advertisement for fear of losing customers to their advertising competitor. Advertising can furthermore raise barriers to entry by creating a strong brand image. Generally, however, the socially detrimental effects of advertising are not thought to be reason for intervention.

In markets in which advertisement is mostly informative, the European Commission should be concerned with marketing and advertisement agreements that aim to reduce competition. Jointly planned campaigns for the commercialization and promotion of products, for example, can provide opportunity and incentive for firms to form other types of agreements restrictive of competition as well. There are additional concerns, for example about the potential foreclosure effects of joint advertising campaigns arising from the exchange of sensitive information. Also, preventing product differentiation through marketing agreements may help create circumstances in which price collusion is more easily sustained. Collusive advertising may thus relate to horizontal price fixing.

B Applicable EU legislation

No special legislation applicable. For applicable legislation see chapter 2, paragraph B.

C Related economics texts

Bishop and Walker (2009), not specifically discussed
Carlton and Perloff (2005), chapter 14
Church and Ware (2000), chapter 17
Martin (1994), chapter 8, paragraph 2
Martin (2002), chapter 9
Motta (2004), not specifically discussed
Tirole (1988), paragraph 7.3
Waldman and Jensen (2001), chapter 12

D Related legal texts

Bellamy and Child (2008), chapter 5, paragraph 8(C)
Jones and Sufrin (2008), chapter 11, paragraph 3(D, iii)
Ritter and Braun (2005), not specifically discussed
Whish (2008), chapter 13, paragraph 9

E Commission decisions in chronological order*

Transocean Marine Paint Association Commission decision 67/454/EEC [1967] OJ L 163/10,
   Case IV/223
EEMO Commission decision 69/90/EEC [1969] OJ L 69/13, Case IV/93
Cematex **Commission decision 71/337/EEC [1971] OJ L 227/26, Case IV/181**
European sugar industry Commission decision 73/109/EC [1973] OJ L 140/17, Case IV/26.918
   (**described in detail as landmark case in section 3.2**) (Martin, 1994, p. 142)
SCPA – Kali und Salz Commission decision 73/212/EEC [1973] OJ L 217/3, Cases IV/791, 1373,
   1374, 1498, 1499, 1500
Gas water-heaters and bath-heaters Commission decision 73/232/EEC [1973] OJ L 217/34, Case
   IV/25.963
Transocean Marine Paint Association Commission decision 74/16/EEC [1974] OJ L 19/18, Case
   IV/223
Papiers peints de Belgique Commission decision 74/431/EEC [1974] OJ L 373/3, Case IV/426
   (Martin, 1994, p. 181)
UNIDI Commission decision 75/498/EEC [1975] OJ L 228/14, Case IV/28.775
Transocean Marine Paint Association Commission decision 75/649/EEC [1975] OJ L 286/24,
   Case IV/223
BPICA Commission decision 77/722/EEC [1977] OJ L 299/18, Case IV/417
EMO Commission decision 79/37/EEC [1979] OJ L 11/16, Case IV/93
Transocean Marine Paint Association Commission decision 80/184/EEC [1980] OJ L 39/73,
   Case IV/223
BPICA Commission decision 82/349/EEC [1982] OJ L 156/16, Case IV/417
Rolled zinc products and zinc alloys Commission decision 82/866/EEC [1982] OJ L 362/40, Case
   IV/29.629
Cematex Commission decision 83/252/EEC [1983] OJ L 140/27, Case IV/181
SMM and T Exhibition Agreement Commission decision 83/666/EEC [1983] OJ L 376/1, Case
   IV/27.492
Zinc Producer Group Commission decision 84/405/EEC [1984] OJ L 220/27, Case IV/30.350
UNIDI Commission decision 84/588/EEC [1984] OJ L 322/10, Case IV/28.775
Wood Pulp Commission decision 85/202/EEC [1985] OJ L 85/1, Case IV/29.725 (Martin, 1994,
   pp. 142–3; Motta, 2004, pp. 211–19)
Roofing Felt **Commission decision 86/399/EEC [1986] OJ L 232/15, Case IV/31.371**

•   Decisions displayed in **bold type** are described in the section. Decisions highlighted with (*) include interesting economic analysis
    by the Commission on the specific topic of the section. Some decisions contain economic reasoning on more than one topic and
    therefore appear in several lists of Commission decisions in chronological order. Reference is made in brackets and **bold type** to the
    relevant section in which the decision is extensively described as a landmark case. When decisions are referenced and/or described
    in some detail in one or more of the economic textbooks, reference in brackets is also made to the relevant part(s) of those
    texts.

VIFKA Commission decision 86/499/EEC [1986] OJ L 291/46, Case IV/28.959

Meldoc Commission decision 86/596/EEC OJ L 348/50, Case IV/31.204

Internationale Dentalschau Commission decision 87/509/EEC [1987] OJ L 293/58, Case IV/31.739

New potatoes Commission decision 88/109/EEC [1988] OJ L 59/25, Case IV/31.735

British Dental Trade Association Commission decision 88/477/EEC [1988] OJ L 233/15, Case IV/31.593

Transocean Marine Paint Association Commission decision 88/635/EEC [1988] OJ L 351/40, Case IV/223

Publishers Association/Net Book Agreements Commission decision 89/44/EEC [1989] OJ L 22/12, Cases IV/27.394, 27.393 (Martin, 1994, pp. 522–3)

Flat Glass Commission decision 89/93/EEC [1989] OJ L 33/44, Case IV/31.906

EMO Commission decision 89/96/EEC [1989] OJ L 37/11, Case IV/93

Sippa Commission decision 91/128/EEC [1991] OJ L 60/19, Case IV/31.559

TACA Commission decision 1999/243/EC [1999] OJ L 95/1, Case IV/35.134

EPI code of conduct Commission decision 1999/267/EC [1999] OJ L 106/14, IV/36.147

P&I Clubs Commission decision 1999/329/EC [1999] OJ L 125/12, Case IV/30.373 (*)

Revised TACA Commission decision 2003/68/EC [2003] OJ L 26/53, Case COMP/37.396/D2

UEFA Commission decision 2003/778/EC [2003] OJ L 291/25, Case COMP/C.2–37.398

Electrical and mechanical carbon and graphite products Commission decision 2004/420/EC [2004] OJ L 125/45, Case COMP/38.359

French beer Commission decision of 29 September 2004, published on DG Comp website on 22 December 2007, Case COMP/C.37.750/B2

Choline chloride Commission decision of 9 December 2004, published on DG Comp website, Case COMP/E-2/37.533

Fine Art Auction Houses Commission decision 2005/590/EC [2005] OJ L 200/92, Case COMP/E-2/37.784 **(described as landmark case in section 2.1)**

F   Economic landmark cases

F.1   *Cematex* Commission decision 71/337/EEC [1971] OJ L 227/26

Relevance: This decision shows the approach adopted since the very beginning of the competition rules implementation by the Commission toward the organization of fairs and expositions. The Commission has always recognized the efficiencies both for producers and consumers of such events even in the presence of limitations regarding the possibility of participation in other similar events. All the efficiencies acknowledged by the Commission are described in this decision, with particular focus on the rationalization of the promoting efforts.

- Case IV/181
- **Decision**: Exemption pursuant to Article 101(3) FEU Treaty for twelve years
- **Decision addressee(s)**:
  - Comité européen des constructeurs de matériel textile (Cematex), *Switzerland*
  - Fachgemeinschaft Textilmaschinen im Verein Deutscher Maschinenbau-Anstalten EV (VDMA), *Federal Republic of Germany*
  - Syndicat des constructeurs belges de machines textiles (SIMATEX), *Belgium*
  - Union des constructeurs de materiél textile de France, *France*
  - TREX British Textile Machinery Organization, *United Kingdom*

  – Associazione di costruttori italiani di macchinario per l'industria tessile, *Italy*
  – Vereniging van Metaal-Industrieën, *the Netherlands*
  – Société Suisse des constructeurs de machines, groupe "Industrie des machines textiles," *Switzerland*

- **Report route:** Application for negative clearance and notification for exemption submitted to the Commission on 25 October 1962 by Cematex
- **Date of the decision:** 24 September 1971
- **Competition Commissioner:** A. Borschette
- **Relevant product market:** Industrial textile machineries and organization of fairs for their exposition
- **Relevant geographical market:** European internal market
- **Description of the case**
  a. **Relevant facts**
     Cematex was an organization set up by trade associations of producers of industrial textile machinery. It combined all the national trade associations from Member States (except Luxembourg) and Switzerland in the same commercial sector.

     One of the statutory functions of Cematex was the organization of an international fair for the exposition of textile machineries and their accessories (ITMA) every four years. Taking part in these events was open to all producers or sellers that were member of one of the national member associations of Cematex and to producers–sellers from other countries irrespective of their affiliation to a national association. Any producer wanting to exhibit at the fair was required to conform to future decisions adopted by the general commissioner in charge of the fair's organization. Furthermore, they were requested to submit themselves to an exclusive participation clause according to which they would refrain from participating in any similar event in Western Europe and in some other neighboring countries either during the year of the exposition or the previous year. The prohibition was extended also to indirect participations. The limitation period for the 1967 and 1971 expositions was extended also to the year following the fair. This supplementary condition was abandoned after the Commission's comments on the contents of the Cematex regulations.

  b. **Origin of the case**
     On 25 October 1962 Cematex submitted to the Commission an application for negative clearance and notification for exemption pursuant to Articles 2 and 4 of Regulation No. 17 to see Article 101(1) FEU Treaty be declared not applicable to the international fair organized for 1963 and to all future similar events or alternatively the same events be declared exempted from the application of Article 101(1) FEU Treaty by virtue of Article 101(3) FEU Treaty.

  c. **Economic analysis**
     This decision is the expression of the Commission's repeated and constant positive approach toward a specific form of collective advertising taking place in exhibitions and fairs which are either organized by association of undertakings (as in this case) or by private parties. Their intent is to promote a certain product and to give the opportunities to all producers to expose their products and to consumers to have an unique occasion to directly see all the different offers on the market.

A fair is thought to give as much informative advertising as possible related to the relevant product. A consumer can see and compare the different offers, and as a result it is harder for producers to give misleading information to consumers. Also the competitive function of advertising is ensured because of the direct confrontation between competing similar products. The assessment given by the Commission has always reflected this approach, when certain conditions are respected.

In this particular decision the Commission recognized the anticompetitive effects deriving from the Cematex regulation for exhibitions and fairs. In particular, it stressed the restrictive consequences of the exclusivity clause which prohibited firms from participating in other similar initiatives each two out of four years. The Commission underlined how that condition was restrictive of competition in the market for the provision of fairs organization services and between producers of textile machineries. Indeed, as the ITMA was the most important sector exposition, the interested producers were *de facto* obliged to participate and at the same time to exclude other fairs from their agenda. This would have been detrimental for marketing and promotional activities and especially for new firms in their attempt to consolidate their position on the market or to penetrate new markets.[97] Due to the extension of the prohibition to indirect participation in other fairs, competition between commercial agents and representatives also suffered restrictions.

Nonetheless the efficiencies generated by the Cematex regulation in terms of rationalization of the fairs' offer and of opportunities presented, in particular, to small and medium-sized producers to advertise and promote their products on a large scale were considered as outweighing the restrictive effects of the same set of rules. In particular, the possibility to expose products in direct confrontation with the (quasi-) totality of competitors would have given increasing stimulus to producers in their commercial efforts and a unique opportunity for companies to advertise and promote their machineries. From a consumers' point of view, large expositions would have offered an overall variety of products, major information about them, and better choice orientation.[98] The efficiencies in terms of costs savings in the organization of the events and better marketing and distribution of the products stemming from the two-year prohibition period were also considered relevant in the assessment of the Cematex regulation.

The Commission's appraisal of the competitive effects of these events remained constant throughout the years. The important condition attached by the Commission in each case for the exemption of the agreement in question (which was clearly ensured by the Cematex regulation) has always been the non-discriminatory nature of the conditions to access the exhibition and/or the fair.

d. Fines, remedies, and conditions enclosed
- Obligations for Cematex to inform the Commission about all future rejections of applications for participation in an ITMA fair.

---

97   See recital II-2-b of the decision.   98   See recital III-1-a of the decision.

e. Further developments of the case

In 1981 (when the twelve-year exemption period was about to expire) a further request for exemption was notified. The exemption was extended for a further twelve years by decision 83/252/EEC [1983] OJ L 140/27, Case IV/181.

F.2 *Roofing Felt* Commission decision 86/399/EEC [1986] OJ L 232/15

Relevance: The Commission assesses an advertising agreement provided for within a broader frame of collusive actions. In such circumstances the common promotion is no longer a positive effort for producers and consumers, but is instead an instrument to reinforce and implement the scope of the collusive agreement entered among the same firms and to further reduce the incentive to compete.

- Case IV/31.371
- **Decision**: Infringement of Article 101(1) FEU Treaty, imposition of fines
- **Decision addressee(s)**:
    - Antwerps Teer en Asphaltbedrijf NV, *Belgium*
    - Compagnie Générale des Asphaltes SA, *Belgium*
    - Lummerzheim & Co. NV, *Belgium*
    - Limburgse Asfaltfabrieken PVBA, *Belgium*
    - Kempisch Asphaltbedrijf NV, *Belgium*
    - De Boer & Co. NV, *Belgium*
    - Vlaams Asfaltbedrijf Huyghe & Co. PVBA, *Belgium*
    - La Société Coopérative des Asphalteurs Belges, *Belgium*
    - International Roofing Company SA, *Belgium*
    - Al-Asfalt NV, *Belgium*
- **Report route:** Complaint lodged with the Commission on 11 November 1983
- **Date of the decision:** 10 July 1986
- **Competition Commissioner:** P. Sutherland
- **Relevant product market:** Roofing felt
- **Relevant geographical market:** Belgium
- **Description of the case**
    ### a. Relevant facts
    All the above-mentioned parties were active in the market for the production of roofing felts. Most of them were also engaged in (mainly) roofing works. All the companies were members of the Société Coopérative des Asphalteurs Belges (Belasco), the Belgian trade association for asphalt producers. Only International Roofing Company SA (IR) and Al-Asfalt NV were not Belasco members.

    Roofing felt producers sell a large part of their production directly to general buildings contractors or roofing contractors. Some of them engage directly in roofing activities, while the rest of the products are supplied to wholesalers or retailers.[99]

    Between January 1978 and April 1984, the members of Belasco engaged in a complex and elaborate agreement with the crucial assistance of the Belasco trade association. First, the agreement allocated quotas precisely indicating the

---

99   See recital 6 of the decision.

amount of raw materials each member was allowed to use in the production of the relevant product. Second, they agreed on price lists and minimum prices to be applied in the supply of roofing felt in Belgium. Furthermore they introduced a ban on making any gift to consumers or selling at a loss and jointly established their system of permitted discounts. Lastly, they decided to defend the collective interests of the members by joint advertising initiatives and with studies on systems to achieve standardization in the production and distribution process.

The agreement aimed at strict monitoring of members' implementation and compliance with the cartel's rules. An accountant was appointed with the task of monitoring compliance with quotas via regular or extraordinary inspections of the firms' premises. The members were also required to provide a monthly report of their purchases and movements of stocks of raw materials and finished products, besides an export activity report. In case of breach of the quota agreement, a system of compensation would have ensured the agreed incomes to those undertakings that could not achieve their volume of sales because of the excessive sales of other members. Penalties were established for other infringements of the rules of the agreement.

It is relevant to note that the Belgian legislation at that time imposed upon producers the obligation to communicate their price increases and allowed associations of undertakings to collectively provide this information on behalf of their members to the public authority. The Belasco members did not fully abide by this rule. Beyond collectively notifying the authority, they also collectively established the timing and size of those increases.

Evidence collected by the Commission during its investigations revealed that during several meetings, most of the discussion between the cartel members had revolved around the discounts to be applied to single or collective customers. The parties had agreed upon the so-called "Belasco price list" and discount rates also covering ancillary products. Therefore, parties were committed to adhere to the list and engaged several times in discussions in the attempt to collectively deal with groups of customers which requested larger discounts than those provided in the list. They also concluded agreements with producers that were not members of Belasco (IR and Al-Asfalt NV) for the application of similar discount rates.

Furthermore, the members "took or planned concerted action against other manufacturers to discourage them from pursuing a price cutting policy and/or to take customers away from them. Concerted action against importers and foreign manufacturers was also proposed or decided."[100] In particular, the companies involved decided first to offer maximum discounts to customers of an undertaking not party to the agreement (IKO) to steal away its customers. Second, they proposed to launch a collective attack in the Netherlands on the source of imports to weaken a particular competitor–dealer that had been relying on those sources. Finally, they also collectively targeted a list of customers and tried to plan strategies to attract them.

100   Recital 59 of the decision.

Moreover, as mentioned above, firms' output of roofing felt was sold under the collective trademark "Belasco." The trade association ran annual advertising campaigns to promote the collective mark. Each single member was then free to advertise the "Belasco" trademark individually, in association with or independently from the advertisement of its own trademarks.[101]

b. Origin of the case

On 11 November 1983 a submission was filed to the Commission and on 8 March 1985 a request was made to treat that submission as a complaint for the purpose of Article 3 of Regulation No. 17. On 14 June 1985 the Commission decided to initiate proceedings.

c. Economic analysis

The agreement analyzed in the decision was undoubtedly anticompetitive and its effects on the regular pattern of commerce in Belgium were relevant. It was seriously restrictive of competition. Its prime object was restrictive and the Commission did not give detailed reasoning to demonstrate the restrictive effects of an agreement fixing price and establishing quotas. As already described above, these kinds of *hardcore* restrictions were always unambiguously considered detrimental to welfare.

Nonetheless the Commission focused on the variety of instruments the agreement had provided for the effective implementation and the support of the cartel. The fact that the members continuously took collective actions to guarantee compliance with the agreed rules was considered and described in detail by the Commission.[102]

The decision is particularly interesting because the Commission clarified its position toward advertising agreements strengthening the already anticompetitive effects of a cartel. As in the Belasco agreement, the common advertising campaigns were not aimed at a common effort for the promotion of certain products or certain categories of products (as in the case of the expositions and fairs described in the previous landmark case). They were, in contrast, primarily aimed at limiting "the scope members had, notwithstanding the extensive standardization of roofing felt in Belgium, for competing with one another through product differentiation."[103]

The Commission confirmed its general positive approach toward advertising agreements but in this case specified the restrictive effects that might derive from them. In fact, the Commission affirmed that when other competitive restrictions are imposed, the aim of common advertising campaigns is no longer the rationalization of the promoting activities with derived cost savings, but it is instead the (likely) elimination of the remaining competition between the parties to the agreement. As the Commission stated "[t]here is reason to believe that the joint advertising was intended to back up the other restrictive features of the Agreement by fostering users' impression of a homogenous product and so limiting the scope members ought to have had to compete by differentiating their products."[104]

---

101 See recitals 67 and 68 of the decision.
102 See in particular recital 74 of the decision.

103 *Idem.*
104 Recital 73 of the decision.

d. **Fines, remedies, and conditions enclosed**
   – The Commission imposed the following total fines:

Comp	Fine (ECU)
Antwerps Teer en Asphaltbedrijf NV	420,000
Compagnie Générale des Asphaltes SA	150,000
Lummerzheim & Co. NV	200,000
Limburgse Asfaltfabrieken PVBA	30,000
Kempisch Asphaltbedrijf NV	75,000
De Boer & Co. NV	75,000
Vlaams Asfaltbedrijf Huyghe & Co. PVBA	50,000
La Société Coopérative des Asphalteurs Belges	15,000

   – Obligations for all the undertakings concerned to bring the infringements to an end and to refrain from entering into any agreement or
   engaging in any concerted practice or measure likely to have a similar
   effect.

e. **Further developments of the case**
   Case 246/86 *Belasco and others* v. *Commission* [1989] ECR 2117, appeal
   dismissed
   The Court stated that "... the joint advertising measures, such as [the] use of
   the Belasco mark, restricted competition in so far as they presented a uniform
   image of products in a sector in which individual advertising may facilitate
   differentiation and therefore competition."[105]

2.8 Agreements on standards

A Introduction

In certain industries, quality or technical standards are important in achieving uniform
and reliable service or interconnectivity of complementary products. Standards on product quality
related to safety, content, and environmental impact can also facilitate consumer choice. From
a consumer welfare perspective, an agreement on a standard may guarantee intercompatibility
between products, improved supply conditions, and better repair services. Where standards have
to newly develop, there are often significant coordination problems that can cause delays in
innovation. Agreements on standards can facilitate the interpenetration of new markets and avoid
the duplication of R&D efforts and costs. If different standards are incompatible, a large share of
consumers may be locked-in to using an inferior product.

In general, it is not obvious whether a competitive selection process will always lead to the
adaptation of the best and most efficient standard. It may therefore be efficient if producers
make agreements on standards. Yet, such agreements risk a distortion of competition, which
may limit the level of differentiation, the creation of new products, and hence consumer choice.

---

105   Recital 30 of the judgment.

Furthermore, coordinated standards may have as their object the foreclosure of competitors and the restriction of market access for potential competitors.

To determine whether or not agreements on standards are overall restrictive of competition is complex, however, and can often only be determined on a case-by-case basis. It involves assessing whether the standard concerned is indeed necessary for a successful launch of the product, what is the degree of restrictiveness or permissiveness imposed by the standard, as well as the scope it gives to non-incumbents and potential entrants to benefit from the standard in a non-discriminatory way. Furthermore, when analysing a standard it is important to know whether there exist viable alternative standards, which may then be disadvantaged as a result of the possibly exclusionary nature of the standard setting agreement. Generally, standard agreements form a competition problem in particular when undertakings ride a hardcore price or market sharing cartel on the back of industry negotiations on standards as a cover.

B   Applicable EU legislation

No special legislation applicable. For applicable legislation see chapter 2, paragraph B. See also Commission Guidelines on the applicability of Article 81 to Horizontal Co-operation Agreements [2001] OJ C 3/2, part 6.

C   Related economics texts

Bishop and Walker (2009), paragraph 5.62
Carlton and Perloff (2005), chapter 13, paragraph 2
Church and Ware (2000), not specifically discussed
Martin (1994), not specifically discussed
Martin (2002), not specifically discussed
Motta (2004), paragraph 4.5.3.2
Tirole (1988), paragraph 10.6
Waldman and Jensen (2001), not specifically discussed

D   Related legal texts

Bellamy and Child (2008), chapter 5, paragraph 8(B)
Jones and Sufrin (2008), chapter 13, paragraph 5(G)
Ritter and Braun (2005), chapter 3, paragraph C(3)
Whish (2008), chapter 15, paragraph 9

E   Commission decisions in chronological order[•]

Transocean Marine Paint Association Commission decision 67/454/EEC [1967] OJ L 163/10, Case IV/223

- [•] Decisions displayed in **bold type** are described in the section. Decisions highlighted with (*) include interesting economic analysis by the Commission on the specific topic of the section. Some decisions contain economic reasoning on more than one topic and therefore appear in several lists of Commission decisions in chronological order. Reference is made in brackets and **bold type** to the relevant section in which the decision is extensively described as a landmark case. When decisions are referenced and/or described in some detail in one or more of the economic textbooks, reference in brackets is also made to the relevant part(s) of those texts.

VVVF Commission decision 69/202/EEC [1969] OJ L 168/22, Case IV/597

Transocean Marine Paint Association Commission decision 74/16/EEC [1974] OJ L 19/18, Case IV/223

Transocean Marine Paint Association Commission decision 75/649/EEC [1975] OJ L 286/24, Case IV/223

Video Cassette Recorders **Commission decision 78/156/EEC [1978] OJ L 47/42, Case IV/29.151**

Transocean Marine Paint Association Commission decision 80/184/EEC [1980] OJ L 39/73, Case IV/223

Uniform Eurocheques Commission decision 85/77/EEC [1985] OJ L 35/43, Case IV/30.717

Irish Banks Standing Committee Commission decision 86/507/EEC [1986] OJ L 295/28, Case IV/31.362

Association Belge des Banques Commission decision 87/13/EEC [1987] OJ L 7/27, Case IV/261

X/Open Group Commission decision 87/69/EEC [1987] OJ L 35/36, Case IV/31.458

ABI **Commission decision 87/103/EEC [1987] OJ L 43/51, Case IV/31.356**

Transocean Marine Paint Association Commission decision 88/635/EEC [1988] OJ L 351/40, Case IV/223

Uniform Eurocheques Commission decision 89/95/EEC [1989] OJ L 36/16, Case IV/31.291

Dutch Banks Commission decision 89/512/EEC [1989] OJ L 253/1, Case IV/31.499

APB Commission decision 90/33/EEC [1990] OJ L 18/35, Case IV/32.302

Banque Nationale de Paris/Dresdner Bank Commission decision 96/454/EC [1996] OJ L 188/37, Case IV/34.607

Nederlandse Vereniging van Banken, Nederlandse Postorderbond, etc. Commission decision 1999/687/EC [1999] OJ L 271/28, Cases IV/34.010, 33.793, 34.234, 34.888

Reims II + 13 Commission decision 1999/695/EC [1999] OJ L 275/17, Case IV/36.748

CECED **Commission decision 2000/475/EC [2000] OJ L 187/47, Case IV.F.1/36.718** (Motta, 2004, pp. 27–8)

Reims II renotification Commission decision 2004/139/EC [2004] OJ L 56/76, Case COMP/C/38.170

F Economic landmark cases

F.1 *Video Cassette Recorders* Commission decision 78/156/EEC [1978] OJ L 47/42

Relevance: The decision represents the first attempt of the Commission to analyze from an economic perspective the effect on competition and further research efforts of agreements on standards. The conclusions reached were inspired by a negative approach toward standard agreements. Nonetheless, they contain the intuitions behind future recognition of possible efficiencies derived from such kind of agreements.

- Case IV/29.151
- **Decision:** Infringement of Article 101(1) FEU Treaty
- **Decision addressee(s):**
    - Blaupunkt Werke GmbH, *Federal Republic of Germany*
    - Bosch-Siemens Hausgeräte GmbH, *Federal Republic of Germany*
    - Grundig AG, *Federal Republic of Germany*
    - Loewe Opta GmbH, *Federal Republic of Germany*

- Norddeutsche Mende Rundfunk KG, *Federal Republic of Germany*
- Schwarzwälder Apparate-Bau-Anstalt SABA-Werke, *Federal Republic of Germany*
- Philips GmbH, *Federal Republic of Germany*
- NV Philips Gloeilampenfabrieken, *the Netherlands*

- **Report route:** Notification for exemption submitted to the Commission on 8 December 1975 by Philips GmbH and five other German undertakings for the agreement on the uniform application of technical standards for the VCR system
- **Date of the decision:** 20 December 1977
- **Competition Commissioner:** R. Vouel
- **Relevant product market:** Video cassettes and video cassette recorders
- **Relevant geographical market:** European internal market
- **Description of the case**
  - a. **Relevant facts**

    All the above-mentioned firms were active in the consumer electronics industry and in the market for cassettes and video cassette recorders. Only Philips and Sony had previously developed marketable video cassette systems for sale in Europe. The two companies held a considerable combined market share in the European internal market of more than 70 percent. The respective systems, however, were technically different and thus incompatible with one another and cassettes could only be played on compatible equipment.

    Due to the necessary compatibility of the cassettes with the system, Philips and Sony had licensed "a number of other firms to exploit their patents in the field of magnetic video recording and replay."[106]

    In particular, Philips had signed with several other undertakings the notified agreement concerning the uniform application of its own technical standards (VCR system) by those other companies. The parties agreed to exclusively use the VCR standards. The consent of all the parties involved was required in order to modify the standards set. The agreement provided that "the parties grant each other royalty-free, non-exclusive and non-transferable licenses under their patents and patent applications affecting compatibility, where this is needed to ensure compatibility."[107] All the associated companies of the signatories would respect the same agreement and benefited from the rights deriving from it. All other companies manufacturing VCR machines were free to join the agreement.

  - b. **Origin of the case**

    On 8 December 1975 Philips and five other German undertakings submitted a notification to the Commission pursuant to Article 4 of Regulation No. 17 to see the agreements on uniform application of technical standards for the VCR system be declared exempted from the application of Article 101(1) FEU Treaty by virtue of Article 101(3) FEU Treaty.

  - c. **Economic analysis**

    The combination of a lack of practice and the economists' ambiguous verdict on the effects of standardization agreements on competition has made this field – i.e. the application of competition theory and rules to such

---

106   Recital 7 of the decision.   107   Recital 12 of the decision.

agreements – one in which the Commission approach has undergone considerable change throughout the years.

This represents the first decision on agreements on standards in which the Commission carried out an analysis of the potential economic restrictions. The Commission's treatment of standard setting agreements was very stringent in the beginning, but it was gradually relaxed in the years following the first decisions on such agreements.

In particular, the Commission held that the exclusivity clause included in the agreement was not necessary for suppliers to adhere to the technical standards for the manufacture of VCR equipment. The Commission considered two factors as restrictive of competition. First, the fact that the companies would have not been allowed to use other systems. Secondly, the effects of the licensing provisions "which in fact amounted to a horizontal complex of licensing agreements which should otherwise have been bilateral."[108] The effects were strengthened in consideration of Philips' position on the market. Furthermore, the Commission focused its attention on the fact that as a result of the preclusion of suppliers to develop and use other systems, potential other and "perhaps better"[109] systems were excluded from the market.

Nonetheless, the Commission accepted the potential of standards agreements in achieving improvements in production and distribution of goods. At the same time it rejected the claim that the agreement at hand would generate such efficiency gains.[110]

Admittedly "the combined technical efforts of the parties could be expected to lead to further rationalization . . . and technical progress"[111] but the restrictions imposed were considered not indispensable for the achievement of those efficiencies. Consequently the agreement was not exempted.

Even if the Commission did not authorize the agreement in this specific case, it recognized both the restrictive effects imposed and the potential benefits expected from this agreement.

As mentioned above, the Commission adopted a more flexible approach in subsequent decisions on technical standards, granting exemptions to agreements that were possibly more restrictive than the VCR agreement. In *X/Open Group* in 1987 it allowed the adoption of a computer standard initially not open to all the companies wishing to enter the agreement (and thus potentially creating a barrier to entry to the PC market) simply on the basis of the promise by the members to make the results available to all actors on the market as soon as possible.[112]

d. Fines, remedies, and conditions enclosed

None.

e. Further developments of the case

None.

---

108   Recital 24 of the decision.
109   Recital 29 of the decision.
110   See recital 29 of the decision.

111   Recital 32 of the decision.
112   See *X/Open Group* Commission decision 87/69/EEC [1987] OJ L 35/36.

F.2 *ABI* Commission decision 87/103/EEC [1987] OJ L 43/51

Relevance: In the sector of financial intermediation that is often the object of standard agreements, the Commission for the first time exempted the agreement even in the presence of clauses providing for the fixing of common commissions for certain services. Those restrictions to competition were considered as indispensable for the attainment of the efficiency-enhancing scope of the agreement. The decision shows the Commission's tendency to adopt an increasingly efficiency-based analysis of such agreements that differs from its early approach.

- Case IV/31.356
- **Decision:** Negative Clearance for part of the agreement and Exemption pursuant to Article 101(3) FEU Treaty for ten years for the remaining part
- **Decision addressee(s):**
    - Associazione Italiana Bancaria (ABI), *Italy*
- **Report route:** Application for negative clearance and notification for exemption submitted to the Commission on 11 October 1984 by ABI for agreements and recommendations concerning the activities of the bank members of the association
- **Date of the decision:** 12 December 1986
- **Competition Commissioner:** P. Sutherland
- **Relevant product market:** Banking and bank services
- **Relevant geographical market:** Italy
- **Description of the case**
    a. **Relevant facts**
       ABI is a non-profit association whose members are banks and financial and credit institutions. Its statutory objects and tasks are the protection of its members' interests and the study and monitoring of issues and problems concerning the banking and financial sector.
       ABI adopted a complex set of agreements and recommendations, binding upon its members, consisting of three categories:
       1. Agreements concerning relations between banks
       2. Agreements concerning the relations between banks and their customers
       3. Recommendations relating to the minimum commission chargeable to customers.[113]
       In particular within the first category there were agreements concerning the following standards:
          - An Italian bills and documents collection and/or acceptance service. The agreement governed the technical aspects of the service with regard to the relations between the banks involved. The agreement also provided for fixed amounts to be transferred to the bank which discovered deviations or what in the agreement was referred to as a case of "dishonour."
          - The service of collecting bank cheques and similar instruments payable in Italy. The agreement laid down the rules and technical procedures for the performance of the service and in particular uniform value dates for the debit and credit of cheques

---

113   For a detailed description of all the agreements and recommendations see recitals 6–9 and 20–29 of the decision.

and other instruments applicable between the banks requesting and/or providing the service and those acting as intermediaries.

- A new, uniform type of lire travellers' cheque. The agreement established rules about the issue, circulation, and payments of the new instrument and proposed standardized types of cheques. Specifically, the agreement set rules on the supply and safekeeping of the cheques, their use within and outside Italy, the reimbursement of cheques used, stolen, lost, destroyed, cancelled, or unused, and on the color and the form of the cheques.

- The inter-bank Bancomat convention establishing the criteria for the creation in Italy of a system of 24-hours automated teller machines (ATMs). The agreement laid down the practical and technical conditions for the setting up of the system, involving *inter alia* conditions of operation, apportionment of administrative expenses among the banks involved, the logo, a location map, the standards for the withdrawal procedure, and the information to be included in the accountancy data transmitted. The Bancomat agreement also included an exclusive clause prohibiting the participating banks to join another network.[114]

In its Statement of Objections, the Commission held that parts of the overall agreements fell outside the scope of application of Article 101(1) (i.e. negative clearance), while others lay within the scope of applicability of Article 101(1). Following the Commission's initial assessment, ABI committed itself to abandon some of the agreements and recommendations that were considered seriously restrictive of competition (i.e. agreements on common criteria for the calculation of interests and commissions for several services) and confirmed the remaining parts of the agreement, including the parts referring to standards described above.[115]

b. **Origin of the case**

On 11 October 1984 ABI submitted to the Commission an application for negative clearance and notification for exemption pursuant to Articles 2 and 4 of Regulation 17 to see Article 101(1) FEU Treaty be declared not applicable to a set of agreements and recommendations concerning the activities of its members or alternatively the same agreements and recommendations be declared exempted from the application of Article 101(1) FEU Treaty by virtue of Article 101(3) FEU Treaty.

c. **Economic analysis**

In the overall assessment of the agreements and recommendations introduced by ABI, the Commission appraised with particular attention the standards setting agreements and partly modified its previous approach. The banking sector has in fact been the object of decisions concerning the setting of standards on several occasions and the decisions of the Commission has in principle always been

---

114   See recitals 20–23 of the decision.
115   For a detailed description of the differences between the overall agreement before and after the issuing of the Commission's Statement of Objections, see recitals 14–19.

favourable to those agreements unless they introduce unnecessarily restrictive clauses or clauses unfair for customers.[116]

In this case the Commission analyzed the effects of the agreement concerning the ATM system. The main purpose of the agreement to standardize and rationalize banking operations was valued positively with regard to both supply- and demand-side efficiencies. At the same time the exclusivity clause and the provision fixing the commissions and the value dates for the remuneration for services were considered restrictive of the individual bank's freedom to establish the conditions for the provision of its services. Nonetheless, in the specific circumstances of the case – since the ATM system would have been limited to the Italian territory – that part of the agreement was cleared due to the non-applicability of Article 101(1) for lack of effect on trade between Member States.

In its account of the other standards agreements, the Commission recognized the restrictive effects for competition arising from them. Due to the fixed commission to be transferred, the clause restricted the ABI members' freedom to determine individually the remuneration for the banking services requested or offered. Consequently also the freedom was effectively being undermined to determine, "in the light of their internal profitability situation . . . their specialization and their business policy,"[117] the conditions applicable to the customers. Accordingly, "consumers no longer have the opportunity otherwise open to them to take advantage of competition in respect of mutual obligations or of deriving any benefit from entrusting to a given institution all the services they require."[118]

Assessing the efficiencies deriving from the agreements – outweighing the restrictive effects – the Commission partially modified its previous approach and considered that the fixing of common commissions, applied specially to harmonized services (cheques), as inherent (i.e. necessary to the attainment of the main positive/pro-competitive purpose) to the agreement on standardized procedures. Referring to the agreements concerning the collection and/or acceptance service of bills and documents and the service of collecting bank cheques, the Commission stated that "the joint and uniform fixing of the remuneration for services is inherent in the collaboration between, on [the] one hand, the bank requesting the service and the

---

116   See also *Uniform Eurocheques* Commission decision 85/77/EEC [1985] OJ L 35/43, *Irish Banks Standing Committee* Commission decision 86/507/EEC [1986] OJ L 295/28, *Association Belge des Banques* Commission decision 87/13/EEC [1987] OJ L 7/27, *Uniform Eurocheques* Commission decision 89/95/EEC [1989] OJ L 36/16, *Dutch Banks* Commission decision 89/512/EEC [1989] OJ L 253/1, *APB* Commission decision 90/33/EEC [1990] OJ L 18/35, *Banque Nationale de Paris/Dresdner Bank* Commission decision 96/454/EC [1996] OJ L 188/37, *Nederlandse Vereniging van Banken, Nederlandse Postorderbond, etc.* Commission decision 1999/687/EC [1999] OJ L 271/28.
      Carlo Bagnasco and others v. *Banca Popolare di Novara and Cassa di Risparmio di Genova e Imperia SpA* (Joined cases C-215/96 and C 216/96) is an example of the ECJ case law on standard agreements in the banking sector. This case concerned the interpretation of Article 101 FEU Treaty, in relation to certain standard bank conditions which the Italian Banking Association imposed on its members when contracts were concluded for current-account credit facilities and the provision of general guarantees. The ECJ held that ". . . standard bank conditions, in so far as they enable banks, in contracts for the opening of a current-account credit facility, to change the interest rate at any time by reason of changes occurring in the money market, and to do so by means of a notice displayed on their premises or in such manner as they consider most appropriate, do not have as their object or effect the restriction of competition within the meaning of Article 81(1) of the Treaty" (see recital 37 of the judgment).
117   Recital 43 of the decision.
118   Recital 44 of the decision.

intervening management companies or category institutes and, on the other hand, the banks called upon to provide the service which makes centralized clearing possible."[119] Accordingly the Commission accepted the fixing of a common price for a certain service as ancillary to the establishment of an efficient standard.

The agreements were considered beneficial for consumer welfare and for the organization of the banking system. In fact, "the simplification and standardization of procedure contribute to improving the provision of . . . services . . . It simplifies the work of each intervening bank. Depending on the stage reached in the procedure, each bank knows exactly what service may be requested of it; moreover regardless of who is operating upstream or downstream, it can plan the conduct of the entire operation. The standardization of operations . . . speeds up the operation, improves the payments system, facilitates the distribution of cheques and instruments and makes for speedier circulation of money. The uniformity of the procedure and the standardization of the operations provided for permit the centralization on management companies or "category institutes" of certain operations, notably the cleaning of credit commissions and debit commissions related to services rendered."[120]

Concerning the beneficial effects produced by each single agreement, the Commission specified that:

  – The agreement on Italian bills and documents collection and/or acceptance service, "replacing paper with magnetic type, or better still online transmission, saves time which would otherwise be wasted in transmitting and checking instruments manually."[121]
  – The agreement on the service of collecting bank cheques and similar instruments payable in Italy, "makes it possible to have a limited number of relationship[s]"[122] avoiding each bank having relations with all other banks by creating a network of relationships.
  – The agreement on a new, uniform type of lire travellers' cheque "contributes to improving the payment system"[123] allowing the use of those uniform cheques outside the country of emission and their cashing in the currency of the country where they would have been used.

In the Commission's view consumers would have benefited from the positive effects deriving from the improved system. Furthermore, the fixed commission for the provision of services would not exceed the optimal level given that it would take into account the interests of both the requiring and the providing banks. In addition the agreements were open to all the banks and financial institutions operating in Italy.

Finally, the Commission considered the level of remaining competition in the sector after the agreement and stated that "the agreements at issue do not directly govern relations between banks and their customers. A possibility of

119 Recital 66 of the decision.
120 Recitals 53–56 of the decision.
121 Recital 57 of the decision.

122 Recital 58 of the decision.
123 Recital 59 of the decision.

competition therefore continues to exist at the level of relations between each bank and its customers."[124]

d. Fines, remedies, and conditions enclosed

Obligation for ABI to inform the Commission about any addition and/or modification made to the agreement and any agreement concluded by the members within the association.

e. Further developments of the case

None.

F.3   *CECED* Commission decision 2000/475/EC [2000] OJ L 187/47

Relevance: Enhancing its case-by-case efficiency-based approach to standard agreements, the Commission also accepts restrictions on the variety of products offered to consumers if this is aimed at increasing the efficiency of the standards and of the remaining products. In particular, the reduced environmental impact of the products is considered as a relevant efficiency possibly deriving from the agreement. The potential further common R&D efforts are also taken into consideration.

- Case IV.F.1/36.718
- **Decision:** Exemption under Article 101(3) FEU Treaty for four years
- **Decision addressee(s):**
    - Conseil Européen de la Construction d'Appareils Domestiques (CECED), *Belgium*
- **Report route:** Application for negative clearance and notification for exemption submitted to the Commission on 22 October 1997 by CECED for agreements concerning the activities of its members
- **Date of the decision:** 24 January 1999
- **Competition Commissioner:** M. Monti
- **Relevant product market:** Domestic washing machines
- **Relevant geographical market:** EEA market
- **Description of the case**
    a. **Relevant facts**
       CECED is an association of manufacturers of domestic appliances and their national trade associations. The manufacturers that signed the notified agreement held roughly 90 percent of the EEA market of washing machines at the time of notification. The market had become saturated and the few large suppliers active on it had strongly rationalized production capacities due to considerable bargaining power on the part of the large distribution chains and buying groups.[125]
       Washing machines sold inside the European internal market are classified according to their energy efficiency into seven categories from A (the most efficient) to G (the least efficient) and have to be labeled accordingly. As the Commission stated, "through the EC energy label, consumers can easily assess the cost-effectiveness of a choice among different energy categories. In addition to general product attributes advertising campaigns often stress energy performance, thereby differentiating products, in a context where

124   Recital 68 of the decision.   125   See recitals 9 and 10 of the decision.

environmentally friendly products attract more and more consumers. Thus, energy-efficiency has an influence on purchasing decisions, and hence on competition between manufacturers."[126] The degree of efficiency of the machines is directly proportional to the amount of technology applied in their production and also to their price even if it is not possible to completely isolate the effects of upgrading energy efficiency on production costs.

In order to promote technological development and also to educate consumers becoming increasingly sensitive to environmentally friendly products, the manufacturers entered into an agreement through CECED according to which the parties would stop producing and/or importing in the internal market for the first period of time, machines belonging to categories E, F, and G, and subsequently also category D machines. The parties agreed upon a monitoring system consisting of a database, which would have been controled by an independent consultant that, in turn, would have reported the compliance level of each firm to CECED. The agreement also included a consumers' education program aiming at the diffusion of broader information concerning "environmentally conscious use of washing machines and [the commitment] to promote a wide dissemination of energy-saving technology ... and techniques."[127]

b. **Origin of the case**

On 22 October 1997 CECED submitted to the Commission an application for negative clearance and notification for exemption pursuant to Articles 2 and 4 of Regulation No. 17 to see Article 101(1) FEU Treaty be declared not applicable to a set of agreements concerning the activities of its members or alternatively the same agreements be declared exempted from the application of Article 101(1) FEU Treaty by virtue of Article 101(3) FEU Treaty.

c. **Economic analysis**

This decision further clarified the Commission's position regarding admissible restrictions of competition in case of efficient (technical) standards adopted by industries or groups of firms. Furthermore it added a new element to the Commission's evaluation given by environmental concerns, i.e. general interest concerns.

The Commission recognized the restrictive effects deriving from the agreement in terms of reduced technical diversity and consumer choice. Simultaneously, the agreement was considered as raising production costs for manufacturers. The Commission stated that "production and unit costs would increase appreciably, albeit not excessively, for those models which need upgrading. Therefore, in the short term, the agreement is likely to increase the price of those models."[128] At the same time, it recognized that the agreement would have affected electricity demand as the technological improvement brought about reduced energy consumption. Notwithstanding those restrictions, the Commission considered the efficiencies and the welfare benefits deriving from the agreement as outweighing the restrictive effects. Firstly, it welcomed the setting of a minimum efficiency standard not implying any quota allocation

---

126 Recital 12 of the decision.   128 Recital 34 of the decision.
127 Recital 22 of the decision.

and/or any specification of the required individual contribution to the attainment of the common target. Had they been introduced as part of the standard setting, the agreement would have been deemed unduly restrictive.

In addition, the Commission analyzed the environmental impact of the agreement and accepted its positive effects. In particular, the Commission underlined the fact that less electricity consumption would have generated, on the one side, more technical efficiency and, on the other, an indirect reduction of pollution from electricity generation.

Furthermore it stated that "the agreement is also likely to focus future research and development on furthering energy efficiencies beyond the current technological limits of category A, thereby allowing for increased product differentiation among producers in the long run."[129]

Concerning the individual economic benefits deriving from the enhanced energy and technology standard, the Commission stated that the expected increase in price would have been balanced "within reasonable pay-back periods" by the savings in electricity bills. The Commission also paid particular attention to the resulting environmental benefits.[130]

Finally, confirming its previous approach the Commission put forward the importance of the openness of the agreement and appraised first its accessibility to all manufacturers and second the absence of special obligations on companies to achieve the common objective and instead the possibility of relying on a variety of technical choices.[131]

It is reasonable to conclude that the Commission maintained its case-by-case approach and expressed the competition concerns that arise around standard setting agreements under certain market conditions and for targeting specific aims. It had prohibited quota restrictions in earlier similar cases already and reaffirmed the importance of the standards being open to all firms willing to adopt them.

d. **Fines, remedies, and conditions enclosed**
None.

e. **Further developments of the case**
None.

129 Recital 50 of the decision.
130 See in particular recital 55 of the decision. The Commission understanding of such a kind of agreement was in line with the CFI (now "the General Court") case law. *Stichting Certificatie Kraanverhuurbedrijf (SCK) and Federatie van Nederlands Kraanbedrijven (FNK)* v. *Commission* (Joined Cases T-213/95 and T-18/96) concerned a foundation who set up a certification system under which it issued certificates to firms which met a range of requirements relating to the management of a crane-hire firm and to the use and maintenance of cranes. The CFI stressed that the *openness* of the system and the *acceptance of equivalent guarantees* offered by other systems were pertinent criteria on which the Commission might rely in order to ascertain whether the prohibition at issue distorted competition. First, the prohibition affects significantly the competitive opportunities of uncertified firms if it is difficult to gain access to the certification system. Secondly, by preventing certified firms from calling on the services of uncertified firms even if they provide guarantees equivalent to those of the certification system, that prohibition cannot be objectively justified by an interest in maintaining the quality of the products and services ensured by the certification system. On the contrary, the failure to accept such guarantees protects certified firms from competition from uncertified firms (see recitals 136 and 137 of the judgment).
131 See recital 65 of the decision.

2.9 Exchange of information

A Introduction

Exchange of information is a very broad category of behavior, ranging from strategic alliances to product launch meetings at trade associations. In general, information feeds the competitive process: more transparent markets help buyers and sellers to find each other and competitive offers better. In fact, the model of perfect competition assumes that all actors, on both the demand and on the supply side, are perfectly informed about market conditions. There can also be a dark side to a transparent market, however: it can facilitate the creation and stabilization of tacit and overt cartel agreements. Direct exchange of firm-specific information between competitors, in fact, can trigger collusion. In addition, continuous insight into the market behavior and underlying private information of rivals allows for monitoring cartel compliance and developing credible punishments for deviation.

Whether or not an exchange of information constitutes a potential competition concern therefore requires a careful case analysis. The more concentrated a market is, for example, the higher can be the risk that the exchange of information facilitates collusion. The type of information also matters. In general, aggregate information regarding the entire market is less likely to be problematic than disaggregate information about strategies and behaviors of individual firms. By reducing information asymmetries, access to aggregate market information can even be beneficial to competition. Also information about the past – although it can be used to design punishments in cartels – is thought to be less problematic than information about future strategies. The way in which the information is exchanged is also relevant. The public communication of information – for example, as part of a market investigation by an independent agency – is often regarded to be less likely to restrict competition than the private exchange of information.

B Applicable EU legislation

No special legislation applicable. For applicable legislation see chapter 2, paragraph B.

C Related economics texts

Bishop and Walker (2009), paragraphs 5.14 – 5.24
Carlton and Perloff (2005), chapter 5, paragraph 2; chapter 11, paragraph 3(ii), and chapter 19, paragraph 3(iii)
Church and Ware (2000), paragraphs 10.1.2, 10.5, and 10.6
Martin (1994), not specifically discussed
Martin (2002), paragraph 10.3
Motta (2004), paragraph 4.2.2
Tirole (1988), paragraphs 6.1 and 9.1.1.1
Waldman and Jensen (2001), chapter 8, paragraph 4

D Related legal texts

Bellamy and Child (2008), chapter 5, paragraph 6
Jones and Sufrin (2008), chapter 11, paragraph 3(D, iv)

Ritter and Braun (2005), chapter 3, paragraph C(7)
Whish (2008), chapter 13, paragraph 8

E   Commission decisions in chronological order•

Quinine Commission decision 69/240/EEC [1969] OJ L 192/5, Case IV/26.623 (Martin, 1994, p. 200)

European sugar industry Commission decision 73/109/EC [1973] OJ L 140/17, Case IV/26.918 **(described in detail as landmark case in section 3.2)** (Martin, 1994, p. 142)

Manufacturers of Glass Containers (IFTRA) **Commission decision 74/292/EEC [1974] OJ L 160/1, Case IV/400**

COBELPA/VNP Commission decision 77/592/EEC [1977] OJ L 242/10, Cases IV/312, 366 (Martin, 1994, p. 183)

Vegetable Parchment Commission decision 78/252/EEC [1978] OJ L 70/54, Case IV/29.176 (Martin, 1994, pp. 183–4)

Central Stikstof Verkoopkantoor Commission decision 78/732/EC [1978] OJ L 242/15, Case IV/26.186

White Lead Commission decision 79/90/EEC [1979] OJ L 21/16, Case IV/29.535

Italian Cast Glass Commission decision 80/1334/EEC [1980] OJ L 383/19, Case IV/29.869 **(described in detail as landmark case in section 2.2)**

Zinc Producer Group Commission decision 84/405/EEC [1984] OJ L 220/27, Case IV/30.350

Wood Pulp Commission decision 85/202/EEC [1985] OJ L 85/1, Case IV/29.725 (*) (Martin, 1994, pp. 142–3; Motta, 2004, pp. 211–19)

Polypropylene Commission decision 86/398/EEC [1986] OJ L 230/1, Case IV/31.149

Meldoc Commission decision 86/596/EEC OJ L 348/50, Case IV/31.204

Fatty Acids **Commission decision 87/1/EEC [1987] OJ L 3/17, Case IV/31.128**

New potatoes Commission decision 88/109/EEC [1988] OJ L 59/25, Case IV/31.735

PVC Commission decision 89/190/EEC [1989] OJ L 74/1, Case IV/31.865

LdPE Commission decision 89/191/EEC [1989] OJ L 74/21, Case IV/31.866

U.K. Tractors Registration Exchange **Commission decision 92/157/EEC [1992] OJ L 68/19, Cases IV/31.370, 31.446**

Cartonboard Commission decision 94/601/EEC [1994] OJ L 243/1, Case IV/33.833

Amino Acids Commission decision 2001/418/EC [2001] OJ L 152/24, Case COMP/36.545/F3

Citric Acid Commission decision 2002/742/EC [2002] OJ L 239/18, Case COMP/E-1/36.604

Interbrew and Alken-Maes Commission decision 2003/569/EC [2003] OJ L 200/1, Case IV/37.614/F3

O2 UK/T-Mobile UK – UK network sharing agreement Commission decision 2003/570/EC [2003] OJ L 200/59, Case COMP/38.370

Methionine Commission decision 2003/674/EC OJ L 255/1, Case C.37.159

3G Network sharing Germany Commission decision 2004/207/EC [2004] OJ L 75/32, Case COMP/38.369

Industrial copper tubes Commission decision 2004/421/EC [2004] OJ L 125/50, Case COMP/38.240

• Decisions displayed in **bold type** are described in the section. Decisions highlighted with (*) include interesting economic analysis by the Commission on the specific topic of the section. Some decisions contain economic reasoning on more than one topic and therefore appear in several lists of Commission decisions in chronological order. Reference is made in brackets and **bold type** to the relevant section in which the decision is extensively described as a landmark case. When decisions are referenced and/or described in some detail in one or more of the economic textbooks, reference in brackets is also made to the relevant part(s) of those texts.

Plasterboard Commission decision 2005/471/EC [2005] OJ L 166/8, Case COMP/E-1/37.152

Monochloroacetic acid Commission decision of 19 January 2005, published on DG Comp website, Case COMP/E-1/37.773

Industrial Thread Commission decision of 14 September 2005, published on DG Comp website, Case COMP/38.337

Industrial bags Commission decision of 30 November 2005, published on DG Comp website, Case COMP/F-3/38.354

Rubber chemicals Commission decision of 21 December 2005, published on DG Comp website, Case COMP/F-1/38.443

Hydrogene peroxide and perborate Commission decision of 3 May 2006, published on DG Comp website, Case COMP/38.620

Acrylic glass producers Commission decision of 31 May 2006, published on DG Comp website, Case COMP/38.645

Copper fittings Commission decision of 20 September 2006, published on DG Comp website, Case COMP/38.121

Steel beams (readopted) Commission decision of 8 November 2006, published on DG Comp website, Case COMP/38.907

Gas insulated switchgear Commission decision of 24 January 2007, published on DG Comp website, Case COMP/38.899

Elevators and escalators Commission decision of 21 February 2007, published on DG COMP website, Case COMP/38.823

Fasteners and attaching machines Commission decision of 19 September 2007, published on DG Comp website, Case COMP/39.168

Car glass producers Commission decision of 12 November 2008, not yet published, Case COMP/39.125

Marine hose producers Commission decision of 28 January 2009, not yet published, Case COMP/39.406

Heat stabilisers Commission decision of 11 November 2009, not yet published, Case COMP/38.589

F   Economic landmark cases

F.1   *Manufacturers of Glass Containers (IFTRA)* Commission decision 74/292/EEC [1974] OJ L 160/1

Relevance: From the very beginning of competition law enforcement the Commission has always been very clear in that exchanges of information on prices are prohibited. The Commission in this decision considers them as eliminating a large part of the risk (consisting in the uncertainty about competitors' actions) faced by firms on the market and also fundamental to the commercial strategy of each firm.[132]

---

132   For a significant example of European judicatures assessment of similar information exchange agreement, see also Case T-1/89 *Rhône-Poulenc SA* v. *Commission*, that clearly shows the CFI's early attitude toward discussions on price increases among competitors. The case concerned meetings during which information was exchanged between competitors about the prices they wished to see charged on the market, the prices they intended to charge, their profitability thresholds, the sales volume restrictions they judged to be necessary, their sales figures, or the identity of their custumers. With regard to this kind of conduct the CFI observed that; ". . . not only did the applicant pursue the aim of eliminating in advance uncertainty about the future conduct of its competitors but also, in determining the policy which it intended to follow on the market, it could not fail to take account, directly or indirectly, of the information obtained during the course of those meetings. Similarly, in determining the policy which they intended to follow, its competitors were bound to take into account, directly or indirectly, the information disclosed to them by the

- For case report, relevant market, relevant facts, origin of the case, obligations, fines, and remedies, and further development of the case, see Case *F.1* in section *2.1*.

    c. Economic analysis

    In this early decision concerning a price fixing and a market sharing agreement in the market for glass containers, the Commission clearly established the principle according to which the exchange of information concerning prices among competitors (in this case also part of a broader agreement) is not allowed and will always be considered as anticompetitive unless a special justification can be given. This approach, concerning only this specific type of information, has been maintained by the Commission throughout the years.

    The IFTRA rules (as described in Case *F.1*, section 2.1) established a very precise monitoring system for the exchange of information which was inherent to the overall agreement because it was necessary for its implementation. The Commission clearly stated that "it is contrary to the provision of Article 85(1) of the EEC Treaty for a producer to communicate to his competitors the essential elements of his price policy such as price lists, the discounts and terms of trade he applies, the rates and date of any change of them and the special exceptions he grants to specific customers. An undertaking which informs its competitors of such elements of its price policy will only do so when certain that, in accordance with the agreement entered into with such competitors in pursuant of the IFTRA rules, they will pursue a similar price policy for deliveries to the market where the undertaking is price leader. By such means the possibility of unforeseen or unforeseeable reactions by competitors is sought to be eliminated, thus removing a large element of the risk normally attaching to any individual action in the market."[133]

F.2 *Fatty Acids* Commission decision 87/1/EEC [1987] OJ L 3/17

Relevance: This decision constitutes the first case in which the Commission considered an exchange of information in isolation, i.e. not in the frame of a broader agreement, as an infringement of competition rules. For the first time the Commission also drew the line between the approach to be taken toward on the one hand exchange of aggregate and statistical data and on the other information on single business.

- Case IV/31.128
- **Decision:** Infringement of Article 101(1) FEU Treaty, imposition of fines
- **Decision addressee(s):**
    - Unilever NV, *the Netherlands*
    - Henkel KGaA, *Federal Republic of Germany*
    - Oleofina SA, *Belgium*
- **Report route:** Commission decision of 15 January 1986 to start a proceedings on its own initiative
- **Date of the decision:** 2 December 1986
- **Competition Commissioner:** P. Sutherland
- **Relevant product market:** Oleochemicals stearine and oleine (fatty acids)

---

applicant about the course of conduct which the applicant itself had decided upon or which it contemplated adopting on the market."[132]

133 Recital 43 of the decision.

- **Relevant geographical market:** European internal market
- **Description of the case**
  ### a. Relevant facts
  Unilever (which was part of the agreement through its division Unichema), Henkel, and Oleofina were the three largest European producers of oleochemicals. They were all large firms with multiple activities in Europe and in the rest of the world. All of them utilized a large part of their production of fatty acid for captive use.

  The European market consisted of forty producers, ranging from very small to very large manufacturers. At the time of the decision the market was suffering structural overcapacity (20–30 percent) and a low or stagnant growth rate; at the same time it was facing growing competition from developing countries.

  In 1976 the European producers of oleochemicals representing 90 percent of the European fatty acid market formed a trade association named the Association des Producteurs d'Acides Gras (APAG) which, in turn, was associated with the European Council of Chemical Manufacturers' Federations (CEFIC). CEFIC rules, in regulating the exchange of aggregate industrial and statistical information among members, explicitly provided for rules ensuring the non-disclosure of information concerning individual companies.

  Following the acquisition of the remaining 50 percent of the capital of a subsidiary that Unilever did not own yet and the resulting internal reorganization, production rationalization and reduction, Unilever approached its two main competitors (i.e. Henkel and Oleofina) in order to conclude with them an agreement concerning the reciprocal exchange of information. In September 1979 they agreed to exchange on a quarterly basis data about their respective total tonnages of stearine and oleine sold to third parties (i.e. excluding those for captive use) and also to provide information about past sales data referring to the period 1976–8. The firms signed the agreement "to enable the participants to monitor possible major changes in their relative positions as a result of any unilateral capacity reduction by Unichema which would follow the acquisition."[134] Another perceived object was to "examine the possible reaction of the market following the takeover . . . and the reorganization."[135]

  After the Commission investigation in 1982 the agreement was ended in January 1983. During its investigation the Commission found Unichema documents which revealed that as a leader in the production of a certain commodity it was entitled to maintain its current market share and that any attempt by its competitors to gain some of its customers via price cutting would have triggered a reaction in other markets and generated a general price instability. It also considered that one of the collective tasks of the main producers was to bear the responsibility of potential capacity reductions.
  ### b. Origin of the case
  On 15 January 1986 the Commission, on its own initiative, adopted a decision to initiate proceedings against the above-mentioned undertakings in respect of exchange of information agreements concluded by them concerning the fatty acid market.

---

134   Recital 14 of the decision.   135   Recital 17 of the decision.

c. Economic analysis

The decision is particularly relevant because it establishes the possibility to infringe competition rules (i.e. Article 101(1) FEU Treaty) through information exchange agreements that are not established in the frame of broader horizontal agreements and that are not simply the instrument for monitoring compliance with other agreements (e.g. market sharing or price fixing). At the same time the decision is also significant because for the first time (in line with the economically based approach already embraced by the ECJ case law)[136] the Commission clearly underlined the difference in the approach that it would adopt in the assessment of statistical and aggregate information exchanges through trade associations and of exchanges of information concerning individual businesses.

The Commission allowed the exchange of aggregate data via a trade association, while stressing the anticompetitive effects stemming from the exchange of data from individual firms such as information on quantities produced and sold.[137] "The regular exchange of information [about individual sales] gave each of the parties the opportunity of identifying the individual business of his two major competitors and thus to measure on a quarterly basis the future performance of that market . . . The exchange, therefore, . . . enables each of the parties to identify more precisely the competitive behavior of the others . . . The agreement thus removed an important element of uncertainty on the part of each of them as to the activities of the others,"[138] the Commission stated.

In the Commission's view, the aim of the agreement was *undoubtedly* to achieve a market stabilization that would have allowed each party to maintain its market share.[139] It would have consequently lessened the intensity of competition among the parties. The stabilization of the market was seen as producing effects largely similar to a market sharing agreement since the parties would have not competed to attract each other's customers. Therefore an agreement establishing exchange of sensible business information had "inherent restrictive effects upon competition although these may not be measurable or even apparent to an observer of the market unaware of the existence of such an agreement."[140] The anticompetitive nature of the agreement was made even clearer by the fact that notwithstanding the opportunity to exchange, within the APAG, information that would have been positively considered by the Commission (i.e. aggregated), the parties decided to enter into a different agreement to exchange other types of information (i.e. disaggregated).

Another relevant aspect of the decision is the fact that the Commission admitted the possibility that historical information may also facilitate collusive behavior between competitors, in particular enabling the parties to determine their respective traditional position on a given market and thus to spot any future deviation from past market behaviours (i.e. changes of strategy.)[141] In the specific circumstances of the case, historical information was relevant because

136 Joined cases 40–48, 50, 54–56, 111, 113 and 114/73 *European Sugar Industry* [1975] ECR 1663.
137 See recitals 34–40 of the decision.
138 Recitals 36 and 37 of the decision.
139 See recital 38 of the decision. Emphasis added.
140 Recital 45 of the decision.
141 See recital 36 of the decision.

it would have increased the effects of the exchange of information about future quantities produced.

d. Fines, remedies, and conditions enclosed
  – The Commission imposed the following total fines:

Company	Fine (ECU)
Unichema	50,000
Henkel	50,000
Oleofina	50,000

e. Further developments of the case
None.

F.3 *U.K. Tractors Registration Exchange* Commission decision 92/157/EEC [1992] OJ L 68/19

Relevance: Relevance of market conditions and type of information exchanged in the analysis of exchange of information agreements. Benchmark rules given by the Commission and confirmation of the case-by-case approach.

- For case report, relevant market, facts finding, origin of the case, economic analysis, obligations, fines and remedies see Case *F.1* in section *2.6*.
  e. Further developments of the case
  Case T-34/92 *Fiatagri UK Ltd and New Holland Ford Ltd* v. *Commission* [1994] ECR II-905, appeal dismissed.
  Case C-8/95P *New Holland Ford* v. *Commission* [1998] ECR I-3175, CFI (now "the General Court") judgment upheld.
  Case T-35/92 *John Deere Ltd* v. *Commission* [1994] ECR II-957, appeal dismissed. The CFI observed that the Commission decision was the first in which the Commission had prohibited an information exchange system concerning sufficiently homogenous products which did not directly concern the prices of those products, but which did not underpin any other anticompetitive arrangement either.[142]
  Furthermore the CFI observed that "a truly competitive market transparency between traders is in principle likely to lead to the intensification of competition between suppliers, since in such a situation, the fact that a trader takes into account information made available to him in order to adjust his conduct on the market is not likely, having regard to the atomized nature of the supply, to reduce or remove for the other traders any uncertainty about the foreseeable nature of its competitors' conduct."[143] On the other hand, the Court considers that general use, as between main suppliers and to their sole benefit and consequently to the exclusion of the other suppliers and of consumers, of exchanges of precise information at short intervals, identifying registered vehicles and the place of their registration is, on a highly concentrated oligopolistic market such as the market in question and on which competition is as a result already greatly reduced and exchange of

142 Recital 51 of the judgment.   143 *Ibid.*

information facilitated, likely to impair substantially the competition which exists between traders. In such circumstances, the sharing, on a regular and frequent basis, of information concerning the operation of the market has the effect of periodically revealing to all competitors the market positions and strategies of the various individual rivals.[144]

Case C-7/95 *John Deere Ltd* v. *Commission* [1998] ECR I-3111, CFI judgment upheld.

144   *Ibid.*

3   Abuse of dominance

A   Introduction

The European competition rules, in particular in Article 102 FEU Treaty, protect against the abuse of a dominant position by firms with monopolistic market power. Monopolists or other undertakings holding significant market power are less restrained in their business decisions than firms operating in a competitive environment. Dominant firms may consequently have the ability to raise prices profitably above competitive levels, or deliver a poorer quality of products.

Neither a dominant position, nor the concept of abuse is well defined in EU competition law. The meaning of the concepts has instead continuously developed over case law: Commission decisions and the rulings of the European Courts. This development has not always been in line with mainstream economic thinking, which has been at the root of controversy and hotly debated abuse cases.

The definition of dominance employed by the ECJ in several judgments is based on two prerequisites: *independence* and *prevention of effective competition*. The ECJ provides a definition of dominance as a position of economic strength enabling a firm to prevent the maintenance of effective competition on the market and to act independently of competitors, customers, and consumers.[1] Complete independence from customers and consumers is hard to imagine. After all, even a monopolist is constrained by the demand curve it faces. The concept of independence from competitors is more useful as a benchmark. A dominant firm can in principle raise prices above competitive levels, as it knows itself safe from rivals that can profitably undercut such prices in a competitive market.

The idea of *prevention of effective competition* used by the European judicature stems from the consideration that only in a market in which no firm is able to exert market power, neither independently nor in combination with its rivals, will competition prevail. The concept of market power is consistently accepted as a valuable benchmark for the definition of dominance.

In EU competition law, a dominant position is not *per se* prohibited or objectionable. Dominance is often the legitimate result of competitive behavior. Firms can have achieved a level of excellence which rivals find impossible to meet. They may implement better R&D programs, enjoy more efficient organization, reap economies of scale, produce internal growth and conducive factors such as their reputation, the degree of product differentiation, unique access to key inputs and/or financial resources and opportunity costs. These strategies are all legitimate – if not desirable – ways for firms to enhance their position to the benefit of consumers. European Competition law is concerned only with the abuse of such a dominant position.

EU case law distinguishes *exclusionary* practises from *exploitative* abuses. The former concern active attempts to prevent competitors from operating in the market. This may, for example, be achieved by using dominance to raise artificial entry barriers, or to credibly threaten with predatory

---

1   See, *inter alia*, Case 27/76 *United Brands Co. and United Brands Continental BV v. Commission* [1978] ECR 207.

prices in response to entry. *Exploitative* abuses are aimed at the exploitation of customers and consumers. Examples are charging excessive prices, and some forms of bundling and tying. These strategies can also be part of an abusive exclusionary strategy, however.

Although the question what exactly constitutes abusive conduct is certainly not uncontroversial, a common classification can be found in the economic literature.[2] This is followed in the organization of material on all cases of dominance analyzed by the Commission in sections in this chapter. Section 3.1 deals with excessive pricing, discriminatory sales conditions and prohibition to resale. Section 3.2 analyzes loyalty discounts and fidelity rebates schemes possibly abusive, while section 3.3 describes cases of predatory pricing. Section 3.4 deals with different types of product bundling and tying. In section 3.5 the few cases in which the Commission has dealt with price squeezing are described. Section 3.6 deals with raising entry barriers by restricting and/or preventing entry. Section 3.7 analyzes refusals to deal, in particular with relation to essential facilities. The last two sections of the chapter deal, respectively, with interoperability issues (3.8) and best price guarantees strategy (3.9).

B Applicable EU legislation

Article 102 FEU Treaty.

See also Commission Notice on the definition of the relevant market [1997] OJ C 372/3.

Commission guidance paper on enforcement priorities in applying Article 82 EC Treaty to abusive exclusionary conduct by dominant undertakings, published on 3 December 2008 on DG Comp website.

C Related economics texts

Bishop and Walker (2009), chapter 6
Carlton and Perloff (2005), chapters 4, 9, and 10
Church and Ware (2000), chapters 2, 4, 5, 6, 20, and 21
Martin (1994), chapters 4, 15, and 16
Martin (2002), chapters 8 and 11
Motta (2004), chapters 2 and 7
Tirole (1988), chapters 1, 3, and 9
Waldman and Jensen (2001), chapter 2, paragraph 6; chapters 10, 11, 14, and 18

D Related legal texts

Bellamy and Child (2008), chapter 10
Jones and Sufrin (2008), chapters 5, 6, and 7
Ritter and Braun (2005), chapter 5
Whish (2008), chapters 5, 17, and 18

---

2   The current debate among scholars on the identification of exclusionary abuses of dominance is at the heart of the Commission guidance paper on enforcement priorities in applying Article 102 FEU Treaty to abusive exclusionary conduct by dominant undertakings.

3.1 Excessive pricing, discriminatory sales conditions, and prohibition to resale

A Introduction

Firms with substantial market power can act as price setters. The most straightforward (ab)use of a dominant position therefore is to raise prices above competitive levels. There are nevertheless only very few abuse cases for excessive prices: the landmark decision in *Chiquita* (1976) and some aspects of the liberalized State monopolies decisions of the 1990s. In practice it is often difficult to assess what would have been the price levels without the abuse. Even when production costs can be attributed to units reasonably well, high prices can sometimes be justified as a natural reward for risky investments, entrepreneurial success, and innovation. Deciding whether a price is excessively high requires an estimation of what the competitive price level would have been. Inaccuracies in the methods to determine competitive counterfactuals make interventions vulnerable to errors and successful appeals. In addition, matters of excessive pricing come very close to price regulation, which is outside the ambit of the competition authorities.

Exploitative price discrimination occurs when a product is sold to different consumers at different prices, which do not reflect differences in the costs of supply. The ability to price discriminate derives from lack of alternative products and the possibility to prevent resale, for which market power is often a prerequisite. There are different types of price discrimination, including supplying each customer at his/her maximum willingness to pay (first-degree price discrimination). More common are imperfect forms of price discrimination. In the case of second-degree price discrimination, firms offer a range of deals to all consumers, inducing them to self-select according to their preferences: examples are rebates and discounts. Third-degree price discrimination occurs when companies apply different prices to consumers having different observable characteristics, such as age or location. The reason that this is possible is that different categories of identifiable and isolated consumers have a different elasticity of demand for the same good or service.

The overall welfare consequences of exploitative price discrimination are ambiguous. Price discrimination may in some cases enhance total welfare, where it leads to an increase in total output. Often when price discrimination is applied, however, this results in lower consumer welfare. More sophisticated forms of price discrimination can be anticompetitive – for example, excluding (downstream) competitors by giving them less favourable business deals. However, price discrimination can also sometimes be a necessary mechanism to recover fixed costs in industries in which these are high and variable costs are low (or zero). It is a difficult task for competition authorities to develop adequate tools to properly distinguish situations in which price discrimination is a competition concern from those in which it is not.

B Applicable EU legislation

No special legislation applicable. For applicable legislation see chapter 3, paragraph B.

C Related economics texts

Bishop and Walker (2009), paragraphs 6.14–6.19 and 6.29–6.40
Carlton and Perloff (2005), chapter 4, paragraph 1; chapter 9 and chapter 10
Church and Ware (2000), paragraphs 2.4, chapter 5

Martin (1994), chapters 4 and 15
Martin (2002), chapter 4
Motta (2004), paragraphs 2.2, 2.3, and 7.4
Tirole (1988), chapters 1 and 3
Waldman and Jensen (2001), chapter 2, paragraph 6 and chapter 14

D Related legal texts

Bellamy and Child (2008), chapter 10, paragraph 4 (B, ii, D and G)
Jones and Sufrin (2008), chapter 7, paragraph 9(A, i and B)
Ritter and Braun (2005), chapter 3, paragraph C(3)
Whish (2008), chapter 18, paragraph 3

E Commission decisions in chronological order[*]

Gema Commission decision 71/224/EC [1971] OJ L 134/15, Case IV/26.760

European sugar industry Commission decision 73/109/EC [1973] OJ L 140/17, Case IV/26.918 (**described in detail as landmark case in section 3.2**) (Martin, 1994, p. 142)

General Motors Continental Commission decision 75/75/EEC [1975] OJ L 29/14, Case IV/28.851 (*)

Chiquita **Commission decision 76/353/EEC [1976] OJ L 95/1, Case IV/26.699** (Bishop and Walker, 2009, 2.03, 3.46, 4.27, 4.3, 6.4, 6.14–6.17; Martin, 1994, pp. 102–3, 417, 438; Motta, 2004, pp. 35, 118, 499)

Michelin Commission decision 81/969/EEC [1981] OJ L 353/33, Case IV/29.491 (**described in detail as landmark case in section 3.2**) (*) (Bishop and Walker, 2009, 6.43; Motta, 2004, pp. 343, 500)

GVL Commission decision 81/1030/EEC [1981] OJ L 370/49, Case IV/29.839

British Telecommunications Commission decision 82/861/EEC [1982] OJ L 360/36, Case IV/29.877

British Leyland Commission decision 84/379/EEC [1984] OJ L 307/11, Case IV/30.615 (*) (Martin, 1994, p. 438)

Tetra Pak II Commission decision 92/163/EEC [1992] OJ L 72/1, Case IV/31.043 (**described in detail as landmark case in section 3.4**) (Bishop and Walker, 2009, 6.01, 6.77, 6.79, 6.109–6.112)

HOV SVZ/MCN Commission decision 94/210/EEC [1994] OJ L 104/34, Case IV/33.941

Irish Sugar Commission decision 97/624/EC [1997] OJ L 258/1, Cases IV/34.621, 35.059

AFS/ADP Commission decision 98/513/EC [1998] OJ L 230/10, Case IV/35.613

Ilmailulaitos/Luftfartsverket Commission decision 1999/198/EC [1999] OJ L 69/24, Case IV/35.767

CFO (Football World Cup) Commission decision 2000/12/EC [2000] OJ L 5/55, Case IV/36.888

- [*] Decisions displayed in **bold type** are described in the section. Decisions highlighted with (*) include interesting economic analysis by the Commission on the specific topic of the section. Some decisions contain economic reasoning on more than one topic and therefore appear in several lists of Commission decisions in chronological order. Reference is made in brackets and **bold type** to the relevant section in which the decision is extensively described as a landmark case. When decisions are referenced and/or described in some detail in one or more of the economic textbooks, reference in brackets is also made to the relevant part(s) of those texts.

Deutsche Post AG – Interception of cross-border mail Commission decision 2001/892/EC [2001] OJ L 331/40, Case COMP/C-1/36.915

Clearstream Commission decision of 2 June 2004, published on DG Comp website, Case COMP/38.096

Telefónica Commission decision of 4 July 2007, published on DG Comp website, Case COMP/38.784 **(described in detail as landmark case in section 3.5)**

F   Economic landmark cases

F.1   *Chiquita* Commission decision 76/353/EEC [1976] OJ L 95/1

Relevance: Landmark decision where the Commission defines its approach toward price discrimination enforced by a dominant firm. In the Commission reasoning the impact that the market integration goal underlying EU competition law has on the Commission assessment is observable. The decision is also important because it represents one of the very few cases in which the Commission deals with excessive pricing.

- Case IV/26.699
- **Decision:** Infringement of Article 102 FEU Treaty
- **Decision addressee(s):**
  – United Brands Company (UBC), *United States of America*
  – United Brands Continental BV (UB Continental), *the Netherlands*
- **Report route:** Submissions filed to the Commission on 27 May 1974
- **Date of the decision:** 17 December 1975
- **Competition Commissioner:** A. Borschette
- **Relevant product market:** Bananas
- **Relevant geographical market:** Belgium, Denmark, Germany, Ireland, Luxembourg, and the Netherlands
- **Description of the case**
  - a. **Relevant facts**
    About a third of the world banana production is imported into the European market. All varieties of bananas are exported and shipped when still green and are then artificially ripened in the country of destination. Ripeners usually belong to the same importers/distributors but there are also some independent ones. The banana market has seen increased branding of the fruit and concomitant intensive sales campaigns and advertising strategies. The practical consequence of the new commercial strategy is that each single banana has to be marked or labeled before leaving the country of production.

    The brand usage was introduced by United Fruit Company in 1967 with the brand "Chiquita." In 1970 UBC was created as a result of the merger between United Fruit Company and American Seal-Kap. UBC was a large company operating in the market for oil, rice, soya beans, several vegetables, a wide range of preserved food products, and also for chemicals, plastics, packaging, rail transport, and telecommunications.

    Because of the restrictive intervention of the American antitrust authority, banana production represented only 18.5 percent of total UBC turnover at the time of the decision. In 1974 UBC's production accounted for 35 percent of total world banana export. It was the largest producer in the world, it had one of the largest shipping fleets, and made use of one of the largest refrigerated containers shipping operators (Salen shipping company). UBC owned a large number of subsidiaries throughout the world. Import and distribution of bananas were organized according to a complex scheme coordinated by three wholly owned subsidiaries representative and responsible for UBC activities in Europe and the Middle East (UB Continental), in Italy (Compagnia Italiana della Frutta SpA), and in the UK (Fyffes Group Ltd).[3] In some countries UBC had its own ripening facilities while in others it conducted enquiries to find private ripeners subject to strict technical requirements and contracted them to ripen and distribute Chiquita-brand bananas. In Germany, for instance, UBC used to sell its bananas mainly through the Scipio group, which owned more than a third of the ripening facilities of the country. In order to promote and protect Chiquita's image, UBC relied on large advertising campaigns carried out at different levels and on strict and rigorous quality controls of all ripeners and selling points. There were specific size and color requirements that had to be met before a banana was branded with the Chiquita name.

UBC was (directly or indirectly) the largest banana seller in all (then) European countries.[4] Between 1971 and 1974 it supplied around 40 percent of the bananas sold in the Community. In the relevant geographic market it had a market share of around 45 percent.[5] Its main competitors active in all EEC national markets were Del Monte and Castle&Cook. Other smaller competitors were active only in some EEC Member States.[6]

Bananas for sale to customers in European Member States were handled by UBC mainly through the ports of Rotterdam and Bremerhaven; there they were loaded onto refrigerated trucks of the buyers (ripeners/distributors). Transport was therefore on their account, the only exception being the bananas for the Irish market which were delivered by UBC in Ireland with a price overcharge to cover transportation costs. "Although its bananas [were] sold f.o.r. Bremerhaven or Rotterdam, the sales price[s] which UBC fixes each week for Chiquita bananas vary substantially according to the Member State where the customer has his business and the bananas are to be retailed . . . the variations are not attributable to any differences in customs duties or transport costs, since these are borne by the distributors/ripeners."[7] The differences in prices charged to the consumers in the different Member States varied considerably and had a spread of up to 138 percent, as the comparison of Danish and Irish prices illustrated.[8] Olesen was the second largest UBC's distributor/ripener in Denmark. It was active also in the distribution of other banana varieties and became in 1969 the exclusive distributor for Dole bananas (produced by Castle&Cook) in Denmark. Subsequently, UBC started reducing the orders placed by Olesen and on October 1973 it informed Olesen that it had terminated the supply of Chiquita bananas. As a consequence, Olesen lost a number of large customers, which had made their business relation with Olesen conditional on the provision

---

3   For details about the distribution/selling system in the different Member States see recitals I-1-3 and I-1-7 of the decision.

4   See recital I-1-7 of the decision.

5   See recital II-A-2 of the decision.

6   *Idem.*

7   Recital I-2-b of the decision.

8   For a more detailed description of the cost structure see recital I-2-b of the decision.

of Chiquita bananas. On February 1975 the supplies were resumed and consequently Olesen withdrew the complaint it had filed to the Commission.

b. Origin of the case

On 27 May 1974 submissions were filed to the Commission by The Tropical Fruit Co., Jack Dolan Ltd, and Banana Importers of Ireland Ltd. On 19 March 1975 the Commission decided to initiate proceedings against UBC.

c. Economic analysis

This decision is of crucial importance in EU competition law enforcement history, because it defined the Commission's rationale concerning price discrimination, the relevance of market integration in its assessment of potential abusive behavior (i.e. prohibition to resale). It also constitutes one of the very few decisions dealing with a case of excessive pricing (besides few other decisions in the 1990s following the liberalization process).

UBC's differentiation in prices charged to customers in different Member States was considered abusive of the dominant position because it was not justifiable on any grounds. Article 102 FEU Treaty clearly prohibits dominant firms from applying dissimilar conditions to similar transactions. The transactions in question were seen as "equivalent" by the Commission. The Commission explained that "[t]he bananas are all freighted in the same ships, are unloaded at the same costs . . . and are of the same variety, of similar quality, packaged in the same way and sold in substantially similar quantities under the same Chiquita brand name."[9] In rejecting the UBC argument according to which the discrimination was justified by the attempt to charge to each part of the market the price it could bear, the Commission seemed to accept the possibility of applying price discrimination similar to *third-degree price discrimination*. Actually the Commission did not reject UBC's argument in theory but just stated that it was not acceptable because "marketing conditions in these Member States are in fact broadly comparable."[10] Therefore there were no differences between different groups of consumers justifying price discrimination. The result of the discrimination was the creation of a system of substantial price differences in each Member State and a competitive disadvantage for distributors/ripeners attempting to sell their bananas outside the Member State in which they were based and for which they received supplies from UBC.

In the Commission's view, the mentioned competitive disadvantage was strengthened by the prohibition imposed on the distributors/ripeners to sell the bananas when still green or to resell them to other ripeners. In practise this prohibition would have obliged all the distributors to operate their own ripening facilities and prevent them from acting as pure resellers. The consequence was to prevent UBC's distributors/ripeners from "entering into competition at resale level with UBC and the other importers/distributors in business on the banana market, since at that stage all trade has to be in green bananas only."[11] The other consequence of the prohibition was a *de facto* prohibition to export (i.e. prohibition to resale and to resale in another Member State) and consequently the maintenance of market segregation

---

9   Recital II-A-3-b of the decision.
10   *Idem.*

11   Recital II-A-3-b of the decision.

between Member States. The Commission's focus on the effect of the abusive conduct on market integration in Europe exemplifies the relevance of the overall goal to achieve a single market in the enforcement and interpretation of EU competition rules.

A further abuse UBC was accused of was its charging of unfair prices to some of its customers. Referring to the ECJ case law, the Commission stated that "a wide variation in price which is not justified on objective grounds can be a determining factor of an abuse."[12] In evaluating the fairness of the prices, the Commission started from the consideration that, for UBC admission, also the prices applied in Ireland were profitable and that those prices were in some instances 100 percent lower than the prices applied in other Member States. This produced a substantial profit. So the first criterion adopted was a comparison of prices applied in different countries. The second was analyzing the so-called "economic value of the product." The Commission stated that the UBC's prices were excessive compared to the economic value of the supplied product and challenged the huge price difference between branded and unbranded bananas which was unjustified with regard to quality and production costs. Therefore, the prices charged were considered unfair and their implementation an abuse of dominance. Even if economists do not always agree concerning the use of the above-mentioned criteria and concerning their ability to analyze the welfare effects of excessive pricing, they agree that it is difficult to establish a definition of what constitutes a fair price. As mentioned above, this case remains a rare example in competition law enforcement history and, therefore, the Commission's position on excessive prices is not easy to evaluate.[13]

The last abuse of which UBC was accused was the refusal to supply Olesen between 1973 and 1975. That conduct was considered abusive particularly because it restricted Olesen's commercial freedom on the banana distribution market.[14]

d. Fines, remedies, and conditions enclosed

- The Commission imposed on UBC a total fine of EUA 1,000,000.
- Obligations for UBC to bring the infringements to an end without delay.
- Obligation for UBC to inform all its distributors/ripeners in the relevant geographical market about the cessation to apply the prohibition to resale green bananas and to inform the Commission about the accomplishment of its obligation not later than 1 February 1976.
- Obligation for UBC to inform the Commission by 20 April 1976 and thereafter twice a year not later that 20 January and 20 July for a period of two years about the prices charged in the relevant geographical market.

---

12 Recital II-A-3-c of the decision.
13 In the case *Port of Helsingborg* brought to its attention, the Commission, rejecting two complaints lodged by port operators, had the occasion to discuss the meaning of "economic value." It noted how the "economic value" cannot be determined only on the basis of costs and that demand-side considerations are also relevant. Moreover, the Commission pointed out the relevance to be given to sunk costs and to opportunity cost in the assessment of the "economic value" of the good considered. See Commission letter related to Case COMP/A.36.570/D3 of 23 July 2004.
14 For a more detailed description of refusal to supply see recital II-A-3-c of the decision. The topic will be broadly examined in section 3.8 of this chapter.

–   The Commission imposed on UBC a periodic penalty payment of EUA 1,000 for each day of delay from the dates stated in the decision in the accomplishment of the obligation to provide information about the prices.

e. Further developments of the case

Case 27/76 *United Brands* v. *Commission* [1978] ECR 207, fines reduction and Commission decision partially annulled. The ECJ found that the Commission had failed to prove that UBC had charged unfair prices. According to the Court, the Commission adopted a debatable basis for the calculation of the prices, did not take into due account some documents produced by UBC, and ultimately failed to demonstrate an excessive profit margin by UBC because it did not analyze the cost structure of the company. Nonetheless, the ECJ confirmed the circumstance that "charging a price which is excessive because it has no reasonable relation to the economic value of the product supplied would [constitute] an abuse. This excess could, *inter alia*, be determined objectively if it were possible for it to be calculated by making a comparison between the selling price of the product in question and its cost of production, which would disclose the amount of the profit margin."[15]

3.2 Loyalty discounts and fidelity rebates

A   Introduction

Discounts and rebates are a common example of second-degree price discrimination. Loyalty discounts and fidelity rebates are often cumulative and progressive, locking customers into exclusive commercial relations with a single seller. This, in turn, may make it difficult for competitors to maintain their customer base and for new entrants to establish themselves in the market. Fidelity discounts can also be abused by a dominant firm to exclude rivals in a manner very similar to tying practises. That is, loyalty discounts and fidelity rebates can be used to discriminate not among final consumers, but among retailers and distributors in order to induce them either to buy more or to break their other supply contracts. This is therefore different from quantity rebates. Fidelity rebates and loyalty discounts may be justified so far as incremental prices are above incremental costs. On the other hand, forcing companies to adopt a uniform price policy might not benefit consumers directly if total output falls as a consequence of the uniform price being raised above the willingness of certain group(s) of consumers to pay.

B   Applicable EU legislation

No special legislation applicable. For applicable legislation see chapter 3, paragraph B.

C   Related economics texts

Bishop and Walker (2009), paragraphs 6.29–6.40
Carlton and Perloff (2005), chapter 10, paragraphs 1 and 3

---

15   Recitals 250 and 251 of the judgment.

Church and Ware (2000), paragraph 5.4.3
Martin (1994), not specifically discussed
Martin (2002), not specifically discussed
Motta (2004), paragraph 7.4, specifically 7.4.1.6
Tirole (1988), paragraph 3.3
Waldman and Jensen (2001), chapter 14, paragraph 6(6)

D   Related legal texts

Bellamy and Child (2008), chapter 10, paragraph 4(B, iii)
Jones and Sufrin (2008), chapter 7, paragraph 6(E)
Ritter and Braun (2005), chapter 5, paragraph D(6 c)
Whish (2008), chapter 18, paragraph 4

E   Commission decisions in chronological order*

European sugar industry **Commission decision 73/109/EC [1973] OJ L 140/17, Case IV/26.918**
(Martin, 1994, p. 142)

Michelin **Commission decision 81/969/EEC [1981] OJ L 353/33, Case IV/29.491** (Bishop and
Walker, 2009, 6.43; Motta, 2004, pp. 343, 500)

Eurofix – Bauco/Hilti Commission decision 88/138/EEC [1988] OJ L 65/19, Cases IV/30.787,
31.488 (**described in detail as landmark case in sections 3.4 and 3.6**) (Bishop and Walker,
2009, 6.64; Martin, 1994, p. 449)

Napier Brown/British Sugar Commission decision 88/518/EEC [1988] OJ L 284/41, Case
IV/30.178 (**described in detail as landmark case in section 3.5**)

BPB Industries PLC Commission decision 89/22/EEC [1989] OJ L 10/50, Case
IV/31.900

Soda-ash – Solvay Commission decision 91/299/EC [1991] OJ L 152/21, Case IV/33.133d (*)
(Motta, 2004, p. 502)

Soda-Ash – ICI Commission decision 91/300/EEC [1991] OJ L 152/40, Case IV/33.133d

British Midland/Aer Lingus Commission decision 92/213/EEC [1993] OJ L 96/34, Case
IV/33.544 (**described in detail as landmark case in section 3.7**)

Cewal, Cowac, Ukwal Commission decision 93/82/EEC [1993] OJ L 34/20, Cases IV/32.448,
32.450 (Bishop and Walker, 2009, 6.106; Motta, 2004, p. 144)

Irish Sugar Commission decision 97/624/EC [1997] OJ L 258/1, Cases IV/34.621, 35.059

Virgin/British Airways Commission decision 2000/74/EC [2000] OJ L 30/1, IV/D-2/34.780 (*)
(Bishop and Walker, 2009, 4.24, 6.01, 6.42, 6.43; Motta, 2004, p. 499)

Deutsche Post AG Commission decision 2001/354/EC [2001] OJ L 125/27, Case
COMP/35.141

• Decisions displayed in **bold type** are described in the section. Decisions highlighted with (*) include interesting economic analysis
  by the Commission on the specific topic of the section. Some decisions contain economic reasoning on more than one topic and
  therefore appear in several lists of Commission decisions in chronological order. Reference is made in brackets and **bold type** to the
  relevant section in which the decision is extensively described as a landmark case. When decisions are referenced and/or described
  in some detail in one or more of the economic textbooks, reference in brackets is also made to the relevant part(s) of those
  texts.

Michelin **Commission decision 2002/405/EC [2002] OJ L 143/1, Case COMP/E-2/36.041**
Soda-Ash/Solvay Commission decision 2003/6/EC [2003] OJ L 10/10, Case COMP/33.133
Soda-Ash/ICI Commission decision 2003/7/EC [2003] OJ L 10/33, Case COMP/33.133
Compagnie Maritime Belge (CEWAL) Commission decision of 30 April 2004, published on DG
  Comp website, Cases COMP/D/32.448, 32.450
Prokent AG – Tomra system Commission decision of 29 March 2006, published on DG Comp
  website, Case COMP/38.113
Intel Commission decision of 13 May 2009, not yet published, Case COMP/37.990

F   Economic landmark cases

F.1   *European sugar industry* Commission decision 73/109/EC [1973] OJ L 140/17

Relevance: The first case in which the Commission dealt with a system of rebates applied by a dominant firm potentially producing exploitative effects for (non-exclusive) customers and exclusionary effects for competitors. The system, based on the granting of rebates only in case of exclusivity contracts with customers and completely unrelated to costs and quantities, was considered abusive by the Commission.

- Case IV/26.918
- **Decision:** Infringement of Article 101 and 102 FEU Treaty
- **Decision addressee(s):**
    - Raffinerie Tirlemontoise SA (RT), *Belgium*
    - Centrale Suiker Maatschappij NV (CSM), *the Netherlands*
    - Cooperatieve Vereniging Suiker Unie UA (SU), *the Netherlands*
    - Westdeutsche Zuckervertriebsgesellschaft mbH & Co. KG, *Federal Republic of Germany*
    - Pfeifer & Langen, *Federal Republic of Germany*
    - Südzucker Verkauf GmbH (SZV), *Federal Republic of Germany*
    - Süddeutsche Zucker AG, *Federal Republic of Germany*
    - Zuckerfabrik Franken GmbH, *Federal Republic of Germany*
    - Sucre-Union SA, *France*
    - Société des Raffineries et Sucreries Say, *France*
    - Société F. Béghin SA, *France*
    - Générale Sucrière SA, *France*
    - Société Nouvelle de Raffinerie Lebaudy-Sommier SA, *France*
    - Groupement d'Intérêt Economique Lebaudy-SUC, *France*
    - Sucres & Denrées SA, *France*
    - Eridania Zuccherifici Nazionali SpA, *Italy*
    - Società Generale di Zuccherifici, *Italy*
    - Cavarzere-Produzioni Industriali, *Italy*
    - Società Italiana per l'Industria degli Zuccheri SpA, *Italy*
    - Romana Zucchero SpA, *Italy*
    - Zuccherificio del Volano SpA, *Italy*
    - Agricola Industriale Emiliana (AIE) SpA, *Italy*
    - SADAM SpA, *Italy*
    - Zuccherificio di Sermide SpA, *Italy*

- **Report route:** Commission decision of 31 May 1972 to start proceedings on its own initiative
- **Date of the decision:** 2 January 1973
- **Competition Commissioner:** A. Borschette
- **Relevant product market:** Raw and white sugar
- **Relevant geographical market:** European internal market
- **Description of the case**
  - a. **Relevant facts**

    This case is a fully fledged investigation carried out by the Commission in the sugar market in Europe. The above-mentioned undertakings were the major sugar producers in Europe and the larger suppliers in their respective countries. Some of the national markets within the (then) EEC were characterised by large overcapacity (i.e. the Belgian and the French markets) while some others (i.e. Italy and the Netherlands) were unable to fully satisfy the national demand and imported from other European countries. In Germany supply and demand were on balance. Luxembourg did not have any sugar production facility and completely depended on imports (mainly from Belgium).

    Since July 1978 the production and the distribution of sugar in the Community had been regulated by Council Regulation No. 1009/67/EC and its implementing measures. Those provisions were considered necessary "to ensure that the necessary guarantees in respect of employment and standards of living [were] maintained for Community growers of sugar beet and sugar cane and to avoid both overproduction of sugar and shortages thereof. The basic machinery set up to achieve these objectives consist[ed] essentially of the fixing of intervention prices and production quota. For each sugar marketing year an intervention price [was] fixed for white sugar produced in the Community, and the Community intervention agencies [were] obliged to purchase at [that] price all quantities of sugar offered to them. However, to avoid the danger of overproduction, this obligation to purchase [was] only to apply within the limits of certain quotas. For this purpose a basic quota and a maximum quota [was] fixed for each sugar undertaking."[16]

    The Community sugar market relied on protectionist measures against other suppliers in the world market where the prices used to be lower than in the EEC. Measures to assist producers in coping with their overproduction were also provided. It was explicitly not the intention of the European regulator to fix market prices in Europe; all actions were intended to support the European sugar producers. The Commission investigation revealed that since the above-mentioned Regulation had come into force collusive agreements existed among producers relating to the sale of sugar for human consumption on the various national markets. The different *concerted practises* adopted by the sugar producers were aimed at ensuring the protection of their respective national markets and consequently restricting competition between certain groups of sugar producers and sellers. The main instruments adopted to effectively implement the practises were:

---

16   Recital I-B-11 of the decision.

– An agreement between a group of national producers in a certain country and producers of overproducing countries (France and Belgium)
for the supply of sugar to be resold under the same conditions as the
"national" sugar.
– The allocation of the purchased sugar among national producers on
the basis of quota.
– The suppliers' undertaking to deliver sugar to other purchasers in the
buying country (not member of the *buying group*) either at a higher
price or conditional on the consent of the *buying group*.

Similar agreements were concluded in Italy, the Netherlands, West
Germany, and South Germany. They caused a strong compression
of natural competition between on the one side, importers of sugar
and national producers and, on the other, between national producers
reaching the agreement with foreign producers (with overcapacity)
and the rest of the producers in that same Member State.[17]

In light of the multiple cartelization of the European sugar industry, the Commission investigation also detected some market power
positions in which the undertakings' behaviors had to be scrutinized
from a dominance perspective. In particular the position of RT on the
Belgian market, of CSM and SU on the Dutch market, and of SZV
on the South German market, and the relations those undertakings
established with their dealers, were investigated by the Commission.
RT imposed restrictions on its Belgian dealers to resell the sugar
only to certain groups of customers and for certain users. CSM and
SU imposed on their Dutch dealers several obligations, among which
were those to maintain similar sale prices for sugar imported from
France and sugar acquired by Dutch producers (i.e. acquired by themselves) and not to undertake any further imports without the consent
of Dutch producers. Finally, SZV imposed on its agents the obligation
not to resell sugar bought from other producers without its consent and
granted them fidelity rebates based on the acquisition of their entire
annual requirement from SZV.

b. **Origin of the case**

On 31 May 1972 the Commission, on its own initiative, adopted a decision to
initiate a proceeding against the above-mentioned undertakings in respect of
agreements concluded by them concerning the sugar market in Europe.

c. **Economic analysis**

This decision deals primarily with a series of cartels established to partition
the European market in several national or subnational markets. This was the
case in Germany in order to protect national producers from foreign competition. Furthermore, the collusive practise led to the allocation of quota in each
single market between the national producers. These practises had the effect of
eliminating (or strongly reducing) competition between national undertakings
and producers that could potentially become importers of sugar into national

---

17   For a detailed description of the cartels established in each relevant geographic area, see recitals from II-A-1 to II-D-3 of the
decision.

markets other than their own (i.e. price fixing and market sharing). Moreover the undertakings involved also entered in tender fixing practises concerning the system of tenders for export refunds for sales to non-member countries which constituted one of the protective measures adopted in Europe for sugar producers active outside the Community.[18]

Furthermore, the Commission considered that RT, CSM, SU, and SZV had abused their dominant positions on the respective national markets by imposing the above-mentioned obligations on their dealers because "[t]he object of these abuses was to limit the principal sources of supply of these dealers, who might have wished to buy sugar for other uses [or to import it freely from other countries], as well as the sources of supply of the dealers' clients."[19]

Next to the size and depth of the investigation carried out by the Commission, this decision is particularly significant because it was the first case in which the Commission had to deal with a system of rebates that could have potentially constituted an abuse of dominance by an undertaking in a given area.

In the specific circumstances of the case, SZV offered annual rebates to those customers that bought all their sugar from them (i.e. in case of exclusive purchasing agreement). SZV threatened that if a customer purchased somewhere else it would lose the annual rebate entirely. Assessing the effects on competition of that system of fidelity rebates, the Commission stated that "the granting of a rebate which does not depend on the amount bought, but only on whether the annual requirements are covered exclusively by the SZV, is an unjustifiable discrimination against buyers who also buy sugar from sources other than SZV. Since the buyers depend for at least part of their supplies on SZV as they have insufficient storage facilities and need regular supplies, the disadvantage of losing the rebate is usually greater than the advantage of buying sugar from outsiders even if they offer it at more favourable prices."[20]

In the Commission's view, the system of rebates was not only discriminatory for non-exclusive buyers, but also highly damaging to competitors. "[I]f the client wishes to buy [part of its requirements] abroad the foreign supplier's price must compensate for the loss of the annual rebate. Such favourable offers [would be], however, practically ruled out."[21] The negative effects on competitors were strengthened by the possibility of the dominant firm controlling customers' purchases from foreign suppliers through fidelity rebates and through information on the average amounts bought annually, which they used to manipulate the business of foreign competitors.

This first assessment of abusive rebates carried out by the Commission recognised the exclusionary effect of such rebates on competitors and thus the negative effects for consumers in the long run. At the same time, the decision disregarded much of the direct discriminatory effects on consumers. Finally, it is also important to note that in the specific case the rebates were completely unrelated to both quantities and costs.

18   See in particular recital II-F of the decision.   20   Recital II-E-1 of the decision.
19   Recital II-E-1 of the decision.   21   *Idem.*

d. Fines, remedies, and conditions enclosed
  – The Commission imposed the following total fines:

Company	Fine (EUA)
Raffinerie Tirlemontoise SA	1,500,000
Sucres & Denrées SA	1,000,000
Société des Raffineries et Sucreries Say	500,000
Société F. Béghin SA	700,000
Générale Sucrière SA	400,000
Eridania Zuccherifici Nazionali SpA	1,000,000
Società Italiana per l'Industria degli Zuccheri SpA	300,000
Cavarzere-Produzioni Industriali	200,000
Agricola Industriale Emiliana (AIE) SpA	100,000
Zuccherificio del Volano SpA	100,000
SADAM SpA	100,000
Cooperatieve Vereniging Suiker Unie UA	800,000
Centrale Suiker Maatschappij NV	600,000
Pfeifer & Langen	800,000
Süddeutsche Zucker AG	700,000
Südzucker Verkauf GmbH	200,000

  – Obligations for the above-mentioned undertakings to bring the infringements to an end.

e. Further developments of the case
Joined Cases 40 to 48, 50, 54 to 56, 111, 113 and 114/73 *Suiker Unie and others* v. *Commission* [1975] ECR 1663, fines reduction, and Commission decision partly annulled mainly to the extent to which it found the parties to have engaged in a concerted practise.

Nonetheless, with regard to the discount scheme, the ECJ confirmed the loyalty rebate to be discriminatory because "different net prices were charged to two economic operators who bought the same amount of sugar from SZV if one of them purchased from another producer as well."[22]

Moreover the ECJ ruled that the loyalty rebate was "likely to limit markets to the prejudice of consumers within the meaning of article 86 (b), because it gave other producers and especially those having their places of business in other Member States no chance or restricted their opportunities of competing with sugar sold by SZV."[23]

F.2 *Michelin* Commission decision 81/969/EEC [1981] OJ L 353/33

Relevance: The Commission analyzes a system of loyalty discounts established individually and selectively for each customer according to sale targets fixed by Michelin. The

---

22 Recitals 522 and 523 of the judgment.   23 Recital 526 of the judgment.

Commission, broadening the reasoning carried out in *European sugar industry*, describes the tying effect and the consequent exclusionary result of such a detailed rebates' scheme.

- Case IV/29.491
- **Decision:** Infringement of Article 102 FEU Treaty
- **Decision addressee(s):**
  - NV Nederlandsche Banden-Industrie Michelin (NBIM), *the Netherlands*
- **Report route:** Complaint lodged with the Commission on 29 July 1977
- **Date of the decision:** 7 October 1981
- **Competition Commissioner:** F. Andriessen
- **Relevant product market:** New replacement tires for trucks and buses
- **Relevant geographical market:** The Netherlands
- **Description of the case**
  - a. **Relevant facts**
    The market for tires is rather diverse and consists of different sorts of tires designed according to the type of vehicle involved. The difference is also reflected in the price per unit. Each type of tyre, in turn, comes in different specifications as to quality, treads, and sizes. For each kind of tyre the separation of original equipment market and replacement market is of fundamental importance. Within the latter, carried out primarily through a large organization of specialized dealers and not directly by the producers, it is important to distinguish between new replacement tires and retread tires. Provided the carcass is in good conditions, used tires can be fitted with a new tread and can thus last up to twice as long. Therefore, new and retreated tires are not considered as interchangeable products since the degree of reliability of the retreads is perceived as much lower then in the case of a new product. Accordingly their price is about 40 percent lower than the price of new tires.

    At the time of the decision, the tyre industry was characterized by high horizontal concentration and dominated by four manufacturers (including the Michelin group). The horizontal concentration was "combined with vertical integration in the form of increasing control of sales channels by the tyre manufacturers."[24]

    Michelin held the largest market share in the European market for new tires. Due to some inventions and to a continuous policy of research and innovation, it had special know-how that, combined with its financial resources, allowed it to have a very large and expanding range of products. NBIM, a subsidiary of the Michelin group responsible for the manufacture and sale of Michelin tires in the Dutch market, held "by far the largest share of the Netherlands market in new replacement tires for trucks and buses."[25] Between 1975 and 1980, 59–65 percent of trucks and buses tires sold in the Netherlands had Michelin tires.

    The tyre market was characterised by readily available price lists. The gross prices NBIM charged its dealers were comparable with the prices for the tires of its main competitors, however the net price was considerably higher because NBIM did not grant discounts as high as those granted by its competitors. "Consequently dealers [used to] pay some 10 to 15 percent more for Michelin

---

24   Recital 10 of the decision.   25   Recital 15 of the decision.

tires than for tires of other makes. This fact [did] not of course have any decisive significance with regard to the price of the various tires to the final consumer."[26]

The discount system applied by NBIM provided for a fixed component added directly to the invoice amount so that the dealer would benefit immediately. The amount was announced by NBIM and was common knowledge (15 percent up to 1977, 22.5 percent in 1978, and 30 percent in 1979). Together with the fixed part of the discount, NBIM used to apply a variable component consisting of various bonuses. The amount of those bonuses was discussed on an individual basis with each dealer during the visit of NBIM representatives. These additional discounts were communicated orally to the dealers and were rarely confirmed by written documents. The bonuses were usually given annually and ranged from 10 to 22 percent in 1977. The bonuses were significantly reduced following the increase of the invoice discount to a maximum of 2 percent in 1979. In 1979 NBIM introduced a system of four-monthly bonuses (0–3 percent) which amounted to roughly one-third of the annual bonus and thus did not significantly alter the overall discounts system.

The system adopted by NBIM's main competitors provided for a (higher) invoice discount ranging from 40 to 60 percent and sometimes to an annual discount which was known beforehand and "was not used as an individualized sale target. Thus, it did not have in any way the character of a 'fidelity' rebate.'"[27]

On the contrary, the bonus granted by NBIM "was established individually for each dealer in accordance with the efforts he has made in distributing Michelin tires, this being measured in terms of *increase* ... of his purchases from NBIM."[28] In practise at the beginning of the year NBIM negotiated with each dealer a "target" to be achieved in order to obtain the discount. NBIM reserved the power to change bonus conditions in the meanwhile should the dealer not meet the target. Furthermore "comparison of the customer[s'] files show[ed] that dealers purchasing very different quantities often received the same bonuses and vice versa, ... The implementation of the bonus schemes was thus flexible, but entirely at the discretion of NBIM."[29] In general the targets were fixed in such a way that the target for a certain year (or the targets during the year in which a system of gradually graduated targets was applied) was higher than the amount purchased the previous year "while the corresponding bonus figure did not in most cases show any increase."[30]

b. Origin of the case

On 29 July 1977 a complaint for the purpose of Article 3 of Regulation 17 was submitted to the Commission on behalf of Bandegroothandel Frieschebrug NV. On 19 February 1980 the Commission decided to initiate proceedings.

c. Economic analysis

In this decision, the Commission analyzed two effects of loyalty rebates, namely the tying effect for consumers and a consequent exclusionary effect for competitors. The Commission decided that the rebates system constituted an

---

26   Recital 18 of the decision.
27   Recital 22 of the decision.
28   Recital 23 of the decision. Emphasis added.

29   Recital 25 of the decision.
30   Recital 24 of the decision.

abuse of a dominant position. "The discount system [was] clearly aimed at tying the dealers closely to NBIM and thus making it difficult for other producers to gain a foothold in the market. The various bonuses [were] related to a sales 'target' which [was] established at the beginning of each annual sales campaign for each dealer, i.e. *on an individual and selective basis*. Even in periods when the economic situation is poor, the 'targets' [were] usually set at a level . . . higher than the purchases made in the previous year. As a result, great pressure [was] put on the dealers to outdo themselves each year in their sales of Michelin tires."[31] According to the Commission the fact that the amount of discount granted by NBIM directly on the invoice of its dealers (the fixed amount) was considerably lower that what was usually granted by its competitors was clear evidence that the "targets" system was [being] used as instrument to put competitors and customers under pressure. The system also enabled NBIM to use other flexible types of discounts such as e.g. annual bonuses and quarterly bonuses to exert pressure. "The outcome of the system applied by NBIM is that to a great extent tyre dealers are deterred from taking advantage of offers made by competitors during the course of the year. In this respect, the bonuses must be regarded as a variant of loyalty rebates. Though they are not linked to an exclusive purchasing requirement . . . NBIM is able through the discount system to ensure that it obtains a maximum percentage . . . of purchases made by dealers."[32]

Another characteristic of the discount system that was contested by the Commission was its alleged discriminatory nature. According to the Commission, since different dealers were granted different discounts for comparable quantities purchased and since "comparable amounts purchased almost never result[ed] in the same or comparable discount being granted,"[33] the discount system could be considered quantitative only "within the strictly individual context of each purchaser. The bonus rates [were] not established on the basis of objective criteria applicable to all purchasers . . . The discounts [were] not comparable to the normal quantity discounts which are customary in the trade and which constitute a reward calculated subsequently according to objective criteria in advance and known to all."[34]

The Commission concluded that "[t]he discount system is of such a nature that it can only be practised by an enterprise in a dominant position. Dealers would never accept this system being imposed by other manufacturers. Michelin's competitors do not therefore use a similar system and are in no position to engage in such practises."[35]

d. Fines, remedies, and conditions enclosed
– The Commission imposed on NBIM a total fine of ECU 680,000.

e. Further developments of the case
Case 322/81 *Michelin* [1983] ECR 3461, fines reduction and Commission decision partly annulled. The abusive nature of the discounts system was confirmed but its discriminatory nature was rejected.

---

31   Recital 38 of the decision. Emphasis added.
32   Recital 44 of the decision.
33   Recital 42 of the decision.
34   *Idem.*
35   Recital 48 of the decision.

The discount system at stake in the first *Michelin* decision was confirmed to be abusive by the ECJ. The ECJ stated that "any system under which discounts are granted according to the quantities sold during a relatively long reference period has the inherent effect, at the end of that period, of increasing pressure on the buyer to reach the purchase figure needed to obtain the discount or to avoid suffering the expected loss for the entire period."[36] "That effect was accentuated still further by the wide divergence between Michelin NV's market share and those of its main competitors."[37] Another factor that was considered by the ECJ was the lack of transparency of Michelin NV's entire discount system, which led to uncertainty among the dealers.

The ECJ did, however, reject the discriminatory nature of the discount system, by stating that "although a system based on individual sales targets fixed or agreed every year for each dealer necessarily involves certain differences between the rates of discount granted to different dealers for the same number of purchases..., it has not been established that such differences in treatment between different dealers are due to the application of unequal criteria and that there are no legitimate commercial reasons capable of justifying them."[38]

Accordingly, the ECJ granted a fine reduction, mainly because the rebate system had not been shown to be discriminatory and the variation in the target discount was considerably less than appeared from the Commission decision. Moreover, according to the ECJ, the Commission had also wrongly interpreted Michelin's customer records and could not support its allegation that the purpose of the sales targets fixed by Michelin was to compel dealers continually to increase the proportion of Michelin tires in their total turnover. The ECJ reduced the fine to ECU 300,000.

F.3 *Michelin* Commission decision 2002/405/EC [2002] OJ L 143/1

Relevance: The Commission, following the ECJ ruling in the first Michelin case, carried out a cost-based analysis of the very complex system of rebates set by Michelin. The economic concept underlying the Commission's reasoning on quantity rebates followed the idea that, in order to not be abusive, incremental prices should not be lower than incremental costs. The decision has been confirmed by the CFI (now "the General Court") and represents the latest development of competition law in Europe regarding rebates.

- Case COMP/E-2/36.041
- **Decision:** Infringement of Article 102 FEU Treaty
- **Decision addressee(s):**
  - Manufacture Française de Pneumatiques Michelin (Michelin), *France*
- **Report route:** Commission decision of 28 June 1999 to start proceedings on its own initiative
- **Date of the decision:** 20 June 2001
- **Competition Commissioner:** M. Monti
- **Relevant product market:** Retreads and new replacement tires for trucks

---

36 Recital 81 of the judgment.   38 Recital 90 of the judgment.
37 Recital 82 of the judgment.

- **Relevant geographical market:** France
- **Description of the case**
  ### a. Relevant facts
  At the time of the decision, Michelin held 18 percent of the world market and competed for world market leadership with Bridgestone and Goodyear. In the EU it was the largest manufacturer, with 32 percent of market share, which was twice the amount of its closest competitor. The market for tires was very concentrated, both worldwide and in Europe. The supply structure varied throughout the EU and accordingly market shares differed across Member States. In France, Michelin held a particularly strong position which was certainly in part due to the substantial goodwill it traditionally enjoyed in its home market.

  The market structure and organization is different in every tyre sector. The detailed account can be found on p. 127 in the description of the first *Michelin* decision.[39] Michelin held more than 50 percent of market share on both relevant product markets for more than twenty years. Other evidences of dominance were Michelin's strong presence on adjacent markets, omnipresent commercial and technical service on the ground, leading position in French distribution channels, and the practise of offering loyalty rebates. It was also able to sell through specialized dealers that were forced to become economically dependent on Michelin. This dependence meant in practise that in light of the strong demand for Michelin tires none of the dealers was able to eliminate Michelin from their product range without losing their credibility. In fact, Michelin was thus an inevitable partner.

  The commercial policy that Michelin implemented in 1980 and followed until 1998 hinged on three strategies:

  1. The general price conditions in France for professional dealers. The price system was based on a list price, i.e. the net price invoiced and a complex system of rebates calculated on the basis of each financial year and usually not paid before the last day of February following the end of the relevant year.

     Between 1980 and 1996, "[t]he rebates provided for in the general conditions of sale were divided into three categories. *Quantity rebates*, rebates for the dealers' service to users ('*service bonus*'), and rebates dependent on increases in new tyre sales ('*progress bonus*'). In addition, dealers exceeding a given Michelin turnover threshold for two financial years in a row were allowed to negotiate a 'commercial cooperation agreement' (known as an 'individual agreement') entitling them to further rebates"[40] and to a more favourable system for the calculation of the general rebates.

     The quantity rebates Michelin offered to a dealer depended on its annual turnover of all Michelin tires except heavy plant tires and retreads which were subject to a different rebate calculation grid. Such a grid indicated the percentage deductible from the list price which was dependent on the turnover achieved in a financial year.

39   See, *supra*, Case F.2 in this section.   40   Recital 56 of the decision.

The second bonus was a service bonus. The *service bonus* "was an additional incentive proposed by Michelin to the specialised dealer 'to improve his equipment and after-sales service.' In reality the degree of cooperation and services offered to Michelin were also taken fully into account when the rates were fixed."[41] To qualify for the bonus a dealer had to achieve a certain minimum threshold and comply with a number of rules to commit to Michelin. Over the years, both the number of commitments and the number of "points" a dealer had to score to obtain the rebate increased. Most of them concerned services affecting customers – such as for instance staff training, proprietary machinery, know-how, and quality of facilities. However, some of the commitments were clearly only in the interest of Michelin, such as the commitments to supply customers with a certain amount of new Michelin products (whose quantity has to be a percentage in relation to the regional share of such products), to provide accurate information on the behavior of the different type of products, and to provide retreading services.

Finally, a third bonus was offered. "The *progress bonus* was intended to reward dealers who agreed at the beginning of the year to undertake in writing to exceed a 'minimum base, fixed by common agreement, depending on past performance and future prospects' and who managed to exceed it. The base was proposed each year and negotiated with the dealer."[42] Michelin used a formula to calculate the bonus. The latter was a function of the truck tyre turnover, the number of tires sold, a rate depending on the dealers' commitments, and the base committed to achieve.[43] The scale of the progress bonus was divided into several steps which were progressively reduced until 1996. Then they were reduced to two steps. Ultimately, the bonus was reduced to a single-step reduction, which applied to the entire turnover whenever the base amount exceeded 20 percent or more of the minimum base.

In 1997 and 1998 Michelin made substantial changes to its sale policy toward dealers following the opening of the Commission investigation, partly as a reaction to amendments to the French legislation prohibiting sales at a loss and also as result of the extensive restructuring of the group carried out in 1996. Firstly, different business conditions were set for various product categories and an altogether different system introduced for new and retreaded tires. Secondly, in the truck tires sector quantity rebates, the service bonus, and the progress bonus were substituted by *invoice rebates*, the *achieved-target bonus*, *end-of-year rebates* and the *multi-product rebate*.

The *invoice rebate* was granted on the basis of the new tires purchased in the preceding year, the average for the preceding two years or for the preceding three years, depending on which was the most

---

41 Recital 60 of the decision. Emphasis added.   43 See recital 69 of the decision.
42 Recital 68 of the decision. Emphasis added.

favourable parameter for the dealer and according to a scale. A dealer wishing to obtain a higher discount was entitled to agree with Michelin upon a "target contract," taking account of the dealer's realistic potential to achieve a higher level of the discount scale in the coming year.

The *achieved-target bonus* was granted and amounted in 1997 and 1998 to 2 percent and 1.5 percent of the invoiced annual turnover, respectively, if the target determined in the "target contract" had been reached. The *end-of-year rebate* was granted according to a scale depending on the relation between the invoice rebate originally granted and the net invoiced turnover. The *multi-product rebate* was granted to dealers who achieved, with all Michelin products, at least 50 percent of their total turnover and who sold a significant number of tires in specific sectors. The rebate was granted on the invoice turnover achieved through new products.

As regards the retreaded truck tires, Michelin adopted a much simpler rebates system – that is, invoice rebates of 5 percent and end-of-year rebates. The practise of the individual agreement remained unchanged in structure even if new scales were adopted.[44]

2. The agreement for optimum use of Michelin truck tires, the "pro agreement", was introduced in 1993 for dealers purchasing new truck tires from Michelin France, and allowed the dealers in question to obtain further rebates. In order to obtain those rebates the dealers were asked to fulfil a number of further obligations.[45]

3. The bilateral business cooperation and service assistance agreement ("The Michelin friends club"). Created in 1990, through the club's membership Michelin allowed its dealers to grant additional financial benefits in return for making numerous commitments. Michelin would have participated in the dealer's financial effort, in particular with a contribution to investment and training, conditional on the attainment of a certain turnover target established at the beginning of each year. Furthermore, Michelin also granted a series of other benefits to the members of the club.[46] Michelin demanded as a condition for membership in turn to commit to a detailed list of obligations. In particular, the communication of highly detailed corporate, financial, and business information; the promotion of Michelin brand and new products together with a commitment not to divert consumer demand away from Michelin tires and to maintain given volumes and market share covered by Michelin products; "to carry a sufficient stock of Michelin products to meet customer demands immediately."[47]

44	For a more detailed description of the rebates system and to see the scales' figures, see recitals 80–95 of the decision.
45	See recitals 97–100 of the decision.
46	For a detailed description of Michelin's contribution to the club, see recitals 104–106 of the decision.
47	Recital 107 of the decision. For a detailed description of the conditions attached to the membership, see the same recital.

b. Origin of the case

On 28 June 1999 the Commission, on its own initiative, adopted a decision to initiate a proceeding against Michelin in respect of the rebate systems adopted by the latter in the relationship with its dealers.

c. Economic analysis

The rebates system analyzed in this decision was complex and implemented through a variety of pricing and discounts schemes. The Commission, on the one hand, considered the system abusive as a whole and, on the other, stated that the single components of it, all abusive considered on a single basis, were strengthened by the overall effects on competition that the entire system (i.e. the cumulative effect of all its parts) produced. Firstly, the system of sale targets present in both the old system (until 1996) and in the new one (1997 and 1998) was considered highly abusive by the Commission due to its loyalty-inducing and tying effects and also to its individualized nature (i.e. based on a dealer-by-dealer basis). In their assessment, the Commission mainly confirmed what had already been stated in the previous *Michelin* case.[48] It strongly condemned the system because "[a]n undertaking in a dominant position cannot require dealers to exceed, each year, their figures for the previous years and thus automatically increase its market shares by taking advantage of its dominant position. [T]he bonus was unfair, because of the requirement imposed by Michelin to increase purchases and because of the insecurity brought about by the individualized determination of the minimum base. The bonus was also loyalty-inducing and market partitioning since it applied only to purchases made from Michelin France."[49] The *progress bonus*, as well as the *achieved-target bonus*, its substitute in the new rebate system, were despite some structural differences regarded as essentially serving the same purpose, namely to deprive the dealer of its option freely to choose its source of supply, threatening him with the loss of the target bonus.

Nevertheless, the most relevant aspect of the Commission's reasoning about rebates is given in the decision with reference to the *quantity rebates*. Recalling the judgment of the ECJ following the appeal proposed by NBIM against the first *Michelin* decision,[50] the Commission stated that "The Court of Justice has ruled against the granting of quantity rebates by an undertaking in a dominant position where the rebates exceed a reasonable period of three months . . . on the grounds that such a practise is not in line with normal competition based on price. Merely buying a small additional quantity of Michelin products made the dealer eligible for a rebate on the whole of the turnover achieved with Michelin and this was greater than the fair marginal or linear return on the additional purchase, which clearly creates a strong buying incentive effect. In the Court's view, a rebate can only correspond to the economies of scale achieved by the firm as a result of the additional purchases which consumers are induced to make."[51]

What the Commission stated in this recital is a prohibition for rebate systems applying the higher percentage of discount to the whole quantity purchased and

48   See case F.2 in this section.
49   Recitals 263 and 264 of the decision.
50   Case 322/81 *Michelin* [1983] ECR 3461.
51   Recital 216 of the decision.

not only to the marginal (additional) quantity. A higher discount awarded due to additional purchases and applied to the entire quantity purchased creates a loyalty effect. The Commission insisted that a legal rebate system would have to provide an effective economic advantage for the customer. It stated that "this system [introduced by Michelin] has as its object and effect the tying of dealers to Michelin and that in providing an advantage not based on any economic service justifying it, the discounts tend to remove or restrict the buyer's freedom to choose his source of supply and thus to bar competitors [from] access to the market."[52] The same reasoning was extended to the *service bonus*, since it "had the same features as the quantity rebates, except that the minimum turnover threshold were imposed by Michelin."[53] This approach recognises the requirement to charge incremental prices above incremental costs in order to avoid exclusionary (i.e. abusive) rebate practises.

The time period to which the system applied (i.e. a year) is relevant because it strengthened the loyalty-inducing effect since "[a]ny system under which rebates are granted according to the quantities sold during a relatively long reference period has the inherent effect, at the end of that period, of increasing pressure on the buyer to reach the purchase figure needed to obtain the discount or to avoid suffering the foreseeable loss for the entire period."[54]

The overall rebate system was also assessed as abusive for some of its other features. The Commission focused particularly on the market partitioning effect due to the fact that only tires purchased from Michelin France were taken into consideration.[55] Among other aspects, the "Michelin friends club" was also considered by the Commission "as a tool to [rigidify] or indeed improv[e] its position on the market."[56] The main purpose of the club was to create close relations with large dealers and impose on them a particularly strict loyalty requirement such as the promotion of the brand, not to divert spontaneous demand toward other brands, and the maintenance of a predetermined (high) market share for Michelin products. In light of the importance of *Michelin*, a "practise of this kind certainly bears no direct relation to any real cost savings to the manufacturer . . . and it can only be a barrier to whatever competition still exists there"[57] and "leaves the dealers completely dependent on Michelin . . . . Any change in the dealer's commercial or strategic policy would leave him open to reprisals on the part of Michelin. Certainly all members of the Club shared the feeling that there could be no turning back,"[58] the Commission emphatically concluded.

d. **Fines, remedies, and conditions enclosed**
   – The Commission imposed on Michelin a total fine of Euro 19.760.000 Euros.
   – An obligation for Michelin to refrain from repeating or continuing similar conducts.

---

52   Recital 227 of the decision.
53   Recital 248 of the decision.
54   Recital 228 of the decision.
55   See recitals 240–247, 271, and 313–314 of the decision.

56   Recital 317 of the decision.
57   Recital 318 of the decision.
58   Recital 326 of the decision.

e. Further developments of the case

T-203/01 *Michelin* v. *Commission* [2003] ECR 4071, appeal dismissed.

The CFI confirmed that a legal rebate system would have to provide an effective economic advantage for the customer. It stated that: "... the Commission was entitled to conclude, in the contested decision, that the quantity rebate system at issue was designed to tie truck tyre dealers in France to the applicant by granting advantages which were not based on any economic justification. Because it was loyalty-inducing, the quantity rebate system tended to prevent dealers from being able to select freely at any time, in the light of the market situation, the most advantageous of the offers made by various competitors and to change supplier without suffering any appreciable economic disadvantage. The rebate system thus limited the dealers" choice of supplier and made access to the market more difficult for competitors, while the position of dependence in which the dealers found themselves, and which was created by the discount system in question, was not therefore based on any countervailing advantage which might be economically justified."[59]

The CFI also confirmed that the reference period to which the quantity rebate system applied was highly relevant. In particular, it ruled that: "It follows from all of the foregoing that a quantity rebate system in which there is a significant variation in the discount rates between the lower and higher steps, which has a reference period of one year, and in which the discount is fixed on the basis of total turnover achieved during the reference period, has the characteristics of a loyalty-inducing discount system."[60]

3.3 Predatory pricing

A Introduction

Dominant firms may try to enhance or maintain their market power by driving (potential) competitors from the market. One of the possible instruments to do so is to use predation strategies. Predatory pricing is a strategy in which an incumbent firm prices below its own costs – thus incurring a loss – in order to inflict (expected) losses upon a (potential) competitor. Initially, such low prices would be good for consumers. In the so-called "recoupment phase," however, once the competitor(s) has left the market to the predator, the remaining dominant firm has the ability to raise its price again above the competitive price level and compensate for the initial loss.

A number of conditions have to be satisfied for predatory pricing to be a possible competition concern. Firstly, the predator must indeed make losses in the short run that cannot be well explained, other than as part of a predation strategy. Secondly, the firm must have the possibility of excluding its actual and/or potential competitors from the market. Thirdly, the alleged predator must actually be able to raise price above cost in the long run in order to recoup them. The latter requires, among other things, that there are sufficiently high (real or perceived) barriers to entry to prevent firms that exited when prices were low to quickly enter the market again in the recoupment phase. Such barriers can in fact be created endogenously by the dominant

---

59   Recital 110 of the judgment.   60   Recital 95 of the judgment.

firm: a possible example is establishing a reputation for reacting strongly to new entry. In addition, it is important to dispose greater financial resources than competitors so as to be able to afford the initial losses ("deep pockets"). This also relates to the situation when large (diversified) enterprises apply predatory prices: they usually do so on one or a small number of submarkets on which they sell their broad range of products, making sufficient margin on the other markets. Furthermore, the present discounted value of the expected long-run profit stream needs to exceed that of the initial losses. In practise, it is often difficult to conclusively determine whether these conditions indeed hold. Companies may complain about the low prices of their rivals, but they also would do so in case of genuine competition. Tests for predatory pricing require insight into the production costs of the alleged predator, which is often very difficult to reliably obtain.

B   Applicable EU legislation

No special legislation applicable. For applicable legislation, see chapter 3 paragraph B.

C   Related economics texts

Bishop and Walker (2009), paragraphs 6.84–6.118
Carlton and Perloff (2005), chapter 11, paragraph 2(1)
Church and Ware (2000), chapter 21
Martin (1994), chapter 16
Martin (2002), paragraph 8.5
Motta (2004), paragraph 7.2
Tirole (1988), paragraphs 9.4–9.8
Waldman and Jensen (2001), chapter 10, paragraphs 3 and 4

D   Related legal texts

Bellamy and Child (2008), chapter 10, paragraph 4 (B, i)
Jones and Sufrin (2008), chapter 7, paragraph 6 (A, B and C)
Ritter and Braun (2005), chapter 5, paragraph D (6, a and b)
Whish (2008), chapter 18, paragraph 6

E   Commission decisions in chronological order•

ECS/Akzo Chemie **Commission decision 85/609/EEC [1985] OJ L 374/1, Case IV/30.698**
(Bishop and Walker, 2009, 6.01, 6.98, 6.108; Motta, 2004, p. 118)
Tetra Pak II Commission decision 92/163/EEC [1992] OJ L 72/1, Case IV/31.043 (**described in detail as landmark case in section 3.4**) (*)(Bishop and Walker, 2009, 6.77, 6.79, 6.108–6.112)
Cewal, Cowac, Ukwal Commission decision 93/82/EEC [1993] OJ L 34/20, Cases IV/32.448, 32.450 (Bishop and Walker, 2009, 6.106; Motta, 2004, p. 144)
Irish Sugar Commission decision 97/624/EC [1997] OJ L 258/1, Cases IV/34.621, 35.059

• Decisions displayed in **bold type** are described in the section. Decisions highlighted with (*) include interesting economic analysis by the Commission on the specific topic of the section. Some decisions contain economic reasoning on more than one topic and therefore appear in several lists of Commission decisions in chronological order. Reference is made in brackets and **bold type** to the relevant section in which the decision is extensively described as a landmark case. When decisions are referenced and/or described in some detail in one or more of the economic textbooks, reference in brackets is also made to the relevant part(s) of those texts.

Deutsche Post AG Commission decision 2001/354/EC [2001] OJ L 125/27, Case COMP/35.141
Wanadoo Interactive **Commission decision of 16 July 2003, published on DG Comp website, Case COMP/38.233** (Bishop and Walker, 2009, 6.108–6.110)
Compagnie Maritime Belge (Cewal) Commission decision of 30 April 2004, published on DG Comp website, Cases COMP/D/32.448, 32.450

F Economic landmark cases

F.1 *ECS/Akzo Chemie* Commission decision 85/609/EEC [1985] OJ L 374/1

Relevance: The decision is the first case ever in which the Commission dealt with predatory pricing. The Areeda and Turner theory (see *infra*) is discussed in the decision and not accepted as a generally valid rule to establish the predatory nature of pricing policies. Following an appeal lodged against the decision, the ECJ stated what still now constitutes the standard approach of European Courts and the Commission to this kind of abuse.

- Case IV/30.698
- **Decision:** Infringement of Article 102 FEU Treaty
- **Decision addressee(s):**
    - Akzo Chemie BV, *the Netherlands*
- **Report route:** Complaint lodged with the Commission on 15 July 1982
- **Date of the decision:** 14 December 1985
- **Competition Commissioner:** P. Sutherland
- **Relevant product market:** Organic peroxide
- **Relevant geographical market:** United Kingdom
- **Description of the case**
    - a. **Relevant facts**
        Akzo Chemie (Akzo) forms, together with its subsidiaries, the chemical and fibres group of the large multinational Akzo NV.
        Organic peroxides are specialty chemicals related to the polymer industry where they are used in several different production processes. Akzo was the leading firm in the organic peroxides market. According to Akzo its dominant position derived, *inter alia*, from strong commercial and technical marketing organization, a complete set of products, strong efforts in R&D, production spread, and market coverage. The major organic peroxide is benzoyl peroxide which is used, e.g., as a flour bleach additive. Within the EEC, at the time of the investigation, that application of benzoyl peroxide was allowed only in the United Kingdom and Ireland. In the British and Irish markets there were only three suppliers of a nearly full range of flour additives: Akzo UK, ECS and Diaflex. Akzo UK was by far the largest supplier of bleaching agents and held in the relevant analyzed period (1979–84) a constant market share of about 50 percent. Moreover, Akzo's dominant position was strengthened by being the only supplier of a full range of products and by a unique economic strength which allowed it to afford a period of economic downturn (i.e. losses). There were three principal customers in the United Kingdom for flour additives: RHM, Spiller, and Allied Mills (the major milling groups). Historically Akzo UK and Diaflex shared RHM's business. Since 1982 Akzo was the only supplier of Spillers. Allied Mills were traditionally (before the dispute that raised the

question underlying the decision) supplied primarily by ECS (two-thirds) as well as by Akzo UK. The Irish market was characterized by customers buying all their requirements from a single supplier and consequently by cross-supplying among suppliers in case of shortfall in production or to cover the needs of a producer for a product it did not produce itself.[61]

"Before the dispute between ECS and Akzo in late 1979, prices of flour additives in the United Kingdom rose steadily in regular increments of 10 percent."[62] Akzo prices were always higher than those charged by its competitors. Nonetheless Akzo did not encounter any resistance to its price increase or to its higher prices (i.e. it did not lose any customers).

The decision of ECS to expand from flour additives to the more profitable plastics usage (of benzoyl peroxide) gave rise to the conducts which ECS complained about. In a meeting with ECS urgently called by Akzo UK, the latter – according to ECS – threatened ECS with price reduction below cost and selective price cuts aimed at ECS customers in the flour additives market in case ECS would not have withdrawn from the plastic market. ECS applied and was granted an injunction under Article 102 FEU Treaty in a hearing at the High Court in London.

Akzo denied the abusive nature of its reaction to ECS entering the plastic market. It claimed that the sales policy adjustment for flour additives was made only to make it more competitive after ECS began the new activity in the plastics sector. The two companies settled out of court. Notwithstanding the settlement, the dispute did not end. "In 1982 ECS complained to the Commission that the behavior complained of had been continued in spite of the undertaking given to the High Court. The gist of ECS' complaint was that Akzo UK had by a process of attrition taken from it its most important customers in the large independent sector as well as certain individual mills in the Allied group, and that it had only managed to keep its remaining customers by reducing prices to the very low price levels quoted by Akzo UK."[63]

The abusive conduct alleged consisted in taking ECS' most important customers by means of below-cost or unreasonably low prices. The Commission's investigations revealed that the price cutting to a below-cost level was part of a deliberate strategy planned in detail by Akzo UK aimed at systematically approaching ECS' customers and offering them a range of flour additives at prices far below those currently applied and involving a considerable loss for Akzo UK. "It [was] evident that Akzo was prepared to allow its flour additive business to be operated at a loss in order to achieve the objective of eliminating or disciplining ECS."[64]

Akzo UK's reply was, once again, that it was only adjusting its prices to a more competitive level as a response to the lower price introduced by ECS, and that its ability to charge lower prices was partly due to its higher efficiency. After having carried out its investigation, the Commission adopted a decision ordering interim measures. It ordered Akzo UK "to return to the profit margins

---

61   For a more detailed description of the UK and Ireland market see recitals 15–22 of the decision.

62   Recital 23 of the decision.

63   Recital 29 of the decision.

64   Recital 35 of the decision.

which it had been applying in the flour additives sector in the United Kingdom immediately before the dispute had arisen with ECS."[65]

In order not to lose any customers to ECS, Akzo adopted an "English clause"[66] with one of the main customers on the British market (Spillers). In practise, following one of the periodical Akzo UK's price increases, Spillers – in the frame of a broader agreement – had contacted ECS to place part of its orders for flour additives with ECS. The response of Akzo UK was to match the ECS price. Furthermore, it agreed with Spillers that it would have offered the lowest price the other suppliers would have proposed, provided that Spillers gave Akzo UK all the information regarding its competitors' offers.

b. Origin of the case

On 15 July 1982 a complaint was filed to the Commission pursuant to Article 3 of Regulation 17 by Engineering and Chemical Supplies Ltd, Gloucester. They complained that Akzo had infringed Article 102 FEU Treaty. On 8 June 1983 the Commission decided to initiate proceedings.

c. Economic analysis

This decision has been particularly important in EU competition law enforcement because it was the first case in which the Commission dealt with a predatory strategy of a dominant firm and because through an appeal lodged against this decision the ECJ expressed what is now the landmark criterion for the assessment of predatory pricing in Europe.

Firstly the Commission, recalling the ECJ judgment in *Hoffmann – La Roche*[67] confirmed that the concept of abuse of dominance encompasses also exclusionary abuses that "influence the structure of the market where, as a result of the very presence of the undertaking in question, the degree of competition was weakened, and which . . . had the effect of hindering the maintenance of the degree of competition still existing in the market or the growth of that competition."[68] Therefore, "Article 86 is not aimed solely at practises which might damage consumers or customers directly but also those which are indirectly detrimental to them through their impact on effective competitive structure."[69] With regard to predatory pricing, this remark seems to be perfectly in line with economic thoughts on the scope of intervention of antitrust agencies in cases of predation – that is, the protection of consumers directly or indirectly harmed by predation.

As to predation itself, the Commission's initial observation was that "Article 86 does not prescribe any cost-based legal rule to define the precise stage at which price-cutting by a dominant firm may become abusive and indeed the broad application of the concept of abuse to different forms of exclusionary behavior would argue against such a narrow test."[70] Therefore, no *per se* rules on abusive prices are provided by EU competition law.

---

65   Recital 30 of the decision.
66   For the economics of "English clause" and related landmark cases see, *infra*, section 3.9 of the book.
67   Case 85/76 *Hoffmann – La Roche* [1979] ECR 461.
68   Recital 74 of the decision referring to Case 85/76 *Hoffmann – La Roche* [1979] ECR 461, recital 91.
69   Recital 73 of the decision.
70   Recital 75 of the decision.

Furthermore, the Commission described the defensive line followed by Akzo which substantially mirrored the theory developed by Areeda and Turner (1975). According to the theory, prices charged by a dominant firm that are below its marginal cost are presumed to be predatory (i.e. abusive, unlawful) while prices above marginal costs are presumed to be lawful. The two authors also suggest using average variable costs (AVCs) as a reliable proxy for marginal cost as marginal costs are difficult to estimate in practise. The rationale behind this theory is that only less efficient firms will be harmed by prices below AVC.

The Commission had two main lines of reasoning. Firstly, Akzo UK failed to comply with the test. What the firm considered as AVC excluded labour, repair, and maintenance which according to Areeda and Turner (1975) should be included in the calculation of AVC. They may in fact exclude only capital cost, property, taxes unaffected by output, and depreciation due to plant obsolescence.

Secondly, the Commission did not accept a *per se* rule such as the one proposed by Areeda and Turner (1975). Rather, the Commission's opinion was that such an approach would fail to take into account the long-term strategic considerations which might underlie price cutting; moreover it did not take into account the element of the discrimination and would consequently permit such results. Also the alternative test proposed during the proceedings by Akzo's economic expert (Professor Yamey) that price cuts should always be allowed if "profit maximizing" in the short term regardless of the damaging effect on competitors, was rejected by the Commission. According to the Commission "a test based on the aggressor's costs alone will not cover all cases of unfair conduct designed to exclude or damage a competitor. Apart from the inherent difficulty of accurately establishing costs, no such test would give sufficient weight to the strategic aspect of price cutting behavior."[71] Thus, according to the Commission prices above AVC are also predatory if the intention to eliminate competitors is demonstrated.[72]

The Commission ruled the price cut adopted by Akzo UK to be of a predatory nature, and found an abuse of a dominant position by charging "unreasonably low prices intended to damage ECS' viability by either taking the customer's business or forcing ECS itself to supply at uneconomic prices in order to keep the business."[73] According to the Commission, what constituted a strengthening factor of the predatory nature of the price cut was its selective nature aimed at attracting regular customers of ECS (while maintaining the usual prices for established customers) and the fact that Akzo UK departed from its previous "pattern . . . of full cost recovery in flour additives."[74] As the Commission stressed in Article 3 of the decision confirming its previous orientation on price discrimination, it did not consider abusive a price discrimination based on objective differences between categories of customers "which reasonably and objectively reflect differences in production and delivery costs attributable

71   Recital 78 of the decision.
72   See in particular recital 79 of the decision.
73   Recital 82 of the decision.
74   Recital 81 of the decision.

to the annual requirement of the customer, order size, and other commercial factors."[75]

The Commission, basing its reasoning on the ECJ judgment in *Continental Can*,[76] held that the abuse on the British and Irish market could constitute an abuse also in the overall European organic peroxide internal market (i.e. admitted the possibility of abusive cross-subsidization). The Commission stated that "a dominant position held in one market may be abused by conduct in a market other than the one in which the dominant position is held."[77] The "English clause" was also considered abusive.[78]

d. Fines, remedies, and conditions enclosed

 - The Commission imposed on Akzo a total fine of ECU 10,000,000.
 - Obligations for Akzo to bring the infringements to an end and to refrain from repeating or continuing similar behaviors.
 - Obligation for Akzo to inform all its customers for flour additives in UK and Ireland which had accepted to obtain the whole of their requirements from Akzo, that such a stipulation was not binding on them, and to inform the Commission about the accomplishment of the obligation before 1 April 1986.
 - Obligation for Akzo to furnish to the Commission a yearly compliance report for a period of five years within the first two months of each year. The report shall list in detail the prices applied to each customer for each flour additive product in the territory of the EEC, include the financial statements for the flour additive, and indicate the criteria adopted for the calculation of costs.
 - The Commission imposed on Akzo a periodic penalty payment of ECU 1,000 for each day of delay from the dates stated in the decision in the accomplishment of the obligations to provide information.

e. Further developments of the case

Case 62/86 *Akzo* v. *Commission* [1991] ECR I-3359, fines reduction and Commission decision partly annulled.

Following an appeal by Akzo against the decision, the ECJ partially modified the Commission's approach and established what is now the benchmark for the assessment of predatory pricing in EU competition law. The adopted decision is a modified version of the Areeda – Turner test and states that "prices below average variable costs . . . must be regarded as abusive. A dominant undertaking has no interest in applying such prices except that of eliminating competitors so as to enable it subsequently to raise its prices by taking advantage of its monopolistic position, since each sale generates a loss, namely the total amount of fixed costs . . . and, at least, part of the variable costs related to the unit produced. Moreover, prices above average variable costs . . . but below average total costs, must be regarded as abusive if they are determined as part of a plan for eliminating a competitor."[79] The ECJ entailed that prices above

---

75 Article 3 of the decision.
76 Case 6/72 *Continental Can* [1973] ECR 215.
77 Recital 85 of the decision.
78 For a detailed description of the economics of the "English clause" (i.e. best price guarantee) and its interpretation given by the Commission, see section 3.10 of this chapter.
79 Case C-62/86 *Akzo* [1991] ECR I-3359, recitals 71 and 72.

average total cost cannot be considered predatory. The *Akzo* test was subsequently confirmed and developed in *Tetra Pak II*, in which the Commission and then the ECJ confirmed the possibility of abusive cross-subsidization and established the principle according to which the Commission is no longer obliged to prove that the dominant firm will recoup its losses in order to consider a price cut as abusive.[80] This approach shows an interpretation of predation apparently focused more on the protection of competitors than on the protection of consumers (and welfare) as such.

The cost-based Areeda – Turner test, as well as the modified version adopted by the ECJ, is controversial amongst economists. Few economists consider it capable of providing a correct description of all markets and possible strategies adopted.

As for the fine reduction, the ECJ stated that "there are three factors which prompt the Court to reduce the fine. Firstly, with regard to the unreasonably low prices that Akzo quoted or granted both to its own customers and to those of ECS, it must be observed that abuses of this kind come within a field of law in which the rules of competition had never been determined precisely. Moreover, the limited effect of the dispute between Akzo and ECS must be taken into account, since the infringement did not significantly affect their respective shares of the flour additives market. It is mentioned in the decision (point 18) that before the dispute ECS had a market share of 35 percent, compared with 30 percent in 1984, while that of Akzo rose from 52 percent to 55 percent. Finally, the Commission was not justified in regarding the infringement of the interim measures decision, consisting in alignments on Diaflex's prices, as an aggravating factor capable of justifying the high amount of the fine. That decision permitted alignment on the prices of any competitor and did not exclude those of Diaflex. Consequently, as soon as the Commission had evidence proving that Diaflex was not a genuine competitor and that the alignments were therefore not made in good faith, it should have exercised the powers to impose sanctions that it had reserved to itself."[81] The fine was reduced to ECU 7,500,000 (25 percent reduction).

F.2   *Wanadoo Interactive* Commission decision of 16 July 2003, published on DG COMP website

Relevance: This decision deals with the abusive conduct of a dominant firm acting in an emerging market and is therefore of particular importance. Further, the Commission made an adjustment to the application of the *Akzo* predation test.

- Case COMP/38.233
- Decision: Infringement of Article 102 FEU Treaty
- **Decision addressee(s):**
  - Wanadoo Interactive, *France*
- **Report route:** Commission decision of 19 December 2001 to start proceedings on its own initiative

---

80   *Tetra Pak II* Commission decision 92/163/EEC [1992] OJ L 72/1, Case IV/31.043.
81   Recital 163 of the judgment.

- **Date of the decision:** 16 July 2003
- **Competition Commissioner:** M. Monti
- **Relevant product market:** Market for high-speed internet access for residential customers
- **Relevant geographical market:** France
- **Description of the case**
    a. **Relevant facts**

    The Commission considers high-speed internet access as a key factor in the development of the European information society.[82] High-speed internet access provides easier, faster access to the internet, further contributing to the spread of e-commerce and development of new electronic forms of distribution. The supply of a commercial digital subscriber line (DSL) service in Europe did not begin until 1999. In France, the use of high-speed internet access presumed residential users to have a telephone line or high-speed access cable and an internet service provider (ISP) subscription enabling them to access the web. Consumers can choose to buy high-speed internet access from a company such as France Télécom or a cable provider and additionally to get an internet subscription.

    During the period covered by the decision Wanadoo was part of the group France Télécom. France Télécom owned the majority of the shares in Wanadoo SA which in turn held up to 99.9 percent of Wanadoo Interactive' capital. Wanadoo SA and its subsidiaries covered all the internet activities and telephone directory business of France Télécom.

    The Commission draws a distinction between two products provided by Wanadoo. First, Wanadoo launched the asymmetric digital subscriber level (ADSL) product where users are directly linked to France Télécom and the ADSL line. When consumers opted for Wanadoo's second product eXtense the company covered all services and used France Télécom's wholesale services.[83] Firstly, to provide an ADSL service companies had to use France Télécom's local access network (LAN). This network, that links all telephone subscribers to its network, in turn is owned by France Télécom. During the period covered by the decision, France Télécom *de facto* controlled all ADSL connections in France.[84]

    The Commission stated that Wanadoo abused its dominant position by charging prices for the ADSL products which failed to cover its variable costs from January 2001 to end of July 2001 and its full costs from August 2001 to October 2002.

    Furthermore, the Commission stressed that internal documents proved the company's strategy to eliminate competitors in the upcoming market of high-speed internet providers.[85] In addition, the company was informed about the legal dangers of their pricing strategy.[86]

    b. **Origin of the case**

    On 19 December 2001 the Commission decided to initiate proceedings after an investigation into the telecommunications sector that was initiated by the Commission's decision of 27 July 1999.

---

82   See recital 1 of the decision.
83   See recital 43 of the decision.
84   See recital 231 of the decision.

85   See recitals 271–284 of the decision.
86   See recital 142 of the decision.

c. **Economic analysis**

To establish the finding of a dominant position of Wanadoo at the retail level the Commission paid a great deal of attention to the specific relationship between France Télécom and Wanadoo. Wanadoo was put in a special position through its link with the France Télécom group by means of commercial and technical deployment facilities and potential financial support. These advantages were of decisive importance in gaining massive penetration of an emerging market. Moreover, Wanadoo Interactive held a huge market share in excess of 50 percent, which needed to be considered as potentially problematic. In addition, the competitors in the market were not able to create a counterweight to Wanadoo.[87]

The technical support through France Télécom transferred an advantage to Wanadoo which its competitors did not have and therefore the Commission regarded it as "a strategic entry barrier . . . and a factor of dominance."[88] Wanadoo Interactive profited from being within a large group by receiving a customized national and regional IP routing facility. Furthermore, Wanadoo Interactive had access to information regarding the suitability of telephone lines for ADSL technology which put them in an advanced position compared to their competitors which had to follow a difficult procedure to adjust to mass marketing, especially large retailers.

Secondly, Wanadoo was represented in all 700 network agencies of France Télécom throughout the whole territory. In *Michelin I* the ECJ concluded that both commercial networks giving direct access to consumers and possibilities of commercial synergies contribute to create a dominant position.[89] Especially in a market of rapid growth and where a new product is being introduced, the possibilities of using an already established distribution network contributed to Wanadoo's dominant position.

The Commission ruled that Wanadoo had abused its dominant position in the high-speed internet service market by practicing below-cost pricing.[90] A predation test is done to distinguish between abusive pricing and just competitive pricing and the Commission applied it in line with the judgments *Akzo* and *Tetra Pak II*.[91] According to the Commission an abuse is assumed where a "non-recovery of average variable costs per unit" takes place.[92]

In this context, the issue of recoupment of losses became relevant to assess the plausibility of an alternative business rationale that could explain the losses concerned. Even though the Commission considered recoupment of losses not to be a precondition for proof of an abuse through predatory pricing in terms of Article 102 FEU Treaty, it investigated the possible recoupment.[93] Wanadoo submitted that the Commission did not take into account the special features

---

87   T-Online France belongs as a subsidiary to Deutsche Telekom but does not have a similar position in France compared to France Télécom. Although AOL France is linked to the AOL group operating more widely at the world level it has held less than 3 percent of the high-speed internet access market in France: see recital 226 of the decision.

88   See recital 237 of the decision.

89   See Case 322/81 *Michelin* [1983] ECR 3461, recitals 55 and 56–58.

90   See recitals 256–299 of the decision.

91   Case C-62/86 *Akzo* [1991] ECR I-3359, recitals 71 and 72; Case C-333/94 *Tetra Pak* v. *Commission* [1996] ECR I-5951, recital 41.

92   See recital 256 of the decision.

93   See recitals 335 and 338 of the decision.

of launching a new product in the calculation of the non-recovery of variable costs. Where a new product is introduced, costs to acquire new customers have to be considered. In Wanadoo's line of reasoning it would have been more advantageous to subject itself to the predation test if the variable costs had been lower. In fact, assuming that the variable costs had been lower, then, compared to the charged prices, predatory pricing would have been more difficult to demonstrate for the Commission.

It is important to note that the Commission made an adjustment to the application of the *Akzo* predation test in exchange for more flexibility.[94] The flexibility of the application is shown by not calculating the variable costs as reported in the company's annual accounts. By contrast, the costs of acquiring customers for Wanadoo's ADSL service were spread over forty-eight months rather than twelve months. Hereby the Commission eased the impact of costumer acquisition costs as a component of variable costs.[95] The costs were treated as a commercial investment to be written off over a realistic customer's lifetime and did not appear at once, which resulted in lower variable costs. This approach was also accepted by the CFI (now "the General Court") in its judgment later on.[96] Even though the Commission applied a more flexible approach as the *Akzo* judgment had adopted, Wanadoo was found guilty of predatory pricing.

The Commission further clarified that the predation concept was also applicable to an emerging market.[97] It refused Wanadoo's statement that the application was merely possible where the complete market had already stabilized. The Commission based its approach on the fact that nothing in Article 102 of the FEU Treaty or in Community case law confirms that an exception for the application of the competition rules to sectors which can be considered as emerging markets, exists.[98] The competition authorities cannot wait until a predatory pricing strategy has led to the elimination of competitors.

The Commission further proved on grounds of internal documents that predatory pricing was part of Wanadoo's strategy to pre-empt competition on the market.[99] The Commission concluded that Wanadoo's policy had to be seen in the context of the objectives of France Télécom.[100] Wandoo's cumulated losses between 2000 and 2002 stood in contrast with the cumulated profits of its parent company, France Télécom.[101] Wanadoo aimed to secure the largest number of subscribers in 2001 even though its price offers were not profitable.[102] Thus, it "clearly and knowingly made a trade off between an objective of minimal profitability which would have made it possible to recoup within a reasonable period the cost of acquiring customers and an objective of ambitious market penetration to the detriment of its competitors."[103]

In light of the definition of the relevant service market, the Commission drew a distinction between high-speed and low-speed internet access and approached

94   See recital 261 of the decision.
95   See recitals 261–262 of the decision.
96   Case T-340/03 *France Télécom* v. *Commission* [2007] ECR II-107, recital 156.
97   See recital 300 of the decision.
98   See recital 301 of the decision.

99   See recitals 110–112 of the decision.
100   See recital 285 of the decision.
101   See recital 288 of the decision.
102   See recital 282 of the decision.
103   See recital 278 of the decision.

them separately.[104] It based the market definition on differences in performance of the products concerned, i.e. that high-speed internet allowed download speeds to be greater than those made with the ISDN technology which resulted further in a difference in price.

It can be assumed that the Commission decided to tackle predatory pricing in the retail market for several reasons, whereas there were also indications of a margin squeeze. First, Wanadoo was not completely vertically integrated because it was not fully owned by Francé Télécom throughout the time period covered by the decision. Besides, the Commission found sufficient evidence of an abuse – for instance, Wanadoo's dominance at the retail level, the charging of prices below average variable costs, and finally a number of internal documents revealing a strategy to force competitors out of the market.

d. Fines, remedies, and conditions enclosed
- The Commission imposed on Wanadoo Interactive a total fine of 10.35 million Euros.
- Obligation for Wanadoo Interactive to end the infringement in so far as it had not done so. Furthermore, to refrain from any behavior having a similar object or effect compared to those examined as infringement.
- Report to the Commission the revenue account for each year.

e. Further developments of the case
Case T-340/03 *France Télécom* v. *Commission* [2007] ECR II-107 and Case Cases T-339/04 *Wanadoo SA* v. *Commission* [2007] ECR II-521. Commission decision upheld.
Case C- 202/07 *France Telecom* v. *Commission*, judgment of 2 April 2009. CFI judgment confirmed.
In particular, the ECJ – overturning the opinion of the Advocate General – held that the CFI was right in confirming that in order to bring a predatory price case the Commission was not required to prove that Wanadoo had the possibility of recouping its losses.

3.4 Bundling and tying

A Introduction

Pure bundling is a business practise in which two products are sold together by the same firm without the possibility for consumers to buy either one of them separately. In case the individual products can also be bought separately, we speak of "mixed bundling." The tying of products refers to a product being sold by a company only if bought together with another product, while the latter (tying) product can also be purchased alone.

Whether or not bundling and tying can cause competition problems very much depends on the case at hand. Bundles and ties can in many circumstances be justified from an efficiency point of view. It would often be very costly and inefficient to sell different complementary components of a more complex product separately. Also, a tying agreement can be an efficient way to solve

---

104   See Case T-340/03 *France Télécom* v. *Commission* [2007] Para 91.

asymmetric information problems. By making sure that complex goods are functioning properly, consumers and firms are better off, as the optimal use of the product is guaranteed.

Competition concerns may arise, however, when the company that is bundling or tying a product to another one is dominant (or has significant market power) in the tying good market. The tie can then be used to price discriminate customers in cases in which part of the components are used by customers at different levels of intensity. Tying the repeat purchase input can make it a metering instrument that can be used to extract surplus from customers. In this way, the dominant firm can lower the price of the tying good and use the sales of the tied good to make overall profits. If as an effect of this strategy there will be more customers willing to buy the tying good (at a lower price) the net effect of tying can be positive on welfare. The typical example used to describe this type of tying is photocopying machines and toner cartridges.

Potential anticompetitive effects of bundling and tying are based on a leverage argument, according to which a firm can abuse its dominance in the tying good's market to restrict (potential) competition in the tied product market in which the firm is not dominant. Market dominance is thus extended to the tied good's market. When products are tied, that is, this may foreclose firms operating in individual components markets. Similarly, bundling and tying can create barriers to entry for producers that are not able to offer the full bundle. Since tying and bundling restrict the consumer's freedom of choice, the conduct could constitute an exploitative abuse of dominance where there are no plausible efficiency gains resulting from the combined sale.

B   Applicable EU legislation

No special legislation applicable. For applicable legislation see chapter 3, paragraph B.

C   Related economics texts

Bishop and Walker (2009), paragraphs 6.63–6.82
Carlton and Perloff (2005), chapter 10, paragraph 2
Church and Ware (2000), paragraphs 5.4.3 and 16.4
Martin (1994), chapter 15, paragraphs 3 and 4
Martin (2002), paragraph 13.2.6
Motta (2004), paragraph 7.3.2
Tirole (1988), paragraphs 3.3 and 8.4
Waldman and Jensen (2001), chapter 14, paragraph 3

D   Related legal texts

Bellamy and Child (2008), chapter 10, paragraph 4 (F, i)
Jones and Sufrin (2008), chapter 7, paragraph 6(H)
Ritter and Braun (2005), chapter 5, paragraph D(5)
Whish (2008), chapter 17, paragraph 3 and chapter 18, paragraph 5

E   Commission decisions in chronological order*

Gema Commission decision 71/224/EC [1971] OJ L 134/15, Case IV/26.760

Eurofix – Bauco/Hilti **Commission decision 88/138/EEC [1988] OJ L 65/19, Cases IV/30.787, 31.488** (Bishop and Walker, 2009, 6.64; Martin, 1994, p. 449)

Napier Brown/British Sugar Commission decision 88/518/EEC [1988] OJ L 284/41, Case IV/30.178 (**described in detail as landmark case in section 3.5**)

London European/Sabena Commission decision 88/589/EEC [1988] OJ L 317/47, Case IV/32.318

Flat Glass Commission decision 89/93/EEC [1989] OJ L 33/44, Case IV/31.906

Tetra Pak II **Commission decision 92/163/EEC [1992] OJ L 72/1, Case IV/31.043** (Bishop and Walker, 2009, 6.77, 6.79, 6.108–6.112)

Van Den Bergh Foods Commission decision 98/531/EC [1998] OJ L 246/1, Cases IV/34.395, 34.073, 35.436

AAMS Commission decision 98/538/EC [1998] OJ L 252/47, Case IV/36.010

TACA Commission decision 1999/243/EC [1999] OJ L 95/1, Case IV/35.134

DSD Commission decision 2001/463/EC [2001] OJ L 166/1, Case COMP/34.493

De Post-La Poste, former Natural Monopoly Commission decision 2002/180/EC [2002] OJ L 61/32, Case COMP/37.859

Microsoft Commission decision 2007/53/EC, summary of the decision published in [2007] OJ L 32/23, full text published on DG Comp website (**described as landmark case in sections 3.6, 3.7, and 3.8**) (Bishop and Walker, 2009, 6.73–6.82, 6.117, 6.134)

F   Economic landmark cases

F.1   *Eurofix – Bauco/Hilti* Commission decision 88/138/EEC [1988] OJ L 65/19

Relevance: This is the first decision in which the Commission dealt with a generally applied tying policy adopted by a dominant firm. The decision describes both the exclusionary effect of tying for actual and potential competitors and the exploitative effect for consumers.

- Cases IV/30.787 and 31.488
- **Decision:** Infringement of Article 102 FEU Treaty
- **Decision addressee(s):**
  - Hilti AG, *United Kingdom*
- **Report route:** Complaints lodged with the Commission on 7 October 1982 and 26 February 1986
- **Date of the decision:** 22 December 1987
- **Competition Commissioner:** P. Sutherland
- **Relevant product market:** Nail guns, Nails, cartridge, and cartridge strips compatible with Hilti nail guns
- **Relevant geographical market:** European internal market
- **Description of the case**

- Decisions displayed in **bold type** are described in the section. Decisions highlighted with (*) include interesting economic analysis by the Commission on the specific topic of the section. Some decisions contain economic reasoning on more than one topic and therefore appear in several lists of Commission decisions in chronological order. Reference is made in brackets and **bold type** to the relevant section in which the decision is extensively described as a landmark case. When decisions are referenced and/or described in some detail in one or more of the economic textbooks, reference in brackets is also made to the relevant part(s) of those texts.

a. Relevant facts

Hilti AG (Hilti) is a large producer of professional building industry equipment, selling worldwide and in all the European Member States. At the time of the decision it was the world leader in the field of nail guns and consumable products for use therein (i.e. nails, cartridge, and cartridge strips). In Europe it used to sell its product either through wholly owned subsidiaries or via exclusive distribution agreements with independent distributors. Eurofix and Bauco (the two complainants) were small-sized companies active on the English market for the production and distribution of nails. In particular Bauco specialized in importing and distributing nails compatible with the Hilti nail guns (nails had to be produced in such a way to fit specific nail guns). Hilti's range of products was protected to a certain extent by patents.

The two complainants informed the Commission about a series of alleged anticompetitive behaviors adopted by Hilti intended to exclude them from the market for nails compatible with Hilti's nail guns. Following its decision to open proceedings and as a result of its investigations, the Commission discovered that Hilti had adopted the following commercial behavior:

1. It had been selling cartridge strips to end users and/or distributors only if purchased with the necessary complements of nails. In particular, in its internal documentation Hilti referred to this policy as to an "embargo on cartridge-only sales." The explanation given for potential refusal to supply cartridge strips without nails was based on the alleged safety risk and concerns about other nails.[105]

2. "In case where Hilti did not carry out the tying described above, it attempted to block the sale of competitors' nails by a policy of reducing discounts for orders of cartridge without nails. The reduction of discounts was not linked primarily to any objective criteria such as quantity but was based substantially on the fact that the customer was purchasing competitors' nails."[106]

3. In reaction to Eurofix's attempt to purchase cartridges without nails outside the United Kingdom to circumvent Hilti's policy, Hilti exerted pressure on its independent distributors outside the United Kingdom not to fulfil export orders (in particular on its Dutch distributor where Eurofix had tried to obtain supplies).[107]

4. Hilti consistently refused to supply independent producers of nails (including the two complainants) with cartridges. At the same time it hindered them from obtaining independent supply of cartridges, either refusing the necessary licenses to independent producers or fixing royalties so high "as to amount to a refusal."[108] At the same time it refused to supply cartridge strips to those clients which might have sold those strips to independent producers of nails.

---

105 See recitals 30–32 of the decision.
106 Recital 33 of the decision.
107 See recitals 35–37 of the decision.

108 Recital 39 of the decision. See also recitals 38, 40, and 41 of the decision.

5. Hilti adopted several discriminatory tactics (not only referring to applied discounts) regarding its customers. The latter were distinguished between supported and non-supported depending on their acceptance of Hilti's direct selling system, of other arrangements, and on the recognition brand loyalty for a family of Hilti's products.[109]

b. Origin of the case

On 7 October 1982 and on 26 February 1985 two complaints were filed to the Commission pursuant to Article 3 of Regulation 17 by Eurofix Limited and Bauco (UK) Ltd. They complained that Hilti AG had infringed Article 102 FEU Treaty. On 9 August 1985 the Commission decided to initiate proceedings.

c. Economic analysis

Hilti was found guilty of several forms of abusive conduct by which it had tried to monopolize the markets it was already dominating. All the conducts described above were aimed at the exclusion of actual competitors from the relevant markets and at preventing entry of potential new competitors. As the Commission stated, "the different aspects of Hilti's commercial behavior were designed to this effect and were aimed at preventing Hilti-compatible cartridge strips from being freely available. Without such availability ... independent producers of Hilti-compatible nails have been severely restricted in their penetration of the market. Furthermore, customers have been obliged to rely on Hilti for both cartridge and nails for their Hilti nail guns."[110]

The Commission described all aspects of Hilti's abusive conduct, focusing in particular on the refusal to supply competitors and the attempts to restrict the entry of new possible actors on the relevant markets. Furthermore the Commission also assessed the inconsistency of the "safety argument" proposed by Hilti to justify its overall behaviour. In particular, the Commission noted how that was an objective never really put forward and pursued by Hilti before the complaints against its abuses.[111]

Concerning the tying policy adopted by Hilti, the Commission noted that "making the sale of patented cartridge strips conditional upon taking a corresponding complement of nails constitutes an abuse of a dominant position... These policies leave the consumer with no choice over the source of his nails and as such abusively exploit him. In addition, these policies all have the object or effect of excluding independent nail makers who may threaten the dominant position Hilti holds. The tying [was] not [an] isolated incident but a generally applied policy."[112] Moreover "in an attempt to reinforce its tying policy in the UK... Hilti... induced its Dutch distributor to stop the supply of cartridge strips. This action foreclosed that source of supply to customers and further had the effect of partitioning the common market."[113] It is interesting to note how the Commission, in the first case in which it described the effects of tying policies, focused its attention on both the exclusionary and the exploitative consequences. This approach is slightly more consumer oriented than purely economic concerns about the exclusionary effects of tying on competitors.

---

109   See recitals 42–47 of the decision.
110   Recital 74 of the decision.
111   See recitals 77–96 of the decision. See also, *infra*, section 3.7 of the book.

112   Recital 75 of the decision.
113   Recital 76 of the decision.

d. Fines, remedies, and conditions enclosed
- The Commission imposed on Hilti a total fine of ECU 6,000,000.
- Obligation for Hilti to bring the infringements to an end and to refrain from repeating or continuing similar conducts.

e. Further developments of the case
Case T-30/89 *Hilti* v. *Commission* [1991] ECR 1439, appeal dismissed.
Case C-53/92 *Hilti* v. *Commission* [1994] ECR I-667, CFI judgment upheld.

F.2 *Tetra Pak II* Commission decision 92/163/EEC [1992] OJ L 72/1

Relevance: The Commission describes tying practises as abusive in themselves and also as generating further abuses. In fact they produce effects on other neighbouring markets where the dominant firm will be able to cross-subsidise aggressive (i.e. predatory) price policies by means of monopoly profits guaranteed by the tying strategy. The effects on both interbrand and intrabrand competition are described.

- Cases IV/31.043
- **Decision:** Infringement of Article 102 FEU Treaty
- **Decision addressee(s):**
  - Tetra Pak International SA, *Switzerland*
- **Report route:** Complaint lodged with the Commission on 7 September 1983
- **Date of the decision:** 24 July 1991
- **Competition Commissioner:** P. Sutherland
- **Relevant product market:** Aseptic and non-aseptic cartons and production machines
- **Relevant geographical market:** European internal market
- **Description of the case**
  ### a. Relevant facts
  The Tetra Pak group (Tetra Pak) is one of the world's leading companies in the field of the packaging of liquid and semi-liquid aliments in cartons. In the packaging industry, the main distinction is between aseptic and non-aseptic packaging. The two products are intended for different types of products and require completely different technical and logistical processes. Therefore, they are considered as different markets. At the time of the decision the aseptic market in Europe was quasi-monopolistic, with Tetra Pak holding a market share of 90–95 percent in both cartons and packaging machines markets. The non-aseptic market was more open to competition but still oligopolistic, with Tetra Pak holding a market share of around 50–55 percent in the markets for cartons and machines. Its main competitor on the non-aseptic market was Elopak (the parent company of the complainant Elopak Italia). "For technological reasons and because of the existence of a large number of patents and restrictive trade practises, barriers to entry into the aseptic market are very high. They are considerably less so in the non-aseptic sector, at least as far as technological barriers are concerned."[114]

  Elopak Italia complained about several aspects of Tetra Pak's trading policy which were considered abusive particularly because restrictive of competitors' possibility to increase their market share and/or to break the monopolistic

114 Recital 18 of the decision.

position of Tetra Pak on the aseptic market. Following the complaint the Commission carried out investigations providing detailed information on Tetra Pak's trading policy in all the Member States where it was active (even if the original complaint referred only to the Italian market). The main features of the dominant firm's strategy can be summarised as follows:

1. Tetra Pak pursued an extensive patent policy covering its entire basic technology as well as slight modifications. Furthermore, it did not grant any manufacturing license around the world for its machines and for cartons within Europe. Its distribution system exclusively consisted of companies belonging to the group and consequently prevented any intrabrand competition.

2. The purchasing/leasing contracts concerning the packaging machines provided a number of clauses basically homogenous in all countries based on the exclusive right of Tetra Pak to control the configuration, the operation, and the maintenance of the supplied machines. Furthermore, in Italy (the country where the complainant operated), purchasers were obliged to inform Tetra Pak of all modifications and improvements to the equipment and to grant Tetra Pak the ownership of any derived intellectual property (IP) right.[115]

3. Concerning the supply of cartons, Tetra Pak also established exclusionary conditions in the contracts with its clients. In particular, it imposed an obligation to use only Tetra Pak cartons in packaging machines and to purchase cartons only from Tetra Pak or from another supplier chosen by Tetra Pak. In Italy an obligation similar to that concerning the IP rights of improved machines was introduced for cartons.[116]

4. The purchasers had to submit regular compliance reports. Furthermore they had to ask for Tetra Pak's authorization if they wanted to resell machines subject to a pre-emption right reserved to Tetra Pak.

5. In case of leasing contracts, similar conditions were included in the agreements and the rent was composed of a "base rent" usually similar to the actual price of the machines, as well as an annual and a monthly production rent.

6. The pricing policy adopted in the sales of cartons showed relevant differences between Member States. The lowest prices were charged in Italy. In the sales of machines, the differences between Member States were also significant (i.e. up to 100 percent in some cases) with the lowest machine sales also being present in Italy. Similar patterns emerged for leasing agreements for machines.[117]

7. The real prices charged for the machines were generally much lower (up to 50 percent) than those appearing in the contracts. There were several methods to reduce them which were often used in conjunction with each other (e.g. the buying up of competitor's machines at inflated prices, trading old Tetra Pak machines at inflated prices,

---

115   See recitals 23–26 of the decision.
116   See recital 27 of the decision.

117   See recitals 52–53 and 57–67 of the decision.

fictional purchases of old machinery then left at the clients' disposal, etc.). These methods were used for granting reduction and discounts. Moreover, an analysis of the net profit margins on sales of machines in Italy showed that they were sold at a loss. This selling at a loss was accompanied by several other steps taken by Tetra Pak to obstruct the distribution of competing machines in Italy and by other activities aimed at monitoring/restricting the activities of competing firms.[118]

8. Tetra Pak took over the Austrian company Selfpack, the German company Zupack, and acquired control over Liquipak in 1970, 1982, and 1986, respectively. They were all active in the packaging sector and in some cases improved Tetra Pack's technique and the know-how.[119]

9. An analysis of the impact of cartons sales and their profitability showed that the aseptic cartons alone represented 80 percent of cartons sales and nearly 70 percent of the group's total turnover. They were by far the most profitable products and, considering Tetra Pak's market share, they faced almost no competition. The non-aseptic products represented 7 percent of the sales and were profitable. One particular type of non-aseptic carton (the Rex carton), a direct competitor on the Italian market of Elopak's non-aseptic carton, was persistently making losses not only in Italy. It was sold at prices below *direct variable costs* and in some years at prices below input costs.[120]

b. Origin of the case

On 7 September 1983 a complaint was filed to the Commission pursuant to Article 3 of Regulation 17 by Elopak Italia srl. It complained that Tetra Pak and its associated companies had infringed Article 102 FEU Treaty. On 9 December 1988 the Commission decided to initiate proceedings.

c. Economic analysis

In analyzing the overall structure of Tetra Pak's commercial policy and its numerous abusive aspects aimed at excluding its competitors from the market and at partitioning the European market on a national basis, the Commission described the central role played by the tying clauses and the effects that they produced on adjacent markets. These tying clauses allowed Tetra Pak to cross-subsidize its anticompetitive sales at a loss of machineries and of non-aseptic cartons in a market where competition was still present. In the Commission's words "Tetra Pak managed to impose . . . certain contractual obligations aimed essentially at binding [customers] to the group and preventing any trade in its products. Using these contractual obligations to limit or even avoid as far as possible any possibilities of inter-brand and intra-brand competition, and due to its completely autonomous production and distribution policy, the group succeeded in imposing a compartmentalization of national market for its products . . . All the conditions for an artificial restriction of competition are met, permitting it, in these sectors where its virtual monopoly is established (in the aseptic market), to pursue a policy of profit maximization . . . to the

---

118   See recitals 68–88 of the decision.   120   See recitals 47–51 of the decision.
119   See recitals 89–91 of the decision.

detriment of consumers: this enables [it] in turn to subsidize, in those sectors where competition still persists . . ., an aggressive and indeed predatory price policy. For this purpose, a number of obligations are imposed on the customer which have no link with the purpose of the contracts, and . . . some of these obligations distort the very nature of those contracts."[121]

In assessing the restrictive effects of the contractual clauses imposed by Tetra Pak, the Commission focused its attention on the anticompetitive nature of the tying obligation imposed upon the customers to acquire only Tetra Pak cartons and only from the same company. The system, strengthened by distribution agreements and patent policy, had the effect of completely excluding both interbrand and intrabrand competition. Such a system "makes the carton market completely dependent on the equipment market and favours the charging of discriminatory prices or indeed loss-making operations on the latter market. On the one hand, the fact that the sales of machines inevitably involved the sales of cartons as well will quite normally encourage the seller, where necessary, to make major concessions which will vary considerably depending on the weight of the partner in negotiations. On the other hand, the prospect of guaranteed income from future carton sales . . . will enable him readily to consider selling equipment at a loss, within the profitability threshold for [combined sales]. The reverse, i.e. the subsidizing of carton sales by profits made on machines sales, is clearly possible too. Although constituting abuses in their own right, [these] clauses may therefore potentially generate further abuses. They place competitors . . . who cannot . . . subsidize possible losses on a given product through profits made on another product, in a very uncomfortable position."[122]

The effect of the tying policy was to completely eliminate competition for the sale of cartons and also of associated products for machines (e.g. spare parts, technical services). Consequently, competition existed only at the moment of supplying equipment because once the machines were sold they implied a lifetime guarantee for Tetra Pak assistance and Tetra Pak cartons. "Tetra Pak thus artificially limit[ed] competition to the area in which its position is strongest because equipment . . . is the area in which its technological lead is greatest and entry barriers are at their highest. This is why Tetra Pak is so attached to the system of tied machine/carton sales. It enables it to secure virtually all its profits (some 95 percent) in the form of income from cartons (as result of their purchase being compulsory) as soon as the machine is placed with the customer. And as far as this latter operation is concerned, the advantage which Tetra Pak obtains from its technological lead may be complemented, if necessary to win an order, by selling or leasing machines at a loss, which in any event will have only a very marginal effect on financial results."[123] Accordingly, in assessing the price policy adopted by Tetra Pak, the Commission considered the sale of both cartons and machines in the non-aseptic sector as predatory because they were made at a loss and hence abusive while noting the predatory potential of such tying clauses.[124]

121   Recitals 105 and 106 of the decision.
122   Recital 117 of the decision.
123   Recital 146 of the decision.
124   See recitals 147–155 of the decision.

Tetra Pak's attempt to justify the exclusive purchasing obligations with arguments based on technical requirements, product liability, public health, synergy effects obtained by R&D, as well as after-sales level and on the protection of its reputation were dismissed by the Commission either because they were unsustainable or because the aims pursued could have been achieved with measures less restrictive of competition and of consumers' choices.[125]

d. Fines, remedies, and conditions enclosed

- The Commission imposed on Tetra Pak a total fine of ECU 75,000,000.
- Obligations for Tetra Pak to bring the infringements to an end and to refrain from repeating or continuing similar behaviors.
- Obligation for Tetra Pak to amend its machines purchase/lease contract in order to eliminate the aspects that were declared abusive by the Commission.
- Obligation for Tetra Pak to guarantee that any difference between the prices charged in different Member States will exclusively depend on market conditions.
- Obligation for Tetra Pak to guarantee its customers the opportunity to freely choose their supplying Tetra Pak subsidiary within the Community.
- Obligation for Tetra Pak to refrain from applying any form of price discrimination and/or predatory pricing as well as discriminatory discounts.
- Prohibition for Tetra Pak to refuse orders from non-end users.
- Obligation for Tetra Pak to inform all acquirers/leasers of machines of the specification which packaging cartons must meet in order to be used on its machines.
- Obligation for Tetra Pak, for a period of five years, to submit a report to the Commission allowing it to assess the compliance of the company with its obligations and prohibitions.

e. Further developments of the case

Case T-83/91 *Tetra Pak* v. *Commission* [1994] ECR II-755, appeal dismissed.

In dismissing the appeal the CFI (now "the General Court") stated that: "the combined effect of the ... clauses at issue ... was an overall strategy aiming to make the customer totally dependant on Tetra Pak for the entire life of the machine once purchased or leased, thereby excluding in particular any possibility of competition at the level both of cartons and of associated products."[126]

The CFI ruled that the resulting system of tied sales could not be objectively justified in the light of commercial usage, since "the tied sale of filling machines and cartons cannot be considered to be in accordance with commercial usage."[127]

Case C-333/94 *Tetra Pak* v. *Commission* [1996] ECR I-595, CFI judgment upheld.

The ECJ confirmed the CFI's judgment and held that the list of abusive practises as set out in Article 102 FEU is not exhaustive, thus even where tied

125 See recitals 118 and 119 of the decision.   127 Recital 137 of the judgment.
126 Recital 135 of the judgment.

sales of two products are in accordance with commercial usage or there is a natural link between the two products in question, such sales may still constitute an abuse.[128]

3.5 Price squeezing

A Introduction

A price squeeze can occur when a firm operates in both an upstream market, where it is dominant, and in the related downstream market, where it faces competition. The vertically integrated firm can abuse its upstream market power to try to exclude its competitors in the downstream market by giving its own subsidiary better terms of trade than its rivals. In particular, the dominant firm can lower the price of its downstream product while at the same time increasing the input price it charges to its downstream competitors, so that the latter cannot profitably meet the consumer prices, with the effect of driving them out of the market. Upstream dominance that can so be abused often relates to a firm controlling an essential facility.[129]

Anticompetitive price squeezes are difficult to identify, in part again because they require insight into the cost structures of different firms. In addition, vertical integration can allow for passed-on efficiency gains that can explain differences in internal and external prices. What appears to be a price squeeze may in fact be competitive pricing in the downstream market. Interfering with competition would then unduly privilege inefficient firms.

B Applicable EU legislation

No special legislation applicable. For applicable legislation see chapter 3, paragraph B.

C Related economics texts

Bishop and Walker (2009), 6.136–6.139
Carlton and Perloff (2005), not specifically discussed
Church and Ware (2000), not specifically discussed
Martin (1994), not specifically discussed
Martin (2002), not specifically discussed
Motta (2004), paragraph 7.3.5
Tirole (1988), paragraph 4.6.2
Waldman and Jensen (2001), chapter 4, paragraph 3(3) and chapter 15, paragraph 3(2)

D Related legal texts

Bellamy and Child (2008), chapter 10, paragraph 4 (E, i)
Jones and Sufrin (2008), chapter 7, paragraph 6(A, xiv)
Ritter and Braun (2005), not specifically discussed
Whish (2008), chapter 18, paragraph 7

---

128   Recital 37 of the judgment.
129   For a description of the economics of essential facilities, see *infra* section 3.8 of the book.

E Commission decisions in chronological order*

General Motors Continental Commission decision 75/75/EEC [1975] OJ L 29/14, Case IV/28.851

Napier Brown/British Sugar **Commission decision 88/518/EEC [1988] OJ L 284/41, Case IV/30.178**

Deutsche Telekom Commission decision 2003/707/EC [2003] OJ L 263/9, Cases COMP/C.1/37.451, 37.578, 37.579 (Bishop and Walker, 2009, 6.138)

Telefónica **Commission decision of 4 July 2007, published on DG Comp website, Case COMP/38.784**

F Economic landmark cases

F.1 *Napier Brown/British Sugar* Commission decision 88/518/EEC [1988] OJ L 284/41

Relevance: The decision constitutes one of the rare cases in which the Commission dealt with vertical squeezing and the first in which it explained the competitive consequences of it in economic terms. To show the abusiveness of the conduct the Commission focused its attention on the differences between the charged prices in case of squeezing and, on the other hand, in case of competitive conduct.

- Case IV/30.178
- **Decision:** Infringement of Article 102 FEU Treaty
- **Decision addressee(s):**
  - British Sugar plc, *United Kingdom*
- **Report route:** Complaint lodged with the Commission on 19 September 1980
- **Date of the decision:** 18 July 1988
- **Competition Commissioner:** P. Sutherland
- **Relevant product market:** Granulated sugar (made from sugar beet or sugar cane)
- **Relevant geographical market:** United Kingdom
- **Description of the case**
  - a. **Relevant facts**
    British Sugar plc (BS) was the largest producer and seller of sugar in the United Kingdom and held the legal monopoly in the production of beet sugar in the United Kingdom under the Sugar Act of 1956. At the time of the decision, BS held 58 percent of the relevant market. Furthermore its dominant position was strengthened by several other elements, in particular by "the inability of its main competitors to compete fully and effectively with it, the barriers to entry existing on the British sugar market, and BS's proven ability to influence the price at which sugar is sold in Britain by unilateral actions."[130]

    Napier Brown and Company Limited (NB) was the largest merchant of sugar in the United Kingdom. It was active in buying and selling sugar both as

---

- Decisions displayed in **bold type** are described in the section. Decisions highlighted with (*) include interesting economic analysis by the Commission on the specific topic of the section. Some decisions contain economic reasoning on more than one topic and therefore appear in several lists of Commission decisions in chronological order. Reference is made in brackets and **bold type** to the relevant section in which the decision is extensively described as a landmark case. When decisions are referenced and/or described in some detail in one or more of the economic textbooks, reference in brackets is also made to the relevant part(s) of those texts.

130   Recital 60 of the decision. For a detailed analysis of BS' position on the relevant market, see recitals 50–60 of the decision.

a merchant of bulk quantities and as a *nominal merchant* (i.e. trying to obtain the best condition for a customer who places an order). NB had traditionally been a customer of BS but decided in October 1983 to enter the retail market for packaged sugar. Soon after, NB encountered several problems in the retail market caused by the practises adopted by BS and brought this to the attention of the Commission, which initiated proceedings against BS.

In its subsequent investigation, the Commission found extensive documentation of the business policy adopted by BS, revealing very clearly its underlying intentions. The Commission ascertained that "BS introduced a policy whereby it intended to visit major outlets for retail sugar and offer to them one or more BS products at excellent prices on the condition that the customer 'de-listed' or refused to stock [NB derived products]."[131] NB had complained about the fact that BS had consistently refused to supply industrial sugar and instead offered only sugar of a different grain that NB found was much more difficult to commercialize. BS justified its policy as having suffered a period of input shortage and a forced adoption of a quota system to equally satisfy all purchasers.

NB also claimed that BS had been undercutting NB's retail sugar prices to (potential) clients "to a level at which it was impossible for a repackager of sugar in the United Kingdom without an internal source of industrial sugar to survive in the long term, thus artificially maintaining an unrealistically low margin between its prices of industrial and retail sugar with the objective of forcing NB out of the market."[132] In its price analysis of the downstream product (the sugar sold at the retail level) the Commission noted that the main difference was the transportation costs. BS, particularly due to its adoption of a delivered price system,[133] could rely on its system for delivering industrial sugar and incurred only limited additional costs while NB had to bear the price for the delivery of industrial sugar from BS plus the transport costs for retail sugar. Based on the costs analysis, the Commission found that BS was offering very low prices to NB's customers, systematically undercutting NB's prices.

A further complaint of NB referred to BS' refusal to supply beet sugar and its frequent substitution with cane sugar. The beet origin was particularly relevant for NB because it was allowed to receive a storage rebate on that quality of sugar from the (then) EEC. The Commission did not find in its investigation any particular difficulty in BS supplying NB with beet sugar.

b. **Origin of the case**

On 19 September 1980 a complaint was filed to the Commission pursuant to Article 3 of Regulation 17 by Napier Brown and Company Limited and other UK sugar merchants. They complained that British Sugar had infringed Article 102 FEU Treaty. The complaint was subsequently amended and extended

---

131   Recital 15 of the decision.
132   Recital 24 of the decision.
133   BS did not offer an ex-factory purchasing option. This was another of the practises whose abusive nature was contested by the Commission: see recitals 32 and 69–72 of the decision.

by Napier Brown and Company Limited in mid-1985. On 3 June 1986 the Commission decided to initiate proceedings.

c.   Economic analysis

The decision deals with several abuses of a dominant position that in the Commission's view BS had committed. The Commission began its investigation with an assessment of the refusal to supply NB with industrial sugar. It found that the alleged shortage period, the consequent quota scheme adopted by BS, and the necessity to substitute industrial sugar with "special grain" sugar were all unnecessary measures put forward to justify a refusal to supply but which had been implemented to provoke NB's withdrawal from the retail sugar market.[134]

The decision is particularly relevant because it is one of the rare cases in which the Commission dealt with a squeezing practise and the first case in which it clearly stated its approach toward that practise. The Commission stated that "[I]n a case such as this, where an undertaking is alleged to be dominant in the markets for the supply of both a raw material and a downstream product, and it is further alleged that the dominant undertaking maintains an artificially low margin between the price of the raw material . . . and the price of the downstream product . . . , the analysis of pricing must be centered upon the differences between the selling price of the dominant companies' raw material and its downstream product prices."[135] With reference to the possible effect of the mentioned price difference on the competitiveness of the downstream market, it added "the minimum at which NB could sell packet sugar in order not to make a loss (using industrial sugar purchased from BS) would be, assuming that it matched BS's efficiency, . . . Thus, with a retail price below . . . NB or any repackager as efficient as BS, had an insufficient margin to repackage and sell sugar for retail sale, even without trying to make a profit"[136]

These considerations were used as benchmark for the assessment of BS' price policy. The Commission after a careful consideration of the parties' costs stated that "[t]he maintaining by [BS] of a margin between the price which it charges for a raw material to the companies which compete with the dominant company in the production of the derived product, which is insufficient to reflect that dominant company's own costs of transformation (in this case the margin maintained by BS between its industrial and retail sugar prices compared to its own repackaging costs) with the result that competition in the derived product is restricted, is an abuse of dominant position."[137] None of BS' competitors on the retail market would have been able to compete with the dominant firm at comparable levels of efficiency.[138]

---

134   For the economics of market power and refusal to supply competitors, see section 3.8 of the book.
135   Recital 25 of the decision.
136   Recital 30 of the decision.
137   Recital 66 of the decision.
138   In *Deutsche Telekom* (Case T 271/03) the CFI stated that "the Community judicature has not yet explicitly ruled on the method to be applied in determining the existence of a margin squeeze . . ." (recital 188 of the judgment). The CFI then in paragraph 191 repeated the formula, as set out by the Commission in its decision in *Napier Brown/British Sugar*, and then ruled in paragraph 192 that: ". . . *any other approach could be contrary to the general principle of legal certainty*" (emphasis added).

Similarly, the refusal to supply NB with beet-origin sugar was considered an abusive conduct because of its discriminatory effect on NB compared to other customers.[139]

d. Fines, remedies, and conditions enclosed
   - The Commission imposed on British Sugar plc a total fine of ECU 3,000,000.

e. Further developments of the case
None.

F.2 *Telefónica* Commission decision 2008/C 83/05 [2007] OJ C 83/06

Relevance: Assessment of margin squeeze by applying the *equally efficient competitor* test. Commission evaluation of differences between predatory and squeezing strategies.

- Case COMP/38.784
- **Decision:** Infringement of Article 102 FEU Treaty
- **Decision addressee(s):**
   - Telefónica SA, *Spain*
   - Telefónica de España SAU, *Spain*
- **Report route:** Complaint lodged with the Commission on 11 July 2003
- **Date of the decision:** 4 July 2007
- **Competition Commissioner:** N. Kroes
- **Relevant product market:** Retail broadband "mass" market, market for wholesale broadband access at regional level, market for wholesale broadband access at national level
- **Relevant geographical market:** Spain

Description of the case

a. Relevant facts

Telefónica is the Spanish telecommunications incumbent and it is the only company operating a nationwide fixed telephone network. Competitors who intend to offer broadband internet access to end users will have to set up an alternative local access network (LAN). The costs and the timeframe for setting up such a network are often exorbitant and setting up such networks is not economically viable for competitors. Alternatively, competitors can use the already existing wholesale broadband access. Two of three available wholesale broadband accesses are exclusively provided by Telefónica, whereas the other is provided by both Telefónica and a competing operator. Still, the latter depends on Telefónica's input to supply the type of wholesale product.

At the end of 2006 consumers used 80 percent of the broadband internet connections via the ADSL service. Hence, it was the main technology used in Spain to provide broadband internet access. In addition, Telefónica is active in providing internet access to end users, i.e. in the downstream market. The Commission found an inequity from September 2001 to December 2006 between Telefónica's upstream and downstream prices. The Commission accused the company of an abuse in form of a margin squeeze and imposed one of the highest ever fines for an Article 102 FEU infringement. The Commission pointed

---

139   See recitals 73–76 of the decision.

out that the great harm caused by Telefónica's practises both to competitors and to end users, and further that the company was able to stop the margin squeeze at any time, justified the large fine.

The decision shows that control of essential inputs such as a broadband internet controlled by a dominant undertaking is decisive to ensure competition on a liberalized market such as the telecommunication sector.

b. Origin of the case

On 11 July 2003 France Télécom España SA lodged a complaint to the Commission. In February 2006 the Commission initiated proceedings.

c. Economic analysis

In the broadband access market it appeared that there was an insufficient spread between Telefónica's prices for wholesale access to competitors and its tariffs for retail broadband access to end users. For that same reason, potential competitors and new entrants were hindered in competing with Telefónica on the market for retail broadband access. Hence, Telefónica was found guilty by the Commission of engaging in a margin squeeze.

Article 102 FEU does not contain a definition of margin squeezing.[140] But in *Deutsche Telekom*[141] the CFI (now "the General Court") confirmed the constitutive elements of margin squeezing by taking over the Commission's decision. According to that decision, a margin squeeze exists if "the difference between the retail prices charged by a [vertically integrated] dominant undertaking and the wholesale prices it charges its competitors for comparable services is negative, or insufficient to cover the product-specific costs to the dominant operator of providing its own retail services on the downstream market."[142]

Firstly, Telefónica is a vertically integrated firm because it is active on the upstream market for wholesale ADSL access to competitors and further on the downstream market by providing broadband access to end users.

Secondly, competitors who wish to provide broadband services to consumers cannot enter the market with an alternative technology but only by contracting wholesale broadband access products owned by Telefónica. Therefore, downstream competitors are dependent on Telefónica's input that can be considered as "essential" for competition on the downstream market.

Thirdly, the Commission found an inconsistency between Telefónica's upstream and downstream prices. The dominant undertaking "imposes on competitors additional efficiency constraints which the incumbent does not have to support in providing its own retail services."[143] Hence, Telefónica can provide its retail services at a price with which its competitors can compete only by not being profitable.

The calculation of the margin squeeze by the Commission is done by the "equally efficient competitor test"[144] that was also applied in *Deutsche*

---

140 Definition in: Notice on the application of the competition rules to access agreements in the telecommunications sector, OJ C 265/2 [1998], recitals 117–118.
141 Case T-27/03 *Deutsche Telekom* v. *Commission* [2008], recital 166.
142 See recital 107 of the Commission decision of 21 May 2003, COMP/C-1/37.451,37.578,37.595 – Deutsche Telekom AG, 2003 OJ L 263.
143 Case T-27/03 *Deutsche Telekom* v. *Commission* [2008], recital 140.
144 See recitals 311–312 of the decision.

Telekom.[145] It tests whether "a competitor having the same cost function at the downstream arm of the vertically integrated company is able to be profitable in the downstream market given the wholesale and retail prices charged by [Telefónica]."[146]

Accordingly, the Commission had to calculate the profitability of an equally efficient competitor. In line with the practise of the ECJ and the Commission in cases dealing with margin squeeze, the "period-by-period" approach was applied to measure profitability.[147] This approach consists of comparing the observed revenues and costs for an annual period.[148] The Commission further applied the discounted cash flow ("DCF") method where also the company's future growth is taken into account. This approach looks "at the profitability of a business over a reasonably long period."[149] Both tests to calculate profitability led to the same result – that an equally efficient company could not provide broadband access profitably given the price that Telefónica had charged. According to the test results the Commission found Telefónica guilty of a margin squeeze between its retail prices and national wholesale prices.[150]

The conditions for margin squeezing and predatory pricing are very similar, i.e. that the downstream price is excessively low relative to the upstream price within both predatory pricing and margin squeezing. But in contrast to predatory pricing, margin squeezing creates losses for consumers not only in the long run but also in the short run.[151] The restriction of competition leads to a higher retail price which eats away at consumer surplus. Furthermore, in a margin squeeze case the dominant company is not necessarily making losses. Predatory pricing, on the other hand, leads to lower consumer prices at least as long as competitors are undercut to force them out of the market.

Under certain market conditions, especially in emerging markets or when launching new products, a company can set prices below its own costs for a period of time.

Nevertheless, the Commission did not accept Telefónica's justification that the downstream losses were caused and justified by necessary investments and efficiencies that benefited the consumers.[152]

Moreover, margin squeezing can have several anticompetitive effects. Although an impact on competition is not a mandatory condition for proving the abusive nature of a margin squeeze, it is part of the present Commission's decision.[153]

Firstly, the dominant firm in the upstream market aims to take advantage of its position in the downstream market. Telefónica's actions forced ADSL competitors to undercut Telefónica's retail prices in order to attract consumers which resulted in losses which could not be recovered within a reasonable

145   Case T-27/03 *Deutsche Telekom* v. *Commission* [2008], recital 107.
146   See recital 315 of the decision.
147   Case C-62/86 *Akzo Chemie* v. *Commission* [1991] ECR I-3359, Paras 64 and 65; Case C-333/94 *Tetra Pak* v. *Commission* [1996] ECR I-5951, Para 40.
148   See recital 328 of the decision.

149   See recitals 329–330 of the decision.
150   See recital 520 of the decision.
151   See recital 558 of the decision.
152   See recitals 619 ff. of the decision.
153   Case T-27/03 *Deutsche Telekom* v. *Commission* [2008], recitals 181–183. See also recitals 543–563 of the decision.

period of time.[154] Hence, competitors were left with a decision to leave the market or make losses.

Secondly, it is anticompetitive if it is a tool to protect a dominant position in the upstream market. When competitors are hindered from establishing themselves on the downstream market, the vertically integrated undertaking may set up barriers to consolidate dominance in the upstream market.

In addition, margin squeezes can have an anticompetitive impact on end users. The Commission stated that Spanish consumers paid higher prices for broadband access than in other European countries. Competition would have driven down retail prices had it not been restricted by Telefónica's practises.[155]

d. Fines, remedies, and conditions enclosed
  – The Commission imposed on Telefónica a total fine of 151,875,000 Euros

e. Further developments of the case
  Case T-336/07 *Telefónica and Telefónica de España* v. *Commission*, pending

3.6 Restricting and/or preventing entry

A Introduction

A firm's decision whether or not to become active in a certain market depends first and foremost on the profits it can expect to make in that market. These depend, among other things, on the (sunk) costs of entry, the reactions of competitors to entry, and long-run profit margins in accommodated market competition. Potential and new entrants are important for the competitiveness of markets. They exert competitive pressure on the incumbent firms, even when there are only few companies actually active in the market. Barriers to entry therefore may be detrimental to the competitive process.

Many types of barriers to entry are essentially exogenous, such as crucial patents or other IP rights, essential facilities, and in some cases economies of scale. In addition, by changing the competitive dynamics or market characteristics, an incumbent firm can create or raise (artificial) barriers to entry. One possible way to try to do this is to invest in excess capacity, in order to reduce the marginal cost of increasing output and to be able to credibly and aggressively react to entry. Another is aiming to modify product demand with an aggressive advertising campaign or with a product proliferation strategy aimed at reducing the available product space for the new entrant's good. In case consumers buy complementary parts of the product they have purchased, the incumbent can raise a barrier to entry for other suppliers by raising or creating the switching cost to discourage consumers switching to entrants. There are other kinds of strategies described in the literature as well, such as lobbying to change government regulation. Yet for most of them, there is neither case law in the EU judicatures nor Commission decisions in which these strategies were found to be anticompetitive.

Several of the types of abuses described in this chapter can also be considered as raising rivals' costs strategies to make entry more difficult. Tying, refusal to deal, squeezing, price discrimination, and preventing interoperability can all be tools to raise rivals' costs of viable

---

154   See recital 546 of the decision.   155   See recital 562 of the decision.

competition to the point where they may decide to exit or not to enter. Yet it is important to keep in mind that certainly not all strategies that potentially raise rivals' costs are necessarily anticompetitive. Large R&D investments, for example, may have this effect, but would rarely be considered anticompetitive.

B   Applicable EU legislation

No special legislation applicable. For applicable legislation see chapter 3, paragraph B.

C   Related economics texts

Bishop and Walker (2009), paragraphs 3.20–3.30 and 7.039–7.045
Carlton and Perloff (2005), chapter 3, paragraph 4; chapter 11, paragraph 1(2)
Church and Ware (2000), paragraph 11.5, chapter 14, paragraph 15.3 and chapter 20
Martin (1994), chapter 4, paragraph 2
Martin (2002), chapter 8; paragraphs 11.3 and 11.4
Motta (2004), paragraphs 7.3, specifically 7.3.1 and 7.3.5
Tirole (1988), chapter 8; paragraphs 9.3 and 9.4
Waldman and Jensen (2001), chapters 5, 10, 11, and 12, paragraph 6

D   Related legal texts

Bellamy and Child (2008), chapter 10, paragraph 4 (C)
Jones and Sufrin (2008), chapter 7, paragraph 8(F)
Ritter and Braun (2005), not specifically discussed
Whish (2008), chapter 5, paragraph 4(B, iii)

E   Commission decisions in chronological order•

General Motors Continental Commission decision 75/75/EEC [1975] OJ L 29/14, Case IV/28.851
Eurofix – Bauco/Hilti **Commission decision 88/138/EEC [1988] OJ L 65/19, Cases IV/30.787, 31.488** (Bishop and Walker, 2009, 6.64; Martin, 1994, p. 449)
Tetra Pak I (BTG-license) **Commission decision 88/501/EEC [1988] OJ L 272/27, Case IV/31.043**
London European/Sabena Commission decision 88/589/EEC [1988] OJ L 317/47, Case IV/32.318
Decca Navigator System Commission decision 89/113/EC [1989] OJ L 43/27, Cases IV/30.979, 31.394
British Midland/Aer Lingus Commission decision 92/213/EEC [1993] OJ L 96/34, Case IV/33.544 **(described in detail as landmark case in section 3.8)**
Magill TV Guide/ITP, BBC, and RTE **Commission decision 89/205/EEC [1989] OJ L 78/43, Case IV/31.851** (Bishop and Walker, 2009, 6.130, 6.131; Motta, 2004, p. 68)

• Decisions displayed in **bold type** are described in the section. Decisions highlighted with (*) include interesting economic analysis by the Commission on the specific topic of the section. Some decisions contain economic reasoning on more than one topic and therefore appear in several lists of Commission decisions in chronological order. Reference is made in brackets and bold type to the relevant section in which the decision is extensively described as a landmark case. When decisions are referenced and/or described in some detail in one or more of the economic textbooks, reference in brackets is also made to the relevant part(s) of those texts.

Tetra Pak II Commission decision 92/163/EEC [1992] OJ L 72/1, Case IV/31.043 (**described in detail as landmark case in section 3.4**) (Bishop and Walker, 2009, 6.77, 6.79, 6.108–6.112)

British Midland/Aer Lingus Commission decision 92/213/EEC [1993] OJ L 96/34, Case IV/33.544 (**described in detail as landmark case in section 3.7**)

French-West African Shipowners' Committees Commission decision 92/262/EEC [1992] OJ L 134/1, Case IV/32.450

Warner – Lambert/Gillette and Bic/Gillette and others Commission decision 93/252/EEC [1993] OJ L 116/21, Cases IV/33.440, 33.486

Sea Containers/Stena Line Commission decision 94/19/EEC [1994] OJ L 15/8, Case IV/34.689 (Bishop and Walker, 2009, 6.121, 6.128–6.130; Motta, 2004, p. 67)

Irish Sugar Commission decision 97/624/EC [1997] OJ L 258/1, Cases IV/34.621, 35.059

Van Den Bergh Foods Commission decision 98/531/EC [1998] OJ L 246/1, Cases IV/34.395, 34.073, 35.436 (*)

GVG/FS Commission decision 2004/33/EC [2004] OJ L 11/17, Case COMP/37.685

Microsoft **Commission decision of 24 March 2004, published on DG Comp website, Case COMP/C-3/37.792** (Bishop and Walker, 2009, 6.73–6.82, 6.117, 6.134)

Prokent AG – Tomra system Commission decision of 29 March 2006, published on DG Comp website, Case COMP/38.113

AstraZeneca **Commission decision of 19 July 2006, published on DG Comp website, Case COMP/37.507** (Motta, 2004, pp. 269–70; Bishop and Walker, 2009, 13.07)

Intel Commission decision of 13 May 2009, not yet published, Case COMP/37.990

F Economic landmark cases

F.1 *Eurofix – Bauco/Hilti* Commission decision 88/138/EEC [1988] OJ L 65/19

Relevance: In this decision the Commission describes a composite strategy adopted by Hilti aimed at preventing entry through different abusive practises complementing the already described tying policy and all aimed at the same exclusionary scope.

- For case report, relevant market, relevant facts, allegation, obligations, fines, and remedies, see Case *F.1* in section *3.4*.
    - **c. Economic analysis**

      In its attempt to prevent the development of independent nail producers Hilti, as described in the relevant facts, adopted a number of strategies to stifle the sale of Hilti-compatible nails on the market. In this decision, the Commission for the first time accepted both the exclusionary (the direct effect) and the exploitative effects of the policy aimed at restricting entry on a certain market.

      Hilti's refusal to supply cartridges to long-standing customers motivated by the concern they would be resold to independent nail producers had "the aim of blocking entry into the market for Hilti-compatible nails."[156] The denial or delaying of licensing legitimately available rights under Hilti's patents for cartridge strips has, in the Commission analysis of Hilti's policy, the same effect. "Despite its legal availability Hilti still tried to prevent any such license coming into existence by the size of the royalty demanded. Internal Hilti documentation

---

156   Recital 77 of the decision.

show[ed] the royalty was not objectively justified but was an attempt to block or at very least unreasonably to delay any such license... Hilti's aim was to prevent competing supplies of cartridge strips in which it [held] a dominant position... This case is all the more serious since Hilti use[d] its position in cartridge strips to prevent competition for nails."[157]

A further instrument used by Hilti to prevent the entrance of new actors on the compatible-nails and on the non-Hilti cartridge strips market was price discrimination. As the Commission stated, "Hilti ha[d] a policy designated to illegally limit the entry into the market of competitors producing Hilti-compatible nails. On several occasions Hilti singled out some of the main customers of these competitors and offered them especially favourable conditions in order to secure their loyalty, going in some cases so far as to give away products free of charge. These conditions were selective and discriminatory in that other customers of Hilti buying similar or equivalent quantities did not benefit from these special conditions. [Those offers] reflected Hilti's pre-established policy of attempting to limit [competitors'] entry into the market for Hilti-compatible nails. [A] selectively discriminatory pricing policy by a dominant firm designed purely to damage the business of, or deter market entry by, its competitors, whilst maintaining higher prices for the bulk of its other customers, is both exploitative of these other customers and destructive of competition."[158]

The Commission's approach confirmed that a conduct which by itself constitutes an abuse of dominance can also artificially raise entry barriers for competitors of dominant firms. Actually in this case refusal to deal and price discrimination were used to obtain the restriction of competition. The use of licenses and royalties to raise entry barriers reflects what economic theory says about the possibility of employing *absolute barriers to entry* in order to restrict the ability of competitors to penetrate the market.

e. **Further developments of the case**

Case T-30/89 *Hilti* v. *Commission* [1991] ECR 1439, appeal dismissed.

The CFI (now "the General Court") upheld the Commission decision. It stated: "... the Court observes that it is clear from the documents before it that at the material time Hilti was not prepared to grant licenses on a voluntary basis and that during the proceedings for the grant of licenses of right it demanded a fee approximately six times higher than the figure ultimately appointed by the Comptroller of Patents. A reasonable trader, as Hilti claims to have been, should at least have realized that by demanding such a large fee it was needlessly protracting the proceedings for the grant of licenses of right, and such behavior undeniably constitutes an abuse."[159]

Furthermore the CFI observed that a selective and discriminatory policy such as that operated by Hilti impairs competition inasmuch as it is liable to deter other undertakings from establishing themselves in the market. The inescapable

---

157   Recital 78 of the decision.
158   Recital 80 of the decision.

159   Recital 99 of the judgment.

conclusion is therefore that the Commission had good reason to hold that such behavior on Hilti's part was improper.[160]

Case C-53/92 *Hilti* v. *Commission* [1994] REC I-667, CFI judgment upheld.

F.2 *Tetra Pak I (BTG-license)* Commission decision 88/501/EEC [1988] OJ L 272/27

Relevance: This case, which would today be considered under the Merger Regulation, was assessed under Article 102 by the Commission before the entry into force of that Regulation in 1989. The takeover of a small competitor and the consequent acquisition of its exclusive technology were considered as raising entry barriers for potential competitors. The Commission, confirming its previous orientation, showed concerns about barriers raised by dominant firms regardless of the instrument used to achieve that goal.

- Case IV/31.043
- **Decision:** Infringement of Article 102 FEU Treaty
- **Decision addressee(s):**
    - Tetra Pak Rausing SA, *Switzerland*
- **Report route:** Complaints lodged with the Commission on 23 and 26 June 1986
- **Date of the decision:** 26 July 1988
- **Competition Commissioner:** P. Sutherland
- **Relevant product market:** Aseptic cartons and production machines
- **Relevant geographical market:** European internal market
- **Description of the case**
    a. **Relevant facts**
        The Tetra Pak group (Tetra Pak) is one of the world's leading companies in the field of the packaging of liquid and semi-liquid aliments in cartons. In the field of packaging the main distinction made is between aseptic and non-aseptic packaging. The two operations are intended for different types of products and require completely different technical and logistical procedures. Therefore, they are considered as different markets. At the time of the decision Tetra Pak held around 90 percent market share in the aseptic market for both cartons and machines (the relevant markets for the decision). The only competitor able to produce machines for aseptic cartons was PKL. Both companies used to exclusively supply cartons for machines they had sold. The large part of the revenue came from the supply of cartons given that each single machine was built to last for several years and to process tens of millions of cartons. "The main technical barriers to enter into the market [were] however in the production and maintenance of the aseptic packaging machines. This requires not only an adequate sterilization technology for the cartons, but also considerable know-how and expertise. This technology and know-how are necessary to produce a reliable machine capable of both operating continuously and maintaining an aseptic environment under dairy conditions. Only such machines will produce packaged liquids of the necessary quality and shelf life."[161]

---

160   Recital 100 of the judgment.   161   Recital 23 of the decision.

In 1981 the public National Research and Development Council (NRDC) assigned to Novus Corp. (a member of the Liquipak Group) an exclusive license for patents and know-how relevant to a certain aseptic filling process for a period of seven years. "It was agreed that the licensor would regard sympathetically a request for continuation of the period of exclusivity provided the licensee had made its best endeavors to meet demand and that such extension did not infringe Article 85. The NRDC retained the right to review the terms of the license in the event of a takeover of the licensee that could operate against the public interest."[162] In 1983 Novus Corp. assigned the license (within its same group) to Liquipak International BV, who dealt with R&D in the field of filling equipment. In 1986 Tetra acquired Liquipak International Inc. a manufacturer and marketer of machines for filling cartons, and in the frame of the same operation, Tetra also acquired Liquipak International BV (and the related exclusive license).

Next to the aseptic packaging system licensed by NRDC, there were at the time of that takeover no other aseptic packaging systems suitable for paper-based cartons but those developed by Tetra Pak and its only competitors PKL (based on the same sterilization process).

b. Origin of the case

On 23 and 26 June 1986 two complaints were filed to the Commission pursuant to Article 3 of Regulation No. 17 by Elopak Group. It complained that Tetra Pak and its associated companies had infringed Article 101 and 102 FEU Treaty. On 24 February 1987 the Commission decided to initiate proceedings.

c. Economic analysis

The analysis made by the Commission is relevant because it addresses the question of raising entry barriers (i.e. abusing the dominant position) by means of the acquisition of an exclusive license and thus a way of strengthening an already existing dominant position. In this decision, the Commission therefore considered the acquisition not only as an abuse of a dominant position but as an *absolute barrier to entry* which was abusive and therefore illegally raising entry barriers

The Commission stated that "[t]his acquisition [of the exclusive license] not only strengthened Tetra's very considerable dominance but also had the effect of preventing, or at very least considerably delaying, the entry of a new competitor into a market where very little if any competition is found."[163]

The Commission applied in this decision the so-called *Continental Can* doctrine of the abusive nature of strengthening an already existing dominant position by means of a takeover of a competitor.[164] In the particular circumstances of the case, the acquisition by Tetra Pak of an important technology *de facto* eliminated all remaining competition on the market and made potential competition in the future very unlikely.

Nowadays this case would be assessed under the Merger Regulation and not under Article 102, but the decision is still relevant because it is indicative of the

---

162   Recital 6 of the decision.
163   Recital 46 of the decision.
164   See Case 6/72 *Continental Can* [1973] ECR 215. See also, *infra*, chapter 8.

Commission's approach toward any possible entry barriers raised in an already dominated market and thus toward the exclusion of remaining competitors. The focus the Commission put on the offsetting effect that market entry can potentially have on attempts of monopolization is particular important.

"Technology [was] the key to entering the market for aseptic milk packaging machines. Technology for the sterilization of cartons (which is the object of the ... patent) is a vital element of the technology necessary to produce aseptic milk packaging machines. The acquisition therefore strengthened Tetra's dominance of the existing competition by reinforcing its technical advantages *vis-à-vis* the minimal competition that remains ... The impact of this acquisition on the market was not hypothetical but very real. The effect in the circumstances of this case was to preclude the possibility of any new competition ... Tetra thereby raised considerably or even insurmountably the barriers to entry. The effect of blocking or delaying the entry of a new competitor is all the more serious in a market such as the present one already dominated by Tetra because a new entrant is virtually the only way at the present time in which Tetra's power over the market could be challenged."[165]

d. Fines, remedies, and conditions enclosed
None.

e. Further developments of the case
Case T-51/89 *Tetra Pak* v. *Commission* [1990] ECR II-309, appeal dismissed.

The CFI (now "the General Court") ruled that "... the presence on the markets in aseptic machines and cartons of only one competitor of Tetra Pak ... and the existence of technological barriers and numerous patents preventing new competitors from entering the market in aseptic machines, contributed to maintaining and strengthening Tetra Pak's dominant position both on the market in aseptic machines and on that in aseptic cartons. Even though ... it was technically possible for competitors to enter the market in aseptic cartons, the lack of available aseptic machines primarily due to Tetra Pak" s policy of tied sales was in practise a serious barrier to access to the market by new competitors."[166]

F.3 *Magill TV Guide/ITP, BBC, and RTE* Commission decision 89/205/EEC [1989] OJ L 78/43

Relevance: In this decision the Commission stated its position toward the relation between IP rights and dominant position. It also clarified the scope of applicability of the *essential facilities doctrine* to IP rights. The case saw a dominant firm restricting entry in a (potential) market for a new product and reserving that market for itself by means of refusing to supply an essential facility.

- Case IV/31.851
- **Decision:** Infringement of Article 102 FEU Treaty
- **Decision addressee(s):**
    - Independent Television Publications Ltd, *United Kingdom*
    - British Broadcasting Corporation, *United Kingdom*
    - BBC Enterprises Ltd, *United Kingdom*

---

165   Recital 47 of the decision.   166   Recital 110 of the judgment.

     – Radio Telefis Eireann, *Ireland*
- **Report route:** Complaints lodged with the Commission on 4 April 1986
- **Date of the decision:** 26 July 1988
- **Competition Commissioner:** P. Sutherland
- **Relevant product market:** Weekly television programmes listing and TV guides
- **Relevant geographical market:** Ireland and Northern Ireland
- **Description of the case**
  a. **Relevant facts**

  Television in the United Kingdom and Ireland was provided by satellite channels and the British Broadcasting Corporation (BBC) and ITV. ITV content was provided by several private contractors, in turn franchised by the Independent Broadcasting Authority (IBA) and Radio Telefis Eireann (RTE). Independent Television Publications Ltd (ITP) was the publisher of journals dealing with the programmes offered by independent television in the United Kingdom (i.e. the programmes offered by ITV).

  The competitor Magill TV Guide Ltd (Magill) was established in order to publish a weekly magazine containing information about the forthcoming TV programmes broadcast by all the channels available for viewers on the Irish and Northern Irish markets. "Following injunctions obtained by ITP, BBC, and RTE, restraining Magill from publishing their advance weekly television listings pending full national proceedings on the right to publish this material, Magill . . . ceased its publishing activities."[167]

  All the above-mentioned broadcasters provided on request the daily newspapers in Ireland and Northern Ireland with weekly listing of the forthcoming TV programmes free of charge in order to advertise their TV programmes. The right of the newspapers to publish that information was restricted by the copyrights protecting the program scheduling. They were bound by the copyright notice accompanying the transmission of the information defining the limit within which the publishers were permitted to reproduce the information.[168]

  At the same time, there was no comprehensive weekly TV guides available on the Irish and Northern Irish markets. Magill's attempt lasted only for a brief period before being interrupted for the reasons stated above. Nonetheless, all the mentioned broadcasters used to publish their individual weekly TV guide, which in the case of BBC and ITP TV guides (*TV Times* and *Radio Times*) were biggest selling weekly journals in the United Kingdom.[169]

  b. **Allegation**

  On 4 April 1986 a complaint was filed to the Commission pursuant to Article 3 of Regulation 17 by Magill. It claimed that ITP, BBC, and RTE had infringed Article 102 FEU Treaty. On 16 December 1987 the Commission decided to initiate proceedings.

  c. **Economic analysis**

  This decision represents a landmark case in EU competition law enforcement for several reasons. It clarified the approach of the Commission toward the relation between intellectual property rights (IPRs) and a dominant position

---

167   Recital 5 of the decision.   169   See recitals 15–18 of the decision.
168   See recitals 8–14 of the decision.

and, at the same time, the scope of applicability of the *essential facilities doctrine* in the sphere of IPRs before further Commission interventions in similar contexts.

The three TV broadcasters were accused of having abused their dominant position on the TV market by denying potential competitors access to a different and new market with likely consumer demand. In effect, the dominant firms refused to supply the program scheduling necessary for access to the market for TV guides which represented the essential facility that gave them control over the downstream market and the opportunity to raise insurmountable entry barriers.

"The impossibility for publishers to produce and publish a comprehensive TV guide result[ed] from the refusal of ITP, BBC and RTE to permit the publication of advance weekly listings as well as from the legal proceedings which ITP, BBC, and RTE institute[d] against those publishers not respecting the terms of the licenses granted and those not granted licenses at all ... Thus, ITP, BBC, and RTE prevent[ed] the meeting of a substantial potential demand existing on the market for comprehensive TV guides."[170] The exclusionary purpose of those practises, as well as their detrimental effect for consumers, for the Commission was clear. It stated that "the ... policies and practises of ITP, BBC, and RTE [were] intended to protect and ha[d] the effect of protecting the position of their individual TV guides, which do not compete with one another or with any other guides. In this connection the Commission considers that the three undertakings [were] perfectly capable ... of playing a major role on the market for comprehensive weekly TV guides, if they so wish[ed] ... By limiting the scope of their licensing policies so as to prevent the production and sale of comprehensive TV guides, however, they restrict competition to the prejudice of consumers ... The Commission takes the view that ... undertakings in a dominant position ... which use that position to prevent the introduction on to the market of a new product ... abuse that dominant position ... A further element of the abuse is that, by virtue of their ... policies and practises, ITP, BBC, and RTE, ... retain[ed] for themselves also the derivative market for weekly TV guides, a market upon which competition could otherwise take place, particularly in relation to weekly comprehensive guides."[171]

From an economic perspective, cases such as *Magill* relate to absolute barriers to entry which constitute an abuse not only on the market where the dominant position is held, but also on a related/dependent market. The Commission established with this decision that under specific circumstances an IPR can be considered as an *essential facility*. Those circumstances were found firstly in the indispensability of the license for carrying out the business in question, secondly in the introduction of a new product in case of granted access to the *facility*, thirdly in the absence of a justification in terms of superior interests to be protected and fourthly in the exclusion of all competition on the derivative market in case of refusal to grant access to the essential facility.

---

170   Recital 23 of the decision. The Commission also specified that the existence of a *substantial potential demand* was derivable from the advantages offered by an omni-comprehensive guide compared with a several distinct guides (also in terms of money savings), from the possibility to offer that product at a reasonable price, and from the experience derived from other Member States.
171   Recital 23 of the decision.

d. Fines, remedies, and conditions enclosed

- Obligations for ITP, BBC, and RTE to bring without delay the infringements to an end.
- Obligation for ITP, BBC, and RTE to supply each other and third parties on request and on a non-discriminatory basis with their individual advanced weekly program listings and to do so requiring, if any, reasonable royalties.
- Obligation for ITP, BBC, and RTE to submit to the Commission for approval proposals of the terms upon which they considered third parties should be permitted to publish the advance weekly program listings.

e. Further developments of the case

Case T-69/89 *RTE* v. *Commission* [1991] ECR II-485, appeal dismissed.

Case T-76/89 *ITP* v. *Commission* [1991] ECR II-575, appeal dismissed.

Joined Cases C-241/91 and 242/91 *RTE, and ITP* v. *Commission* [1995] ECR I-743, CFI judgments upheld. In particular, the ECJ held that the refusal by the owner of an IPR to grant a license cannot in itself constitute abuse of a dominant position.[172] However the exercise of an exclusive right by the proprietor may, in exceptional circumstances, involve abusive conduct.[173]

These circumstances were found in the fact that: (i) the refusal in question concerned a product, the supply of which was indispensible for carrying on the business in question,[174] (ii) such refusal prevented the appearance of a new product for which there was potential consumer demand,[175] (iii) it was not justified by objective considerations,[176] and that (iv) it was likely to exclude all competition in the secondary market for television guides.[177]

F.4   *Microsoft* Commission decision 2007/53/EC, summary of decision published in [2007] OJ L 32/23

Relevance: The Microsoft case is one of the most well-known European abuse of dominance cases. Microsoft was accused of infringing Article 102 on the grounds of both tying and refusal to supply interoperability information. The fine in the decision, at the time it was issued, was the highest fine ever given to a single firm: 497.2 million Euros, but this was further increased by 280.5 million Euros in 2006 and by 899 million Euros in 2008 for non-compliance. The decision was upheld by CFI (now "the General Court") in 2007. The case is a landmark decision with regard to dominant companies having to allow competition, in particular in high-tech industries.

- Case COMP/C-3/37.792
- **Decision:** Infringement of Article 102 FEU Treaty. The infringement is by (a) refusing to supply interoperability information and allowing its use for the purpose of developing and distributing server operating system products and (b) tying the Windows Media Player with the Windows PC Operating System.
- **Decision addressee(s):** Microsoft Corporation, *United States*
- **Report route:** The Commission received a complaint by Sun Microsystems on 10 December 1998. The Commission initiated proceedings on 1 August 2000. The

---

172   Recital 49 of the judgment.
173   Recital 50 of the judgment.
174   Recital 53 of the judgment.

175   Recital 54 of the judgment.
176   Recital 55 of the judgment.
177   Recital 56 of the judgment.

Commission was also concerned about the Windows Media Player (WMP) and, on its own initiative, started proceedings on 29 August 2001 on that matter. The two proceedings were joined in one case.

* **Date of the decision:** 24 March 2004
* **Competition Commissioner:** M. Monti
* **Relevant product market:** PC operating systems, work group server operating systems (for PCs linked together in networks), media players
* **Relevant geographical market:** Worldwide
* **Description of the case**
  a. **Relevant facts**

    Microsoft is a software company, employing some 55,000 people around the world, and one of the largest companies in the world in terms of market capitalization. Sun Microsystems is a provider of network computing infrastructure solutions and employs some 36,100 people around the world. Both companies are present in each of the EEA countries. Sun Microsystems sent a complaint to the Commission on 10 December 1998. It argued that Microsoft enjoyed a dominant position as a supplier of PC operating systems and accused the company of infringing Article 102. It claimed that Microsoft reserved to itself essential information that network computing software products (work group server operating systems) need to interoperate fully with Microsoft PC operating systems. "According to Sun, the withheld interoperability information is necessary to viably compete as a work group server operating system supplier."[178] On 1 August 2000 the Commission initiated proceedings by sending the first Statement of Objections to Microsoft.

    In the meantime (February 2000), the Commission had launched an investigation into Microsoft's conduct on its own initiative. This investigation concentrated upon Microsoft's Windows 2000 generation of PC and work group server operating systems and Microsoft's incorporation of the WMP into its PC operating system products. The two cases were joined. The Commission used market enquiries to gather information and sent requests for information to seventy-five companies (seventy-one responded) using PC and work group server operating systems and to forty-six companies (thirty-three responded) active in areas related to that of the WMP.

    There was already an antitrust case against Microsoft ongoing in the United States. In 1998 the United States and twenty States had filed a case under the Sherman Act against Microsoft. The complaint focused on Microsoft's measures against Netscape's web browser Netscape Navigator and against Sun's Java technologies. There was a threat that Microsoft would have to break itself up, but the United States and Microsoft agreed a settlement on 2 November 2001 that did not include such structural changes.

    There are three relevant product markets discussed in the decision. The first is that of PC operating systems. Microsoft is obviously dominant there with market shares exceeding 90 percent. There are also very high barriers to entry. The second is that of work group server operating systems. Work group server operating systems are operating systems running on central network computers that provide services to office workers around the world in their day-to-day

---

178   Recital 3 of the decision.

work, such as file and printer sharing, security, and user identity management. Microsoft was also found to be a dominant player having some 60–75 percent of the market share. This strong position is enhanced by "strong commercial and technical associative links between the PC operating system market and the work group server operating system market. As a result, Microsoft's dominance over the PC operating system market has a significant impact on the adjacent market for operating systems for work group servers."[179] The third relevant product market is that of media players. A media player is a software product that is able to play back music and video content over the Internet. This product market is a bit different, "the market for streaming media players is not examined as a market where Microsoft might occupy a dominant position at the date of adoption of this Decision, but as a reference market in which to locate the products and vendors that are foreclosed by Microsoft's tying of WMP."[180]

b. Origin of the case

The Commission received a complaint by Sun Microsystems on 10 December 1998 and initiated proceeding on 1 August 2000. The Commission was also concerned about the WMP and, on its own initiative, started proceedings on 29 August 2001 on that matter. The two proceedings were joined in one case.

The Commission accused Microsoft of breaking EU competition law by leveraging its near-monopoly in the market for PC operating systems onto the markets for work group server operating systems and for media players. That is, Microsoft has abused its market power by deliberately restricting interoperability between Windows PCs and non-Microsoft work group servers, and by tying its WMP, a product where it faced competition, with its Windows operating system. This illegal conduct had enabled Microsoft to acquire a dominant position in the market for work group server operating systems, which are at the heart of corporate IT networks, and risked eliminating competition altogether in that market. Microsoft's conduct had also significantly weakened competition on the media player market. The ongoing abuses limited innovation and harmed the competitive process and consumers, having less choice and facing higher prices.

c. Economic analysis

There are two key issues of abuse of dominance in this case. These are refusal to supply (interoperability) and tying. We first discuss refusal to supply. Microsoft had refused Sun information that would enable that company to design work group server operating systems that would fully interoperate with Windows PCs and servers. Microsoft presented IP claims, but for one thing "in order to allow Sun to provide for such seamless integration, Microsoft only had to provide specifications of the relevant protocols, that is to say, technical documentation, and not to give access to the software code of Windows, let alone to allow its reproduction by Sun."[181] Microsoft's refusal to supply was also not limited to Sun, but part of a more general pattern of conduct. The non-disclosures by Microsoft appeared part of a broader strategy designed to shut competitors out of the market. The refusal was also a change in conduct because previously analogous information had been made available to Sun and other companies.

---

179   Recital 17 of the decision.   181   Recital 18 of the decision.
180   Recital 403 of the decision.

The Commission also argued that "disclosure of information of the kind refused by Microsoft was commonplace in the industry."[182] Microsoft's IP claims were also put aside with reference to the Software Directive (Council Directive 91/250/EEC). This Directive restricts the exercise of copyright over software in favor of interoperability.

The second issue was the tying of WMP with the dominant Windows PC operating system. The Commission argued that Windows and WMP were two separate products, but that Microsoft did not give customers the choice to obtain Windows without WMP. This tying was foreclosing competition. The market data already showed an increase in the market share of WMP to the detriment of competing media players. The decision emphasized that "on the basis of the case law of the Court, the Commission is, in particular, not required to prove that competition has already been foreclosed or that there is a risk of the elimination of all competition to establish a tying abuse. Otherwise, antitrust scrutiny in certain software markets would come too late as evidence of market impact could only be demonstrated once the market had 'tipped'."[183] The tying of WMP with the Windows PC operating system artificially reduced the incentives for music, film, and other media companies, as well software developers and content providers, to develop their offerings to competing media players. As a result, Microsoft's tying of its media player product has the effect of foreclosing the market to competitors, and hence ultimately reducing consumer choice, since competing products were set at a disadvantage which was not related to their price or quality.

d. Fines, remedies, and conditions enclosed

- The Commission imposed on Microsoft a total fine of 497,196,304 Euros.
- Microsoft shall within 120 days make the interoperability information available to any undertaking having an interest in developing and distributing work group server operating system products and shall, on reasonable and non-discriminatory terms, allow the use of the interoperability information by such undertakings for this purpose. The information has to be kept updated on an ongoing basis and in a timely matter.
- Microsoft shall within 90 days offer a fully-functioning version of the Windows Client PC Operating System which does not incorporate the Windows Media Player. Microsoft retains the right to offer a bundle of the Windows Client PC Operating System and Windows Media Player.

e. Further developments of the case

Case T-201/04, *Microsoft* v. *Commission* [2007] ECR II-3601, appeal dismissed.

Pending the appeal, Microsoft did not comply with the decision. In particular, Microsoft did not disclose complete and accurate documentation that would allow competing work group servers to achieve full interoperability with Windows PCs and servers.

---

182   Recital 21 of the summary decision.   183   Recital 28 of the summary decision.

For that reason, on 15 December 2005 the Commission ordered Microsoft to fully comply with the decision and imposed a periodic penalty of 2 million Euros per day if the company did not.

On 12 July 2006 the Commission imposed a further 280.5 million Euros fine on Microsoft, for non-compliance with the decision in the time period from 16 December 2005 to 20 June 2006. In addition, the periodic penalty for non-compliance was increased to 3 million Euros per day.

After the CFI, on 17 September 2007, had upheld the Commission decision, on 22 October 2007 Microsoft announced that it would comply and not appeal the decision any longer. Still, there was a further fine for the period of non-compliance between 21 June 2006 and 21 October 2007. This fine amounted to 899 million Euros and was issued on 27 February 2008.

In January 2009 the European Commission announced that it would investigate the bundling by Microsoft of Internet Explorer with Windows Operating Systems. Microsoft was accused of tying and again of abuse of its dominant position. A statement of objections was sent to Microsoft on 15 January 2009. On 16 December 2009, the Commission adopted a decision rendering legally binding commitments offered by Microsoft. In particular, Microsoft committed to offer users of Windows choice among different browsers and to allow computer manufacturers and users the possibility to turn Internet Explorer off. Such a decision formally closed the proceedings.

F.5   *AstraZeneca* Commission decision 2006/857/EC [2005], OJ L 332/24

Relevance: For the first time, the Commission stated that misusing rules and procedures when applying for patents, in order to delay competitors' entry into the market, can constitute an abuse of a dominant position.

- Case COMP/A.37.507/F3
- **Decision:** Infringement of Article 102 FEU Treaty
- **Decision addressee(s):**
  - AstraZeneca AB, *United Kingdom*
  - AstraZeneca Plc, *United Kingdom*
- **Report route:** Joint complaints lodged with the Commission on 12 May 1999
- **Date of the decision:** 15 June 2005
- **Competition Commissioner:** N. Kroes
- **Relevant product market:** Oral formulation of prescription PPIs products (so-called proton-pump inhibitors)
- **Relevant geographical market:** National market in Belgium, Denmark, Germany, Norway, Sweden, the Netherlands, the United Kingdom.
- **Description of the case**
  - a. **Relevant facts**
    The Anglo-Swedish pharmaceutical and healthcare group AstraZeneca brought a new generation of medicine to treat acid-related diseases on to the market. The medicine, called Losec, prevents acid from being pumped into the stomach by means of a specific enzyme. Losec belongs to a class of medicines known as PPIs.[184]

---

184   Proton-pump inhibitors (PPIs) are used for the prevention and long-lasting reduction of gastric acid production. They are the most potent inhibitors of acid secretion available today.

The pharmaceutical sector is heavily regulated, on both the national and on the Community level. To ensure, that only safely proved medicines are marketed in the EU, companies have to apply for a market authorisation. This authorisation can be acquired by the European Medicines Agency (EMA) (centralized procedure) or by the reference Member State (decentralized procedure). After the Committee for Medical Products for Human Use has examined the application pursuant to Article 3 of Regulation No. 762/04, the EMA will issue a market authorisation which is valid for the entire Community. If the reference Member State has issued a market authorisation, an authorisation for the remaining Member States can be received by the mutual recognition procedure laid down in the Regulation.

For generic drugs an abridged procedure to receive market authorisation exists. According to the provisions laid down in Article 4(3) point 8(a)(iii) of Council Directive 65/65[185] a market authorization or an import license can be obtained if the generic is *essentially similar* to the reference product, the *data exclusivity* of the reference product has expired or the original product was authorized and *marketed* in the Member States in which its application is filed.[186]

Furthermore, a pharmaceutical company expects to receive a patent on certain innovations which lasts for up to twenty years. Patent protection is intended to guarantee the recoupment of the R&D investments and a reward for the company's innovative efforts. In order to receive a national or a European patent companies can apply to the national authorities or to the European Patent Office (EPO) which is based in Munich. In addition, in the Community a company can apply for extra protection for pharmaceutical products via Supplementary Protection Certificates (SPCs) under European law that last up to five years after the expiration of the patent. The SPC can also be granted by national authorities but not by the EPO. The SPC regulation[187] contained a transitional period to allow drugs that had gained market authorisation before the coming into force of the regulation but after 1 of January 1985 to get an SPC. However the appointed date was not uniformly applied across the Community.[188]

The Commission accused AstraZeneca of having changed the date of its first market authorisation and thus abused the rules and procedures of the national medicines agencies issuing a market authorisation. The company thus achieved extended patent protection for Losec.

The second abuse by AstraZeneca was found in the selective market deregistration for Losec capsules. Hereby, AstraZeneca intended to block or delay entry by generic firms and parallel traders.

---

185 Council Directive 65/65/EEC of 26 January 1965 on the approximation of provisions laid down by Law, Regulation or Administrative Action relating to proprietary medicinal products, [1965] OJ 22/369, repealed by Article 10 of Directive 2001/83/EC of the European Parliament and of the Council of 6 November 2001 on the Community code relating to medicinal products for human use [2001] OJ L 311/67.

186 See recital 260–261 of the decision.

187 Council Regulation No. 1768/92 of 18 June 1992 concerning the creation of a supplementary protection certificate for medical products, [1992] OJ L 198/1.

188 See Article 19(2) and (3) of Regulation 1768/92; the appointed date for Italy and Belgium was 1 January 1982 while for Denmark and Germany it was 1 January 1988.

b. Origin of the case

On 12 May 1999 a joint complaint was filed to the Commission by Generics (UK) Limited and Scandinavian Pharmaceuticals Generics AB (both part of Merck Generics). They claimed that AstraZeneca had abused its dominant position.

c. Economic analysis

The Commission concluded that AstraZeneca held a dominant position on the product market for oral formulations of PPIs. The definition of the relevant market is important to identify possible competitors which are able to constrain the undertaking's behaviour, prevent it from acting independently from competitive pressure, and further to limit the commission's field of investigation.[189]

The definition of the relevant product market contained in the decision is decisive because it concerns the pharmaceutical market and takes into account the distructiveness of this sector compared to other industries. Firstly, there consists a high degree of public regulation and further a classification system that groups products according to their functional interchangeability, additionally, on the demand side, doctors and not consumers themselves make the key decision which medicine to buy.[190]

Thus, the Commission showed that product price is not the only relevant factor in defining the relevant product market in the pharmaceutical sector. Therefore, the product characteristic – i.e. its therapeutic use and price pattern substitutability – constitute the determining factors. The Commission considered that the prescription of PPIs constitutes a separate product market in every analysis of each market because it "faced no significant competitive constraints from H2 blockers or other products used for treatment of acid-related . . . diseases."[191]

Further, the dominant position of AstraZeneca was identified by the Commission, considering its high market shares, high price of Losec compared to other PPIs, and the patent protecting the capsule formulation of PPI medicines. Moreover, the health authorities according to the Commission were not deemed to dispose of significant buyer power.

The decision states that according to settled case law the application of high market shares is an important parameter in the pharmaceutical sector.[192] Thus, market shares ranging from 75 percent to 87 percent were deemed to prove dominance without further analysis.[193] The Commission applied a country-by-country analysis and found that AstraZeneca's market shares were high over the entire period in the countries concerned.

AstraZeneca was found guilty of two abuses of its dominant position. Firstly, the company had given misleading presentations pursuant to the provisions contained in the SPC Regulation (Article 19) to patent agents, patent offices, and national courts in order to acquire or preserve SPCs for omeprazole.

---

189   See Commission Notice on the definition of the relevant market for the purposes of Community competition law [1997] OJ C 372/3
190   See recital 362 of the decision.
191   See recital 504 of the decision.
192   See recital 515 of the decision.
193   See Case C-85/76 *Hoffmann – La Roche* v. *Commission* [1979], recitals 39 and 41.

AstraZeneca changed the date of its first market authorization in its application for SPC, and hence could obtain SPCs in Germany and Denmark.

In addition, the Commission stated that the concept of abuses does not only apply to behavior in the market but also to the use of public procedures and regulations, i.e. also administrative and judicial processes.[194] Moreover, the Commission clarified that Article 102 FEU Treaty applies also to the ownership of IPRs. The EU rules of competition and remedies still apply although the SPC Regulation provides specific remedies.[195] Nevertheless, "the mere possession and enforcement of a patent or any other intellectual property right against a competitor does not, in principle, violate Article 82 EC Treaty."[196]

The second abuse was found in deregistering Losec capsules in Sweden, Denmark, and Norway after launching a new tablet form for Losec. As shown by internal documents, this approach was intended to prevent entry of generics and parallel trade because generics and parallel trade of products depend on a market authorisation of the original reference product. The Commission acknowledged the commercial freedom of a company when it says "that single acts involving the launch, withdrawal, or requests for deregistration of a pharmaceutical product would not normally be regarded as an abuse."[197] Nevertheless such a business decision should also not contain competitive constraints nor result in foreclosure effects in the market.

The Commission rejected the company's arguments that the legal uncertainty of Community competition law served as an objective justification. It was expected that a major undertaking should hold knowledge or a high degree of awareness of antitrust laws.[198]

d. Fines, remedies, and conditions enclosed

The Commission imposed:
  - On AstraZeneca AB and AstraZeneca Pltc, a total fine of 46,000,000 Euros.
  - On AstraZeneca AB a fine of 14,000,000 Euros.

e. Further developments of the case

Case T-321/05 *AstraZeneca* v. *Commission*, pending

3.7 Refusal to deal and essential facilities doctrine

A Introduction

Each firm is free to choose its business partners and customers to supply. This lies at the very foundation of the freedom of enterprise. Compulsory dealing is usually not subject to contract law. Some competition concerns may nonetheless arise in case of dominant firms refusing to supply certain customers. Through a refusal to supply, an undertaking may attempt to maintain or acquire market power. In particular this strategy can be used to raise entry barriers, to discriminate among customers, or to exclude competitors from downstream markets. This practice, in particular when essential facilities are involved, may result in irreversible exclusion

---

194 See recital 743 of the decision.
195 See recital 744 of the decision.
196 See recital 741 of the decision.

197 See recital 792 of the decision.
198 See recital 904 of the decision.

from the market for firms being denied access to an essential facility at the dominant firm's disposal. Common examples of essential facilities are ports and airport infrastructures, but they may also include IP. It is often difficult to determine conclusively that a certain good or a service is indeed essential for carrying out a certain business. If it is, complex considerations underlie decisions as to whether access should be granted and a refusal to grant access would constitute an abuse of dominance.[199]

For a certain asset to be considered an "essential facility," it is typically required that it is irreproducible or reproducible only under uneconomical conditions. Often a facility is considered essential when viable alternatives to enter the market are lacking or there exists excess capacity in the facility so that granting access would not impose an unreasonable financial burden on the dominant firm. It is also important to distinguish cases in which the ownership of the essential facility is the result of firm's own risk and investment or merely the result of legal monopolies – such as for airports slots before the liberalization of the air transport. In the former case, access should probably be granted more carefully than in the latter.

In some cases, the Commission and the European judicature have considered abusive refusals to supply that did not imply an essential facility. Refusal to supply has been deemed abusive, *inter alia*, where it implied unfair and exclusionary supplying conditions,[200] when it was a retaliatory strategy to punish a customer and protect the dominant firm's commercial interests,[201] or when it implied the refusal to supply a dominant firm's with spare parts for the product distributed.[202]

B Applicable EU legislation

No special legislation applicable. For applicable legislation see chapter 3, paragraph B.

C Related economics texts

Bishop and Walker (2009), paragraphs 3.24–3.25 and 6.119–6.139
Carlton and Perloff (2005), chapter 19, paragraph 4
Church and Ware (2000), not specifically discussed
Martin (1994), not specifically discussed
Martin (2002), not specifically discussed
Motta (2004), paragraphs 2.5.2 and 7.3.4
Tirole (1988), not specifically discussed
Waldman and Jensen (2001), not specifically discussed

---

199   In Bronner (Case C-7/97), the ECJ listed four elements which need to be present before the refusal could constitute an abuse. "... it would still be necessary ... not only that the refusal of the service comprised in home delivery be likely to eliminate all competition in the daily newspaper market on the part of the person requesting the service and that such refusal be incapable of being objectively justified, but also that the service in itself be indispensable to carrying on that person's business, inasmuch as there is no actual or potential substitute in existence for that home-delivery scheme" (recital 41 of the judgment).
    Moreover the ECJ held that "For such access to be capable of being regarded as indispensable, it would be necessary at the very least to establish ... that it is not economically viable to create a second home-delivery scheme for the distribution of daily newspapers with a circulation comparable to that of the daily newspapers distributed by the existing scheme" (recital 46 of the judgment).
200   *Eurofix – Bauco/Hilti* Commission decision 88/138/EEC [1988] OJ L 65/19, Cases IV/30.787, 31.488 (described in sections 3.0 and 3.7) and *Napier Brown/British Sugar* Commission decision 88/518/EEC [1988] OJ L 284/41, Case IV/30.178 (described in section 3.4).
201   *Chiquita* Commission decision 76/353/EEC [1976] OJ L 95/1, Case IV/26.699.
202   *Hugin/Liptons* Commission decision 78/68/EEC [1978] OJ L 22/23, Case IV/29.132.

D Related legal texts

Bellamy and Child (2008), chapter 10, paragraph 4 (F, ii)
Jones and Sufrin (2008), chapter 7, paragraph 7(E)
Ritter and Braun (2005), chapter 5, paragraph D(3, b)
Whish (2008), chapter 17, paragraph 4

E Commission decisions in chronological order•203

ZOJA/CSC-ICI, Commercial Solvents Commission decision 72/457/EEC [1972] OJ L 299/51, Case IV/26.911

Chiquita **Commission decision 76/353/EEC [1976] OJ L 95/1, Case IV/26.699** (Bishop and Walker, 2009, 2.03, 3.46, 4.27, 4.3, 6.04, 6.14–6.17; Martin, 1994, pp. 102–3, 417, 438; Motta, 2004, pp. 35, 118, 499)

ABG/Oil Companies Commission decision 77/327/EEC [1977] OJ L 117/1, Case IV/28.841

Hugin/Liptons Commission decision 78/68/EEC [1978] OJ L 22/23, Case IV/29.132 (Bishop and Walker, 2009, 4.46, 6.21)

British Leyland Commission decision 84/379/EEC [1984] OJ L 307/11, Case IV/30.615 (Martin, 1994, p. 438)

Eurofix – Bauco/Hilti Commission decision 88/138/EEC [1988] OJ L 65/19, Cases IV/30.787, 31.488 **(described in detail as landmark case in sections 3.2 and 3.6)** (Bishop and Walker, 2009, 6.064; Martin, 1994, p. 449)

Napier Brown/British Sugar Commission decision 88/518/EEC [1988] OJ L 284/41, Case IV/30.178 **(described in detail as landmark case in section 3.5)**

Magill TV Guide/ITP, BBC, and RTE **Commission decision 89/205/EEC [1989] OJ L 78/43, Case IV/31.851** (Bishop and Walker, 2009, 6.130, 6.131; Motta, 2004, p. 68)

British Midland/Aer Lingus **Commission decision 92/213/EEC [1993] OJ L 96/34, Case IV/33.544**

Sea Containers/Stena Line Commission decision 94/19/EEC [1994] OJ L 15/8, Case IV/34.689 (Bishop and Walker, 2009, 6.121, 6.128–6.130; Motta, 2004, p. 67)

Frankfurt Airport Commission decision 98/190/EC [1998] OJ L 72/30, Case IV/34.801

Deutsche Post AG – Interception of cross-border mail Commission decision 2001/892/EC [2001] OJ L 331/40, Case COMP/C-1/36.915

GVG/FS Commission decision 2004/33/EC [2004] OJ L 11/17, Case COMP/37.685

Microsoft **Commission decision of 24 March 2004, published on DG Comp website, Case COMP/C-3/37.792** (Bishop and Walker, 2009, 6.73–6.82, 6.117, 6.134)

Clearstream Commission decision of 2 June 2004, published on DG Comp website, Case COMP/38.096

• Decisions displayed in **bold type** are described in the section. Decisions highlighted with (*) include interesting economic analysis by the Commission on the specific topic of the section. Some decisions contain economic reasoning on more than one topic and therefore appear in several lists of Commission decisions in chronological order. Reference is made in brackets and **bold type** to the relevant section in which the decision is extensively described as a landmark case. When decisions are referenced and/or described in some detail in one or more of the economic textbooks, reference in brackets is also made to the relevant part(s) of those texts.

203 Issues of essential facilities are also central in some of the decisions addressed to Member States pursuant to Article 106 FEU Treaty. In those cases a public facility was the object of the Commission's concern. These decisions are listed in chapter 7.

F   Economic landmark cases

F.1   *Chiquita* Commission decision 76/353/EEC [1976] OJ L 95/1

Relevance: In the above described landmark decision the Commission adopted the approach that refusal to supply used as a means to punish a well-established customer for its commercial behavior and to induce a loyalty effect for other customers, particularly where against the same commercial interest of the dominant firm, constitutes an abuse of dominance.

- For case report, relevant market, relevant facts, allegation, obligations, fines and remedies, and further development of the case see Case *F.1* in section *3.1*.
  #### c.   Economic analysis
  Among the several abuses committed by UBC in the frame of its contested commercial policy, the Commission found abusive its refusal to continue to supply its second-largest distributor/ripener in Denmark, Olesen. This commercial conduct was adopted by UBC in response to Olesen becoming the exclusive distributor of the competing banana brand Dole in Denmark and for having run a strong advertising campaign for that competing brand.

  What is interesting about this part of the decision is the Commission's attention to the loyalty effect and the consequent exclusionary effects that a similar behavior would have caused on UBC competitors. On the one side, the refusal to supply Olesen with Chiquita bananas directly damaged the business interests of the firm concerned. Simultaneously, considering Chiquita's importance on the market and its indispensability for many ripeners/distributors, "[t]his would discourage it and other distributors/ripeners from selling competing brands any more, or at least from participating in advertising and sales promotion campaigns for such brands, as is normally the practise in this field. In this manner UBC succeed[ed] in keeping its principal distributor/ripeners within its own marketing network and in preventing its competitors from having access to them."[204]

  UBC's attempts to justify its refusal to supply bananas were not considered persuasive by the Commission firstly because not proportional to Olesen conduct and secondly because the effect that it produced on the market, as a consequence of the *de facto* prohibition to advertise competing brands, was to hamper the effective selling of a competing brand. The Commission stated that "a buyer must be allowed the freedom to decide what are his business interests, to choose the products he will sell, even if they are in competition with each other; in effect to determine his own sales policy. When dealing with a supplier in a dominant position, such buyer may well find it worthwhile to sell several competing products, including those of the dominant firm, and to advertise them, but to an extent which he must remain free to decide for himself."[205]

F.2   *Magill TV Guide/ITP, BBC, and RTE* Commission decision 89/205/EEC [1989] OJ L 78/43

Relevance: As described above, in this decision the Commission recognised, under specific circumstances, IPR as essential facility. Therefore, refusal to supply constitutes an abuse

204   Recital II-A-3-d of the decision.   205   *Idem.*

of dominance because that strategy produces foreclosure effects on the derivative (potential) market.

- See Case *F.3* in section *3.6*.

F.3 *British Midland/Aer Lingus* Commission decision 92/213/EEC [1993] OJ L 96/34

Relevance: In the decision the effects of an economically unjustified refusal to supply by a dominant undertaking producing undue effects on competitor's costs necessary to enter the market and on their revenues are described, as well as the exclusionary effects produced. This is the first decision in which the Commission applied the (quasi-) essential facilities doctrine to the air transport sector that were the object of several further Commission interventions in the frame of the liberalization process.

- Case IV/33.544
- **Decision:** Infringement of Article 102 FEU Treaty
- **Decision addressee(s):**
  - Aer Lingus plc, *Ireland*
- **Report route:** Complaints lodged with the Commission on 26 April 1990
- **Date of the decision:** 26 February 1992
- **Competition Commissioner:** L. Brittan
- **Relevant product market:** London (Heathrow)–Dublin air transport service
- **Relevant geographical market:** United Kingdom and Ireland
- **Description of the case**
  #### a. Relevant facts
  Aer Lingus plc (Aer Lingus) is the Irish flagship company. British Midland Airways Limited (British Midland) was at the time of the decision the main operating company of the Airlines of Britain Holdings plc.

  Before 1989 the only two carriers providing the service on the route between Heathrow and Dublin were Aer Lingus (with around 75 percent of passengers carried) and British Airways (with around 25 percent of passengers carried). After having obtained the authorizations British Midland announced in February 1989 its intention to start services on that route.

  As a result of one of the most important IATA achievements, air transport was organized almost completely by interlining and "voluntary changes" agreement among carriers. About 95 percent of worldwide air transport was characterised by such agreements and refusals to an application were rare. Interlining agreements allow airlines to sell seats on their routes. Effectively, one ticket, issued by one carrier, can consist of different route segments or connection flights performed by different airlines. The effect of the "voluntary changes" agreements is that airlines accept a change of ticket at passengers' request even if the change concerns the segment operated by another carrier. The interlining and "voluntary changes" system is highly important to complement the network of each airline and to improve the offer to clients and in particular to frequent and/or business clients, who need a highly interchangeable interconnectivity. It makes it possible for passengers to easily change the reservations, routings, or airlines mentioned on their tickets. Interlining between airlines is also important for travel agents because it allows them to have at their disposal a wider choice of connections in their activity of issuing tickets and because it reduces the possibility of unused tickets which do not give a right to the commission for the agents.

Aer Lingus and British Midland were linked by a reciprocal interlining and "voluntary changes" agreement. Immediately after British Midland's announcement of entering the Heathrow – Dublin route, Aer Lingus announced the termination of its acceptance of interchangeability of tickets with British Midland on that route and thus the end of the existing agreement. Nonetheless, British Midland started its services and achieved a significant 21 percent market share on the route during its second year of activity.[206]

The services offered on the route between London Heathrow and Dublin were considered as a separate product market because, even with the presence of three other main airports in London offering flights to Dublin, for a large number of passengers the other solutions would have not constituted viable alternatives in terms of frequency and range of connections.[207] Given its substantial market share and a number of contributing factors Aer Lingus held a dominant position on that market.[208]

b. Origin of the case

On 26 April 1990 a complaint was filed to the Commission pursuant to Article 3 of Regulation 17 by British Midland. It complained that Aer Lingus had infringed Article 102 FEU Treaty. On 4 June 1991 the Commission decided to initiate proceedings.

c. Economic analysis

In this decision the Commission illustrated specifically for the first time the effects that an unjustified refusal to supply by a dominant undertaking can have on the entry cost borne by the new or small market actors, particularly in a market with existing high entry barriers.

In the particular circumstances of the case, the Commission stated that "[r]efusing to interline is not normal competition on the merit. Interlining has for many years been accepted industry practise, with widely acknowledged benefits for both airlines and passengers. A refusal to interline for other reasons than problems with currency convertibility or doubts about the creditworthiness of the beneficiary airline is a highly unusual step. [T]he argument that interlining would result in a loss of revenue would not in itself make the refusal legitimate. Aer Lingus has not argued that interlining with British Midland would have a significant effect on its own costs, whereas there is evidence that a refusal to interline would impose a significant handicap on British Midland. [The] duty to interline ... would exist in particular when the refusal or withdrawal of interline facilities by a dominant airline is objectively likely to have a significant impact on the other's airline ability to start a new service or sustain an existing service on account of its effects on the other airline's costs and revenue in respect of the service in question ... When an airline commences a new service, it will normally expect to incur some losses during an initial period,

---

206   See recitals 3–9 of the decision.   208   See recitals 18–23 of the decision.
207   See recital 14 of the decision.

during which it will have to organize the economic operation of its service and to attract sufficient interest from the travel trade and from travellers. It cannot expect to attain the load factors and the revenue necessary to ensure profitable operations from the beginning of the service. Therefore new entry will always be difficult. Denying interline facilities is likely to increase that difficulty. A new entrant without interlining facilities is likely to be considered in this respect as a second-rate airline by travel agents and by travellers alike, ... in particular the well-informed business travellers ... who make a disproportionately large contribution to the revenue of the new entrant; significantly reducing this revenue will have a serious effect on the economics of the new entrant's operations."[209]

Analyzing the concrete effects produced by Aer Lingus' refusal, the Commission noted that "British Midland's load factors are appreciably lower than Aer Lingus' on the same route. The difference to a large extent reflects British Midland's handicap in carrying interline passengers. This implies that passengers ... prefer to play safe and use the service of the airline with the highest frequency. The resulting loss of revenue ... may be estimated at several million ECU per year.

A refusal to interline also hinders the maintenance or development of competition when it imposes a significant cost on competitors. If an incumbent airline operates at high frequency on a route accounts for a very large share of capacity, and refuses to interline with a new entrant on that route, the latter will have a choice. It can either start a low frequency service in order to minimize initial losses, but will then face a long unprofitable start-up period. Alternatively a new entrant can operate a high frequency from the beginning, even though this may not be warranted by its initial market share, so as to attract ... travellers who require high frequencies, ... In both situations a new entrant will face higher start-up costs ...

The fact that British Midland has been able to continue operations notwithstanding the handicap imposed on it by Aer Lingus, ... it does not mean that the refusal had no effect on competition ... The lawfulness of the refusal at the time when it occurred cannot depend on whether the competitor was later willing and able to remain on the route in spite of the disadvantage imposed on it ... Aer Lingus has pursued a strategy which (even if not wholly effective) is both selective and exclusionary and restrict[s] the development of competition ... The refusal to interline in this case essentially consist[s] in the imposition, contrary to normal industry practise, of a significant handicap on a competitor by raising its costs and depriving it of revenue."[210]

In the present case, it is difficult to compare the interlining to an *essential facility*. British Midland was trying to enter the same market rather than a downstream market Nonetheless, in hindsight, the Commission's approach in this decision can be seen as the precursor of the decisions adopted, *inter*

209   Recitals 25–28 of the decision.   210   Recitals 28–30 of the decision.

alia, in the air transport industry that explicitly applied the essential facilities doctrine.[211] The Commission did not condemn the refusal to supply as such, but because of its significant effect on competition and the lack of economic justification.

The airline sector has been subject to several Commission investigations besides the present one. This interest was particularly strong in the liberalization period during the 1990s. The Commission investigated several airline carriers but also Member States and their efforts to abolish the national legal monopolies. Various decisions dealt with the issue of airports as *essential facilities* and the problems that arose around the non-discriminatory and exclusive availability of slots, passengers' registration systems, and luggage handling services. The Commission's approach was largely in line with the economic approach to the question and promoted the policy of opening infrastructural essential facilities to competitors that were not the outcome of private investments or R&D but merely the results of legally awarded exclusivity status.[212]

d. **Fines, remedies, and conditions enclosed**
    - The Commission imposed on Aer Lingus plc a total fine of ECU 750,000.
    - Obligations for Aer Lingus plc to bring the infringements to an end.
    - Obligations for Aer Lingus plc to grant British Midland Airways Limited the authority to issue or complete transportation documents for carriage between London Heathrow and Dublin according to its own tariffs and other provisions as laid down in IATA's resolution on interlining and to effect changes to transportation documents according to the IATA resolution on voluntary changes to tickets.
    - Obligations for Aer Lingus plc to notify the Commission of all the measures taken to comply with its obligations.

e. **Further developments of the case**
    None.

F.4 *Microsoft* Commission decision 2007/53/EC, summary of decision published in [2007] OJ L 32/23

Relevance: As described above Microsoft was accused of infringing Article 102 on the grounds of both tying and refusal to supply interoperability information. The case is particularly significant as it clarifies the conditions under which, according to the Commission, dominant companies have to allow competition and thus deal with competitors, in particular in high-tech industries.

- See Case *F.4* in section *3.6*.

---

211 The term *essential facility* was then formally used for the first time in a formal decision under Article 102 by the Commission in *Sea Containers/Stena Line* Commission decision 94/19/EEC [1994] OJ L 15/8, Case IV/34.689.

212 See, *inter alia*, *Frankfurt Airport* Commission decision 98/190/EC [1998] OJ L 72/30, Case IV/34.801, *British Midland (Zaventem)* Commission decision 95/364/EC [1995] OJ L 12/8 and *Portuguese Airports* Commission decision 1999/199/EC [1999] OJ L 69/31, Case IV/35.703.

3.8 Preventing interoperability of standards and networks

A Introduction

One particular form of refusal to supply can occur when a firm holding a dominant position on one market is present also on the market(s) for complementary product(s) that is competitive. In such circumstances, the dominant firm may be able to leverage power to the complementary goods market by denying compatibility (i.e. interoperability) between the monopolized product and the rival version of the product facing competition. Pursuing this strategy, the dominant incumbent can try to achieve results similar to anticompetitive tying.

Competition concerns have arisen in particular around interoperability in network industries.[213] In such industries, the entry of a new firm may be practically impossible without access to the network of the dominant firm. Nonetheless, a large firm with a relevant network may have few or no incentives at all in granting compatibility to new competitors. This effect is believed to have been operational in some markets for software. The European *Microsoft* case[214] concerned, among other things, the refusal to provide sufficient information to guarantee interoperability between Microsoft's software and that of its (potential) competitors.

B Applicable EU legislation

No special legislation applicable. For applicable legislation see chapter 3, paragraph B.

C Related economics texts

Bishop and Walker (2009), not specifically discussed
Carlton and Perloff (2005), not specifically discussed
Church and Ware (2000), paragraph 16.2
Martin (1994), not specifically discussed
Martin (2002), not specifically discussed
Motta (2004), paragraphs 2.6.3.3 and 7.3.3
Tirole (1988), paragraph 10.6
Waldman and Jensen (2001), not specifically discussed

D Related legal texts

Bellamy and Child (2008), chapter 10, paragraph 4 (F, ii, 10.133)
Jones and Sufrin (2008), chapter 7, paragraph 7(G) and chapter 10, paragraph 9
Ritter and Braun (2005), not specifically discussed
Whish (2008), chapter 17, paragraph 4(A, iii)

---

213 See also, *supra*, section 2.9 of the book.
214 *Microsoft* Commission decision 2007/53/EC, summary of the decision published in [2007] OJ L 32/23, full text published on DG Comp website.

E   Commission decisions in chronological order[•]

Decca Navigator System **Commission decision 89/113/EC [1989] OJ L 43/27, Cases IV/30.979, 31.394**

Microsoft **Commission decision 2007/53/EC, summary of the decision published in [2007] OJ L 32/3** (Bishop and Walker, 2009, 6.73–6.82, 6.117, 6.134)

F   Economic landmark cases

F.1   *Decca Navigator System* Commission decision 89/113/EC [1989] OJ L 43/27

Relevance: A unique decision, until *Microsoft*, in which the Commission described the competitive concerns related to interoperability. There is no in-depth economic analysis in the Commission reasoning, nonetheless the effects of abusive use of interoperability codes by a monopolist are described.

- Cases IV/30.979, 31.394
- **Decision:** Infringement of Article 101 and 102 FEU Treaty
- **Decision addressee(s):**
  – Racal Electronics plc, *United Kingdom*
  – NV Philips Gloeilampenfabrieken, *the Netherlands*
  – Polytechnic Electronics plc, *United Kingdom*
- **Report route:** Complaints lodged with the Commission on 21 December 1983, 26 February 1985, and 9 April 1985
- **Date of the decision:** 21 December 1988
- **Competition Commissioner:** P. Sutherland
- **Relevant product market:** Commercial receivers for Decca Navigator System (DNS, an international radio navigation system) and DNS signals
- **Relevant geographical market:** European internal market (for receivers) and part of Europe where the signals transmitted from Denmark and the United Kingdom can be received (for signals)
- **Description of the case**
  - a. **Relevant facts**

    Racal – Decca Marine Navigation Ltd (Decca), an affiliate of Racal Electronics, was active in the design, manufacturing, and marketing of navigational aids and other electronic devices. The DNS was an international radio system used for navigation at sea, on land, and in the air. It was operated in the whole world and was based on a system of connected land-based stations ("chains") and on receivers put on board the vessel receiving the signals. It was used largely for sea transport. It was applied to all kinds of navigation (ocean-going vessels, commercial ships, coaster and fishing vessels, military ships, and pleasure-boats). The DNS system was at that time the only reliable system operating in the northern part of the Community (between Denmark and the United

---

- Decisions displayed in **bold type** are described in the section. Decisions highlighted with (*) include interesting economic analysis by the Commission on the specific topic of the section. Some decisions contain economic reasoning on more than one topic and therefore appear in several lists of Commission decisions in chronological order. Reference is made in brackets and **bold type** to the relevant section in which the decision is extensively described as a landmark case. When decisions are referenced and/or described in some detail in one or more of the economic textbooks, reference in brackets is also made to the relevant part(s) of those texts.

Kingdom). Until 1983 Decca used to rent its receivers for commercial use and sell those for military use. The market for pleasure-boat receivers was not yet developed because the rental charge demanded was too high for non-commercial boats. "Although the patents on DNS [had] expired, there [were] others barriers to entering into competition in the transmission of signals with a system of such high accuracy, extensive coverage, and wide range as the DSN."[215]

AP Radiotelefon A/S, an affiliate company of the Philips group (AP), and Polythecnic Electronics plc (PE) were two companies active in the sector for navigation system devices. AP started to market its own compact DNS-compatible receiver in 1981, and PE in 1983. As a reaction, Decca immediately started preparing possible countermeasures to maintain its monopoly position. Initially it adopted retaliatory measures against AP consisting in unannounced changes in the transmission frequencies of its DNS signals causing critical disturbances in shipping. After a negotiating period the two firms reached an agreement under which AP would not produce and/or sell receivers for commercial use while Decca would stop its production for receivers for pleasure-boats. For that purpose Decca granted a non-exclusive license to AP for the production of pleasure-boat receivers compatible with DNS signals. Furthermore Decca would have been AP's distributor of pleasure-boat receivers. In its investigation the Commission discovered documents attesting the explicit intention of the parties to "divide the market"; the agreement was actually the instrument to achieve that goal.[216]

Similarly, Decca threatened PE in the initial period with legal proceedings, alleging unfair competition. The parties subsequently entered into an agreement according to which Decca would award a non-exclusive license to PE for the manufacture and supply of pleasure-boat receivers compatible with DNS signals while PE would be excluded from any engagement in the market for receivers for commercial use.[217]

For all other producers of receivers that did not reach an agreement with Decca, a change in the signals denied compatibility of their devices with DNS signals (i.e. formally they were not granted licenses).[218]

Decca had a dominant position on the market for radio signals for navigation systems since it was in the relevant market the only supplier of a reliable and sufficiently sophisticated system. The same dominance was present in the market for receivers. Until AP's attempt to enter the market, Decca enjoyed a monopolistic position. After AP's and PE's commercial efforts to enter the market the dominant position in the market for receivers for commercial use was maintained, given the agreements and the exclusion of further competition by means of signals switching.[219]

b. **Origin of the case**

On 21 December 1983, 26 February 1985, and 9 April 1985 complaints were filed to the Commission pursuant to Article 3 of Regulation 17 by the

215   Recital 8 of the decision.
216   See recital 31 of the decision.
217   See recitals 61–69 of the decision.

218   See in particular for the RS case, recitals 46–56 of the decision.
219   See recitals 91–96 of the decision.

Landesfischereiverband Schleswig-Holstein and Rauff&Søresen. They complained that Racal–Decca Navigator Limited (later Racal–Decca Marine Navigation Ltd) had infringed Article 102 FEU Treaty. On 30 September 1987 the Commission decided to initiate proceedings.

c. Economic analysis

This decision was the only formal decision until the more recent *Microsoft* case[220] in which the Commission dealt with the issue of interoperability. The case deals, as described above, with an attempt to prevent actual and future producers of competing versions of a complementary good from providing that same good by means of artificial technical entry barriers raised by the dominant producer for the producers of the complementary goods.

The explicit aim of Decca's policy to change the DNS signal was to either exclude unlicensed competitors from the market for signal receivers altogether, or at least to frustrate the participants by making participation as costly and complicated as possible. Decca took hostile measures to prevent new entry and was perfectly aware of the effect it would have, as the documents collected during the Commission investigation revealed. The alteration of the signal was considered as the "strongest weapon" to hinder market entrance and to defend its monopolistic position.[221]

The Commission did not provide an extensive description of the economics behind its reasoning but, nonetheless, clearly identified the effects that followed from such a strategy. It stated that "[t]he changes in DNS signals were abusive in that they were deliberately made in such a way as to cause the malfunctioning of the devices sold by unlicensed competitors"[222] and that "[t]he changes were effective and caused losses to customers. In a Philips' report on possible competitors' countermeasures, the conclusion was reached that the adaptation of the device, through the software, would take at least two months from the date of the signal change. The attractiveness of a radio navigator receiver which might malfunction for two months after a signal change is necessarily seriously reduced."[223]

The decision included an overall assessment of all aspects of the agreements and concluded that the agreements reached between Decca and AP and Decca and PE were both anticompetitive. The licensing agreement at hand can be challenged from two different angles. It can either be considered in a horizontal context in which the market sharing agreements clearly constituted horizontal collusion. Or it can be understood in a dominance context in which the agreement is an unlawful attempt to protect a dominant position and reap its benefits which is an abuse of a dominant position. The agreement served only two purposes, first to make Decca the exclusive supplier of commercial receivers

220   See *supra* this section, note 214. Prior to this decision the Commission had also dealt with interoperability issues in 1978 in a case concerning IBM codes. The investigation was closed after the Commission reached an agreement with IBM concerning several issues, among which was the access to source codes. Therefore, the case was not concluded with a formal decision.
221   See recital 27 of the decision.
222   Recital 108 of the decision.
223   Recital 110 of the decision.

and second to shield AP from competition on the market for DNS-compatible receivers for pleasure-boats.[224]

d. Fines, remedies, and conditions enclosed
None.

e. Further developments of the case
None.

F.2 *Microsoft* Commission decision 2007/53/EC, summary of the decision published in [2007] OJ L 32/23

Relevance: As described above, Microsoft was accused of infringing Article 102 on the grounds of both tying and refusal to supply interoperability information. The decision is of prominent importance as it states the conditions under which, according to the Commission, dominant companies have to allow interoperability between operating systems and work group servers provided by other (non-dominant) operators.

* See Case *F.4* in section *3.6*.

3.9 Best price guarantees ("English clauses")

A Introduction

Best price guarantees, also called "English clauses," specify sales conditions between certain parties that are conditional on the sale prices of other parties. The common form is that a buyer of a product who finds a similar product for sale at a lower price from a competing seller retains the right to demand the same low price from the original supplier. There are different varieties of this basic set-up.

The potential anticompetitive effect of best price guarantees lies in that the clauses discourage competition on prices by creating a contractual commitment to neutralize any attempt to steal business from competitors. In addition, the clauses are a source of information about the identity of a company's competitors and their pricing policies. Before buying (part of) its supplies from a different manufacturer offering a better deal, a customer is incentified to inform its current supplier about the offer received and give him the possibility to match that offer and supply the required products instead. For a dominant firm, these agreements can be a means to obtain conditions that are effectively very similar to an exclusive purchasing agreement. They provide the firm with a competitive advantage and the *de facto* exclusion keeps residual firms from competing on the market. Furthermore, when there is competition in a market, the monitoring qualities of best price guarantees can help sustain (tacit) collusion.

B Applicable EU legislation

No special legislation applicable. For applicable legislation see chapter 3, paragraph B.

C Related economics texts

Bishop and Walker (2009), not specifically discussed
Carlton and Perloff (2005), chapter 5, paragraph 2(2)

---

224   See recitals 97–107 and 117–119 of the decision.

Church and Ware (2000), paragraph 10.6
Martin (1994), not specifically discussed
Martin (2002), paragraph 10.6
Motta (2004), paragraph 4.2.3
Tirole (1988), paragraphs 6.1 and 8.4
Waldman and Jensen (2001), chapter 9, paragraph 1(3)

D Related legal texts

Bellamy and Child (2008), chapter 10, paragraph 4 (C, 10.099)
Jones and Sufrin (2008), not specifically discussed
Ritter and Braun (2005), chapter 5, paragraph D(6, c, ii)
Whish (2008), chapter 17, not specifically discussed

E Commission decisions in chronological order*

Vitamins, Hoffmann – La Roche **Commission decision 76/642/EEC [1976] OJ L 223/27, Case IV/29.020** (Bishop and Walker, 2009, 6.01, 6.06, 6.41, 6.112; Martin, 1994, pp. 103–4, 538; Motta, 2004, pp. 34–5, 118, 499)
ECS/Akzo Chemie Commission decision 85/609/EEC [1985] OJ L 374/1, Case IV/30.698 **(described in detail as landmark case in section 3.3)** (Bishop and Walker, 2009, 6.01, 6.98, 6.108; Motta, 2004, p. 118)

F Economic landmark case

F.1 *Vitamins, Hoffmann – La Roche* Commission decision 76/642/EEC [1976] OJ L 223/27

Relevance: In the first decision relating to "English clause" provisions, the Commission described the competitive advantages deriving from such a clause for a dominant firm and of the exclusionary effect produced on competitors. The position of the Commission is particularly focused on the information abusively obtained by the dominant firm through the provision of the clause.

- Case IV/29.020
- **Decision:** Infringement of 102 FEU Treaty
- **Decision addressee(s):**
    - Hoffmann – La Roche Group, *Switzerland*
- **Report route:** Commission decision of 16 July 1975 to start a proceedings on its own initiative
- **Date of the decision:** 9 June 1976
- **Competition Commissioner:** P. Hillery

- Decisions displayed in **bold type** are described in the section. Decisions highlighted with (*) include interesting economic analysis by the Commission on the specific topic of the section. Some decisions contain economic reasoning on more than one topic and therefore appear in several lists of Commission decisions in chronological order. Reference is made in brackets and **bold type** to the relevant section in which the decision is extensively described as a landmark case. When decisions are referenced and/or described in some detail in one or more of the economic textbooks, reference in brackets is also made to the relevant part(s) of those texts.

- **Relevant product market:** Vitamins A, B2, B3, B6, C, E, H
- **Relevant geographical market:** European internal market
- **Description of the case**
  a. **Relevant facts**

     Hoffmann – La Roche was the world leader for the production and the marketing of bulk vitamins. It supplied vitamins for a multitude of different purposes, namely the pharmaceutical market, the food market, and the animal feed market. Although, at the time of the decision, many of its patents had already expired, it still maintained a technological lead over its competitors. This was reflected mostly in the highly developed technical sale services and the highly specialized sales network, as well as in the considerable stockpiles at local level enabling rapid and regular supply of product. In the different vitamins markets (each vitamin constitutes a different product market) its market share ranged from 95 percent in vitamin B6 and H to 47 percent in vitamin A. Its turnover was larger than that of all other producers. The range of vitamins it was able to offer to customers was wider than those of its competitors and fortified Hoffmann – La Roche's dominant position because usually customers bought more than one single vitamin. Furthermore, as market entrance required "large and specialized investment and the programming of capacities over long periods in order to be profitable, it [was] unlikely that the possibility of entry by new competitors to the market would... have an appreciable effect on the position of Roche."[225]

     The main buyers of bulk vitamins were firms in the pharmaceuticals, food, and animal feed industries. Even if part of the demand was by small and medium-sized firms, by far the most important purchasers of vitamins were the large-scale users and multinational groups. The majority of Hoffmann – La Roche's customers was large multinational groups. The sales strategy of Hoffmann – La Roche hinged on exclusive or preferential agreements with its customers. These agreements were named "fidelity agreements" and although they varied considerably from customer to customer they did have the following common features:

     - "purchasers obtain[ed] from Roche all or most of their vitamins requirements in the form of vitamins manufactured by Roche;
     - Roche provide[d] purchasers with all or most of their vitamins requirements at the most favourable price obtaining on the customer's domestic market;"[226]
     - A rebate was granted at the end of the year (or every six months) to those customers that had obtained all or most of their purchased vitamins from Roche. The total of all types of vitamins purchased by the customer was taken into consideration for the calculation of the rebate. The rebates varied across customers;
     - "The so-called 'English' clause provide[d] that customers are to inform Roche if any 'reputable' manufacturer charges a price lower that that charged by Roche..., and if Roche does not lower its price to that level customers are free to obtain supplies from the other

---

225   Recital 21 of the decision.   226   Recital 11 of the decision.

manufacturer without losing the fidelity rebate on their purchases from Roche."[227]

The documentation collected by the Commission during its investigation revealed that Hoffmann – La Roche consciously and intentionally used that system as a means to shield its business from competition.[228]

b. Origin of the case

On 16 July 1975 the Commission, on its own initiative, adopted a decision to initiate a proceeding against Hoffmann – La Roche with respect to agreements concluded by the latter concerning the vitamins market in Europe.

c. Economic analysis

All of the fidelity agreements were considered entirely anticompetitive by the Commission. The conduct of Roche "by its very nature . . . hampers the freedom of choice and equality of treatment of purchasers and restricts competition between bulk vitamins manufacturers in the common market."[229] In particular, the obligation imposed on customers to buy all their requirements from a single supplier eliminated choice and tied customers to Hoffmann – La Roche which barred other vitamins manufacturers from accessing those large and relevant customers. Considering the discount granted on the basis of the total purchases of vitamins (i.e. of all groups of vitamins) and the relevance of the rate of discount granted, entrance for new competitors was made practically impossible.[230]

Besides the assessment of the rebate system, induced loyalty, and exclusivity contractual conditions set by Hoffmann – La Roche, already largely described in the *European sugar industry* case,[231] this decision is particularly interesting also because it gave the Commission the opportunity for the first time to assess the impact on competition of a so-called "English clause" applied by a dominant undertaking in the contractual relations with its customers. The Commission introduced an interpretative approach toward "English clauses" that has not been modified since then, and that has also been confirmed by the Community judicatures.

According to the Commission "[t]he provision known as the 'English clause' is but a very limited relaxation of the system applied by Roche. The argument that this provision in fact leaves the customer free to purchase from the competitors of Roche is belied by the function of the clause. This provision, whilst enabling Roche to learn of the prices offered by its competitors, leaves to Roche the decision whether the customer in question is free to purchase from the competitor offering vitamins at lower price; the customer is free to purchase from the competitor only where Roche decides not to match the price offered . . . It is clear that should the sale in question be of interest to Roche . . . then Roche with its strength in the vitamins market is put in a position to adjust its price

---

227   *Idem.*
228   See recital 12 of the decision.
229   Recital 22 of the decision.
230   See recitals 23 and 24 of the decision.
231   *European sugar industry* Commission decision 73/109/EC [1973] OJ L 140/17, Case IV/26.918. See, *supra*, section 3.2 of the book.

and so preserve exclusivity of supply to the customer in question. It is therefore the decision of Roche in each case, depending on the circumstances, whether to admit partially, or to deny access to, a competitor to the market which Roche has reserved for itself."[232]

d. Fines, remedies, and conditions enclosed

- The Commission imposed on Hoffmann – La Roche a total fine of EUA 300,000.
- Obligations for Hoffmann – La Roche to bring the infringements to an end.

e. Further developments of the case

Case 85/76 *Hoffmann – La Roche* v. *Commission* [1979] ECR 461, fines reduction.

The Court confirmed the Commission's findings with regard to the English clause. The Court stated that: "... the English clause under which Roche's customers are obliged to inform it of more favourable offers made by competitors together with the particulars above mentioned – so that it will be easy for Roche to identify the competitor – owing to its very nature, places at the disposal of the applicant information about market conditions and also about the alternatives open to, and the actions of, its competitors which is of great value for the carrying out of its market strategy."[233]

Moreover the Court observed that the fact that an undertaking in a dominant position requires its customers (or obtains their agreement under contract) to notify it of its competitor's offers, whilst the said customers may have an obvious commercial interest in not disclosing them, is of such a kind as to aggravate the exploitation of the dominant position in an abusive way.[234]

Notwithstanding those findings, the ECJ granted Hoffmann – La Roche a fine reduction due to the Commission's mistakes in evaluating the applicant's dominant position on the market for vitamins in group B3, and the fact that the duration of the infringement was found to be a little over three years and thus less than the five years which the Commission took into consideration in calculating the fine.[235]

---

232 Recital 25 of the decision.
233 Recital 107 of the judgment.

234 Recital 107 of the judgment.
235 Recital 140 of the judgment.

4 Licensing

A Introduction

A license is a legal instrument through which the owner of an intellectual property right (IPR) confers upon another party the right to (temporarily) use its IPR. Licenses are one of several ways to arrange exploitation of an IPR, together with direct exploitation and assignment. The licensing of IPRs is a valuable instrument to both stimulate and disseminate innovation and new technologies. The license mechanism can increase competition by allowing new entrants equal access to high technological standards. Licenses are accordingly generally seen as an expression of dynamic and innovative economies.

In certain circumstances, however, competition concerns related to licensing may arise. In most cases, licensing agreements provide the licensee with a conditional permission to exploit the right in question. Frequently, these concern the protection of confidential information, the meeting of high quality standards in the production or the use of the licensed good, or a protection against the risk of competition from the licensee. These conditions and obligations attached to the agreement can have anticompetitive intent and/or effect. Licensors can, for example, eliminate the possibility that the licensee will compete in one or more of its markets. It can do so by limiting the scope of application or confine territorial application of the IPR. Licensing conditions also often include explicit non-competition clauses or limitations on the licensee's freedom to deal with the licensor's competitors. Assessing the possible anticompetitive impact of such conditions can be problematic, not in the least because IPR licensing often occurs in rapidly evolving highly technological markets, in which the competitive equilibrium has yet to be established.

This chapter consists of two sections. Section 4.1 on Trademarks and branding deals with IPRs that concern external characteristics of products. Section 4.2 on Patents and other intellectual property rights focuses on IPRs of technological innovations and new knowledge, mainly covered by patents, know-how, and copyrights. The majority of competition cases is concerned with the latter category of licensing.

B Applicable EU legislation

Article 101 FEU Treaty.
See also Commission Notice on the definition of the relevant market [1997] OJ C 372/3.

C Related economics texts

Bishop and Walker (2009), paragraphs 5.59–5.63
Carlton and Perloff (2005), chapter 16, paragraph 3

Church and Ware (2000), chapter 18
Martin (1994), chapter 12, paragraph 2
Martin (2002), paragraphs 4.3, 4.4, and 14.6
Motta (2004), paragraph 2.5.1
Tirole (1988), paragraph 10.8
Waldman and Jensen (2001), chapter 13

D Related legal texts

Bellamy and Child (2008), chapter 9, paragraphs 3, 4, and 6
Jones and Sufrin (2008), chapter 10, paragraph 3
Ritter and Braun (2005), chapter 7, paragraphs D(2), E(2 and 4), and F
Whish (2008), chapter 19

4.1 Trademarks and branding

A Introduction

A trademark is a sign or a mark used to identify a certain product or service and to differentiate it from other products and services. The first user of a certain trademark (the one who registers the mark) is granted the right to use it exclusively for an indefinite period of time. All competitors are allowed to produce and supply similar competing goods or services but are banned from using that mark. Unlike other IPRs, a trademark does not necessarily have to bring any novelty or technological enhancement to the product in order to be registered. The idea behind the protection of trademarks is that they are important instruments to identify the reputation and the goodwill of a product and of its manufacturer.

Agreements for the licensing of trademarks are usually concluded in combination with the licensing of other IPRs. This allows the licensee's full exploitation of the IP in question. This can be important to help consumers to establish a link between the licensee's products and the licensed technology. Alternatively, they are often part of broader vertical agreements and particularly common in distribution and franchising agreements.[1]

Competitive concerns that might arise in case of trademark licensing agreements concern territorial exclusivity, non-competition, and market sharing clauses potentially attached to the license.[2]

---

[1] Decisions referring to similar situations, i.e. trademark agreements in the frame of a broader vertical relation between undertakings, are described in the chapter dedicated to vertical restrictions (chapter 5).

[2] In *EMI* v. *CBS* (Case 51/75) the ECJ made some general observations with regard to trademarks and their relevance in competition law. First it observes that a trademark right, as a legal entity, does not possess those elements of contract or concerted practice as referred to in Article 101(1) (recital 26 of the judgment). Nevertheless the exercise of that right might fall within the ambit of the prohibitions contained in the Treaty if it were to manifest itself as the subject, the means, or the consequence of a restrictive practice (recital 27 of the judgment). Moreover the Court states that: "a restrictive agreement between traders within the common market and competitors in third countries that would bring about an isolation of the common market as a whole which, in the territory of the Community, would reduce the supply or products originating in third countries and similar to those protected by a mark within the Community, might be of such a nature as to affect adversely the condition of competition within the common market" (recital 53 of the judgment).

B Applicable EU legislation

Council Directive 89/104/EEC of 21 December 1988 to approximate the laws of the Member States relating to trademarks [1989] OJ L 40/1 (the First Trade Mark Directive).

Council Regulation (EC) No. 40/94 of 20 December 1993 on the Community trademark [1994] OJ L 11/1.

Commission Regulation (EC) No. 2868/95 of 13 December 1995 implementing Council Regulation No. 40/94 on the Community trademark.

For agreements not covered by these legislative provisions, general legislation is applicable (see chapter 4, paragraph B).

C Related economics texts

Bishop and Walker (2009), not specifically discussed
Carlton and Perloff (2005), chapter 7 and chapter 16, paragraph 1
Church and Ware (2000), paragraph 18.3.1
Martin (1994), chapter 8, paragraph 2 and chapter 11
Martin (2002), paragraphs 4.3 and 4.4
Motta (2004), paragraph 2.5.1
Tirole (1988), paragraphs 7.2 and 7.3
Waldman and Jensen (2001), not discussed

D Related legal texts

Bellamy and Child (2008), chapter 9, paragraph 6(A)
Jones and Sufrin (2008), chapter 10, paragraphs 2(B, iii) and 6
Ritter and Braun (2005), chapter 7, paragraphs A(2, f), C(6), and F(2)
Whish (2008), chapter 19, paragraphs 2 and 4

E Commission decisions in chronological order[•]

Nicholas Frères & Vitapro Commission decision 64/502/EEC [1964] OJ L 64/2287, Case IV/95
ASBL Tube d'Acier Soudé Electr. Commission decision 70/346/EEC [1970] OJ L 153/14, Case IV/412 (Martin, 1994, p.182)
Sirdar-Phildar Commission decision 75/297/EEC [1975] OJ L 125/27, Case IV/27.879
INTERGROUP Commission decision 75/482/EEC [1975] OJ L 212/23, Case IV/28.838
Penneys Commission decision 78/193 [1978] OJ L 60/19, Case IV/29.246
Campari **Commission decision 78/253/EEC [1978] OJ L 70/69, Cases IV/117, 171, 172, 856, 28.173**
Toltecs-Dorcet Commission decision 82/897/EEC [1982] OJ L 379/19, Case IV/30.128
Carlsberg Commission decision 84/381/EEC [1984] OJ L 207/26, Case IV/30.129

• Decisions displayed in **bold type** are described in the section. Decisions highlighted with (*) include interesting economic analysis by the Commission on the specific topic of the section. Some decisions contain economic reasoning on more than one topic and therefore appear in several lists of Commission decisions in chronological order. Reference is made in brackets and **bold type** to the relevant section in which the decision is extensively described as a landmark case. When decisions are referenced and/or described in some detail in one or more of the economic textbooks, reference in brackets is also made to the relevant part(s) of those texts.

Velcro/Aplix Commission decision 85/410/EEC [1985] OJ L 233/22, Case IV/4240
Moosehead/Whitbread **Commission decision 90/186/EEC [1990] OJ L 100/32, Case IV/32.736**

F   Economic landmark cases

F.1   *Campari* Commission decision 78/253/EEC [1978] OJ L 70/69

Relevance: This decision represents the first case in which the Commission gave an economically based assessment of the implications deriving from a number of clauses attached to a trademark agreement. All the limitations of competition entailed in those clauses that are considered as necessary and acceptable for the proper implementation of a trademark licensing are described, together with the assessment criteria to be used in the presence of such agreements.

- Cases IV/117, 171, 172, 856, 28.173
- **Decision:** Exemption pursuant to Article 101(3) FEU Treaty for nine years
- **Decision addressee(s):**
    - Davide Campari Milano SpA, *Italy*
    - Ognibeni & Co., *the Netherlands*
    - Hans Prang, *Federal Republic of Germany*
    - Campari France SA, *France*
    - Sovinac SA, *Belgium*
    - Johs. M. Klein & Co., *Denmark*
- **Report route:** Notification for exemption submitted to the Commission on 27 June 1973 by Campari Milano SpA.
- **Date of the decision:** 23 December 1977
- **Competition Commissioner:** R. Vouel
- **Relevant product market:** Alcoholic "bitter" aperitifs
- **Relevant geographical market:** Not indicated
- **Description of the case**
    a. **Relevant facts**
        Campari Milano was the owner of the international trademarks for the alcoholic aperitifs Bitter Campari and Cordial Campari. To promote those brands abroad, Campari Milano set up a network of licensees to produce and commercialize its products. In each European Member State it appointed an exclusive licensee with the exception of the United Kingdom and Ireland where it concluded a contract of exclusive import and distribution.
        The main provisions of the license agreements were as follows:
        - The licensees were granted the exclusive right to use the trademarks for the manufacture of aperitifs in their allotted territory.
        - Campari Milano refrained from manufacturing its aperitifs in the allotted territories.
        - The licensees agreed not to supply competing products.
        - Licensor and licensees undertook to refrain from active sales in the territories assigned to other members of the agreement.
        - All parties were free to take adequate measures to meet unsolicited requests of export within the (then) EEC, under the condition not to undersupply the allotted territory.

- Licensor and licensees were to help buyers willing to export the products in recovering the duties and taxes paid on alcohol.
- The licensees undertook to not export the products outside the EEC.
- Diplomatic corps, ship victuallers, foreign armed forces, and all bodies exempted from the payment of duties on alcohol would have been supplied exclusively with the original Italian product (manufactured by Campari Milano).
- The licensees had the obligation to comply exactly with the licensor's instructions for the manufacture of the products, to buy raw materials meeting certain specifications indicated by the licensor and to buy the secret ingredients – i.e. the secret mixture of herbs exclusively from the licensor.
- The licensees had the obligation not to unveil the secret techniques and recipes used for the production of the products.
- The licensees had the obligation to promote sales and engage in advertising campaigns.
- A council of three arbitrators would have settled disputes.

The license agreements had no provisions concerning the price policies. In each Member State, alcoholic products were subject to national legislation on labeling, advertising limitations, alcoholic contents requirements, and special taxation regimes.

b. **Origin of the case**

On 27 June 1973 Campari Milano SpA submitted to the Commission a notification pursuant to Article 4 of Regulation 17 to see a network of licensing agreements be declared exempted from the application of Article 101(1) FEU Treaty by virtue of Article 101(3) FEU Treaty.

c. **Economic analysis**

In this case the Commission gave a clear and defined example of its policy toward trademark licensing. In particular, the Campari agreements gave the Commission the opportunity to analyze the competitive impact of several clauses enclosed in a trademark licensing agreement which constitute the typical attachments to this kind of agreement. With this decision, the Commission indicated and gave an assessment of all the 'acceptable' limitations that are necessary for the proper, effective, and convenient conclusion of a trademark licensing agreement.

Recognising the freedom of the proprietor of a trademark to license to third parties, the Commission analyzed the restrictive effects produced by the network of exclusive licenses granted. "If [the proprietor of the trademark] undertakes only to allow one single undertaking to use his trademark in a particular territory and to refrain himself from manufacturing products bearing his trademark there, he loses his freedom to respond to other requests for licenses and the competitive advantage to be gained from manufacture by himself in this territory."[3] Furthermore, the non-competition clause and the ban to engage in active sales were also considered particularly restrictive of competition by the Commission. "The exclusion of competing products prevents

---

3 Recital II-A-1 of the decision.

the licensees from marketing such products across borders between Member States, or from making license agreements in relation to such products with undertakings in other Member States."[4] The active sales ban was considered as having a strong restrictive impact on competition, in particular taking into consideration the (individual) production capacity of both the licensor and the licensees.[5]

While the above-mentioned obligations were regarded as restrictive by the Commission, some other provisions were considered functional to the main agreement and without an effect on competition. In particular, all the obligations concerning quality controls over the manufacturing plants and the ingredients utilized for the production (including the purchase obligation of certain secret raw material), the requirement to employ the secret techniques and recipes and the advertising campaigns were considered in no aspect restrictive of competition and instead useful for the proper protection of the IPR in question.[6]

Notwithstanding the restrictive effects caused by some of the clauses enclosed in the licensing agreements, the Commission considered their overall impact on competition positive and, at the same time, their inclusion in the agreements indispensable to create the necessary incentives for the licensees to invest in production and pay the respective royalties. The territorial protection from intrabrand competition granted as well as the prohibition on handling competing products where necessary to permit a "sufficient return on the investment made by each licensee for the purpose of manufacturing the product bearing the trademark under conditions acceptable to the licensor and holder of the trademark, and [to] enable . . . the licensee to increase its production capacity and constantly to improve the already long established distribution network . . . The ban on dealing in competing products also contribute[d] to improving distribution of the licensed products by concentrating sales efforts, encouraging the build-up of stocks and shortening delivery times."[7]

An interesting distinction was made by the Commission between the effects of a non-competition clause in a trademark license and one in a patent license which clarified the Commission's approach toward trademark agreements. The Commission concluded that "[a]lthough a non-competition clause in a licensing agreement concerning industrial property rights based on the result of a creative activity, such as a patent, would constitute a barrier to technical and economical progress by preventing the licensees from taking an interest in other techniques and products, this is not the case with the licensing agreements under consideration here, the aim pursued by the parties, as is clear from the agreement taken as a whole, is to decentralize manufacture within the EEC and to rationalize the distribution system linked to it."[8] The prohibition of selling competing products was thus analysed here with similar criteria as applied in case of vertical exclusive distribution agreements. In the same way, the prohibition of active sales outside the allotted territory and the allocation of certain

4   Recital II-B of the decision.
5   Recital II-A-3 of the decision.
6   Recital II-C of the decision.

7   Recitals III-A-1 and III-A-2 of the decision.
8   Recital III-A-2 of the decision.

special categories of customers (such as diplomatic corps, ship victuallers, foreign armed forces, and duty-free shops) were also considered necessary to concentrate sales efforts and to improve the distribution and supply of the products.

The Commission also took into consideration the resulting increase of the total output on the market. It remarked that the licensing agreement in fact "increased the quantity of Bitter Campari available to consumers and improved distribution, so that consumers benefit directly."[9]

The necessity of restrictions on intrabrand competition were assessed in light of the availability of one or more 'other potential undertakings' in the same market to reach the agreement in the absence of those protections and not of the availability of the same undertaking involved in the actual agreements. This has been the usual approach of the Commission toward restriction of intrabrand competition related to the licensing of IPRs. "In particular none of the licensees and in all probability no other undertaking in the spirituous liquors industry would have been prepared to make the investment necessary for a significant increase in sales of Bitter if it were not sure of being protected from competition from other licensees or Campari Milano itself."[10]

d. Fines, remedies, and conditions enclosed

- Obligations for all the parties to inform the Commission of all the awards made under the arbitration clause attached to the agreement.
- Obligations for all the parties to notify to the Commission, on a yearly basis, the volume of exports of Bitter Campari within the EEC, the cases of refusal to meet orders and the cases of refusal to seek refund of taxes corresponding to declarations made by customers who have exported Campari products within the EEC.

e. Further developments of the case

None.

F.2   *Moosehead/Whitbread* Commission decision 90/186/EEC [1990] OJ L 100/32

Relevance: This decision is relevant because the Commission broadened its previous reasoning and carried out an assessment of the trademark non-challenge clause in competition

---

9   Recital III-B of the decision.
10   Recital III-C of the decision. The Commission's reasoning concerning the exclusive licensing was first tested in *L. C. Nungesser KG and Kurt Eisele* v. *Commission* (Case 258/78). In this case the ECJ first made a distinction between *open* and *not open* exclusive licenses. The so-called "open license" relates solely to the contractual relationship between the owner of the right and the licensee, whereby the owner merely undertakes not to grant other licenses in respect of the same territory and not to compete himself with the licensee on that territory. The "not open" exclusive license relates to an absolute territorial protection, under which the parties to the contract propose, regarding the products and the territory in question, to eliminate all competition from third parties, such as parallel importers or licensees for other territories (recital 53 of the judgment).

The grant of such an open exclusive right could provide an incentive to innovative efforts. The Court stated: "In fact, in the case of a license of breeders' rights over hybrid maize seeds newly developed in one Member State, an undertaking established in another Member State which was not certain that it would not encounter competition from other licensees for the territory granted to it, or from the owner of the right himself, might be deterred from accepting the risk of cultivating and marketing that product; such a result would be damaging to the dissemination of a new technology and would prejudice competition in the Community between new product and similar existing products" (recital 57 of the judgment).

The Court concluded that an open exclusive license, that is to say a license which does not affect the position of third parties such as parallel importers and licensees from third countries, is not in itself incompatible with Article 101(1) of the Treaty (recital 58 of the judgment). With regard to the so-called "not open" licenses the Court stated that it has "consistently held . . . that absolute territorial protection granted to a licensee in order to enable parallel import to be controlled and prevented results in the artificial maintenance of separate national markets, contrary to the Treaty" (recital 61 of the judgment).

law. Within that appraisal, a difference between the consequences of challenging the ownership and challenging the validity of the trademark is made. Trademarks are also scrutinized as a potential barrier to entry.

- Case IV/32.736
- **Decision:** Exemption pursuant to Article 101(3) FEU Treaty for ten years
- **Decision addressee(s):**
    - Moosehead Breweries Limited, *Canada*
    - Whitbread and Company plc, *United Kingdom*
- **Report route:** Notification for exemption submitted to the Commission on 2 June 1988 by Whitbread and Company plc and Moosehead Breweries Limited
- **Date of the decision:** 23 March 1990
- **Competition Commissioner:** L. Brittan
- **Relevant product market:** Lager beer
- **Relevant geographical market:** United Kingdom
- **Description of the case**
    a. **Relevant facts**
       The two parties were both active in the beer market. Moosehead Breweries Limited (Moosehead) was a manufacturer, seller, and distributor of beer in Canada, while Whitbread and Company plc (Whitbread) was a brewer operating a large number of public houses in England. The two undertakings made an agreement concerning the manufacture of the beer sold by Moosehead in Canada and other countries outside Europe under the trademark "Moosehead." The product was a non-premium lager beer but had, according to the parties, a particular taste typical of Canadian lager beers. According to the agreement "Moosehead grant[ed] to Whitbread the sole and exclusive right to produce and promote, market, and sell beer manufactured for sale under the name 'Moosehead' in the licensed territory [United Kingdom, Isle of Man and the Channel Islands], using Moosehead know-how. Whitbread pa[id] to Moosehead a royalty for this exclusive right."[11] The agreement provided for a number of specifications and obligations that can be summarized as follow:
          - Whitbread had the obligation to comply with the type and quality of raw material indicated by Moosehead.
          - The licensee would not engage in active sales outside the allotted territory but was free to receive unsolicited orders from outside it.
          - Whitbread undertook to not produce for the period of validity of the agreement any other Canadian beer.
          - Whitbread agreed to sell the product only under the trademark 'Moosehead' and to use the same trademark only in relation to the contract product.
          - The ownership of the trademark was shared between the two parties under the UK trademark law and Whitbread had the exclusive right to use it. At the same time Whitbread agreed to observe all the conditions attached to the trademark and not to challenge the ownership and the validity of the trademark.

---

11   Recital 7–2 of the decision.

> – Moosehead would have provided the licensee with the know-how necessary for the production of the beer and Whitbread would have complied with the directions and specifications indicated by Moosehead.

b. Origin of the case

On 2 June 1988 Whitbread and Company plc and Moosehead Breweries Limited submitted to the Commission a notification for exemption pursuant to Article 4 of Regulation No. 17 to see the exclusive license agreement be declared exempted from the application of Article 101(1) FEU Treaty by virtue of Article 101(3) FEU Treaty.

c. Economic analysis

The assessment given by the Commission regarding the potentially restrictive clauses of the trademark licensing agreement between the parties substantially reflects the same consideration already described in the previous landmark decision about trademarks.[12]

What is interesting in this decision is the difference made by the Commission between different trademark non-challenge clauses, as well as the description of the potential use of the IPR attached to the trademark to raise entry barriers.

The Commission stated that "in general terms, a trademark non-challenge clause can refer to the ownership and/or the validity of a trademark:

> – The ownership of a trademark may, in particular, be challenged on grounds of the prior use or prior registration of an identical trademark. A clause in an exclusive trademark license agreement obliging the licensee not to challenge the ownership of a trademark ... does not constitute a restriction of competition within the meaning of Article 85(1). Whether or not the licensor or licensee has the ownership of the trademark, the use of it by any other party is prevented in any event, and competition would thus not be affected.
> – The validity of a trademark may be contested on any ground under national law, and in particular on the ground that it is generic or descriptive in nature. In such an event, should the challenge be upheld, the trademark may fall into the public domain and may thereafter be used without restriction by the licensee and any other party.
>
> Such a clause may constitute a restriction of competition ... because it may contribute to the maintenance of a trademark that would be an unjustified barrier to entry into a given market.
>
> Moreover in order for any restriction of competition to fall under Article 85(1), it must be appreciable. The ownership of a trademark only gives the holder the exclusive right to sell products under that name. Other parties are free to sell the product in question under a different trademark or tradename. Only when the use of a well-known trademark would be an important advantage to any company entering or competing in any given market and the absence of it constitutes therefore a significant barrier to entry, would this clause

---

12   See recitals 15–1 to 15–3 and 16 of the decision. See also, *supra, Campari* Commission decision 78/253/EEC [1978] OJ L 70/69 in Case F.1 of this section.

which impedes the licensee to challenge the validity of the trademark constitute an appreciable restriction of competition."[13]

Considering the market conditions and the novelty of the trademark introduced by Whitbread in the United Kingdom, the Commission did not consider "Moosehead" as a trademark possibly raising entry barriers.

d. Fines, remedies, and conditions enclosed
None.

e. Further developments of the case
None.

4.2 Patents and other intellectual property rights

A Introduction

A patent confers a non-permanent right to the maker of a newly invented product, process, design, or substance to prevent others from using, reproducing, or marketing the product covered by the patent and its derivatives. Patents are granted for actual inventions, but not for abstract ideas. The exclusive rights are granted for a limited period of time, which is usually twenty years. After the patent expires others can use the information enclosed in the patent.

Patents represent the strongest form of legal protection of intellectual properties. They confer (near-) monopoly power to the inventor of a truly unique product to commercially exploit the invention. Patents prevent the production of similar products, substances, designs, and the use of similar processes by other competing suppliers.

Another form of IPR is copyright. Copyright protects intellectual creations such as literature, music, and other artistic works from unauthorized exploitation by third parties. In the EU such protection is awarded for the lifetime of the author plus seventy years. Unlike patents, a copyright protects the holder only against copying, and not against the possibility that someone else might independently create the same idea. Copyright protection therefore is longer, but also narrower and shallower in scope.

Know-how is technically not protected under IPR provisions. Nonetheless it is usually treated in licensing agreements as if it were an IPR. Know-how is a set of practical information that is neither patented nor registered in any other form. It usually takes the form of a (business) secret and is kept confidential.

The first aim in granting IPRs is to provide incentives and means for creative expression, innovation, and research. The ability to charge prices above the direct cost of production, at least for the period for which the intellectual product is protected, enables the inventor to recover the R&D cost or other risky investments made in the invention process. Without IPRs, competition from imitators would imply that fixed costs cannot be covered from market revenues, which could effectively take away the incentive to invent. An optimal design of patents therefore considers the inevitable trade off between the necessity to provide proper incentives for innovation, and the social benefits from the dissemination of innovations and competition between different producers

---

13   Recital 15–4 of the decision. Emphasis added.

that would benefit consumers. The efficient breadth, depth, and length of IPR protection to be granted may differ between different industries.

B   Applicable EU legislation

Commission Regulation No. 772/2004 on the application of Article 81(3) of the Treaty to categories of technology transfer agreements [2004] OJ L 123/11 (Block Exemption Regulation of Technology Transfer Agreements).

Commission Guidelines on the Application of Article 81 of the Treaty to Technology Transfer Agreements [2004] OJ C 101/2.

For agreements not covered by the Block Exemption Regulation, general legislation is applicable (see chapter 4; paragraph B).

C   Related economics texts

Bishop and Walker (2009), not specifically discussed
Carlton and Perloff (2005), chapter 16
Church and Ware (2000), paragraphs 18.2 and 18.3
Martin (1994), chapter 12, paragraph 2
Martin (2002), paragraph 14.6
Motta (2004), paragraphs 2.4.3.3 and 2.5.1
Tirole (1988), chapter 10
Waldman and Jensen (2001), chapter 13, paragraph 5

D   Related legal texts

Bellamy and Child (2008), chapter 9, paragraphs 4(A) and 6
Jones and Sufrin (2008), chapter 10, paragraph 2(B, ii)
Ritter and Braun (2005), chapter 7, paragraphs A(2), C(1–5, 7), and E
Whish (2008), chapter 19, paragraphs 2, 3, and 4

E   Commission decisions in chronological order•

Burroughs-Delplanque Commission decision 72/25/EEC [1972] OJ L 13/50, Case IV/5400
Burroughs/Geha-Werke Commission decision 72/26/EEC [1972] OJ L 13/53, Case IV/5405
Davidson Rubber Co Commission decision 72/237/EEC [1972] OJ L 143/31, Cases IV/6964, 17.448, 17.545, 18.673, 26.858, 26.890
Raymond-Nagoya Commission decision 72/238/EEC [1972] OJ L 143/39, Case IV/26.813
Kabelmetal-Luchaire **Commission decision 75/494/EEC [1975] OJ L 222/34, Case IV/21.353**
Bronbemaling/Heidemaatschappij **Commission decision 75/570/EEC [1975] OJ L 249/27, Case IV/28.967**

•   Decisions displayed in **bold type** are described in full in the section. Decisions highlighted with (∗) include interesting economic analysis by the Commission on the specific topic of the section. Some decisions contain economic reasoning on more than one topic and therefore appear in several lists of Commission decisions in chronological order. After each mention, reference is made in brackets and **bold type** to the relevant section in which the decision is extensively described as a landmark case. When decisions are referenced and/or described in some detail in one or more of the economic textbooks, reference in brackets is also made to the relevant part(s) of those texts.

AOIP/Beyrard Commission decision 76/29/EEC [1976] OJ L 6/8, Case IV/26.949

Breeders' Right-Maize Seed Commission decision 78/823/EEC [1978] OJ L 286/23, Case IV/28.824

Vaessen/Moris Commission decision 79/86/EEC [1979] OJ L 19/32, Case IV/29.290

Gema Statutes Commission decision 82/204/EEC [1982] OJ L 94/12, Case IV/29.971

Windsurfing International Commission decision 83/400/EEC [1983] OJ L 229/1, Case IV/29.395 (*)

Schlegel/CPIO Commission decision 83/622/EEC [1983] OJ L 351/20, Case IV/30.099

Velcro/Aplix Commission decision 85/410/EEC [1985] OJ L 233/22, Case IV/4240

Breeders's Right: Roses Commission decision 85/561/EEC [1985] OJ L 369/9, Case IV/30.017

Boussois/Interpane Commission decision 87/123/EEC [1987] OJ L 50/30, Case IV/31.302

Rich Products/Jus-Rol Commission decision 88/143/EEC [1988] OJ L 69/21, Case IV/31.206

Delta Chemie/DDD Commission decision 88/563/EEC [1988] OJ L 309/34, Case IV/31.498

Decca Navigator System Commission decision 89/113/EC [1989] OJ L 43/27, Cases IV/30.979, 31.394

British Midland/Aer Lingus Commission decision 92/213/EEC [1993] OJ L 96/34, Case IV/33.544 (**described in detail as landmark case in section 3.8**)

Coapi Commission decision 95/188/EC [1995] OJ L 122/37, Case IV/33.686

PMI-DSV Commission decision 95/373/EC [1995] OJ L 221/34, Case IV/33.375

Eurovision Commission decision 2000/400/EC [2000] OJ L 151/18, Case IV/32.150 (*)

UEFA Commission decision 2001/478/EC [2001] OJ L 171/12, Case COMP/37.576 (*)

Eco-Emballages Commission decision 2001/663/EC [2001] OJ L 233/37, COMP/34.950

International Federation of the Phonographic Industry Commission decision 2003/300/EC [2003] OJ L 107/58, Case COMP/C2/38.014

UEFA **Commission decision 2003/778/EC [2003] OJ L 291/25, Case COMP/C.2–37.398**

ARA, ARGEV, ARO Commission decision of 16 October 2003, published on DG Comp website, Cases COMP/D3/35.470 to 35.473

Telenor, Canal +, Canal Digital Commission decision of 29 December 2003, published on DG Comp website, Case COMP/C-2/38.287

F   Economic landmark cases

F.1   *Kabelmetal-Luchaire* Commission decision 75/494/EEC [1975] OJ L 222/34

Relevance: The Commission has always recognized the IPR holder's freedom in choosing the subjects to whom (possibly) to grant a license. Nonetheless, in this decision, the Commission expressed concerns about possible partitioning and exclusionary effects deriving from some clauses attached to the licensing agreement.

- Case IV/21.353
- **Decision:** Exemption pursuant to Article 101(3) FEU Treaty for thirty-three months
- **Decision addressee(s):**
    - Kabel und Metallwerke Gutehoffnungshütte AG, *Federal Republic of Germany*
    - Ets Luchaire SA, *France*
- **Report route:** Notification for exemption submitted to the Commission on 2 February 1963 by Kabel und Metallwerke Neumeyer AG
- **Date of the decision:** 18 July 1975
- **Competition Commissioner:** R. Vouel

- **Relevant product market:** Techniques for the manufacturing of steel parts with cold-extrusion process
- **Relevant geographical market:** Not indicated
- **Description of the case**
  a. **Relevant facts**
  Kabel und Metallwerke Gutehoffnungshütte AG (Kabelmetal) had developed and patented a number of special techniques for the creation of steel parts from the cold-extrusion process. Kabelmetal licensed its patent to a large number of firms across Europe. The object of that licensing agreement was not the basic extrusion process, not patented and thus accessible to all firms, but the specific techniques developed for the production and shaping of parts. The main users of those products were the mechanical engineering industry, the motor industry, and the electrical industry.[14]

  One of the licensee firms was Ets Luchaire SA (Luchaire). It concluded a licensing agreement with Kabelmetal whose main provisions were as follows:
    – Exclusive license agreement in France for the manufacture of all products in which production Kabelmetall used its secret and patented manufacturing techniques.
    – The exclusive right granted to Luchaire to sell those products in some non-Member States (Spain and Portugal) and the prohibition for Luchaire to sell in other non-Member States other than Spain and Portugal.
    – Non-exclusive right granted to Luchaire to sell the same products in all Member States.
    – Agreement on the reciprocal exchange of information concerning the application of the licensed techniques.
    – Luchaire undertook to grant Kabelmetal a non-exclusive license for all potential improvements related to the licensed processes discovered and patented by the licensee.
    – Luchaire would have paid royalties for the license. At the same time Kabelmetal undertook to not grant anybody better conditions and terms for licensing agreements concerning the same object.[15]

  b. **Origin of the case**
  On 2 February 1963 Kabel und Metallwerke Neumeyer AG (later to become Kabel und Metallwerke Gutehoffnungshütte AG) submitted to the Commission a notification pursuant to Article 4 of Regulation 17 to see a patent and know-how licensing agreement concluded with Ets Luchaire SA be declared exempted from the application of Article 101(1) FEU Treaty by virtue of Article 101(3) FEU Treaty.

  c. **Economic analysis**
  The Commission concerns arising in patent licensing agreements are not much different from those arising in other IPR licensing issues, including trademarks. As described in the previous section of this chapter, the Commission recognizes the freedom of an IPR holder to choose her licensees, but is concerned about the possible partitioning and exclusionary effects that might derive from exclusivity

---

14   See recital I-1 of the decision.   15   See recital I-2 of the decision.

clauses attached to the agreements in question. The former aspect emerges very clearly in this decision from the obligation imposed by the Commission upon the parties. It concerned an originally drafted agreement different from the one assessed in the decision to eliminate a clause prohibiting the licensee to export the products from France (the exclusivity territory of the licensee) to other Member States.[16]

In assessing the competitive impact of the licensing agreement, referring to the effect on other potential licensee's competitors willing to use the exclusively licensed technology, the Commission stated that "[i]f the patent holder... undertakes to restrict the use of his inventions to one single firm in a specified territory, he is no longer able to make agreements with other applicants for licenses; such an undertaking on the part of the holder is not of *the essence of the patent*; such an exclusive license... may be a restriction of competition. [T]he exclusive manufacturing agreement granted by Kabel-metal, apart from restricting Kabelmetal's freedom, seriously affect [ed] the position of others... who might wish to apply the techniques in question, since they are prevented from using these techniques within the common market."[17] Even without clarifying the exact meaning of the "essence of the patent," the Commission voiced the concerns that arose. Other contractual clauses were not considered restrictive of competition but instead conducive to the proper and full implementation of the patentee's rights.[18]

The Commission evaluated the efficiencies generated by the exclusive agreement and weighed them against the mentioned restrictive effects. The Commission's approach toward the licensing of patents, even if it would be modeled and further specified throughout the years, and even if its economically oriented setting would be specified as well, as reflected in several legislative measures,[19] is already concerned about the effects on the market outcome that the agreement would produce. This is true at least with reference to interbrand competition. When the Commission stated that "[t]his provision has therefore enabled another manufacturer within the EEC to use improved techniques for machines steel parts – techniques which... make possible considerable savings in raw material and the production of high-quality finished products,"[20] it showed concerns about the whole of the Community production's increase and improvement as result of the licensing agreement.

The territorial protection granted to the licensee was considered indispensable for the attainment of that goal. The Commission stated that "to grant Luchaire exclusive rights contributes to promoting economic progress, since *it made possible the licensing agreement* in question by guaranteeing Luchaire a sufficient return on its investment by virtue of the territorial advantages it derives from the exclusion of any other firm which might be interested

---

16 See recital 15 of the decision.
17 Recital 6 of the decision. Emphasis added.
18 See recital 8 of the decision.
19 For the currently applicable legislation, see paragraph B. The current Block Exemption Regulation on Technological Transfer Agreements is, compared with previous legislative measures applicable to this kind of agreement, an expression of the more economically oriented approach adopted by the Commission.
20 Recital 10 of the decision.

in manufacturing on the basis of the licensor's techniques."[21] It then added, with a reasoning reflecting the approach adopted in the appraisal of clauses eliminating intrabrand competition in case of IPR licensing (see the *Campari* decision, section 4.1), that "[g]iven the investment required to apply Kabelmetal's techniques and to promote sales of products manufactured by extrusion process,... Kabelmetal would have been unable to get any interested firm in the EEC to apply the techniques it possessed at that time, or indeed any new development involving fresh investment, had it not given an undertaking that other firms would be unable to compete with it directly by manufacturing the products in question using the same protected or secret techniques in the territory covered by the licensing agreement. The protection which this territorial advantage gives against the risk of insufficient use of production capacity that has had to be created could not be attained by measures which would restrict competition to a lesser degree."[22]

d. **Fines, remedies, and conditions enclosed**
    – Obligations for the parties to inform the Commission of all judgments given under the arbitration clause.
e. **Further developments of the case**
    None.

F.2 *Bronbemaling/Heidemaatschappij* Commission decision 75/570/EEC [1975] OJ L 249/27

Relevance: Confirming and specifying its approach the Commission assessed the exclusionary effects deriving from clauses of exclusivity included in the agreement, as well as their negative consequences affecting market outcome.

- Case IV/28.967
- **Decision:** Infringement of Article 101 FEU Treaty
- **Decision addressee(s):**
    – NV Heidemaatschappij Beheer, *the Netherlands*
    – Landdevelopment and Reclamation Company (Lareco) BV, *the Netherlands*
    – BV Grondboorbedrijf J. Mos, *the Netherlands*
    – De Ruiter Boringen en Bemalingen BV, *the Netherlands*
    – Reinders-Wessemius Grondboorbedrijven BV, *the Netherlands*
- **Report route:** Notification for exemption submitted to the Commission on 6 August 1974 by NV Heidemaatschappij Beheer, Lareco BV, BV Grondboorbedrijf J. Mos, De Ruiter Boringen en Bemalingen BV, and Reinders-Wessemius Grondboorbedrijven BV
- **Date of the decision:** 25 July 1975
- **Competition Commissioner:** R. Vouel
- **Relevant product market:** System for the installation of well-point drainage systems
- **Relevant geographical market:** the Netherlands
- **Description of the case**
    a. **Relevant facts**
        NV Heidemaatschappij Beheer (HB) filed a patent application concerning "a process for the installation of a well-point drainage system consisting of filter

tubes connected to pumps and of a well-point drainage system installed in this way."[23] During the procedure for the granting of the patent, three firms – A. H. Steenberger BV, De Ruiter BV, and Grondboorbedrijf J. Mos – opposed the awarding of the patent. They claimed that the process submitted for patenting was already used by them and that they were already manufacturing equipment as a result of it. The patent would have granted an undue monopoly to the holder, excluding them from the use of the system.

They subsequently reached an agreement with HB according to which they would have withdrawn their opposition to the patent in return for a license granted to each one of them. The agreement also included a clause according to which HB would refrain from granting further identical or similar licenses to other firms in the Netherlands without the agreement of the majority of all parties to the agreement (i.e. HB and the three licensees). The agreement was effectively implemented when two outside firms applied for a license and were rejected by such a majority.[24]

b. **Origin of the case**

On 6 August 1974 the above-mentioned undertakings submitted to the Commission a notification pursuant to Article 4 of Regulation 17 to see the patent licensing agreements between each one of them and Heidemaatschappij Beheer be declared exempted from the application of Article 101(1) FEU Treaty by virtue of Article 101(3) FEU Treaty.

c. **Economic analysis**

In this decision, the Commission was faced with a situation in which the process subject to the procedure for granting the patent was already known and used by several undertakings. The Commission confirmed and specified its approach concerning exclusive clauses included in licensing agreements. Here it applied it to a case where efficiencies of exclusive licenses seemed not very realistic and where total market output could have been negatively affected.

For this reason, the Commission held that "The provisions objected [to] [i.e. the provided necessity of licensees' approval to grant further licenses] do not contribute to improving the production or distribution of goods or to promoting technical or economic progress. On the contrary, by allowing the number of firms authorised to exploit the patented process to be restricted they hinder wider use of the process and prevent know-how from being enriched by a broader range of experience. This process is already well known and widely used in the Netherlands; confining its exploitation to a limited number of licensees has no beneficial economic effect such as might be expected of an exclusive license having the prime purpose of facilitating penetration of a new market . . . Far from allowing consumers a fair share of the benefits derived by the firms concerned from the agreements, the agreements hinder the development of competition and prevent users from being supplied on more favourable terms . . . Moreover, contracts for major projects frequently stipulate that . . . no other process can

---

23 Recital I of the decision.   24   Recital I of the decision.

be used [therefore] undertakings which are not licensed to exploit the patented process cannot tender."[25]

d. Fines, remedies, and conditions enclosed

None.

e. Further developments of the case

None.

F.3 *UEFA* Commission decision 2003/778/EC [2003], OJ L 291/25

Relevance: This decision illustrates a way to balance exclusive rights for selling media rights in the sport sector with a broader access of broadcasters as well internet and telephone operators and their compatibility with European Competition rules.

- Case COMP/C.2–37.398
- **Decision:** Exemption pursuant to Article 101(3) FEU Treaty for seven years
- **Decision addressee(s):**
    - Union des Associations Européennes de Football, *Switzerland*
- **Report route:** Notification for exemption submitted to the Commission on 1 February 1999 by UEFA and amended on 13 May 2002.
- **Date of the decision:** 23 July 2003
- **Competition Commissioner:** M. Monti
- **Relevant product market:** Upstream market for the sale and acquisition of free-TV, pay-TV, and pay-per-view rights; downstream markets on which TV broadcasters compete for advertising revenue depending on audience rates, and for pay-TV/pay-per-view subscribers; upstream market for wireless/3G/UMTS rights, Internet rights, and video-on-demand rights; upstream and downstream market for the other commercial rights (sponsorship, suppliership and product licensing)
- **Relevant geographical market:** EU Member States' national markets
- **Description of the case**
    a. **Relevant facts**

    UEFA is an association of national football associations registered in Switzerland. At the time of the decision the UEFA counted fifty-one members, twenty-one located in the EEA. The association holds sole jurisdiction to organise or abolish international tournaments in Europe among which is the UEFA Champions League. The Champions League is a tournament organised every year between the top European football clubs. The media rights for the three qualifying rounds are sold by the members of the association or football clubs themselves whereas the joint selling arrangement applies only to the UEFA Champions League stage and final knockout phases. Within a joint selling agreement, sports clubs transfer their media rights to their respective sports association which then sells these rights as a bundled product to a particular broadcaster.

    On 19 February 1999 UEFA notified rules, regulations, and implementing decisions with regard to its joint selling arrangement to the Commission. After the statement of objections by the Commission on 18 July 2001 including the rejection of exemption under Article 101(1) FEU Treaty, UEFA amended the

---

25   Recital III of the decision.

arrangement. The Commission especially criticised the former arrangement that UEFA was selling all Champions League TV rights in one single package to only one broadcaster for several years in a row. This procedure constituted only one single source of supply and was found by the Commission to restrict competition between broadcasters.[26] Moreover, other sources such as internet or phone operators were excluded from access to a broadcast of the matches because they were exclusively shown on TV. The Commission found that this procedure further reduced the development of digital sport services and the new products of mobile phones which was moreover not in the interest of broadcasters, clubs, consumers, and fans.

The amended joint selling arrangement included the following main provisions focusing on the reduction of UEFA's exclusive rights to sell media rights:[27]

- The broadcasting rights for matches within the UEFA Champions League are transferred to UEFA except those of the three qualifying matches.
- UEFA's main TV rights will be split into two packages for free-TV and pay-TV, each including two matches per night.
- If UEFA does not manage to sell the media rights by a certain cut-off date, the individual football clubs are entitled to market the matches themselves.
- In addition to UEFA, the football clubs are entitled to show Champions League's content on the internet and to provide it to operators using, for instance, the UMTS technology.
- Individual football clubs gain the right to use archive content.
- The rights will be sold for a period of no longer than three years by UEFA through a public tender procedure in which all broadcasters are allowed to submit bids.

b. Origin of the case

On 1 February 1999 UEFA submitted to the Commission a notification pursuant to Article 4 of Regulation 17 to see a joint selling arrangement relating to the selling of television broadcasting rights and amended on 13 May 2002 declared exempted from the application of Article 101(1) FEU Treaty by virtue of Article 101(3) FEU Treaty.

c. Economic analysis

Sport is subject to EU law, and more specifically to competition rules, to the extent that it constitutes an economic activity within the meaning of Article 3 of the FEU Treaty.[28] The regulations of the UEFA Champions League contain the rules for the purchase of the commercial rights that were granted to UEFA. In assessing the impact of the joint selling arrangement, the Commission found that it restricts competition because UEFA holds an exclusionary position with regard to sell jointly the commercial rights of the UEFA Champions League.[29]

---

26   See recital 19 of the decision.
27   See recitals 26–54 of the decision.

28   See recital 105 of the decision.
29   See recital 114 of the decision.

The Commission stated that "the media rights…relate to all types of media rights and are not restricted to the rights of specific markets. As such, the restrictive effects of UEFA's joint selling arrangement are capable of manifesting themselves on any of the markets where the rights be used."[30] Individual football clubs are thus excluded from marketing the commercial rights individually. As a consequence, commercial operators are forced to purchase the relevant rights under the conditions and prices set up by the joint selling body.

The Commission concluded that the joint selling arrangement restricted competition in the upstream market where rights owners – for example, sports associations – sell their rights to broadcasters. Furthermore, competition in the downstream broadcasting market was restricted since football events play an important role in competition for advertisers or for subscribers for pay-TV and pay-per-view TV.[31]

In assessing the conditions for exemption under Article 101(3) FEU Treaty, the Commission weighed the efficiencies gained by the joint selling arrangement against its restrictive effects.

The Commission accepted the following efficiencies resulting from a joint selling arrangement: the creation of a single point of sale and branding.

Firstly, through the sale of a package of media rights business operations are facilitated.[32] If package rights are sold to a single media operator, transaction costs are reduced and hence, efficiencies are created. Moreover, a single point of sale is essential because no individual football club can foresee how far it will proceed in the tournament, and thus is unable to sign a commercial contract for selling its commercial rights.[33] A single point of sale is further attractive if an international competition such as the UEFA Champions League takes place because it benefits the planning of the program schedule and allows media operators to broadcast the league as a whole.[34] Besides consumers this procedure additionally enables broadcasters to plan commercial, technical, and programming plans for a whole football season.[35]

Secondly, the selling of the rights to an entire tournament according to the Commission provides the chance to establish a brand. The joint selling procedure guarantees the uniformity and consistency of the product's quality.[36] The media operator can establish a brand for that tournament, increasing its recognition among consumers and, hence, broadening distribution. In contrast to the joint selling of media rights, football clubs cannot package the rights from different football clubs into one package that would appear like an UEFA Champions League branded product.[37]

The Commission concluded that restrictions were indispensable to ensure a product of high quality representing the UEFA Champions League objectively and independently.[38] Moreover, they are indispensable to provide the tournament to viewers as a whole. The Commission considered further that clubs

---

30   See recital 113 of the decision.
31   See recital 116 of the decision.
32   See recital 139 of the decision.
33   See recital 140 of the decision.
34   See recital 145 of the decision.

35   See recital 149 of the decision.
36   See recital 154 of the decision.
37   See recital 162 of the decision.
38   See recital 174 of the decision.

do not possess the ability to sell on their own behalf exactly the same rights compared to the UEFA Champions League package which is jointly sold. On the other hand, clubs do have the possibility of individual sales. They can sell the media rights if UEFA has not found demand for them and this leads to competition between UEFA and the football clubs.

d. Fines, remedies, and conditions enclosed
- Condition that football clubs may sell their live TV rights to free-TV broadcasters if there is no reasonable offer from any pay-TV broadcaster.

e. Further developments of the case
None.

5 Vertical restrictions

A Introduction

Vertical agreements are concluded between companies at different levels of the supply chain. They are widely used when there are frequent vertical business interactions. Few firms produce inhouse all their required inputs and are active in all stages of the production process, up to and including the specialised distribution of the final goods and services. Vertical agreements between independent firms can often create cost efficiencies, enhanced production efficiency, or an improved allocation of products on the market. In particular, they can help prevent double mark-ups, free-riding among either producers or retailers, and the promotion of investments in service and the certification of quality. Vertical agreements are therefore common and efficient in many production chains.

Vertical agreements may, however, also restrain trade and so have anticompetitive effects. The imposition of maximum prices, for example, may protect downstream market power. Vertical restraints are also known to restrict entry for new competitors – for instance, by preventing access to distributors – and reduce either intrabrand or interbrand competition, or both. These anticompetitive effects of vertical agreements are discussed in the literature and have been identified by competition authorities including the European Commission.

To assess the possible anticompetitive effects of vertical agreements properly, it is important to understand the type and degree of competition at all relevant levels of the production chain. Indeed, the restrictive effects of vertical restraints are typically produced horizontally from one layer of production to another. To balance the potential pro- and anticompetitive effects of vertical agreements requires a careful case-by-case assessment of market conditions.

Section 5.1 discusses exclusive agreements resulting in foreclosure of the market. Section 5.2 deals with territorial exclusivity and parallel import/export-bans. These types of agreements are of particular concern in Europe, because they go against the internal market objective. Section 5.3 deals with Resale Price Maintenance (RPM), which has consistently been considered as anticompetitive in Europe. Bundling and tying are discussed in section 5.4. Section 5.5 is about selective distribution systems, which have rarely raised competition concerns with the European Commission. Section 5.6 discusses franchising and section 5.7 discounts and rebates. In several sections, reference is made to relevant parts of chapter 3, where vertical agreements relate to possible abuses of dominance.

B Applicable EU legislation

Regulation 2790/1999 on the application of Article 81(3) of the Treaty to categories of vertical relations and concerted practices [1999] OJ L 336/21 (Block Exemption Regulation on

Vertical Agreements). For vertical restraints not covered by the Block Exemption Regulation on Vertical Agreements, Article 101 FEU Treaty is applicable.

Commission Guidelines on Vertical Restraints [2000] OJ C 291/1.

Commission Notice on the definition of the relevant market for the purposes of Community competition law [1997] OJ C 372/3.

C Related economics texts[1]

Bishop and Walker (2009), paragraphs 5.34–5.55
Carlton and Perloff (2005), chapter 12
Church and Ware (2000), chapter 22
Martin (1994), chapter 17
Martin (2002), chapter 13
Motta (2004), chapter 6
Tirole (1988), chapter 4
Waldman and Jensen (2001), chapter 15

D Related legal texts

Bellamy and Child (2008), chapter 6
Jones and Sufrin (2008), chapter 9
Ritter and Braun (2005), chapter 4
Whish (2008), chapter 16

5.1 Exclusive dealing and market foreclosure

A Introduction

There are various types of exclusive dealing contracts. An exclusive purchasing agreement is an agreement through which a retailer undertakes to purchase his demand for a certain product only from one supplier and refrains from doing business with competing suppliers of the same good. This type of agreement can ensure that the manufacturer appropriates a specific investment made by avoiding free riding and stimulating the maximum effort of a retailer in the commercialization and advertisement of its products. In an exclusive distribution agreement, a manufacturer supplies only one or a few chosen retailers in a given territory. These agreements may improve the quality of service – for example, through product-specific staff training and facilitated customer feedback. Many cases dealt with by the Commission involved combinations of exclusive purchasing and distribution in one agreement.

---

1   In many of the textbooks referred to in this book, the economics of vertical relation are described following a distinction between intrabrand and interbrand competition. The effect of this categorization is that many restraints described in independent sections of this book are touched upon several times throughout the chapter(s) of each book dedicated to vertical restraints. This is the reason why in many sections following this introductory section about vertical restraints, the reference is made to the entire chapter(s) of the books and not to a specific paragraph/section.

In addition to the potential anticompetitive effects of the type of contracts here discussed, exclusive dealing contracts often impede firms' entry into foreign Member State economies, which can hinder the objective of the "creation and implementation of the internal market." In particular, this is so when the contracts have evolved nationally over many years and involve sharing arrangements concerning the surplus.

B Applicable EU Legislation

No special legislation applicable. For applicable legislation see Chapter 5, paragraph B.

C Related economics texts

Bishop and Walker (2009), paragraphs 5.34–5.55
Carlton and Perloff (2005), chapter 12, paragraph 3
Church and Ware (2000), paragraph 22.3.2
Martin (1994), chapter 17
Martin (2002), paragraph 13.2.5
Motta (2004), chapter 6, specifically paragraph 6.4.1
Tirole (1988), paragraph 4.4.1
Waldman and Jensen (2001), chapter 15, paragraph 3

D Related Legal Texts

Bellamy and Child (2008), chapter 6, paragraphs 4(A, B) and 6(A, 6.139–6.140 and B, 6.143–6.158)
Jones and Sufrin (2008), chapter 9, paragraph 4(B, iii, b, and c)
Ritter and Braun (2005), chapter 4, paragraph B(5, a, d, and 6)
Whish (2008), chapter 16, paragraph 6(G, i, ii, and iii)

E Commission decisions in chronological order*

Bendix & Meertens and Straet Commission decision 64/344/EEC [1964] OJ L 64/1426, Case IV/12.868
Deutsche Philips GmbH Commission decision 73/322/EEC [1973] OJ L 293/40, Case IV/27.010 **(described in detail as landmark case in section 5.3)**
Frubo 74/433/EEC [1974] OJ L 237/16, Case IV/26.602
Stoves and Heaters (Haarden- en Kachelhandel) Commission decision 75/358/EEC [1975] OJ L 159/22, Case IV/712
Reuter/BASF **Commission decision 76/743/EEC [1976] OJ L 254/40, Case IV/28.996**
Junghans Commission decision 77/100/EEC [1977] OJ L 30/10, Case IV/5715

•   Decisions displayed in **bold type** are described in the section. Decisions highlighted with (*) include interesting economic analysis by the Commission on the specific topic of the section. Some decisions contain economic reasoning on more than one topic and therefore appear in several lists of Commission decisions in chronological order. Reference is made in brackets and **bold type** to the relevant section in which the decision is extensively described as a landmark case. When decisions are referenced and/or described in some detail in one or more of the economic textbooks, reference in brackets is also made to the relevant part(s) of those texts.

Centraal Bureau voor de Rijwielhandel Commission decision 78/59/EEC [1978] OJ L 20/18, Case IV/147

Cauliflowers Commission decision 78/66/EEC [1978] OJ L 21/23, Case IV/28.948

Liebig Spices **Commission decision 78/172/EEC [1978] OJ L 53/20, Case IV/29.418**

Zanussi Commission decision 78/922/EEC [1978] OJ L 322/36, Case IV/1576

BP KEMI-DDSF Commission decision 79/934/EEC [1979] OJ L 235/20, Case IV/29.021

Cane Sugar Supply Agreements Commission decision 80/183/EEC [1980] OJ L 39/64, Case IV/29.266

The Distillers Co. Ltd – Victuallers Commission decision 80/789/EEC [1980] OJ L 233/43, Case IV/26.528 (Bishop and Walker, 2009, 1.08)

Cafeteros de Colombia Commission decision 82/860/EEC [1982] OJ L 360/31, Case IV/30.077

Schlegel/CPIO Commission decision 83/622/EEC [1983] OJ L 351/20, Case IV/30.099

Nutricia Commission decision 83/670/EEC [1983] OJ L 376/22, Cases IV/30.389, 30.408 (*)

Aluminium Commission decision 85/206/EEC [1985] OJ L 92/1, Case IV/26.870

Peugeot Commission decision 86/506/EEC [1986] OJ L 295/19, Case IV/31.143

ARG/Unipart Commission decision 88/84/EEC [1988] OJ L 45/34, Case IV/31.914

Bloemenveilingen Aalsmeer Commission decision 88/491/EEC [1988] OJ L 262/27, Case IV/31.379

National Sulphuric Acid Association Commission decision 89/408/EEC [1980] OJ L 190/22, Case IV/27.958 (*)

IJsselcentrale and others Commission decision 91/50/EEC [1991] OJ L 28/32, Case IV/32.732

Scottish Nuclear, Nuclear Energy Agreement Commission decision 91/329/EEC [1991] OJ L 178/31, Case IV/33.473

Distribution of Packages Tours 1990 World Cup Commission decision 92/521/EEC [1992] OJ L 326/31, Cases IV/33.378, 33.384

Schoeller Lebensmittel GmbH and Co. KG Commission decision 93/405/EEC [1993] OJ L 183/1, Case IV/31.533 (Motta, 2004, pp. 391–8)

Langnese-Iglo GmbH Commission decision 93/406/EEC [1993] OJ L 183/19, Case IV/34.072 (*) (Motta, 2004, pp. 391–8)

Van Den Bergh Foods **Commission decision 98/531/EC [1998] OJ L 246/1, Cases IV/34.395, 34.073, 35.436**

FEG and TU Commission decision 2000/117/EC [2001] OJ L 39/1, Case IV/33.884

PO/Yamaha Commission decision of 16 July 2003, published on DG Comp website, Case COMP/37.975

Telenor, Canal +, Canal Digital Commission decision of 29 December 2003, published on DG Comp website, Case COMP/C-2/38.287

F   Economic landmark cases

F.1   *Reuter/BASF* Commission decision 76/743/EEC [1976] OJ L 254/40

Relevance: The Commission describes the effect on competition of "non-competition obligations." The Commission approach toward this type of limitation in vertical relations tends to recognize their necessity in order to protect the investments made and the market value of the (possibly) transferred technology, know-how, and goodwill. The appropriability of the benefits underlying the conclusion of the vertical agreement are also taken into consideration in the assessment of the potentially restrictive effect of the exclusive dealing clauses.

- Case IV/28.996
- **Decision:** Infringement of Article 101 FEU Treaty
- **Decision addressee(s):**
    - BASF Aktiengesellschaft, *Federal Republic of Germany*
    - Dr. Gottfried Reuter, *Federal Republic of Germany*
    - Gottfried Reuter Holding GmbH, *Switzerland*
- **Report route:** Complaint lodged with the Commission on 27 January 1975 by Dr. Gottfried Reuter
- **Date of the decision:** 26 June 1976
- **Competition Commissioner:** G. M. Thomson
- **Relevant product market:** Polyurethanes
- **Relevant geographical market:** European internal market
- **Description of the case**
    a. **Relevant facts**
        The product object of the decision are synthetic products used for the manufacture of a variety of final products in a number of industries such as motor, construction, shipbuilding, and mechanical engineering. The semi-finished products could already be used at different stages of the production so that different materials and/or products were available.[2]

        At the time of the decision and in the years preceding 1976, the market for polyurethanes was in continuous and rapid expansion. Bayer was by far the largest supplier of the European market and only a limited number of competitors were active in Europe. Among those, BASF Aktiengesellschaft (BASF) was a manufacturer operating in most stages of polyurethanes transformation that had adopted a policy aimed at strengthening its position in the markets for the other production stages by joint venture companies with other producers and by the acquisition of the Elastomer Group (Elastomer). The latter was a group formed by many companies active as "system formulator" in a variety of research, development, and construction activities connected to the polyurethanes market. Half of Elastomer's shares were held by Dr. Reuter, a researcher chemist specializing in polyurethanes. The remaining 50 percent of the shares in Elastomer AG, on which Dr. Reuter held an option to purchase, were held by the Investitions- und Handelsbank Zurich (IHB).

        Dr. Reuter reached an agreement with BASF according to which he would have exercised his option on the IHB shares and transferred them to BASF. At the same time Reuter granted BASF an irreversible option to acquire the 50 percent of shares he already owned. After the share transfer was concluded, Reuter would also transfer all know-how and technology in the relevant field to Glasurit (a BASF subsidiary).

        The agreement was completed by a clause stating that "Dr. Reuter shall for a period of eight years from the signing of this contract refrain from engaging directly or indirectly in any activity in Germany or elsewhere in the relevant field; he shall form no new firms of his own in this field nor own any firms

---

2   See recital I-1 of the decision.

or shares in firms, nor maintain or enter into any contractual association with third parties, nor act as employee, adviser or in any similar function."[3]

Furthermore the parties agreed that "Dr. Reuter may continue R&D activities [only] on manufacturing processes for isocyanates and ployether polyols and may commercialize the result of his R&D by issuing licenses . . . However, he shall not hold shares in companies operating plants using their own processes."[4]

In addition Dr. Reuter guaranteed not to reveal to any third party for a period of eight years any protected or unprotected know-how, information, and experience related to the field nor any relevant non-public information concerning the Elastomer business.[5]

b. Origin of the case

On 27 January 1975 Dr. Gottfried Reuter filed to the Commission a complaint for the purpose of Article 3 of Regulation 17. The Commission decided to initiate proceedings.

c. Economic analysis

This decision exemplifies the Commission's approach to "non-competition clauses." These kinds of obligations are often included as a contractual condition in vertical relations and are particularly common in cases of vertical integration. In the present case, the effect on competition was even strengthened by the transfer of ownership, technology, and know-how in addition to the explicit non-compete clause protecting the business that BASF acquired through the transaction.

In its appraisal of non-compete clauses, the Commission developed an approach aimed at one of three goals. Firstly, it committed to trying to protect the value of an acquisition made by one of the contractors. Secondly, it committed to protect the investment made by one of the contract partners. Thirdly, it protected the ability of the contractor to reap the benefits underlying the vertical agreement. These commitments thus led the Commission to regularly clear a number of agreements for a limited period of time to allow for the anticipated benefits to materialize, subject to a continued reassessment of whether the alleged benefits were indeed being reaped.

In the present decision, the Commission established a general principle applying to non-compete obligations stating that "[w]hen the material assets of a business are sold it is not normally necessary to protect the purchaser by imposing a prohibition on competition on the seller. In the present case, however, the sale included goodwill and know-how; indeed these items constituted a substantial part of the asset transferred. In order to determine whether Article 85(1) applies to the non-competition clause in the agreement, it is above all necessary to examine how far the clause is essential to the preservation of the transferred worth of the undertaking and it exceeds what is necessary for such preservation."[6]

---

3   Recital I-3 of the decision. The contractual clause referred to is indicated in the decision as Clause IX.
4   *Idem*. The contractual clause referred to is indicated in the decision as Clause X.
5   See recital I-3 of the decision. The contractual clause referred to is indicated in the decision as Clause XI.
6   Recital II-3 of the decision. Accordingly the ECJ, with regard to the general non-compete obligation in [*Pronuptia*], stated that
     " . . . , the franchisor must be able to communicate his know-how to the franchisees and provide them with the necessary assistance in order to enable them to apply his methods, without running the risk that know-how and assistance might benefit competitors, even indirectly. It follows that provisions which are essential in order to avoid that risk do not constitute restrictions on competition for the purposes of Article 85(1). That is also true of a clause prohibiting the franchisee, during the period of validity of the contract

The Commission looked at the three potentially restrictive components of the contracts given by first, the appropriability of the investment, second by the transfer of technology and know-how, and third, of course, the explicit non-compete clause.

As to the first element of its analysis, it stated that "[i]t is recognised that it may be necessary in certain cases to provide safeguards to ensure the effective performance of an agreement. These may take the form of a contractual non-competition clause in case where not only the material assets of an undertaking but also its commercial goodwill, including relations with customers, are to be transferred to the purchaser. In such a case, it is essential to prevent a seller from re-acquiring his old customers either directly or indirectly through cooperation with the purchasers' competitors in the periods immediately following the transfer... This protection must be limited to the period required by an active competitive purchaser for him to take over undiminished the undertaking's market position such as it was at the time of the transfer. Account must be taken of such organizational problems as may arise until the newly acquired firm has been integrated into the purchaser's undertaking or group."[7]

The same reasoning was adopted with reference to the transfer of know-how and technologies. The Commission laid the basis for the appropriability of the benefits associated with the agreement by means of protecting the buyer's newly acquired know-how. This was done by protecting it from ongoing attempts of the seller of know-how to continue to exert competitive pressure on the acquirer. This was consequential to the fact that "the transfer of technical know-how in connection with the sale of an undertaking does not automatically preclude any further activity on the part of the seller based on such know-how. The opportunity of using know-how which is unknown to competitors is, like goodwill, a competitive advantage."[8]

For the same reasons listed above in case of transfer of goodwill, protection against competition from the seller was considered justified for a limited period of time. "In determining the duration of the non-competition clause, the factors particularly to be taken into account are the nature of the transferred know-how, the opportunities for its use, and the knowledge possessed by the purchaser... A distinction must be made between know-how existing at the date of transfer and new or further developments by the transferrer based on or in connection with the transferred know-how."[9]

In this specific case, the Commission considered that the non-competing obligation used by the acquirer was exceeding what was necessary for achieving the "legitimate object", i.e. the full appropriation of the commercial value of the transfer.[10]

---

and for a reasonable period after its expiry, from opening a shop of the same or a similar nature in an area where he may compete with a member of the network. The same may be said of the franchisee's obligation not to transfer his shop to another party without the prior approval of the franchisor; that provision is intended to prevent competitors from indirectly benefiting from the know-how and assistance provided. Case 161/84 *Pronuptia de Paris GmbH* v. *Pronuptia de Paris Irmgard Schillgallis*, recital 16.

7   *Idem.*
8   *Idem.*
9   *Idem.*
10   Recital II-4 of the decision.

It was particularly the use of an exclusive non-commercialized R&D clause which the Commission considered to be excessively restrictive for a successful takeover and timely know-how and technology transfer, and held that in place of such a clause BASF could by means of "active management in a relatively short time" cope with the "difficulties in reorganizing these fully operational [acquired] undertakings."[11]

The Commission further clarified that "in no circumstances may an obligation to keep know-how secret from third parties, imposed on the transfer of an undertaking, be used to prevent the transferrer, after the expiry of the reasonable term of a non-competition clause, from competing with the transferee by means of new and further developments of such know-how. Nor can it be said that a non-competition clause of a particularly long duration would be justified by the high costs incurred by BASF in taking over the undertaking."[12]

d. Fines, remedies, and conditions enclosed

– Obligations for all the parties to bring the infringement to an end.

e. Further developments of the case

None.

F.2 *Liebig Spices* Commission decision 78/172/EEC [1978] OJ L 53/20

Relevance: Confirming its generally positive approach toward vertical exclusive relations in consideration of the efficiencies produced in the distribution and commercialization of products as well as of their common use in commercial practise, the Commission – in the specific circumstances of the case – detected the anticompetitive effects of exclusive purchasing agreements involving all the large distributors active in the sale of the relevant products. The foreclosure effects for competitors and the absence of beneficial effect for consumers are described.

- Case IV/29.418
- **Decision:** Infringement of Article 101 FEU Treaty
- **Decision addressee(s):**
    – Brooke Bond Liebig Ltd, *United Kingdom*
    – Brooke Bond Liebig Benelux NV, *Belgium*
    – GB-Inno-BM SA, *Belgium*
    – Delhaize Frères et Cie., *Belgium*
    – Le Lion SA, *Belgium*
    – Sarma Penney Ltd, *Belgium*
- **Report route:** Commission decision of 24 June 1977 to start proceedings on its own initiative
- **Date of the decision:** 21 December 1977
- **Competition Commissioner:** R. Vouel
- **Relevant product market:** Packaged spices for domestic consumption
- **Relevant geographical market:** Belgium

---

11   Recital II-4-b of the decision.   12   Recitals II-4-c and II-4-d of the decision.

- **Description of the case**
  - a. **Relevant facts**

    At the time the present decision was adopted, the Belgian market for spices was characterized by fast growth and the presence of four big producers together holding around 85 percent of the market share. They were Brooke Bond Liebig (Liebig), India, Ducros, and Topo. Liebig's share accounted for 39 percent of the Belgian spices market in 1976. Its market share was almost twice the size of that of its closest competitor; its growth rate was also much larger than that of other large producers.

    The food distribution system in Belgium consisted of a host of food stores selling a wide variety of goods including spices and a small group of large self-service stores which accounted for roughly 73 percent of the total turnover of all food stores despite the fact that they represented merely 16 percent of the selling points. Although very limited in number, the super- and hypermarkets made up about 52 percent of total sales among the self-service stores. The three largest supermarkets chains in Belgium were GB-Inno-BM, Delhaize Frères et Cie., Le Lion, and Sarma Penney. Together they achieved almost 60 percent of Liebig's sales in Belgium which represented around 30 percent of the entire Belgian market.

    The above-mentioned three distribution chains all concluded a distribution agreement with Liebig, according to which:
    - The distributors undertook to sell only Liebig spices except spices sold under their own brand name.
    - The distributors accepted the obligation to sell at prices determined by Liebig under the condition that the same price would have been adopted also by other retailers.
    - The distributors were to display Liebig's products in a number of illuminated shelves, positioned above items of common consumption (such as sugar and oil), and always in a more prominent position than the same spices of the distributor's brand.
    - Liebig would have granted annual rebates and sales incentives, and would have guaranteed a minimum profit agreed upon with each distributor. In case the distributor would have not achieved the established profit, the manufacturer would have paid the difference. Furthermore Liebig would have provided the distributors with display units and ensured direct supply so as to avoid the need for the supermarkets to have large stocks.
  - b. **Origin of the case**

    On 31 May 1972 the Commission, on its own initiative, adopted a decision to initiate proceedings against the above-mentioned undertakings in respect of agreements concluded by them concerning the spices market in Europe.
  - c. **Economic analysis**

    The Commission's approach toward exclusive dealings agreements has been, since the very beginning of EU competition law enforcement, aware of the distinctiveness of these kinds of agreement, of their common use in the distribution of the products at retail level, and of the efficiencies they can generate. One of the first Block Exemption Regulations establishing an automatic exemption under Article 101(3) of categories of agreement was in fact the regulation adopted by the Commission in 1967 that exempted – under certain conditions – the exclusive purchasing agreements and the exclusive distribution agreements by the application of Article 101(1).[13]

In this decision, however, the Commission, insisting on the inapplicability of the special legislation, provided for an analysis of the agreements in question that showed its approach toward exclusive dealing agreements and potential beneficial or restrictive effects. Clearly, although it was not a "pure" exclusive purchasing agreement because it permitted the supermarkets to sell their own branded spices, the agreement restricted interbrand competition by preventing distributors from selling other brands than Liebig.

Interestingly, the Commission interpreted the substantial financial rewards in the form of rebates, RPM, and a pre-determined profit that were built into the obligation as means to pay the distributors to exclude competing brands from their shelves. It remarked that "[t]he financial return therefore also restricts competition."[14]

Similarly, the Commission made it clear that the restriction of interbrand competition "prevent[ed] the distributors concerned from exercising their freedom of choice in respect of the purchase and resale of spices by binding them to a single supplier, [f]urthermore they are also such as to restrict competition between spice producers by prohibiting the producers of other brands from selling their own spices through the distributors in question."[15]

The assessment was based on an analysis of the special characteristics of first, the product, second, the distribution system, and, third, the market as a whole.[16] On the basis of this three-pronged approach, the Commission concluded that the agreement imposed a severe restriction of competition and decided against an exemption. "[S]pices for domestic consumption are marketed in very large ranges which can only be adequately introduced and sold in large self-service stores. The large self-service store offers the best setting for the sale of spices, since it is the only place where a large number of consumers can see, familiarize themselves with, and purchase new varieties. [T]he presentation of such a range requires space, proper equipment, supporting services, and a publicity effort which an independent retailer can rarely provide. [S]uch a retailer is generally not interested in offering the entire range . . . The importance of these stores

---

13   Commission Regulation No. 67/67/EEC [1967] OJ 57/849, cited also in recital 25 of the decision.
14   Recital 17 of the decision.
15   Recital 18 of the decision.
16   This is in line with the case-law on exclusive supply agreements. In *Stergios Delimitis* v. *Henninger Bräu AG* (Case C-234/89), in determining the effect of an agreement, the ECJ stated that first the relevant market had to be defined, as both a product market and as a geographical market (see recitals 16–18 of the judgment). Furthermore and in order to assess whether the existence of the exclusive supply agreement impedes access to the market, the ECJ found it necessary to examine the nature and extent of those agreements in their totality, comprising all similar contracts tying a large number of points of sale to several national producers (see recital 19 of the judgment). "The effect of those networks of contracts on access to the market depends specifically on the number of outlets thus tied to national producers in relation to the number of public houses which are not so tied, the duration of the commitments entered into, the quantities of beer to which those commitments relate, and on the proportion between those quantities and the quantities sold by free distributors" (see recital 19 of the judgment). Moreover "account must be taken of the conditions under which competitive forces operate on the relevant market. In that connection it is necessary to know not only the number and the size of producers present on the market, but also the degree of saturation of that market and customer fidelity to existing brands, for it is generally more difficult to penetrate a saturated market in which customers are loyal to a small number of large producers than a market in full expansion in which a large number of small producers are operating without any strong brand names" (see recital 22 of the judgment).

is borne out by the fact that although they represent only 1 percent of the total number of food retailers in Belgium, they account for 30 percent of the distribution of spices in the Belgian market. [Therefore t]he Liebig competitors would make a more pronounced and effective impact and be in a position to expand sales to a greater degree if they had access to the few major distributors rather than having to deal with a large number of smaller retailers. It therefore follows that if a producer is prevented from introducing his brands into the premises of the distributors concerned, his opportunities to canvass for sales and above all to launch his product on the Belgian market are appreciably restricted."[17]

A further consideration of the Commission concerned Liebig's market power. In light of its prominent position in the relevant market, the effect of preventing expansion and entry made the agreement a more serious restriction than, for example, in a more easily penetrable market.[18]

The appraisal of this agreement is consistent with economic theory concerning exclusive supply agreements because it bears on the foreclosure effect associated with exclusive dealing contracts when they are concluded with all (relevant) distributors. Consistently, the Commission stated "these agreements have the effect of excluding other brands without providing the undertakings concerned or consumers with the advantages *normally* expected from an exclusive agreement [and] have adverse effects on distribution, in that they prevent the distribution of several brands at the exact point where such distribution could be made in the most favorable conditions."[19]

These advantages that in the Commission's view were "normally" to be expected from such agreements are listed in the relevant Regulation mentioned above. In particular, they concern the improvement of distribution and the potential to overcome sales conflicts arising from multiple contacts and legal relations, but also the potentially increased promotion of sales and more intensive marketing activities. Similarly, they can be a guarantee for the continuity of supplies, but also for the suppliers themselves they can be a way for small and medium sized firms (SMEs) to enter and compete in new markets.[20]

d. **Fines, remedies, and conditions enclosed**
–   Obligation for the parties to put an end to the infringement.

e. **Further developments of the case**
None.

F.3   *Van den Bergh Foods* Commission decision 98/531/EC [1998] OJ L 246/1

Relevance: The case is an example of the increased economic approach of the Commission toward vertical restraints and exclusivity. An exclusivity clause may significantly restrict competition when used by a dominant firm. The exclusive distribution system is an infringement

17   Recital 21 of the decision.
18   *Idem*. In *Stergios Delimitis* v. *Henninger Bräu AG* (Case C-234/89), with regard to market power the ECJ stated that the "market position of the contracting parties must be taken into consideration. That position is not determined solely by the market share held by the brewery and any group to which it may belong, but also by the number of outlets tied to it or to its group, in relation to the total number of premises for the sale and consumption of drinks found in the relevant market" (recital 25 of the judgment).
19   Recitals 25 and 26 of the decision. Emphasis added.
20   See preamble of Regulation 67, *supra* n. 13.

of both Article 101 and 102, since it combines vertical restraints in the form of current freezer-cabinet agreements with client retailers and the abuse of a dominant position inducing other retailers to also opt for such agreements.

- Cases IV/34.395, IV/34.073, IV/35.436
- **Decision:** Infringement of Articles 101 and 102 FEU Treaty. Ceasing of infringements and informing retailers that the exclusivity provisions are void.
- **Decision addressee(s):** Van den Bergh Foods Ltd, *Ireland*
- **Report route:** Complaint filed to the Commission on 18 September 1991 (IV/34.073), complaint filed to the Commission on 22 July 1992 (IV/34.395), notification to the Commission on 8 March 1995 (IV/35.436)
- **Date of the decision:** 11 March 1998
- **Competition Commissioner:** K. Van Miert
- **Relevant product market:** Single wrapped items of impulse ice cream
- **Relevant geographical market:** Ireland
- **Description of the case**
    a. **Relevant facts**

    Van den Bergh Foods Ltd, formerly known as HB Ice Cream Ltd (HB) was the largest seller of impulse ice-cream products in Ireland. The company had "a policy under which it makes freezer cabinets available to retail outlets stocking its ice-cream products on the basis of cabinet exclusivity."[21] Retailers with an HB cabinet were not allowed to use it to stock impulse ice-cream products by other producers. This exclusive distribution system strenghtened HB's market position. HB achieved a market share for impulse ice cream in Ireland of about 85 percent, with only two competitors, Mars Ireland (Mars) and Valley Ice Cream (Valley), achieving both about 6 percent, with more than tiny market shares. HB's practise of supplying freezer cabinets to retailers subject to a condition of exclusivity was not unique, it was "widely employed by ice-cream manufacturers and distributors throughout Europe."[22]

    Master Foods Ltd, trading as Mars Ireland, was the first to lodge a complaint with the Commission against HB because the latter provided freezer cabinets to a large number of retailers in return for exclusivity in stocking the wrapped ice cream. Mars claimed that competition was restrained since access could not be gained to a sizeable number of retail outlets in this way. A similar complaint was lodged by Valley one year later. This company went into liquidation in 1997, before the date of the decision. In May 1992, there was an Irish High Court ruling allowing for supplier-exclusive cabinets and Mars and Valley followed HB in amending their cabinet agreements to make them exclusive as well.

    Retail outlets have limited space for the siting of freezer-cabinets. These freezers are necessary to store impulse ice cream and very few of them are retailer-owned. The manufacturers lend the freezer cabinets to the retailer free on loan and subject to freezer-cabinet agreements, meaning that the retailer has to use the freezers exclusively for the storage of the supplier's products. HB has for many years made freezer-cabinets available to retailers. The retailer does not have to pay a rent for this and maintenance and repair is also performed by

21 See recital 1 of the decision. 22 See recital 21 of the decision.

HB. Maintaining cabinet ownership and exclusivity has been a strategic goal for HB.[23]

Exclusivity is an issue since the vast majority (87 percent)[24] of retail outlets is not willing to use up further space to install another freezer for impulse ice cream. When asked if prepared to exchange the existing HB cabinet with one from another ice-cream supplier, 82 percent said they were not prepared to do so. The key reasons being "the popularity and leadership position of HB and contentment with the present arrangement."[25] Some 72 percent of all retail outlets selling impulse ice cream had at least one HB cabinet, leaving Mars (14 percent), Nestle (10 percent), and Valley (10 percent) far behind.[26]

The contractual provisions in the cabinet agreements restricted the ability of the contracting retailers to stock and offer for sale impulse products from competing suppliers. Retailers were unlikely to exchange a HB cabinet for one by another supplier given the overwhelming strength of HB's position on the relevant market. In addition, they were also unlikely to acquire and maintain their own cabinet, because of higher costs and inconvenience. The likelihood of installing an additional freezer-cabinet next to a HB one was also small, given the limited retail space in many outlets and the strength of HB on the relevant market, implying little extra sales from an additional cabinet. Hence, interbrand competition was claimed by Mars and Valley to be severely limited.

b. Origin of the case

On 18 September 1991, Mars filed a complaint under Article 3 of Regulation 17. This was followed on 22 July 1992 by a similar complaint by Valley. On 29 July 1993 the Commission provisionally concluded that HB had infringed both Article 101 and 102. HB contested this view and the Commission allowed HB to come with proposals to modify its distribution arrangements. On 8 March 1995, these were notified to the Commission and on 15 August 1995 the Commission announced its intention to take a favourable view toward HB's notified arrangements. The Commission revised its expressed intention because of lack of results of the altered arrangements and on 22 January 1997 sent a new statement of objections to HB.

c. Economic analysis

The decision has both elements of vertical restraints (exclusivity clause) and abuse of dominance. Therefore, it is ruled under both Article 101 and 102. The exclusivity provision in HB's freezer-cabinet agreements relating to outlets where the only freezer-cabinets in place have been provided by HB, constitutes an infringement of Article 101(1). HB's inducement to retailers to enter into cabinet agreements subject to a condition of exclusivity by offering and maintaining cabinets at no direct charge, constitutes an infringement of Article 102.

Competing suppliers were foreclosed from access to those outlets with HB freezer-cabinet agreements. Entry to the market was virtually impossible; foreclosure in the Irish market was as much as 89 percent.[27] "This incumbency

---

23 See recitals 65–68 of the decision.
24 See recital 97 of the decision.
25 See recital 104 of the decision.

26 See recital 91 of the decision.
27 See recital 114 of the decision.

advantage has ensured that the only new entrants to the relevant market in recent times have had 'deep pockets': Mars, Häagen Dazs and Nestlé."[28] The market entry of Mars had led HB to insist on freezer exclusivity as a means of checking the effective entry and expansion of a new rival.

The vertical restraint led to the inability of retailers to exercise their commercial freedom of choice. It was made very unattractive for retailers not to have a HB cabinet. HB's exclusive distribution system led to a serious distortion of the competitive landscape because of the dominant position of the firm. Other firms had similar freezer-cabinet agreements but their impact was much smaller than that of HB. The market was continuously dominated by one firm for a long time, having some four-fifths of the market. The proposed revised distribution arrangements in 1995 were first seen by the Commission as "an opportunity for a far-reaching structural change in the market."[29] In no way did this result materialize.

The position of HB on the relevant market for single wrapped impulse ice cream was so dominant not only because of a very large market share, but also because HB was part of the powerful Unilever group. HB also had an extensive product range. It was very attractive for retailers to enter into freezer-cabinet agreements with HB and HB was not only aware of this but targeted it. HB's competitors thus found market penetration and expansion very difficult. The Commission states that "An undertaking in a dominant position has a special responsibility not to allow its conduct to impair genuine undistorted competition in the common market."[30]

d.   Fines, remedies, and conditions enclosed

Van den Bergh Foods Ltd had to cease the infringements and the exclusivity provisions had to be declared void.

e.   Further developments of the case

Case T-65/98 *Van der Bergh Foods* v. *Commission* [2003] ECR II-4653. Commission decision upheld.

Case C-552/03 *Unilever Bestfoods (anciennement Van der Bergh Foods)* v. *Commission* [2006] ECR I-9091. Appeal dismissed.

5.2   Territorial exclusivity and parallel import/export bans

A   Introduction

Territorial exclusivity is a special form of an exclusive dealing agreement that attracts the European Commission's special attention as a potential territorial partitioning of the European Member States. The constitutional objective of installing and implementing a single market in Europe lies at the heart of the above-mentioned concern that by means of territorial exclusivity agreements the European market will remain artificially separated. This is also the reason why the rules against parallel import bans are strictly enforced by the Commission. Import ban clauses are commonly included in exclusive distribution agreements and oblige each exclusive distributor to

---

28   See recital 191 of the decision.   30   See recital 267 of the decision.
29   See recital 246 of the decision.

respect the exclusivity of the territory allotted by the manufacturer to other distributors and not to jeopardize the artificially created "monopolistic area" with parallel imports. At the same time, the prevention of arbitrage among retailers – that is, parallel imports from cheaper areas to areas where prices are higher – can constitute an important instrument to guarantee the effectiveness of the territorial restriction clauses.

B Applicable EU legislation

No special legislation applicable. For applicable legislation see chapter 5, paragraph B.

C Related economics texts

Bishop and Walker (2009), paragraphs 5.34–5.55
Carlton and Perloff (2005), chapter 12, paragraph 3
Church and Ware (2000), paragraphs 22.2.2, 22.2.3, and 22.2.4
Martin (1994), chapter 17, paragraph 1
Martin (2002), paragraph 13.1
Motta (2004), paragraphs 6.1, 6.2.2, and 6.2.5
Tirole (1988), paragraph 4.3
Waldman and Jensen (2001), chapter 15, paragraph 3 and chapter 19, paragraph 4(3)

D Related legal texts

Bellamy and Child (2008), chapter 6, paragraph 4(B, I, 6.053–6.061)
Jones and Sufrin (2008), chapter 9, paragraph 4(B, ii, a and iii, c)
Ritter and Braun (2005), chapter 4, paragraph B(3 and 5, a)
Whish (2008), chapter 16, paragraph 6(F)

E Commission decisions in chronological order•

Grosfillex & Fillistorf Commission decision 64/233/EEC [1964] OJ L 64/915, Case IV/61
Grundig-Consten Commission decision 64/566/EEC [1964] OJ L 64/2545, Case IV/3344 (*)
    (Martin, 1994, pp. 64, 181, 530)
Dru-Blondel Commission decision 65/366/EEC [1965] OJ L 65/2194, Case IV/3036
Hummel-Isbecque Commission decision 65/426/EEC [1965] OJ L 65/2581, Case IV/2702
Maison Jallatte Commission decision 66/5/EEC [1966] OJ L 66/37, Case IV/22.491
Rieckermann /AEG-Elotherm Commission decision 68/376/EEC [1968] OJ L 276/25, Case
    IV/23.077
Christiani and Nielsen Commission decision 69/195/EEC [1969] OJ L 165/12, Case IV/22.548
Kodak Commission decision 70/332/EEC [1970] OJ L 147/24, Case IV/24.055

• Decisions displayed in **bold type** are described in the section. Decisions highlighted with (*) include interesting economic analysis by the Commission on the specific topic of the section. Some decisions contain economic reasoning on more than one topic and therefore appear in several lists of Commission decisions in chronological order. Reference is made in brackets and **bold type** to the relevant section in which the decision is extensively described as a landmark case. When decisions are referenced and/or described in some detail in one or more of the economic textbooks, reference in brackets is also made to the relevant part(s) of those texts.

Omega Commission decision 70/488/EEC [1970] OJ L 242/22, Cases IV/3213, 10.498, 11.546, 12.992, 17.394, 17.395, 17.971, 18.772, 18.888

Pittsburgh Corning Europe-Formica Belgium-Hertel Commission decision 72/403/EEC [1972] OJ L 272/35, Cases IV/26.876, 26.892, 26.894

WEA-Filipacchi Music Commission decision 72/480/EEC [1972] OJ L 303/52, Case IV/26.992

Deutsche Philips GmbH Commission decision 73/322/EEC [1973] OJ L 293/40, Case IV/27.010 **(described in detail as landmark case in section 5.3)**

Advocaat Zwarte Kip Commission decision 74/432/EEC [1974] OJ L 237/12, Case IV/28.374

Duro-Dyne/Europair Commission decision 75/74/EEC [1975] OJ L 29/11, Case IV/560

Goodyear Italian/Euram Commission decision 75/94/EEC [1975] OJ L 38/10, Case IV/23.013

Stoves and Heaters (Haarden- en Kachelhandel) Commission decision 75/358/EEC [1975] OJ L 159/22, Case IV/712

Miller International Schallplatten GmbH Commission decision 76/915/EEC [1976] OJ L 357/40, Case IV/29.018

Gero-Fabriek Commission decision 77/66/EEC [1977] OJ L 16/8, Case IV/24.510

Theal/Watts Commission decision 77/129/EEC [1977] OJ L 39/19, Case IV/28.812

Centraal Bureau voor de Rijwielhandel Commission decision 78/59/EEC [1978] OJ L 20/18, Case IV/147

BMW Belgium NV and Belgian BMW dealers **Commission decision 78/155/EEC [1978] OJ L 46/33, Case IV/29.146**

Arthur Bell and Sons Ltd **Commission decision 78/696/EEC [1978] OJ L 235/15, Case IV/29.440**

Teacher and Sons Commission decision 78/697/EEC [1978] OJ L 235/20, Case IV/28.859

Breeders' Right-Maize Seed Commission decision 78/823/EEC [1978] OJ L 286/23, Case IV/28.824

Zanussi Commission decision 78/922/EEC [1978] OJ L 322/36, Case IV/1576

Kawasaki Commission decision 79/68/EEC [1979] OJ L 16/9, Case IV/29.430

Pioneer Commission decision 80/256/EEC [1980] OJ L 60/21, Case IV/29.595

Johnson and Johnson Commission decision 80/1283/EEC [1980] OJ L 377/16, Case IV/29.702

Hennessey-Henkell Commission decision 80/1333/EEC [1980] OJ L 383/11, Case IV/26.912

Italian Flat Glass Commission decision 81/881/EC [1981] OJ L 326/32, Case IV/29.988 (*) (Bishop and Walker, 2009, 5.07, 5.14; Martin, 1994, pp. 178–9)

Moët & Chandon Commission decision 82/203/EEC [1982] OJ L 94/7, Case IV/30.188

Hasselblad Commission decision 82/367/EEC [1982] OJ L 94/7, Case IV/25.757

National Panasonic Commission decision 82/853/EEC [1982] OJ L 354/28, Case IV/30.070 (*)

Ford Werke AG Commission decision 83/560/EEC [1983] OJ L 327/31, Case IV/30.696

Polistil/Arbois Commission decision 84/282/EEC [1984] OJ L 136/9, Case IV/30.658

John Deere Commission decision 85/79/EEC [1985] OJ L 35/58, Case IV/30.809

Aluminium Commission decision 85/206/EEC [1985] OJ L 92/1, Case IV/26.870

Whiskey and Gin Commission decision 85/562/EEC [1985] OJ L 369/19, Case IV/30.570 (*)

Sperry New Holland Commission decision 85/617/EEC [1985] OJ L 376/21, Case IV/30.839

Peugeot Commission decision 86/506/EEC [1986] OJ L 295/19, Case IV/31.143

Tipp-Ex Commission decision 87/406/EEC [1987] OJ L 222/1, Cases IV/31.192, 31.507

Sandoz Commission decision 87/409/EEC [1987] OJ L 222/28, Case IV/31.741

Fisher Price/Quaker Oats Ltd Toyco Commission decision 88/86/EEC [1988] OJ L 49/19, Case IV/31.017

Konica Commission decision 88/172/EEC [1988] OJ L 78/34, Case IV/31.503

Film Purchases by German Television Commission decision 89/536/EEC [1989] OJ L 284/36, Case IV/31.734

Bayo-n-ox Commission decision 90/38/EEC [1990] OJ L 21/71, Case IV/32.026

Bayer Dental Commission decision 90/645/EEC [1990] OJ L 351/46, Case IV/32.877

D'Ieteren motor oils Commission decision 91/39/EEC [1991] OJ L 20/42, Case IV/32.595

IJsselcentrale and others Commission decision 91/50/EEC [1991] OJ L 28/32, Case IV/32.732

Gosme/Martell-Dmp Commission decision 91/335/EEC [1991] OJ L 185/23, Case IV/32.186

Viho/Toshiba Commission decision 91/532/EC [1991] OJ L 287/39, Case IV/32.879

Eco System/Peugeot Commission decision 92/154/EEC [1992] OJ L 66/1, Case IV/33.157

Newitt/Dunlop Slazenger Commission decision 92/261/EEC [1992] OJ L 131/32, Case IV/32.290 (Bishop and Walker, 2009, 5.40)

Viho/Parker Pen Commission decision 92/426/EEC [1992] OJ L 131/32, Case IV/32.725

Distribution of Railway Tickets by Travel Agents Commission decision 92/568/EEC [1992] OJ L 366/47, Case IV/33.585

Ford Agriculture Commission decision 93/46/EEC [1993] OJ L 20/1, Case IV/31.400

Schoeller Lebensmittel GmbH and Co. KG Commission decision 93/405/EEC [1993] OJ L 183/1, Case IV/31.533 (Motta, 2004, pp. 391–8)

Langnese-Iglo GmbH Commission decision 93/406/EEC [1993] OJ L 183/19, Case IV/34.072 (*) (Motta, 2004, pp. 391–8)

Zera/Montedison and Hinkens/Stähler Commission decision 93/554/EEC [1993] OJ L 272/28, Cases IV/31.550, 31.898

Tretorn & others Commission decision 94/987/EEC [1994] OJ L 378/45, Cases IV/32.948, 34.590

BASF Lacke & Farben AG, Accinauto SA Commission decision 95/477/EC [1995] OJ L 272/16, Case IV/33.802

Bayer (ADALAT) Commission decision 96/478/EC [1996] OJ L 201/1, Case IV/34.279/F3 (Motta, 2004, p. 497)

Novalliance/Systemform Commission decision 97/123/EC [1997] OJ L 47/11, Case IV/35.679

VW-Audi Commission decision 98/273/EC [1998] OJ L 124/60, Case IV/35.733

Sicasov Commission decision 1999/6/EC [1999] OJ L 4/27, Case IV/35.280

Nathan-Bricolux Commission decision 2001/135/EC [2001] OJ L 54/1, Case COMP.F.1/36.516

Opel Commission decision 2001/146/EC [2001] OJ L 59/1, Case COMP/36.653 (*)

Glaxo Wellcome, Aseprofar and Fedifar, Spain Pharma, BAI, EAEPC **Commission decision 2001/791/EC [2001] OJ L 302/1, Cases COMP/36.957, 36.997, 37.121, 37.138, 37.380** (Bishop and Walker, 2009, 1.08, 5.40; Motta, 2004, p. 497)

Central Parts/JCB Commission decision 2002/190/EC [2002] OJ L 69/1, Case COMP.F.1/35.918

Mercedes Benz Commission decision 2002/758/EC [2002] OJ L 257/1, Case COMP/36.264

Omega/Nintendo + 1 Commission decision 2003/675/EC [2003] OJ L 255/33, COMP/35.587

PO/Yamaha Commission decision of 16 July 2003, published on DG Comp website, Case COMP/37.975

Souris/Topps Commission decision of 26 May 2004, published on DG Comp website, Case COMP/C-3/37.980

SEP and Others/Automobiles Peugeot Commission decision of 5 October 2005, published on DG Comp website, Cases COMP/F-2/36.623, 36.820, 37.275

F   Economic landmark cases

F.1   *BMW Belgium NV and Belgian BMW dealers* Commission decision 78/155/EEC [1978] OJ L 46/33

Relevance: Absolute export prohibition and territorial prohibition included in, otherwise allowed, selective distribution agreements eliminate intrabrand competition, create artificial protection against natural price competition among retailers, and are ultimately detrimental for consumers. Even if territorial protection (i.e. the partitioning of the internal market) has always been of great concern for the Commission, this is the first decision in which the reasoning was based on the production or otherwise of efficiencies on the market.

- Case IV/29.146
- **Decision:** Infringement of Article 101 FEU Treaty
- **Decision addressee(s):**
    - BMW Belgium NV, *Belgium*
    - Autohandel O. Cocquyt NV, *Belgium*
    - Etn. W. Jorssen, *Belgium*
    - Garage Hindrickx, *Belgium*
    - Pvba J. Siau-Vermeesch, *Belgium*
    - Ets. J. De Smeth, *Belgium*
    - Ets. Jo Vallè, *Belgium*
    - Ets. J. Depotter, *Belgium*
    - Garage J. Wiliquet Sprl, *Belgium*
    - Ets. Rajans SA, *Belgium*
    - Garage Verhaeren, *Belgium*
    - S. C. Dewilde Motor, *Belgium*
    - Ets. Autogamas Sprl, *Belgium*
    - Ets. Houyoux, *Belgium*
    - Garage Léon Louyet Sprl, *Belgium*
    - Station Albert 1er SA, *Belgium*
    - Sprl Auto Service, *Belgium*
    - Ets. A. Petit & Co. SA, *Belgium*
    - Ets. Lean Blaise Sprl, *Belgium*
    - Ets. Cuisinier, *Belgium*
    - Ets. Briot Sprl, *Belgium*
    - Garage Georges Antoine, *Belgium*
    - Garage Hubert Scaillet, *Belgium*
    - Ets. Ferracin, *Belgium*
    - Ets. Le Stop, *Belgium*
    - Autobedrijf De Ruysscher, *Belgium*
    - Garage W. Termont-Vermeire, *Belgium*
    - NV Centrauto, *Belgium*
    - Garage R. Geurts & Zn Pvba, *Belgium*
    - Etn. Dekkers, *Belgium*
    - Etn. J. Vandeperre Pvba, *Belgium*
    - J. Sebrechts, *Belgium*
    - Garage van Avondt & Zn Pvba, *Belgium*

- Garage A. Ottevaere, *Belgium*
- Ceres-Leterme Pvba, *Belgium*
- Garage St Christophe Pvba, *Belgium*
- Garage Vangoidsenhoven, *Belgium*
- Garage Moderne-Ghyselinck, *Belgium*
- Garage R. Kellens-Behiels, *Belgium*
- Garage S. De Mey, *Belgium*
- Etn. J. & M. Sels Pvba, *Belgium*
- Garage Tanghe Pvba, *Belgium*
- Pvba Gebr. Van den Bulck, *Belgium*
- Pvba De Kempische Molen, *Belgium*
- Garage Aalbrecht W., *Belgium*
- Etn. Erco NV, *Belgium*
- Garage A. Liesens, *Belgium*
- Garage Centrum Mottoul, *Belgium*

- **Report route:** Complaints lodged with the Commission on 24 November 1975 by Automobilimporte C. Heuer and on 9 December 1975 by MGH Motorgesellschaft mbH
- **Date of the decision:** 23 December 1977
- **Competition Commissioner:** R. Vouel
- **Relevant product market:** BMW cars and spare parts
- **Relevant geographical market:** Belgium
- **Description of the case**
  a. **Relevant facts**
     In January 1975, BMW Belgium notified to the Commission a selective distribution agreement to be set up with its retailers on Belgian territory. The agreement largely reflected the provisions contained in the selective distribution agreements adopted by BMW in Germany for which the main reason for exemption, in the Commission's reasoning, was the absence of any export prohibition.[31]

     Since the prices for BMW cars in Belgium were significantly lower than those charged in other countries, the interstate sales from Belgium achieved a considerable level. This practise was called to the attention of BMW's Head Office in Munich which, in a letter to BMW Belgium, reminded it of the contractual obligation valid for all retailers to not sell any vehicle to unauthorized dealers or resellers. At the same time, BMW Munich reminded it that the export of vehicles through authorised dealers or the sale to final customers did not constitute a breach of contractual obligations. Nonetheless, BMW Munich noted how the achieved level of imports of BMW vehicles from Belgium to Germany was disrupting local (i.e. German) retailers and was harming the relation with some of them.[32]

     As a reaction to that letter, BMW Belgium directly addressed all retailers in Belgium with a circular that in particular stated that:
       - There was no reason to sell abroad in a period of shortage in supplies like that the Belgian BMW dealers were facing.

31   The decision in question is *BMW AG* Commission decision 75/73/EEC [1975] OJ L 29/1, Case IV/14.650. The decision is extensively described in section 5.5 of the book.
32   See recital 3 of the decision.

- Sales to unauthorised dealers were absolutely prohibited and would constitute a serious breach of the distribution agreement.
- Following that communication, in September 1975, BMW Belgium addressed a further circular to the retailers which they were supposed to accept and sign. The forty-eight retailers listed above signed the circular which made the following statements addressed to the retailers:
- If Belgian retailers sold abroad BMW Munich would have to either consider Belgian prices too low or to consider the stocks excessive and react accordingly.
- The consequences of those considerations would have been a cut in the supplies of vehicles unless prices were raised again.
- Sales made abroad had several disadvantages for the retailers operating them. There was a concern that the foreign customers "will never come to your workshop; will never buy parts or accessories from you; will never give you the opportunity to make a further profit on a car sold to you in part exchange; will never, as many customer[s] in your territory, give you any reason to expect an opportunity to sell them a second or a third BMW."[33]
- The sales abroad would have created an overall problem in the distributors' network and would have consequently justified a reduction in the number of cars supplied to the Belgian market.
- The only solution proposed was then the elimination of all the sales outside Belgium, on the one side, as a form of solidarity for and protection of the network and, on the other, as a means to restore BMW Munich confidence in the Belgian dealers.

The position envisaged by BMW Belgium in the circular was reinforced by an opinion addressed to the dealers by the Belgian BMW Dealers' Advisory Committee, which concluded its statement saying that "the only advice it has to offer in this case is 'No more sales outside Belgium'."[34]

In February 1976, following complaints from some agents acting on behalf of non-Belgian clients trying to buy BMW vehicles in Belgium and as a result of requests for interlocutory injunctions, BMW Belgium addressed to the retailers a further letter in which it clarified the intention of the previous circular of September 1975. In the new circular it stated that the interpretation of the previous communication as instructions for dealers and as a prohibition to export was a misinterpretation of the real intentions underlying the document. According to BMW Belgium it was in fact aimed exclusively at reinforcing the prohibition to resale to unauthorised dealers and resellers.[35]

b. Origin of the case

On 24 November and 9 December 1975 respectively, Automobilimporte C. Heuer and MGH Motorgesellschaft mbH filed to the Commission two

---

33   Recital 4.4 of the decision.   35   See recitals 8–11 of the decision.
34   *Idem.*

complaints for the purpose of Article 3 of Regulation 17 concerning the distribution agreements between BMW Belgium and its dealers. On 3 November 1976 the Commission decided to initiate proceedings.

c. Economic analysis

The commercial practices envisaged by the circular of September 1975 were considered anticompetitive and gave the Commission the possibility to state unequivocally its position on total territorial restriction and bans on parallel imports. The Commission never denied the possibility for some firms to rely, in certain commercial sectors, on selective distribution agreements[36] and/or on exclusive distribution agreements.[37] What the Commission has instead always rejected as restrictions of competition not justifiable by any deriving efficiencies were clauses impeding interstate trade and therefore, artificially separating the European market.[38]

The Commission regarded the restriction of intrabrand competition resulting from the clauses banning parallel import as detrimental for consumers and their possibility to freely choose suppliers in Europe as well as strongly reducing price competition between dealers (i.e. the possibility to charge monopoly prices). The approach is in line with the concerns about territorial exclusivity expressed in the economic literature.

In a previous decision concerning BMW's selective distribution system in Germany, the Commission had already stated that under export prohibitions "consumers were not granted a fair share of the benefits which might otherwise result from exclusive dealing agreements, as the export prohibitions led to a form of territorial protection enabling different retail prices to be charged in the various countries of the common market."[39] By reference to it, the Commission further specified that decision, and stated in the present decision that it would "exempt selective distribution agreement . . . only if there is no other restriction on the freedom of consumers to buy new cars anywhere in the common market or to effect such purchases by agents. An exemption always requires an examination as to whether potential competition remains between all the selected dealers in the common market, so that they are compelled through competitive pressures to react to each other's price structures and to respond to low prices quoted by other dealers. The export prohibition concerned in these proceedings sought to eliminate such pressures and insulate the market operated by Belgian dealers for new BMW vehicles from the markets operated by other dealers for these vehicles in the common market."[40]

---

36   See, *infra*, section 5.5 of the book.
37   See, *supra*, section 5.1 of the book.
38   This is in line with the ECJ's case law on territorial exclusivity. In *Grundig-Consten* (Joined cases 56 and 58/64) the ECJ ruled that " . . . an agreement between producer and distributor which might tend to restore the national divisions in trade between Member States might be such as to frustrate the most fundamental objections of the Community. The treaty, whose preamble and content aim at abolishing the barriers between states, and which in several provisions gives evidence of a stern attitude with regard to their reappearance, could not allow undertakings to reconstruct such barriers. Article 81(1) is designed to pursue this aim, even in the case of agreements between undertakings placed at different levels in the economic process."
39   *BMW AG* Commission decision 75/73/EEC [1975] OJ L 29/1, Case IV/14.650, recital 12.
40   Recital 21 of the decision.

d. Fines, remedies, and conditions enclosed
- The Commission imposed the following total fines:

Company	Fine (EUA)
BMW Belgium	150,000
5 garages[41]	2,000
3 garages[42]	1,500
39 garages[43]	1,000

e. Further developments of the case
Joined Cases 32, 36–82/78 *BMW Belgium and others* v. *Commission* [1979] ECR 2435, appeal dismissed.

The Court confirmed the Commission decision and stated that the agreements had as their object the prevention, restriction, or distortion to an appreciable extent of competition within the common market in respect of a product of a particular make.[44] "By attempting to partition the markets, as regards the export of products of a particular make, those agreements were also capable of affecting the trade between Member States, within the meaning of Article 81(1)."[45]

F.2 *Arthur Bell and Sons Ltd* Commission decision 78/696/EEC [1978] OJ L 235/15

Relevance: In this decision the Commission further strengthened its approach toward absolute parallel import bans. It stated that in case parallel import is profitable from a cost perspective, bans imposed by supply/distribution agreements constitute undue restrictions of competition not producing any balancing efficiencies. The Commission focused its attention in particular on the elimination of any competitive pressure on distributors that would have been present in the absence of parallel import ban.

- Case IV/29.440
- **Decision:** Infringement of Article 101 FEU Treaty
- **Decision addressee(s):**
  - Arthur Bell and Sons Ltd, *United Kingdom*
- **Report route:** Commission decision of 21 September 1977 to start a proceedings on its own initiative
- **Date of the decision:** 28 July 1978
- **Competition Commissioner:** R. Vouel
- **Relevant product market:** Whisky

---

41 Autohandel O. Cocquyt NV, Etn. W. Jorssen, Garage Hindrickx, Pvba J. Siau-Vermeesch, and Ets J. De Smeth.
42 Ets. Jo Vallè, Ets. J. Depotter, and Garage J. Wiliquet Sprl.
43 Ets. Rajans SA, Garage Verhaeren, S. C. Dewilde Motor, Ets. Autogamas Sprl, Ets. Houyoux, Garage Léon Louyet Sprl, Station Albert 1er SA, Sprl Auto Service, Ets. A. Petit & Co. SA, Ets. Lean Blaise Sprl, Ets. Cuisinier, Ets. Briot Sprl, Garage Georges Antoine, Garage Hubert Scaillet, Ets. Ferracin, Ets. Le Stop, Autobedrijf De Ruysscher, Garage W. Termont-Vermeire, NV Centrauto, Garage R. Geurts & Zn Pvba, Etn. Dekkers, Etn. J. Vandeperre Pvba, J. Sebrechts, Garage van Avondt & Zn Pvba, Garage A. Ottevaere, Ceres-Leterme Pvba, Garage St Christophe Pvba, Garage Vangoidsenhoven, Garage Moderne-Ghyselinck, Garage R. Kellens-Behiels, Garage S. De Mey, Etn. J. & M. Sels Pvba, Garage Tanghe Pvba, Pvba Gebr. Van den Bulck, Pvba De Kempische Molen, Garage Aalbrecht W., Etn. Erco NV, Garage A. Liesens, and Garage Centrum Mottoul.
44 Recital 31 of the judgment.
45 Recital 32 of the judgment.

- **Relevant geographical market:** United Kingdom
- **Description of the case**
  ### a. Relevant facts
  Arthur Bell and Sons Ltd (Bell) was a large British company engaged in distilling, blending, and distributing whisky. It was the second largest seller of Scotch whisky in the United Kingdom and its most famous brand was the best-selling Scotch whisky brand there.

  Bell adopted standardised conditions of sale with all its customers in the United Kingdom (wholesalers, supermarkets, and brewers). They provided that "[t]he acceptance of the invoice by the purchaser binds him that whisky supplied in bond shall not be offered directly or indirectly by subsale or otherwise for exportation outside Great Britain."[46] Due to very high excise duties imposed by UK legislation, at the moment in which the spirits were removed from bond, their export under bond (which is precisely what was prohibited by Bell's sales conditions) was the only potentially profitable possibility of export.[47]

  ### b. Origin of the case
  On 21 September 1977 the Commission, on its own initiative, adopted a decision to initiate a proceedings in respect of Bell's conditions of sale pursuant to Article 3(1) of Regulation No. 17.

  ### c. Economic analysis
  This decision confirmed the Commission's approach toward export (i.e. parallel import) prohibitions attached to a distribution and/or purchasing agreement. It further strengthened the Commission's approach because it established the principle that in as far as from a cost perspective the possibility to engage in parallel imports is potentially profitable and therefore to an extent encourages competition, bans imposed by supply/distribution agreements are anticompetitive and non-justifiable from an efficiency perspective.

  As mentioned above, due to the very high and non-reimbursable excise duties imposed by the United Kingdom for alcohol exports, only Scotch whisky bought under bond could potentially be exported and sold at competitive prices in other Member States. The provision preventing the export of Bell's whisky bought under bond was for the Commission clearly aimed at restricting competition.[48] Bell submitted that parallel imports under profitable conditions were highly unlikely to occur due to the higher prices charged by Bell to intermediate customers in the United Kingdom compared with the price charged to distributors in other Member States. Therefore, according to Bell the prohibition to export whisky bought under bond would have not produced any effective impact on competition.

  The Commission responded to these claims by arguing firstly that "[i]t may indeed have been difficult at certain periods for parallel importers of Bell's Scotch whisky bought in the United Kingdom to undercut Bell's distributors in other European countries. Since distributors are said to have higher distribution costs than parallel importers, these difficulties would have depended in particular on the extent to which such higher costs of the distributors were below the time-to-time differences between the two Bell price levels."[49]

---

46   Recital I-2-c of the decision.
47   See recital I-2-3 of the decision.

48   See recital II-1-c of the decision.
49   Recital II-1-c of the decision.

That said, although the Commission gave some merit to the claim that it was potentially possible to compete at a profitable level with the distributors in other countries, it emphasized at the same time that besides the difficulties in parallel import commerce due to the described factual differences in trade conditions "[t]he prohibition under consideration, however, prevented all trade customers and their purchaser from exercising any actual or potential competition with dealers in Bell's Scotch whisky in other European countries. In particular, they were prevented even from potentially exercising pressure on distributors so that the latter would have been induced to minimize their distribution costs and confine themselves to reasonable margins. [T]he export prohibition prevented all 2,400 trade customers from exporting and competing with the numerous dealers in whisky in other European countries. Many of these trade customers are of considerable importance and were willing and able to engage in export activities, and also numerous dealers in other European countries were potential buyers of Scotch whisky resold by United Kingdom trade customers."[50]

Even if without the prohibition effective obstacles to parallel trade had persisted, the prohibition would not have been justified, because it would undoubtedly have reduced further any potentially remaining competitive pressure on distributors.

d. Fines, remedies, and conditions enclosed
  – Obligation for Arthur Bell and Sons Ltd to bring the infringement to an end.

e. Further developments of the case
None.

F.3 Glaxo Wellcome, Aseprofar and Fedifax, Spain Pharma, BAI, EAEPC Commission decision 2001/791/EC [2001] OJ L 302/1

Relevance: The case is an example of restricting parallel trade by using a dual pricing system for prescription drugs. Parallel trade is impeded by charging lower prices to wholesalers if they sell in Spain versus when they export these products – for example, to the United Kingdom. The sales conditions are an infringement of Article 101, restraining competition "by object." Glaxo Wellcome introduces a range of economic arguments for its vertical distribution system but the Commission does not allow the requested negative clearance nor exemption. The case has clear connections to earlier cases such as *Sandoz* (IV/31.741) from 1987 and *Volkswagen* (COMP/35.733) from 1998.

- Cases COMP/36.957 (notification), COMP/36.997, COMP/37.121, COMP/37.138, and COMP/37.380 (complaints).
- **Decision:** Infringement of Article 101 FEU Treaty.
- **Decision addressee(s):** GlaxoSmithkline plc, *United Kingdom*
- **Report route:** Notification to the Commission on 6 March 1998 (Case IV/36.957), subsequent complaints lodged with the Commission by Aseprofar and Fedifar (Case IV/36.997), by Spain Pharma (Case IV/37.121), by Bundesverband der Arzneimittel-Importeure (BAI) (Case IV/37.138), and by the European Association of Euro Pharmaceutical Companies (EAEPC) (Case IV/37.380).

---

50   Recital II-1-d of the decision.

- **Date of the decision:** 8 May 2001
- **Competition Commissioner:** M. Monti
- **Relevant product market:** Prescription drugs
- **Relevant geographical market:** Spain and all other European Member States
- **Description of the case**
  - a. **Relevant facts**

    Glaxo Wellcome SA (GW), is the Spanish subsidiary of Glaxo Wellcome plc, from 2000 onwards part of GlaxoSmithkline plc. The pharmaceutical company is a major global player. GW develops, manufactures, and markets medicines in Spain. GW notified new sales conditions for Spanish wholesalers on 6 March 1998 to enter into force three days thereafter. The sales conditions contain a Clause 4 discriminating between prices charged to wholesalers reselling the products to Spanish pharmacies or hospitals and those charged to wholesalers exporting the products. The latter prices exceed those applied for domestic resales. The new sales conditions were sent to eighty-nine wholesalers, of whom seventy-five accepted the conditions.[51] The new sales conditions apply in total to eighty-two pharmaceutical products, all prescription drugs.[52] These include fifteen product combinations (some in different packages) of eight drugs considered by GW as "prime candidates for parallel trade between Spain and the United Kingdom: Becotide, Beconase, Becloforte, Flixotide, Imigran, Lamictal, Serevent and Ventolin."[53] GW has substantial market shares in the relevant markets for these eight drugs.

    Three wholesaler associations and one wholesaler lodged complaints with the Commission. "All complainants regard Clause 4 of GW SA's new sales conditions as an agreement that puts in place a system of dual pricing impeding parallel trade."[54] The associations were the Spanish wholesaler associations Aseprofar and Fedifar, the German association of importers of pharmaceutical products BAI, and the EAEPC, representing national associations of importers and exporters of pharmaceutical products. The individual wholesaler which complained was Spain Pharma SA, a Spanish wholesaler with three-quarters of its turnover derived from exports to other Member States. GW initially suspended supply to wholesalers that did not subscribe to the new sales conditions, among them Spain Pharma SA and three members of Aseprofar; GW tracked down wholesalers that the company suspected of exporting products that should have stayed in Spain according to Clause 4. The sales conditions were, however, suspended on 26 October 1998 due to interim measures by the Spanish competition defense tribunal. GW then supplied the products to all wholesalers for the (low) Clause 4A prices instead of the higher Clause 4B prices. GW afterwards refrained from implementing the sales conditions again.

    Price differences for pharmaceutical products between different Member States create opportunities for parallel trade. The share of intra-Community trade in prescription drugs is limited, though "estimated to have increased over a period of 12 years (1985 to 1997) from 0.5 percent to 2 percent of total sales." The parallel import market share is relatively important only for

---

51   See recital 12 of the decision.
52   See recital 13 of the decision.
53   See recital 15 of the decision.
54   See recital 105 of the decision.

three Member States: the United Kingdom (4–8 percent), Denmark (9 percent), and The Netherlands (10–12 percent).[55] These countries have medium-to-high pharmaceutical prices, whereas Spain has relatively low prices. Spain and the United Kingdom differ in their (reimbursement) systems of determining prescription drug prices. Spain fixes maximum prices, taking into account the complete cost, including R&D costs. Firms may apply for price increases afterwards. The United Kingdom has a pharmaceutical price regulation scheme (PPRS) using a target return on capital (of 21 percent). UK pharmacists may benefit from parallel trade since they receive a fixed reimbursement fee based on the manufacturer's list price. This is intensified by a "claw back" discount of 4–5 percent to take savings into account made by pharmacists through purchasing cleverly (e.g. by parallel trade).

In each of GW's fifteen product combinations the Spanish prices are below the EU average and in each of them the UK prices are above the EU average, sometimes substantially so (more than 20 percent). Hence, parallel trade may cause loss of sales revenue to GW, the extent of which cannot be "refined" and "data provided may not be reliable" according to GW.[56]

b. Origin of the case

GW argues that Clause 4 is "not intended to block sales by distributors established in Spain to countries outside Spain."[57] Still, it argues that parallel trade may hinder the funding of R&D and delay new product introduction. GW maintains that "Spain creates a distortion of competition because its system of maximum wholesale prices which aims at reducing the national healthcare budget puts at risk the policy of other Member States, including the United Kingdom, which consider adequate R&D investment to be a priority."[58] GW also argues that shortages in Spain may arise due to exporting.

The four complainants complain that the dual-pricing system is "per se illegal" and that parallel trade may benefit consumers.[59] The allegation by the Commission is "that the new sales conditions have as their object and effect to restrict competition and affect trade between Member States to an appreciable extent."[60]

c. Economic analysis

The decision centers around the use of a dual-pricing system by GW to restrict parallel trade of its products from Spain to the United Kingdom. GW admits that the system is "intended to reduce the incentive for Spanish traders to engage in parallel trade of prescription medicines purchased at the low levels set by the Spanish Government."[61] The high Clause 4B prices prevent or limit parallel trade in a large majority of cases. They produce the effect of an export ban. Export bans and dual-pricing systems are considered to restrict "competition 'by object'."[62] Hence, there would not be a need for an economic assessment of the actual effects.

The Sandoz pharmaceutical company received a fine by the Commission in 1987 since it displayed the words "export prohibited" on the sales invoices (case IV/31.741). This is an obvious analogy to an export ban. A similar dual-pricing

---

55 See recitals 29–34 of the decision.
56 See recital 71 of the decision.
57 See recital 21 of the decision.
58 See recital 80 of the decision.

59 See recital 105 of the decision.
60 See recital 189 of the decision.
61 See recital 116 of the decision.
62 See recital 124 of the decision.

case was the early *Distillers* case (IV/28.282) from 1978 where different prices were charged for export and for UK consumption. A more recent case is the reduction by Volkswagen of the bonus granted to retailers in case of exports (COMP/35.733).

The latter case is interesting since in the car sector national price regulations are also important and "these companies have not been able to rely on the difference between national regulations to justify restrictions on parallel trade."[63] Pharmaceutical companies may even be less affected by national regulation since they "are always involved in the regulatory process governing their sales price."[64] They have negotiating power and "the Spanish regulatory authorities expressly allow pharmaceutical companies to propose prices which fully reflect their R&D costs."[65]

Parallel trade constitutes only a relatively small part of pharmaceutical sales and, therefore, will hardly affect funding for R&D. The limited influence of parallel trading can also be seen in the persistence of price differences across countries even in the presence of parallel trade. The appreciation of the pound sterling was important in increasing parallel trade between Spain and the United Kingdom. "Although the absolute volume of Spanish-sourced imports increase[d], their share of all imports into the United Kingdom remained stable. It must therefore be concluded that the appreciation of [the] British pound attracted imports from all sources without the alleged discrepancies between the Spanish and UK regulatory systems playing any material role in this process."[66] And then, even if there are distortions of competition due to national regulations, this should "be tackled by Community-wide harmonization measures" and not by restricting parallel trade.[67]

R&D was found not to have suffered with GW's loss of revenue. Firstly, the loss was insignificant relative to GW's R&D expenditure and, secondly, R&D grew very strongly even in a period of parallel trade in the 1980s and 1990s.

d.   Fines, remedies, and conditions enclosed
–   GW SA had to cease the infringement. It was not allowed to have dual pricing.

e.   Further developments of the case
Case T-168/01 *GlaxoSmithKline Services* v. *Commission* [2006] ECR II-2969. The CFI (now "the General Court") decided on 27 September 2006. The decision by the Commission was partially annulled. The CFI argued that the Commission did not take proper account of the specifics of the pharmaceutical sector. Because of national regulations the CFI claims that parallel trade may not necessarily reduce prices. The CFI is also critical about the Commission's analysis with regard to the possibility that sales conditions may contribute to innovation. Financing of pharmaceutical innovation is vital for business survival and GW could allocate the surplus obtained to R&D. The Commission is asked to reconsider the request for exemption.

Joined Cases C-501, 513, 515, and 519/06 *Glaxo SmithKline and Others* v. Commission. Appeal dismissed. The ECJ decided on 8 October 2009.

63   See recital 127 of the decision.
64   See recital 132 of the decision.
65   See recital 133 of the decision.
66   See recital 143 of the decision.
67   See recital 148 of the decision.

5.3 Resale price maintenance

A Introduction

Resale price maintenance (RPM) is a practise in which a supplier suggests the price that its purchasers, retailers, should charge for its products. These "adviced prices" may be accompanied by the implicit threat to refuse to supply to a customer who prices differently. A distinction between two different forms of RPM is made in the literature. In one form, a price ceiling is set. In another form, the downstream prices are explicitly fixed.

A price ceiling is quite generally accepted as a normal business practise, without imposing undue restrictions on competition. When fixed-price RPM is employed by upstream firms holding market power, however, it may be an effective instrument to maintain higher than competitive prices and to avoid renegotiations that could lead to output expansion and price reduction. Other possible effects of RPM stem from its potential to facilitate collusion among producers in the upstream market, reducing interbrand competition by creating price transparency at the retail level that can make it easier to monitor (tacit) price agreements. In addition, RPM can help to eliminate intrabrand competition on price. In theory, this latter effect may also produce positive welfare effects in as far as it constitutes means to eliminate free-riding problems and to make retailers compete on elements other than price. In many cases, however, the restrictive effects on competition may outweigh the limited efficiencies that RPM can yield.

B Applicable EU legislation

RPM in the form of retail price fixing is considered a so-called hard core restrictions in EU competition law. The most important effect of this negative assessment is the exclusion of RPM from the scope of applicability of the Block Exemption Regulation on Vertical Agreements. Therefore vertical agreements providing for RPM have to be normally assessed under Article 101 FEU Treaty.[68]

C Related economics texts

Bishop and Walker (2009), paragraphs 5.34–5.55
Carlton and Perloff (2005), chapter 12, paragraphs 3 and 5
Church and Ware (2000), paragraphs 10.6 and 22.2
Martin (1994), chapter 17, paragraph 1
Martin (2002), paragraphs 13.1 and 13.2
Motta (2004), paragraphs 4.2.3, 6.2.2, 6.2.5, and 6.3.2
Tirole (1988), chapter 4
Waldman and Jensen (2001), chapter 15, paragraph 3(1)

D Related legal texts

Bellamy and Child (2008), chapter 6, paragraph 4(B, I, 6.050–6.052)
Jones and Sufrin (2008), chapter 9, paragraphs 2(C, iv, b, and c) and 4(B, ii, b)

---

68   RPM is explicitly indicated as a *hardcore* restriction, making the generalized exemption inapplicable to such agreements in Article 4(a) of Regulation No. 2790/1999 on the application of Article 81(3) of the Treaty to categories of vertical relations and concerted practices [1999] OJ L 336/21 (Block Exemption Regulation on Vertical Agreements) and in Article 4(1)(a) of Commission Regulation No. 772/2004 on the application of Article 81(3) of the Treaty to categories of technology transfer agreements [2004] OJ L 123/11 (Block Exemption Regulation of Technology Transfer Agreements).

Ritter and Braun (2005), chapter 4, paragraph B(3 and 6)

Whish (2008), chapter 16, paragraph 7(D, i)

E   Commission decisions in chronological order•

Pittsburgh Corning Europe-Formica Belgium-Hertel Commission decision 72/403/EEC [1972] OJ L 272/35, Cases IV/26.876, 26.892, 26.894

Deutsche Philips GmbH **Commission decision 73/322/EEC [1973] OJ L 293/40, Case IV/27.010**

Stoves and Heaters (Haarden- en Kachelhandel) Commission decision 75/358/EEC [1975] OJ L 159/22, Case IV/712

Gero-Fabriek Commission decision 77/66/EEC [1977] OJ L 16/8, Case IV/24.510

Centraal Bureau voor de Rijwielhandel Commission decision 78/59/EEC [1978] OJ L 20/18, Case IV/147

Liebig Spices Commission decision 78/172/EEC [1978] OJ L 53/20, Case IV/29.418 (**described in detail as landmark case in section 5.1**)

Breeders' Right-Maize Seed Commission decision 78/823/EEC [1978] OJ L 286/23, Case IV/28.824

Hennessey-Henkell Commission decision 80/1333/EEC [1980] OJ L 383/11, Case IV/26.912

VBBB/VBVB Commission decision 82/123/EEC [1982] OJ L 54/36, Case IV/428 (Martin, 1994, p. 532)

D'Ieteren motor oils Commission decision 91/39/EEC [1991] OJ L 20/42, Case IV/32.595

Distribution of Railway Tickets by Travel Agents Commission decision 92/568/EEC [1992] OJ L 366/47, Case IV/33.585

Novalliance/Systemform Commission decision 97/123/EC [1997] OJ L 47/11, Case IV/35.679

Volkswagen Commission decision 2001/711/EC [2001] OJ L 262/14, Case COMP/F-2/36.693

Central Parts/JCB Commission decision 2002/190/EC [2002] OJ L 69/1, Case COMP.F.1/35.918

PO/Yamaha Commission decision of 16 July 2003, published on DG Comp website, Case COMP/37.975 (*)

F   Economic landmark cases

F.1   *Deutsche Philips GmbH* Commission decision 73/322/EEC [1973] OJ L 293/40

Relevance: Resale price maintenance (RPM) has always been considered as an anti-competitive practise by the Commission with the exception of price ceilings. In the specific circumstances of this early decision the Commission described the effect on competition deriving from the combination of RPM with a parallel import ban. The presence of special national provisions allowing the common fixing of resale prices is irrelevant in the assessment of the effect of RPM on competition.

- Case IV/27.010
- **Decision:** Infringement of Article 101 FEU Treaty

• Decisions displayed in **bold type** are described in the section. Decisions highlighted with (*) include interesting economic analysis by the Commission on the specific topic of the section. Some decisions contain economic reasoning on more than one topic and therefore appear in several lists of Commission decisions in chronological order. Reference is made in brackets and **bold type** to the relevant section in which the decision is extensively described as a landmark case. When decisions are referenced and/or described in some detail in one or more of the economic textbooks, reference in brackets is also made to the relevant part(s) of those texts.

- **Decision addressee(s):**
  - Deutsche Philips GmbH, *Federal Republic of Germany*
- **Report route:** Commission decision of 26 July 1972 to start proceedings on its own initiative
- **Date of the decision:** 5 October 1973
- **Competition Commissioner:** A. Borschette
- **Relevant product market:** Domestic appliances, televisions, experimental apparatus, lamps, and electric shavers
- **Relevant geographical market:** Not indicated
- **Description of the case**
  - **a. Relevant facts**

    A number of clauses in the terms of delivery and payment adopted by Deutsche Philips GmbH (Philips), in the frame of the contractual relations with its German dealers, concerned the prices to be charged at retail level, the possibility for retailers to engage in exports and in parallel imports, and limitations to horizontal supplies among retailers or distributors.

    In particular those terms provided for:
      - The obligation for retailers to sell to consumers products that were the object of the agreement in case of domestic appliances, electric shavers, lamps, and experimental apparatus only at the price indicated by Philips. The obligation was valid also for products sold to consumers outside Germany.
      - The same obligation (i.e. the RPM) in case of products purchased not directly from Philips but instead from other domestic or foreign suppliers.
      - The obligation for wholesalers and retailers to sell electric shavers abroad only under explicit permission granted by Philips.
      - The prohibition for wholesalers to supply other wholesalers or to sell directly to consumers and the prohibition for retailers to supply other retailers or wholesalers.

    All the described clauses characterizing the vertical relations between Philips and its German wholesalers and retailers were the target of the Commission investigation, which was merely initiated to search for export bans in the contractual conditions.

  - **b. Origin of the case**

    On 26 July 1972 the Commission, on its own initiative, adopted a decision to initiate a proceeding against Deutsche Philips GmbH for price agreements concluded by them concerning the electrical goods market in Europe.

  - **c. Economic analysis**

    Cases of RPM have consistently been considered anticompetitive and are very unlikely to satisfy the conditions for exemption listed in Article 101(3) FEU Treaty. The Commission's position toward RPM has always been unambiguous and RPM in EU competition law is, as in other jurisdictions, *de facto* prohibited. The main concern of the Commission in all the decisions regarding RPM clauses is the complete elimination of intrabrand competition on price, the consequent possibility of collusion among retailers, and thus the restriction of the possibility of choice between competitive alternatives for consumers. Another strong concern of the Commission is the risk that RPM may be used in combination with export or parallel import prescriptions, as a tool to artificially divide and isolate the internal market.[69]

This early decision is explicative of the Commission's position, particularly because it was adopted in the frame of a national legislation (i.e. a particular German law) that still permitted price maintenance for certain products (including the relevant products). The Commission firstly noted how the imposition of the resale price exceeded, also for sales operated outside Germany, what was allowed by German law and certainly constituted a restriction of competition in Member States other than Germany.[70] Furthermore, "the German retailers were obliged to observe the fixed prices applying in Germany when reselling goods covered by the agreement and imported from another European country into Germany. This reimport price fixing thus prevented the German retailer from entering into competition with other German retailers regarding prices when reselling reimported goods in Germany. This reimport price fixing cannot be justified by the fact that it serves to protect the price fixing which is legally permitted in Germany . . . The fact that vertical price fixing is allowed in a given Member State is not sufficient justification for exempting measures designed to preserve this price fixing from the scope of Article 85(1) . . . Clearly it should not be overlooked that retailers in Germany did not, as a result of the reimport price fixing, lose the possibility of purchasing products in other EEC countries on more favorable terms, notably at lower purchase prices. However, the only advantage to be gained from this would be an increase in dealers' trading margins without the dealers being able to pass this advantage on to consumers in the form of lower prices, and thereby increase sales and obtain new customers. At any rate the competitive position at the retail stage – as regards the prices, which were decisive for the consumer – would be the same as in the case of protection by means of export or reimport ban."[71]

Even in cases in which the national legislator still considered RPM as not problematic with regard to certain products, any further restriction in the freedom of downstream firms of choosing prices was considered as strongly restrictive of competition by the Commission. This assessment given to RPM clauses in vertical agreements has been continuously and consistently confirmed in Commission decisions thereafter.

---

69   In this regard, see also the ECJ case law on RPM. In *Vereniging ter Bevordering van het Vlaamse Boekwezen, VBVB, and Vereniging ter Bevordering van de Belangen des Boekhandels, VBBB*, v. *Commission* (Joined cases 43/82 and 63/82) the ECJ ruled that a restrictive system whose effect is to deprive distributors of all freedom of action as regards the fixing of the selling price up to the level of the final price to the consumers, infringes Article 101(1) FEU Treaty (see recital 45 of the judgment). Another example of the ECJ's unambiguous approach toward RPM is *Pronuptia de Paris GmbH* v. *Pronuptia de Paris Irmgard Schillgallis* (Case 161/84), where it ruled that "provisions which impair the franchisee's freedom to determine his own prices are restrictive of competition" (recital 25 of the judgment).

70   See recital II-2-b of the decision.

71   Recital II-2-c of the decision. In *Fédération nationale de la coopération bétail and viande (FNCBV) and Others* v. *Commission* (Joined cases T-217/03 and T-245/03), the CFI had held that, by its very nature, an agreement concluded by federations representing farmers and federations representing slaughterers fixing minimum prices for certain categories of cows, with the aim of making them binding on all traders in the market in question, has the object of restricting competition, *inter alia* by artificially limiting the commercial negotiating margin of farmers and slaughterers and distorting the formation of prices in the markets in question.

   d. **Fines, remedies, and conditions enclosed**
        – The Commission imposed on Deutsche Philips GmbH a total fine of
          EUA 60,000.
   e. **Further developments of the case**
        None.

5.4 Bundling and tying

A Introduction

   The economics of bundling and tying has been described in section 3.4 as an abuse of
dominance.[72] Its application as a vertical restraint relates directly to that use. Tying can be an
instrument for price discrimination, and strategic deterrence of entry. A typical example of a
restrictive tie in a vertical relation is the obligation imposed upon the tenant of a public house to
exclusively purchase beer (or other alcoholic products, the *tying good*) from the producer that
will lease to the tenant the premises (the *tied good*) to carry out its commercial activity. Such
contracts can be restrictive of competition in markets that are not characterized by dominance of
one or more firms.

B Applicable EU legislation

No special legislation applicable. For applicable legislation see chapter 5, paragraph B.

C Related economics texts

Bishop and Walker (2009), paragraphs 6.63–6.82
Carlton and Perloff (2005), chapter 10, paragraph 2
Church and Ware (2000), paragraphs 5.4.3, 16.4, and 22.3.1
Martin (1994), chapter 15, paragraphs 3 and 4
Martin (2002), paragraph 13.2.6
Motta (2004), paragraph 7.3.2
Tirole (1988), paragraphs 3.3 and 8.5
Waldman and Jensen (2001), chapter 14, paragraph 3

D Related legal texts

Bellamy and Child (2008), chapter 6, paragraph 6(A, 6.141) and chapter 10, paragraph 4(F, i)
Jones and Sufrin (2008), chapter 7, paragraph 6(H)
Ritter and Braun (2005), chapter 5, paragraph D(5)
Whish (2008), chapter 17, paragraph 3

---

72   The landmark decisions described in section 3.4 are *Eurofix-Banco/Hilti* Commission decision 88/138/EEC [1988] OJ L 65/19 and
     Tetra Pak II Commission decision 92/163/EEC [1992] OJ L 72/1.

E   Commission decisions in chronological order•

SSI Commission decision 82/506/EEC [1982] OJ L 232/1, Cases IV/29.525, 30.000

Carlsberg Commission decision 84/381/EEC [1984] OJ L 207/26, Case IV/30.129

Bloemenveilingen Aalsmeer Commission decision 88/491/EEC [1988] OJ L 262/27, Case IV/31.379

Whitbread Commission decision 1999/230/EC [1999] OJ L 88/26, Case IV/35.079/F3 (*)

Bass Commission decision 1999/473/EC [1999] OJ L 186/1, Case IV/36.081/F3

Scottish and Newcastle Commission decision 1999/474/EC [1999] OJ L 186/28, Case IV/35.992/F3

Inntrepreneur, Spring Commission decision 2000/484/EC [2000] OJ L 195/49, Cases IV/36.456/F3

Visa International Commission decision 2002/914/EC [2002] OJ L 318/17, Case COMP/29.373 (*)

Gaz de France/ENI Commission decision of 26 October 2004, published on DG Comp website, Case COMP/38.662 (*)

MasterCard Multilateral Interchange Fees Commission decision of 19 December 2007, published on DG Comp website, Case COMP/34.579

F   Economic landmark cases

The landmark Commission decisions on bundling and tying are described in section 3.4.

5.5   Selective distribution systems

A   Introduction

Selective distribution agreements limit the number of retailers that are licensed to sell certain good(s) or service(s). Subject to fulfilling qualitative and/or quantitative requirements prescribed by the nature of the product, certain distributors can be selected as exclusive dealers at the manufacturer's discretion. This type of vertical restraint certainly reduces intrabrand competition among retailers in limiting the number of authorized outlets. It can be an instrument to pursue efficiencies in the distribution system of the kind discussed in the introduction to the chapter. In particular, retailers may need to incur substantial costs from advertising activities, customer services provided to their clients, or special offers or special services required by the manufacturer of the products. Without selective distribution systems, some retailers may free ride on costly services provided by others.

Selective distribution agreements are typically adopted to market branded luxury, and/or highly technological goods. The manufacturer of these kinds of products is often interested in selling its products only in outlets which have some trained and expert personnel that reflect the brand's

---

•   Decisions displayed in **bold type** are described in the section. Decisions highlighted with (*) include interesting economic analysis by the Commission on the specific topic of the section. Some decisions contain economic reasoning on more than one topic and therefore appear in several lists of Commission decisions in chronological order. Reference is made in brackets and **bold type** to the relevant section in which the decision is extensively described as a landmark case. When decisions are referenced and/or described in some detail in one or more of the economic textbooks, reference in brackets is also made to the relevant part(s) of those texts.

image. In particular when there is an important after-sales market, specialized personnel can be essential to the development of a market and the choice of distributors constitutes an essential part of the marketing strategy adopted by a manufacturer.

B   Applicable EU legislation

No special legislation applicable. For applicable legislation see chapter 5, paragraph B.

C   Related economics texts

Bishop and Walker (2009), paragraphs 5.34–5.55
Carlton and Perloff (2005), chapter 12, paragraph 3(1)
Church and Ware (2000), not specifically discussed
Martin (1994), chapter 11, paragraph 3
Martin (2002), paragraph 13.2.3
Motta (2004), paragraphs 6.1, 6.2.2, 6.2.3, and 6.2.4
Tirole (1988), chapter 4
Waldman and Jensen (2001), chapter 15, paragraph 3(2)

D   Related legal texts

Bellamy and Child (2008), chapter 6, paragraph 5
Jones and Sufrin (2008), chapter 9, paragraphs 4(B, iii, d) and 5(C, vi, d)
Ritter and Braun (2005), chapter 4, paragraph B(5, b and 10, e)
Whish (2008), chapter 16, paragraph 5(G, iv)

E   Commission decisions in chronological order•

Omega Commission decision 70/488/EEC [1970] OJ L 242/22, Cases IV/32.13, 10.498, 11.546, 12.992, 17.394, 17.395, 17.971, 18.772, 18.888 (*)
Du Pont de Nemours (Deutschland) Commission decision 73/196/EEC [1973] OJ L 194/27, Case IV/14.111
BMW AG **Commission decision 75/73/EEC [1975] OJ L 29/1, Case IV/14.650**
SABA **Commission Decision 76/159/EEC [1976] OJ L 95/1, Case IV/847** (Martin, 1994, pp. 530–1)
Junghans Commission decision 77/100/EEC [1977] OJ L 30/10, Case IV/57.15
BMW Belgium NV and Belgian BMW dealers Commission decision 78/155/EEC [1978] OJ L 46/33, Case IV/29.146 **(described in detail as landmark case in section 5.2)**
Krups Commission decision 80/489/EEC [1980] OJ L 120/26, Case IV/28.553

•   Decisions displayed in **bold type** are described in the section. Decisions highlighted with (*) include interesting economic analysis by the Commission on the specific topic of the section. Some decisions contain economic reasoning on more than one topic and therefore appear in several lists of Commission decisions in chronological order. Reference is made in brackets and **bold type** to the relevant section in which the decision is extensively described as a landmark case. When decisions are referenced and/or described in some detail in one or more of the economic textbooks, reference in brackets is also made to the relevant part(s) of those texts.

AEG-Telefunken Commission decision 82/267/EEC [1982] OJ L 117/15, Case IV/28.748 (Martin, 1994, pp. 531, 536)

Murat Commission decision 83/610/EEC [1983] OJ L 348/20, Case IV/30.668

SABA's EEC Distribution System Commission decision 83/672/EEC [1983] OJ L 376/41, Case IV/29.598

IBM PC Commission decision 84/233/EEC [1984] OJ L 118/24, Case IV/30.849

Grohe sales system Commission decision 85/44/EEC [1985] OJ L 19/17, Case IV/30.299

Ideal-Standard Sales System Commission decision 85/45/EEC [1985] OJ L 20/38, Case IV/30.261

Grundig Commission decision 85/404/EEC [1985] OJ L 233/1, Case IV/29.420

Ivoclar Commission decision 85/559/EEC [1985] OJ L 369/1, Case IV/30.846

Villeroy and Bosch Commission decision 85/616/EEC [1985] OJ L 376/15, Case IV/30.655

Vichy Commission decision 91/153/EEC [1991] OJ L 75/57, Case IV/31.624

IATA Passenger Agency Programmes Commission decision 91/480/EEC [1991] OJ L 258/18, Case IV/32.659

IATA Cargo Agency Programmes Commission decision 91/481/EEC [1991] OJ L 258/29, Case IV/32.792

Yves Saint-Laurent Parfums Commission decision 92/33/EEC [1992] OJ L 12/24, Case IV/33.242

Parfums Givenchy **Commission decision 92/428/EEC [1992] OJ L 236/11, Case IV/33.542**

Grundig (distribution system) Commission decision 94/29/EEC [1994] OJ L 20/15, Case IV/29.420 (*)

F   Economic landmark cases

F.1   *BMW AG* Commission decision 75/73/EEC [1975] OJ L 29/1

Relevance: The Commission from the beginning of competition law enforcement has recognized that efficiencies may derive from a selective distribution agreement. In this early decision, after having recognized the efficiencies deriving from the agreement, the Commission set some limits for the (anticompetitive) restrictions on the dealers' freedom to be possibly included in such agreements. Absolute territorial protection for dealers was considered as non-admissible and the necessary objective application of the dealership's selection criteria was stated.

- Case IV/14.650
- **Decision:** exemption pursuant to Article 101(3) FEU Treaty for five years
- **Decision addressee(s):**
    - Bayerische Motoren Werke AG, *Federal Republic of Germany*
- **Report route:** Notification for exemption submitted to the Commission on 31 January 1963 by Bayerische Motoren Werke AG (BMW)
- **Date of the decision:** 13 December 1974
- **Competition Commissioner:** A. Borschette
- **Relevant product market:** BMW products
- **Relevant geographical market:** Germany
- **Description of the case**
    - a.   **Relevant facts**
        BMW entered into distribution agreements in Germany with a selected number of main dealers and retailers. The agreements were all concluded on the basis

of standard forms disposed by BMW and submitted to the Commission for exemption.

According to those standard agreements each BMW dealer would have acted as representing the interest of BMW within the territory assigned to him but conducting independent business on his own account and risk. Furthermore each party (main dealer or retailer) undertook with the other contractual party (either BMW or the BMW main dealer) the following obligations:

- To operate a business satisfying BMW's requirements concerning premises, equipment, and technical and commercial management.
- To operate a service department and an after-sale service and a workshop responding to BMW's requirements, to employ qualified staff, and to ensure they would receive further training as required.
- To sell a quantity of products corresponding at least to the estimated demand and sales potential of the territory in question.
- Not to sell BMW products to unauthorised dealers.
- Not to operate branches or outlets outside their own allotted territory and to advertise in other territory only after having promoted sales and after-sales services in their own territory. The freedom to sell outside the allotted territory was guaranteed.
- Not to sell or resell either as an independent dealer or as some other manufacturers' agent products competing with BMW vehicles and products. The obligation might have been disregarded under BMW authorization which in any case should have taken into due account the economic circumstances of the dealer requiring the authorization.
- To follow BMW's instructions in the advertisement of the products. This obligation did not extend to prices and sales conditions.
- To obtain BMW's consent in order to participate in fairs and exhibitions.
- To maintain a stock of goods sufficient to satisfy expected demand.
- To grant a guarantee in the same terms as the guarantee granted by BMW and to ensure assistance to all BMW clients regardless of the dealer from where the vehicle had been acquired.
- To provide BMW with all the information required about the commercial position of the dealer, the market situation, and the sales trends.
- To use the BMW trademark without any addition or alteration.[73]
  In addition to the above-listed contractual obligations, the main dealers also had the obligation to conclude, interrupt, or terminate any retail agreement without the consent of BMW and to conclude or interrupt retail agreements upon BMW's request.[74]

BMW undertook with main dealers and the latter with retailers to deliver products in accordance with the conditions of sale and delivery published by BMW and to not appoint further main dealers or retailers

---

73 See recital 3 of the decision. 74 See recital 4 of the decision.

in the territory, nor to change the territory without giving the interested parties sixty days' notice.[75]

Moreover BMW agreed with regard to main dealers not to undertake direct sales to consumers with the exception of a few listed categories, to guarantee products in accordance with the condition of sale and delivery, and to reimburse dealers for expenses incurred for services provided under guarantee and free services obligations.[76]

b. Origin of the case

On 31 January 1963 BMW submitted to the Commission a notification pursuant to Article 4 of Regulation 17 to see its standard forms of contract adopted in Germany for the sale of its products be declared exempted from the application of Article 101(1) FEU Treaty by virtue of Article 101(3) FEU Treaty.

c. Economic analysis

This decision reveals that the Commission had a positive approach toward selective distribution agreements and has always recognized the efficiency reasons that can lie beneath the adoption of such a commercial strategy since the beginning of EU competition law enforcement.

The reasoning of the Commission recognizes the efficiencies and the economies of scale deriving from selective distribution agreements and, as far as the criteria for the selection of the dealers are applied objectively and in a non-discriminatory way, it recognizes that the restrictions imposed upon competition by these practices are outweighed by the efficiencies deriving from them.

The Commission described the restrictive effects on competition that would have derived by BMW's set of agreements. In particular the Commission underlined the exclusion from the system of all potential dealers willing to sell BMW's product but not ready to offer all the additional services required by the distribution contract, the further restriction of dealers' opportunity to join the network deriving from BMW's right also to exclude dealers from the system in cases where the latter were able to satisfy all the requirements. Further restrictions were considered as deriving from the exclusion of the possibility for all non-members of the dealership system to sell BMW products, from limiting the main dealers to freely select the retailers ("result[ing] in main dealers having little scope, when appointing retail dealers to follow their own views on sales policy where these differ from those of BMW,"[77]) from the restriction of BMW's direct sales to final consumers, and from the limitation of the advertising campaign in territories other than the allotted one.[78] The Commission considered some other of the obligations included as conditions for the dealership as non-restrictive of competition.[79]

Notwithstanding those restrictive effects arising from the selective distribution system, the Commission recognized the efficiencies resulting from it and considered those efficiencies more significant than the restrictions and the system necessary to guarantee proper services in the sale of such complex goods as

75   See recital 5 of the decision.
76   See recital 6 of the decision.
77   Recital 13 of the decision.
78   See recitals 13–19 of the decision.
79   See recitals 20–22 of the decision.

cars. In assessing the possible positive effects generated by the agreements, the Commission stated it "is prepared to accept that such a system may contribute to improving both the production and distribution of goods and to promoting technical progress. Limiting the number of dealers can be regarded as more beneficial, so far as it is based on the requirement by BMW of minimum standards for selection and continued employment of dealers. By such means the following can in particular be ensured:

  – that BMW motor vehicles are received and stored in technically perfect conditions ...;
  – that both maintenance and preparation and also services carried out under guarantee and extended free service are not only sufficiently available but are also of an adequate quality for the consumers ...;
  – that any modifications to vehicles that become necessary may be carried out ...;
  – that sufficient plant, equipment, and BMW-trained personnel are available for the provision of the above services ...;
  – that the store of spare parts is adequate in range and quality ...;
  – that BMW may rapidly and fully inform its appointed dealers of technical problems as they arise ...."[80]

The possibility for BMW to directly appoint new dealers and to reserve the right to refuse retailers of the main dealers, even if not based on "universally predictable and objective criteria,"[81] was recognized by the Commission as an important element facilitating the overall rationalization of the system and consequently as improving the offered services. "The cooperation between BMW and its dealers, which goes beyond the mere marketing of products, provides ... a method of rationalizing the sale and services of BMW vehicles and parts and thereby provides a better service to the consumers than a system of free marketing to which such cooperation is not attached. Motor vehicles, products of limited life, high cost and complex technology, require regular maintenance by specially equipped garages or service depots, because their use can be dangerous to life, health and property and can have a harmful effect on the environment. It is therefore of importance that those responsible for the maintenance of vehicles have access to the latest technical knowledge which the manufacturer has acquired in the development and construction of the vehicle. Moreover, continual cooperation between BMW and its main dealers may assist BMW in the preparation of its maintenance instructions and training programmes, and may also lead indirectly to improvements in the design of vehicles."[82]

The exclusion by BMW of direct sales to customers was considered as important for the organization and concentration of BMW's marketing activity, the improvement of sales promotion by the appointed dealers, and as rationalizing distribution as a whole.[83]

---

80 Recitals 23 and 24 of the decision.
81 Recital 24 of the decision.

82 Recital 24 of the decision.
83 See recital 26 of the decision.

Concerning the non-competition clause included in the agreements, the Commission noted, "the advantages of this clause outweigh its disadvantages. Since in principle appointed BMW dealers have to concentrate their efforts in selling ... BMW products, it may be expected that technical expertise and advice are provided for BMW vehicles and parts and that competition between the products of the different manufacturers of motor vehicles and parts [i.e. inter-brand competition] is strengthened at the different levels of distribution."[84]

According to the Commission the overall system set by BMW would have therefore produced advantages for consumers and would have not eliminated competition at the distribution level.[85]

An important condition for the possibility of organizing selective distribution agreements, which is derivable from this decision, was the non-inclusion in the agreements of clauses creating artificial territorial protection such as export ban and parallel import ban clauses, or clauses providing for the absolute prohibition to resell outside a certain territory. The Commission, as already described in section 5.2, has always considered such clauses highly anticompetitive and not satisfying the conditions that Article 101(3) FEU Treaty requires for exemption.[86]

d. **Fines, remedies, and conditions enclosed**

    – Obligation for BMW to submit an annual report to the Commission indicating, on the one side, any case of refusal to conclude a distribution agreement in Germany and any termination or modification of the existing ones and, on the other, any case of refusal of a BMW distributor in Germany to sell competing products.

e. **Further developments of the case**

    None.

F.2   *SABA* Commission Decision 76/159/EEC [1976] OJ L 95/1

Relevance: Besides the qualitative requirements demanded by the producer of distributors in order to be part of its distribution system, which constitute the typical content of a selective distribution agreement, the Commission in this decision exempted also quantitative restraints imposed upon selected distributors since they were considered necessary for the achievement of the efficiencies deriving from the agreement. The decision fully confirms the constant positive approach of EU competition law toward selective distribution agreements.

---

84   Recital 28 of the decision.
85   Within the assessment made of other notified selective distribution agreements in the following years, the Commission has exempted several and different qualitative requirements included in those agreements and has, on a case-by-case basis, appraised the derived efficiencies and the effectiveness of those requirements for their achievement. An interesting instance was given in *Parfums Givenchy* (Commission decision 92/428/EEC [1992] OJ L 236/11, Case IV/33.542). In that decision the Commission exempted a selective distribution agreement in which one of the requirements in order to become a Givenchy distributor was to sell in the outlets a certain number of competing luxury products (i.e. a multi-branding obligation). According to the Commission, the requirement was "intended to maintain a distribution system based on the sale of Givenchy products alongside other competing luxury brands, which ensures that retailers are able to run a specialized business that is capable of offering consumers a wide range of competing products and thereby attract customers. This also helps to ensure the enhanced presentation of the contract goods whilst stimulating inter-brand competition ... The clause ... gives customers the opportunity to compare a range of competing products when making a purchase. [It] is necessary in order to attract and retain the loyalty of consumers who expect to find, in each retail outlet, a specialized commercial environment allowing them to choose from a range of competing brands. [Furthermore] authorized Givenchy retailers are able to take advantage of interbrand competition" (Recitals II-B-2, 4 and 5 of the decision).
86   See recitals 11 and 12 of the decision.

- Case IV/847
- **Decision:** exemption pursuant to Article 101(3) FEU Treaty from December 1972 until July 1980 for the Sole Distribution Agreement and from February 1975 to July 1980 for other agreements listed in the decision
- **Decision addressee(s):**
    - SABA (Schwarzwälder Apparate-Bau-Anstalt August Schwer und Söhne GmbH), *Federal Republic of Germany*
    - A. Loschetter & Fils, *Luxembourg*
    - Ets. Fr. Drion, *Belgium*
    - SABA Netherlands NV, *the Netherlands*
- **Report route:** Notifications for exemption submitted to the Commission by SABA.
- **Date of the decision:** 15 December 1975
- **Competition Commissioner:** A. Borschette
- **Relevant product market:** Trade in electronic equipment for domestic leisure purposes
- **Relevant geographical market:** European internal market
- **Description of the case**
    a. **Relevant facts**
    SABA (a television, radio, and tape-recording equipment manufacturer) set up a complex and multi-level distribution system in order to sell its entire range of products throughout the European market.

    SABA based its distributive organization on different types of dealers, signing distribution and cooperation agreements with each of them. Those agreements provided for some common provisions aimed at the sales and promotion of its products and simultaneously for some specific obligations depending on the level of distribution concerned.

    According to the distribution agreements as well as to the so-called cooperation agreements, the dealers (wholesalers, sole distributors, and specialist retailers) were asked to fulfill a set of both qualitative and quantitative requirements.

    In particular all the dealers had to:
    - Trade from specified shops for the sales.
    - Participate in the creation and consolidation of the SABA sales network.
    - Participate in the SABA service system, particularly through qualified staff for after-sales services.
    - Supply goods for resale within the common market only to SABA dealers and personally check that the dealer asking for supplies had been appointed by SABA as member of the distributive network.
    - Keep stock of serial numbers of resold articles and data about the purchasers.
    - Not export and/or re-import SABA products to and from countries outside the (then) EEC.

    The sole distributors were given the exclusive right to market the relevant products within their allotted territories (on a national base) but at the same time they subscribed to further obligations, according to which:
    - They would not manufacture and market competing products.
    - They would not carry out active sales outside their allotted territories.

- They would achieve a certain minimum turnover from the SABA products sales.
- They would place binding advanced orders for each sales period.
- They would notify any cost incurred in their territory.

Furthermore the specialist retailers had to:

- Trade from premises suitable for properly advertising and displaying SABA products.
- Stock the SABA range as fully as possible and in case of direct purchases from SABA a complete range of products.

Special further restrictive obligations concerning minimum related turnover and – as a result of amendments following the Commission's observations on the restrictive nature of some provisions included in an earlier version of the agreement – prohibition of direct sales to consumers unless they were business consumers, were established for wholesalers in the Federal Republic of Germany.

No restrictions at all were imposed in the agreements regarding the selling prices (there was no RPM) and the possibility to enter into cross-supplies and/or return-supplies agreements among members of the distribution network.[87]

b. Origin of the case

On 19 December 1962, 12 February 1963, 20 June 1969, 31 July 1972, and 22 July 1974 SABA submitted to the Commission several notifications pursuant to Article 4 of Regulation 17 to see its Conditions of Sale, distributorship agreements for wholesalers and retailers, and a cooperation agreement with retailers and wholesalers be declared exempted from the application of Article 101(1) FEU Treaty by virtue of Article 101(3) FEU Treaty.

c. Economic analysis

The Commission approach toward selective distribution system (see also the previous case in this section, *BMW AG*) has always been in line with economic literature that recognizes this type of vertical restraint – although restrictive of intrabrand competition among products' dealers – as a tool to avoid free-riding in the marketing of high-brand products (the typical example is luxury goods), to guarantee product quality certification, and to provide incentives at the retail level for the provision of better customer services and for new investment in the provision of services.

Confirming its previous orientation, the Commission stated that the "application of purely qualitative tests such as the technical qualifications of dealers and specialist knowledge of their staff, participation of wholesalers in the creation of a distribution network and services system, the suitability of trading premises and adequacy of customer services ... would generally exclude from the SABA distribution system only those dealers not capable of selling electronic equipment for domestic leisure purposes in a manner satisfactory to the consumer or of providing the necessary service ... To be market [ed] adequately, trained personnel must be available to sell the goods from premises suitable for their display, stocking, and demonstration. Dealers must also be in a position to

---

87   See recitals 1–18 of the decision.

provide guarantee and after-sales services."[88] All these requirements – together with the provisions related to the German wholesalers considered as part of a legitimate allocation of functions and the obligation upon the sole distributors to notify all the territory-incurred costs – do not constitute restrictions of competition under Article 101(1) EC Treaty.[89]

In contrast to its previous approach, the Commission for the first time exempted even provisions of the distribution agreements which were by their own nature quantitative rather than qualitative (in the specific case the six-monthly supply contracts, the minimum turnover requirement, and the stock range obligation).[90]

Notwithstanding the recognized anticompetitive nature of those contractual clauses,[91] the Commission assessing their effects under Article 101(3) FEU Treaty qualified them as indispensable for the achievement of the following pro-competitive and economically efficient aims:

- A better planning of SABA production and sales policy, in particular to ensure continuity of supply and rationalization of manufacturing and marketing.
- Obligation for SABA – in the frame of the cooperative relation with its dealer – to offer goods at a reasonable price, suitable for the market, and appropriate to the particular local requirements of local consumers.
- A better and more intensive exploitation of the market and the promotion of sales.
- An improvement in the distribution of the relevant products.
- An improvement in the services offered to consumers (continuity of supplies, adaptation to local requirements, broader range of stocked goods, pass-on to consumers of benefits achieved by the manufacturer and dealers).[92]

d. Fines, remedies, and conditions enclosed
- Submission by SABA of annual reports to the Commission setting out all cases of: refusal to appoint a dealer or withdrawal of such an appointment, refusal to conclude a supply contract with a SABA dealer or withholding of supplies, exercising the right to inspect the register of serial numbers of a dealer.

---

88   Recital 28 of the decision.
89   See recitals 27–28 and 34–36 of the decision.
90   The Commission had already exempted in an earlier decision a selective distribution system set by Omega that provided for a limitation of the number of selling points (i.e. a closed selective distribution system). The motivation given by the Commission for the exemption was that the limitation of the selling points would have guaranteed each retailer with enough turnover to enable them to make an effort to promote sales and customer services (*Omega* Commission decision 70/488/EEC [1970] OJ L 242/22, Cases IV/32.13, 10.498, 11.546, 12.992, 17.394, 17.395, 17.971, 18.772, 18.888). The same approach was followed in the landmark decision *BMW AG* described on p. 252 in this section. In this sense, it can be said that the Commission had already allowed quantitative restrictions (the number of outlets) not based on qualitative criteria. What is actually intended in the present decision on quantitative restrictions are obligations imposed upon the retailers to achieve quantitative results in their sales activities. In this sense, it can be said that those described in the current decision are inside-the-distribution system quantitative restrictions, while those referred to in *Omega* are out-of-the-system quantitative restrictions.
91   "These obligations ensure a high degree of dependence by dealers on SABA. They lead to the exclusion of those undertakings meeting the qualitative criteria of appointment but which are not in a position or not willing to comply with these additional obligations," recital 29 of the decision.
92   See recitals 26–27, 29, and 38–46 of the decision.

e. Further development of the case.

Case 26/76 *Metro* v. *Commission (SABA I)* [1977] ECR 1875, appeal dismissed. In this landmark judgment the ECJ, confirming the Commission's decision, gave a substantive interpretation of what EU competition law allows in case of selective distribution agreement and what is instead prohibited. The ECJ also carried out an analysis of wholesalers' role in the market for domestic electronic equipments and their importance for final consumers.[93]

F.3   *Parfums Givenchy* Commission decision 92/428/EEC [1992] OJ L 236/11

Relevance: The decision states that a selective distribution network can be exempted under the condition that qualitative or product-related criteria are applied in a non-discriminatory manner. The Commission further dealt with the issue of whether the condition to carry a sufficient number of competing brands (known as a multibranding obligation) can be exempted under Article 101(3) of the Treaty.

- Case No. IV/33.542
- **Decision:** Application of exemption of Article 101(3) of the EEC Treaty for five years
- **Decision addressee(s):**
    - Parfums Givenchy SA, *France*
- **Report route:** Application for exemption was submitted by Givenchy on 19 March 1990.
- **Date of the decision:** 24 July 1992
- **Competition Commissioner:** L. Brittan
- **Relevant product market:** Luxury cosmetic products
- **Relevant geographical market:** European internal market
    #### Description of the case
    #### a. Relevant facts
    Parfums Givenchy SA (Givenchy) belongs to the Louis Vuitton Moët-Hennessy group and is active on the market for luxury products including luxury perfumery products, leather goods, cognac, spirits, haute couture, and fashion accessories. Givenchy operated with a selective distribution system for luxury cosmetic products in the Member States. Retailers were selected by Givenchy or its exclusive agents on the basis of a number of criteria. The standard agreement that bound Givenchy and the authorized network dealers included quantitative and qualitative requirements. The company notified the standard agreement to the Commission including the following obligations:
    - To provide trained sales personnel, and further attendance at training organized by Givenchy.
    - Retailers have to cooperate in advertising and promotion activities.
    - Products could only be sold in a shop's display that fitted the prestige of the products.
    - To provide optimal storage for the product's preservation.
    - To sell a sufficient number of products from competing brands.
    - To display and sell Givenchy's products exclusively on the premises covered by the contract.
    - To refrain from engaging in the active sale of a product that had not yet been launched in the retailer's territory.

---

93   See in particular recitals 20–22 and 46–50 of the judgment.

    – To achieve a minimum amount of annual purchases from Givenchy or its exclusive agents.[94]

    No restrictions at all were imposed in the agreements regarding resale product prices and the possibility to enter into cross-supply between members of the distribution network.[95] The contracts were concluded for a duration of one year.

b. Origin of the case

On 19 March 1990 Parfums Givenchy SA submitted to the Commission a notification pursuant to Article 19(3) of Regulation 17 to see its standard agreement of selective distribution adopted in the Member States exempted from the application of Article 101(1) FEU Treaty by virtue of Article 101(3) FEU Treaty.

c. Economic analysis

    In line with its previous decisions, as well as with ECJ case law, the Commission recalled that "a selective distribution system necessarily affects competition in the common market. However, it has always been recognized that certain products which are not ordinary products or services have properties such that they cannot properly be supplied to the public without the intervention of specialized distributors."[96] The Commission recognizes in its decision that certain conditions are essential for the sales of luxury products and also for the consumer to preserve the developed reputation as high-quality products marketed under a well-known brand.

    The Commission analyzed certain conditions that were included in the standard-form distribution contract of Givenchy and their restrictive effects on competition. The Commission acknowledged that for the sales of luxury products trained personnel is necessary and additionally constitute an advantage for consumers in choosing a product that suits their tastes and requirements. It further recognized that marketing under a well-established brand is an essential factor on competition and enables the manufacturer to maintain its position in the market.[97] The Commission concluded that these selection criteria do not restrict competition or the retailer's choice of which products he wants to sell.

    Further, the Commission looked at those conditions that could not be qualified as being of a "qualitative nature." In particular, the Commission underlined the exclusion from the network of those retailers that were willing to carry Givenchy's products but were not authorized. The requirement that the retailer had to achieve a minimum annual purchase set by Givenchy or its exclusive agents was regarded as restricting competition because it "goes beyond the requirements regarding the technical qualification of retailers or their sales staff."[98] Moreover, the Commission found that obligations such as carrying competing brands and refraining from selling a product constituted limitations creating restrictions on competition. The Commission regarded obligations – for instance, the checking of the authorized retailers' invoices by Givenchy – as monitoring measures to maintain the tightness and homogeneity of the distribution network.[99]

---

94   See recitals I.C.a.i-viii of the decision.
95   See recitals I.C.c. and I.C.e. of the decision.
96   Case C-107/82 *AEG* v. *Commission* [1983], ECR 3151, recital 13.

97   See recital II.A.5 of the decision.
98   See recital II.A.6.b. of the decision.
99   See recital II.A.7.i of the decision.

Regardless of restrictive effects arising from the selective distribution system, the Commission underlined that the efficiencies deriving from the system and the required maintenance of the market position as a luxury brand dominated the restrictions. It recognized the brand image as a key factor in competition and pointed out that, in this separate market segment, a consumer's decision was essentially based on the brand. By conditions such as the minimum purchase requirement, Givenchy can ensure continuous supplies and, furthermore, it allows the company to concentrate on the most effective retailers. The Commission additionally recognized that the carrying of competing brands enabled Givenchy to attract customers that were interested in high-quality brands. This condition is further necessary, according to the Commission, to "attract and retain the loyalty of consumers who expect to find, in each retail outlet, a specialized commercial environment."[100] In this way, it can also be ensured that the retailer runs a business that is "capable of offering consumers a wide range of competing brands and thereby attract customers." [101] This requirement stimulates interbrand competition rather than restricting it.

The requirement to refrain from selling a product in a Member State where it has not yet been launched, is of crucial importance for the manufacturer to test a new product on the market.

The Commission especially stressed the advantages for consumers that the system creates, namely "that the luxury product is not becoming an everyday product as a result of a downgrading of its image and a decrease in the level of creation."[102] Furthermore, consumers are left with a wide choice in the shops that are required to sell competing brands.

According to the Commission, the distribution network set by Givenchy enables retailers to take advantage of interbrand competition and since no anticompetitive clauses are included in the standard form, competition would not be eliminated. As a consequence, the Commission stated that the conditions for exemption within the meaning of Article 101(3) of the Treaty are fulfilled.

d. Fines, remedies, and conditions enclosed
– Obligation for Givenchy to submit every two years a report to the Commission including the total amount of purchases of Givenchy achieved by all the authorized retailers, price increases, the launching of new products or the withdrawal of old products, the number of authorized retailers and the amounts set annually by the company or its exclusive agents pursuant to the minimum annual purchases requirement.

e. Further developments of the case
Case T-87/92 *BVBA Kruidvat* v. *Commission* [1996] ECR II-01931. Appeal dismissed. Kruidvat filed a second appeal to the ECJ (C-70/97 *BVBA Kruidvat* v. *Commission* [1998] ECR I-07183), dismissed.

Case T-88/92 *Groupement d'achat Edouard Leclerc* v. *Commission* [1996] II-01961. The decision of the Commission was partially annulled. The CFI (now "the General Court") argued that the Commission did not take proper account

100   See recital II.B.4 of the decision.   102   See recital II.B.3 of the decision.
101   See recital II.B.2 of the decision.

of all restrictions of the exclusive distribution agreement. In general, the CFI confirmed that shop location, trained personnel, the sale of products potentially detracting from Givenchy's image, etc., were all reasonable conditions in such an agreement. The scale of other activities carried out in the outlet, however, was not in itself a reason not to grant the distributor status to a retail shop.

5.6 Franchising

A Introduction

Franchising is a particular form of vertical relations through which a franchisor sells a business model to one or more franchisees. Sometimes the franchisor sells only the right to use its trademark or its brand. Usually a franchising agreement includes both intellectual property rights (IPRs) such as patents and trademarks, as well as commercial actions and business strategies. The latter can include, *inter alia*, advice on advertising, choice of location, store design, selling strategies, and accounting methods. The franchisor often also provides commercial and technical assistance and training to the franchisee to ensure that its business methods are properly implemented and its goodwill maintained and protected. The franchisee agrees to respect the business manners established by the franchisor and to run its activities accordingly.

Franchising agreements can help eliminate double marginalization. They can also be important instruments to penetrate new markets by the franchisor without having to make substantial investments fully independently. The relationship between franchisor and franchisee(s) is based on reciprocal trust and efforts made in order to make the business profitable. The franchisor has an interest in high franchise revenues as its fee is proportional; it may give additional incentives to the franchisee by allowing the latter to keep the bulk of extra profits. At the same time, the franchisee has an interest in the way the overall franchisor's business is run. In particular, the franchisee is interested in the maintenance of the reputation and goodwill of the brand, which directly affect its own sales. It is therefore interested in the performance of all other franchisees and in the effective provision of services and assistance by the franchisor.

Franchising agreements clearly constitute limitations of the franchisee's freedom to establish its business and conduct it in its preferred way. Nonetheless, they can be important to stimulate interbrand competition and to expand the reputation and the business network of the franchisor. In certain types of markets, franchise agreements are a common marketing instrument – for example, in fast-food restaurants, gas stations, and car dealership agreements.

Franchising agreements typically provide for a franchise fee plus a percentage on sales that the franchisee will pass on to the franchisor. Such non-linear pricing strategies can create economies of scale, as well as an incentive for the franchisee to buy more products from the franchisor to benefit from volume discounts. What usually causes further concerns for competition authorities in franchising are the combined vertical restraints that may be attached to the main agreement. These can include exclusive supply agreements, non-compete clauses, exclusive (or selective) distribution agreement, RPM, and territorial restrictions.

B Applicable EU legislation

No special legislation applicable. For applicable legislation see chapter 5, paragraph B.

C Related economics texts

Bishop and Walker (2009), not specifically discussed
Carlton and Perloff (2005), chapter 12, paragraphs 3(1) and 4

Church and Ware (2000), not specifically discussed
Martin (1994), chapter 15, paragraph 3
Martin (2002), not specifically discussed
Motta (2004), paragraphs 6.1, 6.2.1.1, 6.2.3.1, and 6.3.1
Tirole (1988), chapter 4 and paragraphs 8.2.3
Waldman and Jensen (2001), chapter 15, paragraph 2 and chapter 19, paragraph 4(2)

D Related legal texts

Bellamy and Child (2008), chapter 6, paragraph 7
Jones and Sufrin (2008), chapter 9, paragraph 4(B, iii, e)
Ritter and Braun (2005), chapter 4, paragraph B(5, c)
Whish (2008), chapter 16, paragraph 5(G, v)

E Commission decisions in chronological order[•]

Yves Rocher **Commission decision 87/14/EEC [1987] OJ L 8/49, Cases IV/31.428, 31.429, 31.430, 31.431, 31.432**
Pronuptia Commission decision 87/17/EEC [1987] OJ L 13/39, Case IV/30.937 (*)
Computerland Commission decision 87/407/EEC [1987] OJ L 222/12, Case IV/32.034
Service Master Commission decision 88/604/EEC [1988] OJ L 332/38, Case IV/32.358
Charles Jourdan Commission decision 89/94/EEC [1989] OJ L 35/31, Case IV/31.697

F Economic landmark case

F.1 *Yves Rocher* Commission decision 87/14/EEC [1987] OJ L 8/49

Relevance: In the first decision in which the Commission dealt with a franchising agreement, the Commission showed a general positive propensity toward such agreements. It recognised the efficiencies deriving from the franchise network and considered as indispensable many of the clauses attached to it that might have limited competition to a certain (limited) extent. The only franchise clause considered as unjustifiably restrictive of competition (i.e. not inherent to the agreement) was the territorial protection granted.

- Cases IV/31.428, 31.429, 31.430, 31.431, 31.432
- **Decision:** exemption pursuant to Article 101(3) FEU Treaty for seven years
- **Decision addressee(s):**
    – Société d'études de chimie et de thérapie appliqués Laboratoires de Cosmétologie Yves Rocher, *France*
- **Report route:** Application for negative clearance and notification for exemption submitted to the Commission on 15 January 1985 by Société d'études de chimie et de thérapie appliqués Laboratoires de Cosmétologie Yves Rocher
- **Date of the decision:** 17 December 1986

• Decisions displayed in **bold type** are described in the section. Decisions highlighted with (*) include interesting economic analysis by the Commission on the specific topic of the section. Some decisions contain economic reasoning on more than one topic and therefore appear in several lists of Commission decisions in chronological order. Reference is made in brackets and **bold type** to the relevant section in which the decision is extensively described as a landmark case. When decisions are referenced and/or described in some detail in one or more of the economic textbooks, reference in brackets is also made to the relevant part(s) of those texts.

- **Competition Commissioner:** A. Borschette
- **Relevant product market:** Cosmetic products
- **Relevant geographical market:** Not indicated
- **Description of the case**
  - a. **Relevant facts**

      Société d'études de chimie et de thérapie appliqués Laboratoires de Cosmétologie Yves Rocher (Yves Rocher) was a company active in the market for the production, distribution, and marketing of cosmetic products. It was active in every segment of the relevant market (beauty products, alcohol-based perfumes, hair-care products, and toiletries). The market was characterized by a large number of producers none of them holding significant market power. The products were sold either through general retail outlets or specialized retail shops. Yves Rocher's selling policy in Europe combined mail orders and about 1,000 franchised retailers active in seven Member States and directly supplied either by Yves Rocher or by a wholly owned subsidiary.

      The franchisees were selected by Yves Rocher according to their "personality, their apparent overall aptitude for running a cosmetic retailing business and their performance in the training programme."[103] All contracts were concluded personally and there was an explicit prohibition for franchisees to transfer or assign the contract without written authorization of the franchisor.

      The main provisions of the standard franchising agreement adopted by Yves Rocher were as follows:
      - The franchisee undertook to employ a sufficient number of qualified staff.
      - The franchisor would have carried out a preliminary market and location study and proposed a district; the franchisee, under Yves Rocher authorization, would have then established the precise shop location. The latter would have been defined in the contract together with the ban to change it without previous consent from the franchisor.
      - The franchisee received territorial protection in a certain area both from other franchisees' activities and from Yves Rocher.
      - Yves Rocher granted the franchisees the right to use its sign, trademark, design, and models.
      - Yves Rocher undertook to transfer to the franchisees its know-how concerning every aspect of the franchise business and in particular technical, commercial, promotional, publicity, administrative and financial matters, staff training, and general administration.
      - Yves Rocher would have organized a training session before the opening of the beauty center (the retail shop) and further training during the agreement. It would have furthermore put at the franchisees' disposal all its technical knowledge in order to make the retail points operate in accordance with its policy and image.
      - The franchisees were required to employ uniform trading methods, all indicated in a manual provided by Yves Rocher. In particular in their centers they were supposed to use uniform standards in interior design, lighting, fitting-out (all at Yves Rocher expense), layout and

103   Recital 16 of the decision.

furnishing, presentation of products, sales techniques, publicity campaigns, nature and quality of beauty treatments offered, accounts, and insurance.
- All franchisees were obliged not to enter into business with any other competing product or firm. They also had to sell only products carrying the Yves Rocher trademark, for one year after the end of the contract, at least in their exclusive territory.
- Franchisees paid an initial fee and a periodic fixed proportion of publicity costs.
- Franchisees were authorized to buy the products also from other franchisees, besides directly from Yves Rocher. They were nonetheless banned from supplying non-authorized resellers.

b. Origin of the case

On 15 January 1985 Yves Rocher submitted to the Commission an application for negative clearance and a notification for exemption pursuant to Articles 2 and 4 of Regulation 17 to see Article 101(1) FEU Treaty be declared not applicable to the standard form for franchise contracts or alternatively the same standard form be declared exempted from the application of Article 101(1) FEU Treaty by virtue of Article 101(3) FEU Treaty.

c. Economic analysis

This decision constitutes the first case (together with *Pronuptia*)[104] in which the Commission dealt with a franchising agreement. It also demonstrates the permissive approach of the Commission and more in general of EU competition law toward franchising agreements. The Commission recognized the peculiar nature of this type of distribution organization, all its benefits for the development of commerce and competition, for an improved commercialization of the products in question and also for consumers. The Commission's approach recognizes the efficiencies produced by franchising agreements.

Under the specific circumstances of the case, the Commission found that many of the contractual clauses did not restrict competition at all and therefore fell outside the scope of application of Article 101. A franchise network was generally considered as a positive and pro-competitive organization. Accordingly, the majority of the contractual clauses attached to it were considered on the one side as inherent restrictions without which the agreement would have not been concluded and, on the other, as the logical consequences of the franchising structure. In particular, the obligations to exploit IPRs and know-how in a certain manner were considered as "inherent in the very existence of its right in its intellectual creations."[105]

The same assessment was made about Yves Rocher's freedom to choose its franchisees. "It is logically entitled to choose its partners freely and turn down applicants who do not, in its view, have the personal qualities and business qualifications which it requires for the application of the formula it has developed."[106]

---

104   *Pronuptia* Commission decision 87/17/EEC [1987] OJ L 13/39, Case IV/30.937. The two decisions were adopted the same day, 17 December 1986.
105   Recital 40 of the decision.
106   Recital 41 of the decision.

Similar considerations motivated the decision to find the clauses concerning the choice of the shop location, all the obligations concerning the setting and the decoration of the shop as well as those related to interior lay-out and trading methods non-restrictive in nature.[107]

The non-compete clause, as well as the obligation not to carry out competing activity for the duration of the contract (and for one further year after its expiration date), were considered inherent in the nature of the distribution agreement and "indispensable to protect the know-how and assistance provided by the franchisor. By their nature, the know-how and assistance provided are of a kind which could be used for the benefit of other beauty product or services, which would, even if only indirectly, enable competitors to benefit from the trading methods employed. Other means to avoid same risks might not be as effective."[108] The same reasoning was applied to the remaining obligations provided for in the franchising agreements.

After having given an interpretation of the clauses that normally (i.e. inherently) substantiate this kind of agreements, the Commission found that – among the ones it assessed – the territorial protection granted to each franchisee constituted a form of market sharing between franchisor and franchisees which was further reinforced by the prohibition imposed upon franchisees not to open a second shop outside their assigned territory. Those clauses were therefore restrictive of competition under Article 101(1). In assessing the beneficial effects deriving from that restriction and possibly outweighing the negative results, the Commission gave its view of the nature of the franchise. "The Franchise contracts go beyond mere distribution agreements, for the franchisor undertakes to grant rights to use its identifying marks and its proven trading methods with a view to the application of an original and changing distribution formula. [F]ranchise contracts contribute to improving the distribution of the goods in question, since they help the producer to penetrate new markets by enabling him to expand his network without having to undertake any investment in the fitting-out of new shops. Moreover, the development of a chain of identical retail outlets strengthens competition *vis-à-vis* large retail organizations with a branch network. By its policy of selection and training . . . Yves Rocher increases inter-brand competition and accordingly improves the structure of cosmetic distribution. The close integration of independent traders within the Yves Rocher network leads to a rationalization of distribution through a standardization of trading methods covering every aspect of retailing. The direct nature – there being no wholesalers – of the relation . . . facilitates consumer feedback and the adjustment of supply to a constantly changing demand. [Furthermore t]he grant to franchisees of an exclusive territory . . . enables them to pursue a more intensive policy of selling Yves Rocher products by concentrating on their allotted territory . . . Territorial exclusivity also simplifies planning and ensures the continuity of supplies."[109]

A certain degree of territorial protection was considered necessary because "none of the Yves Rocher franchisees would, in all probability, have agreed to undertake the investment needed to set up an independent business had he

---

107   See recitals 42–45 of the decision.
108   Recital 47 of the decision.

109   Recitals 58–60 of the decision.

not been certain of receiving a degree of protection against competition from another Center set up in his territory by the franchisor or other franchisee."[110] Also consumers would have benefited by the wide range of cosmetics from the same brand readily available and from the effort made by the franchisees "motivated by the desire for maximum efficiency."[111]

d. Fines, remedies, and conditions enclosed

– Obligation for Yves Rocher to submit an annual report to the Commission indicating the current recommended retail prices and prices to be paid by franchisees in the Member States in which it had established a franchising network.

e. Further developments of the case

None.

5.7 Discounts and rebates

A Introduction

The economics and potential anticompetitive use of discounts and rebates have been described in section 3.2. In case of vertical relations they can constitute an incentive to strengthen the exclusive links already existing between manufacturer and retailer(s).

B Applicable EU legislation

No special legislation applicable. For applicable legislation see chapter 5, paragraph B.

C Related economics texts

Bishop and Walker (2009), paragraphs 6.29–6.40
Carlton and Perloff (2005), chapter 10, paragraphs 1 and 4

---

110   Recital 63 of the decision.
111   Recital 61 of the decision. In ruling on the Commission decision in the *Pronumptia* case (87/17/EEC, mentioned above), the ECJ followed the same line of reasoning and stated that "the franchisor must be able to communicate his know-how to the franchisees and provide them with the necessary assistance in order to enable them to apply his method, without running the risk that that know-how and assistance might benefit competitors, even indirectly. It follows that provisions which are essential in order to avoid that risk do not constitute restrictions on competition for the purposes of article 81(1)." Moreover the ECJ ruled that the same applies for a clause prohibiting the franchisee, during the period of validity of the contract and for a reasonable period after its expiry, from opening a shop of the same or a similar nature in an area where he may compete with a member of the network. The same may be said of the franchisee's obligation not to transfer his shop to another party without the prior approval of the franchisor; that provision is intended to prevent competitors from indirectly benefiting from the know-how and assistance provided.
       Furthermore, and with regard to territorial protection, the ECJ stated that a provision which obliges the franchisee to sell goods covered by the contract only in the premises specified therein, prohibits the franchisee from opening a second shop. A combination of provisions of that kind results in a sharing of markets between the franchisor and the franchisees or between franchisees and thus restricts competition within the network. A restriction of that kind constitutes a limitation of competition for the purposes of article 101(1) if it concerns a business name or symbol which is already well known. The ECJ confirmed the Commission's finding that a certain degree of territorial protection is necessary. The ECJ stated that "a prospective franchisee would not take the risk of becoming part of the chain, investing his own money, paying a relatively high entry fee and undertaking to pay a substantial annual royalty, unless he could hope, thanks to a degree of protection against competition on the part of the franchisor and other franchisees, that his business would be profitable." However, such a consideration is only relevant to an examination of the agreement in the light of the conditions laid down in article 101(3). See Case 161/84, *Pronuptia de Paris GmbH* v *Pronuptia de Paris Irmgard Schillgallis*.

Church and Ware (2000), paragraph 5.4.3
Martin (1994), not specifically discussed
Martin (2002), not specifically discussed
Motta (2004), paragraph 7.4, specifically 7.4.1.6
Tirole (1988), paragraph 3.3
Waldman and Jensen (2001), chapter 14, paragraph 6(6)

D   Related legal texts

Bellamy and Child (2008), chapter 10, paragraph 4(B, iii)
Jones and Sufrin (2008), chapter 7, paragraph 6(E)
Ritter and Braun (2005), chapter 5, paragraph D(6,c)
Whish (2008), chapter 18, paragraph 4

E   Commission decisions in chronological order•

Liebig Spices **Commission decision 78/172/EEC [1978] OJ L 53/20, Case IV/29.418**
BP KEMI-DDSF Commission decision 79/934/EEC [1979] OJ L 235/20, Case IV/29.021
SSI Commission decision 82/506/EEC [1982] OJ L 232/1, Cases IV/29.525, 30.000

F   Economic landmark case

F.1   *Liebig Spices* Commission decision 78/172/EEC [1978] OJ L 53/20

Relevance: In the frame of the exclusive purchasing agreement described above, the Commission found that rebates used as form of reimbursement for non-dealing with other competing suppliers would strengthen the (already) anticompetitive effect of the exclusive dealing agreement.

- For case report, relevant market, facts finding, allegation, economic analysis, obligations fines and remedies, and further development of the case, see Case *F.2* in section *5.1*.

• Decisions displayed in **bold type** are described in the section. Decisions highlighted with (*) include interesting economic analysis by the Commission on the specific topic of the section. Some decisions contain economic reasoning on more than one topic and therefore appear in several lists of Commission decisions in chronological order. Reference is made in brackets and **bold type** to the relevant section in which the decision is extensively described as a landmark case. When decisions are referenced and/or described in some detail in one or more of the economic textbooks, reference in brackets is also made to the relevant part(s) of those texts.

6 Joint ventures and alliances

A Introduction

Joint ventures and alliances are forms of cooperation that undertakings, often active on the same relevant market, can use to achieve common market objectives. In an alliance, undertakings coordinate their activities and so partially integrate their commercial interests. A joint venture is a separate company, created for a special purpose and typically fully owned by the mother company(ies). Joint ventures are often used for the joint development, exploitation, and commercialization of a new technology or product. Such cooperative efforts carried out by the undertakings can generate and promote efficiencies in different ways and contribute to welfare. Common examples of the possible beneficial effects of joint ventures are concentrated research efforts, rationalized distributive and commercial structures, and the provision of a better-structured set of services.

Joint ventures and alliances can also raise serious anticompetitive concerns. The firms involved may use their cooperation agreements as a vehicle to exchange information and coordinate actions beyond what would strictly be necessary for achieving efficiency gains. That is, their cooperation may induce collusion. Typically, when competing firms involved in the venture cooperate, their market power increases and it is not always straightforward to tell whether that increase was brought about by synergies or restrictive clauses in the agreement and the stifling of competition. Hence, joint ventures and alliances should come under close scrutiny by the competition authorities, especially when market power was already significant before the setting up of the joint venture. An example of this would be distribution joint ventures, for which there is a potential risk of price coordination. The possible clearance of proposals for joint ventures and alliances therefore has to rest on careful analysis of any case-specific competition concerns.

This chapter consists of three sections. In section 6.1, research and development (R&D) joint ventures are discussed, toward which the Commission's approach has always been positive, and it includes special legislation applicable to such agreements. Section 6.2 is about marketing, selling, distribution, and production joint ventures. These have been considered more critically by the Commission. Section 6.3 discusses strategic and technological alliances. The Commission recently independently classified certain kinds of such long-lasting agreements as "strategic alliances."

B Applicable EU legislation

In the system of EU competition law joint ventures are divided into two main categories: concentrative full-function joint ventures (considered as partial mergers) and cooperative joint ventures. The criteria for the assessment of joint ventures' nature are set out in the Commission's consolidated jurisdictional notice on mergers.[1]

The concentrative joint ventures are assessed under the provisions of the Merger Regulation.[2]

The cooperative aspects of the concentrative joint ventures are assessed according to the criteria of Article 101 FEU Treaty within the regulatory frame of the Merger Regulation.[3]

Cooperative joint ventures and alliances are assessed under Article 101 FEU Treaty.

In the evaluation of the joint ventures, the Commission's notice on horizontal agreements is relevant because it shows the Commission's approach toward these kinds of agreements. See Commission Guidelines on the applicability of Article 81 to horizontal co-operation agreements [2001] OJ C 3/2.

C Related economics texts

Bishop and Walker (2009), paragraph 5.56
Carlton and Perloff (2005), chapter 16, paragraphs 2, 3, and 4
Church and Ware (2000), chapter 18
Martin (1994), chapter 12
Martin (2002), chapters 12 and 14
Motta (2004), paragraph 4.5
Tirole (1988), chapter 10, specifically 10.8
Waldman and Jensen (2001), not discussed

D Related legal texts

Bellamy and Child (2008), chapter 7
Jones and Sufrin (2008), chapter 13
Ritter and Braun (2005), chapter 3, paragraph C and chapter 6, paragraph D
Whish (2008), chapter 15

6.1 R&D joint ventures

A Introduction

In a joint venture in R&D, two or more firms can coordinate their research efforts and cooperate to develop new products or technologies. This allows the firms to avoid duplicative research efforts and investment and create economies of scale and scope. In addition, joint ventures

---

1 Commission consolidated jurisdictional notice under Council Regulation (EC) No. 139/2004 on the control of concentrations between undertakings, published on 10 July 2007 on DG Comp website. The consolidated jurisdictional notice has replaced the previous four jurisdictional notices. There were: Commission Notice on the concept of full-function joint venture [1998] OJ C 66/1; Commission Notice on the concept of concentration [1998] OJ L C 66/5; Commission Notice on the concept of undertakings concerned [1998] OJ C 66/14; Commission Notice on calculation of turnover [1998] OJ C 66/25.

2 See Article 3(4) of Council Regulation 139/2004 on the control of concentration between undertakings [2004] OJ L 24/1. Full-function joint ventures are assessed under the Merger Regulation and no longer pursuant to Article 101 FEU Treaty since an amendment introduced to the first Merger Regulation of 1989 by Regulation (EC) No. 1310/97 of 30 June 1997 amending Regulation (EEC) No. 4064/89 etc. on the control of concentrations between undertakings [1997] OJ L 40/17.

3 Article 2(4) EC Merger Regulation.

are means to solve at least partly the structural problems associated with the dissemination or protection of knowledge. Joint ventures can thereby provide a strong incentive to invest in research programs and so raise the total level of research activity.

An important characteristic that distinguishes private R&D from other commercial activities is that research generates spillover effects from which rivals in the sector can benefit. New knowledge has public good aspects. When intellectual property rights (IPR) protection is not watertight, *ex ante*, this aspect of knowledge can weaken a firm's incentive to engage in R&D. Independent companies may choose to wait for others to commit to research programs first, in an attempt to free ride on the effort and exploit the results. A related characteristic of R&D effort is that it can be wasteful if duplicative. In particular when IPR protection is strong, so that concurrent R&D investments can be large, R&D joint ventures can pool efforts and so help avoid duplication of costs with proper research coordination and, at the same time, direct and equal access to the results of the joint effort.

R&D joint ventures also carry, however, serious anticompetitive risks. Particularly in oligopolistic markets, they can actually slow down the pace of innovation – for example, when the leading firms in the market have an interest to exploit a given level of technological development and protract the emergence of innovative challengers to their product. The close cooperation in a joint venture can also facilitate collusive behavior in marketing and commercialization operations, or tempt incumbents to strategically use R&D as a tool to raise entry barriers and rivals' cost.

B   Applicable EU legislation

The EU competition law approach to R&D joint ventures is based on a generalized exemption from application of Article 101(1) FEU Treaty in case of limited market power of the undertakings concerned, which is extended also to the joint production and marketing phase. The relevant normative provisions are contained in Regulation No. 2659/2000 on the application of Article 81(3) of the EC Treaty to categories of research and development agreements [2000] OJ L 304/7 (R&D Block Exemption Regulation, which replaced the original R&D Block Exemption Regulation of 1984).

For R&D joint ventures not covered by the R&D Block Exemption Regulation, general legislation on joint ventures will be applicable (chapter 6, paragraph B).

See also Commission Guidelines on the Applicability of Article 81 to horizontal co-operation agreements [2001] OJ C 3/2, part 2.

C   Related economics texts

Bishop and Walker (2009), paragraph 2.36
Carlton and Perloff (2005), chapter 16, paragraphs 2 and 3
Church and Ware (2000), chapter 18
Martin (1994), chapter 12, paragraph 3
Martin (2002), paragraphs 14.3.2 and 14.4.5
Motta (2004), paragraphs 4.5.2 and 4.5.4
Tirole (1988), chapter 10, specifically 10.8
Waldman and Jensen (2001), not specifically discussed

D Related legal texts

Bellamy and Child (2008), chapter 7, paragraph 5
Jones and Sufrin (2008), chapter 13, paragraphs 4 and 5(C)
Ritter and Braun (2005), chapter 3, paragraph C(2) and chapter 6, paragraph D
Whish (2008), chapter 15, paragraph 5

E Commission decisions in chronological order*

Henkel/Colgate Commission decision 72/41/EEC [1972] OJ L 14/14, Case IV/26.917 (Martin, 1994, p.380)

Rank/Sopelem Commission decision 75/76/EEC [1975] OJ L 29/20, Case IV/26.603

United Reprocessors GmbH Commission decision 76/248/EEC [1976] OJ L 51/7, Case IV/26.940/a

KEWA Commission decision 76/249/EEC [1975] OJ L 51/15, Case IV/26.940/b

De Laval-Stork Commission decision 77/543/EEC [1977] OJ L 215/11, Case IV/27.093 **(described in detail as landmark case in section 6.2)**

GEC-Weir Sodium Circulators Commission decision 77/781/EEC [1977] OJ L 327/26, Case IV/ 29.428 (*)

Sopelem/Vickers Commission decision 78/251/EEC [1978] OJ L 70/47, Case IV/29.236

Beecham/Parke, Davis **Commission decision 79/298/EEC [1979] OJ L 70/11, Case IV/28.796** (Martin, 1994, p.376)

Sopelem/Vickers Commission decision 81/1066/EEC [1981] OJ L 391/1, Case IV/29.236

Amersham Buchler Commission decision 82/742/EEC [1982] OJ L 314/34, Case IV/30.517

Carbon Gas Technologie Commission decision 83/669/EEC [1983] OJ L 376/17, Case IV/29.955

BP/Kellogg Commission decision 85/560/EEC [1985] OJ L 369/6, Case IV/30.971

Optical Fibres **Commission decision 86/405/EEC [1986] OJ L 236/30, Case IV/30.320**

Enichem/ICI **Commission decision 88/87/EEC [1988] OJ L 50/18, Case IV/31.846**

Olivetti/Canon Commission decision 88/88 [1988] OJ L 52/51, Case IV/32.306

Bayer/BP Chemicals Commission decision 88/330/EEC [1988] OJ L 150/35, Case IV/32.075

BBC Brown Boveri Commission decision 88/541/EEC [1988] OJ L 305/33, Case IV/32.368

Continental/Michelin Commission decision 88/555/EEC [1988] OJ L 272/27, Case IV/32.173

Alcatel/ANT Nachrichtentechnik Commission decision 90/46/EEC [1990] OJ L 32/19, Case IV/32.006

Elopak/Metal box-Odin Commission decision 90/410/EEC [1990] OJ L 2009/15, Case IV/32.009 (*)

Konsortium ECR 900 Commission decision 90/446/EEC [1990] OJ L 228/31, Case IV/32.688

KSB/Goulds/Lowara/ITT Commission decision 91/38/EEC [1991] OJ L 20/42, Case IV/32.363 (*)

Eirpage Commission decision 91/562/EEC [1991] OJ L 306/22, Case IV/32.737

FIAT/Hitachi Commission decision 93/48/EEC [1993] OJ L 20/10, Case IV/33.031

• Decisions displayed in **bold type** are described in the section. Decisions highlighted with (*) include interesting economic analysis by the Commission on the specific topic of the section. Some decisions contain economic reasoning on more than one topic and therefore appear in several lists of Commission decisions in chronological order. Reference is made in brackets and **bold type** to the relevant section in which the decision is extensively described as a landmark case. When decisions are referenced and/or described in some detail in one or more of the economic textbooks, reference in brackets is also made to the relevant part(s) of those texts.

Ford/VW Commission decision 93/49/EEC [1993] OJ L 20/14, Case IV/33.814 (*) (Bishop and Walker, 2009, 5.58; Motta, 2004, pp.15–16)

Bayer/BP Chemicals Commission decision 94/384/EEC [1994] OJ L 174/34, Case IV/32.075

Pasteur Merieux-Merck Commission decision 94/770/EEC [1994] OJ L 309/1, Case IV/34.776

Asahi/Saint-Gobain Commission decision 94/896/EEC [1994] OJ L 354/87, Case IV/33.863

Fujitsu AMD Semiconductor Commission decision 94/823/EEC [1994] OJ L 341/66, Case IV/34.891

Philips-Osram Commission decision 94/986/EEC [1994] OJ L 378/37, Case IV/34.252

Phoenix/GlobalOne Commission decision 96/547/EEC [1996] OJ L 239/57, Case IV/35.617

Iridium Commission decision 97/39/EEC [1997] OJ L 16/87, Case IV/35.518

British Interactive Broadcasting/Open **Commission decision 1999/781/EC [1999] OJ L 312/1, Case IV/36.539**

GEAE/P&W Commission decision 2000/182/EC [2000] OJ L 58/16, Case IV/36.213

F   Economic landmark cases

F.1   *Beecham/Parke, Davis* Commission Decision 79/298/EEC [1979] OJ L 70/11

Relevance: EU competition law has always been in favor of common efforts carried out by firms to increase R&D. This decision shows the efficiency-based approach of the Commission toward R&D joint ventures. Possible efficiencies deriving from such joint ventures are described in accordance with the economic literature and concerns are expressed about the possible restriction of post-innovation competition.

- Case IV/28.796
- **Decision:** Exemption pursuant to Article 101(3) FEU Treaty for ten years
- **Decision addressee(s):**
    - Beecham Group Limited, *United Kingdom*
    - Parke, Davis and Company, *United States*
- **Report route:** Notification for exemption submitted to the Commission on 28 January 1974 by Beecham Group Limited
- **Date of the decision:** 17 January 1979
- **Competition Commissioner:** R. Vouel
- **Relevant product market:** Trade in pharmaceutical products for therapeutic applications
- **Relevant geographical market:** Not indicated
- **Description of the case**
    a. **Relevant facts**
       Beecham and Parke, Davis and Company were medium-sized manufacturers of pharmaceutical products active in the fields of research and production–distribution of pharmaceuticals.
       Beecham operated a number of subsidiaries and facilities throughout Europe and although Parke, Davis owned subsidiaries only in France, Belgium, and Italy, they were both operating at a European-wide level.
       The two companies did considerable pharmaceutical research pursuing different programs but neither of them reached the research intensity of their competitors which appropriated up to 15% of total turnover to R&D.

The two companies accordingly decided to set up a joint research program which was "aimed at creating a new product which will differ in therapeutic application from all existing products . . . for . . . the long-term prophylactic treatment of impairment of blood circulation."[4]

R&D in the pharmaceutical industry is very costly due to the massive investment needed, and also time-consuming due to long periods of extensive testing. Consequently, R&D is risky and notwithstanding the massive R&D efforts, many products fail to reach the market.

As with most of the research programs, R&D of the new product that Beecham and Parke, Davis pursued required costly long-term investment, i.e. extended over ten years costing $20 million.[5]

The two companies set up a joint venture company combining their research efforts to share the costs of R&D, bear the risk, and jointly develop a product. Both companies retained their own research team, but agreed to commonly plan the details, scope, and direction of their projects; to exchange all details of the work carried out under the common program; and keep all related information, know-how, and data confidential. After the research phase, they would have jointly planned the development program and equally shared its costs. They were free to leave the common development plan and pursue independent research. What is more, the remaining party would have had to share any further results of its development effort under a licensing agreement at the latter's request.

According to the modified version of the agreement following the Commission's observations, both parties would retain the right to apply for patents (although an obligation to grant license in favor of the other party in case of an individual patent was provided in the agreement) and autonomously produce and market the invention resulting from the common research activity.

Notwithstanding their commercial independence, they would have fully exchanged "information on improvements to the production of the drugs and pharmaceutical forms, including all change in methods, for a period of 10 years from the first marketing of a product."[6]

b. **Origin of the case**

On 28 January 1974 Beecham Group Limited submitted a notification to the Commission pursuant to Article 4 of Regulation No. 17 to see the Joint Research and Development Agreement entered into by it with Parke, Davis be declared exempted from the application of Article 101(1) FEU Treaty by virtue of Article 101(3) FEU Treaty.

c. **Economic analysis**

The Commission has generally looked favorably at R&D agreements within the internal market given their potential for technological and scientific progress in Europe.

The initial approach toward cooperative R&D joint ventures was to permit them provided that they were not unnecessarily restrictive of post-innovation activities (an orientation formally expressed in the Notice concerning

---

4   Recital 4 of the decision.   6   Recital 17 of the decision.
5   Recital 4 of the decision.

agreements, decisions, and concerted practices in the field of cooperation between enterprises of 1968).[7]

Indeed, as in this case, the Commission recognized the potential restrictive and anticompetitive effects of the cooperation. In particular it focused its attention on the potential negative effects on competition of the fully and detailed disclosure of information during the entire research, developing, and (envisaged ten-year) production phase. It stressed how the exchange of all results of the R&D activities would have impeded the attainment of a competitive advantage by one of the parties and how the tendency to concentrate all research efforts in the joint project stifled investments in other possible independent research.

The Commission acknowledged the economic and social welfare benefits of R&D cooperation, accepting the inherent competitive restrictions. In particular, in its assessment of the notified agreement under Article 101(3) FEU Treaty the Commission recognized the importance of the joint venture as an incentive for the research activities of the parties. The Commission, recognizing the risks and the costs the parties would face in individual research projects, stated that they were "considerably reduced by [the] decision to recommence... former individual research in the form of collaboration in the use of... specialized facilities and complementary expertise in this and in related fields [and that] the pooling of the research capacities and efforts of both parties [was] a major factor in providing... a reasonable likelihood of success."[8] Even the avoidance of duplication of research expenditures, the timely and superior commercialization of new products (technical progress), and thus ultimately the benefit for consumers, were recognized as positive effects of the joint venture, offsetting the derived restriction of competition.

There were two important elements that prompted the Commission to exempt the agreement under Article 101(3) FEU Treaty. The first was the guarantee that the parties were free to manufacture and market the product after the innovation phase "wherever, in whatever quantities and under whatever conditions, trademarks, and prices they individually consider appropriate."[9] This condition for the exemption is congruent with the Commission's initial approach to R&D joint ventures, which paid particular attention to the non-restriction of competition in the production, commercialization, and distribution phase. Secondly, the Commission took account of the fact that the parties would not have been able by means of their cooperation to eliminate further competition from the pharmaceutical market, that was described as a highly competitive market.[10] This approach reflected warnings from economists for abuse of R&D programs to raise entry barriers for potential entrants.

d. **Fines, remedies, and conditions enclosed**
None.

e. **Further developments of the case**
None.

---

7   Notice, concerning agreements, decisions, and concerted practises in the field of cooperation between enterprises [1968] OJ C 75/3.

8   Recital 37 of the decision.
9   Recital 42 of the decision.
10 See recitals 45–46 of the decision.

F.2 *Optical Fibres* Commission Decision 86/405/EEC [1986] OJ L 236/30

Relevance: Confirming its overall positive approach to R&D joint ventures, the Commission in this decision analyzed the potential restrictive effects of a network of interrelated joint ventures in an oligopolistic market. The decision stressed the importance of the rapid introduction of new technology in the European market as result of the joint venture.

- Case IV/30.320
- **Decision:** Exemption pursuant to Article 101(3) FEU Treaty for fifteen years
- **Decision addressee(s):**
    - Corning Glass Works, *United States*
    - BICC plc, *United Kingdom*
    - Siemens AG, *Germany*
    - Optical Fibres, *United Kingdom*
    - Siecor GmbH, *Germany*
- **Report route:** Two different notifications submitted to the Commission by Corning Glass Works and other affiliated companies on 17 March 1981 (for agreements related to the United Kingdom) and 24 June 1983 (for the joint venture in France)
- **Date of the decision:** 14 July 1986
- **Competition Commissioner:** P. Sutherland
- **Relevant product market:** Optical fibres and optical cables
- **Relevant geographical market:** not indicated
- **Description of the case**
    a. **Relevant facts**

    Corning Glass Works was a US corporation with several subsidiaries in Europe active in the manufacture and sale of different products and in particular of glass and ceramic products, which made a path-breaking invention when they developed optical fibres in 1970. At the time it was suggested that they could possibly be used for communication purposes and replace the previous types of cables. To protect its technology, Corning registered several patents in all major countries of the world including most of the European Member States.

    In order to develop the use of the optical fibres in the production of optical cables, Corning set up joint development agreements with several leading European cable producers for the communication sector. The general agreements were composed of joint venture agreements, patent, and know-how agreements through which Corning granted the joint venture a non-exclusive license under its (corresponding) national patent.

    The agreement was such that Corning would provide the necessary technology (the optical fibres) and the joint venture partners would produce fibre cables. They would have subsequently sold the fibre cables mainly to telecommunication companies in the Member States which had been their regular customers in the past.

    The cooperation with the main cable producers was essential for Corning to enter the (then) EEC markets because as "[a] new entrant in the telecommunication market [it] faced strong local purchasing policies on the part of most European PTTs."[11]

According to the joint venture agreements, the European partners were entitled to additional supplies of optical fibres from Corning. In addition they were free to buy from competing producers. The agreement also granted them the right to actively sell outside their own territory covered by other joint ventures. By contrast, they would have been limited to passive sales outside their own territory if Corning had appointed an exclusive licensee for the production of optical fibres there. Finally, the agreement did not contain so-called "safeguard clauses" under which any possible improvements made by the joint ventures were to be licensed to Corning.[12]

b. **Origin of the case**

On 17 March 1981 Corning submitted a notification to the Commission pursuant to Article 4 of Regulation 17 to see the joint development agreement and all the related agreements entered into in the United Kingdom be declared exempted from the application of Article 101(1) FEU Treaty by virtue of Article 101(3) FEU Treaty. The same was done for the German agreements and the joint venture in France on 24 June 1984.

c. **Economic analysis**

In this case, none of Corning's European partners was an actual or potential competitor on the market of optical fibres production, because they were active in the complementary market of the production of cables. Even though they could have potentially developed their own research projects, at the time it was much more likely that they would be using the technology provided by the American company. Given this background, none of the agreements would individually raise any competition concerns, particularly because the absence of safeguard clauses prevented foreclosure of the market. All in all, third parties were not harmed or restrained in an anticompetitive way.

What makes this case interesting is that the Commission investigated whether the crucial and powerful position Corning assumed connecting several parallel joint ventures active on the same market was likely to lead to collusive behavior. "The creation of a network of interrelated joint ventures with a common technological provider in an oligopolistic market"[13] was considered detrimental for the competitiveness of the market, the reason being that the market was already highly concentrated with few producers of optical fibres. In light of this, the Commission held that Corning as the *de facto* joint venture exclusive supplier of the technology in question exerted considerable influence on their business decisions. Compared to a state in which the joint ventures were able to compete freely, the Commission concluded that such "technological dependence"[14] in which the joint ventures found themselves potentially led to collusion among the joint ventures under Corning's direction. Consequently, the Commission recognized the restrictive effects caused by this type of network effect.

12 Recital 69 of the decision.
13 Recital 48 of the decision.
14 Recital 49 of the decision.

The Commission's analysis of the joint ventures' network is only part of the overall assessment which ultimately led it to exempt the entire group of agreements pursuant to Article 101(3) because it found that its benefits outweighed its negative effects. In markets such as the optical fibres market, in which development of new and improved technologies is fast-paced, the agreements scrutinized in the decision were indispensable to promote technical progress and to allow a reduction of research costs and thus to enhance consumer benefits. This line of reasoning is consistent with the usually more favorable approach of the Commission toward R&D joint ventures.

What materializes in this decision and what appears to constitute the new approach of the Commission is in fact a general policy for the development of a European industry and its relations with other industrialized countries. According to the Commission, the agreements at hand were particularly important to "enable the European companies to withstand competition from non-Community producers, especially in the USA and Japan, in an area of fast-moving technology."[15]

This approach aimed at the increase in total welfare in the long term for the entire European optical fibres industry, rather than a short-term gain for the related telecommunications and television broadcasting industries as well as for European consumers.

d. Fines, remedies, and conditions enclosed
  – Prohibition for the parent undertakings of the joint ventures and the joint ventures themselves to disclose to other joint ventures or parent companies information concerning prices, costs, sales, production, marketing plans, or any other competitive information related to the relevant product market.
  – Obligation for each joint venture to submit an annual report to the Commission indicating: total annual production and sales figures; information about customers within the EEC, the charged prices and supplied quantities for orders exceeding 100 km; prices and delivery terms agreed between the joint ventures and their parent undertakings.

e. Further developments of the case
None.

F.3 *Enichem/ICI* Commission Decision 88/87/EEC [1988] OJ L 50/18

Relevance: The Commission's positive assessment about R&D joint ventures is confirmed and reinforced where such agreements are instruments to achieve efficient reorganization of industries and elimination of overcapacity.

- Case IV/31.846
- **Decision:** Exemption pursuant to Article 101(3) FEU Treaty for five years
- **Decision addressee(s):**
  – Enichem SpA, *Italy*
  – Imperial Chemical Industries plc, *United Kingdom*
  – European Vinyls Corporation, *Belgium*

---

15 Recital 59 of the decision.

- **Report route:** Application for negative clearance and notification for exemption submitted to the Commission by Enichem SpA and Imperial Chemical Industries plc
- **Date of the decision:** 22 December 1987
- **Competition Commissioner:** P. Sutherland
- **Relevant product market:** Vinyl chloride monomer (VCM) and all types of polyvinylchloride (PVC)
- **Relevant geographical market:** European internal market
- **Description of the case**
    a. **Relevant facts**
       Enichem (an Italian company active in several markets of the energy sector and one of the largest petrochemical European companies) and ICI (a British company operating in several industries with its main business in chemicals products) set up a joint venture (called EVC) to join R&D efforts concerning VCM/PVC products and to market and sell them.
       The main purpose of the joint enterprise was the rationalization of previous independent operations relating to the relevant products. They aimed at restructuring their business to "regain competitiveness and progressively reduce losses."[16] The agreement provided for an extensive shutting down of production capacity which corresponded to a relevant share of the estimated overcapacity in the internal market at that time. They would have achieved their objectives in particular through the shutting down of the oldest and least efficient plants.
       They intended to share R&D facilities and personnel but remain two separate organizations jointly owning the results of the rationalized R&D efforts coordinated by the joint venture.
       Enichem and ICI dedicated the entire capacity of their plants for the manufacture of the relevant products to the joint venture, supplying it with all the necessary raw materials (at a commonly set price for at least 90 percent of the requirements), services, utilities, and assistance.
       Enichem did not have interests in other companies involved in the VCM/PVC production, while ICI had (more or less) relevant interests in four competing companies inside and outside the internal market. ICI also had interests in the downstream PVC processing companies.
    b. **Origin of the case**
       On 26 March 1986 Enichem SpA and Imperial Chemical Industries plc submitted an application to the Commission for negative clearance and a notification for exemption pursuant to Articles 2 and 4 of Regulation 17 to see Article 101(1) FEU Treaty be declared not applicable to the joint venture or alternatively the joint venture be declared exempted from the application of Article 101(1) FEU Treaty by virtue of Article 101(3) FEU Treaty.
    c. **Economic analysis**
       In this case the reasoning of the Commission focused on the compatibility of the joint venture's purpose with its current industrial policy that at that time was

---

16   Recital 18 of the decision.

in favor of industrial reorganization and reduction of structural overcapacity. The petrochemical industry was suffering from a general overcapacity and thus the Commission welcomed the coordinated, swift, and thorough rationalization of Enichem's and ICI's related businesses which otherwise would have not individually occurred.

The Commission clearly recognized the restriction of competition imposed by the creation of the joint venture and highlighted three aspects. Firstly, it was concerned about the continued cooperation among two of the largest companies in the petrochemical sector. Secondly, the first point was aggravated by the fact that Enichem and ICI were actual and potential competitors and competitors of EVC in the production of the relevant products. Thirdly, the Commission voiced its concern about the reduction of production capacity inherent in the agreement declared by the parent companies.

Notwithstanding these apprehensions, the Commission welcomed the measures facilitating a massive capacity reduction in response to a depressed market demand and to a structural industry overcapacity. Moreover, the Commission's reasoning was motivated by the consideration that the joint venture would have enabled the two parent companies to carry out their reorganization without disadvantaging consumers. This concerned both the range of available products, which is particularly relevant for the competitiveness of the companies in the PVC market, and the perpetuation of a competitive level of product supply and quality maintenance.

The Commission applied an industrial policy criterion in favor of a reduction or elimination of industry overcapacity. As mentioned above, Enichem's and ICI's overcapacity accounted for a large share of the market overcapacity, which meant that the exemption was aimed at reorganization of the industry and, in particular, at large and favorable reorganization of the two companies involved. The importance attributed to the industry reorganization by the Commission is understandable if one considers that the effect of the joint venture was the creation of the strongest actor on the petrochemical European market. Indeed summing up their market shares, ICI and Enichem would have achieved a market share of 22–23 percent in the PVC market and consequently "the anticompetitive impact . . . could [have] been significant, particularly on a market characterized by a tendency toward tighter oligopoly."[17] The balance between the strongly conflicting goals of allowing for the development of a competitive market and of imposing extensive reorganization of the industry that was struck by the Commission is exemplified by the definition it gave of residual competitiveness of the market which it considered to be still *workable*.[18] Although the concept is not fully clear it indicates a level of competitiveness below the level of unfettered competitive conditions. This decision was accompanied by a number of attached conditions and obligations.

---

17 Recital 48 of the decision.
18 *Idem.*

d. Fines, remedies, and conditions enclosed

- Divestiture of all direct and indirect interests in competing producers or distributors within the internal market, with the exception of pure financial interests.
- Submission of an annual report by the joint venture and the parent companies to the Commission indicating: capacity closures, change of production and distribution of the relevant products, production and sales of each product by the joint venture, and (where possible) by parties in the common market and in each Member State as well as the output quantities consumed internally.
- Communication to the Commission of each initiative of the joint venture, the parent companies, or their subsidiaries with reference to the relevant product market or upstream and/or downstream markets.
- Communication to the Commission in advance of any renewal, extension in scope or nature, amendment, or addition to the exempted agreement.

e. Further developments of the case
None.

F.4 *British Interactive Broadcasting/Open* Commission decision 1999/781/EC [1999] OJ L 312/1

Relevance: Sufficient economic reasoning for imposing conditions on a joint venture became increasingly relevant after the CFI (now "the General Court") judgment in 1998 in the *European Night Services* case. The current case of a joint venture in digital interactive television in the United Kingdom by four parties shows such an increased sophistication of economic reasoning. The Commission seeks to safeguard competition and prevent early leadership resulting in premature foreclosure. The proposed joint venture was strongly dependent on two of the parties: BSkyB and British Telecom and, as such, not fully functional in nature.

- Case IV/36.539
- **Decision:** Exemption for a period of seven years for the joint venture, under ten conditions
- **Decision addressee(s):**
  - BT Holdings Ltd, *United Kingdom*
  - British Sky Broadcasting Ltd, *United Kingdom*
  - Midland Bank plc, *United Kingdom*
  - Matsushita Electric Europe Ltd, *United Kingdom*
- **Report route:** Notification to the Commission on 13 June 1997
- **Date of the decision:** 15 September 1999
- **Competition Commissioner:** K. Van Miert
- **Relevant product market:** Digital interactive television services, pay-television service, and customer-access telecommunications infrastructure.
- **Relevant geographical market:** United Kingdom
- **Description of the case**
  ### a. Relevant facts
  Four companies joined to create a joint venture company, British Interactive Broadcasting Ltd (BiB), in order to provide digital interactive television

services to consumers in the United Kingdom. The joint venture became known as Open, being the name of the interactive television platform. BiB's parent companies were BSkyB, British Telecom (BT), Midland Bank, and Matsushita Electric Europe, which held a shareholding of 32.5%, 32.5%, 20%, and 15%, respectively.[19] BiB was created both to develop the infrastructure necessary for digital interactive television services and to provide such e-commerce services. BiB also provided services such as email and computer game play. An important element of the infrastructure was a digital set-top box.

BT was the former UK telecommunications monopolist and has a very high share of residential fixed telecommunication lines. BSkyB is a pay-television broadcaster and its services are delivered by satellite or cable. The company has a particularly strong market position in the pay-television market. Midland Bank is part of the HSBC group and provides a range of banking and financial services in the United Kingdom. Matsushita Electric Europe is part of the Matsushita Electric Industrial group operating worldwide and a designer, developer, and manufacturer of electronic and electrical products and technology.

BiB will be active mainly on the digital interactive television services market and on the related technical services market. However, BSkyB and BT are present in a number of markets closely connected to these two. The digital interactive television services comprise a broad range of services including home banking, home shopping, game play, email, and internet access. At the time "in the United Kingdom only some 25% of households have a personal computer and fewer than half of these are equipped with a modem,"[20] so the new service provided a benefit to consumers.[21] BSkyB had a very strong position on the pay-television market. It dominated the satellite pay-television market and was the key supplier of film and sports channels, the latter essential to be successful as a pay-television operator. BSkyB had "more than 90% of the pay-television rights to first-run major films" and sports rights contracts to "almost all national league football, rugby football, cricket, golf and boxing."[22] This means that, even though there are pay-television competitors like cable operators, they "have no choice but to purchase BSkyB's film and sports channels."[23] The competitors also use technical services through Sky Subscribers Services Ltd (SSSL). BT has a strong position on the customer access telecommunications infrastructure market. It largely owns the residential fixed lines network in the United Kingdom. Next to BT's traditional copper network there are the cable networks of the cable operators, that at the time "pass 48% of homes in the United Kingdom."[24]

The joint venture agreement contained a range of clauses, some of which implied exclusivity. An example is that in the originally notified joint venture "it was a condition of purchase of a BiB subsidised set-top box that consumers subscribed to BSkyB's digital pay-television service for a minimum contract term of 12 months."[25] BT was granted exclusivity to supply to BiB all

19   See recital 94 of the decision.
20   Recital 21 of the decision.
21   Recital 163 of the decision.
22   Recitals 73 and 78 of the decision.
23   Recital 79 of the decision.
24   Recital 89 of the decision.
25   Recital 120 of the decision.

telecommunications requirements for a period of three years. BiB also granted Midland Bank a ten-year exclusivity for the transaction management system. The interactive set-top box Digibox was designed with BSkyB's proprietary interface instead of a common interface. BSkyB's specifications for the Digibox also allowed only its own electronic programming guide. The joint venture agreement furthermore contained a subsidy-recovery mechanism to compensate for the subsidized set-top boxes. The main sources of revenue for BiB to recover the costs were "derived at the wholesale level, rather than direct from end-users."[26] Lastly, there were non-competition provisions for the four parties.

Certain features of the proposed joint venture agreement were changed after the Commission informed parties of its concerns. A new version of the agreement was signed on 4 August 1998. This new agreement contained a more limited non-competition provision, no longer exclusivity for the electronic programming guide, and no need to subscribe to BSkyB's pay-television service. In addition, a legal separation into two companies has been arranged in order to increase transparency: one for the (recovery of) subsidies of set-top boxes and one for the creation and operation of BiB's interactive services.

b.   **Origin of the case**

The Commission argued that "BSkyB and BT's participation in BiB results in an appreciable restriction of competition on the market for digital interactive television services" (recital 140). BT and BSkyB were potential competitors prior to the BiB joint venture. These companies even themselves argued that "the main telecommunications operators (other than BT) could become competitors to BiB."[27]

Nevertheless, an exemption was granted.

c.   **Economic analysis**

There are four reasons given for granting an exemption in this case. Firstly, it was believed to lead to "an improvement in the distribution of goods and technical and economic progress."[28] The parties would be able to overcome the current technological limitations of both satellite broadcast technology and the copper telecommunications network. Secondly, consumers could benefit from the availability of the new service, especially those consumers who have no PC and/or no access to the internet. Third, one of the non-competition provisions, a prohibition for the four parties to hold more than a 20% interest in a competing company, was considered indispensable for the success of the joint venture. BT and BSkyB could have provided some form of interactive services on their own. "However, by cooperating together in BiB they are able to provide a better service and to do so more quickly."[29] The success of the joint venture would be threatened "in case of a transfer to a competitor of the unique ideas and strategies, which are being developed by the parties in BiB."[30]

The final reason is that under these conditions competition would not be eliminated. There are cable networks that have plans to introduce digital

26   Recital 113 of the decision.
27   Recital 143 of the decision.
28   Recital 159 of the decision.
29   Recital 166 of the decision.
30   Recital 167 of the decision.

interactive television services. Nevertheless, BSkyB and BT have very important market positions protected by barriers to entry. The risk of eliminating competition can be reduced when "competition to BT comes from the cable networks, that third parties are ensured sufficient access to BiB's subsidized set-top boxes and to BSkyB's film and sport channels, and that set-top boxes other than BiB's set-top box can be developed in the market."[31] BT has, for example, agreed to divest itself of its existing cable network interests in the United Kingdom. Competition from the cable segment can therefore be safeguarded.

d. Fines, remedies, and conditions enclosed

The parties cooperated with the Commission by amending the joint venture agreement. The remedies helped alleviate the Commission's concerns. The conditions extend these remedies further for the exemption to be granted.

e. Further developments of the case

There was no appeal. BSkyB increased its shareholding in Open from 32.5% to 80.1% one year after the exemption was granted. BT remained the only other party, with a 19.9% shareholding.

6.2 Marketing, selling, distribution, and production joint ventures

A Introduction

Firms may cooperate through joint ventures aimed not at innovation but at common production and/or marketing of products. Typically, these are limited cooperation agreements between otherwise competing companies in some specific parts of the sectors in which they are active. When the costs of production, distribution, and the marketing of a certain product are high, these kinds of joint ventures can bring about cost savings and so improve efficiency. Joint ventures can assume many different forms – focusing, for example, on the limited joint distribution of several products manufactured by different firms, joint marketing, distribution and selling of separately produced goods, or joint production of a good previously independently produced by competing firms. The efficiency gains possibly achieved by such (post-innovation) joint ventures are general direct costs savings, but can also include a reduction of environmental risks, an improved quality of the final products, capacity expansion, and ensuing consumer benefits.

Within the context of the joint venture meetings, however, there is the possibility to exchange information, which can raise serious anticompetitive concerns of potential collusion in strategic decisions. Concentrated markets are particularly vulnerable to such restrictions on the natural competitive conditions of the market, even when only tacitly coordinated. The risk of collusion in (post-innovation) joint ventures means that they are regarded with reservations by the competition authorities. The assessment of these agreements has to strike a balance between possible beneficial effects and a possible foreclosure of the market. In particular, the authorities conducting the investigation have to preserve the economic autonomy of the parties and avoid the elimination of competition between joint venture members.

---

31   Recital 170 of the decision.

B Applicable EU legislation

Regulation No. 2658/2000 on the application of Article 81(3) of the EC Treaty to categories of specialization agreements [2000] OJ L 304/3 (Specialization Agreements Block Exemption Regulation).

For agreements not covered by the Specialization Agreements Block Exemption Regulation, general legislation on joint ventures will be applicable (chapter 6, paragraph B).

See also Commission Guidelines on the applicability of Article 81 to horizontal co-operation agreements [2001] OJ C 3/2, parts 3–5.

C Related economics texts

Bishop and Walker (2009), paragraph 5.56
Carlton and Perloff (2005), chapter 16, paragraph 3
Church and Ware (2000), not specifically discussed
Martin (1994), not specifically discussed
Martin (2002), not specifically discussed
Motta (2004), paragraph 4.5.1
Tirole (1988), not specifically discussed
Waldman and Jensen (2001), not specifically discussed

D Related legal texts

Bellamy and Child (2008), chapter 7, paragraphs 6 and 7(A)
Jones and Sufrin (2008), chapter 13, paragraph 5(D, E, F)
Ritter and Braun (2005), chapter 3, paragraph C(3, 5, 6, 9) and chapter 6, paragraph D
Whish (2008), chapter 15, paragraphs 6 and 8

E Commission decisions in chronological order*

Alliance des constructeurs français Commission decision 68/317/EEC [1968] OJ L 201/1, Case IV/25.140
Cobelaz-usines de synthèse Commission decision 68/374/EEC [1968] OJ L 276/13, Case IV/565
Cobelaz-cokeries Commission decision 68/375/EEC [1968] OJ L 276/19, Case IV/507
CFA Commission decision 68/377/EEC [1968] OJ L 276/29, Case IV/666
SEIFA Commission decision 69/216/EEC [1969] OJ L 173/8, 704, Case IV/25.410
Supexie Commission decision 71/22/EEC [1971] OJ L 10/12, Case IV/337
SAFCO Commission decision 72/23/EEC [1972] OJ L 13/44, Case IV/23.514 (Martin, 1994, pp.182–3)
Rank/Sopelem Commission decision 75/76/EEC [1975] OJ L 29/20, Case IV/26.603
SHV-Chevron Commission decision 75/95/EEC [1975] OJ L 29/20, Case IV/26.872 (*)

•   Decisions displayed in **bold type** are described in the section. Decisions highlighted with (*) include interesting economic analysis by the Commission on the specific topic of the section. Some decisions contain economic reasoning on more than one topic and therefore appear in several lists of Commission decisions in chronological order. Reference is made in brackets and **bold type** to the relevant section in which the decision is extensively described as a landmark case. When decisions are referenced and/or described in some detail in one or more of the economic textbooks, reference in brackets is also made to the relevant part(s) of those texts.

United Reprocessors GmbH Commission decision 76/248/EEC [1976] OJ L 51/7, Case IV/26.940/a

Vacuum Interrupters Ltd Commission decision 77/160/EEC [1977] OJ L 48/32, Case IV/27.442 (*)

De Laval-Stork **Commission decision 77/543/EEC [1977] OJ L 215/11, Case IV/27.093**

GEC-Weir Sodium Circulators Commission decision 77/781/EEC [1977] OJ L 327/26, Case IV/29.428

WANO Schwarzpulver Commission decision 78/921/EEC [1978] OJ L 322/26, Case IV/29.133

Beecham/Parke, Davis Commission decision 79/298/EEC [1979] OJ L 70/11, Case IV/28.796 (**described in detail as landmark case in section 6.1**) (Martin, 1994, p.376)

Floral Commission decision 80/182/EEC [1980] OJ L 39/51, Case IV/29.672 (**described in detail as landmark case in section 2.5**)

Vacuum Interrupters Ltd Commission decision 80/1332/EEC [1980] OJ L 383/1, Case IV/27.442

Langenscheidt/Hachette Commission decision 82/71/EEC [1982] OJ L 39/25, Case IV/29.972

Amersham Buchler Commission decision 82/742/EEC [1982] OJ L 314/34, Case IV/30.517

Rockwell/IVECO **Commission decision 83/390/EEC [1983] OJ L 224/19, Case IV/30.437**

VW/MAN Commission decision 83/668/EEC [1983] OJ L 376/11, Case IV/29.329

Mitchell Cotts/Sofiltra Commission decision 87/100/EEC [1987] OJ L 41/31, Case IV/31.340 (*)

Enichem/ICI Commission decision 88/87/EEC [1988] OJ L 50/18, Case IV/31.846 (**described in detail as landmark case in section 6.1**)

Olivetti/Canon Commission decision 88/88 [1988] OJ L 52/51, Case IV/32.306

De Laval-Stork Commission decision 88/110/EEC [1988] OJ L 59/32, Case IV/27.093

IVECO-Ford Commission decision 88/469/EEC [1988] OJ L 230/39, Case IV/31.902

United International Pictures **Commission decision 89/408/EEC [1989] OJ L 190/22, Case IV/30.566**

Cekacan Commission decision 90/535/EEC [1990] OJ L 299/64, Case IV/32.681

Screensport/UER Commission decision 91/130/EEC [1991] OJ L 63/32, Case IV/32.524

Eirpage Commission decision 91/562/EEC [1991] OJ L 306/22, Case IV/32.737

FIAT/Hitachi Commission decision 93/48/EEC [1993] OJ L 20/10, Case IV/33.031

Ford/VW Commission decision 93/49/EEC [1993] OJ L 20/14, Case IV/33.814 (Motta, 2004, pp.15–16)

Astra Commission decision 93/50/EEC [1993] OJ L 20/23, Case IV/32.745 (*)

Exxon/Shell **Commission decision 94/322/EEC [1994] OJ L 144/20, Case IV/33.640**

ACI Commission decision 94/594/EEC [1994] OJ L 224/28, Case IV/34.518

Night Services Commission decision 94/663/EEC [1994] OJ L 259/20, Case IV/34.600

Pasteur Merieux-Merck Commission decision 94/770/EEC [1994] OJ L 309/1, Case IV/34.776

Fujitsu AMD Semiconductor Commission decision 94/823/EEC [1994] OJ L 341/66, Case IV/34.891

Eurotunnel Commission decision 94/894/EEC [1994] OJ L 354/66, Case IV/32.490

International Private Satellite Partners Commission decision 94/895/EEC [1994] OJ L 354/75, Case IV/34.768

Asahi/Saint-Gobain Commission decision 94/896/EEC [1994] OJ L 354/87, Case IV/33.863

Philips-Osram Commission decision 94/986/EEC [1994] OJ L 378/37, Case IV/34.252

Lufthansa/SAS Commission decision 96/180/EC [1996] OJ L 54/28, Case IV/35.545 (*) (Bishop and Walker, 2009, 5.57; Motta, 2004, pp.81, 104, 269)

Phoenix/GlobalOne Commission decision 96/547/EC [1996] OJ L 239/57, Case IV/35.617

Iridium Commission decision 97/39/EC [1997] OJ L 16/87, Case IV/35.518

TPS Commission decision 1999/242/EC [1999] OJ L 90/6, Case IV/36.237

P&O Stena Line Commission decision 1999/421/EC [1999] OJ L 163/61, Case IV/36.253

Cegetel + 4 Commission decision 1999/573/EC [1999] OJ L 218/14, Case IV/36.592

Télécom Développement Commission decision 1999/574/EC [1999] OJ L 218/24, Case IV/36.581

British Interactive Broadcasting/Open **Commission decision 1999/781/EC [1999] OJ L 312/1, Case IV/36.539**

Identrus Commission decision 2001/696/EC [2001] OJ L 249/12, Case IV/37.462

F   Economic landmark cases

F.1   *De Laval-Stork*, Commission Decision 77/543/EEC [1977] OJ L 215/11

Relevance: For the first time in this decision the Commission carried out an overall economically oriented analysis of the possible pro-competitive and anticompetitive effects arising from a marketing and production joint venture.

* Case IV/27.093
* **Decision:** Exemption pursuant to Article 101(3) FEU Treaty for nine years
* **Decision addressee(s):**
    – De Laval Turbine International Incorporated, *United States*
    – Koninklijke Machinefabriek Stork BV, *the Netherlands*
    – Stork Roterende Werktuigen BV, *the Netherlands*
    – De Laval-Stork VOF, *the Netherlands*
* **Report route:** Notification for exemption submitted to the Commission on 2 March 1973 by Stork Roterende Werktuigen BV
* **Date of the decision:** 25 July 1977
* **Competition Commissioner:** R. Vouel
* **Relevant product market:** Turbines, centrifugal compressors, and industrial pumps.
* **Relevant geographical market:** Not indicated.
* **Description of the case**
    a. **Relevant facts**
       Stork Roterende Werktuigen BV (Stork) is a company active in the production of industrial pumps and is a wholly owned subsidiary of Koninklijke Machinefabriek Stork BV (KMS) which is part of a large Dutch group (Verenigde Machinefabrieken) worldwide active in a number of industries related to the pump market and to the production of turbines and compressors.
       De Laval Turbine International Incorporated (a wholly owned subsidiary of De Laval Turbine Incorporated which is controlled by the large conglomerate Transamerica Corporation) is a company active on the European market in the production of compressors, turbines and pumps.
       The two companies set up a joint venture agreement (signed also by KMS) to enable the products transferred by the parent companies to the joint venture with their existing designs to be "designed, redesigned, manufactured and marketed [aiming to] increase De Laval International's penetration of the European market and to expand the business of KMS in the fields of compressors and industrial turbines."[32]

---

32   Recital 3 of the decision.

The joint venture was signed for a (renewable) period of five years.

The parent companies would have provided the joint venture with all the necessary facilities (in terms of cash, know-how, licenses, plants, offices, and staff). Specifically, the parties signed a license agreement for compressors, turbines, and pumps, and a know-how and industrial property licensing agreement granting exclusivity to the joint venture within the territory of the (then) EEC and in several other territories. Particular provisions were introduced to regulate the eventualities of the joint venture's dissolution and one party's withdrawal from the joint venture business (those provisions were the object of the described remedies and conditions attached to the decision).

The relevant market was characterized by a client-based production adjusted according to the requests of each single order and customer. Therefore, two products were never identical. Both companies were part of very large groups with business interests all over the world (and particularly in the case of De Laval) and their joint sales through the joint venture would have constituted only a part of the aggregate sales of their respective groups.

b. Origin of the case

On 2 March 1973 Stork Roterende Werktuigen BV submitted a notification to the Commission pursuant to Article 4 of Regulation 17 to see the joint venture agreement entered into by Stork with De Laval Turbine International Incorporated be declared exempted from the application of Article 101(1) FEU Treaty by virtue of Article 101(3) FEU Treaty.

c. Economic analysis

In this decision the Commission carried out an analysis of the pro-competitive and anticompetitive effects generated by the joint venture and enumerated the possible benefits and restrictions deriving from a production and marketing joint venture.

The Commission identified the following restrictions arising from the Laval-Stork agreement. Firstly, it objected to the coordination of the marketing and production policies, and secondly, the lack of competition between the parent companies. Thirdly, it expressed concerns about the absence of autonomous costs and pricing decisions deriving in particular from the permanent reciprocal consultation and exchange of information. More generally, the independence of the parties' competitive behavior would have been removed, along with the uncertainty about future actions of the parties, which were considered a crucial characteristic of competitive markets.

The above-mentioned effects were aggravated because the members had been actual or obvious potential competitors on all of the markets concerned. Consequently, the joint venture agreement was an indispensable tool neither for De Laval International to enter the European market nor to allow KMS to extend its business activities to the product in question. The Commission's assessment was confirmed by the fact that the parent companies showed their actual capacity to act independently as well as in competition with each other in related product and neighboring geographical markets.

Notwithstanding the considerable negative impact of the joint venture on the competitive structure of the market that the Commission established, it exempted the agreement albeit subject to some conditional measures, concluding that the positive effects outweighed the restrictive ones.

In the view of the Commission, the joint venture was instrumental to achieve the following:

- An easier, faster, and more effective interpenetration of the European market for De Laval International with a significant reduction of the necessary investment costs and related risks.
- An efficient reorganization and expansion of KMS' turbine and compressor business.
- The avoidance of "uneconomic capacity . . . thus [enabling] the parties to reach optimal size in relation to market conditions"[33] through the coordination of the investment.
- A significant reduction of the ratio of fixed costs to total costs likely subsequently to lead to lower final prices.
- Improved, more regular, and quicker services, combined with a better ability to take account of their specific requirements for particular products to the benefit of consumers.

d. Fines, remedies, and conditions enclosed

- The exclusivity of the patents and know-how granted by the parent companies to the joint venture has to be considered as not preventing the possibility of each of the parents directly dealing with customers' orders in case the joint venture was not able to satisfy such orders.
- The parents have to be able to continue (after the expiring of the three years' limitation period following the dissolution of the joint venture) to benefit from patents and know-how granted to the joint venture provided that that knowledge is indispensable for the exploitation of patents and know-how jointly acquired through the joint venture.
- The parents must be free to export the products manufactured under granted patents and know-how to the internal market and non-Member States.
- The parents must be free to use the know-how deriving from the common production notwithstanding the prohibition (after the expiring of the three years' limitation period following the dissolution of the joint venture) to make exact copies of the products.
- Obligation for the parent companies to inform the Commission of any change and addition to the joint venture agreement.
- Obligation for the parent companies to submit every two years to the Commission a report about the activities of the joint venture.
- Obligation for the parents to inform the Commission of any new activity undertaken by the parties individually or together with any other company active on the relevant market subject of the decision which might strengthen their position and restrict the competitiveness of the relevant market.

---

33   Recital III-10 of the decision.

e. **Further developments of the case**
   With *De Laval-Stork* Commission decision 88/110/EEC [1988] OJ L 59/32,
   Case IV/27.093, the Commission renewed the exemption for a further twenty
   years.

F.2 *Rockwell/Iveco* Commission Decision 83/390/EEC [1983] OJ L 224/19

Relevance: The Commission in this decision stressed the importance of analyzing
the market structure and features in order to assess the effects on competition of the joint
venture.

* Case IV/30.437
* **Decision:** Exemption pursuant to Article 101(3) FEU Treaty for eleven years
* **Decision addressee(s):**
    - Iveco Industrial Vehicles Corporation BV, *the Netherlands*
    - Rockwell International Corporation, *United States*
    - Omevi Officine Meccaniche Veicoli Industriali SpA, *Italy*
* **Report route:** Notification for exemption submitted to the Commission on 18 August
  1981 by Rockwell International Corporation and Iveco Industrial Vehicles Corpora-
  tion BV
* **Date of the decision:** 13 July 1983
* **Competition Commissioner:** F. Andriessen
* **Relevant product market:** Rear drive axles for trucks.
* **Relevant geographical market:** Not indicated.
* **Description of the case**
    a. **Relevant facts**
       Rockwell is a leading US company in the market for the supply of rear drive
       axles for trucks. It is also engaged in the broader production of automotive
       components.
           Iveco is a company belonging to the Italian Fiat Group active in the pro-
       duction of commercial vehicles. At the time of the decision it operated four
       plants for manufacturing axles. It supplied the group and satisfied the demand
       for axles while not making external sales to third parties.
           In order to save the start-up costs of setting up a new axle manufacturer,
       the two companies set up a joint venture for the production and distribution of
       axles that would have used the already existing plants and facilities Iveco had in
       Europe. According to the intentions of the parent companies, Rockwell would
       have been able to penetrate the European market through the joint venture.
       In fact, it would have been nearly impossible for a new entrant to survive
       on the new market without a strong partner purchasing the larger part of the
       initial production. The European market was not made up of independent
       axle manufacturers supplying the truck producers but instead consisted of
       (wholly owned) axle manufacturer business units producing specifically for
       truck fabrication.
           At the same time, Iveco would have had access to Rockwell's axle technology
       to avoid expensive R&D projects. Rockwell would have licensed its technology
       to the joint venture, the former in turn would have received all the improvements
       in the transferred technology made by the latter.

The parties agreed also on the fact that Iveco together with all its subsidiaries would entirely meet their requirements with joint venture axles and that the joint venture would be the non-exclusive distributor of the axles produced by Rockwell and one of the Iveco subsidiaries in addition to the axles produced by the joint venture itself.

b. Origin of the case

On 18 August 1981 Rockwell International Corporation and Iveco Industrial Vehicles Corporation BV submitted to the Commission a notification pursuant to Article 4 of Regulation 17 to see the joint venture agreement they had entered into to be declared exempted from the application of Article 101(1) FEU Treaty by virtue of Article 101(3) FEU Treaty.

c. Economic analysis

In this decision the Commission largely confirmed its earlier stance (see e.g. the previous case in this section *De Laval-Stork*) on production and distribution joint ventures. In addition, the focus of this decision lay on the market structure and its features. The assessment of the joint ventures's exemption under Article 101(3) accepted the imposition of anticompetitive restrictions through the agreement as necessary to allow for the parties to achieve an efficient and sufficiently rapid penetration of the market.

The Commission expressed awareness of the restrictions arising from the agreement and objected to the coordination of marketing and production policies and the fact that the parent companies would cease to compete with each other. However, despite the negative impact of the joint venture upon the competitive structure of the market, the Commission exempted the agreement because it recognized that "the advantages resulting from this cooperation outweigh considerably the harmful effects it entails."[34]

In this case, the Commission broadened its analysis beyond the efficiency gains in the form of a reduction of investment costs and related risk, the technological advances and broader range of products, a better and more efficient use of plant capacity, and the rationalization of production. The Commission also pointed out a likely pass-on of the savings in production costs to the consumers and the arising of consumer benefits due to the improved technology. These efficiencies, already discussed in the previous landmark case, were described as encompassing the peculiar characteristics of this relevant market, i.e. the existence of very high entry barriers for new entrants. In light of the above-mentioned preference of truck producers to manufacture their own axles, the entrance into the market called for "a considerable marketing and sales effort. A precondition for the commercial success of the JVC is the willingness of other truck manufacturers to cease at least part of their own axle production. A decision such as this with far-reaching business implications requires exhaustive and protracted negotiations ... These particular difficulties in obtaining customers and the necessary expenditure in time and effort and technical considerations militate in favor of the need for joint marketing through the JVC."[35] The prohibitions on competition imposed on the parties and the restrictions

---

34   Recital II-11 of the decision.   35   Recital II-10 of the decision.

on investment plans introduced were also considered as indispensable for the achievement of the joint venture's aims.

The Commission's analysis concludes that the penetration and the ensuing growth of an underdeveloped market resulting in a clearer separation between truck producers and single components producers were realistic and sufficiently beneficial to justify the restrictions necessary for their accomplishment.

d. Fines, remedies, and conditions enclosed

- Provision of measures regulating the case of dissolution of the joint venture and ensuring that the parties will be able to use the technical know-how in possession of the joint venture up to that point and necessary for the separate continuation of the production.
- Obligations for the parties to notify to the Commission any amendment or addition to the agreement and any awards by arbitration tribunals.

e. Further developments of the case
None.

F.3 *Exxon/Shell* Commission Decision 94/322/EC [1994] OJ L 144/20

Relevance: In this decision the Commission relied upon the efficient introduction of a more efficient technology in Europe together with environmental considerations as reasons to exempt a joint venture between two strong competitors that would have been considered restrictive of competition in absence of those described efficiencies. The decision confirmed the fact that the Commission considers joint ventures as privileged instruments to enhance and improve market conditions in Europe.

- Case IV/33.640
- **Decision:** Exemption pursuant to Article 101(3) FEU Treaty for ten years
- **Decision addressee(s):**
    - Exxon Chemical International Inc., *Belgium*
    - Shell International Chemical Company, *United Kingdom*
- **Report route:** Application for negative clearance and notification for exemption submitted to the Commission on 21 November 1991 and 29 May 1992 by Exxon Chemical International Inc. and on 2 December 1991 and 10 June 1992 by Shell International Petroleum Company and Shell Netherlands Chimie SA
- **Date of the decision:** 18 May 1994
- **Competition Commissioner:** K. Van Miert
- **Relevant product market:** Linear low-density polyethylene and High-density polyethylene.
- **Relevant geographical market:** European internal market.
- **Description of the case**
    ### a. Relevant facts
    Exxon Chemical Polymers SNS is an incorporated company of the Exxon Group, a multinational group whose main business activities are in energy production and distribution.

    Shell Chimie SA is an incorporated company of the Shell Group, a multinational group active in the oil, natural gas, chemicals, coal, and metals businesses.

The two companies set up a 50/50 joint venture (named Cipen) for the production of linear low-density polyethylene (LLDPE) and of high-density polyethylene (HDPE). The two products are not fully interchangeable. They were to be sold independently by the two partners, together with other similar products of their own respective productions.

The joint venture was signed for a (renewable) period of fifteen years.

The overall agreement was composed of several agreements aimed at the detailed and precise organization of all the aspects of Cipen's activities and of the parties' cooperation within the joint venture. In particular, the parties signed the *Joint venture agreement* setting out the basic outline of the joint venture. Furthermore they signed the *Group of economic interest constitution*, stipulating the main purposes of Cipen and the instruments at its disposal for their achievement (general meeting, sole director and controller). In order to regulate the day-to-day management and other important issues they signed the *Internal and operating rules*. Among other things these rules regulated possible new investment (joint investment and separate investments), costs sharing, and supplies. The parties also signed a *Plant utilization agreement* fixing the production rights of each party (the production hours to be shared according to the parties' interest in Cipen) and a *Construction, operating and services agreement*. Finally the parties signed two supply contracts regulating the reciprocal provision of ethylene and butane.

The relevant markets were oligopolistic, characterized by a considerable degree of price transparency and a certain stability of production capacities and market shares. The two parties were among the leading suppliers in both the LLDPE and the HDPE market and disposed of more than 20 percent of the European total production capacity at the moment of the joint venture starting up.

b. Origin of the case

On 21 November 1991 and 29 May 1992 Exxon Chemical International and on 2 December 1991 and 10 June 1992 Shell International Petroleum Company Limited and Shell Netherlands Chimie SA submitted to the Commission an application for negative clearance and a notification for exemption pursuant to Articles 2 and 4 of Regulation No. 17 to see Article 101(1) FEU Treaty be declared not applicable to the joint venture or alternatively the joint venture be declared exempted from the application of Article 101(1) FEU Treaty by virtue of Article 101(3) FEU Treaty.

c. Economic analysis

The joint venture agreement was assessed according to the then new Commission Notice concerning the assessment of cooperative joint ventures.[36]

In this decision the Commission reasserted its previous approach toward production (and marketing) joint ventures and listed the possible anticompetitive

---

36   Commission Notice concerning the assessment of cooperative joint ventures pursuant to Article 85 of the EEC Treaty, OJ C 43/2. The Notice had been published on 16 February 1993. The joint venture was considered cooperative (instead of concentrative) because "it does not perform all the functions of an autonomous economic entity, and gives rise to coordination of competitive behavior by the parents both between themselves in relation to the joint venture (point 10 of the Commission Notice)" (recital 41 of the decision).

effects arising from them. Also in this case, the joint venture would have led to coordination of the investment plans and of the production activities of the parent companies; a likely coordination of the competitive behavior at the distribution level (with particular relation to the prices) and an overall coordination (also due to the flow of information between the parent companies) of the production plans as a whole (i.e. also outside the joint venture). The Commission particularly stressed the "central role of the independence of business operators with respect to their business decisions which must be subject to reciprocal influence."[37]

Considering the fact that the parent companies were two of the strongest actors on the relevant product markets, the restrictive effects would have been strengthened.

However, despite the negative impact of the joint venture on the competitive structure of the market the Commission exempted the agreement. It concluded that its positive effects justified the restrictions conditionally on the imposition of a number of measures.

Besides the efficiency gains already described in the previous landmark cases, the Commission focused its attention on the fact that the joint venture would have introduced a new technology in Europe (an LLDPE/HDPE plant using the Unipol technology). That technology would have guaranteed a high degree of flexibility and efficiency. The presence of LLPDE at low cost would have "[encouraged] the costumers to convert ageing extrusion equipment... This would result in a reduction of customers' use of raw materials, their costs, and the volume of plastic wastes."[38]

Another important positive effect highlighted by the Commission was the avoidance of health and environmental risks connected with the transport of ethylene (avoided as an effect of the implementation of one of the supply contracts) together with the implementation of alternative technologies. Finally, in the Commission's view, the impact on the remaining competitors guaranteed that effective competition was not eliminated.

d. Fines, remedies, and conditions enclosed
  – Obligation for Exxon and Shell to inform the Commission in advance of any renewals, amendments, or additions to the agreement and of stopping or terminating the production of the joint venture.
  – Obligation for each party to submit, on a yearly basis, a report to the Commission concerning the activities related to the production and sale of LLPDE, and HPDE.
  – Obligation for the parents to inform the Commission of any possible change in capacity within or outside the Group of Economic Interest.
  – Obligation for the parent companies to answer to any possible request of information from the Commission.

e. Further developments of the case
None.

---

37   Recital 54 of the decision.   38   Recital 67 of the decision.

6.3 Strategic and technological alliances

A Introduction

Since the second half of the 1990s, the Commission identified strategic alliances as a separate category of economic conduct. They are defined as an organizational arrangement that governs contracts between separate firms. Unlike joint ventures, they do not lead to a newly created economic unit. The degree of collaboration of alliance contracts varies extensively. Alliances range from loose implicit contracts on licensing and explicit contracts that involve joint work of a business unit, to coordination of resources, industrial processes, and management of the participating companies, which enables a form of close cooperation usually only achieved by a full merger. As with R&D joint ventures, strategic alliances can constitute an important tool for capital investments which would not be sustainable for a single firm.

The efficiency gains that derive from these kinds of alliances arise from the coordination and the harmonization of the members' networks and technologies. The typical organization can potentially bring about superior technologies, increased quality and variety of the offered services, and costs savings. All these efficiency gains could raise welfare and therefore be beneficial to consumers without leading to a merger among the parties.

However, a very intense and close coordination of activities in the production of goods and the development or marketing of services raises potentially very serious competition concerns. Collusion and foreclosure of the market for new entrants will be lurking when the cooperation goes as far as coordination of prices, capacities, and offers to customers. Alliances could lead to an increase of combined market power, so that the incumbents obtained more possibilities to tighten their restrictions of competition and raise entry barriers.

The assessment of strategic and technological alliances requires striking a balance between permitting their potentially beneficial effects and preventing risks of foreclosure of the market. Here, taking account of the specific nature of markets that are more likely to be affected by such risks, such as the telecommunications sector and the air transport sector, is important.

B Applicable EU legislation

No special legislation applicable. For applicable legislation see chapter 6, paragraph B.

C Related economics texts

Bishop and Walker (2009), not specifically discussed
Carlton and Perloff (2005), not specifically discussed
Church and Ware (2000), not specifically discussed
Martin (1994), not specifically discussed
Martin (2002), not specifically discussed
Motta (2004), not specifically discussed
Tirole (1988), not specifically discussed
Waldman and Jensen (2001), not specifically discussed

D Related legal texts

Bellamy and Child (2008), chapter 7, paragraph 7(C, D, E)
Jones and Sufrin (2008), not specifically discussed

Ritter and Braun (2005), chapter 3, paragraph C(8)
Whish (2008), not specifically discussed

E   Commission decisions in chronological order•

BT/MCI Commission decision 94/579/EC [1994] OJ L 223/36, Case IV/34.857
Olivetti/Digital Commission decision 94/771/EC [1994] OJ L 309/24, Case IV/34.410 (*)
Atlas Commission decision 96/546/EC [1996] OJ L 239/23, Case IV/35.337
Unisource Commission decision 97/780/EC [1997] OJ L 318/1, Case IV/35.830 (*)
Uniworld Commission decision 97/781/EC [1997] OJ L 318/24, Case IV/35.738
Unisource Commission decision 2001/143/EC [2001] OJ L 52/30, Case IV/36.841 (*)
Austrian Airlines/Lufthansa Commission decision 2002/746/EC [2002] OJ L 242/25, Case IV/37.730
Air France/Alitalia Commission decision of 7 April 2004, published on DG Comp website, Case COMP/38.284/D2 (*)

F   Economic landmark case

F.1   *BT/MCI* Commission Decision 94/579/EC [1994] OJ L 223/36

Relevance: In this decision the positive effects of a strategic and technological alliance in the telecommunications sector are analyzed in view of the liberalization and globalization of the relevant market. It represents a landmark decision because for the first time the Commission recognized a global alliance as a separate type of agreement distinct from joint ventures and at the same time provided an economic assessment of the efficiencies deriving from such alliances.

- Case IV/34.857
- **Decision:** Exemption pursuant to Article 101(3) FEU Treaty for seven years
- **Decision addressee(s):**
    - British Telecommunications plc, *United Kingdom*
    - MCI Communications Corporation, *United States*
- **Report route:** Application for negative clearance and notification for exemption submitted to the Commission on 18 September 1993 by British Telecommunications and MCI
- **Date of the decision:** 27 July 1994
- **Competition Commissioner:** K. Van Miert
- **Relevant product market:** Value-added and enhanced telecommunications services for intensive users
- **Relevant geographical market:** Global market

•   Decisions displayed in **bold type** are described in the section. Decisions highlighted with (*) include interesting economic analysis by the Commission on the specific topic of the section. Some decisions contain economic reasoning on more than one topic and therefore appear in several lists of Commission decisions in chronological order. Reference is made in brackets and **bold type** to the relevant section in which the decision is extensively described as a landmark case. When decisions are referenced and/or described in some detail in one or more of the economic textbooks, reference in brackets is also made to the relevant part(s) of those texts.

- **Description of the case**
  a. **Relevant facts**

    British Telecommunications (BT) is the former UK monopolist telecommunications operator (TO) and supplies all kinds of telecommunications services and equipment for private and business customers. At the moment of the decision BT was the world's fourth largest TO.

    Its partner MCI was "a telecommunications common carrier in the United States of America providing a broad range of US and international voice and data communications services including long-distance telephone, record communications, and electronic mail services to and from the US ... MCI is the second largest long-distance operator in the United States of America after AT&T and the world's fifth largest in terms of traffic."[39]

    The decision dates from the time when Europe was undergoing a period of widespread liberalization of the, until then, monopolized telecommunications markets.

    In order to become a pre-eminent actor in the emerging market of enhanced and value-added telecommunications services for multinational companies, the two undertakings made an agreement to start up a joint venture named Newco and allow BT the acquisition of a 20 percent stake in MCI, making BT the largest single shareholder in MCI).[40]

    Newco was expected to offer a set of global services initially based on the services already offered by the parent companies. These would include in particular data services, value-added application services, traveler services, intelligent network services and VSAT network services, and services for the outsourcing of the customers' network. Those services were supposed to be provided cross-border and globally. These product features would have constituted a novelty in a market so far characterized by national monopolies and national TOs with different incompatible networks, not laid out to provide cross-border services. The ongoing rapid convergence of telecommunications and information technology (together with the liberalization and globalization of the market) was envisaged to accelerate the creation and development of globally provided services.

    According to the overall agreement establishing the global alliance, Newco would have sold its products to the parent companies which would distribute them exclusively – MCI in the Americas and BT in the rest of the world.[41] Furthermore the parents agreed to obtain from Newco all requirements for global products. The parent companies then introduced between themselves and vis-à-vis Newco a non-compete clause.[42] The parties and the joint venture also created a reciprocal license agreement according to which each parent granted to Newco "irrevocable, perpetual, non-exclusive, non-transferable licenses to use the technical information solely for the purposes of the business [and]

---

39 Recital 4 of the decision.
40 BT owned 75.1% of Newco share capital and MCI owned 24.9% of it.
41 Notwithstanding the non-compete clause, Newco was recognized in its possibility to sell global products directly to customers.
42 Nonetheless the joint venture agreement ensured "that in case of deregulation of the US/UK (and vice versa) route for the provision of international voice services, BT and MCI will receive from each other the necessary support to compete." Recital 25 of the decision.

Newco grants to each parent company, upon request, similar licenses to use the technical intellectual property rights of Newco."[43]

b. Origin of the case

In 1993 BT and MCI notified a concentration pursuant to the Merger Regulation. The Commission concluded that none of the notified transactions constituted a concentration and so informed the parties by decision of 13 September 1993. Consequently, the parties converted that notification into an application for negative clearance and notification for exemption pursuant to Article 2 and Article 4 of Regulation 17 to see Article 101(1) FEU Treaty be declared not applicable to the agreements or alternatively the same agreements be declared exempted from the application of Article 101(1) FEU Treaty by virtue of Article 101(3) FEU Treaty. The application and the notification were submitted on 18 September 1993.

c. Economic analysis

The decision is a landmark decision because it is the first time the Commission recognized a global alliance as a separate type of agreement distinct from a joint venture and in which it provided an economic assessment of the efficiencies deriving from it.

According to the Commission the parent companies were "potential competitors of Newco and of each other in respect of the global products to be offered by Newco and actual competitors in the overall telecommunications market."[44] Since the parent companies were active in fields similar to the relevant product market and had the financial, technological, and logistic capacities to enter the relevant market on their own, Newco could not be considered as the only objectively available means to successfully enter the relevant market. The alliance would have eliminated competition between the parents in the provision of telecommunications services not only on an international basis but also on a national basis due to the non-compete clause. In fact due to the "loss of rights" clause the undertakings agreed to not interfere with their respective core business in their respective geographical areas (the Americas for BT and outside the rest of the world for MCI); had they interfered, they would have lost certain rights.[45] This agreement practically partitioned the market and eliminated all incentives for each party to start up local companies and activities notwithstanding the fact that both of them had already been involved in relevant business in each other's geographical area before the alliance.[46] An additional concern was the combination of, on the one hand, Newco's organizational structure, through which the parties could have pooled their IPRs and cross-license each other and the joint venture on an exclusive basis allowing a continuous exchange of information, and, on the other hand, the isolation of the Community market though BT's exclusive right to distribute Newco's products.

Aware of the restrictions arising from the alliance, the Commission nonetheless concluded that the efficiencies generated by the agreements outweighed the negative effects. Indeed "the combination of BT and MCI technologies

---

43 Recital 26 of the decision.
44 Recital 34 of the decision.

45 See recital 32 of the decision.
46 See recital 42 of the decision.

will allow Newco to offer new services, . . . cheaply and of a more advanced in nature than either BT or MCI would have been capable of providing alone; . . . in addition . . . Newco could allow the Community's most important companies to achieve levels of telecommunications performance on an international level currently only available at some national/local level, that could enable them to better withstand global competition."[47] The Commission also remarked the considerable cost savings derived from operations carried in a single network, which simultaneously increased the efficiency with which Newco's products and services could be distributed.

Furthermore the Commission held that the non-compete clause and the obligation to buy all requirements for global products were ancillary to the creation and successful operation of the joint venture. The exclusive distribution agreement and the "loss of rights" clause were considered indispensable for the positive result of the alliance and for the proper protection of parent companies' software otherwise – without such a sort of territorial limitation – unprotected under IP law.[48] In light of these considerations, the fact that strong competitors would be present even after the alliance was allowed and all suppliers faced "substantial bargaining power of customers,"[49] the Commission concluded that the overall effect of the alliance was positive for the European telecommunications market.

d. Fines, remedies, and conditions enclosed
None.

e. Further developments of the case
None.

---

47   Recital 53 of the decision.
48   "The 'loss of rights' . . . are indispensable in particular as a means of permitting confidence between the parent companies to grow and, consequently, to permit the necessary transfer of technology so as to allow Newco to succeed." Recital 62 of the decision. Nonetheless the Commission made the "loss of rights" clauses exempted subject to a limitation period of five years (instead of seven like the rest of the alliance). The intent was to avoid too strict and inseparable an interconnection between each other's technologies that would have prevented the entrance of the parties in each market with their own proprietary technology.
49   Recital 58 of the decision.

7 Restrictions to competition by Member States

A Introduction

The FEU Treaty sets out rules to prevent distortions of competition in Europe and pursues that aim, regardless of the material author of the behavior that triggers the anticompetitive effects. Even though the competition rules (Articles 101 and 102) are addressed to undertakings, Member States may distort competition in various direct and indirect ways as well. In particular, states can allocate exclusive rights to undertakings that would effectively provide these companies with positions of dominance or (near-) monopoly.

In order to prevent this, the FEU Treaty imposes several obligations on the European Member States.[1] The prominent set of obligations is imposed on the Member States by Article 106(1). It requires Member States to abstain from enacting or maintaining in force measures that are contrary to the rules of the Treaty. This holds in particular with regard to measures that may conflict with rules on competition in cases where the Member States grant special or exclusive rights to undertakings. The provisions of Article 106(1) permit Member States to create privileged firms or (legal) monopolies or to award respective rights, under the condition that the States adhere in those cases to the Treaty rules (on competition). The role played by the Court of Justice (ECJ) in the interpretation of Article 106 and of the derived obligations for Member States has been crucial. The ECJ has repeatedly ruled upon the relation existing between competition rules and the provision of services of general economic interest and between dominant position and legal monopolies. Moreover, the ECJ has consistently held that a correct interpretation of Articles 102 and 106 implies that firms which were granted (legal) monopolies or privileges are in a position of dominance on the (national) market, which is not as such incompatible with Article 102.

---

1 Perhaps the single most relevant obligation upon Member States is to loyally cooperate in the achievement of the European Union tasks stated in Article 4(3) EU Treaty, which states that "Pursuant to the principle of sincere cooperation, the Union and the Member States shall, in full mutual respect, assist each other in carrying out tasks which flow from the Treaties." When read in conjunction with Articles 101 and 102, this has led the European Courts to state that "it must be pointed out that Articles [101 and 102] of the Treaty *per se* are concerned only with the conduct of undertakings and not with national legislation. The Court has consistently held, however, that Articles [101 and 102] of the Treaty, in conjunction with Article [4(3)], require the Member States not to introduce or maintain in force measures, even of a legislative nature, which may render ineffective the competition rules applicable to undertakings. Such would be the case ... if a Member States were to require or favor the adoption of agreements, decisions or concerted practices contrary to Article [101] or to reinforce their effects, or to deprive its own legislation of its official character by delegating to private traders responsibility for taking decisions affecting the economic sphere", Case 267/86 *Van Eycke* v. *Aspa* [1988] ECR 4769, recital 16. On the development of the 'useful effect doctrine', see also Case 13/77 *INNO* v. *ATAB* [1977] ECR 2115; Case 136/86 *BNIC* v. *Aubert* [1987] ECR 4789; Case C-185/91 *Reiff* [1993] ECR I-5801; Case C-245/91 *Ohra* [1993] ECR I-5851; and Case C-35/99 *Arduino* [2002] ECR I-1529. Other obligations for Member States aimed at the maintenance of competitive conditions in the internal market are set in Articles 34–36 (free movement of goods) and Article 56–62 (free provision of services), Article 37 (monopolies), Articles 107–109 (State aid), Articles 110–113 (non discriminatory taxation).

Member States are instead in breach of the combined disposal of Articles 102 and 106 where the undertakings in question, by merely exercising the exclusive rights or privileges granted by national legislation, infringe Article 102.[2]

Article 106(2) FEU Treaty provides an important exception to the general principle laid out in the first paragraph of the same article. In Article 106(2), it is stated that firms entrusted with the provision of services of general economic interest are bound by rules on competition in so far as the respect of those rules "does not obstruct the performance, in law or in fact, of the particular tasks assigned to them". The only limit to the restriction is given by the *interest of the Community*, which must not be jeopardized by the development of the trade that occurs due to the application of the exception pursuant to Article 106(2). Again, the current interpretation given to Article 106(2) is the result of plentiful ECJ case-law.[3]

The notion of "services of general economic interest" frequently recurs in case law[4] and recent legislative interventions at European level.[5] Such services are a very sensitive issue since they represent an important instrument for Member States to implement, e.g., their social policy. Accordingly, Article 14 FEU Treaty acknowledges a place for services of general economic interest in the shared values of the Union and their role in promoting social and territorial cohesion. At the same time they may imply restrictions of competition in the national markets and therefore distortions of competition in the internal market. Their sensitive nature is recognized by the ECJ who stated that "[I]n allowing, in certain circumstances, derogations from the general rules of the Treaty, Article [106(2)] of the Treaty seeks to reconcile the Member States' interest in using certain undertakings, in particular in the public sector, as an instrument of economic or fiscal policy with the Community's interest in ensuring compliance with the rules on competition and preservation of the unity of the common market".[6]

The Commission is empowered by Article 106(3) to ensure compliance with the provisions of Article 106 via decisions and directives addressed to Member States. The Commission has made extensive use of these powers during the 1990s, when the internal market was subject to widespread liberalization.

---

2   The precise meaning to be attributed to the relation between Articles 102 and 106 is still debated and subjected to continuous interpretation and refinements through the Courts. It is for instance not absolutely clear how national provisions leading/inducing/imposing breaches of Article 102 upon undertakings granted with exclusive rights should be treated. Indeed, the mentioned rather ambiguous expressions (leading/inducing/imposing) have been used by the ECJ in several leading judgments and still hold for further clarifications. See in particular Case C-260/89 *ERT* [1991] ECR I-2925; Case C-41/90 *Höfner & Elser* v. *Macroton*[1991] ECR I- 1979; Case C-179/90 *Porto di Genova* [1991] ECR I-5889.

3   The interpretation of Article 106(2), the limits and conditions to its applicability, the concept of *obstruction* to the performance of services of general economic interest, the consequences of such exception upon the (allowed) limits of competitive restrictions in other activities carried out by the same undertakings and not covered by public service obligations (i.e. cross-subsidization), have been the object of several jurisprudential interventions and are still to be entirely clarified. An in-depth analysis of the case law development and of all policy implications attached to it exceeds the scope of this book, nonetheless for some reference to the most significant Courts decisions, see *inter alia* Case C-393/92 *Almelo* v. *Ijsselmij* [1994] ECR I-1477; Case C-320/91 *Corbeau* [1993] ECR I-2533; Case C-115–117/97 *Brentjens* [1999] ECR I-6025; Case C-475/99 *Ambulanz Glöckner* [2001] ECR I-8089.

4   In particular Case C-280/00 *Altmark Trans and Regierungspräsidium Magdeburg* [2003] ECR I-7747 on limits of applicability of State Aid rules to services of general economic interest.

5   See in particular Commission Decision 2005/842/EC on the application of Article 106(2) to State aid in the form of public service compensation granted to certain undertakings entrusted with the operation of services of general economic interest [2005] OJ L 312/67.

6   Case C-115–117/97 *Brentjens* [1999] ECR I-6025, recital 103.

B Applicable EU legislation

Articles 3(3) and 4(3) EU Treaty; Articles 14, 102, and 106 FEU Treaty.

For services of general economic interest, see:

Commission Directive 80/723/EEC of 25 June 1980 on the transparency of financial relations between Member States and public undertakings [1980] OJ L 195/35.

Commission Communication on services of general interest in Europe [2001] OJ C 17/4.

Community framework for State aid in the form of public service compensation 2005/C 297/04 [2005] OJ C 297/4.

Commission Directive 2005/81/EC of 28 November 2005 amending Directive 80/723/EEC on the transparency of financial relations between Member States and public undertakings as well as on financial transparency within certain undertakings [2005] OJ L 312/47.

Commission Decision 2005/842/EC on the application of Article 86(2) to State aid in the form of public service compensation granted to certain undertakings entrusted with the operation of services of general economic interest [2005] OJ L 312/67.[7]

C Related economics texts

Bishop and Walker (2009), paragraph 1.01
Carlton and Perloff (2005), chapter 4, paragraph 3(2) and chapter 20
Church and Ware (2000), paragraph 4.1.1.1
Martin (1994), not specifically discussed
Martin (2002), not specifically discussed
Motta (2004), not specifically discussed
Tirole (1988), not specifically discussed
Waldman and Jensen (2001), chapter 1, paragraph 4 and chapter 20

D Related legal texts

Bellamy and Child (2008), chapter 11
Jones and Sufrin (2008), chapter 8
Ritter and Braun (2005), chapter 9
Whish (2008), chapter 6

E Commission decisions in chronological order[•]

Greek Insurance Commission decision 85/276/EEC [1985] OJ L 152/25
Canary Islands Commission decision 87/359/EEC [1987] OJ L 194/28

---

7   EU (competition) law also plays a significant role in the regulation of markets that used to be State monopolies. See in particular sector-specific legislation concerning energy, electricity, gas, postal services, telecommunications, and transports. The relevant legislation and its evolution over time since the liberalization process in the 1990s until today can be found on DG Comp website. See http://ec.europa.eu/comm/competition/index_en.html.

•   Decisions displayed in **bold type** are described in the section. Reference is made in brackets and **bold type** to the relevant section in which the decision is extensively described as a landmark case. When decisions are referenced and/or described in some detail in one or more of the economic textbooks, reference in brackets is also made to the relevant part(s) of those texts.

Provision in the Netherlands of express delivery services **Commission decision 90/16/EEC [1990] OJ L 10/47**

Provision in Spain of express courier services Commission decision 90/456/EEC [1990] OJ L 233/19, Case IV/31.990

Rødby Commission decision 94/119/EEC [1994] OJ L 55/52

British Midland (Zaventem) Commission decision 95/364/EC [1995] OJ L 12/8

GSM Italia Commission decision 95/489/EC [1995] OJ L 280/49

Telecom Eireann **Commission decision 97/114/EC [1997] OJ L 41/8**

GSM Spain Commission decision 97/181/EC [1997] OJ L 76/19

Additional implementation periods to Portugal Commission decision 97/310/EC [1997] OJ L 133/19

Additional implementation periods to Luxembourg Commission decision 97/568/EC [1997] OJ L 234/7

Additional implementation periods to Spain Commission decision 97/603/EC [1997] OJ L 243/48

Additional implementation periods to Greece Commission decision 97/607/EC [1997] OJ L 245/6

Broadcasting television Flanders Commission decision 97/606/EC [1997] OJ L 244/18

Italian ports legislation Commission decision 97/744/EC [1997] OJ L 301/17

Tariffs for piloting in the Port of Genoa Commission decision 97/745/EC [1997] OJ L 301/27

Portuguese Airports Commission decision 1999/199/EC [1999] OJ L 69/31, Case IV/35.703

AENA Commission decision 2000/521/EC [2000] OJ L 208/36, Case COMP/35.737

Consorzio risposta and consorzio recapitali Commission decision 2001/176/EC [2001] OJ L 63/59, Case COMP/37.721

Snelpd/France, La Poste Commission decision 2002/344/EC [2002] OJ L 120/19, Case COMP/37.133

Germany – Restriction on mail preparation Commission decision of 20 October 2004, published on DG Comp website, Case COMP/C.38.745/B2

Greece – Quasi-exclusive access to lignite in the electricity market Commission decision of 5 March 2008, published on DG COMP website, Case COMP/38.700

Slovakian postal legislation Commission decision of 7 October 2008, published on DG Comp website, Case COMP/F-1/39.562

F   Economic landmark cases

F.1   *Provision in the Netherlands of express delivery services* Commission decision 90/16/EEC [1990] OJ L 10/47

Relevance: In this decision, the Commission for the first time established a link between national provisions concerning State monopolies and the derived, practically inevitable, abuses of a dominant position for the undertaking involved. Consequently the obligations of the State to comply with the obligations deriving from Article 106 are particularly relevant in light of the potentially consequent infringements of Article 102. The conditions for the application of the exception for services of general economic interest pursuant to Article 106(2) are also described. Even if annulled by the ECJ on procedural grounds (breach of right of defence), the concepts in the decision indicate the Commission's approach against anticompetitive conducts in the postal service markets.

- **Decision:** Infringement of Article 106(1) FEU Treaty (read in conjunction with Article 102)
- **Decision addressee(s):**
  - Kingdom of the Netherlands
- **Report route:** Commission initiative pursuant to Article 106(3) FEU Treaty
- **Date of the decision:** 20 December 1989
- **Competition Commissioner:** L. Brittan
- **Relevant product market:** Provision of express delivery postal services
- **Relevant geographical market:** The Netherlands
- **Description of the case**
  a. **Relevant facts**
  PTT Post BV was the postal service company in the Netherlands and at the time of the decision wholly owned by the Dutch State. As a monopolist, it provided the basic postal services under the public service obligations. In exchange for the public services carried out, PTT Post was the only undertaking entitled to set up and operate post boxes and to issue postage stamps accompanied by other minor privileges.

    The law adopted in October 1988 disciplining the postal services in the Netherlands prohibited all undertakings other than PTT Post from providing express delivery postal services for letters weighing up to 500 gs unless the undertakings were registered, offered a significantly better service than that provided by PTT Post, and provided services at a price not below a certain threshold amount fixed by law. The minimum price limit was not applicable to PTT Post and was in fact set by the national legislator above the rates charged by some private express delivery service providers before the adoption of the new law.

    The market for express deliveries differs from that for basic postal services in that transport is quicker and usually offered in combination with additional services. The service responds to the needs of the business community, which requires timely deliveries and which are not as sensitive to additional associated cost. The express delivery services are therefore not interchangeable with the regular postal services and the two services are not competing.

  b. **Origin of the case**
  By the letter of 7 November 1988 the Commission expressed its concerns about the conflict of the drafted postal law of the Netherlands with competition rules. Once the law was adopted the Commission invited the Netherlands to produce further information and to express its opinion about possible incompatibility of the approved legislation with Community law. The Commission warned the Netherlands of the possible adaptation of a decision pursuant to Article 106(3) in case its concerns were confirmed.

  c. **Economic analysis**
  According to the Commission the effect of the law was to extend the dominant position of PTT Post from the market for regular postal services

(in which it operated as a monopolist) to the separate market for express services. Furthermore, the consequence of the exclusivity for express delivery services provided for less than *fl.* 11.90 (the minimum price limit set by decree) was also to extend the dominant position to the remaining part of the same market for express deliveries.

As the Commission noted "[c]ompetition on the remaining part of the market does not exclude such a dominant position since PTT Post BV is able to adopt a market strategy which takes no account of that competition, without thereby suffering any detrimental effects. There will be no constraints on any strategies PTT Post BV adopts with regard to the express delivery service it offers major customers since its competitors will not be able to offer discounts below the legal minimum."[8] As a result, the number of service providers and the quality of the services would be negatively affected. In fact, competitors would not have been able to offer a full set of services and would have suffered a clear disadvantage.

In this regard the Commission stated that "[t]he Netherlands post office can take advantage of the fact that it alone is able to provide services for less than the minimum price in order to provide its customers with other services at a price approaching their marginal cost, whereas its competitors will have to charge all their collection and transport costs against solely those services not covered by the monopoly. By reserving the market for express deliveries at a price below the legal minimum to the Post Office, the Netherlands are creating discrimination even in the services that are not reserved."[9]

By the same token, the attempt carried out by the Netherlands to justify the measure under the exception provided for in Article 106(2) was dismissed by the Commission. In fact, it noted that there was no risk of jeopardizing the provision of the service of general economic interest (i.e. the regular postal service) by opening the separate and mostly unrelated market for express deliveries to competition. Therefore the extension of the position of dominance was unnecessary to achieve that goal or meet the requirement. Furthermore "the financial viability of the post office"[10] would have not been at risk. In fact the substantial advantages PTT Post could reap and the economies of scale it could achieve using its staff and infrastructures in the provision of a variety of services would have guaranteed the profitability of the business. Opening the market to express deliveries competitors would not have obstructed the provision of this service of public economic interest.

Since in case of dominant firms, the reservation of a market for ancillary activities which might be carried out by another undertaking constitutes an abuse of dominant position; and since that abuse was the consequence of a piece of national legislation, the law in question was considered incompatible with Article 106(1) interpreted in conjunction with Article 102.

---

8   Recital 11 of the decision.
9   Recital 14 of the decision. The Commission in the same recital also noted that the requirement of a better service (compared to PTT Post's) as a condition necessary in order to continue to provide the service would create legal uncertainty for competitors because once PTT Post became able to offer the same standards of quality they would have been obliged to leave the market.
10   Recital 17 of the decision.

d. Fines, remedies, and conditions enclosed
- Obligation for the Netherlands to inform the Commission within two months about the measures adopted to comply with the decision.

e. Further developments of the case
Case C-48/90, 66/90 *PTT Nederland* v. *Commission* [1992] ECR I-565. The Commission decision was annulled since the Court recognized a breach of the right of the defense of the Netherlands deriving from the incomplete notification of the statement of objections.

F.2 *Telecom Eireann* Commission decision 97/114/EC [1997] OJ L 41/8

Relevance: This decision is the landmark case for a number of subsequent decisions occurring in the frame of the so-called "liberalization period" (during the 1990s) in which the Commission, through the powers conferred to it by Article 106(3), assumed an important role in the implementation of a European-wide policy (and the legislative measures) to liberalize and regulate sectors characterized by State monopolies and regulate them. Also relevant in this decision is the detailed market analysis carried out in order to justify the acceptance of the Irish requests and the modification in the interpretation of the condition for applicability of the exception pursuant to Article 106(2) in line with ECJ case law.

- **Decision:** Additional period for the implementation of a Commission Directive granted to Ireland.
- **Decision addressee(s):**
  - Ireland
- **Report route:** Request for additional implementation periods submitted by the Irish Government to the Commission
- **Date of the decision:** 27 November 1996
- **Competition Commissioner:** K. Van Miert
- **Relevant product market:** Voice telephony services and underlying network infrastructures
- **Relevant geographical market:** Ireland
- **Description of the case**
  ### a. Relevant facts
  In 1990 the Commission adopted the Directive 90/338/EEC[11] on competition in the market for telecommunication services which was subsequently partly amended by the Commission Directive 96/2/EC[12] with regard to provisions regulating mobile and personal communications. The two directives were adopted in order to liberalize the provision of telecommunication services in the Member States that were until that time provided by State monopolies and consequently characterized by a complete absence of competition.

  Each Member State was granted a period of time to implement each of the liberalizing measures provided in the directives. The same directives specified the Commission obligation to grant additional implementation periods upon request of single Member States when the request referred to an extension of

---

11 Commission Directive 90/338/EEC of 28 June 1990 on competition in the market for telecommunication services [1990] OL L 192/10.

12 Commission Directive 96/2/EC of 16 January 1996 amending Directive 90/338/EEC with regard to mobile and personal communications [1996] OJ L 20/59.

exclusive rights granted to a company entrusted with the provision of services of general economic interests. In light of the characteristics of its national market for telecommunication services and of the universal services carried out by Telecom Eireann (i.e. services of general economic interest), the Irish Government made use of that option and demanded from the Commission more time for the implementation of several of the obligations with which it was forced to comply under the mentioned directives.

The Irish Government asked for a two-year extension of the deadline until January 2000, to comply with the rule for the abolition of the exclusive rights granted to Telecom Eireann (the national telecom company) as regard the provision of voice telephony and underlying network infrastructure. It also asked for a three-years extension of the deadline for the lifting of restrictions present in the already liberalized telecommunication services and in particular the network services, the granting of access to and maintenance of infrastructures, and services for the sharing of the network and important facilities.

The Irish Government justified its request by the significant capital investment (and debts) incurred by Telecom Eireann in preceding years for the development of the network and the consequent constraints suffered in the ability to achieve the "necessary structural adjustments, particularly of tariffs, because of those high debt levels, the high cost of delivering telecommunications services in Ireland, and Telecom Eireann's high cost-structure."[13] As a consequence, Telecom Eireann needed, according to the Irish Government, further structural adjustments in order to be able to effectively compete in a fully competitive market. Among others, the structural modifications to be achieved concerned further development of the Irish telecommunication network, the adjustment of Telecom Eireann's tariff structure, further developments of Telecom Eireann home and international services, and adjustment in its cost and management structure in order to change it into a "market-driven and customer-focused organization."[14]

b. Origin of the case

On 15 May 1996 the Irish Government delivered to the Commission requests for an additional implementation period for the implementation of Directive 90/338/EEC[15] on competition in the market for telecommunication services which was later partly amended by Commission Directive 96/2/EC.

c. Economic analysis

After having recognized the public economic interest nature of the services provided by Telecom Eireann in the Irish market for telecommunication, the Commission observed that "[t]he question which falls to be considered is therefore the extent to which the requested temporary exclusion of all competition from other economic operators is necessary in order to allow the holder of the exclusive right to continue performing its task of general interest and in particular to have the benefit of *economically acceptable conditions*. The main

---

13   Recital 2-2.1 of the decision.
14   Recital 2-2.2 of the decision.
15   Commission Directive 90/338/EEC of 28 June 1990 on competition in the market for telecommunication services [1990] OL L 192/10.

starting point for such an examination must be the premise that the obligation to perform the . . . services [of general economic interest] in conditions of economic equilibrium presupposes that it will be possible to offset less profitable sectors against the profitable sectors and hence justifies a restriction of competition from individual undertakings where the economically profitable sectors are concerned."[16]

The Commission reasoned that had those restrictions not been imposed, competitors would turn to other more profitable sectors, leaving the undertaking entrusted with the public service obligation at a significant competitive disadvantage.

The concept of *financial viability* used by the Commission in the previous landmark case is here broadened and specified and it follows the interpretation given to the conditions of applicability of Article 106(2) in several interventions of the European Courts. According to the ECJ "it is not necessary in order for the conditions for the application of Article 90(2) of the Treaty to be fulfilled, that the financial balance or economic viability of the undertaking entrusted with the operation of a service of general economic interest should be threatened. It is sufficient that, in the absence of the rights at issue, it would not be possible for the undertaking to perform the particular tasks entrusted to it . . . under *economically acceptable conditions*"[17] The actual meaning of the expression *economically acceptable conditions* is still the object of debate and different interpretation.[18]

In its assessment of the consequences resulting from granting exclusive rights to Telecom Eireann, the Commission noted that besides ensuring a universal voice telephony and telecommunication network, the company was able to finance more cheaply investments for the digitalization of the network but at the same time to maintain "higher tariffs and less efficient cost structure – in particular due to overstaffing – than it would be in a competitive environment."[19]

Considering then the specific arguments produced by Ireland to sustain the request for additional periods and the alleged necessary structural adjustments, the Commission considered them in the light of three different circumstances, namely the need for further balancing of the tariffs, the low telephone density characterizing the Irish market and the high debt and cost structure of Telecom Eireann.

In its assessment of Telecom Eireann's actions taken in the first phase of the liberalization period and of the effort made by the firm to achieve efficiencies and to allow the opening up of the market to competitors, the Commission carried out a detailed analysis of the current conditions of the Irish market for telecommunications.

---

16 Recitals 12 ands 13 of the decision. Emphasis added.
17 Case C-115–117/97 *Brentjens* [1999] ECR I-6025, recital 107. Emphasis added.
18 Another important distinction made by the Commission concerning the conditions for the applicability of the exception pursuant to Article 106(2) regarded the provision – by the company entrusted with the provision of services of general economic interest – of specific services dissociable from the service of general interest, not necessary for the performance of the latter and that therefore do not constitute the object of exclusive rights, see recital 15 of the decision. In this, the Commission fully acknowledged the principle stated by the ECJ in recital 19 of the leading case *Corbeau*, see *supra* note 3.
19 Recital 19 of the decision.

Concerning the first-mentioned circumstance, i.e. the rebalancing of the tariffs, the Commission considered firstly the ongoing efforts made by Ireland to level the tariffs and bring prices closer to costs, secondly the effort to decouple more and more the price charged from the distance of the communication facilitated by technological advances, and thirdly the adjustments made to align revenues and costs. With successful liberalization at stake, the Commission considered it reasonable to grant Telecom Eireann extra time to prepare the firm for a fully competitive market, because had entry by other foreign providers been allowed prematurely, the progress that had been made in the meanwhile would have been seriously jeopardized.[20]

Similar considerations recognizing the ongoing efforts in the direction of making the company more efficient, increasingly productive, with better-dimensioned staff, as well as in reducing the debt and structurally modifying the financial situation, were made by the Commission in its assessment of the Irish market. The investments made in the previous year and the necessity for additional time in order to fully recoup them were taken into due consideration. All the above-mentioned considerations concerning the Irish market existed in relation to the two other indicated benchmarks, namely debt and cost structure and the density of telephony lines on the Irish market. These additional results led the Commission to conclude that it was necessary to grant the Irish telecom company additional implementation periods (also regarding the deadline for lifting the restrictions on already liberalized markets).[21]

These decisions, that were subsequently also adopted with respect to other Member States similarly asking for extensions of their liberalization efforts, showed, on the one hand, the appreciation by the Commission of the difficulties encountered by both Member States and companies in liberalizing long-lasting State monopolies. At the same time they demonstrate the rigorous liberalization policy and the continuous effort demanded by the Commission to achieve intermediate targets in all aspects of the telecommunication industry and create competitive markets.

d. Fines, remedies, and conditions enclosed

- Obligation for the Irish Government to publish all measures necessary for lifting the restriction on the liberalized telecommunication services (network, infrastructure, and facilities and sites sharing).
- Obligation for the Irish Government to publish before 1 April 1998 and to adopt before 1 November 1998 all measures intended to be adopted in order to fully implement competition in the relevant telecommunication markets by 1 January 2000.
- Obligation for the Irish Government to notify to the Commission before 1 January 1999 the draft licenses for voice telephony and/or underlying network providers.
- Obligation for the Irish Government to publish before 1 April 1999 the licensing conditions for all services and the interconnection charges in accordance with the relevant European Directives.

---

20   See recitals 22–27 of the decision.   21   See in particular recitals 28–36 of the decision.

- Obligation for the Irish Government to grant before 1 November 1999 licenses in order to make possible the provision under competitive conditions of voice telephony and of unrestricted interconnection of mobile networks.
- Obligation for the Irish Government to inform the Commission about all the measures adopted in order to achieve the required transparency concerning the Telecom Eireann's involvement in investments outside Ireland and to avoid further extension (due to statutory protection) of Telecom Eireann's dominant position in the public payphone market and on the TV cable market.

e. Further developments of the case

None.

8 Mergers and acquisitions

A Introduction

Mergers and acquisitions (M&As) can have important effects on competitive conditions. At the same time, they can generate significant efficiencies, and so are often a natural part of industry evolution. In economic theory, an important distinction is made between horizontal, vertical, and conglomerate mergers. In horizontal mergers, there is a distinction between two types of possible anticompetitive effects: unilateral effects and coordinated effects. In vertical mergers, there are concerns about upstream or downstream foreclosure of rivals as part of the strategic considerations to merge. In conglomerate mergers, there may be combinations of these concerns at play.

Empirical reviews of the *ex post* effects of mergers on profitability, sales, and market shares have found that the economic effects of mergers can vary considerably from case to case.[1]

The FEU Treaty does not provide any specific rule expressly installing merger control in Europe. Consequently, until the adoption of the first Merger Regulation in 1989,[2] the control of potential anticompetitive effects of mergers could be achieved only by application of Article 101 and Article 102. As a result, the merging parties did not have a strict obligation to notify their merger plans to the Commission. Only by means of a broad interpretation of the Treaty provisions could anticompetitive mergers be controlled. Article 102, in particular, was utilized as an instrument to challenge possible abuses of dominance after the strengthening of an already dominant position via acquisition of competitors in markets in which competition is not sufficiently protected by, for example, low barriers to entry and supply-side substitution.

At the request of the Commission, in 1963 a number of experts investigated the problem of concentrations in the common market. On the basis of the experts' report the Commission in 1966 published its "Memorandum on the Concentration of Enterprises in the Common Market,"[3] in which it argued for the creation of a system of *ex ante* control of concentrations in Europe. The Memorandum concluded that the absence of such a system inhibited an effective competition control in Europe.

The first attempt by the Commission to effectively implement merger control in Europe was in the *Continental Can* case on the basis of an extensive application of Article 102. After the adoption

---

1 See, for example, Gugler *et al.* (2003).
2 Council Regulation (EEC) No. 4064/89 etc. of 21 December 1989 on the control of concentrations between undertakings [1989] OJ L 395/1, subsequently amended by Council Regulation (EC) No 1310/97 of 30 June 1997 amending Regulation (EEC) No. 4064/89 etc. on the control of concentrations between undertakings [1997] OJ L 40/17.
3 In EEC Competition Series Studies, no. 3.

of the *Continental Can* decision[4] in 1972 – a decision that was later substantially confirmed by the ECJ – the *ex post* applicability of Article102 to mergers strengthening dominant positions was established. Subsequently, the Commission adopted a legislative proposal for a merger control regulation in 1973. After extensive debate and several rejections by the Council, the first Merger Regulation was approved in 1989.

The 1989 Merger Regulation was substantially revised, resulting in the publication of a new Merger Regulation in 2004.[5] The regulation widened the scope for application to more undesired restrictive effects of mergers. Particularly, while in the first regulation only concentration creating or strengthening a dominant position with a consequent impediment of effective competition was prohibited, under the new Article 2(3) of the Merger Regulation, no merger – at least for non-coordinated effects[6] – would be cleared by the Commission which in any way significantly impedes effective competition in the internal market (the SIEC test).[7] The new approach endorsed in the Merger Regulation acknowledged, therefore, the need to be able to prohibit welfare-decreasing mergers, even when they do not create dominant positions.[8]

The Merger Regulation[9] as well as the ensuing Commission Guidelines[10] reflect developments in legal and economic thinking about M&As. These came to stress, among other things, that concentration is not always a suitable measure for competition, in particular not in bidding markets and markets that are contested by supply-side substitution or potential entrants. Also, there was increasing regard for the importance of countervailing power, potential competition, and the likely dynamic future developments of markets, on the basis of which parties could have mergers approved that would raise competition concerns strictly from the point of view of market share analysis. Furthermore, the horizontal merger guidelines include possibilities for merging parties to invoke an efficiency argument for mergers that raise antitrust concerns.[11] The non-horizontal merger guidelines recognize the efficiency benefits that can come from the vertical integration of business, while at the same time offering a coherent structure to assess anticompetitive concerns related to the input foreclosure and customer foreclosure strategies that may underlie vertical merger plans.

4   See *infra*.
5   Council Regulation (EC) No 139/2004 on the control of concentrations between undertakings [2004] OJ L 24/1.
6   Recital 25 of the introduction of the Merger Regulation states: "... The notion of "significant impediment of effective competition" in Article 2(2) and (3) should be interpreted as extending, beyond the concept of dominance, only to anticompetitive effects of a concentration resulting from the non-coordinated behavior of undertakings which would not have a dominant position on the market concerned."
7   The scope of the applicability of the so-called SIEC test (Significant Impediment of Effective Competition) was subject to wide debate in Europe. For guidelines on the intended use by the Commission of the SIEC test, see Commission Guidelines on the assessment of horizontal mergers under the Council Regulation on the control of concentration between undertakings [2004] OJ C 31/5.
8   In *T-Mobile Austria/tele.ring* the Commission has, as result of the application of the SIEC test, for the first time raised concerns related to the merger between two firms that would have not created or strengthened a dominant position but that nonetheless, was considered likely to produce non-coordinated effects on the market. The merging companies were the second and the third largest operators on the market and even after the merger would have not become the market leader. The Commission cleared the merger following the submission of commitments by the parties. See *T-Mobile Austria/tele.ring* Commission decision of 26 April 2006, Case COMP/M.3916.
9   See Article 2(1)(b) of the Merger Regulation(s) cited above.
10 Guidelines on the assessment of horizontal mergers under the Council Regulation on the control of concentration between undertakings [2004] OJ C 31/5, and Guidelines on the assessment of non-horizontal mergers under the Council Regulation on the control of concentrations between undertakings [2008] OJ C 265/6.
11 Guidelines on the assessment of horizontal mergers under the Council Regulation on the control of concentration between undertakings [2004] OJ C 31/5, points 76–88.

The Merger Regulation applies only to mergers that satisfy a double jurisdictional test. Firstly, the Regulation intends to control concentrations that result in a "lasting change in the control of the undertakings concerned and therefore in the structure of the market."[12] Control over the merging entity is deemed to occur when undertaking(s) can exercise *decisive influence* on it. The interpretation given to the concepts of concentration, change in control on a lasting basis, and decisive influence is defined in Article 3 of the Regulation. Secondly, since the Regulation applies only to mergers affecting the structure of the internal market, only those having a *Community dimension* are appraised under the Regulation rules. The concept of "Community dimension" is defined in Article 1 according to a turnover criterion and its allocation among a (minimum) number of Member States.[13]

Since the 1989 Merger Regulation entered into force, the Commission has adopted in total over 3,500 merger decisions at different procedural stages. The sheer volume of decisions makes it impossible to present all merger cases using the methodology so far adopted for the book. There are simply too many European merger decisions to classify and systematically describe all of them by economic rationale. Instead, we present a selected number of the Commission's merger decisions to reflect its merger policy in two parts. The first part of the chapter deals with all decisions concerning mergers adopted before the 1989 Merger Regulation entered into force. This relatively small set of merger cases illustrates the Commission's merger control *avant la lettre*, revealing its relevance for later regulatory developments and enforcement practices. The full set of merger decisions adopted before 1989 is listed.

The second part of the chapter presents a select sample of merger decisions more recently adopted by the European Commission that are particularly interesting from the point of view of economic analysis. These decisions have been selected as illustrations of the current approach in the assessment of effects of merger on competition. In many cases, their fate on appeal before the European Courts has been decisive in defining the current approach under EU law toward M&As, for example the level of legal and economic proof required in the analysis of the competitive impact of a merger. In particular, section 8.1 discusses unilateral effects and section 8.2 coordinated effects in horizontal mergers. Section 8.3 considers vertical and conglomerate mergers. Section 8.4 presents cases on minority acquisitions while section 8.5 discusses cases in which specific economic defenses were mounted, in particular the failing firm defense and the efficiency defense. Section 8.6 concludes this chapter with cases selected for their interesting remedies. See also annex III for a list of all blocked merger cases.

B Applicable EU legislation

Council Regulation (EC) No 139/2004 on the control of concentrations between undertakings [2004] OJ L 24/1.

---

12   Recital 20 of the Merger Regulation cited above.
13   "A concentration has a Community dimension where: (a) the combined aggregate worldwide turnover of all the undertakings concerned is more than EUR 5,000 million; and (b) the aggregate Community-wide turnover of each of at least two of the undertakings concerned is more than EUR 250 million, unless each of the undertakings concerned achieves more than two-thirds of its aggregate Community-wide turnover within one and the same Member State. A concentration that does not meet the thresholds laid down in paragraph 2 has a Community dimension where: (a) the combined aggregate worldwide turnover of all the undertakings concerned is more than EUR 2,500 million; (b) in each of at least three Member States, the combined aggregate turnover of all the undertakings concerned is more than EUR 100 million; (c) in each of at least three Member States included for the purpose of point (b), the aggregate turnover of each of at least two of the undertakings concerned is more than EUR 25 million; and (d) the aggregate Community-wide turnover of each of at least two of the undertakings concerned is more than EUR 100 million, unless each of the undertakings concerned achieves more than two-thirds of its aggregate Community-wide turnover within one and the same Member State." Articles 1(2) and 1(3) of the Merger Regulation cited above.

Guidelines on the assessment of horizontal mergers under Council Regulation on the control of concentration between undertakings [2004] OJ C 31/5.

Guidelines on the assessment of non-horizontal mergers under the Council Regulation on the control of concentrations between undertakings [2008] OJ C 265/6.

Commission Notice on the definition of the relevant market [1997] OJ C 372/3.

Commission Notice on remedies acceptable under Council Regulation (EC) No 139/2004 and under Commission Regulation (EC) No 802/2004 [2008] OJ C 267/1.

Commission Notice on restrictions directly related and necessary to concentrations ("ancillary restraints") [2005] OJ C 56/2005.

Commission consolidated jurisdictional notice under Council Regulation (EC) 139/2004 on the control of concentrations between undertakings, published on 10 July 2007 on DG Comp website.[14]

C Related economics texts

Bishop and Walker (2009), chapter 7
Carlton and Perloff (2005), chapter 2, paragraph 2 and chapter 19, paragraph 3(5)
Church and Ware (2000), chapter 23
Martin (1994), chapters 9 and 10
Martin (2002), chapter 12
Motta (2004), chapters 5 and 7
Tirole (1988), paragraphs 4.6.2.1, 9.5, 9.6, and 9.7
Waldman and Jensen (2001), chapter 4

D Related legal texts

Bellamy and Child (2008), chapter 8
Jones and Sufrin (2008), chapter 12
Ritter and Braun (2005), chapter 6
Whish (2008), chapters 20, 21, and 22

E Commission decisions in chronological order (adopted before 1989)•

Continental Can Company **Commission decision 72/71/EEC [1972] OJ L 7/25, Case IV/26.811**
SHV-Chevron Commission decision 75/95/EEC [1975] OJ L 29/20, Case IV/26.872
Reuter/BASF Commission decision 76/743/EEC [1976] OJ L 254/40, Case IV/28.996

---

14 The consolidated jurisdictional notice has replaced the previous four jurisdictional notices. There were Commission Notice on the concept of full-function joint venture [1998] OJ C 66/1; Commission Notice on the concept of concentration [1998] OJ L C 66/5; Commission Notice on the concept of undertakings concerned [1998] OJ C 66/14; Commission Notice on calculation of turnover [1998] OJ C 66/25.

• Decisions displayed in **bold** are described in the section.

Mecaniver/PPG Commission decision 85/78/EEC [1985] OJ L 35/54, Case IV/30.666
Tetra Pak I (BTG-license) Commission decision 88/501/EEC [1988] OJ L 272/27, Case IV/31.043
Metaleurop SA Commission decision 90/363/EEC [1990] OJ L 179/41, Case IV/32.846

F   Economic landmark case

F.1   *Continental Can Company* Commission decision 72/71/EEC [1972] OJ L 7/25

Relevance: In the absence of specific rules enabling the Commission to conduct merger control, the Commission established in this landmark decision the principle according to which the strengthening of a dominant position via a merger with a competing firm can constitute an abuse of dominance under specific market circumstances.

- Case IV/26.811
- **Decision:** Infringement of Article 102 FEU Treaty
- **Decision addressee(s):**
    - Continental Can Company Inc., *United States of America*
- **Report route:** Commission decision of 9 April 1970 to start proceedings on its own initiative
- **Date of the decision:** 9 December 1971
- **Competition Commissioner:** A. Borschette
- **Relevant product market:** Metal packaging materials
- **Relevant geographical market:** Germany and Benelux
- **Description of the case**
    - a. **Relevant facts**
        Continental Can Company Inc. (Continental Can) was the world's largest producer of metal packaging and a relevant producer of paper and plastic packaging as well as of the machinery required for their production. Since at the time of the decision, Continental Can held an 85.8% stake in its German competitor Schmalbach-Lubeca-Werke AG (SLW), which was the main producer of light metal packaging in Europe and itself held a dominant position on the German market for several metal package products, Continental Can was considered to have effectively acquired control over SLW.

        At the same time, Continental Can made a takeover bid for the shares of Thomassen and Drijver-Verblifa NV (TDV) via its wholly owned holding company Europemballage Corporation and acquired 91.1% of TDV equity as a result. Prior to the takeover, TDV had already been Continental Can's licensee for the Netherlands and was the largest producer of metal packaging in the Benelux countries. Furthermore, Continental Can had transferred all its interests in SLW to Europemballage Corporation, further strengthening the relation between SLW and TDV.

        Moreover Continental Can owned majority or minority equity participations in some thirty companies operating in the same production sector and had stipulated licensing and technical assistance agreements with fifty-one companies operating in the packaging industry.

b. Origin of the case

On 9 April 1970 the Commission adopted on its own initiative a decision to initiate proceedings against Continental Can and its holding company Europemballage Corporation in respect of the acquisition by the latter of the majority of the share capital of its competitor Thomassen and Drijver-Verblifa NV.

c. Economic analysis

This decision is of paramount importance in EU competition law enforcement, because the Commission asserted the principle that in the absence of specific rules explicitly appointing powers to conduct merger control, it could conduct an *ex post* control on mergers between companies dominating a certain market via Article 102 FEU. As a result the "acquisition of control over a competitor" and the consequent strengthening of a dominant position might constitute an abuse of dominance in its own right irrespective of any other abusive conduct in which the dominant firm may have been engaged.

This ground-breaking decision was upheld by the ECJ in the appeal brought by Continental Can and became known as the *Continental Can Doctrine*. With regard to the fact that firms were not obliged to notify their acquisitions, the doctrine constituted the primary foundation upon which EU merger control rested until the entry into force of the first Merger Regulation.

The Commission stated that in some circumstances the acquisition of majority participations in a competing firm by a dominant firm could constitute an abuse of dominance. According to the Commission the strengthening effect that derives would further reduce the already low degree of competitiveness on the dominated market. The described effect is even stronger when the acquired rival company is itself in a very strong position in its market (as was the case with TDV in the Benelux) and where such a market is potentially in tough competition with the market dominated by the acquiring firm (as in the case of the Benelux market and the German market).[15]

The Commission concluded in its assessment of the acquisition that its effect was the elimination of any residual competition between two large firms that had until that moment been competing with each other. In the absence of the takeover – had they not been constrained by the dominant position of Continental Can – TDV could have constituted an important alternative for German users given TDV's capacities and productivity, and the closeness of the two geographical areas involved. Similarly, purchasers in the Benelux countries would have been affected by the irreversible change of supply and a reduction of possible alternatives to TDV's supplies.[16]

The finding of an abusive effect of the strengthening of the dominant position was reinforced by the absence of supply substitutability, which was in particular due to the size, structure, and impact (or lack thereof) of the few remaining small competitors.[17]

The Commission's reasoning was confirmed by the ECJ which clarified that "[t]he restraint of competition which is prohibited if it is the result of

15   See recitals 22–25 of the decision.   17   See recital 30 of the decision.
16   See recital 29 of the decision.

behavior falling under Article 85, cannot become permissible by the fact that such behavior succeeds under the influence of a dominant undertaking and results in the merger of the undertakings concerned. In the absence of explicit provisions one cannot assume that the Treaty, which prohibits in Article 85 certain decisions of ordinary association of undertakings restricting competition without eliminating it, permits in Article 86 that undertakings, after merging into an organic unity, should reach such a dominant position that any serious chance of competition is practically rendered impossible . . . In any case Articles 85 and 86 cannot be interpreted in such a way that they contradict each other, because they serve to achieve the same aim."[18]

d. Fines, remedies, and conditions enclosed
  − Obligations for Continental Can to bring the infringements to an end and to submit to the Commission proposals aimed at the full implementation of the injunction.

e. Further developments of the case
In Case 6/72 *Europemballage Corporation and Continental Can Company Inc. v. Commission* [1975] ECR 215, the decision was annulled for lack of sufficient legal substantiation of the allegation in the Commission's reasoning. Nonetheless the ECJ confirmed the idea that the strengthening of a dominant position by the acquisition of a rival can constitute abusive conduct.

8.1 Horizontal mergers: unilateral effects

A Introduction

Unilateral effects of a horizontal merger result from the reduced number of independent competitors that remain after two (or more) of them integrate their business objectives. In principle, both the merged entity and its remaining rivals obtain some market power and potential to raise prices to the detriment of consumers in the presence of fewer or weaker competitive constraints. That is, with fewer competitors in the market, firms in imperfectly oligopolistic competition can often realize higher mark-ups. Even though the relationship between market concentration and the ability to price above costs is not straightforward, the competition authorities usually take the pre-merger level of concentration in the market and the change of concentration due to the merger into consideration when assessing the merger for approval. Concentration is typically measured by the Herfindahl–Hirschman Index (HHI), which is the sum of the squared market shares of all firms active in the relevant market. Its absolute level is typically used in combination with the change in the HHI that would obtain if the merger were consummated, ΔHHI.[19] In addition,

18   Case 6/72 *Europemballage Corporation and Continental Can Company Inc. v. Commission* [1975] ECR 215, recital 25.
19   In EU merger control the general principle given by the Commission in the Horizontal Merger Guidelines is that a post-merger HHI below 1,000 is unlikely to identify horizontal concerns deriving from the merger; when the HHI is between 1,000 and 2,000, a ΔHHI above 250 is considered as possibly causing competitive concerns; in case of HHIs above 2,000, ΔHHI above 150 shows that a merger is likely to create competitive concerns. These measures are considered by the Commission as indicative of its general approach that can be modified depending on the special circumstances of the case. See Guidelines on the assessment of horizontal mergers under the Council Regulation on the control of concentration between undertakings [2004] OJ C 31/5, points 19–21. The US merger guidelines of 1982 used comparable numbers with the US Department of Justice likely to challenge mergers in case of a combination of a (postmerger) HHI of above 1,800 and a ΔHHI of above 100.

the assessment of unilateral market power can include analyses of entry barriers, countervailing power, and demand variables.

B Applicable EU Legislation

No special legislation applicable. For applicable legislation see Chapter 8 paragraph B.

C Related economics texts

Bishop and Walker (2009), chapter 7, paragraphs 7.19–7.38
Carlton and Perloff (2005), chapter 2, paragraph 2 and chapter 19, paragraph 3(5)
Church and Ware (2000), chapter 23
Martin (1994), chapters 9 and 10
Martin (2002), chapter 12
Motta (2004), chapters 5 and 7
Tirole (1988), paragraphs 4.6.2.1, 9.5, 9.6, and 9.7
Waldman and Jensen (2001), chapter 4

D Related legal texts

Bellamy and Child (2008), chapter 8, paragraph 4(D)
Jones and Sufrin (2008), chapter 12, paragraph 5(D, iii, c)
Ritter and Braun (2005), chapter 6
Whish (2008), chapters 20, paragraph 6(B, I, a) and 21, paragraph 5(C, ii, a)

E Selection of commission decisions in chronological order•

Aerospatiale-Alenia/De Havilland **Commission decision 91/619/EEC [1991] OJ L 334/42, Case IV/M.053** (Martin, 2004, pp. 327–9; Bishop and Walker, 2009, 7.05 and 7.88)
Volvo/Scania **Commission decision 2001/403/EC [2000] OJ L 143/74, Case COMP/M.1672** (Motta, 2004, p. 239, n. 24, and 295; Bishop and Walker, 2009, 15.26–15.28 and 15.38)
SEB/Moulinex **Commission decision SG (2002) D/228087 of 8 January 2002, non-opposition notice in OJ C 49/18, Case COMP/M.2621**

F Economic landmark cases

F.1 *Aerospatiale-Alenia/De Havilland* **Commission decision 91/619/EEC [1991] OJ L 334/42**

Relevance: The decision represents the first prohibition decision in the history of merger control in Europe. The merger was held under the Merger Regulation to strengthen the dominant

---

•   For this section, instead of a complete list of Commission decisions in chronological order, we present only a selection of merger decisions that have been significant for the development of European merger control. Decisions displayed in **bold type** are described in the section. Reference is made in brackets and **bold type** to the relevant section in which the decision is extensively described as a landmark case. When decisions are referenced and/or described in some detail in one or more of the economic textbooks, reference in brackets is also made to the relevant part(s) of those texts.

position of Aerospatiale-Alenia and to generate unilateral effects incompatible with the common market. Among other arguments, the Commission relied in its reasoning heavily on the high combined post-merger market share. In this decision the Commission also rejected an efficiency defense made by the parties. The Commission was reported to have been strongly divided over this decision.[20]

- Case IV/M.053
- **Decision:** Prohibition decision pursuant to Article 8(3) of the Merger Regulation
- **Decision addressee(s):**
  - Aerospatiale SNI, *France*
  - Alenia-Aeritalia&Selenia Spa, *Italy*
- **Report route:** Notification of the proposed concentration on 13 May 1991
- **Date of the decision:** 2 October 1991
- **Competition Commissioner:** L. Brittan
- **Relevant product market:** Regional turboprop aircraft with 20 to 70 seats
- **Relevant geographical market:** Global market excluding China and Eastern Europe
- **Description of the case**
  a. **Relevant facts**

  Aerospatiale SNI (Aerospatiale) is a French company active in the civil and military aviation industries. Alenia-Aeritalia (Alenia) is an Italian company also active in the aviation industries. The two companies jointly control the European group Avions de Transport Regionale (ATR), set up in 1982 to jointly design, develop, manufacture, and sell regional transport aircraft. De Havilland is a Canadian division of Boeing and is engaged exclusively in the production of regional turboprop aircraft. Aerospatiale and Alenia wanted to jointly buy De Havilland and run the company through a jointly controlled operating company.

  In defining the relevant product market, the Commission distinguished three submarkets. It distinguished between small turboprop aircraft with 20–39 seats; medium aircraft with 40–59 seats, and large aircraft with 60 or more seats.[21] The Commission analysis was based on four observations. Firstly, the majority of the competitors asked during the investigation agreed with the segmentation into the three submarkets. Secondly, the aircraft offered on the market tended to cluster around the different number of seats indicated by the Commission. What is more, each of the main producers in any segment of the market was also present in the other segments with a different and competing product. This implied that the products belonged to different markets. Finally, a certain degree of supply-side substitutability existed but could only effectively influence market behavior in the medium/long term.[22]

  In calculating the market share of the firms involved, the Commission took into account not only future orders, as suggested by the parties, but also existing aircraft and discontinued aircraft types still present on the market and in use. As a result, in the post-merger market Aerospatiale and Alenia together with De

---

20   See, e.g., Reynolds, M. (1991), "The de Havilland Case: A Watershed for EC Merger Control," *International Financial Law Review*, December 1991, 21–23.

21   See recitals 8–12 of the decision.   22   See in particular recitals 13 and 14 of the decision.

Havilland would have achieved 64 percent of the world market and 72 percent of the European market in the 40–59 seat segment. Similarly, they would have acquired 76 percent of the global market and 74 percent of the European large aircraft market. Adding the three segments together and treating them as one market, the merging parties would have had 50 percent of the global market excluding China and Eastern Europe and 65 percent of the European market.[23]

b. Origin of the case

On 13 May 1991, pursuant to Article 4 of Regulation 4064/89, Aerospatiale and Alenia-Aeritalia notified to the Commission the proposed joint acquisition of De Havilland's assets. On 12 June 1991, with a formal decision, the Commission found the envisaged merger as possibly strengthening a dominant position and initiated proceedings pursuant to Article 6(1)(c) of the Merger Regulation.

c. Economic analysis

In its assessment of the effect of the concentration on competition, the Commission firstly considered the increase in market share of the parties. In the medium and large aircraft segments of the market, another concern that arose was that next to the very high combined market share of the parties, the closest competitor (Fokker) held a mere 22 percent of the market. In the face of a growing trend in the market toward larger aircrafts, the merger gave the significant advantage to the merging parties of higher flexibility concerning prices and sales strategy.[24]

Another significant unilateral effect produced by the merger would have been the elimination of De Havilland as a competitor. Until that time the latter was indeed the most successful competitor of ATR in terms of aircraft sold and had an increasingly flourishing business. It could have been a significant competitor for Alenia and Aerospatiale, as observed in the acquirers' pre-merger review of De Havilland.[25]

Another effect of the concentration would have been that the merging entity would be the only one able to offer a full range of products on the market. This would give ATR/De Havilland a significant advantage over all competitors. Statements made during the oral hearing confirmed that "[f]rom the demand side, airlines derive cost advantages from buying different types from the same seller."[26] Moreover the Commission noted that "according to a study submitted by the parties, it is argued that the inability of a manufacturer to offer a full range of seating capacities under the same umbrella may harm the demand for other existing aircraft of that manufacturer . . . One of the stated main strategic objectives of the parties in acquiring De Havilland is to obtain full coverage of the whole range of commuter aircraft [which will] reduce considerably the risk associated with future demand."[27]

At the same time the Commission maintained that "ATR would considerably broaden its customer base after the concentration"[28] and that the remaining competitors in the medium and large sectors were relatively weak.[29] Based on finding such market conditions, the Commission concluded "the new entity

23 See recitals 21–26 of the decision.
24 See recitals 28–30 of the decision.
25 See recital 31 of the decision.
26 Recital 32 of the decision.

27 Recital 32 of the decision.
28 Recital 33 of the decision.
29 See recitals 34–42 of the decision.

could act to a significant extent independently of its competitors and customers, and would thus have a dominant position on the commuter market."[30]

Nonetheless the Commission recognized that "a concentration which leads to the creation of a dominant position may however be compatible with the common market . . . if there exists strong evidence that this position is only temporary and would be quickly eroded because of [the] high probability of strong market entry."[31] Therefore the Commission went on to verify if there were entry barriers in the market. Based on evidence showing the maturity of the market, the Commission found that even actors already present in a related industry would face high barriers to develop a new commuter aircraft, in that such plans would require high sunk costs and delays in getting the required approval to design and test the aircraft and to receive regulatory approval. The overall period required for the research, production and distribution of the product would not be shorter than six–seven years, which would have increased the risk for new entrants. As the Commission noted "a new manufacturer may come too late into the market to catch the expected period of relatively high demand."[32] The presence of such high sunk costs and of the risk in entering the market made new entry very unlikely "in the foreseeable future."[33]

In this early merger decision, the Commission also took into consideration the efficiency defense by the merging parties. As reported in the decision "[t]he parties argue that one of their objectives in acquiring De Havilland is to reduce costs. The potential cost savings arising from the concentration which have been identified amount to only some 5 million ECU per year. [These] would arise from rationalizing parts procurement, marketing and product support."[34] In that regard, the Commission observed that regardless of any consideration of the relevance of those cost savings for the assessment of the concentration under the Merger Regulation, those savings were of "negligible impact on the overall operation"[35] and could have been achieved simply by better management. Moreover the operation would have not contributed to increasing technical and economic progress as required by Article 2(1)(b) of the Merger Regulation in order to constitute a potential efficiency argument. To the contrary, the creation of a strong actor likely to become a monopolist in the future would have affected consumers by a significant reduction in the product choice.[36] Therefore the Commission rejected the proposed efficiency argument and declared, for the first time in the history of merger control in Europe, the concentration incompatible with the common market.

d. **Fines, remedies, and conditions enclosed**
None.

e. **Further developments of the case**
None.

F.2   *Volvo/Scania* Commission decision 2001/403/EC, [2001] OJ L 143/74

Relevance: The decision illustrates the Commission's analysis of a single-firm dominance in a mature market. While analyzing the effect of the proposed merger the Commission

---

30   Recital 51 of the decision.
31   Recital 53 of the decision.
32   Recital 56 of the decision. See also recital 55 of the decision.
33   Recital 63 of the decision.

34   Recital 65 of the decision.
35   Recital 65 of the decision.
36   See recitals 68 and 69 of the decision.

puts more emphasis on unilateral effects as the key factor to support a finding of dominance. Nevertheless, the Commission assessment is focused not only on unilateral effects. The Commission stressed that Volvo and Scania were each other's closest competitors.

- Case COMP/M.1672
- **Decision:** Concentration declared incompatible with the common market and the functioning of the EEA Agreement
- **Decision addressee(s):**
    – AB Volvo, *Sweden*
- **Report route:** Notification of the proposed concentration on 22 September 1999
- **Date of the decision:** 14 May 2000
- **Competition Commissioner:** M. Monti
- **Relevant product market:** Heavy trucks and buses
- **Relevant geographical market:** National market in Denmark, Finland, Ireland, Norway, and Sweden.
- **Description of the case**
    a. **Relevant facts**

    Volvo and Scania are both leading companies in the manufacturing of buses, marine, and industrial engines. Volvo also sells trucks whereas Scania focuses on heavy trucks.[37] Volvo acquired within an agreement on 6 August 1999 a controlling stake in Scania. Volvo notified the concentration to the Commission. It explained that the rationale of the merger would be to sustain competition in emerging markets for heavy trucks and buses.[38]

    To define the relevant product market, the Commission divided the truck market into separate submarkets: the market for light duty trucks (below 5 tonnes), medium duty trucks (5–16 tonnes) and heavy trucks (above 16 tonnes).[39] Firstly, technical requirements, like the number of axles or the engine type, differ between trucks with a tonnage lower than 16 tonnes and trucks with a tonnage above 16 tonnes. Different technical configurations are linked to higher requirements on durability and operating costs. Secondly, those technical configurations are of key importance for the buyer and therefore also marketed to different categories of customer. In addition, different production lines are used for the production, which relates to the existence of different product markets. In defining the relevant geographical market, the Commission focused on the segment of heavy trucks in the markets of Sweden, Norway, Finland, Ireland, and Denmark.[40] It concluded that the market for heavy trucks is still national, for several reasons: firstly, there exist price divergences between Member States.[41] Even though significant price differences do also exist between neighboring countries, the purchase of trucks is still made on a national level.[42] The Commission points out that "if the market were wider than national it would be reasonable to assume that buyers of heavy-trucks would take advantage of the existing price differences and buy . . . in [a] neighboring country."[43] Secondly, customer preferences and technical requirements differ between Member States.[44] Furthermore, the importance of a distribution and

---

37 See recitals 4 and 5 of the decision.
38 See recital 7 of the decision.
39 See recitals 14–18 of the decision.
40 See recital 31 of the decision.

41 See recital 43 of the decision.
42 See recital 38 of the decision.
43 See recital 49 of the decision.
44 See recitals 50–57 of the decision.

service network points in the same direction as the abovementioned factors that the relevant geographical market is national. In addition, the required truck-rollover test in Sweden was taken as an argument that the Scandinavian country constitutes a national market.

The bus market was also taken into account by the Commission. In contrast to Volvo's view, the Commission considered the relevant product market not as a single market for all buses but distinguished between city buses, intercity buses, and touring coaches.[45] Furthermore, the Commission stated that the markets are still of national scope.

b. Origin of the case
On 22 September 1999 Volvo notified to the Commission pursuant to Article 4 of the Regulation (4064/89, as amended by Regulation 1310/97) to acquire control over the whole of Scania AB by purchasing shares. On 25 October 1999, after concluding that the concentration would create or strengthen a dominant position, the Commission initiated Phase II pursuant to Article 6(1)(c) of the Merger Regulation.

c. Economic analysis
The Commission emphasizes that the crucial question in the assessment of the compatibility of the merger with the common market is "whether or not the proposed merger will lead to the creation or strengthening of a dominant position."[46] As key factors in this assessment the Commission used the market position of the undertakings concerned and their economic and financial power. It determined the creation or strengthening of a dominant position by using factors such as market shares, customer purchasing power, and entry barriers. In addition, an econometric study was requested in order "to measure what effect the merger would have on prices charged to heavy truck drivers."[47] This study attempted to act as a supplement to the way the market power was measured by the Commission, particularly in markets with a fragmented customer structure. Volvo, in contrast, argued that the Commission could not rely on this study. The Commission refrained subsequently from taking the results of the study into account.

To elaborate on the effect of the merger on competition, the Commission distinguished between the effect on the heavy truck market and the bus market. Firstly, the Commission stressed that the two undertakings were their respective closest competitors, for several reasons. Both are known for high-quality products and further for offering a global service network.[48] Moreover, both are Swedish firms. In addition the market positions had been stable within 1989–99 and there existed a symmetry between the market positions of the companies.[49]

Secondly, the Commission considered the increased market shares of the parties operating in the heavy truck market. The market shares of Scania and Volvo were calculated on a national market level. According to the Commission's analysis a dominant position on the markets for heavy trucks would be created in Sweden, Norway, Finland, and Ireland and, further, there were strong indications that this would be the case in Denmark as well.[50] The joint market share of the firms concerned would have been in the 49%–91% range

45 See recitals 220 and 225 of the decision.
46 See recital 71 of the decision.
47 See recital 72 of the decision

48 See recital 80 of the decision
49 See recitals 80–83 of the decision.
50 See recital 213 of the decision.

in Sweden, Denmark, Norway, Finland, and Ireland.[51] Taking the very strong market position of both undertakings into account the Commission stressed that "it is not likely that other truck manufacturers will exercise a significant competitive pressure on the parties."[52]

Possible unilateral effects caused by the concentration would be barriers for competitors to entry. An entry barrier was considered by the Commission in the form of the importance of a service network for truck manufacturers. A service network is essential for a truck manufacturer because its existence plays a role in the customers' purchase decision. As indicated by competitors, purchasers of heavy trucks need service points throughout the entire country, and service operated only in the main cities would not be sufficient.[53]

For new entrants the establishment of a whole service network at the beginning of its market activity might be only run with losses. Volvo and Scania could take advantage of their existing widespread network in the countries concerned.[54] Furthermore, in a post-merger situation the market share gap between the new undertaking and its closest competitors would increase and, hence, weaken such a possible countervailing power.

Another unilateral effect of the merger would be the newly created position to raise prices. Brand and customer loyalty are typical characteristics of the truck market. Both Volvo and Scania are known for their high-quality products. The merged undertaking could profit from this loyalty and raise prices.[55]

In addition, the merger would have had a strong impact on the bus market by creating the second largest bus manufacturer in Europe after DaimlerChrysler.[56] The Commission stated that the proposed concentration of Volvo and Scania would create a dominant position on the markets for touring coaches in Finland and the United Kingdom, for city and intercity buses in Sweden, Finland, Norway, and Denmark and further for city buses in Ireland.[57]

Pursuant to Article 8(2) of the Merger Regulation, Volvo proposed modifications on 21 February 2000 to ensure the adoption of a decision of clearance. For the heavy trucks and bus market Volvo proposed to open up the dealer and service network of Scania and Volvo in Sweden, Norway, Finland, and Denmark and for Volvo in Ireland.[58] Further, it proposed the divestiture of Volvo's 37% stake in Bilia AB, a distributor in the Nordic countries. The proposal included efforts to contact the Swedish Government in order to ensure abolition of the Swedish cab crash test that was considered to constitute an entry barrier for competitors to the Swedish market. Nevertheless, the Commission concluded "following contact with market participants, . . . that the proposed undertakings are insufficient to resolve competitive concerns resulting from the elimination of Volvo's main competitor, Scania."[59]

The Commission analyzed those proposals according to the effect they would have on the market. First, the proposal to abolish the Swedish cab crash test was considered to have little impact on the competitive situation.[60] Even though the vertical link to Bilia AB would be removed by the divestiture of Volvo's shares,

51 See recitals 105, 153, 165, and 186 of the decision.
52 See recital 108 of the decision.
53 See recital 83 of the decision.
54 See recital 134 of the decision.
55 See recital 110 of the decision.

56 See recital 214 of the decision.
57 See recital 331 of the decision.
58 See recital 332 of the decision.
59 See recital 338 of the decision.
60 See recital 339 of the decision.

the dependence between Bilia AB and Volvo would remain. The opening up of the service network was considered as an insufficient incentive to have an effect on the behavior of dealers to take an additional brand or even switch to another brand.[61] Furthermore, the proposed non-discrimination against dealers which took a new brand was criticised since it could not be monitored effectively. The same arguments apply to the proposal to open up the service network in the bus market.

A second proposal of Volvo on 7 March 2000 was dismissed by the Commission according to Article 18(2) of Regulation (EC) No. 447/98 because it had not been filed within the required three-month time limit.

d. Fines, remedies, and conditions enclosed

The Commission blocked the merger.

e. Further developments of the case

Volvo got permission by the Commission to acquire Renault Vehicule Industriels less than half a year later (Case IV/M.1980). Scania was recently acquired by Volkswagen and also in this case there was non-opposition (Case COMP/M.5157). Beforehand, MAN sought to take over Scania and got permission (CASE COMP/M.4336) but ended its hostile bidding.

F.3 *SEB/Moulinex* Commission decision SG (2002) D/228087 of 8 January 2002, non-opposition notice in OJ C 49/18

Relevance: Current Commission and CFI (now "the General Court") assessment of non-coordinated (unilateral) effects of mergers and possibility for the Commission to condition the approval of a proposed concentration on the implementation of behavioral remedies.

- Case COMP/M.2621
- **Decision:** Clearance decision with commitments and obligations enclosed pursuant to Article 6(2) of the Merger Regulation
- **Decision addressee(s):**
    - SEB SA, *France*
    - Moulinex SA, *France*
- **Report route:** Notification of the proposed concentration on 13 November 2001
- **Date of the decision:** 8 January 2002
- **Competition Commissioner:** M. Monti
- **Relevant product market:** Small electrical household appliances
- **Relevant geographical market:** National market in Austria, Belgium, Denmark, Finland, Germany, Greece, Italy, Norway, Spain, the Netherlands, Portugal, Sweden, United Kingdom, and Ireland
- **Description of the case**
    a. Relevant facts
    SEB and Moulinex are French companies active worldwide in the development, production, and marketing of small electrical household appliances.

    On September 2001 bankruptcy proceeding were initiated against the Moulinex group before the Tribunal de Commerce of Nanterre in France. According to French law administrators were appointed to assess whether

---

61 See recitals 341–348 of the decision.

Moulinex should have continued its business, transferred it to third parties, or liquidated it. The Administrators did not consider the continuation of the business activities viable and accordingly decided to find a purchaser for all or part of the business. SEB put forward a proposal to acquire part of the Moulinex business related to small electrical household appliances. The interest of SEB was in particular for the right to exploit the trademark Moulinex in respect of all the products concerned, the acquisition of part of the production facilities and some of the Moulinex' marketing companies. The Tribunal de Commerce accepted the offer made by SEB. The concentration was then notified to the Commission pursuant to the Merger Regulation.

The Commission in a Phase I investigation, found that each category of small electric household appliances – given their characteristics and level of demand substitutability – could constitute a distinct product market and that therefore the analysis was to be carried out for each group of products. The Commission identified thirteen product categories. In particular, deep friers and skillets; mini-ovens, toasters, sandwich and waffle makers, appliances for the preparation of an informal meal, electric barbecues and indoor grills, rice and steam cookers, electric filter coffee machines, kettles, espresso machines, blenders and mixers, irons and ironing stations, and personal care appliances.[62] A national definition of the relevant geographic market was judged by the Commission to be the most suitable.[63]

b. Origin of the case

On 13 November 2001, pursuant to Article 4 of Regulation 4064/89 (as amended by Regulation 1310/97), SEB notified to the Commission the proposed acquisition of certain assets of Moulinex' business. On 5 December 2001 the parties to the concentration proposed commitments to the Commission and, in response to concerns expressed by the Commission, revised their initial commitments on 18 December 2001. Finally, as a result of observations submitted by interested third parties, the merging companies further modified the commitments made to the Commission.

c. Economic analysis

The Commission initially stated that trademarks are one of the most important factors influencing consumers' choice and are therefore one the most relevant elements of competition between manufacturers of the relevant products. It consistently pointed out that both SEB and Moulinex invested significant amounts in maintaining the reputation of their own trademarks.[64]

At the end of its Phase I investigation the Commission concluded that the notified concentration raised serious doubts as to its compatibility with the common market on a number of markets for kitchenware. In particular the Commission found that in Portugal, Greece, Belgium, and the Netherlands where, prior to the concentration, SEB and Moulinex held independently significant positions in the small household electric appliances sector,[65] the situation of SEB would have been strengthened by the addition of Moulinex and the transaction would have led to a combination of (large) market shares with respect to a large

---

62 See recitals 16 and 25 of the decision.
63 See recital 30 of the decision.

64 See recitals 36–39 of the decision.
65 See the table in recital 31 of the decision.

number of the categories of products concerned. According to the Commission assessment, market power would be increased by a portfolio of several trademarks that was unmatched by any of the competitors such as Philips or Braun.[66] Similar concerns, more specifically the substantial change in the competition conditions in the relevant markets, were expressed in relation to the Austrian, Danish, Norwegian, German, and Swedish market. Regarding the other national markets, no concerns were expressed. For each national market about which concerns had been expressed, the Commission carried out a detailed analysis of the impact on competition of the concentration on every single product market. The Commission evaluation was based on the examination of market shares of the undertakings involved in the merger in every single product market and also, in some countries, on the assessment of the strengthening effect that the portfolio power would have generated. The possibility to create or strengthen a dominant position was – following a quantitative analysis – (mainly) determined at a combined market power of more than 40 percent.[67] According to the Commission's analysis the notified transaction raised serious doubts as to the compatibility with the common market, as regards the possibility to exercise market power and reduce competition and welfare, in a series of markets.[68]

Nevertheless, after repeated consultation with the merging firms and third interested parties and several successively wider sets of commitments offered by the merging parties, the Commission found that the serious doubts as to the compatibility of the concentration with the internal market could be overcome since those commitments constituted a direct and immediate response to the competition problems identified. Accordingly the Commission cleared the merger on condition that the parties fulfilled the following agreed behavioral commitments:

- The commitment to grant an exclusive license to sell household electrical appliances under the Moulinex trademark for a period of five years covering the thirteen product categories constituting the relevant product markets;
- The commitment not to market products bearing the Moulinex trademark in the countries concerned during the term of the license and for a further period of three years following the expiry of the license;
- The commitment not to market models of Moulinex products under a trademark other than Moulinex in the territories in respect of which the licensee or licensees have concluded a supply contract or been granted an industrial property license;
- The commitment to enter into supply agreements (at a supply price corresponding to the industrial cost price plus the general costs

---

66 See recitals 43–47 of the decision.
67 See recitals 45–82 for Portugal, Greece, Belgium, and the Netherlands, and recitals 83–127 for Germany, Austria, Denmark, Sweden, and Norway.
68 In particular Germany for deep friers and barbecues/grills; Austria for deep friers and informal meals; Belgium for food mixers, espresso machines, kettles, toasters, informal meals, barbecues/grills, irons, and ironing stations; Denmark for deep friers and portable ovens; Greece for deep friers, kettles, sandwich/waffle makers, espresso machines, and food mixers; Norway for deep friers and portable ovens; the Netherlands for deep friers, espresso machines, mini ovens, informal meals, barbecue/grills, irons, and ironing stations; Portugal for deep friers, toasters, coffee and espresso machines, kettles, mini ovens, sandwich/waffle makers, informal meals, barbecue/grills and informal meals; Sweden for deep friers. See recital 128 of the decision.

associated with production and delivery of the products to the licensee) with, and/or grant licenses covering, industrial property rights in respect of all products concerned, with the exception of food mixers in Germany, to any licensee requesting such a contract or license;

– The commitment to pursue the general policy of the development of new models and to maintain the full economic and competitive value of the Moulinex trademark in each of the nine States concerned until the conclusion of the license agreements;

– The commitment to enter into exclusive trademark licensing agreements for the nine countries in question within the period specified the commitments agreement;

– The commitment relating to approval of the licensee or licensees by the Commission;

– Compliance with any suggestion useful for the fulfilment of the commitments or the performance of Moulinex'/SEB's task which may be made by the representative of the licensees.[69]

d. **Fines, remedies, and conditions enclosed**

As described in section c of this landmark decision the Commission made the approval of the proposed concentration conditional on the parties fulfilling a number of (listed) commitments.

e. **Further developments of the case**

In Case T-114/02 *BaByliss* v. *Commission* [2003] ECR II-1279, BaByliss – a competitor of SEB and Moulinex also interested in the acquisition of the latter – brought an action to the CFI (now "the General Court") in April 2002 seeking the annulment of the Commission's clearance decision.[70] The applicant put forward several pleas in law, claiming in particular, among other requests, that the Commission had erred in its assessment of the effectiveness of the proposed commitments in overcoming the competitive restraints caused by the merger and that the Commission had authorized the merger without any commitments in markets where serious concerns about unilateral effects arise.

As regard to the first claim, the plaintiff claimed in particular that commitments of a behavioral nature (like those proposed by the parties and accepted by the Commission) mainly concerning the (exclusive) use of the Moulinex trademark were not able to overcome the serious doubts on the compatibility of the merger with the common market. On this point, the CFI stated "[a]lthough a sale of assets is often the most suitable corrective measure for easily remedying a competition problem, particularly in the case of horizontal overlap, the possibility cannot in principle be ruled out that a license agreement may be suitable for remedying identified competition problems ... It is common ground that trademarks are of vital importance in the sector affected by the concentration and are one of the main factors in the final consumers' choice."[71] The Court also noted the relevance of the Commission requirements to the parties "on the

---

69   See recital 146 of the decision.
70   Another competitor that objected was Philips, in case T-119/02 *Royal Philips Electronics* v. *Commission* [2003] ECR II-1433. The claims were dismissed by the CFI.
71   Recitals 170 and 173 of the judgment.

status of the licensee and required the license holder or holders to be . . . viable and independent and to be in possession of the competence necessary to provide active and effective competition on the market concerned."[72] Confirming the validity of the Commission's assessment of the commitments' effectiveness in restoring effective competition and the Commission's discretion in carrying out economic analysis, the Court ruled that in the circumstances of the case "the commitments cannot be considered to be of such an extent and complexity that the Commission found it impossible to determine with the requisite degree of certainty that effective competition would be restored in the market, because the final version of the commitments reflects in large measure the objections of the third parties. For the same reason, the commitments accepted by the Commission were sufficiently specific to enable the Commission to assess all details."[73]

Having stated its position on the potential possibility for behavioral commitments to eliminate the competition restrictions caused by a concentration, the CFI also pointed out that in the specific circumstances of the case the particular (binding) remedies accepted by the Commission were effectively able to overcome the competition problems. To strengthen the already mentioned importance of trademarks in consumers' choices in the affected markets, the CFI pointed out the fact that many producers had chosen to outsource the production of their goods and to retain brands and marketing teams. Moreover since the average life of small electrical household appliances was commonly considered to be three years "a trademark license for a term of five years accompanied by a commitment by SEB not to market any such appliances under the Moulinex trademark for a further three years is likely to enable the licensees to induce customers of Moulinex products to migrate to their own brand."[74]

Concerning the claim that the Commission – in its unconditional clearance decision – did not sufficiently consider the competitive risks brought by the concentration in Spain, Italy, Finland, United Kingdom, and Ireland, the Court questioning the Commission's approach to the question raised several problematic issues.

Firstly, the CFI held that it is correct to analyze the overlapping effect generated by the merger in terms of market share held by the merging parties on the same market – as the Commission did – and that the absence of any significant overlap could be considered as overcoming serious doubts even in case of the already existing dominant position of one of the two merging firms. However it would not follow from that that a market share overlapping between 0 and 10 percent could be considered as insignificant and as always excluding possible competitive restriction and in particular the creation or strengthening of a dominant position. In some circumstances those market conditions might actually create competitive concerns and, consequently, should have been scrutinized more thoroughly.[75]

Secondly, the CFI criticized the approach used by the Commission in assessing the competitors' countervailing power. The analysis focused on markets in which the parties' market share was (above) 40 percent (considered as the

---

72   Recital 174 of the judgment.
73   Recital 178 of the judgment.
74   Recital 193 of the judgment.
75   See recitals 316–327 of the judgment.

threshold for possible competition problems). Therein, the mere "presence of competitors is likely to modify, or even eliminate, the combined entity's dominant position only if those competitors hold a strong position which acts as a genuine counterweight."[76] "[T]he market[s] in question are markets with a rather oligopolistic structure and several undertakings have both [an] extensive product range and a pan-European presence."[77] E.g., next to SEB and Moulinex, are Philips, Bosch, Braun, and De Longhi. In any given market such brands may appear, however this itself does not justify the conclusion that the concentration raises no doubts for that market. Only with sufficient market shares could they act as counterweights. The CFI indicates that the same applies to firms having a wide product range but small geographical range and vice versa.

Moreover, the CFI challenged the Commission's interpretation of the consequences the range effect would have on the market. According to the Commission's position (expressed in its reply to the Court's written question), the range effect implies that where the merging parties held a dominant position in a product market(s) that together represents a marginal part of their turnover, the resulting entity would not be induced to exercise market power because it would be the object of retaliation in other product markets where it did not have a dominant position and that represented a larger part of its total turnover.

Starting from the assumption that each product market constitutes a distinct market, the principle expressed is that each market is to be assessed independently and any exception of that principle must be based on specific and consistent evidence. In the case of the alleged range effect, the existence of the mechanism underlying such a concept should be demonstrated. The Court consequently held that the Commission had failed to sufficiently demonstrate its conclusions. In particular it noted "[I]t is common ground that the two parties to the concentration each had a strong position in numerous markets and owned several well-known brands. In addition to resulting in the aggregation of market shares, the concentration had the effect of enlarging the brand portfolio and the number of markets where SEB and Moulinex were present, thus enhancing their market power, particularly in relation to retailers . . . The situation envisaged by the Commission of a conflict between SEB/Moulinex and the retailers is no more plausible than that of an agreement between them to maximize their respective interest. Moreover, the Commission has not even shown how its underlying assumption, namely a price increase by SEB/Moulinex, necessarily affects the retailers' interests and thereby induces them to penalize SEB/Moulinex. When questioned by the Court on the economic principles underlying the range effect factor, the Commission admitted that it had no economic study available to it on the subject."[78] Moreover the Court pointed out that the Commission had focused on only one single type of anticompetitive act the merging parties had allegedly committed, namely the price rise. The Court noted how economies of scale and rationalizing measures deriving from

76 Recital 329 of the judgment.
77 Recitals 329–330 of the judgment.

78 Recitals 355–359 of the judgment.

the merger could have allowed the new entity to grant retailers a larger margin in return for de-listing of competitors. The Commission was obliged to analyze this possibility.

As a result, the CFI annulled the Commission decision in relation to the markets in Italy, Spain, Finland, United Kingdom, and Ireland.

In response to the CFI's annulment, in *SEB/Moulinex* Commission decision 2005/408/EC [2003] OJ L 138, the Commission in turn carried out an in-depth analysis of the national markets for which the initial assessments had been objected to by the CFI.

The Commission divided the product markets into three main categories: markets where the parties had a market share of less than 25 percent, markets with non-significant horizontal overlaps, and markets with a combined market share in excess of 25 percent. The competitive analysis focused mainly on the last-mentioned because in the first two categories the market conditions were considered as not conducive to creating or strengthening a dominant position.

Regarding the markets with significant overlap and an aggregate market share exceeding 25 percent, the Commission analyzed for each concerned market firstly the supply side and thus the presence of competitors with strong international presence and portfolio range products, secondly the structure of the demand and the forms of distribution employed (mainly hypermarket, department stores, and specialist stores), and finally the potential for Moulinex to regain the market position held before the bankruptcy proceedings, the ensuing market share decline, and brand disruption.

The Commission decided not to oppose the proposed merger in any of the scrutinized national markets (Italy, Spain, Finland, United Kingdom and Ireland) and to declare it compatible with the common market.

8.2   Horizontal mergers: coordinated effects

A   Introduction

Coordinated effects of mergers relate to an increase in concentration in the market, which may increase the likelihood of tacit and overt collusion in the entire industry. The reduction of the number of independent actors in the market due to the merger may create market conditions in which it is easier for the remaining firms to engage in collusion. The main concern is that either the reduction of the number of actors alone, or the more symmetric distribution of their assets, or a combination of these two factors, allows the post-merger market participants to coordinate their actions with considerably more ease. Relevant factors in relation to this are structural factors recognized to facilitate collusion such as a small number of firms, barriers to entry, cross-ownerships and other links among competitors, symmetry in the cost structure, dimension, and organization of the firms, product homogeneity, and absent or weak buying power. These are further discussed in chapter 2. In addition, the availability of information and the transparency of rivals' strategies are seminal to the success of collusive agreements. Mergers can greatly influence these conditions.

B   Applicable EU legislation

No special legislation applicable. For applicable legislation see chapter 8, paragraph B.

C Related economics texts

Bishop and Walker (2009), chapter 7, paragraphs 7.49–7.75
Carlton and Perloff (2005), chapter 2, paragraph 2 and chapter 19, paragraph 3(5)
Church and Ware (2000), chapter 23
Martin (1994), chapters 9 and 10
Martin (2002), chapter 12
Motta (2004), chapters 5 and 7
Tirole (1988), paragraphs 4.6.2.1, 9.5, 9.6, and 9.7
Waldman and Jensen (2001), chapter 4

D Related legal texts

Bellamy and Child (2008), chapter 8, paragraph 4(E)
Jones and Sufrin (2008), chapter 12, paragraph 5(D, iii, d)
Ritter and Braun (2005), chapter 6
Whish (2008), chapters 20, paragraph 6(B, I, b) and 21, paragraph 5(C, ii, b)

E Selection of commission decisions in chronological order*

Nestlé/Perrier Commission decision 92/553/EEC [1992] OJ L 356/1, Case IV/M.190 (**described in detail as landmark case in section 8.6**) (Bishop and Walker, 2009, 4.30, 4.34, 7.70, 10.02, 10.11, 10.20, 16.15, 16.16; Motta, 2004, pp. 279–86 and pp. 104, 109, 119, 120, 271, 277)
Gencor/Lonrho Commission decision 97/26/EC [1997] OJ L 11/30, Case IV/M.619 (Bishop and Walker, 2009, 7.70, 10.02, 10.32, 10.61, 10.63; Motta, 2004, pp. 37, 119, 272)
***Airtours/First Choice* Commission decision 2000/276/EC [1999] OJ L 93/1, Case IV/M.1524** (Bishop and Walker, 2009, 4.34, 7.06, 7.72, 10.19; Motta, 2004, pp. 120, 272–73)
***Sony/BMG* Commission decision 2005/188/EC [2004] summary of the decision in OJ L 62/30, Case COMP/M.3333** (Bishop and Walker, 2009, 7.51, 7.74 and 10.02)

F Economic landmark cases

F.1 *Airtours/First Choice* Commission decision 2000/276/EC [1999] OJ L 93/1

Relevance: Landmark case in which a prohibition decision adopted by the Commission under the Merger Regulation was annulled by the CFI (now "the General Court") for the first time. The reason for the annulment was the lack of sufficient economic reasoning substantiating the assessment of the merger-deriving collective dominance. This CFI judgment was one of the driving forces behind the far-reaching reform of the Merger Regulation of 2004, the adoption of the Horizontal Mergers Guidelines, and the resulting policy change from collective dominance to coordinated effects.

• For this section, instead of a complete list of Commission decisions in chronological order, we present only a selection of merger decisions that have been significant for the development of European merger control. Decisions displayed in **bold type** are described in the section. Reference is made in brackets and **bold type** to the relevant section in which the decision is extensively described as a landmark case. When decisions are referenced and/or described in some detail in one or more of the economic textbooks, reference in brackets is also made to the relevant part(s) of those texts.

- Case IV/M.1524
- **Decision:** Prohibition decision pursuant to Article 8(3) of the Merger Regulation
- **Decision addressee(s):**
  - Airtours plc, *United Kingdom*
- **Report route:** Notification of the proposed concentration on 29 April 1999
- **Date of the decision:** 22 September 1999
- **Competition Commissioner:** M. Monti
- **Relevant product market:** Supply to tour operators of seats on charter flights to short-haul destinations
- **Relevant geographical market:** United Kingdom and Ireland
- **Description of the case**
  a. **Relevant facts**

  Airtours plc is a British company mainly active in the supply of package holidays and in the tour operator business. In April 1999 it notified to the European Commission its intention to acquire the entire share value of one of its competitors, British First Choice plc.

  The Commission decided to open an investigation procedure because it suspected that the proposed merger gave raise to serious doubts as to its compatibility with the common market.

  b. **Origin of the case**

  On 29 April 1999, pursuant to Article 4 of Regulation 4064/89 (as amended by Regulation 1310/97), Airtours notified to the Commission the proposed acquisition of all the shares of First Choice. In its decision of 3 June 1999 the Commission found the envisaged merger as possibly creating a dominant position and decided to open the investigation in accordance with Article 6(1)(c) of the Merger Regulation. On 7 September 1999 the applicant submitted a set of commitments in accordance with Article 8(2) of the Merger Regulation in order to answer to the competition concerns which had been raised by the Commission.

  c. **Economic analysis**

  The Commission considered that the notified concentration would lead to the creation of a collectively dominant position in the relevant market in the United Kingdom on the part of Airtours/First Choice, Thomson Travel Group plc, and the Thomas Cook Group Limited. The Commission rejected the argument brought by the parties according to which in order for collective dominance to be envisaged the parties should have engaged in some form of active (i.e. explicit) collusion. The Commission, recalling the CFI's stance in *Gencor/Lonrho*,[79] stated that in order to have tacit collusion it is sufficient for the parties to adapt their conducts to market conditions causing parallel behavior whereby the oligopoly becomes dominant and an anticompetitive market outcome is generated.[80]

  The Commission substantiated its assessment with an in-depth structural analysis of the UK market for tour operators. The general characteristics of the market for short-haul operations were the necessity to operate at a high level of

---

79   *Gencor/Lonrho* Commission decision 97/26/EC [1997] OJ L 11/30, Case IV/M.619.
80   See recitals 51–56 of the decision.

capacity utilization in order to maintain the operations profitably (the tour operators' margins were estimated at around 7 percent) and the necessity to closely match demand and supply and reduce to the minimum the unsold products due to the fact that holiday packages are a peculiar form of perishable goods that completely lose their value immediately after the departure date. The operators' capacity plans are therefore typically fixed 12–18 months in advance and only a few changes are possible due to the inflexibility of many commitments with suppliers. Only by planning months in advance can the operators obtain low and thus attractive prices for their holiday packages and so reduce the risk of unsold holidays.[81] Another important characteristic of the market throughout Europe and especially in the United Kingdom, according to the Commission analysis, was the vertical integration of tour operators both upstream with charter airline operators and downstream with travel agents. The possession of an in-house charter airline as well as of a preferential distribution channel such as a travel agency would create "a number of competitive advantages for the tour operator concerned, in addition to creating another source of income and control of a major cost element."[82]

The Commission investigation of the UK market resulted in the finding of an oligopolistic structure of the relevant market in which the four substantial and integrated tour operators would have been reduced to three after the merger (Airtours/First Choice, Thomson, and Thomas Cook) and in which the gap between the larger actors and the small fringe ones would have been substantially widened. Moreover, due to being vertically separated and lacking bargaining power *vis-à-vis* charter airline operators, the small operators would have been hindered in exerting significant competitive pressure on the larger suppliers and could not have "obtain[ed] the benefits of scale and scope of the larger ones."[83]

Having delineated the (oligopolistic) structure of the market, the Commission proceeded with the analysis of the main market characteristics that would have facilitated the creation and maintenance of collective dominance and which would have been strengthened by the proposed merger. The Commission firstly turned its attention to product homogeneity. According to the Commission "package holiday products . . . are fundamentally similar. They all involve the 'packaging' of the two key elements (travel and accommodation) and they all depend on bulk buying – i.e. a measure of standardization – to produce the economies of scale and scope that enable them to be marketed at a lower price than the equivalent 'bespoke' holiday (i.e. where each element is arranged and contracted for individually)."[84]

Another feature of the market that militated in favor of coordinated effect was the low demand growth which, according to the Commission would not have been "likely to provide a stimulus to competition within the foreseeable future."[85] Moreover the Commission also focused its analysis on what it defined as "the low price sensitivity," meaning that even though the price was certainly

---

81 See recitals 59–66 of the decision.
82 Recital 68 of the decision.
83 Recital 78 of the decision. See also recitals 72–85 of the decision.
84 Recital 88 of the decision.
85 Recital 93 of the decision.

an important parameter in consumer choices, "it is also clear that people are nonetheless willing to pay a certain amount more for their holidays if prices rise generally . . . which also confirms that a collective exercise of market power could increase prices and profits. It is the supply/demand balance which determines the profitability of the market rather than the level of sales as such. Due to the barriers to growth facing the small independent operators, this implies in particular that the integrated operators could increase the overall level of prices, if they were to behave in a parallel way."[86]

Also the similarity in the cost structure[87] and the degree of transparency[88] characterizing the market in both the planning and in the selling season constituted collusive factors. The transparency of the competitors' strategies was particularly evident in the planning period, for three reasons. Firstly, the four major operators had contacts with the same hotels and (extra) charter flights providers. Secondly, capacity choices were transparent because adopted not *ex novo* but most of the time on the basis of the sales in the previous year adopted to the forecast demand of the coming season. Finally, the substantial capacity additions could not be kept confidential but had to be made public (e.g. in case of publicly listed companies). Once the catalogues were launched, the almost complete publication of their respective prices and commercial conditions further increased the transparency in the market. Transparency was practically made complete by the mutual dependency between the main operators "due to the impact on market conditions of the overall level of capacity put on the market for a season."[89] According to the Commission, given the described capacity rigidities, the high degree of transparency would make it even more likely that the four major suppliers would have undersupplied the market.

The competitive assessment of collective dominance deriving from the proposed merger was completed by the assessment of the high entry barriers existing for potential competitors due primarily to the difficulty "to access, on reasonable terms and conditions, airline seats and to distribution through travel agencies,"[90] and to the compelling need to vertically integrate (i.e. access to distribution) in order to be competitive on the market.[91] Finally, the complete absence of buying power on the part of the individual consumers was considered as a further element facilitating a tacitly collusive outcome in this highly concentrated market.[92]

On the basis of all the previous considerations and taking into account the competitive trends in the past showing a rapid consolidation (and vertical integration) in the industry, the Commission declared the merger between Airtours and First Choice incompatible with the common market.

d. Fines, remedies, and conditions enclosed
None.

e. Further developments of the case
In Case T-342/99 *Airtours* v. *Commission* [2002] ECR II-2585, an action was brought by Airtours seeking the annulment of the Commission decision

86 Recital 98 of the decision.
87 See recitals 99 and 100 of the decision.
88 See recitals 102–113 of the decision.
89 Recital 142 of the decision.

90 Recital 116 of the decision.
91 See recitals 114–123 of the decision.
92 See recitals 124–126 of the decision.

prohibiting the merger. In its assessment of the case, the CFI (now "the General Court") upheld the applicant's pleas and annulled the Commission's decision. The Court harshly criticized the Commission's analysis of the evidence and findings and in an unprecedented manner characterized the decision as "vitiated by a series of errors of assessment."[93] The Courts substantiated its judgment with a systematic critical assessment of all the findings upon which the Commission had based its decision.

Initially the CFI confirmed and clarified the cumulative conditions necessary for the finding of a collective dominance, namely the ability for the member of the oligopoly to know how the others behave and monitor their compliance with the common strategy (i.e. transparency of the market); the sustainability over time of the coordination, relating to the existence of retaliatory means to deter defection; and the inability for competitors and consumers to jeopardize the result of the coordinated action.[94]

The Court then moved on to demonstrate the inconsistency of the Commission's argument with the mentioned conditions. Firstly the CFI challenged the Commission's description of the relevant market as static and characterized by the absence of competition. The Court noted how the interpretation of the data presented in the UK Monopolies and Merger Commission (MMC) study given by the Commission, and on which it had based its findings (and which was based on strong empirical evidence and data collection), was incorrect since the MMC had described the market until 1997 as dynamic, characterized by keen competition and no significant barriers to entry. The evidence the Commission presented to show the rapid horizontal and vertical integration of the market since 1997 were not considered as significant by the CFI.[95]

In particular, "as regards horizontal concentration, it is apparent from the documents before the Court . . . that the development, between 1996 and 1999, of the market shares of Thomson, Airtours, and First Choice does not prove that their shares of the short-haul market have increased significantly."[96] Also the interpretation given of the historical data on firms' market shares was challenged by the CFI, which pointed out how the stability over time of market shares can be interpreted as a factor conducive to collective dominance "inasmuch as it facilitates division of the market instead of fierce competition"[97] and that, on the other hand, the volatility of market shares deriving from numerous acquisitions made by the main actors in the scrutinized period was not considered by the Commission which rather described it as a sign of market stagnation and did not consider the possible competition against similar-sized (large) competitors it could have triggered.[98]

Similarly, the finding of low demand growth and its steady pace in the market was challenged by the CFI. The Court pointed out how the Commission evaluation was based "on an incomplete and incorrect [assessment] of the dat[a] submitted to it during the administrative procedure."[99] The Court noted how the Commission had failed to show exact results from the data provided in

---

93   Recital 294 of the judgment.
94   See recital 62 of the judgment.
95   See recitals 93–101 of the judgment.
96   Recital 102 of the judgment and the data provided therein.

97   Recital 111 of the judgment.
98   See recitals 109–120 of the judgment.
99   Recital 127 of the judgment.

the study on *forecasting holiday demand*, particularly where it ascribed to the market an average growth of about 3.7 percent per annum and a high volatility of growth. Also the level of market growth in the two years preceding the notification was misinterpreted and its analysis inaccurate. The CFI showed data on the high level of demand volatility and found that it would "render[s] the creation of [a] collective dominance position more difficult. Conversely stable demand . . . is a relevant factor indicative of the existence of a collective dominant position, in so far as it makes deviations from the common policy (that is, cheating) more easily detectable, by enabling them to be distinguished from capacity adjustment intended to respond to expansion or contraction in a volatile market."[100]

The CFI dedicated much time and effort to the aspect of market transparency. The Court examined carefully the detailed plans of Airtours for a number of different destinations and, after having observed that "each of the large integrated tour operators has to deal with thousands different prices because of the various programmes offered [and that thus] tacit agreements on all those prices would be impossible,"[101] concluded that the capacity decisions were not simply made – as the Commission had concluded – by readjusting the previous year's capacity by a certain percentage. As the Court clearly stated "an examination of the data shows that the planning cycles does not simply run from year to year . . . Top-down considerations take account of the key factors influencing holiday demand, such as economic activity, exchange rates, and consumer confidence . . . Bottom-up considerations are based on a detailed analysis of existing product offerings, starting with, for example, consideration of gross and net margins by flights and accommodation unit[s] for each resort."[102] The decisions were taken on a package-by-package basis. The data showed a wide variety of different changes in the strategies compared to the previous year's capacity, with cases of large reductions (10 percent) and cases of big increases (up to 25–30 percent). Other elements of the Commission's evaluation of the overall market transparency were also strongly disputed. The major tour operators hardly used the same hotels, due also to the different strategies of each hotel. Decisions about airline seats were taken after the capacity planning stage and so would not increase transparency. The Court found that the Commission had wrongly concluded that the high degree of transparency made the market conducive to collective dominance. The section on transparency is particularly significant for the rigor with which the Court approached the question, which indicates the importance given to transparency as an essential condition for collective dominance to be realized.[103]

The Court also urged for a coherent approach regarding the existence of retaliation mechanisms when existence of collective dominance is assumed. In those cases "the prospective analysis of the market . . . must also assess it dynamically, with regard in particular to its internal equilibrium, stability, and the question as to whether any parallel anticompetitive conduct to which it might give rise is sustainable over time . . . The Commission must not

100 Recital 139 of the judgment. The interpretation of the data given by the Court is in recitals 140–142.
101 Recital 158 of the judgment.
102 Recital 161 of the judgment.
103 See recitals 148–182 of the judgment.

necessarily prove that there is a specific retaliation mechanism involving a degree of severity, but it must none the less establish that deterrents exist."[104]

Finally, concerning the potential capacity of small competitors and consumers to exercise competitive restraints and thus jeopardize the tacitly collusive outcome of the market, the CFI noted how the crucial question in the assessment of that aspect is not whether the numerous small competitors are able to achieve the same size and capacity of the largest actors on the market but rather if they "taken as a whole, can respond effectively to a reduction in capacity put on to the market by the large tour operators to a level below estimated demand by increasing their capacity to take advantage of the opportunities inherent in a situation of overall under-supply and whether they can thereby counteract the creation of a collective dominant position."[105] The same reasoning was adopted concerning the customers and their inability to exercise buying power. Challenging the Commission's argument, the Court stated "the fact that consumers do not have significant buyer power because they act in isolation must not be confused with the question of whether they would be able to react to a price rise brought about by the large tour operators restricting capacity put onto the market to an anticompetitive level... It is not disputed that consumers make comparisons before purchasing a holiday."[106]

F.2 *Sony/BMG* Commission decision 2005/188/EC [2004] summary of the decision in OJ L 62/30

Relevance: For the first time a decision clearing a merger is annulled by the CFI for misinterpretation of market data and manifest error in the assessment of the circumstances characterizing the relevant market. The decision, together with the appeal judgment, is also important for the focus on market transparency in an oligopolistic market and the implications that should be derived from such a market condition.

- Case COMP/M.3333
- **Decision:** Clearance decision in Phase II investigation pursuant to Article 8(2) of the Merger Regulation
- **Decision addressee(s):**
    - Bertelsmann AG, *Germany*
    - Sony Corporation of America, *United States*
- **Report route:** Notification of the proposed concentrative joint ventures on 9 January 2004
- **Date of the decision:** 19 July 2004
- **Competition Commissioner:** M. Monti
- **Relevant product market:** Recorded music products, online music supply, music publishing
- **Relevant geographical market:** National markets of the European Member States

---

104 Recitals 192 and 195 of the judgment. 106 Recital 274 of the judgment.
105 Recital 213 of the judgment.

- **Description of the case**
  - a. **Relevant facts**

    Bertelsmann is an international media company involved in worldwide activities including music recording and publishing, books, magazine and newspaper publishing, radio, and television. Its activities in the recorded music market are carried out through the wholly owned subsidiary BMG, which owns several music labels.

    Sony is a worldwide active multinational company operating in the market for recording and publishing of music, and in the production of consumer electronics and entertainment media. Sony also owns several music labels.

    The two companies, in their notification to the Commission, communicated the intention to merge their global recorded music business through the creation of three (or more) equally owned (50–50) joint ventures whose activity would have been the discovery and developments of new artists and subsequent publication and marketing activities.

  - b. **Origin of the case**

    On 9 January 2004, pursuant to Article 4 of Regulation 4064/89 (as amended by Regulation 1310/97), Bertelsmann and Sony notified to the Commission the proposed concentration by which they intended to merge their global recorded music business. In its decision of 12 February 2004 the Commission found the envisaged merger as possibly creating a dominant position and decided to open an investigative procedure in accordance to Article 6(1)(c) of the Merger Regulation.

  - c. **Economic analysis**

    Having defined three relevant product markets, the Commission focused its analysis on whether the joint venture(s) would have created or strengthened a dominant position in each and every one of the indicated markets.

    The markets for recorded music and its publication are dominated by five large record companies (the so-called majors), namely Sony, Bertelsmann, EMI, Warner, and Universal. The merger would have implied a further reduction in the number of dominant actors, with the minor (independent) labels holding 15–20 percent of market share.

    The investigation into the effect of the merger on the competitiveness of the markets was based on the analysis of the price developments in the relevant European markets in light of the Commission's intention to base the decision on the processing and evaluation of large data sets. The Commission in particular analyzed whether the five majors had coordinated their prices in the main national markets of France, United Kingdom, Germany, Italy, and Spain during the previous three–four years. In particular, the Commission analyzed the existence of possible coordination in the mentioned markets of average net prices, published prices to dealers (PPDs), gross and net price ratios, invoice discounts, and retrospective discounts. The prices taken into consideration were those of the top 100 albums for each quarter since they represented at least 70–80 percent of total sales.[107]

    The Commission found that net wholesale prices of the five majors showed a certain degree of homogeneity in all the countries considered, but the

---

107   See recitals 69–73 of the decision.

Commission did not consider those similarities as sufficient for establishing price coordination in the past. Yet the PPDs adopted by the majors are published in catalogues and are thus also publicly available for competitors. Price alignments were found in all the analyzed countries and the Commission took the possibility of price coordination into account. Moreover, net transaction prices were found to be closely linked to the mentioned PPDs with consequent stable net to gross price ratios over time.

Even if the detailed and in-depth analysis of prices provided strong evidence of coordination in all national markets, the existence of collective dominance was excluded in light of the analysis of the discounts applied by the five majors. The Commission found that, in particular relating to invoice discounts that constituted the most relevant aspect of companies' discount policy, differences between the majors existed (on a 3–5 percent scale) as well as differences from album to album. According to the Commission the differences in discount policy impeded the existence of a collective dominance notwithstanding the noted price homogeneity.[108]

The market analysis of the smallest EEA countries (i.e. the Netherlands, Sweden, Ireland, Austria, Belgium, Denmark, Finland, Norway, Portugal, and Greece) showed similar results, mainly because the market structure was found to be comparable to the larger countries that were scrutinized more deeply.[109]

The Commission then carried out a qualitative analysis of product homogeneity and market transparency. The Commission adopted the position of Sony/BMG in regarding recorded music as a heterogenous product with reference to the content (while the format and the pricing strategies appeared to be homogenous). The Commission achieved these results notwithstanding the circumstance that price differentiation regarding genres or type of album did not always occur and the relation between recording companies and distributors were quite stable and persistent. As for the transparency of the market, besides the publication of the mentioned catalogues, the Commission also stressed the publication of hit charts and sales data and the practically public nature of the applied PPD. Nonetheless the Commission regarded the heterogeneity of content, the differences in applied discounts, and the structure and nature of the discount campaigns as having enough impact to make the market non-transparent (and thus excluding the existence of a collectively dominant position). Furthermore, the Commission went on to investigate the presence of retaliatory mechanisms. It specifically focused on the possibility of excluding potential cheaters from mechanisms for the granting of mutual licenses for hit compilation albums constituting an important source of sales. The Commission did not find any evidence concerning the actual implementation of that retaliation.[110]

Therefore, the Commission concluded stating that "the proposed concentration does not create nor strengthen a dominant position as a result of which

108 For the detailed pricing and discount analysis of the   109 See recitals 119–154 of the decision.
     national markets see recitals 74–108 of the decision.   110 See recitals 109–118 of the decision.

effective competition would be significantly impeded in the common market or in a substantial part of it."[111]

d. Fines, remedies, and conditions enclosed
None.

e. Further developments of the case
In Case T-464/04 *Impala* v. *Commission* [2004] ECR II-2289, the Independent Music Publishers and Labels Association (Impala) brought an action to the CFI seeking the annulment of the Commission's decision, claiming that the Commission had made manifest errors of assessment in not recognizing that the proposed merger would have led to collective dominance in all the product markets scrutinized.

The CFI (now "the General Court") took the occasion to reiterate its position on the type of analysis required in case of collective dominance, stating that it had to be case-specific, based on solid evidence and future oriented (i.e. not confined to the analysis of past market behavior).[112]

The Court focused its attention particularly on the Commission's findings about the lack of market transparency. It stressed the peculiar circumstance that all the factors of the markets described by the Commission pointed toward transparency. The Court arrived at the same result regarding the price lists and applied discounts. The same kind of consideration was made by the CFI regarding the structure of the PPDs where the Court was intrigued by the Commission's conclusions that the alignment was quite evident. Finally regarding the discounts the Court noted how the Commission's observations did not advocate the finding of an opaque market but were simply proof that discounts were less transparent than other price elements. In particular, it noted that the decision did "not provide the slightest information as regards their nature, the circumstances in which they are granted or their actual importance for net prices, or their impact on the transparency of prices."[113]

The Court found that the data on campaign discounts did not appear to be sufficiently consistent, reliable, or relevant and that in general the Commission had made a manifest error of assessment.[114]

Particularly relevant in the judgment is the Court's statement on the interpretation of the price homogeneity that the Commission had found and deemed not sufficient to establish coordinated conduct. The CFI said that "close alignment of prices over a long period, especially if they are above a competitive level, together with other factors typical of a collective dominant position, might in the absence of an alternative reasonable explanation, suffice to demonstrate the existence of a collective dominant position, even where there is no firm direct evidence of strong market transparency, as such transparency may be presumed in such circumstances."[115]

---

111   Recital 183 of the decision.
112   See in particular recitals 245–254 of the judgment.
113   Recital 318 of the judgment.
114   The Court's assessment of Commission findings about market transparency is carried out carefully and in detail in recitals 278–459 of the judgment.
115   Recital 252 of the judgment.

Regarding the deterrent mechanisms, the Court found their existence sufficient for the existence of collective dominance without the necessity, as assumed
by the Commission, to demonstrate their factual implementation.[116]

Accordingly, the Court annulled the Commission's decision for inadequate
reasoning and manifest error in the assessment of the elements at the base of
the same decision.[117]

Following the annulment of the decision, the case was re-notified to the
Commission on 31 January 2007 and the Commission started a new assessment
of the transaction. On 1 March 2007, the Commission opened an in-depth
investigation and on 3 October 2007 it confirmed its approval of the proposed
transaction.

Moreover, in Case C-413/06P *Bertelsmann and Sony Corporation of America*
v. *Impala* [2008] OJ C 223/7, the ECJ set aside the judgment of the CFI in the
case *Impala* v. *Commission* and referred the case back to the CFI.

In making its assessment, the ECJ first stated that in the case of an alleged
creation or strengthening of a collective dominant position the Commission
is obliged to assess whether the concentration at issue will lead to a situation
in which effective competition in the relevant market is significantly impeded
by the undertakings which are parties to the concentration and one or more
other undertakings which together, in particular because of correlative factors
which exist between them, are able to adopt a common policy on the market in
order to profit from a situation of collective economic strength, without actual
or potential competitors, let alone customers or consumers, being able to react
effectively.[118]

The ECJ continued by observing that "such correlative factors include, in
particular, the relationship of interdependence existing between the parties to a
tight oligopoly within which, on a market with the appropriate characteristics,
in particular in terms of market concentration, transparency and product homogeneity, those parties are in a position to anticipate one another's behavior and
are therefore strongly encouraged to align their conduct on the market in such a
way as to maximise their joint profits by increasing prices, reducing output, the
choice or quality of goods and services, diminishing innovation or otherwise
influencing parameters of competition."[119]

Secondly and with regard to tacit coordination, the ECJ observed that such
coordination is more likely to emerge if competitors can easily arrive at a common perception as to how the coordination should work, and, in particular,
of the parameters that lend themselves to being a focal point of the proposed
coordination. It is moreover necessary to determine whether such coordination
is sustainable. With regard to sustainability, the ECJ stated that (i) the coor-
dinating undertakings must be able to monitor to a sufficient degree whether

116   See recitals 463–474 of the judgment.
117   In this decision and in particular with the statement concerning the interpretation to be given to price parallelism in specific
      circumstances, the CFI added an additional element in its interpretation of the burden of proof required to demonstrate the
      existence of collective dominance. After the *Airtours* case that was considered as setting a very high standard for the
      demonstration of coordinated effects, this judgment set the same high standard of proof *a contrario* – that is in case the evidence is
      strongly in favor of the actual existence of collective dominance – in order to demonstrate its non-existence.
118   Recital 120 of the judgment.
119   Recital 121 of the judgment.

the terms of the coordination are being adhered to; (ii) there must therefore be sufficient market transparency for each undertaking concerned to be aware of the way in which the market conduct of each of the other participants in the coordination is evolving; (iii) there must be some form of credible deterrent mechanism that can come into play if deviation is detected; and (iv) the reactions of outsiders, such as current or future competitors, and also the reactions of customers, should not be such as to jeopardise the results expected from the coordination.[120]

The ECJ stressed that it is of great importance, in applying those criteria, to avoid a mechanical approach involving the separate verification of each of those criteria taken in isolation, while taking no account of the overall economic mechanism of a hypothetical tacit coordination.[121]

Thus the assessment of, for example, the transparency of a particular market should be carried out using the mechanism of a hypothetical tacit coordination as a basis. The ECJ ruled that "it is only if such a hypothesis is taken into account that it is possible to ascertain whether any elements of transparency that may exist on a market are, in fact, capable of facilitating the reaching of a common understanding on the terms of coordination and/or of allowing the competitors concerned to monitor sufficiently whether the terms of such a common policy are being adhered to. In that last respect and in order to analyze the sustainability of a purported tacit coordination, it is necessary to take into account the monitoring mechanisms that may be available to the participants in the alleged tacit coordination in order to ascertain whether, as a result of those mechanisms, they are in a position to be aware, sufficiently precisely and quickly, of the way in which the market conduct of each of the other participants in that coordination is evolving."[122]

The ECJ ruled that in the case before it the CFI, in carrying out its analysis of those parts, did not have regard to a postulated monitoring mechanism forming part of a plausible theory of tacit coordination.[123]

8.3   Vertical and conglomerate mergers

A   Introduction

Vertical and conglomerate mergers are mergers between firms operating at different levels of the production chain. Vertical mergers occur within a single chain of production and distribution from the initial input suppliers, via all intermediate layers adding value, to the final consumer. Companies can vertically merge upstream as well as downstream. Conglomerate mergers are those between undertakings in different production or distribution chains and/or in less closely related markets. A company may diagonally acquire an upstream or downstream company in a production chain that serves a different relevant market. Conglomerate mergers

---

120   Recital 123 of the judgment; the ECJ also stated that these conditions are in conformity with the conditions laid down by the CFI in recital 62 of its judgment in *Airtours v. Commission*.
121   Recital 125 of the judgment.
122   Recital 126 of the judgment.
123   Recital 130 of the judgment.

therefore can have less obvious anticompetitive effects. Vertical mergers can generate efficiency gains, in particular gains related to the elimination of double mark-ups. Conglomerate mergers can help organize a better allocation of products on the market, a pooling of experience and IPRs, or more efficient marketing. On the other hand vertical and conglomerate mergers are known to carry the risk of vertical foreclosure strategies. That is, an upstream firm with significant market power may want to integrate vertically downstream to reduce downstream competition by raising rival retailers' costs and so aim to foreclose them. Likewise the acquisition of an upstream firm by a dominant downstream company can have the aim of reducing the access of independent upstream companies to customers. That is, such foreclosure strategies can leverage market power vertically. The European Commission's Guidelines on the assessment of non-horizontal mergers recognize these potential competition risks and lay out methods to evaluate their potential impact and concern.[124]

B   Applicable EU legislation

No special legislation applicable. For applicable legislation see chapter 8, paragraph B.

C   Related economics texts

Bishop and Walker (2009), chapter 8
Carlton and Perloff (2005), chapter 2, paragraph 2 and chapter 19, paragraph 3(5)
Church and Ware (2000), chapter 23
Martin (1994), chapters 9 and 10
Martin (2002), chapter 12
Motta (2004), chapters 5 and 7
Tirole (1988), paragraphs 4.6.2.1, 9.5, 9.6, and 9.7
Waldman and Jensen (2001), chapter 4

D   Related legal texts

Bellamy and Child (2008), chapter 8, paragraph 4(F)
Jones and Sufrin (2008), chapter 12, paragraph 5(D, viii)
Ritter and Braun (2005), chapter 6
Whish (2008), chapters 20, paragraph 6(B, i, c) and 21, paragraph 5(D)

E   Selection of commission decisions in chronological order[•]

Worldcom/MCI Commission decision 99/287/EC [1999] OJ L 116/1, Case COMP/M.1069

---

124   Guidelines on the assessment of non-horizontal mergers under the Council Regulation on the control of concentrations between undertakings [2008] OJ C 265/6.
•   For this section, instead of a complete list of Commission decisions in chronological order, we only present a selection of merger decisions that have been significant for the development of European merger control. Decisions displayed in **bold type** are described in the section. Reference is made in brackets and **bold type** to the relevant section in which the decision is extensively described as a landmark case. When decisions are referenced and/or described in some detail in one or more of the economic textbooks, reference in brackets is also made to the relevant part(s) of those texts.

MCI Worldcom/Sprint Commission decision 2003/790/EC [2003] OJ L 300/1, Case COMP/M.1741 (Bishop and Walker, 2009, 7.82, 7.83, 12.11, 12.18; Motta, 2004, p.267)

Tetra Laval/Sidel Commission decision 2004/124/EC [2004] OJ L 43/13, Case COMP/M.2416 (Bishop and Walker, 2009, 4.38, 6.77, 7.06, 8.32, 8.37; Motta, 2004, p.273)

General Electric/Honeywell Commission decision 2004/134/EC [2004] OJ L 48/1, Case COMP/M.2220 (Bishop and Walker, 2009, 6.77, 7.06, 8.01, 8.38–8.42, 13.11; Motta, 2004, pp.37, 115, 120, 275, 277, 378–91)

GE/Amersham **Commission decision 2004/C 74/04 [2004] non-opposition notice in OJ C 74/5, Case COMP/M.3304** (Bishop and Walker, 2009, 7.03, 8.37–8.41)

Google/DoubleClick **Commission decision 2005/590/EC [2005] summary of the decision in OJ C 184/10 [2008]** (Bishop and Walker, 2009, 8.01, 8.06, 8.29)

Schneider/Legrand Commission decision 2004/275/EC [2004] OJ L 101/1, Case COMP/M.2283

ENI/EDP/GDP **Commission decision 2005/801/EC [2004] summary of the decision in OJ L 302/69, Case COMP/M.3440**

F   Economic landmark cases

F.1   *GE/Amersham* Commission decision 2004/C 74/04 [2004] non-opposition notice in OJ C 74/5

Relevance: In this decision the Commission delineates its approach to conglomerate mergers. In particular, it clarifies the conditions under which conglomerate mergers involving complementary goods can be challenged as a means of leveraging market power from one (dominated) market to another (non-dominated one). The decision constitutes a prime example of the more economic approach adopted by the Commission that focused on the effective ability to leverage market power by the merging entity, and on its incentives to do so. Potential portfolio power is accordingly analyzed for its effective possibility to produce restrictive effects on competition.

- Case COMP/M.3304
- **Decision:** Non-opposition decision in Phase I investigation pursuant to Article 6(1)(b) of the Merger Regulation
- **Decision addressee(s):**
    - General Electric Company, *United States*
- **Report route:** Notification of the proposed acquisition on 8 December 2003
- **Date of the decision:** 21 January 2004
- **Competition Commissioner:** M. Monti
- **Relevant product market:** Diagnosis imaging equipment (DI) and diagnostic pharmaceuticals (DP)
- **Relevant geographical market:** Not indicated
- **Description of the case**
    - a. **Relevant facts**
        General Electric (GE) is a US company active in various manufacturing, technological, and service businesses. GE is specifically involved in the business of medical systems and specializes in medical diagnostic imaging instruments and related services and products.
        Amersham is a healthcare and life sciences company mainly acting in the production of diagnosis pharmaceuticals and in the manufacture and discovery

of biopharmaceuticals and drug discovery. The proposed operation aimed at the acquisition of sole control of Amersham by GE.

b. Origin of the case

On 8 December 2003, pursuant to Article 4 of Regulation 4064/89 (as amended by Regulation 1310/97), GE notified to the Commission the proposed concentration by which it intended to acquire sole control over Amersham. After examination of the proposed concentration the Commission found that it did not raise serious doubts as to its compatibility with the common market.

c. Economic analysis

This decision has been adopted after the much debated case *General Electric/Honeywell*,[125] where the Commission was called to assess the effect on competition of a conglomerate merger. After all the discussion that followed that controversial decision, in *GE/Amersham* the Commission further consistently clarified its approach toward conglomerate mergers.

In its assessment of the market structure, the Commission verified that in the DI market there was a sufficient number of suppliers able to exert pressure on GE and thus to ensure competition in the market. In a number of national markets GE held significant market power (i.e. in excess of 40 percent), even if according to the parties that was not necessarily a sign of dominance.[126]

As for the DP market, Amersham faced some rivals with similar market shares and a number of small competitors. On a European scale it did not have a dominant position, but that would have been different for some of the national markets had they been analyzed separately. Yet even there, the parties insisted on the competitiveness of the market.[127]

Since the relevant products were complements, the Commission excluded the existence of horizontal overlapping in the concentration and focused its attention on "whether or not the merged entity may acquire . . . the ability and the economic incentive to foreclos[e] competition, by leveraging its pre-merger market power from one market to another through exclusionary practices, such as bundling and/or tying."[128]

Regarding the possibility of commercial bundling – that is, the possibility for GE to offer its customer a complete bundled set of DI and DP products

125   *GE/Honeywell* Commission decision of 3 July 2001 [2001] OJ L 48/1, Case COMP/M.2220.
126   The parties substantiated their position, focusing on the competitive pressure exercised on those markets by the buying power of hospitals, the ease of switching suppliers and equipment, and also given the bidding nature of the market. See recitals 19–23 of the decision.
127   According to the merging parties, competition in the market was shown by the downward price evolution and price competition between firms. Moreover, the merging firms claimed that Amersham held a very strong market position only in niche markets. See recitals 24–28 of the decision.
128   Recital 31 of the decision. This assessment is in line with the CFI's case law on conglomerate mergers. In *Tetra Laval BV* v. *Commission* (Case T-5/02), the CFI stated that "it is necessary first to determine whether a merger transaction creating a competitive structure which does not immediately confer on the merged entity a dominant position may nevertheless be prohibited under Article 2(3) of the Regulation, when in all likelihood it will allow that entity, as a result of leveraging by the acquiring party from a market in which it is already dominant, to obtain in the relatively near future a dominant position on another market in which the party acquired currently holds a leading position, and when the acquisition in question has significant anticompetitive effects on the relevant markets" (recital 148 of the judgment).
     Moreover the CFI, by way of example, states that "in a case where the markets in question are neighboring markets and one of the parties to a merger transaction already holds a dominant position on one of the markets, the means and capacities brought together by the transaction may immediately create conditions allowing the merged entity to leverage its way so as to acquire, in the relatively near future, a dominant position on the other market" (recital 151 of the judgment).

post-merger at a lower price than the sum of the prices of the single components – the Commission first noted that many of the interviewed competitors and customers had pointed out that strategy as being uncommon in the market due to "significant differences in the procurement procedures and supply chain . . . as well as a completely different procurement timeline."[129]

Despite the third-party reservations, the Commission clearly defined the conditions for leveraging power to be possible and to be anticompetitive. The Commission stated "[f]or commercial bundling to result in foreclosure of competition it is necessary that the merged entity is able to leverage its pre-merger dominance in one product to another complementary product. In addition, for such strategy to be profitable, there must be a reasonable expectation that rivals will not be able to propose a competitive response, and that their resulting marginalization will force them to exit the market. Finally, once rivals have exited the market, the merged firm must be able to implement unilateral price increases and such increases need to be sustainable in the long term, without being challenged by the likelihood of new rivals entering the market or previously marginalized ones re-entering the market."[130]

Accordingly, the Commission went on to verify the concrete existence of those conditions. It found that none of the two merging firms held a dominant position in their respective pre-merger markets. It also noted that there were a sufficient number of effective competitors that would have been able to respond to any attempt of bundling with counterstrategies, and that market conditions would not lead to the foreclosure of competitors when the strategy had been adopted. On the contrary, due to the global presence of rivals and their involvement in all product markets concerns, the effect could have been the erosion of part of their market share in some national market in the short term but not globally and on a permanent basis. Furthermore, the Commission noted in assessing the possible long-term effects of the envisaged strategy that entry barriers were not significant and that consequently in the long term new entry (or re-entry) would have been the most likely response and thus high prices would have not been left unchallenged. The absence of entry barriers was caused by the fact that no local manufacturing facilities were required to sell products in an area because a sales/distribution organization was sufficient.[131]

The Commission also considered whether the concentration might have led to foreclosure as result of technical tying. In the pre-merger market for DP, DI equipments worked with all types of available DP. The concerns potentially arising after the merger were the possible interruption of the interconnectivity of the merged entity's product with the rivals' ones, and a co-defined time-to-market advantage consisting in the possibility to "internalize the knowledge of development plans in DI equipment and DPs carried out by each one of the merging parties."[132] The Commission's approach was again based on the assessment of the ability and incentives to adopt such a strategy. The Commission intended to investigate the likelihood of the merged firm developing new DP products tailored to work exclusively or more efficiently with GE

129   Recital 35 of the decision.
130   Recital 37 of the decision.
131   See recitals 38–42 of the decision.
132   Recital 45 of the decision.

equipment. The investigation concluded that there was no such risk. The market, also according to all the actors consulted, needed tighter cooperation between DI and DP developers based on a non-exclusive cooperation; furthermore the market was thus far characterized by the absence of any (actual or future) interoperability issues. Finally all the main competitors of Amersham carried out large research programs that would have rendered the tying attempt unprofitable because other and newer DP products would have been offered on the market. Also the possibility of realizing time-to-market advantages was considered unlikely, particularly because it would be "very difficult and against the current process of scientific discovery for the developer of a new product to keep development plans away from publicity."[133]

The Commission also considered the economic incentives the merging firms would have had in adopting such a strategy and concluded that technical tying would not have been profit maximizing because "withholding competitors from access to data would deny the merger entity significant sales of Amersham's products to the installed base of competing DI equipment."[134]

The decision represents certainly the most clear and straightforward example of the Commission's economically based approach toward leveraging after conglomerate mergers. It is also a clear case of using a long-term consumer welfare standard in making the trade off between short-term effects and long-term effects of a concentration.

d. Fines, remedies, and conditions enclosed
None.
e. Further developments of the case
None.

F.2 *ENI/EDP/GDP* Commission decision 2005/801/EC [2004] summary of the decision in OJ L 302/69

Relevance: In a market characterized by high concentration due to the presence of historic (State) monopolies, vertical integration between producing and distributing companies can strengthen the dominant position of the incumbent(s). According to the Commission's interpretation of those market circumstances, vertical integration might provide competitive advantages in terms of access to input and other sensitive information concerning rivals, more favorable access to natural resources and to existing infrastructure. This decision represents one of the rare cases of a vertical merger blocked.

- Case COMP/M.3440
- **Decision:** Prohibition decision pursuant to Article 8(3) of the Merger Regulation
- **Decision addressee(s):**
    - EDP – Energias de Portugal, *Portugal*
    - ENI SpA, *Italy*
- **Report route:** Notification of the proposed merger on 9 July 2004
- **Date of the decision:** 9 December 2004
- **Competition Commissioner:** N. Kroes

---

133 Recital 57 of the decision.   134 Recital 59 of the decision.

- **Relevant product market:** Supply of electricity to large industrial customers (high and medium voltage) and supply of electricity to smaller industrial, commercial, and domestic customers (low voltage); supply of gas to power producers and supply of gas to local distribution companies.
- **Relevant geographical market:** Portugal
- **Description of the case**
  - a. **Relevant facts**

    Energias de Portugal (EDP) is the incumbent electricity company in Portugal and also active in the gas and electricity market in Spain as the owner of Hidrocantabrico. EDP is a listed company and 30 percent of its shares are owned by the Portuguese State.

    ENI is a company active worldwide in the exploration and production of oil and natural gas. It is also involved in the supply, distribution, and trade in natural gas. The latter activities are carried out through participation in a number of companies with transportation capacities active on the market for natural gas.

    Gas de Portugal (GDP) is the incumbent gas company in Portugal and, through a number of subsidiaries, covers all the levels of the gas production and distribution chain in Portugal. Before the proposed merger it was jointly controlled by the Portuguese State and ENI through the controlling company Galp Energia.

    Rede Electrica Nacional (REN) controls the energy grid in Portugal and in that market acts as a single buyer of electricity. The proposed operation aimed at granting joint control over GDP to ENI and EDP and, at the same time, at transferring (after a transitory period) the gas transmission network to REN (which was already, as mentioned, the electricity grid operator).

    The operation was envisaged within the frame of the Second Gas Directive and the exemption granted to Portugal that allowed the Portuguese State to liberalize the gas market at least by 2007 for non-residential customers and by 2009 for all customers.[135]

  - b. **Origin of the case**

    On 9 July 2004, pursuant to Article 4 of Regulation No. 4064/89 (as amended by Regulation No. 1310/97), Energias de Portugal SA and ENI SpA notified to the Commission the proposed concentration by which they intended to acquire joint control over Gas de Portugal SGPS SA by way of purchase of shares. In its decision of 12 August 2004 the Commission concluded that the notified operation raised serious doubts as to its compatibility with the common market and decided to open the investigative procedure in accordance to Article 6(1)(c) of the Merger Regulation.

  - c. **Economic analysis**

    The in-depth investigation carried out by the Commission made clear that EDP held a dominant position on the wholesale market for electricity in Portugal. In 2003 EDP held 70 percent of generation capacity and was the largest importer

---

135   Directive 2003/55/EC of the European Parliament and of the European Council of 26 June 2003 concerning common rules for the internal market in natural gas repealing Directive 98/30/EC [2003] OJ L 176/57.

of electricity.[136] Furthermore, EDP's generation portfolio would have remained unequaled after the abolition of the Power Purchase Agreements (PPA) in 2005, still in force at the time of the decision.[137]

After the expiring of the PPA a *stranded cost scheme* has been put in place to compensate existing power generators for any possible loss they might have incurred due to the termination of the PPA. The scheme favors incumbents. On the demand side EDP holds almost the entirety of the distribution of electricity in Portugal and the role the EDP's controlled distribution company (EDP Distribução) would have in the (future) regulated market would have strengthened that position. As matter of fact, as the Commission noted, "EDP Distribução . . . will, as the regulated retailer, take over the function of procuring energy for the regulated market, which currently accounts for 90% of the consumption in Portugal. In the absence of special rules regulating the purchasing behavior of [EDP Distribução] the latter will, in all likelihood, purchase electricity from its own generating company (EDP) through intra-group bilateral agreements."[138] On the supply side the addition of new capacity in the near future, namely the new gas fired power-plant (TER), will be significant in EDP's already wide portfolio in terms of electricity produced (its capacity since 2006 corresponds to 20 percent of the total electricity consumption in Portugal) and strategic territorial location.[139] As regards potential capacity increases of competitors, the Commission considered them to be improbable and, in one case, controlled or at least influenced by EDP.[140] Moreover, neither the pace of demand growth was certain enough to allow predictions on future construction of new capacity facilities nor would the level of imports have been sufficient to challenge EDP's dominant position.[141]

After having established EDP's dominance in the pre-merger market, the Commission assessed both the horizontal and vertical effects stemming from the proposed merger that would have strengthened that dominant position.

The main horizontal effect was the elimination of the main potential competitor in the electricity market, that is GDP itself. The Commission considered the gas incumbent as having a strong incentive to enter the electricity market and as being in a perfect strategic position to successfully do so. These conclusions were supported by the consideration of GDP's access to competitive gas resources that confers significant advantages in the electricity and gas-fired power plants, and of the fact that GDP, as a Portuguese company, could have relied on its brand and gas customers network.[142]

136 Recitals 283–287 of the decision.
137 The PPA provided for REN to be the single buyer of electricity at the wholesale level and for the same company to acquire electricity from a group of bound generators that engaged in the supply electricity to REN – on behalf of the public electricity system – on an exclusive basis for a term of more than twenty years and under a fixed price formula; 83 percent of electricity supplied in Portugal was supplied through the exclusive PPA between REN and the power producers. The PPA were expected to expire in 2005.
138 Recital 299 of the decision.
139 See recitals 302–304 of the decision.
140 See recitals 305–320 of the decision.
141 See recitals 325–334 of the decision.
142 See recitals 335–364 of the decision.

Regarding the non-horizontal effects, the Commission firstly underlined the possibility that EDP would have had to access sensitive information about the input gas costs of (current and future) competitors. Accordingly it would be able to price in such a way as to foreclose its rivals. At the same time information about rivals' daily gas nomination, i.e. "the information, given one day in advance, about the volume of gas that the [electricity production plant] plans to consume on an hourly basis,"[143] would also be disclosed to EDP. Given the relevance of gas supply for understanding the (planned) production pattern, that information would give a significant advantage to EDP.[144]

Secondly, as a consequence of the proposed transaction EDP would have the ability and the incentive to maintain favored access to natural gas and the consequent possibility to use that access to the detriment of actual and potential competitors. As for the high-pressure gas network, EDP would have the opportunity for a rather long temporary period (19.5 months) to influence the strategy and the management of the network (i.e. the company Transgas) and to take advantage of strategic information concerning the network operating features *vis-à-vis* its competitors. Furthermore it would be in the position to use the first existing access point to Portugal (i.e. the pipeline through Algeria, Morocco, Spain, and Portugal) at full capacity in order to prevent competitors from using any freed capacity and to thus impede the possibility for competitors to import a stable and permanent level of gas. Furthermore, the only gas terminal present in Portugal and operated by GDP would, as result of the merger, be controlled by EDP. Consequently competitors willing to access the terminal would be forced to contact GDP/EDP and contract the access conditions with them. Moreover, the high level of uncertainty concerning the announced transfer of infrastructures and transport rights to REN would not ensure that gas requirement to electricity producers would be provided by an entity different from GDP/EDP and when gas supply was to be restricted GDP would favor EDP to the detriment of rivals. All these described market circumstances would allow EDP to raise rivals' costs. In the same way, and particularly against the background of the need for competitors to purchase gas from GDP and the slow pace of the liberalization process in Portugal, EDP could also directly raise the price of gas supplied to competitors.[145]

Similar considerations were made concerning the retail market for electricity, where EDP held 92 percent market share in volume and where GDP constituted, for reasons similar to those expressed in the wholesale market analysis, the most significant potential competitor.

The assessment of the gas market led to similar conclusions. GDP was a legal monopolist and the merger would have strengthened its dominance in a number of markets, particularly due to the foreclosure of potential competitors to supply gas to the only local distributor company and also to large industrial companies and small customers.

---

143   Recital 369 of the decision.
144   See recitals 368–379 of the decision.

145   See recitals 380–432 of the decision.

The parties submitted a variety of commitments to respond to the Commission concerns about the compatibility of the merger with the common market.[146]

The Commission analyzed the effect those commitments would have had on each of the markets concerned. With particular reference to the wholesale electricity market, the parties offered measures aimed at ensuring the entry of competitors, at the same time avoiding the divesting of generation assets. They offered not to build new generation plants and to lease part of EDP's capacity for a limited period of time. The measures were considered highly inadequate to compensate the significant reduction of competition deriving from the loss of GDP as a competitor. In particular, the leased capacity would have accounted for no more than 4 percent of total generation capacity in Portugal. What is more, the leasing agreement could have been interrupted without ensuring the survival of effective competitors. At same time EDP was entitled to know in real time the costs and volumes of electricity that the lessee could market. All those circumstances, according to the Commission, made it very unlikely that the lessee could exercise any influence on the market and any significant competitive constraint on EDP. Moreover the commitment not to build new generation plants was likely to end without achieving the goal of allowing the entry of new actors on the market. The rest of the (minor) proposed commitments were also considered insufficient to re-establish effective competition on the market.

With reference to the vertical concerns expressed by the Commission, it accepted the proposed ownership unbundling of the (only) Portuguese terminal for gas, but the attached conditions were seen as hindering the full and effective implementation of unbundling. In particular, the possibility given to EDP subsidiaries active in Spain to book further capacity before the transfer and to the merging parties to do the same after the merger, would have impeded third parties from effectively building sufficient capacity. Similarly, the other proposed measures aimed at ensuring access to additional capacity to competitors were considered as neither timely, nor economically viable, nor sufficiently enduring to be acceptable.

The commitments offered to eliminate concerns on the retail market for electricity supply and on the natural gas market were also considered by the Commission as generating very few positive effects and unlikely to guarantee a competitive environment in the affected markets.[147] Accordingly, the Commission prohibited the proposed concentration.

d. **Fines, remedies, and conditions enclosed**
   None.

e. **Further developments of the case**
   Case T-87/05 *EDP – Energias de Portugal SA* v. *Commission* [2005] ECR II-16, appeal dismissed.

---

146 To see the precise list and content of the commitments submitted see recitals 610–649, 739–740 and 842–854 of the decision.

147 For an extensive view of the assessment the Commission gave of the proposed commitments see recitals 650–738, 741–841, and 855–912.

F.3   *Google/DoubleClick* Commission decision 2005/590/EC [2005] summary of the decision in OJ C 184/10 [2008]

Relevance: In this decision, the Commission carried out a far-reaching analysis of potential effects on competition of a proposed vertical merger. The Commission elaborated several possible foreclosure strategies of the merged entity and concluded that the concerns put forward by third parties were unjustified.

- Case COMP/M.4731
- **Decision:** Clearance decision in Phase II investigation pursuant to Article 8(2) of the Merger Regulation
- **Decision addressee(s):**
    - Google Inc., *United States*
- **Report route:** Notification of the proposed merger on 21 September 2007
- **Date of the decision:** 11 March 2008
- **Competition Commissioner:** N. Kroes
- **Relevant product market:** Online advertising space
- **Relevant geographical market:** EEA market
- **Description of the case**
    a. **Relevant facts**
    Google is a US company and has become the most well-known internet search engine that offers its services for users free of charge. The company collects almost all of its revenues from online advertising. Thus, it provides space for advertisements on its websites and on partner websites. It is also listed on the stock exchange. Google is moreover a direct provider for ad spaces whereas DoubleClick provides ad serving tools.

    DoubleClick is positioned on the opposite side of the market, where it develops and provides online advertising services – for instance, placement of advertisements on websites – to website publishers, advertisers, and advertising agencies. Online advertisements can be sold directly or through intermediation platforms that match advertisers with publishers providing suitable ad space. Those intermediation platforms can provide bundled or unbundled sales. Google offers with its AdSense network ad serving technology and intermediation services as bundled. On 13 April 2007 Google and DoubleClick agreed that the latter company would be acquired.

    The definition of the relevant product market in the online advertising industry is complex. The Commission drew a distinction between online and offline advertising. Online advertisements are paid for on the grounds of how many internet viewers have really established a contact with the ad – i.e. result-focused – whereas offline advertising is paid for on the grounds of how many consumers might see the advertisement.[148] Online advertisements can appear in text ads or more advanced display ads. Moreover, online advertisements can be sold directly or through an intermediate platform that matches advertisers with publishers. The Commission did not define the market further on the basis of the variety of forms of online advertisement or on the ground of different sales channels. A precise definition of the relevant product market was omitted

---

148   See recital 46 of the decision.

because the Commission concluded that the concentration would not give rise to competition concerns.

b. Origin of the case

On 21 September 2007, pursuant to Article 4 of the Merger Regulation, Google notified the proposed concentration to the Commission. Even though the transaction did not have a Community dimension, at least five Member States (Germany, Spain, Greece, Portugal, and United Kingdom) were affected and agreed to refer the case to the Commission pursuant to Article 4(5) of the Merger Regulation. On 13 November 2007, the Commission raised serious doubts as to the compatibility of the proposed merger with the common market and with the functioning of the EEA Agreement and decided to initiate a proceeding under Article 6(1)(c) of the Merger Regulation.

c. Economic analysis

The Commission considered the relationship between Google and DoubleClick as vertical on the grounds of the following arguments: firstly, the two companies were not direct competitors because they were acting in different markets. After the agreement of a publisher to sell ad space to an advertiser, ad serving technology is required. Suppliers of ad serving space and those of ad serving solutions sell complementary but not overlapping products. Google is present in the market for the provision of online advertising space whereas DoubleClick is not and concentrates on providing digital marketing technology.[149]

Secondly, the ad serving services constitute a very small part of the total costs of unbundled solutions.[150] Thus, a possible price increase in DoubleClick's ad serving tools after the merger probably would not lead to a switch of publishers and advertisers toward the unbundled solutions provided by Google. The Commission concluded rather that such a price increase would lead to publishers and advertisers switching to competing suppliers.

Further, DoubleClick faced other competitors in the market for ad service solutions that constrained the company's pricing.[151] On the advertiser side a competitor held a market share of 35%, equal to that of DoubleClick.[152] In addition, on the publisher side there are two competitors that are present with a market share of around 20% each.[153] Hence, these sides "are able to exert a significant competitive constraint on DoubleClick in the ad serving market."[154]

The Commission investigated further if the merged entity would implement foreclosure strategies. The complaints voiced that DoubleClick could raise its prices for its ad serving solutions after the constraint constituted by the threat of switching to the Google's AdSense bundled solution would have been removed by the merger.[155] DoubleClick's ad serving technology is substitutable with the bundled solution provided by Google. This would lead to an increase in total cost to an advertiser of purchasing display ad space. Google provides display ads placement through its AdSense network. The price increase would lead to some diversion of demand to Google that would be internalized by the

149   See recital 192 of the decision.
150   See recitals 195–202 of the decision.
151   See recital 194 of the decision.
152   See recitals 121–122 of the decision.

153   See recital 128 of the decision.
154   See recital 206 of the decision.
155   See recital 198 of the decision.

merged entity. As said, the cost of ad serving technology represents only a very small part of the total costs of unbundled solutions. Even significant price variations for ad serving tools are unlikely to lead to switching to other forms of advertisements.[156] As the degree of substitution between DoubleClick's ad serving tools and Google's intermediation is limited, the Commission concluded that "it is therefore very unlikely that the parties would have unilateral incentives to increase prices after the merger."[157] The consequence of a price increase would rather be that DoubleClick would lose clients because of the substantial competition mentioned above.[158]

Moreover, those products are clearly differentiated to some extent. It is therefore unlikely that Google's bundled solution and an unbundled solution that includes DoubleClick's display ad serving solution as an additional component constitute close substitutes. The Commission concluded that both solutions do not exert a significant competitive constraint on each other.[159] Therefore, a unilateral price increase would not be profitable for the new entity.

Furthermore, the Commission verified the likelihood of DoubleClick attempting to foreclose the market for intermediation platforms (competing with AdSense) by exercising its market power in the market for ad serving technology. DoubleClick could have raised the price for its ad services where not combined with Google's ad networks, so reducing the inventory available to other networks.

In line with the Non-Horizontal Merger Guidelines – according to which, in order for a merger to be blocked, the new entity has to have both the incentive and the ability to foreclose[160] – the Commission did not consider DoubleClick as having such an opportunity. In fact, DoubleClick possibly faced competitive constraints and did not possess the market power to implement a successful foreclosure strategy.[161] High switching costs to alternative competitors could also hinder customers to react on price increases. Nonetheless, DoubleClick's contracts last only two years, which is viewed as rather short-term compared to other ad serving providers.[162] Moreover, the Commission distinguishes a dynamic in the ability to switch to and from DoubleClick. Advertisers consider the total cost of purchasing ad space whereas publishers consider the total profit from selling such space. Only a substantial price increase of ad serving when used with a competing ad network could lead to a significant switch between ad networks.[163]

Therefore, the Commission concluded that "the proposed concentration would not significantly impede effective competition in the common market or in a substantial part of it."[164]

---

156   See recital 201 of the decision.
157   See recital 202 of the decision.
158   See recital 203 of the decision.
159   See recitals 212–221 of the decision.
160   Guidelines on the assessment of non-horizontal mergers under the Council Regulation on the control of concentrations between undertakings [2008] OJ C 265/6.
161   See recital 296 of the decision.
162   See recital 297 of the decision.
163   See recital 299 of the decision.
164   See recital 367 of the decision.

    d. Fines, remedies and conditions enclosed
    None.
    e. Further developments of the case
    None.

8.4 Minority acquisitions

A Introduction

While they are not the main concern of the competition authorities, minority or partial acquisitions can potentially cause antitrust problems. These concerns are structurally similar to unilateral and coordinated effects in case of (horizontal) mergers. Companies that own the partial equity of competing firms have incentives to adjust their market behavior according to the alignment of business objectives that result from (cross-)minority shareholdings. Essential for the evaluation of these effects are the ownership and control structures of the companies involved. When control is relatively strong, even when ownership is partial, minority shareholdings can facilitate (tacit) collusion. In particular, minority participations may weaken the incentive to cheat on a collusive agreement. The reason for this is that if competitors are partially self-owned, defection profits are reduced.

The control of possible anticompetitive effects of partial acquisitions is not part of the scope of application of the Merger Regulation, which applies only to operations bringing about a lasting change in the control of the undertakings concerned. By this is meant the possibility to exercise "decisive influence."[165] Therefore, if minority participation does not entail a significant change in control, the only legal instrument applicable remains Article 101 FEU, at least for agreements between undertakings.[166] The Commission's interpretation of the competitive effects of minority participation has changed over time. In part due to the small number of cases in which the Commission has had to assess the effects of minority participation, no uniform Commission approach to minority acquisitions has been formulated yet. Minority acquisition concerns have usually been analyzed in the frame of a broader merger assessment.

This section includes all formal Commission decisions in minority acquisitions. Several decisions adopted pursuant to Article 101 and 102 dealing with minority acquisitions in firms' equity are described in detail.

B Applicable EU legislation

No special legislation applicable. For applicable legislation see chapter 8, paragraph B.

---

165   See Article 3 of the Merger Regulation above.

166   With regard to this issue, the Commission states in its guidelines on horizontal agreements that "[t]he present guidelines do not, however, address all possible horizontal agreements. They are only concerned with those types of cooperation which potentially generate efficiency gains, namely agreements on R&D, production, purchasing, commercialisation, standardisation, and environmental agreements. Other types of horizontal agreements between competitors, for example on the exchange of information or on minority shareholdings, are to be addressed separately," Commission Guidelines on the applicability of Article 81 to horizontal co-operation agreements [2001] OJ C 3/2, point 10. Nonetheless, the Commission has so far not published guidelines or notices aimed at providing coherent criteria for the analysis of minority shareholdings agreement under Article 101 FEU Treaty.

C Related economics texts

Bishop and Walker (2009), chapter 7
Carlton and Perloff (2005), chapter 2, paragraph 2 and chapter 19, paragraph 3(5)
Church and Ware (2000), chapter 23
Martin (1994), chapters 9 and 10
Martin (2002), chapter 12
Motta (2004), chapters 5 and 7
Tirole (1988), paragraphs 4.6.2.1, 9.5, 9.6, and 9.7
Waldman and Jensen (2001), chapter 4

D Related legal texts

Bellamy and Child (2008), chapter 8, paragraph 6(C)
Jones and Sufrin (2008), chapter 12, not specifically discussed
Ritter and Braun (2005), chapter 6
Whish (2008), chapters 20, 21, and 22, not specifically discussed

E Commission decisions in chronological order°

Warner – Lambert/Gillette and Bic/Gillette and others **Commission decision 93/252/EEC [1993] OJ L 116/21, Cases IV/33.440, 33.486**
BT/MCI Commission Decision 94/579/EC [1994] OJ L 223/36, Case IV/34.857 **(described in detail as a landmark case in section 6.3)**
Olivetti/Digital Commission Decision 94/771/EC [1994] OJ L 309/24, Case IV/34.410
Phoenix/GlobalOne Commission decision 96/547/EC [1996] OJ L 239/57, Case IV/35.617

F. Economic landmark case

F.1 *Warner-Lambert/Gillette and Bic/Gillette and others* Commission decision 93/252/EEC [1993] OJ L 116/21

Relevance: In this decision, the Commission set the conditions under which a minority participation in competitors' equity capital can constitute an abuse of dominance and a restriction of the already limited competitiveness of the market. In doing so it applied and interpreted the *Philip Morris* doctrine established earlier by the ECJ. By means of this decision the Commission clarified that minority acquisition can be anticompetitive not only with regard to horizontal agreements between undertakings but also in the context of dominant firms.

- Cases IV/33.440, 33.486
- **Decision:** Infringement of Articles 101 and 102 FEU Treaty

---

° Decisions displayed in **bold type** are described in the section. Reference is made in brackets and **bold type** to the relevant section in which the decision is extensively described as a landmark case. When decisions are referenced and/or described in some detail in one or more of the economic textbooks, reference in brackets is also made to the relevant part(s) of those texts.

- **Decision addressee(s):**
  - The Gillette Company, *United States*
  - Eemland Holdings NV, *the Netherlands*
- **Report route:** Complaints filed to the Commission on 12 February and 14 March 1990 by Warner–Lambert Company and BIC SA, respectively; application for negative clearance and notification for exemption submitted to the Commission on 23 February 1990 by the Gillette Company for investment in and relationship with Eemland.
- **Date of the decision:** 10 November 1992
- **Competition Commissioner:** L. Brittan
- **Relevant product market:** Razors and razor blades
- **Relevant geographical market:** European internal market
- **Description of the case**
  - a. **Relevant facts**

    Stora Kopparbergs Bergslags (Stora) was a Swedish company that held a host of consumer product trademarks, among which was the trademark for Wilkinson Sword selling a variety of shaving and toiletry products. The Gillette Company (Gillette) is a US company with worldwide business in the development, manufacture, and sale of personal care products and in particular of shaving products, accounting for half of the group's sales. Eemland Holdings NV (Eemland) was the holding company used for transactions subject of this decision and which had since its creation in 1988 not been active in the relevant market.

    At the time of the decision Gillette was considered the dominant firm because it had a very strong market position, holding 70% of market share in the Community in terms of value of the sales. Wilkinson Sword, by contrast, held a mere 13 percent, and was struggling with a number of problems. Its situation was such that "[a]part from being highly concentrated, the market also exhibit[ed] considerable barriers to entry. These barriers consist of significant economies of scale on the production level, the importance of advertising and the considerable resources and expertise of the established manufacturers."[167]

    By a series of agreements Eemland bought the consumer product division from Stora including the Wilkinson Sword products. In turn it sold the Wilkinson Sword business that was outside the (then) EEC and the United States to Gillette and retained the business inside the EEC and the United States.

    The financial operation was carried out via Eemland, which was no more than a shell company financed by several investors including Gillette (via its subsidiary Gillette UK Limited) using a mixture of equity and loan capital. Gillette held 22 percent of the issued equity capital but did not have voting rights or other rights in the governance of the company. It did, however, acquire very crucial pre-emption and conversion rights and options in Eemland.[168]

    Among a number of agreements entered into by Gillette with Eemland, a clause by which Gillette agreed to indemnify Eemland, Stora, and investors against losses arising from antitrust proceedings relating to the Wilkinson Sword business was signed. The investment and overall agreement became the subject of an investigation, in the United States, of the Department of Justice,

---

167   Recital 9 of the decision.
168   For a more detailed description of Eemland corporate structure see recitals 13–16 of the decision.

as result of which Gillette was prohibited from acquiring any further interest in Eemland.

b. Origin of the case

On 12 February 1990 a complaint was filed to the Commission by the Warner-Lambert Company under Article 3 of Regulation 17 concerning the sale of the Wilkinson Sword wet-shaving business and alleging Gillette and Eemland infringement of Article 101(1) and Gillette infringement of Article 102. A similar complaint relating to the same matter was filed by BIC SA in March 1990.

On 23 February 1990 the Gillette Company submitted an application for negative clearance and notification for exemption to the Commission to see Article 101(1) FEU Treaty be declared not applicable to its agreements with and investments in Eemland or alternatively the same agreements and investments be declared exempted from the application of Article 101(1) FEU Treaty by virtue of Article 101(3) FEU Treaty.

c. Economic analysis

This decision is important because it represented the first case in which the Commission applied and further interpreted the principle established by the ECJ in the landmark judgment *Philip Morris* concerning minority participation in competitors' equity capital.[169]

The ECJ in *Philip Morris* stated firstly that "[a]lthough the acquisition by one company of an equity interest in a competitor does not in itself constitute conduct restricting competition, such an acquisition may nevertheless serve as an instrument for influencing the commercial conduct of the companies in question so as to restrict or distort competition on the market on which they carry on business... in particular where... the investing company obtains legal or de facto control of the commercial conduct of the other company or where the agreement provides for commercial cooperation between the companies or create[s] a structure likely to be used for such cooperation. That may also be the case where the agreement gives the investing company the possibility of reinforcing its position at a later stage and taking effective control of the other company. Account must be taken not only of the immediate effects of the agreement but also of its potential effects and of the possibility that the agreement may be part of a long-term plan."[170]

Secondly, regarding undertakings in a dominant position, the ECJ stated that the acquisition of a minority shareholding in a competing company could constitute an infringement of Article 102 if it confers some influence on the commercial policy of the competitor. In the particular circumstances of the case, however, the Court did not identify this kind of infringement.[171]

Comparing that interpretation of Article 102 with the one given by the Commission in *Gillette*, it may be concluded that the ECJ carried out an interpretative analysis of the criteria formulated by the Commission. This made

---

169   Joined Cases 142/84 and 156/84 *BAT* v. *Commission* [1987] ECR 4487.
170   *BAT* v. *Commission*, above recitals 37–39.
171   "An abuse of [dominant] position can only arise where the shareholding in question results in effective control of the other company or at least in *some influence* on its commercial policy." *Idem*, recital 65. Emphasis added.

Article 102 more likely to be applicable in circumstances dealing with the acquisition of minority participations and the strengthening of an existing dominant position.

Referring to the ECJ's case law regarding the abuse of dominant position[172] (although surprisingly without making reference to the *Continental Can Doctrine*[173]) the Commission found that Gillette had abused its dominant position by influencing the structure of the relevant market, thus restricting competition.

In its appraisal the Commission cited *Philip Morris* and the "*some influence*" doctrine.[174] Even if Gillette's possibilities of influencing the commercial conduct of both Eemland and Wilkinson Sword were much less likely to be effectively used because of the absence of any voting rights in Wilkinson Sword's assembly, the Commission considered the equity participation as possibly influencing Eemland's commercial choices. "Gillette has not only become a major shareholder in Eemland but has also become its largest creditor and has acquired important pre-emption and conversion rights and options in Eemland. The position of Gillette is a matter which the management of Eemland will be obliged to take into account and consequently it is a factor which will influence the commercial conduct of Eemland. It follows that Gillette will have at least some influence on Eemland's commercial policy."[175]

The Commission underlined the differences between the circumstances of the case and those that brought the ECJ to clear the agreement in *Philip Morris*. In particular the fact that it was the dominant firm acquiring minority participation in the rival's equity and not vice versa, as in *Philip Morris*, where a minority shareholding of the dominant firm was acquired by a competitor, led the Commission to conclude that Gillette did have power to influence Eemland's conduct. This assumption "cannot be disregarded simply because of the absence of voting rights and other usual shareholders' rights or because of Gillette's covenant not to exert or attempt to exert any influence over the Board or any member of the Board. Gillette is also a major creditor of Eemland [and the latter] cannot reasonably be expected to ignore this financial dependence on Gillette... In addition, Gillette has important pre-emption and conversion rights and options in Eemland. These rights ensure that no other competitor on the market such as Warner-Lambert or BIC can improve its competitive position through the acquisition of Eemland."[176] Those rights *de facto* impeded Eemland also from entering in a merger and/or joint venture agreement without Gillette's approval. Eemland's debt structure limited its competitive possibility (e.g. its ability to engage in adequate effective campaigns) and from that position of weakness and the derived lessening of competition, Gillette would have benefited as the dominant firm, according to the Commission. Similarly also the annulment of any technological competitive advantage Wilkinson Sword

---

172   Case 322/81 *Michelin* v. *Commission* [1983] ECR 3369   174   Recital 24 of the decision.
       and Case 85/76 *Hoffman-La Roche* v. *Commission* [1979]   175   *Idem.*
       ECR 461.   176   Recitals 25 and 26 of the decision.
173   Case 6/72 *Continental Can* above.

might have had before the agreement would have advantaged and strengthened the position of Gillette.

It is interesting to note that the Commission considered a loan (and thus financial dependence) as equivalent to cross-shareholding between competitors. The approach appears economically sensible as far as there is strong reciprocal interest in the economic success of the other company.

d. Fines, remedies, and conditions enclosed
- Obligations for Gillette and Eemland to bring the infringements to an end and to transmit to the Commission proposals aimed at the accomplishment of the injunction.
- Obligation for Gillette to dispose of its equity interest in Eemland and its interest as a creditor of Eemland.

e. Further developments of the case
None.

8.5   Economic defense arguments

A   Introduction

In recent years, the level of economic analysis applied in merger decisions of the European Commission has become more sophisticated. It has long been possible for a company acquiring another to merge into a highly concentrated market to mount a failing firm defense. To determine whether indeed without the takeover the acquired company would have disappeared from the market as an independent competitor requires rather deep economic analysis. The likely unilateral effects of a horizontal merger that leads to the elimination of one or more independent competitors can be analyzed in the structure of oligopoly models, fitted to the sector under scrutiny by using applied econometrics. Furthermore, the 2004 Merger Guidelines include possibilities for merging parties to invoke an efficiency argument for mergers that raise antitrust concerns. Indeed, it requires in principle that the potential anticompetitive effects of the merger are weighed against possible merger-specific efficiencies.

The most commonly argued such merger efficiencies result from economies of scale and scope, the creation of synergies in R&D, distribution and marketing, and administrative cost savings. In order to be admissible in the overall assessment of the effects of the merger on competition, an efficiency defense has to show convincingly that the claimed efficiencies can be achieved only by way of the merger and not in a less restrictive way. In addition, credible efficiencies will have to affect marginal and/or variable costs rather than fixed costs because the latter are not likely to be passed on to consumers. It is usually complicated to conduct an analysis of the future effects of a merger and thus competition authorities are urged to perform complex assessments which, however, imply a certain degree of discretion.

This section describes a number of cases in which a seminal economic defense argument for a proposed merger was made.

B   Applicable EU legislation

No special EU legislation applicable. For applicable legislation see chapter 8, paragraph B.

C Related economics texts

Bishop and Walker (2009), chapter 7, paragraphs 7.76–7.81, 7.87–7.88
Carlton and Perloff (2005), chapter 19, paragraph 3(5)
Church and Ware (2000), not specifically discussed
Martin (1994), not specifically discussed
Martin (2002), not specifically discussed
Motta (2004), chapter 5, specifically paragraphs 5.2 and 5.6.2
Tirole (1988), paragraph 9.7
Waldman and Jensen (2001), chapter 20

D Related legal texts

Bellamy and Child (2008), chapter 8, paragraphs 4 (g)(ii) and (iii)
Jones and Sufrin (2008), chapter 12, paragraphs (vi) and (vii)
Ritter and Braun (2005), chapter 6, paragraph 2(d)
Whish (2008), chapter 21, paragraph (c)(v) and chapter 22, paragraph (c)(vii)

E Commission decisions in chronological order•

Volvo/Scania **Commission decision 2001/403/EC [2000] OJ L 143/74, Case COMP/M.1672**
(Motta, 2004, p.239, n. 24, and 295; Bishop and Walker, 2009, 15.26–15.28 and 15.38)
NewsCorp/Telepiú **Commission decision 2004/311/EC [2004] OJ L 110/73, Case COMP/ M.2876**
Kornäs/AssiDomän Cartonboard **Commission decision 2006/C209/05 [2006] summary of the decision OJ C 209/12, Case COMP/M.4057**

F Economic landmark cases

F.1 *Volvo/Scania* Commission decision 2001/403/EC, [2001] OJ L 143/74

Relevance: The parties claimed economies of scale as a reason to merge. The decision is one of the most prominent examples of how the Commission can assess the (unilateral) effects of the proposed merger on the basis of a market simulation analysis. The decision shows how such an experiment can support a finding of dominance.

- For case report, relevant market, facts finding, allegation, economic analysis, obligations fines and remedies, and further development of the case, see Case *F.2* in section *8.1.*

F.2 *NewsCorp/Telepiú* Commission decision 2004/311/EC [2004] OJ L 110/73

Relevance: Even though the claimed "failing firm defense" was rejected by the Commission, the financial difficulties of the target undertaking were taken into account. The decision further states the strict requirements of the concept of the "rescue merger" but illustrates that

---

• Decisions displayed in **bold type** are described in the section. Reference is made in brackets and **bold type** to the relevant section in which the decision is extensively described as a landmark case. When decisions are referenced and/or described in some detail in one or more of the economic textbooks, reference in brackets is also made to the relevant part(s) of those texts.

the Commission can also take a more flexible approach and include the financial situation of undertakings in their analysis.

- Case COMP/M.2876
- **Decision**: Clearance decision with commitments and obligations enclosed in a Phase II investigation pursuant to Article 8(2) of the Merger Regulation.
- **Decision addressee(s)**:
    - The News Corporation Ltd, *United States*
- **Report route**: Notification of the proposed concentration on 16 October 2002.
- **Date of the decision**: 2 April 2003
- **Competition Commissioner**: M.Monti
- **Relevant product market**: Pay-TV
- **Relevant geographical market**: Italy
- **Description of the case**
    a. **Relevant facts**
    The News Corporation Limited Australia (NewsCorp) is an Australian media group with activities in the United States, Canada, Europe, Australia, Latin America, and the Pacific Basin. Telepiú Spa (Telepiú) is an Italian pay-TV company which also operates via digital satellite and to a lesser extent via cable since 1996. Stream Spa was a second TV platform which at the time of the decision operated only in digital technology. After the Commission's authorisation[177] in 2000, Stream became a joint venture of NewsCorp and Telecom Italia on a 50–50 basis by a shareholders' agreement.[178] NewsCorp notified to the Commission that it would acquire control of the whole of Telepiú and Stream by purchasing shares.[179] The activities of both undertakings would be merged in a combined satellite pay-TV platform. Telecom Italia would further hold a minority stake with a maximum share of 19.9% in this newly combined pay-TV platform.

    b. **Origin of the case**
    On 16 October 2002, pursuant to Article 4 of Regulation No. 4064/89 (as amended by Regulation No. 1310/97), the undertaking NewsCorp notified to the Commission the proposed concentration. On 29 November 2002, the Commission started investigations in accordance with Article 6(1)(c) of the Merger Regulation after finding that the concentration possibly created a dominant position. On 13 March 2003, the applicant submitted a set of commitments in accordance with Article 8(2) and 10(2) of the Merger Regulation in order to respond to the competition concerns which had been raised by the Commission.

    c. **Economic analysis**
    In assessing the effect of the proposed concentration the Commission found that "the merger will lead to substantial horizontal overlaps in a number of markets which are vertically related."[180] Before the merger Telepiú was already holding a dominant position on the pay-TV market in Italy and further in the

---

177   *Telekom Italia/News Television Stream* Commission decision SG(2000)D/104578 [2000] non-opposition notice in OJ C 66/14, Case COMP/M.1978.
178   See recital 9 of the decision.
179   See recital 1 of the decision.
180   See recital 78 of the decision.

market for the acquisition of exclusive rights for premium films.[181] Through the establishment of a combined platform of Stream and Telepiú a monopoly would be formed in the Italian pay-TV market. Additionally, the Commission found that a quasi-monopolistic situation would be created in acquisition markets.[182] Moreover, it was concluded that there would be almost no competition left in the affected markets after the merger without further conditions ensuring the openness of the market.[183] The Commission considered that the rise of future competitive constraints was unlikely in a post-merger situation without additional requirements and concluded that the merger would actually lead to the creation of a dominant position for Telepiú.[184]

Even if it created market dominance, the merger could be considered as not problematic in that sense if the target firm – here, Stream – constitutes a failing firm. In applying the concept of the failing firm defense, the Commission analyzed firstly, if Stream as "failing firm" would in the "in the near future be forced out of the market if not taken over by another undertaking."[185] The parties claimed that Stream would not become profitable as a stand-alone entity. The Commission did not follow the claim by the parties concerned because there were indications that Stream's financial situation could be improved by better management and an increased effort to combat piracy.[186] The Commission was further confronted with the fact that the acquirer of the failing firm, NewsCorp, was actually one of its parent companies. It was unlikely that the entire firm – in the present case, NewsCorp – would exit the market. It thus appeared that Stream's withdrawal from the pay-TV market would be a management decision to dispose of the business activity which did not meet the expectations of the firm's managing board.[187]

Secondly, the Commission inquired whether there was a less anticompetitive purchaser and concluded that the parties could not prove the existence of such a rival.[188]

Thirdly, the Commission required NewsCorp to show that the assets to be purchased would inevitably exit the market in the absence of the merger. Furthermore, the Commission stressed that a requirement of the claim of a failing firm defence is that the deterioration of the competitive structure through the merger is at least no worse than in the absence of the merger.[189] In case of Stream's bankruptcy, the rights would be returned to the rights holders, who would probably sell them to Telepiú. Thus, the third condition was met. The three conditions are cumulative and, hence, it was not sufficient to consider Stream as a failing firm if only one requirement is proven. The Commission concluded that "NewsCorp has not been able to demonstrate that there is no causal link between the concentration and the effect on competition because

181   See recitals 80 and 144 of the decision.
182   See recital 150 of the decision.
183   See recitals 103–113 the decision.
184   See recital 204 of the decision.
185   See recital 207 of the decision. See also Guidelines on the assessment of horizontal mergers [2004] OJ C 31/5, pp. 89–91.

186   See recital 213 of the decision.
187   See recital 214 of the decision.
188   See recital 217 of the decision.
189   See recital 209 of the decision.

conditions of competition can be expected to deteriorate to a similar or identical extent even without the concentration in question."[190]

Although the Commission rejected the application of the failing firm defence it considered, among other things, the "chronic financial difficulties" of Telepiú and Stream. Here, the Commission has taken a more flexible approach to the concept of the failing firm. It considered that the conditional authorization of the concentration would rather lead to the benefit of consumers than the disruption that would have been caused by the likely closure of Stream which was the smaller and weaker operator of the two.

d. **Fines, remedies, and conditions enclosed**

NewsCorp offered a number of commitments to remove the competition concerns:[191]

- Access to content, such as blockbuster movies, football matches, and other sport rights in the market.
- Access to platform and to technical services that are essential for actual or potential competitors to broadcast by satellite without having to set up their own platform and thus, prevent an entry barrier.
- Divestitures of Telepiù's digital and analogue terrestrial broadcasting activities and further not to enter into any further DTT activities either as network or as retail operator.
- Effective implementation of the conditions through a private arbitration procedure that involves on one side a private arbitration system and on the other side the Italian Community Authority on key issues.
- The commitments will be in force until 31 December 2011.[192]

According to the Commission, the submitted commitments were sufficient to resolve the concerns of a creation of a dominant position by ensuring lower entry barriers and creating conditions for competition.

e. **Further developments of the case**

None.

F.3 *Korsnäs/AssiDomän Cartonboard* Commission decision 2006/C209/05 summary of the decision OJ C 209/12 [2006]

Relevance: Efficiency defense. In this decision the Commission analyzed in detail the arguments put forward by the party that the merger would generate efficiencies. Regardless of the considered efficiencies the decision was to a greater extent influenced by facts such as buyer power, increased competition outside the EEA, and the fact that the two companies were not each other's closest competitors.

- Case COMP/M.4057
- **Decision:** Non-opposition decision in a Phase I investigation pursuant to Article 6(1)(b) of the Merger Regulation.
- **Decision addressee(s):**
  - Korsnäs AB, *Sweden*

---

190   See recital 221 of the decision.
191   See recitals 225–260 of the decision.

192   See recital 260 of the decision

- **Report route:** Notification of the proposed merger on 31 March 2006
- **Date of the decision:** 12 May 2006
- **Competition Commissioner:** N. Kroes
- **Relevant product market:** Production and sale of liquid packaging boards
- **Relevant geographical market:** EEA market
- **Description of the case**
  - a. **Relevant facts**

    Korsnäs is a producer of paper board and especially liquid packaging board. Further, it is a wholly owned subsidiary of a Swedish holding company with equity interests in several companies. The acquired undertaking, AssiDomän Cartonboard Holding AB (AD Cartonboard), is also a paper board producer that operates in liquid and non-liquid packaging board.[193] AD Cartonboard is wholly owned by Sweden's largest forest owner, that is in turn owned by the Swedish state. The main customer of both undertakings is Tetra Pak, whose purchases accounted for 90–100% in 2005.[194]

    In defining the relevant product market, the Commission distinguished between markets for liquid and non-liquid packaging boards because of product characteristics, different supply structures, and customer structures.[195] The products differ in printability, stiffness or smell. A high specialization leads to a limited number of qualified suppliers. Moreover, the customer structure for non-liquid packaging board is more fragmented. The Commission concluded that "it is not necessary to reach a definitive position as to the question of possible narrower product markets as the proposed transaction does not raise competition concerns under any conceivable product market definitions."[196]

    Even though there were some characteristics indicating a worldwide product market, the relevant geographical market was found to be EEA-wide because of low volumes of imports into the EEA, the importance for just-in-time (JIT) deliveries and transport costs for converters.[197]

  - b. **Origin of the case**

    On 31 March 2006, a notification of the proposed merger pursuant to Article 4 following a referral to Article 4(5) of the Merger Regulation was received by the Commission. The undertaking Korsnäs AB acquired control within the meaning of Article 3(1)(b) of the Merger Regulation of the whole of the company AD Cartonboard by purchasing shares.

  - c. **Economic analysis**

    In determining the impact of a merger the Commission took substantiated and likely efficiencies into account as an additional factor to outweigh anticompetitive effects arising from the merger.

    With regard to the market structure for liquid packaging board which is characterized by the existence of one large (StoraEnso) and two smaller suppliers (Korsnäs and AD Cartonboard), with the new entity the second largest supplier in the EEA would be created whereas StoraEnso would remain the leading

---

193   See recital 3 of the decision.
194   See recitals 2 and 3 of the decision.
195   See recitals 9 and 10 of the decision; *Enso/Stora/Scaldia* [2005] OJ C189/9, Case COMP/M.1225, recital 41.
196   See recital 22 of the decision.
197   See recital 24 of the decision.

company.[198] Thus, the Commission concluded that the concentration would not result in the creation of a single dominant firm. The Commission further considered competitive effects resulting from the merged entity. A possible price increase caused by less competition in the EEA among the two remaining liquid packaging boards suppliers had not been uncovered by the Commission. It took into consideration that both companies do not have an overlapping product portfolio and thus, are not each other's closest competitors.[199] The enlarged portfolio would rather enable the new entity to compete more effectively with the much larger supplier, StoraEnso. In addition, the Commission found that there was enough countervailing power by customers, for instance Tetra Pak, and that other suppliers would react to possible price increases by the new entity with an increase in production and thus make price increases for the merged entity or StoraEnso unprofitable.[200] This is possible because there is a significant degree of supply-side substitutability between products of the new entity and other consumer packaging boards. Moreover, the Commission concluded that future competitive constraints from non-EEA competitors needed to be considered as a growing trend toward competitive production of liquid packaging boards outside the EEA.

Furthermore, the Commission evaluated efficiencies brought forward by the party. According to the Horizontal Merger Guidelines,[201] the efficiencies created by the merger might counteract the effects on competition and the potential harm to consumers. However, in order to accept an efficiency defense, the following cumulative conditions must be satisfied: the efficiencies have to be merger-specific, verifiable, and benefit consumers.[202]

Efficiencies are merger-specific if they are a direct consequence of the notified merger and cannot be achieved by less, but also practically achievable, less anticompetitive alternatives.[203] Firstly, substantial synergies as a result of the merger, such as saving input costs, reducing personnel and improvement of production efficiencies, were expected to result from the concentration. The Commission stated that the claimed efficiencies were estimated to amount to 0–5 percent of the merged entity's net sales, and held them to be substantial.[204]

Secondly, efficiencies in innovation and technological progress were claimed to result from the merger. The merged entity will be enabled to realize R&D efficiencies and benefit from implementing best practices across the two production sites.[205]

The Commission emphasized that the new entity would be allowed to compete more effectively with StoraEnso because of its larger product portfolio than Korsnäs and Cartonboard separately.[206] The allocation of production among

---

198   See recital 28 of the decision.
199   See recital 34 of the decision.
200   See recitals 42–53 of the decision.
201   Guidelines on the assessment of horizontal mergers under the Council Regulation on the control of concentration between undertakings [2004] OJ C 31/5, pp. 5–18.
202   *Idem*, p. 78.
203   Guidelines on the assessment of horizontal mergers, *ibidem*, p. 85.
204   See recital 57 of the decision.
205   See recital 58 of the decision.
206   See recitals 60–63 of the decision.

the increased portfolio of machines was considered by the Commission to enable the new entity to increase production and, hence, be more beneficial to consumers.

In order to demonstrate that the efficiencies were beneficial to customers, the merging parties presented a term sheet agreement between Korsnäs and Tetra Pak including specific provisions for deliveries for 2006–9 conditional upon the implementation of the merger with Cartonboard.[207] The term sheet agreement underlined how crucial customer support would be for the outcome of the Commission's decision. Moreover, the term sheet agreement was considered as an earnest that the claimed efficiencies were to be realized immediately after the completion of the transaction.

The Commission agreed that "it appears realistic to assume that the allocation of production among the increased portfolio of machines will indeed allow the merged entity to increase overall production . . . In light of the above mentioned term sheet agreement with Tetra Pak and on the general absence of concern about the transaction among customers . . . the parties have sufficiently established that this category of efficiencies is likely to occur and be passed on to consumers."[208] In addition, the claimed efficiencies were believed to be sufficiently probable so as to be materialized in the future.[209]

The Commission considered claimed efficiencies as one of several factors for the unconditional approval in this 3 to 2 merger case.

d. **Fines, remedies, and conditions enclosed**
   None.

e. **Further developments of the case**
   None.

8.6 Merger remedies

A Introduction

Pursuant to the Merger Regulation, the Commission might declare mergers compatible with the internal market (i.e. approve them) conditionally on the compliance with some precisely identified remedies (and enclosed conditions and obligations).[210] Similar powers rest with the competition authorities in the relevant jurisdictions. Remedies are usually divided into two main categories: structural remedies and behavioral remedies. Structural remedies involve changes in the ownership of existing businesses, relating to both entire and partial ownership. Structural remedies, to use the words of the CFI (now "the General Court"), "prevent once and for all, or at least for some time, the emergence or strengthening of the dominant position previously

---

207   See recital 59 of the decision.
208   See recital 63 of the decision.
209   Guidelines on the assessment of horizontal mergers, *ibidem*, pp. 86–8.
210   See Articles 6(2) and 8(2) of Merger Regulation cited above, *supra*, n. 2. In particular, in both Phase I and II of the merger procedure, the firms involved in the merger – particularly where the Commission has already expressed some competitive concerns for the operation – can propose remedies and commit to comply with them. The Commission can, if it considers the proposed commitments appropriate to overcome the concerns and to make the concentration compatible with the common market, declare those commitments binding upon the undertakings in an official decision. The Commission can also attach to its decision conditions and obligations aimed at the undertakings' compliance with their commitments.

identified by the Commission and do not, moreover, require medium or long term monitoring measures."[211]

The most significant example of structural remedies is the divestiture of a business.[212] This can be an efficient remedy particularly in situations in which the merger creates overlaps in particular (geographical) areas or areas of activity. In Europe, divestitures are accepted by the Commission as a viable instrument to eliminate anticompetitive effects of a merger if the divested assets constitute a viable business and are acquired by a suitable purchaser able to be an effective competitor of the merging entity. This is in line with an effective use and surveillance over the use of divesting instruments as a solution to eliminate the restrictive effects of a concentration.

It has to be noted, though, that the use of divestitures can create problems. Authorities should be particularly wary of the fact that the selling firm has a strong incentive to sell to a buyer that is unlikely to be a viable competitor, one which is neither able to efficiently use the sold assets independently from the seller nor generally one that is able to jeopardize its market power. Asymmetry of information between buyer and seller about the value and the functions of the divested assets might facilitate such behavior. Competition authorities should exercise control over such potential side effects of divestitures. Simultaneously, authorities should not discard concerns about the coordinated effects of the divestiture lightly.

Behavioral remedies impose restrictions on the exercise of property rights and usually consist in commitments to grant access to certain goods or infrastructure (e.g. in case of essential facilities) or to terminate ongoing exclusive agreements. Unlike structural remedies, behavioral remedies require constant monitoring and regulatory actions by the competition authorities, otherwise they could be easily duped by the merging firms.[213] Their implementation and monitoring requires a constant analysis of the industry at hand. The Commission has made use of behavioral remedies where structural remedies were not deemed suitable. In its Notice on acceptable remedies, the Commission explicitly mentions termination of exclusive agreements and access to necessary infrastructure or key technology.[214]

B   Applicable EU legislation

No special legislation applicable. For applicable legislation see chapter 8, paragraph B.

C   Related economics texts

Bishop and Walker (2009), chapter 7
Carlton and Perloff (2005), chapter 2, paragraph 2 and chapter 19, paragraph 3(5)
Church and Ware (2000), chapter 23
Martin (1994), chapters 9 and 10
Martin (2002), chapter 12
Motta (2004), chapters 5 and 7
Tirole (1988), paragraphs 4.6.2.1, 9.5, 9.6, and 9.7
Waldman and Jensen (2001), chapter 4

---

211   Case T-102/96 *Gencor* v. *Commission* [1999] ECR II-753, recital 319.
212   An example of a structural remedy, given by the CFI in *Gencor*, was "a commitment to reduce the market share of the entity arising from a concentration by the sale of a subsidiary," see Case T-102/96 *Gencor* v. *Commission* [1999] ECR II-753, recital 319.
213   See Case T-102/96 *Gencor* v. *Commission* [1999] ECR II-753, recital 319.
214   See Commission Notice on remedies acceptable under Council Regulation (EC) 139/2004 and under Commission Regulation (EC) No. 802/2004 [2008] OJ C 267/1.

D Related legal texts

Bellamy and Child (2008), chapter 8, paragraph 3(D)
Jones and Sufrin (2008), chapter 12, paragraph 5(G)
Ritter and Braun (2005), chapter 6
Whish (2008), chapters 20, paragraph 6(E) and 21, paragraph 6

E Selection of commission decisions in chronological order[*]

Nestlé/Perrier **Commission decision 92/553/EEC [1992] OJ L 356/1, Case IV/M.190** (Bishop
   and Walker, 2009, 4.30, 4.34, 7.70, 10.02, 10.11, 10.20, 16.15, 16.16; Motta, 2004, pp. 279–86
   and 104, 109, 119, 120, 271, 277)
Boeing/McDonnell Douglas **Commission decision 97/816/EC [1997] OJ L 336/16, Case
   IV/M.877** (Bishop and Walker, 2009, 3.13, 12.07, 12.08, 12.11; Motta, 2004, pp.115, 119,
   120)
SEB/Moulinex **Commission decision SG (2002) D/228087 of 8 January 2002 non-opposition
   notice in OJ C 49/18, Case COMP/M.2621**
Vodafone Airtouch/Mannesmann **Commission decision 2003/C 300/06 [2003] non-opposition
   notice in OJ C 300/10, Case IV/M.1795** (Bishop and Walker, 2009, 7.82, 7.83)

F Economic landmark cases

F.1 *Nestlé/Perrier* Commission decision 92/553/EEC [1992] OJ L 356/1[215]

   Relevance: This decision represents the first merger case in which the Commission
challenged the proposed concentration on the argument that it would have created collective
dominance. The merger was cleared subject to the significant divestitures (structural remedies)
proposed by Nestlé and made binding upon the parties by the Commission.

- Case IV/M.190
- **Decision:** Clearance decision with commitments and obligations enclosed in a Phase II
  investigation pursuant to Article 8(2) of the Merger Regulation
- **Decision addressee(s):**
    – Nestlé SA, *Switzerland*
- **Report route:** Notification of a public bid for the acquisition of 100 percent shares of
  Source Perrier SA on 25 February 1992
- **Date of the decision:** 22 July 1992
- **Competition Commissioner:** L. Brittan
- **Relevant product market:** Bottled mineral waters
- **Relevant geographical market:** France

- [*] For this section, instead of a complete list of Commission decisions in chronological order, we only present a selection of merger
   decisions that have been significant for the development of European merger control. Decisions displayed in **bold type** are
   described in the section. Reference is made in brackets and **bold type** to the relevant section in which the decision is
   extensively described as a landmark case. When decisions are referenced and/or described in some detail in one or more of the economic
   textbooks, reference in brackets is also made to the relevant part(s) of those texts.
- 215 The full text of this decision is only available in French. An English translation of the document is available on Euro-Lex website
   at: http://eur-lex.europa.eu/LexUriServ/LexUriServ.do?uri=CELEX:31992D0553:EN:HTML.

- **Description of the case**
  a. **Relevant facts**

Nestlé SA (Nestlé) is a Swiss company active in a number of markets in the food industry throughout the world. Source Perrier SA (Perrier) is a French company involved in the production and distribution of bottled mineral water.

The proposed operation aimed at the acquisition of control by Nestlé over Perrier via a public bid for the totality of the Perrier shares launched by a subsidiary of Nestlé (Demilac). Simultaneously Nestlé concluded an agreement with French firm BSN according to which the Volvic source of Perrier would have been sold to BSN if Nestlé had acquired control of Perrier.[216]

In the definition of the relevant product market the main issue was to decide if the mineral source water, as proposed by the parties, was part of the same market together with non-alcoholic refreshment drinks. Starting from the assumption that "a limited substitutability in terms of functionality alone is not sufficient to establish substitutability in competition terms," the Commission made a qualitative analysis of the potential product substitutability both from a demand and a supply perspective. From the demand side, water and soft drinks responded to different needs and perceptions for customers. Water was associated with the idea of natural product, purity, and a healthy life; its consumption responds to basic needs, and it is bought regularly by consumers for daily use and in large quantities. On the contrary, soft drinks tend to be consumed much more occasionally and usually are used to satisfy a particular taste pleasure.

The Commission substantiated its view applying the Small but Significant and Non-Transitory Increase in Price (SSNIP) test. It stated "three main factors indicate that it cannot be reasonably expected that an appreciable non-transitory increase in the price of source waters compared with that of soft drinks would lead to a significant shift of demand from source waters to soft drinks for reasons of price only."[217] In particular, the Commission focused on the substantial price difference in absolute terms between the two categories of products that constantly characterized the market. In addition, it noted how the strong advertising investment by water producers focusing on an image of a natural, pure, and healthy product which did not belong to other beverage products, substantiated the lack of substitutability between water and soft drinks in the consumers' image. Finally the manufacturers' price evolution over the previous five years had been very different for water and soft drinks. The retailers consulted during the investigations confirmed the differentiation of the markets.

From the supply-side perspective, the production of mineral water was subject to a number of regulatory constraints. Producers needed an authorization and were required to bottle the water at the source. The latter requirements implied that, unlike many soft drinks producers, water producers could not grant trademark licenses to independent bottlers and then resell the product under the original brand name. In case of water the brand name is only associated with the source. Soft drinks producers did not have any of these constraints and, in addition, none of them was active on the market for mineral water production. Moreover the Commission noted how the price strategies followed different

216   Recital 9 of the decision.   217   Recital 13 of the decision.

logics. All these market features, and the production, regulatory, and marketing constraints, pointed toward a very limited supply-side substitutability. It would have been very difficult, if not impossible, to convert a water bottling plant into a production plant for soft drinks, and vice versa.[218] Notwithstanding some differences in price, the Commission refrained from partitioning the relevant product market into submarkets for sparkling, still, and flavored water.

As for the relevant geographical market, the Commission determined France as the relevant area, basing its assessment on the fact that the transportation costs for water at that time were very high, that the demand in different EU Member States was very different in nature, and that trade flows in the Community (besides export from Belgium) was of minor relevance. In addition, the maturity and concentration of the French market, together with the high costs related to the potential reimport of water, also made it complicated to penetrate for (potential) competitors in terms of access to the distribution system. An additional impediment for foreign competitors would have been the large amount of investments made by the three main national producers (Nestlé, Perrier, BSN) for advertising their brand waters over a number of years. The establishment of a new brand would have required large sunk investments and a long time.[219]

The market was highly concentrated. According to the data provided by Nestlé and reproduced by the Commission in its decision, the three main national water suppliers held a market share of 82.3 percent of the French bottled water market by value and nearly 75 percent by volume. The remaining suppliers mainly operated at a local level.[220]

b. Origin of the case

On 25 February 1992, pursuant to Article 4 of Regulation 4064/89 (as amended by Regulation 1310/97), Nestlé notified a public bid for 100 percent of the shares of Perrier that was launched by Demilac, a subsidiary jointly controlled by Nestlé and Banque Indosuez. By formal decision the Commission imposed the suspension of the concentration pursuant to Article 7(2) of the Merger Regulation. When Nestlé acquired the majority of the shares in Perrier it was prohibited from exercising the corresponding rights pursuant to Article 7(3) of the Merger Regulation. On 25 March 1992, with a formal decision, the Commission found that the acquisition raised serious doubts as to its compatibility with the single market and initiated proceedings pursuant to Article 6(1)(c) of the Merger Regulation.

c. Economic analysis

Emanating from the high degree of concentration in the market, the Commission analyzed further post-merger market features to assess the impact of the proposed acquisition in terms of competition.

Firstly, the Commission noted that even if the parties claimed to operate at the maximum of their capacities, each of the two large national post-merger suppliers would dispose of significant idle capacity readily available in case of

218 See recitals 15–18 of the decision.   220   See recitals 49–59 of the decision.
219 See recitals 21–34 of the decision.

a positive demand shock. "After the merger and the sale of Volvic to BSN, the two suppliers would have a considerable number of sources, the overall free capacity of which would by far exceed the total water market volume . . . and each of these two suppliers would have at least one major still mineral water source with huge free capacity compared to the overall market volume and all other local supplier[s]. They would thus be in a position to respond to an increase in demand without any capacity limitation."[221]

The Commission then turned to the market's high transparency. "Even without the merger a narrow oligopoly of three suppliers exists between whom price competition is considerably weakened and for whom the degree of market transparency is very high."[222] Prices had been increasing in a parallel fashion in the preceding five years[223] and the cross-price elasticity of demand for national still waters was relatively low due to high brand loyalty.[224] In addition, the market transparency was fortified if not safeguarded by the three producers routinely publishing price lists and rebates systems and the fact that each producer received monthly sales figures per brand from the Chamber of Commerce.[225]

As acknowledged by the same parties, the cost structures of the three firms were very similar. Furthermore, the competitive pressure exercised by remaining local suppliers (none of whom reached 10 percent of the national market), given their dimension, a number of structural disadvantages they had compared to the big producers, their sales volume, and financial strength, could not constitute a significant constraint for the remaining two post-merger companies.[226]

The Commission decided that even though the merging parties submitted that the ten largest customers, being the distribution groups, accounted for almost 70 percent of the three firms' total turnover, and the first four taking half of all sales, the bargaining power of the big distribution chains was still relatively low. This was due to the fact that none of them represented more than 15 percent of the total turnover of the three firms and that the demand side was in any case characterized by the presence of a large number of other purchasers. Furthermore the mineral water market showed a strong brand loyalty by final consumers. Therefore, bid distributors could not afford not to sell for long periods one of the well-known brand because that would have caused them large losses. Bargaining power was thus even more diminished by these circumstances. Given the post-merger brands portfolio of each of the two companies, in practise none of the distributors – even considering their lasting practise to grant discounts on the basis of the whole volume purchased – would have been in a position to operate on the market without the products of Nestlé-Perrier and BSN.[227]

The emergence of potential competitors was also very unlikely due to the very high entry barriers the Commission had already described in the definition

221   Recital 54 of the decision.
222   Recital 57 of the decision.
223   See recital 59 of the decision.
224   See recitals 60 of the decision.

225   See in particular recital 62 of the decision.
226   See recitals 64–76 of the decision.
227   See recitals 77–89 of the decision.

of the relevant geographic market (e.g. a mature market, high brand loyalty, difficulty in accessing the distribution network).[228]

All these considerations led the Commission to conclude that "the proposed merger between Nestlé and Perrier would create a duopolistic dominant position which would significantly impede effective competition on the French bottled water market."[229] The Commission supported its argument by highlighting that the French market for mineral water had developed instruments of transparency facilitating tacit collusion, that companies had developed "instruments to control and monitor each other's behavior,"[230] and that R&D played only a minor role in such a mature market.[231]

d. Fines, remedies, and conditions enclosed

Nestlé offered a number of commitments to meet the requirements of the Commission to facilitate the entry of a viable competitor able to exert some competitive pressure on Nestlé and BSN behavior.

- Nestlé agreed to sell a number of mineral and spring water brands with sufficient capacity for bottling 3 millions liters per year.
- It agreed not to reveal sales data for the past twelve months to any trade association as long as the market remained oligopolistic.
- It agreed to maintain separate from its own operations all assets and interests acquired in Perrier until the divesting operation was completed and during the same period not to make any structural change in Perrier's business without prior Commission approval. At the same time it would have made all steps to ensure that Perrier's assets were maintained separate.
- During the period of separate holding, Nestlé was to prevent Perrier management from transferring any business secrets, know-how, or other industrial information and/or secrets.
- Concerning the acquirer of the divested assets, Nestlé should have been financially strong and experienced enough as to develop a nationwide distribution organization and to adequately promote the acquired brands. It also needed to be completely financially, structurally, and personally unrelated to Nestlé, Perrier, BSN, their subsidiaries and any individual related to them.[232]

According to the Commission, full compliance with the proposed commitments would have allowed the acquirer of the divested assets to have almost 20 percent of the water capacity previously owned by the three national suppliers, to rely on a number of well-established brands, and to gain a guaranteed foothold in major retail stores. This would have created a viable new competitor able to effectively constrain Nestlé-Perrier and BSN in their market behavior.

---

228 See recitals 90–107 of the decision.
229 Recital 108 of the decision. The Commission then explained why the dominance test provided by Article 2(3) of the Merger Regulation was applicable not only to single-firm dominance but also to cases of collective dominance. This decision was the first case in which the collective dominance test was applied. See recitals 110–116 of the decision.
230 Recital 122 of the decision.
231 See recitals 120–130 of the decision.
232 See recital 136 of the decision.

Consequently the merger would be compatible with the common market and cleared.

e. Further developments of the case
None.

F.2   *Boeing/McDonnell Douglas* Commission decision 97/816/EC [1997] OJ L 336/16

Relevance: In the post-merger market only two global actors would have remained active. The Commission raised serious doubts about the compatibility of the concentration with the internal market. This decision is a prime example of how in duopolistic markets competition can be left undistorted. The Commission did, however, not clear the merger until Boeing had proposed a variety of remedies to open the market to competition.

- Case IV/M.877
- **Decision:** Clearance decision with commitments and obligations enclosed in a Phase II investigation pursuant to Article 8(2) of the Merger Regulation
- **Decision addressee(s):**
  - The Boeing Company, *United States*
- **Report route:** Notification of the proposed concentration on 18 February 1997
- **Date of the decision:** 30 July 1997
- **Competition Commissioner:** K. Van Miert
- **Relevant product market:** Large commercial jet aircrafts
- **Relevant geographical market:** Global market
- **Description of the case**
  a. **Relevant facts**
      Boeing is a publicly traded US corporation producing commercial and military aircraft as well as space aircraft. McDonnell Douglas is also a publicly traded US corporation and it is mainly active in four different areas: military aircraft; missile, space, and electronic systems; commercial aircraft; and financial services. In December 1996 the two companies reached an agreement by which McDonnell Douglas would have become a wholly owned subsidiary of Boeing.

      In the pre-merger market there were three worldwide competitors for the production of large commercial aircrafts: Boeing, Airbus, and McDonnell Douglas. Producers of smaller-size aircrafts were not considered competitors but rather as supplying a different market. Similarly Russian aircraft "are not to be included either, since . . . it appears that they do not yet constitute a real alternative, for reasons of reliability, after-sales service and public image."[233] The customers were mainly airline companies and leasing companies (leasing jets to airlines), the latter serving no more than 20 percent of demand from airlines. Clearly, demand for jet aircraft is driven by the demand for air transportation.

      The figures provided by the parties in the notification revealed that the overall world market share of Boeing was 64 percent, Airbus held a 30 percent market share while McDonnell Douglas supplied the remaining 6 percent. The merging parties also provided data about the average market share for the period

---

233   Recital 30 of the decision.

1987–96 (Boeing 61 percent, Airbus 27 percent, McDonnell Douglas 12 percent). The market repartition in the EEA was by and large split up the same way. Within the EEA area in 1996 Boeing held 61 percent market share, Airbus 37 percent, McDonnell Douglas 2 percent (the 1987–96 average market share in the EEA was 54 percent for Boeing, 34 Percent for Airbus, 12 percent for McDonnell Douglas).[234]

Besides the market share held, a number of other market conditions militated in favor of Boeing enjoying a dominant position on the relevant market. Firstly, all actors in the industry agreed that a number of segments could be identified in the overall market for jet aircraft. The segmentation was identified on the basis of the crafts' seating capacity. Within the "narrow-body" category, crafts were distinguished between airplanes with 100–120 and those with 120–200 seats. The "wide-body" segment included airplanes with a seating capacity of 200–320 seats, 320–400, seats and more than 400 seats. Boeing had a competitive advantage over its rivals as it was the only firm able to offer customers a complete range of aircraft, and it was the only one operating in all segments of the market. Similarly, the fleets operated worldwide consisted predominantly of Boeing-produced airplanes. It was found that roughly 60 percent of the currently flying crafts came from Boeing.[235] Moreover, Boeing could rely on a number of exclusive deals concluded with some major commercial airlines (e.g. American, Delta, and Continental). In addition, as recognized by the notifying parties, "there are massive barriers to entry to this market. Initial development and investment costs are huge . . . The production process itself is characterized by very significant learning curve effects and economies of scale and scope, which must be attained if a new entrant is to compete effectively over time."[236]

The market structure described led the Commission to conclude that "Boeing already enjoys a dominant position on the overall market for large commercial aircraft as well as on the markets for narrow-body and wide-body aircraft."[237]

b. **Origin of the case**

On 18 February 1997, pursuant to Article 4 of Regulation 4064/89 (as amended by Regulation 1310/97), Boeing notified to the Commission the proposed concentration by which it intended to acquire sole control over McDonnell Douglas. After examination of the proposed concentration, by a decision of 19 March 1997, the Commission found that it did raise serious doubts as to its compatibility with the common market and initiated proceedings pursuant to Article 6(1)(c) of the Merger Regulation.

c. **Economic analysis**

The proposed concentration, from the Commission's perspective, would have strengthened Boeing's dominant position. As an immediate result of the merger, Boeing would have increased its market share in the overall market for large commercial aircrafts from 64 percent to 70 percent. This market share increase would have also granted Boeing monopoly in the smallest narrow-body segment of aircraft (100–120 seats) in addition to the monopoly already held in the largest-aircraft segment of the market.

---

234 See recitals 28–37 of the decision.
235 See recitals 38–46 of the decision.
236 Recital 49 of the decision.
237 Recital 52 of the decision.

Moreover, the acquisition of the activities of McDonnell Douglas by Boeing would have reduced the number of competitors from three to two and granted Boeing all the competitive potential of McDonnell Douglas. According to the Commission, even if the current position on the market of McDonnell Douglas was relatively small and it was no longer a truly independent seller of new aircraft, the company's competitive influence in the past – resulting from the enquiry conducted by the Commission among thirty-one operating airlines – used to be larger. The skills and competitive potential held by McDonnell Douglas if integrated in the Boeing group could have had a significant impact on the market. In fact, once part of the group Boeing could decide to invest heavily in the extension of (some) of the McDonnell Douglas product lines. Furthermore Boeing would increase its share in the fleet in service from 60 percent to 84 percent and would consequently increase its long-term relations with customers. Another important competitive advantage Boeing would derive from the merger was the possibility to use McDonnell Douglas' capacity. This would grant Boeing greater elasticity in adopting its production to demand shocks and, above all, it would allow access to engineers for its commercial aircraft development and production which is a rare and expensive input. Finally, the acquisition of McDonnell Douglas would increase Boeing's capacity to enter into exclusive agreements with airlines. Indeed, Boeing might begin to conclude deals encompassing its own and the acquired company's aircraft, spare parts, and services. This would increase the bargaining power of Boeing considering that in the pre-merger market most of the airlines had separate agreements with the two companies.[238]

Furthermore, in the Commission's view "[t]he overall effects resulting from the take-over of [McDonnell Douglas'] defence and space business would lead to a strengthening of Boeing's dominant position."[239] The Commission listed a number of advantages for Boeing deriving from the acquisition of McDonnell Douglas' military and space business. Firstly, Boeing would acquire the financial resources of McDonnell Douglas and enormously increase its overall financial strength, becoming the largest integrated aerospace company in the world.

Secondly, considering that the acquired company was the world's leading producer of military aircraft, the large increase in military and space activities would give Boeing much greater access to R&D activities that in the United States are largely financed by the Government. Unlike other industries, in fact, the defense industry is publicly funded for around 60 percent of its R&D activities, amounting to 12–14 percent of net industry sales. Moreover, in the United States the "defense and space developmental programmes are normally performed under cost/reimbursement-type contracts"[240] that refund companies for all incurred costs plus award or incentive fees agreed between the companies and the Government. The operation would increase the number of R&D contracts in the defense sector for Boeing, and thus the access to public funds.

---

238 See recitals 53–71 of the decision.
239 Recital 72 of the decision.

240 Recital 87 of the decision.

The Commission added that the increase in the defense R&D activities would grant Boeing a number of general competitive advantages and in particular the possibility to transfer "technology developed under public funding to the commercial sector"[241] and a great increase in the number of technical personnel boosting know-how, particularly in the areas of design and manufacturing processes. Furthermore "[I]n a high-technology industry such as commercial aircraft manufacturing, intellectual property, whether patented or in the form of unpatented know-how, is extremely important for the competitive potential of the players in the market. The combination of the world's leading manufacturer of commercial aircraft with the world's leading manufacturer of military aircraft will lead to the combination of two large portfolios of intellectual property."[242]

In a third instance, the Commission noted that Boeing's power *vis-à-vis* suppliers of goods and services such as components, structural parts, and engines would have notably increased as result of the acquisition. Many suppliers of Boeing and McDonnell Douglas in the pre-merger market achieved 50 percent of their sales from supplies to the two aircrafts manufacturers. The merger would have certainly increased the buying power of the post-merger entity and at the same time weakened the competitive position of Airbus.[243]

d. Fines, remedies, and conditions enclosed

In order to remove the competition concerns, Boeing offered the Commission a number of commitments.

- Boeing undertook to maintain for ten years the commercial aircrafts division of McDonnell Douglas (DAC) in a separate legal entity and would provide the Commission with certified reports describing DAC's business performance and results.
- It committed to providing customer supports for DAC aircraft at the same level provided for Boeing aircraft. It also agreed not to withhold or threaten to withhold support for DAC aircraft or impose penalties with respect to support for its DAC aircraft in case an operator proposed to purchase aircraft from other manufacturers.
- It also committed not to use its privileged access to existing DAC aircraft orders to leverage its opportunities and persuade current DAC operators to purchase Boeing aircraft.
- Concerning its exclusive contractual relations with airlines, Boeing undertook not to sign any new exclusive agreement until 1 August 2007 unless other manufacturers offered such an agreement first. It also agreed not to enforce its exclusivity rights with American, Delta, and Continental.
- Concerning intellectual property and the spillover effect from the defense business to the commercial sphere, Boeing "will, upon request by a commercial aircraft manufacturer, license on a non-exclusive, reasonably royalty-bearing basis, any "government-funded patent" which could be used in the manufacture or sale of commercial jet

---

241   Recital 92 of the decision.   243   See recitals 104–108 of the decision.
242   Recital 102 of the decision.

aircraft. Boeing will also license the know-how related to such a patent which is necessary for the full, effective, and rapid exploitation of the patent."[244] All disputes concerning royalties and the government-funded nature of a patent would be submitted to an independent arbitration and Boeing agreed to transmit on a yearly basis to the Commission the list of all its unexpired patents.

- To increase transparency in the defense R&D projects in which it participates, Boeing would submit for ten years an annual report containing all detailed information about every funded R&D project in which it was involved, together with information about the application made in commercial aircrafts of that year's R&D results and the new patents obtained.

- In response to the Commission's concerns about the possibility for Boeing to leverage its supply relations to discriminate against other manufacturers, Boeing submitted not to "exert or attempt to exert undue or improper influence on its suppliers, directly or indirectly, by promising an increase in supplies or subcontracted R&D activities, threatening to decrease supplies or subcontracted R&D activities, or leveraging in any other way its own supply relationships."[245]

The Commission considered the proposed commitments as appropriate to remove its competition concerns. In particular, it noted how "Boeing's enhanced capability to enter into exclusive agreements will become irrelevant in the foreseeable future given that Boeing is not allowed to enter into future exclusive agreements for a period of 10 years. Furthermore, the abandonment of the exclusivity rights in the three existing exclusive agreements will remove the foreclosure of the market resulting from the exclusivity."[246] Operating DAC as a separate legal entity and the commitment not to leverage the product support for the DAC fleet would have further eliminated concerns about the horizontal overlapping with the activities of McDonnell Douglas and the acquisition of additional competitive potential.

According to the Commission, nonetheless the strengthening of the dominant position deriving from the large increase in defense and space business, the agreement on intellectual property rights licensing, and the commitments on transparency and supply relations duly limited the possibility for Boeing to exercise market power.[247]

e. **Further developments of the case**
    None.

---

244 Recital 117 of the decision.
245 Recital 119 of the decision. For detailed description of all commitments offered by Boeing, see recitals 114–119 of the decision.
246 Recital 121 of the decision.
247 See recital 122 of the decision.

F.3   *SEB/Moulinex* Commission decision SG (2002) D/228087 of 8 January 2002
non-opposition notice in OJ C 49/18

Relevance: Current Commission and CFI assessment of non-coordinated (unilateral) effects of mergers and possibility for the Commission to condition the approval of a proposed concentration on the implementation of behavioral remedies.

- For case report, relevant market, facts finding, origin of the case, economic analysis, obligations, fines and remedies, and further development of the case see Case *F.3* in section *8.1*.

F.4   *Vodafone Airtouch/Mannesmann* Commission decision 2003/C 300/06 [2003]
non-opposition notice in OJ C 300/10

Relevance: The Commission decision in *Vodafone Airtouch/Mannesmann* illustrates the significance of commitments to safeguard the competitiveness of markets. It underscores the importance of addressing also undeveloped markets, which might be pre-emptively foreclosed to competitors by a firm with market power in a related market. The decision also shows the Commission's concern for the creation of Europe-wide telecommunications services.

- Case IV/M.1795
- **Decision:** Non-opposition decision in a Phase I investigation pursuant to Article 6(1)(b) of the Merger Regulation
- **Decision addressee(s):**
    - Vodafone Airtouch plc, *United Kingdom*
- **Report route:** Notification of the proposed acquisition on 14 January 2000
- **Date of the decision:** 12 April 2000
- **Competition Commissioner:** M. Monti
- **Relevant product market:** Mobile telecommunications services, advanced seamless pan-European telecommunications services, mobile handsets and mobile telephony network equipment
- **Relevant geographical market:** United Kingdom for mobile telephone services, not indicated for other relevant product markets
- **Description of the case**
    a. **Relevant facts**
       Vodafone Airtouch Plc (Vodafone) is a publicly traded UK-based company operating mobile telecommunications networks and providing the related services. Vodafone's main business is in the operation of cellular radio networks. It has interests in mobile communications companies in ten EU Member States. Mannesmann is a German-based engineering and telecommunications company whose main activity relates to mobile and fixed line telephony. It also has business and commercial interests in a number of EU countries. In 1999 Mannesmann had purchased Orange, a company active in the mobile telephony network and related services in the United Kingdom, an acquisition that had been approved by the Commission.
       By way of a public bid, Vodafone tried to acquire sole control over Mannesmann by purchasing all its shares. The formal offer was accepted by 98.62 percent of Mannesmann shareholders.

b. **Origin of the case**

On 14 January 2000, pursuant to Article 4 of Regulation 4064/89 (as amended by Regulation 1310/97), Vodafone notified to the Commission the public bid announced on 20 December 1999 by which it intended to acquire sole control over Mannesmann. On 22 February 2000, the Commission declared the notification incomplete for lack of substantial information linked to the product market. On 29 February 2000, Vodafone completed the notification. After examination of the proposed concentration the Commission found that it did not raise serious doubts as to its compatibility with the common market.

c. **Economic analysis**

The UK market for mobile telecommunications services had four operators. In the post-merger market, Vodafone would have had sole control of two of them with a combined market share of 53.6 percent (Vodafone 33.2 percent and Orange 20.4 percent). The only other large competitor would have been BT Cellnet with 27 percent. The fourth operator, One2One, had 17.4 percent market share. Market entry is legally restricted since all operators need a license from the national regulator in order to enter the market, and the ability of the regulator to grant new licenses is limited by the scarcity of frequencies.

The merged entity, with its shareholdings in other mobile operators, would have captured nearly 70 percent of the Belgian telecommunications services as a result of the notified concentration. That market share was more than twice as large as the share of its closest and only competitor. According to the Commission, in both the Belgian and UK market the concentration raised serious doubts as to its compatibility with the common market.

In the market for the provision of seamless pan-European mobile telephony services the merging entity would have been in a unique position throughout Europe. Vodafone–Mannesmann would have had controlling interests in mobile operators in eight Member States and joint control of mobile operators in three other EU countries. It would have held 30 percent of all European mobile telephony subscriptions. Consequently, the merging entity would have been the only supplier able to quickly implement the technology required for the provision of advanced seamless services on such a large scale. The Commission observed that "with the difficulties involved in agreeing on the modification of the existing network configuration, centralized management solutions, and cost and profit allocation will make it exceedingly difficult, if not highly unlikely, for third parties to replicate, by agreement, the merged entity's network in the near future."[248] Indeed, it was estimated that the competitors of the merging parties would have needed between three and five years to replicate a similar integrated network by means of contractual arrangements. It was also conceded that such a large-scale undertaking is not only time-consuming and expensive but also "fraught with regulatory delays, *inter alia*, the need for regulatory approval and in many instances the need for important divestments due to anticompetitive overlaps."[249] As a whole, Vodafone's rivals could probably not have overcome the obstacles posed by the separation of the existing networks.

---

248   Recital 40 of the decision.   249   Recital 41 of the decision.

The Commission's assessment of the post-merger market focused also on the enhanced potential of Vodafone–Mannesmann to abuse its dominance and eliminate competitors from the market. The merged entity would have been the only mobile operator "able to meet in the short to medium term... the demand for advanced pan-European services given its ability to overcome technical and commercial barriers to create a truly pan-European integrated network. The merged entity would be the only mobile operator able to capture future growth through new customers... This situation is likely to entrench the merged entity [in] a dominant position on the emerging pan-European market for internationally mobile customers."[250] The necessity for other firms also to have access to Vodafone's network in order to be able to provide (new) customers with advanced services in countries where they would have otherwise no access, gave Vodafone – according to the Commission – the possibility "either to refuse access to its network or to allow access on terms and conditions which will make third party offerings unattractive or simply not competitive."[251] In addition, Vodafone would have potentially disposed of a unique buying power *vis-à-vis* the manufacturers of handsets to "negotiate design functionalities which will not be available to competing operators."[252]

The Commission concluded its analysis stating that the concentration would have led to the creation of a dominant position on the market for the provision of seamless European mobile telecommunications services and therefore opposed the merger.

d. Fines, remedies, and conditions enclosed

In order to remove the concerns expressed by the Commission, Vodafone submitted a number of commitments to alter the nature of the concentration in such a way as to make it compatible with the common market and the requirements imposed under the Merger Regulation.

Concerning the competitive overlap in the UK and Belgian markets, Vodafone agreed to:

- Demerge Orange from the Mannesmann group by selling all Orange shareholdings held by Mannesmann or a member of the group to a stand-alone company. Vodafone assured the Commission that it would execute the demerger as soon as possible or at the latest before a deadline set by the Commission (the final date).

- A jointly appointed Trustee assigned to guarantee the viability and value of the divested assets would monitor the entire divestiture. The Trustee would also exercise Vodafone's "voting rights in respect of Mannesmann's shares so far as such voting affects Orange and [monitored] that the rights whether direct or indirect which Vodafone Airtouch has as a shareholder in Orange are exercised on an independent arm's lengths basis until completion of the sale."[253]

- Vodafone agreed not to dispose of any Orange licenses, database, intellectual property, specialized personnel, or customers, or to pass any confidential information to Orange. Similarly, the Trustee was

250   Recitals 44 and 45 of the decision.   252   Recital 47 of the decision.
251   Recital 46 of the decision.   253   Recital 56 of the decision.

forbidden to give any confidential information about Orange to Vodafone.

Concerning the Commission's doubts about the creation of a dominant position in the market for the provision of seamless mobile communications services
in Europe, Vodafone submitted commitments to give competitors undiscrim-
inated access to the integrated network for a period of three years and to
provide advanced mobile services to competitors' customers. These undertakings "cover exclusive roaming agreements, third parties" access to roaming
arrangements, third partie[s'], access to wholesale arrangements, standards
and SIM-cards, and a set of implementing measures aimed at ensuring their
effectiveness,"[254] including a mechanism for fast dispute resolution in case of
any disagreement.

The Commission considered the array of commitments offered by Vodafone
as sufficient to create the condition for other firms to compete with Vodafone on
the pan-European market for mobile services and at the same time to stimulate
the creation of rivals' own networks. The Commission concluded that "the
undertakings will thus have a structural effect on the market in that they will
make it possible to preserve a competitive structure of supply."[255]

e. **Further developments of the case**
None.

---

254   Recital 58 of the decision.
255   Recital 60 of the decision. For a detailed analysis of the commitments offered by Vodafone, see the commitments proposal
      attached to the decision.

ANNEX I

Decisions related to procedural issues

Listed below are Commission decisions adopted pursuant to Article 11 (Commission's right to ask information) and Articles 15–16 (Commission's right to impose fines) of Council Regulation No. 17: First Regulation Implementing Articles 85 and 86 of the Treaty [1962] OJ 13/204, English special edition OJ [1959–62] 87.

Since May 2004, Regulation No. 17 has been substituted by Council Regulation No. 1/2003 on the implementation of the rules on competition laid down in Articles 81 and 82 of the Treaty [2003] OJ L 1/1. The new Regulation's articles corresponding to Articles 11, 15, and 16 mentioned above are now Articles 18 (request of information), 23, and 24 (imposition of fines).

The new articles significantly modified the content of the previous ones. The differences between the two Regulations are nonetheless beyond the scope of this book. For what is relevant here, one can consider the two sets of articles as the legal basis underlying the adoption of the decisions mentioned in this annex.

CICG-Zeiv/ZPÜ Commission decision 71/85/EEC [1971] OJ L 34/13, Case IV/26.792

Albra-Brasserie Espérance Commission decision 71/257/EEC [1971] OJ L 161/2, Case IV/399

Union des Brasseries Commission decision 71/258/EEC [1971] OJ L 161/6, Case IV/399

Brasserie MAES Commission decision 71/259/EEC [1971] OJ L 161/6, Case IV/399

Asphaltoïd-Keller Commission decision 71/268/EEC [1971] OJ L 161/32, Case IV/239

SIAE Commission decision 71/375/EEC [1971] OJ L 254/15, Case IV/26.909

Rodenstock Commission decision 72/396/EEC [1972] OJ L 267/17, Case IV/8.818, 8.822

Misal Commission decision 72/397/EEC [1972] OJ L 267/20, Case IV/24.171

CSV Commission decision 76/593/EEC [1976] OJ L 192/27, Case IV/26.186

Theal/Watts Commission decision 77/129/EEC [1977] OJ L 39/19, Case IV/28.812

Vereinigung deutscher Freiformschmieden Commission decision 78/24/EEC [1978] OJ L 10/32, Case IV/356

RAI/UNITEL Commission decision 78/516/EEC [1978] OJ L 157/39, Case IV/29.559

Fides Commission decision 79/253/EEC [1979] OJ L 57/33, Case IV/372

AM&S Europe Ltd Commission decision 79/670/EEC [1979] OJ L 199/31, Case IV/379

Fabbrica Pisana Commission decision 80/334/EEC [1980] OJ L 75/30, Case IV/400

Fabbrica Lastre Sciarra Commission decision 80/335/EEC [1980] OJ L 75/35, Case IV/400

Comptoir commercial d'importation Commission decision 82/53/EEC [1982] OJ L 27/31, Case IV/30.211

Telos Commission decision 82/124/EEC [1982] OJ L 58/19, Case IV/29.895

Fire insurance (D) Commission decision 82/174/EEC [1982] OJ L 80/36, Case IV/30.307

National Panasonic (Belgique) Commission decision 82/260/EEC [1982] OJ L 113/18, Case IV/512

National Panasonic France Commission decision 82/465/EEC [1982] OJ L 211/32, Case IV/511

Fédération Nationale Chaussure de France Commission decision 82/756/EEC [1982] OJ L 319/12, Case IV/528

Castrol Commission decision 83/205/EEC [1983] OJ L 114/26, Case IV/30.735

Olympic Airways Commission decision 85/121/EEC [1985] OJ L 46/51, Case IV/31.163

Secretama Commission decision 91/55/EEC [1991] OJ L 35/23, Case IV/32.450

Baccarat Commission decision 91/213/EEC [1991] OJ L 97/16, Case IV/33.300

UKWAL Commission decision 92/237/EEC [1992] OJ L 121/45, 32448, Case IV/32.450

CSM Commission decision 92/500/EEC [1992] OJ L 305/16, Cases IV/33.638, 33.791

MEWAC Commission decision 93/47/EEC [1993] OJ L 20/6, Case IV/32.447

Akzo Chemicals BV Commission decision 94/735/EEC [1994] OJ L 294/31, Case IV/34.887

Anheuser-Busch Inc./Scottish and Newcastle Commission decision 2000/146/EC [2000] OJ L 49/37, Case IV/34.237/F3

E.ON Energie AG Commission decision of 30 January 2008, published on DG Comp website, Case COMP/B-1/39.326

Microsoft Commission decision of 27 February 2008, published on DG Comp website, Case COMP/C-3/34.792

Table of landmark decisions described in the book

2 Horizontal constraints

2.1 Price fixing cartels

Manufacturers of glass containers (IFTRA) Commission decision 74/292/EEC [1974] OJ L 160/1
Vitamins Commission decision 2003/2/EC [2003] OJ L 6/1
Fine Art Auction Houses Commission decision 2005/590/EC [2005] OJ L 200/92

2.2 Market sharing, quota cartels, and specialization agreements

Jaz Peter I Commission decision 69/242/EEC [1969] OJ L 195/5
Italian Cast Glass Commission decision 80/1334/EEC [1980] OJ L 383/19
BPCL/ICI Commission decision 84/387/EEC [1984] OJ L 212/1
Seamless steel tubes Commission decision 2003/382/EC [2003] OJ L 140/1

2.3 Bid-rigging and tender fixing

Building and Constructions in the Netherlands Commission decision 92/204/EEC [1992] OJ L 92/1

2.4 Structural crises cartels

Synthetic Fibres Commission decision 84/380/EEC [1984] OJ L 207/17

2.5 Export cartels

DECA Commission decision 64/599/EEC [1964] OJ L 64/2761
Floral Commission decision 80/182/EEC [1980] OJ L 39/51

2.6 Trade associations

U.K. Tractors Registration Exchange Commission decision 92/157/EEC [1992] OJ L 68/19

2.7 Marketing and advertising agreement

Cematex Commission decision 71/337/EEC [1971] OJ L 227/26
Roofing felt Commission decision 86/399/EEC [1986] OJ L 232/15

2.8   Agreements on standards

Video Cassette Recorders Commission decision 78/156/EEC [1978] OJ L 47/42
ABI Commission decision 87/103/EEC [1987] OJ L 43/51
CECED Commission decision 2000/475/EC [2000] OJ L 187/47

2.9   Exchange of information

Manufacturers of Glass Containers (IFTRA) Commission decision 74/292/EEC [1974] OJ L 160/1
Fatty Acids Commission decision 87/1/EEC [1987] OJ L 3/17
U.K. Tractors Registration Exchange Commission decision 92/157/EEC [1992] OJ L 68/19

3   Abuse of dominance

3.1   Excessive pricing, discriminatory sales condition, and prohibition of resale

Chiquita Commission decision 76/353/EEC [1976] OJ L 95/1

3.2   Loyalty discounts and fidelity rebates

European sugar industry Commission decision 73/109/EEC [1973] OJ L 140/17
Michelin Commission decision 81/969/EEC [1981] OJ L 353/33
Michelin II Commission decision 2002/405/EC [2002] OJ L 143/1

3.3   Predatory pricing

ECS/AKZO Chemie Commission decision 85/609/EEC [1985] OJ L 374/1
Wanadoo Interactive Commission decision of 16 July 2003, published on DG Comp website

3.4   Bundling and tying

Eurofix – Bauco/Hilti Commission decision 88/138/EEC [1988] OJ L 65/19
Tetra Pak II Commission decision 92/163/EEC [1992] OJ L 72/1

3.5   Price squeezing

Napier Brown/British Sugar Commission decision 88/518/EEC [1988] OJ L 284/41
Telefónica Commission decision of 4 July 2007, published on DG Comp website

3.6   Restricting and/or preventing entry

Eurofix – Bauco/Hilti Commission decision 88/138/EEC [1988] OJ L 65/19
Tetra Pak I (BTG-license) Commission decision 88/501/EEC [1988] OJ L 272/27
Magill TV Guide/ITP, BBC, and RTE Commission decision 89/205/EEC [1989] OJ L 78/43
Microsoft Commission decision of 24 March 2004, published on DG Comp website
AstraZeneca Commission decision of 19 July 2006, published on DG Comp website

3.7 Refusal to deal and essential facilities doctrine

Chiquita Commission decision 76/353/EEC [1976] OJ L 95/1
Magill TV Guide/ITP, BBC, and RTE Commission decision 89/205/EEC [1989] OJ L 78/43
British Midland/Aer Lingus Commission decision 92/213/EEC [1992] OJ L 96/34
Microsoft Commission decision of 24 March 2004, published on DG Comp website

3.8 Preventing interoperability of standards and networks

Decca Navigator System Comm. decision 89/113/EEC [1989] OJ L 43/27
Microsoft Commission decision of 24 March 2004, published on DG Comp website

3.9 Best price guarantees ("English Clauses")

Vitamins, Hoffmann – La Roche Commission decision 76/642/EEC [1976] OJ L 223/27

4 Licensing

4.1 Trademarks and branding

Campari Commission decision 78/253/EEC [1978] OJ L 70/69
Moosehead/Whitbread Commission decision 90/186/EEC [1990] OJ L 100/32

4.2 Patents and other intellectual property rights

Kabelmetal-Luchaire Commission decision 75/494/EEC [1975] OJ L 222/34
Bronbemaling V./Heidemaatschappij Commission decision 75/570 EEC [1975] OJ L 249/27
UEFA Commission decision 2003/778/EC [2003] OJ L 291/25

5 Vertical restraints

5.1 Exclusive dealing and market foreclosure

Reuter/BASF Commission decision 76/743/EEC [1976] OJ L 254/40
Liebig Spices Commission decision 78/172/EEC [1978] OJ L 53/20
Van Den Bergh Foods Commission decision 98/531/EC [1998] OJ L 246/1

5.2 Territorial exclusivity and parallel import/export bans

BMW Belgium NV and Belgian BMW dealers association Commission decision 78/155/EEC
   [1975] OJ L 46/33
Arthur Bell and Sons Ltd Commission decision 78/696/EEC [1978] OJ L 235/15
Glaxo Wellcome, Aseprofar and Fedifar, Spain Pharma, BAI, EAEPC Commission decision
   2001/791/EC [2001] OJ L 302/1

5.3 Resale price maintenance

Deutsche Philips GmbH Commission decision 73/322/EEC [1973] OJ L 293/40

5.4 Bundling and tying

None

5.5 Selective distribution system

BMW AG Commission decision 75/73/EEC [1974] OJ L 29/1
SABA Commission decision 76/159/EEC [1976] OJ L 95/1
Parfums Givenchy Commission decision 92/428/EEC [1992] OJ L 236/11

5.6 Franchising

Yves Rocher Commission Decision 87/14/EEC [1987] OJ L 8/49

5.7 Discounts and rebates

Liebig Spices Commission decision 78/172/EEC [1978] OJ L 53/20

6   Joint ventures and alliances
6.1 R&D joint ventures

Beecham/Parke, Davis Commission decision 79/298/EEC [1979] OJ L 70/11
Optical fibres Commission decision 86/405/EEC [1986] OJ L 236/30
Enichem/ICI Commission decision 88/87/EEC [1988] OJ L 50/18
British Interactive Broadcasting/Open Commission decision 1999/781/EC [1999] OJ L 312/1

6.2 Marketing, selling, distribution, and production joint ventures

De Laval-Stork Commission decision 77/543/EEC [1977] OJ L 215/11
Rockwell/IVECO Commission decision 83/390/EEC [1983] OJ L 224/19
Exxon/Shell Commission decision 94/322/EEC [1994] OJ L 144/20
British Interactive Broadcasting/Open Commission decision 1999/781/EC [1999] OJ L 312/1

6.3 Strategic and technological alliances

BT/MCI Commission Decision 94/579/EC [1994] OJ L 223/36

7   Restrictions to competition by Member States

Provision in the Netherlands of express delivery services Commission decision 90/16/EEC [1990] OJ L 10/47
Telecom Eireann Commission decision 97/114/EC [1997] OJ L 41/8

8   Mergers and acquisitions

Continental Can Company Commission Decision 72/21/EEC [1972] OJ L 7/25

8.1   Horizontal mergers: unilateral effects

Aerospatiale-Alenia/De Havilland Commission decision 91/619/EEC [1991] OJ L 334/42
Volvo/Scania Commission decision 2001/403/EC [2000] OJ L 143/74
SEB/Moulinex Commission decision 2005/408/EC [2003] OJ L 138

8.2   Horizontal Mergers: coordinated effects

Airtours/First Choice Commission decision 2000/276/EC [1999] OJ L 93/1
Sony/BMG Commission decision 2005/188/EC [2004] summary of the decision in OJ L 62/30

8.3   Vertical and conglomerate mergers

GE/Amersham Commission decision 2004/C 74/04 [2004] non-opposition notice in OJ C 74/5
ENI/EDP/GDP Commission decision 2005/801/EC [2004] summary of the decision in OJ L
   302/69
Google/Double Click Commission decision 2008/C184/06 [2008] summary of the decision in
   OJ C 184/51

8.4   Minority acquisitions

Warner – Lambert/Gillette and Bic/Gillette and others Commission Decision 93/252/EEC [1993]
   OJ L 116/21

8.5   Economic defense arguments

Volvo/Scania Commission decision 2001/403/EC [2001] OJ L 143/74
NewsCorp/Telepiú Commission decision 2004/311/EC [2003] OJ L 110/73
Korsnäs/AssiDomän Cartonboard Commission decision 2006/C 209/05 [2006] summary of the
   decision in OJ C 209/12

8.6   Merger remedies

Nestlé/Perrier Commission decision 92/553/EEC [1992] OJ L 356/1
Boeing/McDonnell Douglas Commission decision 97/816/EC [1997] OJ L 336/16
SEB/Moulinex Commission decision 2005/408/EC [2003] OJ L 138
Vodafone Airtouch/Mannesmann Commission decision 2003/C 300/06 [2003] non-opposition
   notice in OJ C 300/10

Table of mergers blocked by the European Commission in chronological order

Aerospatiale-Alenia/De Havilland **Commission decision 91/619/EEC [1991] OJ L 334/42, Case IV/M.053**

MSG Media Services Commission decision 94/922/EC [1994] OJ L 364/1, Case IV/M.469

Nordic Satellite Distribution Commission decision 96/177/EC [1996] OJ L 53/20, Case IV/M.490

RTL/Veronica/Endemol ('HMG') Commission decision 96/346/EC [1996] OJ L 134/32, Case IV/M.553

Gencor/Lonrho Commission decision 97/26/EC [1997] OJ L 11/30, Case IV/M.619

Kesko/Tuko Commission decision 97/277/EC [1997] OJ L 110/53, Case IV/M.784

Saint Gobain/Wacker Chemie/Nom Commission decision 97/610/EC [1997] OJ L 247/1, Case IV/M.774

Blokker/Toys "R" Us (II) Commission decision 98/663 [1998] OJ L 316/1, Case IV/M.890

Bertelsmann/Kirch/Première Commission decision 1999/153/EC [1999] OJ L 53/1, Case IV/M.993

Deutsche Telekom/Betaresearch Commission decision 1999/154/EC [1999] OJ L 53/31, Case IV/M.1027

Airtours/First Choice **Commission decision 2000/276/EC [1999] OJ L 93/1, Case IV/M.1524**

Volvo/Scania **Commission decision 2001/403/EC [2001] OJ L 143/74, Case COMP/M.1672**

SCA/Metsä Tissue Commission decision 2003/156/EC [2003] OJ L 57/1, Case COMP/M.2097

MCI Worldcom/Sprint Commission decision 2003/790/EC [2003] OJ L 300/1, Case COMP/M.1741

General Electric/Honeywell Commission decision 2004/134/EC [2004] OJ L 48/1, Case COMP/M.2220

CVC/Lenzing Commission decision 2004/237/EC [2004] OJ L 82/20, Case COMP/M.2187

Schneider/Legrand Commission decision 2004/275/EC [2004] OJ L 101/1, Case COMP/M.2283

ENI/EDP/GDP **Commission decision 2005/801/EC [2004] summary of the decision in OJ L 302/69, Case COMP/M.3440**

Tetra Laval/Sidel Commission decision 2004/124/EC [2004] OJ L 43/13, Case COMP/M.2416

Ryanair/Aer Lingus M.4439, summary of the decision published in [2008] OJ C 4719

Table of landmark merger decisions described in the book in alphabetical order

Aerospatiale-Alenia/De Havilland Commission decision 91/619/EEC [1991] OJ L 334/42, Case IV/M.053

Airtours/First Choice Commission decision 2000/276/EC [1999] OJ L 93/1, Case IV/M.1524

Boeing/McDonnell Douglas Commission decision 97/816/EC [1997] OJ L 336/16, Case IV/M.877

ENI/EDP/GDP Commission decision 2005/801/EC [2004] summary of the decision in OJ L 302/69, Case COMP/M.3440

GE/Amersham Commission decision 2004/C 74/04 [2004] non-opposition notice in OJ C 74/5, Case COMP/M.3304

Google/Double Click Commission decision 2008/C184/06 [2008] summary of the decision in OJ C 184/51, Case COMP/M.4731

Inco/Falconbridge Commission decision 2007/163/EC [2006] summary of the decision in OJ L 72/18, Case COMP/M.4000

Korsnäs/AssiDomän Cartonboard Commission decision 2006/C 209/05 [2006] summary of the decision in OJ C 209/12, Case COMP/M.4057

Nestlé/Perrier Commission decision 92/553/EEC [1992] OJ L 356/1, Case IV/M.190

NewsCorp/Telepiú Commission decision 2004/311/EC [2003] OJ L 110/73, Case COMP/M.2876

SEB/Moulinex Commission decision 2005/408/EC [2003] OJ L 138, Case COMP/M.2621

Sony/BMG Commission decision 2005/188/EC [2004] summary of the decision in OJ L 62/30, Case COMP/M.3333

Vodafone Airtouch/Mannesmann Commission decision 2003/C 300/06 [2003] non-opposition notice in OJ C 300/10, Case IV/M.1795

Volvo/Scania Commission decision 2001/403/EC [2000] OJ L 143/74, Case COMP/M.1672

Table of antitrust decisions in alphabetical order[1]

3G Network sharing Germany Commission decision 2004/207/EC [2004] OJ L 75/32, Case COMP/38.369

AAMS Commission decision 98/538/EC [1998] OJ L 252/47, Case IV/36.010

ABG/Oil Companies Commission decision 77/327/EEC [1977] OJ L 117/1, Case IV/28.841

ABI **Commission decision 87/103/EEC [1987] OJ L 43/51, Case IV/31.356**

ACEC-Berliet Commission decision 68/319/EEC [1968] OJ L 201/7, Case IV/26.045

ACI Commission decision 94/594/EEC [1994] OJ L 224/28, Case IV/34.518

Acrylic glass producers Commission decision of 31 May 2006, published on DG Comp website, Case COMP/38.645

Additional implementation periods to Greece Commission decision 97/607/EC [1997] OJ L 245/6

Additional implementation periods to Luxembourg Commission decision 97/568/EC [1997] OJ L 234/7

Additional implementation periods to Portugal Commission decision 97/310/EC [1997] OJ L 133/19

Additional implementation periods to Spain Commission decision 97/603/EC [1997] OJ L 243/48

Advocaat Zwarte Kip Commission decision 74/432/EEC [1974] OJ L 237/12, Case IV/28.374

AEG-Telefunken Commission decision 82/267/EEC [1982] OJ L 117/15, Case IV/28.748

AENA Commission decision 2000/521/EC [2000] OJ L 208/36, Case COMP/35.737

AFS/ADP Commission decision 98/513/EC [1998] OJ L 230/10, Case IV/35.613

Air France/Alitalia Commission decision of 7 April 2004, published on DG Comp website, Case COMP/38.284/D2

Akzo Chemicals BV Commission decision 94/735/EEC [1994] OJ L 294/31, Case IV/34.887

Albra-Brasserie Espérance Commission decision 71/257/EEC [1971] OJ L 161/2, Case IV/399

Alcatel/ANT Nachrichtentechnik Commission Decision 90/46/EEC [1990] OJ L 32/19, Case IV/32.006

Alliance des constructeurs français Commission decision 68/317/EEC [1968] OJ L 201/1, Case IV/25.140

Aluminium Commission decision 85/206/EEC [1985] OJ L 92/1, Case IV/26.870

Aluminium fluoride producers Commission decision of 25 June 2008, not yet published, Case COMP/39.180

AM&S Europe Ltd Commission decision 79/670/EEC [1979] OJ L 199/31, Case IV/379

Amersham Buchler Commission decision 82/742/EEC [1982] OJ L 314/34, Case IV/30.517

Amino Acids Commission decision 2001/418/EC [2001] OJ L 152/24, Case COMP/36.545/F3

Anheuser-Busch Inc./Scottish and Newcastle Commission decision 2000/146/EC [2000] OJ L 49/37, Case IV/34.237/F3

---

1   Landmark decisions described in the book are displayed in **bold type**.

Bitumen in the Netherlands Commission decision of 13 September 2006, published on DG Comp website, Case COMP/38.456

Bitumen suppliers Commission decision of 3 October 2007, not yet published, Case COMP/ 38.710

Bloemenveilingen Aalsmeer Commission decision 88/491/EEC [1988] OJ L 262/27, Case IV/ 31.379

BMW AG **Commission decision 75/73/EEC [1975] OJ L 29/1, Case IV/14.650**

BMW Belgium NV and Belgian BMW dealers association **Commission decision 78/155/EEC [1978] OJ L 46/33, Case IV/29.146**

Bomée-Stichting Commission decision 75/781/EEC [1975] OJ L 329/30, Case IV/256

Boussois/Interpane Commission decision 87/123/EEC [1987] OJ L 50/30, Case IV/31.302

BP KEMI-DDSF Commission decision 79/934/EEC [1979] OJ L 235/20, Case IV/29.021

BP/Kellogg Commission Decision 85/560/EEC [1985] OJ L 369/6, Case IV/30.971

BPB Industries PLC Commission decision 89/22/EEC [1989] OJ L 10/50, Case IV/31.900

BPCL/ICI **Commission decision 84/387/EEC [1984] OJ L 212/1, Case IV/30.863**

BPICA Commission decision 77/722/EEC [1977] OJ L 299/18, Case IV/417

BPICA Commission decision 82/349/EEC [1982] OJ L 156/16, Case IV/417

Brasserie MAES Commission decision 71/259/EEC [1971] OJ L 161/6, Case IV/399

Breeders'Rights-Maize Seed Commission decision 78/823/EEC [1978] OJ L 286/23, Case IV/28.824

Breeders' Right: Roses Commission decision 85/561/EEC [1985] OJ L 369/9, Case IV/30.017

British Dental Trade Association Commission decision 88/477/EEC [1988] OJ L 233/15, Case IV/31.593

British Interactive Broadcasting/Open **Commission decision 1999/781/EC [1999] OJ L 312/1, Case IV/36.539**

British Leyland Commission decision 84/379/EEC [1984] OJ L 307/11, Case IV/30.615

British Midland/Aer Lingus **Commission decision 92/213/EEC [1993] OJ L 96/34, Case IV/33.544**

British Midland (Zaventem) Commission decision 95/364/EC [1995] OJ L 12/8

British Sugar Commission decision 1999/210/EC [1999] OJ L 76/1, Cases IV/33.708, 33.709, 33.710, 33.711

British Telecommunications Commission decision 82/861/EEC [1982] OJ L 360/36, Case IV/29.877

Broadcasting television Flanders Commission decision 97/606/EC [1997] OJ L 244/18

Bronbemaling/Heidemaatschappij **Commission decision 75/570/EEC [1975] OJ L 249/27, Case IV/28.967**

BT/MCI **Commission Decision 94/579/EC [1994] OJ L 223/36, Case IV/34.857**

Building and Constructions in the Netherlands **Commission decision 92/204/EEC [1992] OJ L 92/1, Cases IV/31.571, 31.572**

Burroughs-Delplanque Commission decision 72/25/EEC [1972] OJ L 13/50, Case IV/5400

Burroughs/Geha-Werke Commission decision 72/26/EEC [1972] OJ L 13/53, Case IV/5405

Cafeteros de Colombia Commission decision 82/860/EEC [1982] OJ L 360/31, Case IV/30.077

Calcium carbide and magnesium based reagents Commission decision of 22 July 2009, not yet published, Case COMP/39.396

Campari **Commission decision 78/253/EEC [1978] OJ L 70/69, Cases IV/117, 171, 172, 856, 28.173**

Canary Islands Commission decision 87/359/EEC [1987] OJ L 194/28

Clima Chappee-Buderus Commission decision 69/241/EEC [1969] OJ L 195/1, Case IV/26.625
CNSD Commission decision 93/438/EEC [1993] OJ L 203/27, Case IV/33.407
Coapi Commission decision 95/188/EC [1995] OJ L 122/37, Case IV/33.686
Cobelaz-cokeries Commission decision 68/375/EEC [1968] OJ L 276/19, Case IV/507
Cobelaz-usines de synthèse Commission decision 68/374/EEC [1968] OJ L 276/13, Case IV/565
COBELPA/VNP Commission decision 77/592/EEC [1977] OJ L 242/10, Cases IV/312, 366
Coffee Terminal Market Association Ltd Commission decision 85/565/EEC [1985] OJ L 369/31, Case IV/27.592
Compagnie Maritime Belge (CEWAL) Commission decision of 30 April 2004, published on DG Comp website, Cases COMP/D/32.448, 32.450
Comptoir commercial d'importation Commission decision 82/53/EEC [1982] OJ L 27/31, Case IV/30.211
Computerland Commission decision 87/407/EEC [1987] OJ L 222/12, Case IV/32.034
Concordato Incendio Commission decision 90/25/EEC [1990] OJ L 15/25, Case IV/32.265
Concrete reinforcing bar Commission decision of 30 September 2009, not yet published, Case COMP/37.956
Consorzio risposta and Consorzio recapitali Commission decision 2001/176/EC [2001] OJ L 63/59, Case COMP/37.721
Continental Can Company **Commission decision 72/71/EEC [1972] OJ L 7/25, Case IV/26.811**
Continental/Michelin Commission Decision 88/555/EEC [1988] OJ L 272/27, Case IV/32.173
Convention chaufourniers Commission decision 69/152/EEC [1969] OJ L 122/8, Cases IV/242, 295
Copper fittings Commission decision of 20 September 2006, not yet published, Case COMP/38.121
Copper plumbing tubes Commission decision 2006/485/EC [2006] OJ L 192/21, Case C.38.069
CSM Commission decision 92/500/EEC [1992] OJ L 305/16, Case IV/33.638, 33.791
CSV Commission decision 76/593/EEC [1976] OJ L 192/27, Case IV/26.186
Davidson Rubber Co Commission decision 72/237/EEC [1972] OJ L 143/31, Cases IV/6964, 17.448, 17.545, 18.673, 26.858, 26.890
De Laval-Stork **Commission decision 77/543/EEC [1977] OJ L 215/11, Case IV/27.093**
De Laval-Stork Commission decision 88/110/EEC [1988] OJ L 59/32, Case IV/27.093
De Post-La Poste, former Natural Monopoly Commission decision 2002/180/EC [2002] OJ L 61/32, Case COMP/37.859
DECA **Commission decision 64/599/EEC [1964] OJ L 64/2761, Case IV/71**
Decca Navigator System **Commission decision 89/113/EC [1989] OJ L 43/27, Cases IV/30.979, 31.394**
Delta Chemie/DDD Commission decision 88/563/EEC [1988] OJ L 309/34, Case IV/31.498
Deutsche Philips GmbH **Commission decision 73/322/EEC [1973] OJ L 293/40, Case IV/27.010**
Deutsche Post AG Commission decision 2001/354/EC [2001] OJ L 125/27, Case COMP/35.141
Deutsche Post AG – Interception of cross-border mail Commission decision 2001/892/EC [2001] OJ L 331/40, Case COMP/C-1/36.915
Deutsche Telekom Commission decision 2003/707/EC [2003] OJ L 263/9, Cases COMP/C.1/37.451, 37.578, 37.579
D'Ieteren motor oils Commission decision 91/39/EEC [1991] OJ L 20/42, Case IV/32.595
Distribution of Packages Tours 1990 World Cup Commission decision 92/521/EEC [1992] OJ L 326/31, Cases IV/33.378, 33.384

Gas water-heaters and bath-heaters Commission decision 73/232/EEC [1973] OJ L 217/34, Case IV/25.963

Gaz de France/ENI Commission decision of 26 October 2004, published on DG Comp website, Case COMP/38.66

GEAE/P&W Commission Decision 2000/182/EC [2000] OJ L 58/16, Case IV/36.213

GEC-Weir Sodium Circulators Commission decision 77/781/EEC [1977] OJ L 327/26, Case IV/29.428

Gema Commission decision 71/224/EC [1971] OJ L 134/15, Case IV/26.760

Gema Statutes Commission decision 82/204/EEC [1982] OJ L 94/12, Case IV/29.971

General Motors Continental Commission decision 75/75/EEC [1975] OJ L 29/14, Case IV/28.851

Germany – Restriction on mail preparation Commission decision of 20 October 2004, published on DG Comp website, Case COMP/C.38.745/B2

Gero-Fabriek Commission decision 77/66/EEC [1977] OJ L 16/8, Case IV/24.510

GISA Commission decision 72/478/EEC [1972] OJ L 303/45, Cases IV/89, 26.349

Glaxo Wellcome, Aseprofar and Fedifar, Spain Pharma, BAI, EAEPC **Commission decision 2001/791/EC [2001] OJ L 302/1, Cases COMP/36.957, 36.997, 37.121, 37.138, 37.380**

Goodyear Italian/Euram Commission decision 75/94/EEC [1975] OJ L 38/10, Case IV/23.013

Gosme/Martell-Dmp Commission decision 91/335/EEC [1991] OJ L 185/23, Case IV/32.186

Graphite Electrodes Commission decision 2002/271/EC [2002] OJ L 100/1, COMP/E-1/36.490

Greece – Quasi-exclusive access to lignite in the electricity market Commission decision of 5 March 2008, published on DG COMP website, Case COMP/38.700

Greek Ferries Commission decision 1999/271/EC [1999] OJ L 109/24, Case IV/34.446

Greek Insurance Commission decision 85/276/EEC [1985] OJ L 152/25

Grohe sales system Commission decision 85/44/EEC [1985] OJ L 19/17, Case IV/30.299

Grosfillex & Fillistorf Commission decision 64/233/EEC [1964] OJ L 64/915, Case IV/61

Groupement des Cartes Bancaires Commission decision of 17 October 2007, published on DG Comp website, Case COMP/38.606

Grundig (distribution system) Commission decision 94/29/EEC [1994] OJ L 20/15, Case IV/29.420

Grundig-Consten Commission decision 64/566/EEC [1964] OJ L 64/2545, Case IV/3344

Grundig Commission decision 85/404/EEC [1985] OJ L 233/1, Case IV/29.420

GSM Italia Commission decision 95/489/EC [1995] OJ L 280/49

GSM Spain Commission decision 97/181/EC [1997] OJ L 76/19

GVG/FS Commission decision 2004/33/EC [2004] OJ L 11/17, Case COMP/37.685

GVL Commission decision 81/1030/EEC [1981] OJ L 370/49, Case IV/29.839

Hard Haberdashery-Needles Commission decision of 26 October 2004, published on DG Comp website, Case F-1/38.338

Hasselblad Commission decision 82/367/EEC [1982] OJ L 94/7, Case IV/25.757

Heat Stabilisers Commission decision of 11 November 2009, not yet published, Case COMP/38.589

Henkel/Colgate Commission Decision 72/41/EEC [1972] OJ L 14/14, Case IV/26.917

Hennessey-Henkell Commission decision 80/1333/EEC [1980] OJ L 383/11, Case IV/26.912

HOV SVZ/MCN Commission decision 94/210/EEC [1994] OJ L 104/34, Case IV/33.941

Hudson's Bay/Dansk Pelsdyravlerforening Commission decision 88/587/EEC [1988] OJ L 316/43, Case IV/31.424

Hugin/Liptons Commission decision 78/68/EEC [1978] OJ L 22/23, Case IV/29.132

Hummel-Isbecque Commission decision 65/426/EEC [1965] OJ L 65/2581, Case IV/2702

Hydrogene peroxide and perborate Commission decision of 3 May 2006, published on DG Comp website, Case COMP/38.620

IATA Cargo Agency Programms Commission decision 91/481/EEC [1991] OJ L 258/29, Case IV/32.792

IATA Passenger Agency Programms Commission decision 91/480/EEC [1991] OJ L 258/18, Case IV/32.659

IBM PC Commission decision 84/233/EEC [1984] OJ L 118/24, Case IV/30.849

Ideal-Standard Sales System Commission decision 85/45/EEC [1985] OJ L 20/38, Case IV/30.261

Identrus Commission decision 2001/696/EC [2001] OJ L 249/12, Case IV/37.462

IFTRA Commission decision 75/497/EEC [1975] OJ L 228/3, Case IV/27.000

IJsselcentrale and others Commission decision 91/50/EEC [1991] OJ L 28/32, Case IV/32.732

Ilmailulaitos/Luftfartsverket Commission decision 1999/198/EC [1999] OJ L 69/24, Case IV/35.767

IMA Rules Commission decision 80/1071/EEC [1980] OJ L 318/1, Case IV/25.077

Industrial and medical gases Commission decision 2003/355/EC OJ L 123/49, Case COMP/E-3/36.700

Industrial bags Commission decision of 30 November 2005, published on DG Comp website, Case COMP/F-3/38.354

Industrial copper tubes Commission decision 2004/421/EC [2004] OJ L 125/50, Case COMP/38.240

Industrial Thread Commission decision of 14 September 2005, published on DG Comp website, Case COMP/38.337

Industrieverband Solnhofener Natursteinplatten eV Commission decision 80/1074/EEC [1980] OJ L 318/32, Case IV/197

Inntrepreneur, Spring Commission decision 2000/484/EC [2000] OJ L 195/49, Cases IV/36.456/F3

Intel Commission decision of 13 May 2009, not yet published, Case COMP/37.990

Interbrew and Alken-Maes Commission decision 2003/569/EC [2003] OJ L 200/1, Case IV/37.614/F3

INTERGROUP Commission decision 75/482/EEC [1975] OJ L 212/23, Case IV/28.838

International Energy Agency Commission decision 83/671/EEC [1983] OJ L 376/30, Case IV/30.525

International Energy Agency Commission decision 94/153/EEC [1994] OJ L 68/35, Case IV/30.525

International Federation of the Phonographic Industry Commission decision 2003/300/EC [2003] OJ L 107/58, Case COMP/C2/38.014

International Petroleum Exchange of London Ltd Commission decision 87/2/EEC [1987] OJ L 3/27, Case IV/30.439

International Private Satellite Partners Commission decision 94/895/EEC [1994] OJ L 354/75, Case IV/34.768

International Removal Services Commission decision of 11 March 2008, not yet published, Case COMP/38.543

Internationale Dentalschau Commission decision 87/509/EEC [1987] OJ L 293/58, Case IV/31.739

IPTC Belgium Commission decision 83/667/EEC [1983] OJ L 376/7, Case IV/30.671

Iridium Commission decision 97/39/EC [1997] OJ L 16/87, Case IV/35.518

Irish Banks Standing Committee Commission decision 86/507/EEC [1986] OJ L 295/28, Case IV/31.362

Marine hose producers Commission decision of 28 January 2009, not yet published, Case COMP/39.406

MasterCard Multilateral Interchange Fees Commission decision of 19 December 2007, published on DG Comp website, Case COMP/34.579

Mecaniver/PPG Commission decision 85/78/EEC [1985] OJ L 35/54, Case IV/30.666

Meldoc Commission decision 86/596/EEC [1986] OJ L 348/50, Case IV/31.204

Mercedes Benz Commission decision 2002/758/EC [2002] OJ L 257/1, Case COMP/36.264

Metaleurop SA Commission decision 90/363/EEC [1990] OJ L 179/41, Case IV/32.846

Methionine Commission decision 2003/674/EC [2003] OJ L 255/1, Case C.37.159

Methylglucamine Commission decision 2004/104/EC [2004] OJ L 38/18, Case COMP/E-2/37.978

MEWAC Commission decision 93/47/EEC [1993] OJ L 20/6, Case IV/32.447

Michelin **Commission decision 81/969/EEC [1981] OJ L 353/33, Case IV/29.491**

Michelin II **Commission decision 2002/405/EC [2002] OJ L 143/1, Case COMP/E-2/36.041**

Microsoft **Commission decision 2007/53/EC, Summary of the decision published in [2007] OJ L 32/23, full text published on DG Comp website**

Microsoft Commission decision of 27 February 2008, published on DG Comp website, Case COMP/C-3/34.792

Milchförderungsfonds Commission decision 85/76/EEC [1985] OJ L 35/35, Case IV/28.930

Miller International Schallplatten GmbH Commission decision 76/915/EEC [1976] OJ L 357/40, Case IV/29.018

Misal Commission decision 72/397/EEC [1972] OJ L 267/20, Case IV/24.171

Mitchell Cotts/Sofiltra Commission decision 87/100/EEC [1987] OJ L 41/31, Case IV/31.340

Moët & Chandon Commission decision 82/203/EEC [1982] OJ L 94/7, Case IV/30.188

Monochloroacetic acid Commission decision of 19 January 2005, published on DG Comp website, Case COMP/E-1/37.773

Moosehead/Whitbread **Commission decision 90/186/EEC [1990] OJ L 100/32, Case IV/32.736**

Murat Commission decision 83/610/EEC [1983] OJ L 348/20, Case IV/30.668

Napier Brown/British Sugar **Commission decision 88/518/EEC [1988] OJ L 284/41, Case IV/30.178**

Nathan-Bricolux Commission decision 2001/135/EC [2001] OJ L 54/1, Case COMP.F.1/36.516

National Panasonic (Belgique) Commission decision 82/260/EEC [1982] OJ L 113/18, Case IV/512

National Panasonic Commission decision 82/853/EEC [1982] OJ L 354/28, Case IV/30.070

National Panasonic France Commission decision 82/465/EEC [1982] OJ L 211/32, Case IV/511

National Sulphuric Acid Association Commission decision 80/917/EEC [1980] OJ L 260/24, Case IV/27.958

National Sulphuric Acid Association Commission decision 89/408/EEC [1980] OJ L 190/22, Case IV/27.958

Navewa–Anseau Commission decision 82/371/EEC [1982] OJ L 167/17, Case IV/29.995

Netherlands beer producers Commission decision of 18 April 2007, published on DG Comp website, Case COMP/37.766

Nederlandse Cement-Handelsmaatschappij Commission decision 72/68/EEC [1972] OJ L 22/16, Case IV/595

Nederlandse Vereniging van Banken, Nederlandse Postorderbond, etc. Commission decision 1999/687/EC [1999] OJ L 271/28, Case IV/34.010, 33.793, 34.234, 34.888

New potatoes Commission decision 88/109/EEC [1988] OJ L 59/25, Case IV/31.735

Newitt/Dunlop Slazenger Commission decision 92/261/EEC [1992] OJ L 131/32, Case IV/32.290

Nicholas Frères & Vitapro Commission decision 64/502/EEC [1964] OJ L 64/2287, Case IV/95

Night Services Commission decision 94/663/EEC [1994] OJ L 259/20, Case IV/34.600

Novalliance/Systemform Commission decision 97/123/EC [1997] OJ L 47/11, Case IV/35.679

Nuovo CEGAM Commission decision 84/191/EEC [1984] OJ L 99/29, Case IV/30.804

Nutricia Commission decision 83/670/EEC [1983] OJ L 376/22, Cases IV/30.389, 30.408

O2 UK/T-Mobile UK – UK network sharing agreement Commission decision 2003/570/EC [2003] OJ L 200/59, Case COMP/38.370

Olivetti/Canon Commission decision 88/88 [1988] OJ L 52/51, Case IV/32.306

Olivetti/Digital Commission decision 94/771/EC [1994] OJ L 309/24, Case IV/34.410

Olympic Airways Commission decision 85/121/EEC [1985] OJ L 46/51, Case IV/31.163

Omega Commission decision 70/488/EEC [1970] OJ L 242/22, Cases IV/32.13, 10.498, 11.546, 12.992, 17.394, 17.395, 17.971, 18.772, 18.888

Omega/Nintendo + 1 Commission decision 2003/675/EC [2003] OJ L 255/33, COMP/35.587

Opel Commission decision 2001/146/EC [2001] OJ L 59/1, Case COMP/36.653

Optical Fibres **Commission Decision 86/405/EEC [1986] OJ L 236/30, Case IV/30.320**

P&I clubs Commission decision 85/615/EEC [1985] OJ L 376/2, Case IV/30.373

P&I Clubs Commission decision 1999/329/EC [1999] OJ L 125/12, Case IV/30.373

P&O Stena Line Commission decision 1999/421/EC [1999] OJ L 163/61, Case IV/36.253

Pabst and Richardz/BNIA Commission decision 76/684/EEC [1976] OJ L 231/24, Case IV/28.980

Papier Mince Commission decision 72/291/EEC [1972] OJ L 182/24, Case IV/642

Papiers peints de Belgique Commission decision 74/431/EEC [1974] OJ L 373/3, Case IV/426

Parfums Givenchy **Commission decision 92/428/EEC [1992] OJ L 236/11, Case IV/33.542**

Pasteur Merieux-Merck Commission decision 94/770/EEC [1994] OJ L 309/1, Case IV/34.776

Penneys Commission decision 78/193 [1978] OJ L 60/19, Case IV/29.246

Peroxygen Products Commission decision 85/74/EEC [1985] OJ L 35/1, Case IV/30.907

Peugeot Commission decision 86/506/EEC [1986] OJ L 295/19, Case IV/31.143

Philips-Osram Commission decision 94/986/EEC [1994] OJ L 378/37, Case IV/34.252

Phoenix/GlobalOne Commission decision 96/547/EC [1996] OJ L 239/57, Case IV/35.617

Pioneer Commission decision 80/256/EEC [1980] OJ L 60/21, Case IV/29.595

Pirelli-Dunlop Commission decision 69/477 [1969] OJ L 323/21, Cases IV/24.470, 24.471

Pittsburgh Corning Europe-Formica Belgium-Hertel Commission decision 72/403/EEC [1972] OJ L 272/35, Cases IV/26.876, 26.892, 26.894

Plasterboard Commission decision 2005/471/EC [2005] OJ L 166/8, Case COMP/E-1/37.152

PMI-DSV Commission decision 95/373/EC [1995] OJ L 221/34, Case IV/33.375

PO/French Beef Commission decision 2003/600/EC [2003] OJ L 209/12, Case COMP/C.38.279/F3

PO/Organic peroxides Commission decision of 10 December 2003, published on DG Comp website, Case COMP/E-2/37.857

PO/Yamaha Commission decision of 16 July 2003, published on DG Comp website, Case COMP/37.975

Polistil/Arbois Commission decision 84/282/EEC [1984] OJ L 136/9, Case IV/30.658

Polypropylene Commission decision 86/398/EEC [1986] OJ L 230/1, Case IV/31.149

Portuguese Airports Commission decision 1999/199/EC [1999] OJ L 69/31, Case IV/35.703

Power transformers producers Commission decision of 7 October 2009, not yet published, Case COMP/39.129

Preinsulated Pipes Commission decision 1999/60/EC [1999] OJ L 24/1, Case IV/35.691

Preserved Mushrooms Commission decision 75/77/EEC [1977] OJ L 29/26, Case IV/27.039

Professional videotape producers Commission decision of 20 November 2007, published on DG Comp website, Case COMP/38.432

Prokent AG – Tomra system Commission decision of 29 March 2006, published on DG Comp website, Case COMP/38.113

Pronuptia Commission decision 87/17/EEC [1987] OJ L 13/39, Case IV/30.937

Provision in Spain of express courier services Commission decision 90/456/EEC [1990] OJ L 233/19, Case IV/31.990

Provision in the Netherlands of express delivery services **Commission decision 90/16/EEC [1990] OJ L 10/47**

PRYM-BEKA Commission decision 73/323/EEC [1973] OJ L 296/24, Case IV/26.825

Publishers Association/Net Book Agreements Commission decision 89/44/EEC [1989] OJ L 22/12, Cases IV/27.394, 27.393

PVC Commission decision 89/190/EEC [1989] OJ L 74/1, Case IV/31.865

PVC Commission decision 94/599/EEC [1994] OJ L 239/14, Case IV/31.865

Quantel International – continuum/Quantel SA Commission decision 92/427/EEC [1992] OJ L 235/9, Cases IV/32.800, 33.335

Quinine Commission decision 69/240/EEC [1969] OJ L 192/5, Case IV/26.623

RAI/UNITEL Commission decision 78/516/EEC [1978] OJ L 157/39, Case IV/29.559

Rank/Sopelem Commission decision 75/76/EEC [1975] OJ L 29/20, Case IV/26.603

Raw tobacco Italy Commission decision of 20 October 2005, published on DG Comp website, Case COMP/C.38.281/B2

Raw tobacco Spain Commission decision of 20 October 2004, published on DG Comp website, Case COMP/C.38.238/B2

Raymond-Nagoya Commission decision 72/238/EEC [1972] OJ L 143/39, Case IV/26.813

Reims II + 13 Commission decision 1999/695/EC [1999] OJ L 275/17, Case IV/36.748

Reims II renotification Commission decision 2004/139/EC [2004] OJ L 56/76, Case COMP/C/38.170

Rennet Commission decision 80/234/EEC [1980] OJ L 51/19, Case IV/29.011

Reuter/BASF **Commission decision 76/743/EEC [1976] OJ L 254/40, Case IV/28.996**

Revised TACA Commission decision 2003/68/EC [2003] OJ L 26/53, Case COMP/37.396/D2

Rich Products/Jus-Rol Commission decision 88/143/EEC [1988] OJ L 69/21, Case IV/31.206

Rieckermann /AEG-Elotherm Commission decision 68/376/EEC [1968] OJ L 276/25, Case IV/23.077

Rockwell/IVECO **Commission decision 83/390/EEC [1983] OJ L 224/19, Case IV/30.437**

Rødby Commission decision 94/119/EEC [1994] OJ L 55/52

Rodenstock Commission decision 72/396/EEC [1972] OJ L 267/17, Case IV/8.818, 8.822

Rolled zinc products and zinc alloys Commission decision 82/866/EEC [1982] OJ L 362/40, Case IV/29.629

Roofing Felt **Commission decision 86/399/EEC [1986] OJ L 232/15, Case IV/31.371**

Rubber chemicals Commission decision of 21 December 2005, published on DG Comp website, Case COMP/F-1/38.443

SABA **Commission Decision 76/159/EEC [1976] OJ L 95/1, Case IV/847**

SABA's EEC Distribution System Commission decision 83/672/EEC [1983] OJ L 376/41, Case IV/29.598

SAFCO Commission decision 72/23/EEC [1972] OJ L 13/44, Case IV/23.514

Sandoz Commission decision 87/409/EEC [1987] OJ L 222/28, Case IV/31.741

SAS Maersk Air and Sun-Air Commission decision 2001/716/EC [2001] OJ L 265/15, Case COMP/D.2 37.444

Schlegel/CPIO Commission decision 83/622/EEC [1983] OJ L 351/20, Case IV/30.099

Schoeller Lebensmittel GmbH and Co. KG Commission decision 93/405/EEC [1993] OJ L 183/1, Case IV/31.533

SCK/FNK Commission decision 95/551/EC [1995] OJ L 312/79, Cases IV/34.216, 34.179, 34.202

Scottish and Newcastle Commission decision 1999/474/EC [1999] OJ L 186/28, Case IV/35.992/F3

Scottish Nuclear, Nuclear Energy Agreement Commission decision 91/329/EEC [1991] OJ L 178/31, Case IV/33.473

Scottish Salmon Board Commission decision 92/444/EEC [1992] OJ L 246/37, Case IV/33.494

SCPA – Kali und Salz Commission decision 73/212/EEC [1973] OJ L 217/3, Cases IV/791, 1373, 1374, 1498, 1499, 1500

Screensport/UER Commission decision 91/130/EEC [1991] OJ L 63/32, Case IV/32.524

Sea Containers/Stena Line Commission decision 94/19/EEC [1994] OJ L 15/8, Case IV/34.689

Seamless steel tubes **Commission decision 2003/382/EC [2003] OJ L 140/1, Case IV/E-1/35.860-B**

Secretama Commission decision 91/55/EEC [1991] OJ L 35/23, Case IV/32.450

SEIFA Commission decision 69/216/EEC [1969] OJ L 173/8, 704, Case IV/25.410

SEP and Others/Automobiles Peugeot Commission decision of 5 October 2005, published on DG Comp website, Cases COMP/F-2/36.623, 36.820, 37.275

Service Master Commission decision 88/604/EEC [1988] OJ L 332/38, Case IV/32.358

SHV-Chevron Commission decision 75/95/EEC [1975] OJ L 29/20, Case IV/26.872

SIAE Commission decision 71/375/EEC [1971] OJ L 254/15, Case IV/26.909

Sicasov Commission decision 1999/6/EC [1999] OJ L 4/27, Case IV/35.280

Siemens/Fanuc Commission decision 85/618/EEC [1985] OJ L 376/29, Case IV/30.739

Sippa Commission decision 91/128/EEC [1991] OJ L 60/19, Case IV/31.559

Sirdar-Phildar Commission decision 75/297/EEC [1975] OJ L 125/27, Case IV/27.879

Slovakian postal legislation Commission decision of 7 October 2008, published on DG Comp website, Case COMP/F-1/39.562

SMM and T Exhibition Agreement Commission decision 83/666/EEC [1983] OJ L 376/1, Case IV/27.492

Snelpd/France, La Poste Commission decision 2002/344/EC [2002] OJ L 120/19, Case COMP/37.133

SNPE-LEL Commission decision 78/571/EEC [1978] OJ L 191/41, Case IV/29.453

SOCEMAS Commission decision 68/318/EEC [1968] OJ L 201/4, Case IV/129

Soda-Ash – ICI Commission decision 91/300/EEC [1991] OJ L 152/40, Case IV/33.133d

Soda-ash – Solvay Commission decision 91/299/EC [1991] OJ L 152/21, Case IV/33.133d

Soda-Ash/Solvay Commission decision 2003/6/EC [2003] OJ L 10/10, Case COMP/33.133

Soda-ash – Solvay/CFK Commission decision 91/298/EEC [1991] OJ L 152/1, Case IV/33.133b

Soda-ash – Solvay/CFK Commission decision 2003/5/EC [2003] OJ L 10/1, COMP/33.133-B

Soda-ash – Solvay/ICI Commission decision 91/297/EEC [1991] OJ L 152/1, Case IV/33.133a

Soda-Ash/ICI Commission decision 2003/7/EC [2003] OJ L 10/33, Case COMP/33.133

Sodium chlorate paper bleach producers Commission decision of 11 June 2008, not yet published, Case COMP/38.695

Sodium gluconate Commission decision of 2 October 2001, not yet published, Case COMP/36.
756

Sodium gluconate Commission decision of 29 September 2004, published on DG Comp website,
Case COMP/36.756

Sopelem/Langen Commission decision 72/24/EEC [1972] OJ L 13/47, Case IV/26.418

Sopelem/Vickers Commission decision 78/251/EEC [1981] OJ L 391/1, Case IV/29.236

Sorbates Commission decision of 1 October 2003, published on DG Comp website, Case
COMP/E-1/37.370

Souris/Topps Commission decision of 26 May 2004, published on DG Comp website, Case
COMP/C-3/37.980

Speciality graphite/PO Commission decision of 17 December 2002, published on DG Comp
website, Case COMP/37.667

Sperry New Holland Commission decision 85/617/EEC [1985] OJ L 376/21, Case IV/30.839

SSI Commission decision 82/506/EEC [1982] OJ L 232/1, Cases IV/29.525, 30.000

Steel beams (readopted) Commission decision of 8 November 2006, published on DG Comp
website, Case COMP/38.907

Stichting Baksteen Commission decision 94/296/EEC [1994] OJ L 131/15, Case IV/34.456

Stichting Certificatie Kraanverhuurbedrijf and FNK Commission decision 94/272/EEC [1994]
OJ L 117/30, Case IV/B-2/34.179

Stoves and Heaters (Haarden- en Kachelhandel) Commission decision 75/358/EEC [1975] OJ L
159/22, Case IV/712

Sugar Beet Commission decision 90/45/EEC [1990] OJ L 31/32, Case IV/32.414

Supexie Commission decision 71/22/EEC [1971] OJ L 10/12, Case IV/337

Synthetic Fibres **Commission decision 84/380/EEC [1984] OJ L 207/17, Case IV/30.810**

Synthetic rubber Commission decision of 29 November 2006, published on DG Comp website,
Case COMP/38.638

Synthetic rubber producers Commission decision of 23 January 2008, not yet published, Case
COMP/38.628

TACA Commission decision 1999/243/EC [1999] OJ L 95/1, Case IV/35.134

Tariff Structures Combined transport of goods Commission decision 93/174/EEC [1993] OJ L
73/38, Case IV/34.494

Tariffs for piloting in the Port of Genoa Commission decision 97/745/EC [1997] OJ L 301/27

Teacher and Sons Commission decision 78/697/EEC [1978] OJ L 235/20, Case IV/28.859

TEKO Commission decision 90/92/EEC [1990] OJ L 13/34, Case IV/32.408

Télécom Développement Commission decision 1999/574/EC [1999] OJ L 218/24, Case IV/
36.581

Telecom Eireann **Commission decision 97/114/EC [1997] OJ L 41/8**

Telefónica **Commission decision of 4 July 2007, published on DG Comp website, Case
COMP/38.784**

Telenor, Canal +, Canal Digital Commission decision of 29 December 2003, published on DG
Comp website, Case COMP/C-2.38.287

Telos Commission decision 82/124/EEC [1982] OJ L 58/19, Case IV/29.895

Tetra Pak I (BTG-license) **Commission decision 88/501/EEC [1988] OJ L 272/27, Case
IV/31.043**

Tetra Pak II **Commission decision 92/163/EEC [1992] OJ L 72/1, Case IV/31.043**

The Distillers Co. Ltd – Victuallers Commission decision 80/789/EEC [1980] OJ L 233/43, Case
IV/26.528

Vereeniging van Cementhandelaren Commission decision 72/22/EEC [1972] OJ L 13/34, Case
IV/324

Vereinigung deutscher Freiformschmieden Commission decision 78/24/EEC [1978] OJ L 10/32,
Case IV/356

Vichy Commission decision 91/153/EEC [1991] OJ L 75/57, Case IV/31.624

Video Cassette Recorders **Commission decision 78/156/EEC [1978] OJ L 47/42, Case
IV/29.151**

VIFKA Commission decision 86/499/EEC [1986] OJ L 291/46, Case IV/28.959

Viho/Parker Pen Commission decision 92/426/EEC [1992] OJ L 131/32, Case IV/32.725

Viho/Toshiba Commission decision 91/532/EC [1991] OJ L 287/39, Case IV/32.879

Villeroy and Boch Commission decision 85/616/EEC [1985] OJ L 376/15, Case IV/30.655

Vimpoltu Commission decision 83/361/EEC [1983] OJ L 200/44, Case IV/30.174

Virgin/British Airways Commission decision 2000/74/EC [2000] OJ L 30/1, IV/D-2/34.780

Visa International Commission decision 2002/914/EC [2002] OJ L 318/17, Case COMP/29.373

Vitamins **Commission decision 2003/2/EC [2003] OJ L 6/1, Case COMP/E-1/37.512**

Vitamins, Hoffmann – La Roche **Commission decision 76/642/EEC [1976] OJ L 223/27, Case
IV/29.020**

Volkswagen Commission decision 2001/711/EC [2001] OJ L 262/14, Case COMP/F-2/36.693

VW-Audi Commission decision 98/273/EC [1998] OJ L 124/60, Case IV/35.733

VW/MAN Commission decision 83/668/EEC [1983] OJ L 376/11, Case IV/29.329

VVVF Commission decision 69/202/EEC [1969] OJ L 168/22, Case IV/597

Wanadoo Interactive **Commission decision of 16 July 2003, published on DG Comp website,
Case COMP/38.233**

WANO Schwarzpulver Commission decision 78/921/EEC [1978] OJ L 322/26, Case IV/29.133

Warner-Lambert/Gillette and Bic/Gillette and others Commission decision 93/252/EEC [1993]
OJ L 116/21, Cases IV/33.440, 33.486

Wax producers Commission decision of 1 October 2008, not yet published, Case COMP/39.181

WEA-Filipacchi Music Commission decision 72/480/EEC [1972] OJ L 303/52, Case IV/26.992

Welded Steel Mesh Commission decision 89/515/EEC [1989] OJ L 260/1, Case IV/31.553

Whiskey and Gin Commission decision 85/562/EEC [1985] OJ L 369/19, Case IV/30.570

Whitbread Commission decision 1999/230/EC [1999] OJ L 88/26, Case IV/35.079/F3

White Lead Commission decision 79/90/EEC [1979] OJ L 21/16, Case IV/29.535

Wild-Leitz Commission decision 72/128/EEC [1972] OJ L 61/27, Case IV/26.844

Windsurfing International Commission decision 83/400/EEC [1983] OJ L 229/1, Case IV/29.395

Wood Pulp Commission decision 85/202/EEC [1985] OJ L 85/1, Case IV/29.725

X/Open Group Commission decision 87/69/EEC [1987] OJ L 35/36, Case IV/31.458

Yves Rocher **Commission decision 87/14/EEC [1987] OJ L 8/49, Cases IV/31.428, 31.429,
31.430, 31.431, 31.432**

Yves Saint-Laurent Parfums Commission decision 92/33/EEC [1992] OJ L 12/24, Case IV/33.242

Zanussi Commission decision 78/922/EEC [1978] OJ L 322/36, Case IV/1576

Zera/Montedison and Hinkens/Stähler Commission decision 93/554/EEC [1993] OJ L 272/28,
Cases IV/31.550, 31.898

Zinc phosphate Commission decision 2003/437/EC [2003] OJ L 153/1, Case COMP/E-1/37.027

Zinc Producer Group Commission decision 84/405/EEC [1984] OJ L 220/27, Case IV/30.350

ZOJA/CSC-ICI, Commercial Solvents Commission decision 72/457/EEC [1972] OJ L 299/51,
Case IV/26.911

Bibliography

Areeda, P. and D. F. Turner (1975), "Predatory Pricing and Related Practices under Section 2 of the Sherman Act," *Harvard Law Review*, 88, 697–733

Aigner, G., O. Budzinski, and A. Christiansen (2006), "The Analysis of Coordinated Effects in EU Merger Control: Where Do We Stand After *Sony/BMB* and *Impala*?," *European Competition Journal*, 2(2), 311–36

Baker, J. B. (2003), "The Case for Antitrust Enforcement," *Journal of Economic Perspectives*, 17, 27–50

Bellamy, C. W. and G. D. Child (2008), *European Community Law of Competition*, 6th edn. Oxford University Press, Oxford

Bishop, S. and M. Walker (2009), *The Economics of EC Competition Law: Concepts, Applications and Measurements*, 2nd edn., Thomson Sweet & Maxwell, London

Bos, I. and M. P. Schinkel (2006), "On the Scope for the European Commission's 2006 Fining Guidelines under the Legal Maximum Fine", *Journal of Competition Law and Economics*, 2(4), 673–82

Carlton, D. W. and J. M. Perloff (2005), *Modern Industrial Organization*, 4th edn., Pearson Addison Wesley, Upper Saddle River, NJ

Carree, M., A. M. Günster, and M. P. Schinkel (2010), "European Antitrust Policy 1957–2004: An Analysis of Commission Decisions," *Review of Industrial Organization*, forthcoming 2010

Church, J. and R. Ware (2000), *Industrial Organization: A Strategic Approach*, Irwin McGraw–Hill, Singapore

Corwin, E. D. (1992), "Trends in Enforcement of the Antimonopoly Laws," in *Antitrust and Regulation*, Edward Elgar, London, 110–18

Davies, S. W., L. N. Driffield, and R. Clarke (1999), "Monopoly in the UK: What Determines Whether the MMC Finds Against the Investigated Firms?," *Journal of Industrial Economics*, 47, 263–83

Duso, T., K. P. Gugler, and B. Yurtoglu (2006), "How Effective is European Merger Control?", *WZB*, Markets and Politics Working Paper, No. SP II 2006–12

European Commission (1972), *I Report on Competition Policy 1971*, Office for Official Publications of the European Communities, Luxembourg

  (1973), *II Report on Competition Policy 1972*, Office for Official Publications of the European Communities, Luxembourg

  (1982), *XI Report on Competition Policy 1981*, Office for Official Publications of the European Communities, Luxembourg

  (1987), *XVI Report on Competition Policy 1986*, Office for Official Publications of the European Communities, Luxembourg

  (1994), *XXIII Report on Competition Policy 1993*, Office for Official Publications of the European Communities, Luxembourg

  (1999), *XXVIII Report on Competition Policy 1998*, Office for Official Publications of the European Communities, Luxembourg

  (2004), *XXXIII Report on Competition Policy 2003*, Office for Official Publications of the European Communities, Luxembourg

  (2007a), *Report on Competition Policy 2005*, Office for Official Publications of the European Communities, Luxembourg

  (2007b), *Report on Competition Policy 2006*, Online version.

Gallo, J. C., K. G. Dau-Schmidt, J. L. Craycraft, and C. J. Parker (1994), "Criminal Penalties under the Sherman Act: A Study of Law and Economics", *Research in Law and Economics*, 16, 171–83

(2000), "Department of Justice Antitrust Enforcement, 1955–1997: An Empirical Study", *Review of Industrial Organization*, 17, 75–133

Geradin, D. and D. Henry (2005), "The EC Fining Policy for Violations of Competition Law: An Empirical Review of the Commission Decisional Practice and the Community Courts' Judgments", *European Competition Journal*, 1(2), 401–73

Ghosal, V. and J. C. Gallo (2001), "The Cyclical Behavior of the Department of Justice Antitrust Enforcement Activity", *International Journal of Industrial Organization*, 19, 27–54

Gual, J. and N. Mas (2005), "Industry Characteristics and Anti-Competitive Behaviour: Evidence from the EU", *University of Barcelona*, Working Paper

Gugler, Klaus, Dennis Mueller, Burcin Yurtoglu, and Christine Zulehner (2003), "The Effects of Mergers: An International Comparison," *International Journal of Industrial Organization*, 21, 625–53

Harding, C. and A. Gibbs (2005), "Why go to Court in Europe? An Analysis of Cartel Appeals 1995–2004", *European Law Review*, 30, 349–62

Harrington, J. E., Jr. (2006), "How Do Cartels Operate?", *Foundations and Trends in Microeconomics*, 2(1), 1–105

Jones, A. and B. Sufrin (2008), *EC Competition Law*, 2nd edn., Oxford University Press, Oxford

Jones, C. and M. van der Woude (2006), *EC Competition Law Handbook*, 17th edn., Thomson Sweet & Maxwell, London

Korah, V. (2006), *Cases and Materials on EC Competition Law*, 3rd edn., Hart Publishing, Portland, OR

Kovacic, W. E. and C. Shapiro (2000), "Competition Policy: A Century of Economic and Legal Thinking", *Journal of Economic Perspectives*, 14(1), 43–60

Lauk, M. (2002), "Econometric Analysis of the Decisions of the German Cartel Office", *Technische Universität Darmstadt, Working Paper*

Lin, P., R. Baldev, M. Sandfort, and D. Slottje (2005), "The US Antitrust System and Recent Trends in Antitrust Enforcement", *Journal of Economic Surveys*, 14, 255–306

Lindsay, A. (2006), *The EC Merger Regulation: Substantive Issues*, 2nd edn., Thomson Sweet & Maxwell, London

Lyons, B. R. (2004), "Reform of European Merger Policy", *Review of International Economics*, 12, 246–61

Martin, S. (1994), *Industrial Economics: Economic Analysis, and Public Policy*, Macmillan, New York

(2002), *Advanced Industrial Economics*, 2nd edn., Blackwell, Oxford

(2007), "The Goals of Antitrust and Competition Policy", in W. D. Collins (ed.), *Issues in Competition Law and Economics*, American Bar Association, 2007, Chicago, IL

Monti, G. (2007), *EC Competition Law*, Cambridge University Press, Cambridge

Motta, M. (2004), *Competition Policy: Theory and Practice*, Cambridge University Press, New York

Nillsen, T. (1997), "On the Consistency of Merger Policy", *Journal of Industrial Economics*, 45, 89–100

Posner, R. A. (1970), "A Statistical Study of Antitrust Enforcement", *Journal of Law and Economics*, 13, 365–419

(2001), *Antitrust Law*, 2nd edn., University of Chicago Press, Chicago

Ritter, L. and W. D. Braun (2005), *European Competition Law: A Practitioner's Guide*, 3rd edn., Kluwer Law International, London

Roeller, L. H. and O. Stehmann (2005), "The Year 2005 at DG Competition: The Trend towards a More Effects-Based Approach", *Review of Industrial Organization*, 29, 281–304

Russo, F. (2006), "Abuse of Protected Position? Minority Shareholdings and Restriction of Markets' Competitiveness in the European Union," *World Competition*, 29(4), 607–33

Stephan, A. (2009), "An Empirical Assessment of the Leniency Notice", *Journal of Competition Law and Economics*, 5, 537–61

Tirole, J. (1988), *The Theory of Industrial Organization*, MIT Press, Cambridge, MA

Vogelaar, F. O. W. (2007), *The European Competition Rules; Landmark Cases of the European Courts and the Commission*, 2nd edn., Europa Law Publishing, Groningen

Waldman, D. E. and E. J. Jensen (2001), *Industrial Organization: Theory and Practice*, 2nd edn., Addison Wesley Longman, Upper Saddle River, NJ

Whish, R. (2008), *Competition Law*. Oxford University Press. Oxford

Index

For EU product safety concerns, contact us at Calle de José Abascal, 56–1°, 28003 Madrid, Spain or eugpsr@cambridge.org.